THE
STRUCTURE
OF THE
EAST GERMAN
ECONOMY

CENTER FOR INTERNATIONAL STUDIES

MASSACHUSETTS INSTITUTE OF TECHNOLOGY

THE
STRUCTURE
OF THE
EAST GERMAN
ECONOMY

WOLFGANG F. STOLPER

WITH THE ASSISTANCE OF
KARL W. ROSKAMP

HARVARD UNIVERSITY PRESS

Cambridge, Massachusetts

1960

Publication of this book has been aided
by a grant from the Ford Foundation.

Distributed in Great Britain by Oxford University Press, London

Library of Congress Catalog Card Number 60–13295

Printed in the United States of America

To the memory of my parents.

PREFACE

WHEN the present study was begun under the auspices of the Center for International Studies at the Massachusetts Institute of Technology in the summer of 1955, my purpose was to find out and describe the way an advanced economy developed under communist rule. East Germany was chosen because more material was openly available for that area than for other satellites, even though no East German statistical abstract had yet been published and though *Statistische Praxis* (the monthly journal corresponding to our *Survey of Current Business*) had not yet been developed to a very useful stage.

As the study progressed, it became evident that something more exciting could be done: a systematic comparison of all aspects of a communist and a western democratic economy. Since my methods in calculating the performance of the East German economy — the core of the study — are identical with West German practices, comparisons can be made industry by industry, economic sector by economic sector, and frequently even product by product.

Thus, although the bulk of the book describes the most industrially advanced Soviet satellite, the calculations required make possible also a detailed, meaningful comparison of a free and a communist economy. The reader may doubt my word; nonetheless I want to state that I had no idea of the outcome of this comparison until the final calculations were made.

In the absence of official statistics, my first task consisted in compiling as many as possible of the available data on outputs of individual commodities, prices, and so on, from East German daily newspapers, speeches, and weekly and monthly publications, and from West German sources. The publication of East German Statistical Yearbooks and other official East German sources made this initial labor superfluous but not useless, for, by the time official data had become plentiful, a workable method of dealing with them had been developed.

I have accepted official figures whenever given in numerical units or by weight; and, since the meaning of any figure is determined by the methods by which it is calculated, I have given as explicit as possible an account of the way the figures were arrived at. Moreover, since the East German figures are used as a basis for my own calculations, which conform wherever possible to methods developed by Western economists, it has been necessary also to explain these methods in detail. These explanations should make it possible for any other researcher to duplicate the steps I have taken if he wishes to do so. Anyone objecting to my methods or results can thus pinpoint my errors, explain precisely where I went wrong, and estimate quantitatively the difference that alternative assumptions would have made in the end result.

The detail is, then, of the essence of the study. Although it hardly makes reading to keep one awake at night, following it through its labyrinthine course will enable the reader to acquire a clear picture not only of the results of my calculations but also of the structure of the East German economy. Decisions as to what prices to use, or what inputs to allow for, and so on, are not based simply on statistical procedures but insofar as possible on what is known of the workings of the East German economy.

In order not to overburden the book with calculations, the tables have been reproduced in abbreviated form. Wherever possible each table includes: first, the basic East German figures — official — on which my own calculations are based; second, the final estimate of output measured by gross value added; and, third, the corresponding West German index where possible. For interested scholars there is available a supplemental hectographed pamphlet containing tables showing each step of the calculations.*

All calculations have been made in German prices of the year 1936 and in West German prices of the year 1950. The choice of years was dictated by the desire to make comparisons with West Germany. The West German index of industrial production was originally based on 1936 prices and has since been recalculated with 1950 prices. Unfortunately, West German calculations of the gross national product (GNP) are available only in 1936 and 1954 prices. It is possible, however, to adjust the calculations of the West German GNP to make them roughly comparable with my calculations of the East German GNP in 1950 prices.

Where feasible I have revised all figures to take account of the latest available data, and the tables have been brought up to 1958 where possible. Time did not permit, however, the rewriting of the complete manuscript in order to discuss the latest developments in detail.

All care has been taken to avoid errors in calculation and transcription, but human fallibility makes it possible, of course, that some have

* Supplement can be purchased from the Publications Office, Center for International Studies, Massachusetts Institute of Technology.

crept into the final results. More serious is the fact that frequently rather broad assumptions have had to be made — the inevitable risk of working with communist statistics. The necessity for constantly having to make the best possible decisions, which nevertheless are arbitrary to an uncomfortable degree, is simply an occupational hazard that writers on communist economies have learned to take with a sense of humor.

A word must be said about the terms used. The term "East Germany" has not the same meaning in Germany itself as it has in this country. Officially, the German Federal Republic confronts the German Democratic Republic, and the term "East Germany" is used to refer to the areas east of the Oder-Neisse line. But it has seemed best to neglect political predilections in favor of common usage. We are interested in an East-West comparison, and hence I refer to the two parts of Germany as East and West Germany. I have tried to be as objective as is humanly possible, and in the calculations I have leaned over backward to give East Germany the benefit of the doubt. This, I feel, is quite consistent with the fact that the reader will have little difficulty in discovering where my sympathies lie.

The arrangement of the book is straightforward. The analysis of the population and labor force in Part I is basic to any understanding of the problems faced by the East German planners. The continuous loss of population is also a sign of the performance of the economy. Part II is a detailed account of the official East German methodology, necessary because not only terminology but also concepts differ in communist and market economies; and even more necessary because "facts" in economics are only rarely so simple that it becomes unnecessary to know just how they were arrived at. Since the East German methodology leaves much to be desired even from the standpoint of the planned economy itself, it becomes necessary to define one's own approach to the analysis of the data. In Part III, therefore, the approach used in this study is outlined and justified. This is followed by the calculation of industrial output (Part III), the output attributable to agriculture (Part IV), and the output attributable to the other sectors of the economy (Part V). The data as a whole are discussed in Part VI, in which the GNP of East Germany by sectoral origin and by use is estimated and compared with the West German performance.

The variety of lengths of the individual parts or chapters was dictated by the material. I have tried to squeeze as much out of the material as possible, but I have made no attempt to derive something from nothing or to guess where there was no basis for guessing.

The Introduction, which was written last, as is proper, contains some material that is not included elsewhere, in particular on the foreign trade of East Germany and her integration into the Soviet bloc.

The book contains an evaluation of the two rival systems as it emerged in my mind from the perusal of the facts. There are, however, a number of additional chapters that might have been but were not written: a chapter on the organization of planning and of the various economic sectors, a fuller discussion of the organization, planning, and structure of the foreign trade of East Germany, and a discussion of the price system. As far as the first is concerned, the information essential to the present study — a detailed calculation of the GNP of East Germany along Western lines — is presented, but there was not time for more. As for the second, I hope at a later date to present some work on foreign trade and on an analysis of investments under the First and Second Five Year Plans.

The third missing chapter is the story of a failure. Originally, I hoped to calculate the East German GNP not only in West German prices of 1936 and 1950 but also in West German and East German current prices. In this way I hoped to develop sectoral price indices. Unfortunately, not enough information on East German prices was available to make this project feasible, and it had to be abandoned.

I am indebted to more people than can be mentioned without making the acknowledgments read like a telephone book. It is only fitting that I should mention first Professor Max F. Millikan, Director of the Center for International Studies. Nor is this politic politeness. The study was undertaken at his suggestion, but he left the content and the development to me. A more patient director of any group cannot be imagined; and the complete freedom to work in ideal surroundings has contributed substantially to what merits the book may have.

High on the list is the Deutsche Institut für Wirtschaftsforschung in Berlin and its director, Dr. Ferdinand Friedensburg, Dr. Ferdinand Grünig and in particular Dr. Gerhard Abeken, who helped in numerous ways. Starting with suggestions as to sources, they willingly gave their time to discuss the difficulties and help me clarify the issues; they made critical comments and suggested solutions to vexing problems. The publications of the Institute have been particularly useful and are acknowledged in numerous places.

The Bundesministerium für gesamtdeutsche Fragen, through the interest of Secretary of State Franz Thedieck and Dr. Leimbach, opened its extensive archives to me. Thus I was able to find already prepared a collection of material from the East German press and an excellent collection of books, pamphlets, and documents. All of them were available from their publishers, but it saved months of work to find them collected and sorted and ready for use. Particular mention should be made also of Dr. Paula Kläb, who, remembering our common membership in Schumpeter's seminars in Bonn, helped a fellow student find and analyze material. Dr. Rudolf Richter of the University of Frankfurt helped me to sift literally cubic meters of interesting material.

Professor Matthias Kramer and Dr. Konrad Märkel helped me with their extensive knowledge of agricultural problems. Professor Kramer let me use his manuscript before publication. The calculations of the GNP attributable to agriculture would have been impossible without their help and advice or without the discussions I had with Dr. Werner Klatt in London and Professor Gerschenkron at Harvard.

Dr. Franz Rupp's analytical skill and knowledge helped immeasurably in putting facts into perspective. Professor Bruno Gleitze, whose basic *Ostdeutsche Wirtschaft* provides the starting point for any calculation of the Soviet German industrial output in 1936, gave generously of his time.

At the Free University of Berlin and its Ost-Europa Institut, Professor Karl Thalheim and Dr. Wolfgang Förster helped with discussions, provided me with facts, discussed problems with me, and placed their library and archives at my disposal. And at the United States Mission in Berlin, Mr. David Klein and Mrs. Eugenie Zawadski helped substantially in numerous ways. Professor Erich Welter and his staff at the University of Mainz, Dr. Walter Bauer, and many others in Germany too numerous to mention have helped greatly.

In this country, Dr. Fred Sanderson of the Department of State helped me to get started. At a later date, Professors Abram Bergson, Alexander Gerschenkron, and Horst Mendershausen helped by discussing many problems with me. Since the calculations raised many technologically intricate problems outside the realm in which an economist is competent, even with the aid of technical handbooks, the assistance given by Professors Thomas B. King (Metallurgy), Walter C. Schumb (Chemistry), Milton C. Shaw (Mechanical Engineering), and Charles N. Satterfield (Chemical Engineering), all at the Massachusetts Institute of Technology, was essential. In Geneva, Mr. Gunnar Myrdal, Mr. Hal B. Lary, and particularly Mr. Nicholas Plesz drew my attention to publications I had missed, made critical comments, and checked errors in interpretation.

Unfortunately for me, Mr. Peter Wiles of Oxford received the manuscript too late to make possible my incorporating more than a few of his suggestions and criticisms. In particular I regret that time did not permit the expansion of the "non-productive services" section of Chapter 19, but the appendix on Services which follows Chapter 19 in Part V is the direct result of his suggestions. On the other hand, I do not at this time feel that I could make an independent estimate of reparations payments as he also wished me to do.

As with the chapters that seemed possible but were not written, so there are also acknowledgments that seem likely but will not be forthcoming. The most important of these, perhaps, should be to the East German Central Statistical Office. Since I was interested in as objective a study as possible, I was anxious to get East German criticisms, not indeed as to my methodology with which they would naturally disagree, but on the interpretation and possible omission of data. I consequently offered to send copies of the first draft to East Berlin with the understanding that it would be criticized and that some gaps in my information would be closed. I wrote to this effect to East Berlin, received a polite answer offering critical help, and sent four copies. When no criticism came, I wrote again and received a polite reply that unfortunately the pressure of work in East Berlin and the size and detail of my study made any thorough criticism of it impossible. There the matter rested, except that I should add that the statistical abstracts that finally did appear went a long way to fill the gaps in my information (without, however, changing the end result of the calculations very much). I mention this correspondence to show that I have at least tried. If East German critics should read this study, they ought at least to know that they had a chance to make their views known beforehand.

A few people must be mentioned specially. Mr. Karl Roskamp has been a devoted and imaginative collaborator throughout the study. His contributions were varied and many; it is only proper that his name should appear on the title page. Miss Elizabeth Terlingen did the nerve-wracking work of typing, proofreading, and catching mistakes in the first and the final draft. Her efficiency kept me working very hard. My wife retyped the whole manuscript in more than one version, becoming a highly proficient typist in the course of a somewhat dubious entertainment. She also helped me with calculations and recalculations. Mrs. Jean Clark, Mr. Richard W. Hatch, and Mrs. Dorothy Rowland did the meticulous editorial work and labored hard to make the book more readable. Professor Everett Hagen tried his best to make the tables consistent.

Finally, and in many ways most important, I have to thank Professor Theodor Heuss, first President of the German Federal Republic, who, for purely personal reasons, took an interest in the study and introduced me to many persons in a manner which opened doors that would normally have been closed to me.

WOLFGANG F. STOLPER

Ann Arbor, Michigan
June 1959

CONTENTS

PART FIVE

**CONSTRUCTION, TRANSPORTATION
AND COMMUNICATION,
AND TRADE**

PART SIX

**THE GROSS NATIONAL PRODUCT
OF EAST GERMANY**

TABLES

THE
STRUCTURE
OF THE
EAST GERMAN
ECONOMY

Short forms of titles used in the text*

Agriculture and Food Handbook — *Statistisches Handbuch für Landwirtschaft und Ernährung*

Direktive — *Direktive für den zweiten Fünfjahrplan zur Entwicklung der Volkswirtschaft in der Deutschen Demokratischen Republik, 1956 bis 1960*

German Yearbook — *Deutschland Jahrbuch*

Materialien — *Materialien zur Wirtschaftslage in der Sowjetischen Zone*

Neuberechnung — *Neuberechnung des Index der industriellen Nettoproduktion*

Production Statistics of 1936 — *Gesamtergebnisse der amtlichen Produktionsstatistik*

Reichs Statistical Yearbook — *Statistisches Jahrbuch des Deutschen Reiches*

Rules of Thumb for Agriculture — *Faustzahlen für die Landwirtschaft*

Statistical Handbook of Germany — *Statistisches Handbuch von Deutschland*

Statistical Practice — *Statistische Praxis*

Statistical Rules of Thumb — *Landwirtschaftliche Richtzahlen und Hinweise (Faustzahlen) für den Berater und praktischen Landwirt*

Statistical Yearbook of the German Democratic Republic — *Statistisches Jahrbuch der Deutschen Demokratischen Republik*

Statistical Yearbook of the German Federal Republic — *Statistisches Jahrbuch für die Bundesrepublik Deutschland*

Statistics Quarterly — *Vierteljahreshefte zur Statistik*

* For abbreviations used in the notes and tables, see p. 55.

ECONOMIC DEVELOPMENT UNDER A COMMUNIST SIGN

ONLY rarely in economics do we deal with even an approximation to laboratory conditions, and rarely if ever are comparable sets of data available. It is particularly difficult to make meaningful comparisons of national economies. Thus, any interpretation of the growth rates in the Soviet Union and in the United States is bedeviled by the fact that the Soviet Union started as a backward nation when the United States was already the most important industrial complex in the world. The economy of the communist German Democratic Republic, which is here referred to as East Germany, offers a unique example for a meaningful East-West comparison. For, with the division of Germany in 1945 and the coup in Czechoslovakia in 1948, a centralized planned economy and a communist regime have, for the first time in history, been instituted in industrially advanced areas.

Historically, the attraction of communism has been greatest in the underdeveloped areas, where a forced industrialization program accompanied by revolutionary changes in the social structure has been defended as the only means of breaking the fetters of a corrupt feudal society, of imperialist exploitation, and of crushing poverty. Such at least is the defense of communism made by Milovan Djilas in *The New Class*.[1] Whatever one may think of Djilas' interesting analysis of the emergence of totalitarian regimes with centrally planned economies in Russia, Yugoslavia, and other backward areas of the world — and I for one do not consider it an adequate economic analysis, although perhaps adequate psychologically — it is certainly completely inapplicable to East Germany — and, for that matter, to large parts of Czechoslovakia. These areas were by no stretch of the imagination underdeveloped countries.

No matter what tests are applied to East Germany, it is and has long been among the most highly developed regions of the earth. Before the communist seizure, the percentage of the labor force in agriculture was relatively low and that in industry high; illiteracy was all but unknown; German schools and universities were world renowned; average per capita incomes were high; industries were diversified and renowned for the quality of their output, names like Zeiss in optics and Breitkopf and Härtel in music publishing (to take two entirely different examples) were universally known and respected. To be sure, there were some *Junkers* in Mecklenburg, and 36.6 per cent of the total acreage was in farms of 50 hectares or more in East Germany compared with only 11.2 in West Germany, and in general, farms tended to be larger in East Germany (see below Table 98); but there are "underdeveloped" and "backward" areas even within the United States.

Thus the preconditions for the success of the planned economy existed in the area which became East Germany. In fact, since it was an industrially advanced nation rather than a backward peasant economy that became communist, it should present almost a case study of what Marx envisaged. No terror, no concentration camps, no concentration of power in the hands of the New Class, no central planning, no artificial reduction in living standards were required to transform an already advanced and highly developed economy. The planned economy in East Germany must, as it were, stand on its own feet; its achievements or failures can be reasonably compared with the achievements and failures of advanced market economies.

Certainly a most meaningful comparison can be made between East Germany and the Federal German Republic. The iron curtain which divides the Federal German Republic of the North, West, and South from East Germany divides what is in effect a historical, cultural, and, until recently, political unit. Institutions, people, traditions, tastes — all were common to the various sections of Germany, and the people on both sides of the iron curtain consider themselves and will, for some time to come, go on considering themselves members of one nation no matter what their political and other institutional arrangements happen to be. Not only their history, language, family ties, cultural past, and political fortunes but also the economic structure of the two areas were similar before the war.

As Table 1 indicates, the percentage of the labor force in both agriculture and industry (including producing artisans) was somewhat higher in the area of the Soviet Occupation Zone (that is, East Germany, excluding East Berlin) than in the area of the Federal Republic (which does not include West Berlin). Presumably the distribution of the labor force among the various economic sectors was the same in East and West Berlin.

Moreover, factor endowments were similar — although the differences in detail are, of course, important. Both areas have plenty of lignite and potash, but East Germany lacks soft coal of cokeable quality, which the Federal Republic has in abundance in the Ruhr; neither area has iron ore of good quality; the copper ores of East Germany, although the only

Table 1

Per cent distribution of active population by economic sectors,
Federal Republic and Soviet Zone, 1939

Economic sector	Area of Federal Republic		Area of Soviet Zone[c]
	Including individuals without occupation[a]	Excluding individuals without occupation[b]	
	(1)	(2)	(3)
Agriculture and forestry	17.9	20.0	22.0
Industry (including artisans)	40.4	46.0	48.0
Trade and commerce	...	...	17.0
Trade, commerce, banking, and insurance	14.0	16.0	...
Public and private services	15.9	18.0	13.0
Individuals without occupation	12.1	...	...
Total	100.0	100.0	100.0

Sources: Soviet Zone: *SJBR*, 1955, p. 527, Table 3. Federal Republic: *SJBR*, 1955, p. 109, Table VII. 1. (For abbreviations used in the Tables, see p. 456.

[a] *Unabhängige Berufslose* — pensioners, *rentiers*, etc.

[b] Per cent recalculated from col. 1, after omitting number of individuals without occupation.

[c] Soviet Zone — East Germany, excluding East Berlin; East Germany (officially, German Democratic Republic) includes East Berlin. See note in Preface concerning usage in this book.

worthwhile deposits in Germany, have been insufficient even for domestic needs; and Southern Germany, in the Federal Republic, has water power, which is scarce in East Germany. Basically, the differences in factor endowments are almost completely limited to the dissimilarities in the available coal and water power.

There is one further difference that should be mentioned although it is only partly a natural phenomenon. West Germany has in the Rhine River and its ocean ports an important cheap highway; the eastern waterways system, for political reasons, is not as usable. The Elbe and Oder Rivers have their outlets in Hamburg and Stettin, and the Oder has become a border river. The extensive canal system, developed for the needs of a greater integrated Germany, is now of less value than before the division.

Thus the area of East Germany has become more of a railway economy than before, and a much higher percentage of freight must be transported over relatively expensive land routes rather than cheaper water routes. But, to repeat, this is a consequence of partition only to the extent that partition also leads to national and regional isolation.

Partition created similar problems with respect to the industrial structure, which closely followed factor endowments. (These problems will be discussed in detail in the chapters on industrial production.) The differences may be summarized as follows. The basic location factors in both parts were skilled labor, and the differences were essentially caused by the availability of soft coal or lignite. For example, heavy industries based on soft coal were concentrated in the Ruhr and in what is now the Polish Upper Silesian Basin, and other industries based on soft coal, such as coal tar dyes were also found in West Germany; but East Germany had all the heavy industries based on lignite — notably, heavy chemicals, synthetic rubber, and synthetic gasoline. Moreover, since lignite is an excellent base for the generation of electricity, the area of East Germany was a heavy power producer, and industries based on power such as aluminum and magnesium production, were concentrated there — in spite of the absence of hydroelectric power in any quantity. For the rest, the area of East Germany excelled in the production of precision machinery and in manufacturing, from textile machinery to textiles and clothing, from optics to publishing, from cars to office machinery, details of which are discussed in Part III.

In spite of the basic similarities of the two areas that became East Germany and the Federal Republic, the fact that East Germany has developed substantially less than West Germany can hardly be disputed. We may well ask: What accounts for the differences in development? To what extent are they the result of the different economic and political systems? To what extent did they just happen? To what extent are policies that have nothing to do with the system per se responsible?

It was almost inevitable that the division of a closely integrated economy like prewar Germany should cause difficulties — it is as if Detroit were to be cut off from both the market for cars and the supplies of steel. Yet it is not clear a priori why the wounds of division should have been healed so much faster and so much more efficiently in West Germany than in East Germany. The Potsdam Agreement intended that Germany should be treated as a unit. The fact that the occupying powers had fundamentally different *Weltanschauungen* made a division almost inevitable, and the currency reforms in East and West Germany in June 1948 only put the seal on developments that started in 1945.

Failure to treat Germany as an economic unit undoubtedly led to differences in development. But this is, as it were, only a permissive event. Other problems created by the division caused the final results. Without implying anything about their relative importance we may list three main points: different occupation policies, different domestic economic policies, and different foreign economic integrations.

Soviet occupation policy did not adhere for long to the restrictions on industry laid down by the Potsdam Agreement — if it paid any attention to them at all. From the very beginning, such strategic goods as synthetic gasoline and rubber were produced wholly for the Russians, while the Western powers continued to handicap themselves by adhering to the restrictions. To be sure, the effect of the industry limitations imposed by the Potsdam Agreement and of dismantling were probably more psychological than real, since the growth of West German output did not on the whole run into capacity shortages until about 1950. The fact is, however, that unlike the Western Allies the Soviet Union made strenuous efforts to get production going in those lines which were of interest to her while dismantling the rest. Hence the output of lignite, rubber, and gasoline recovered to prewar levels fairly early, and it may well be that in the days before currency reform production progressed more rapidly in East Germany than in West Germany.

The first crucial factor in the occupation policies relates to reparation payments. In West Germany resources were soon poured into the economy to help it on its way; in East Germany reparations payments, estimated by West German sources to have been as high as 25 per cent of production in any given year, continued at least through 1953.

Before this estimate is dismissed as impossibly high, two facts should be noted. In an article on economic development and economic policy in Denmark published in April of 1955,[2] Carl Iverson estimated Nazi exploitation of Denmark at 15 per cent of GNP; and Denmark was, if anything, more gently treated by the Nazis than the other occupied countries. Surely, the Soviet Union might well have taken as much as a quarter in East Germany. Second, our estimates of the uses of GNP indirectly support this estimate of Soviet exploitation. Between 1950 and 1952 gross investment in plant, equipment, and housing cannot have been much more than 13 to 14 per cent of GNP, excluding personal services; by 1954 it was about 18 per cent, and later perhaps as high as 20 to 25 per cent. On the other hand, in 1950 consumption cannot have been much more than 33 to 40 per cent of GNP, and even in 1953, the year of the June uprising (the first of the uprisings in the satellite world), it cannot have been more than 50 per cent. This leaves a very large part for "other" uses, which include, of course, an export surplus (in the form of reparations) and the government sector, as this term is understood in West Germany.

Thus the calculations of the uses of GNP, presented in detail in the last chapter, support what is qualitatively well known — that the exploitation of the area of East Germany was as severe as could be designed and tolerated. Even with great sacrifices in standards of living, investments remained low, and even if the planned economy had been faultlessly efficient, the reparations policies would have resulted in far less production than would otherwise have been attained.

The planned economy did not, of course, work faultlessly. Since, from what can be observed in East Germany, the methods as well as some of the aims were undoubtedly inefficient *even from the standpoint of the planned economy itself*, it is a miracle that so much was achieved. Communist planners have begun to realize that there is something to be said for the price mechanism as a planning device and that too much physical planning in too great detail (which is referred to as *Tonnenideologie*) is inefficient. The original price system of East Germany has therefore been reformed and made more sensible, at least to the extent that it is internally more consistent.

We shall give here three examples of faulty planning in the past and the corrections which have since been instituted. In the agricultural sector the double-price system and the low prices paid to peasants offered no incentives; and greatly detailed physical planning led to an inefficient use of the soil, for the peculiarities of a particular farm could hardly be allowed for centrally. Prices paid to farmers have been raised substantially, and the detailed regulation of planting and of keeping animals have been abolished. Instead, more use is made of economic incentives. To be sure, things do not yet work smoothly. Even in 1959 we find an example of "schematic impositions" by administrative action:

> The council of Born County (*Kreis*) prescribes — without paying attention to local differences or consulting with the persons involved — that 9 per cent of the acreage is to be devoted to corn [maize]. Such a method of working (which also can still be found in other counties) contradicts the principles of the socialist style in the state apparatus and has bad repercussions on the enterprises and the economy. Thus the agricultural cooperative Auterwitz . . . during 1958 was forced to plow under 14 hectares of alfalfa — a crop which is particularly suitable to local conditions — in order to fulfill the corn quota.[3]

Although it is difficult to determine how many individual complaints were made, it is clear that the planners have modified the "working style of the state apparatus" and that agricultural performance is likely to be improved.

A second example relates to the price systems used. (In Part II the systems of prices used to measure output are discussed in detail.) The case against the price system used during the First Five Year Plan was not only that it corresponded to no real prices but also that it sometimes had the perverse effect of causing the index of production to increase most where in West Germany a comparable index would have declined. This mistake has been at least partially corrected.

A third example relates to the concepts of gross production used not only to measure output but also to derive operational results for the working of the planned economy. "Gross production" is intended to measure the total output of the economy, and, indeed, "total product" is sometimes used as a synonym; but the word "total" is used in so wide a sense that no inter-industry or inter-plant flows, and in many cases even intraplant flows are excluded. (This concept is discussed in detail in Part II.)

It is by no means clear why anyone would want to know the "total product of society." When this figure is used to measure the fulfillment of a plan or the productivity of labor, it has certain damaging effects on the planned economy itself. Since purchased materials are part of gross production, it pays a plant to increase the material content of what it produces, to hoard materials, and, in fact, to use materials as wastefully as possible.

The planners have become aware of this problem. Some have suggested doing away with the concept of "gross production" entirely; others do not wish to go that far — mainly for ideological reasons. In any case, a figure of the nature of net value added is now being calculated and used in planning.

But in this area the planned economy still requires substantial improvement. True, plans formulated now are more general, and plant directors have more freedom to decide how they wish to fulfill their part in the plan. Nevertheless, although they must meet the requirements not only of the gross production plan but also of the assortment plan, they will, if they find it impossible to fulfill both, prefer to meet the gross production goals.

Thus it becomes quite possible that a plan is overfulfilled at the same time that there are shortages that were not planned, as in the following instance:

In spite of overfulfillment of the plan, in spite of an increase of production by a fifth, there is much that is not in order. Neither the plan of final production nor of the production of spare parts was fulfilled either in timing or as to assortment. What good is it if an additional DM 5 million worth or more of spare parts is produced but not in the desired assortment? Thus the plan goal of spare parts for tractors and motors was not reached. . . . In the manufacture of agricultural machinery — and in other branches of machine construction — we frequently find the following tendencies: If parts for assembly are only intermittently delivered to a plant, it will use pieces planned as spare parts. This practice is as damaging as the other one, to offset a shortage of production in one line by producing an equal value of other goods.[4]

Again, it is difficult to say what all these complaints amount to, but they highlight shortcomings of the system of planning itself that might, somewhat epigrammatically, be referred to as the revenge of the price system. Planners are aware of the problem, but thus far they are attacking it only in part — by increasing the use of "economic levers," by adding to the number of plans that must be fulfilled simultaneously, or by increasing "political" and "economic" education.

It is startling to observe in East Germany a tendency to favor large projects and an attempt to heal the wounds of partition by "removing disproportionalities," as the communist phrase goes, by building up as full a complement of industries as feasible. It is puzzling to see these attempts and the a priori justifications offered for them. After all, it is not self-evident why even small areas such as East Germany should attempt to have as diversified an industrial structure as possible, or why large projects are endowed with special virtues not enjoyed by smaller undertakings.

The emphasis during the first two Five Year Plans (1951–1955, 1956–1960) has been on big projects, key projects, integrated projects, and heavy industry. When the war ended, there were observers who feared that the Soviet Union would try to become the major producer in heavy and key industries and would try to make over the satellite economies into feeder areas of light and "unessential" industries. Nothing of the kind happened (although one can be sure that Soviet control was not less strict for this reason).

It is possible that big projects are somehow associated in the mind of the communist planner with the creation of the industrial proletariat that is to form the social and class basis of the regime, but in East Germany an industrial proletariat did in fact exist before the advent of the conqueror. (If this were a reason, it would be somewhat reminiscent of our own advertisements assuring one that executives have large vocabularies; hence one can become an executive by developing a large vocabulary.)

It is more likely that the emphasis on big projects and heavy industries has other roots. Certainly a few big projects are easier to plan than many small ones; also, the problem of control is reduced. In a system that distrusts the market mechanism and, to start with, has tried to plan in physical rather than in value terms, big integrated projects have much to recommend them. Furthermore, in a capital-poor country big projects *seem* like a good way to economize scarce resources. (Oskar Lange, in writing on the economic program in Poland, pointed out that in fact the scarce resources there were squandered.[5]) It can also be observed that the planned economy in East Germany during the first half of the 1950's worked with minimal inventories in the hands of individual plants and always strained itself to the utmost. This is quite consistent with high inventory accumulation by the central authorities.

The explanation for this peculiar state of affairs undoubtedly is to be found in a combination of reasons, and I would put the factor of control high on the list. The individual manager wants to control as much as he can. Since he is responsible to the authorities for fulfilling his plan and therefore does not wish to depend too much on outside deliveries, he himself will tend to welcome the opportunity to produce parts that might otherwise be purchased outside the firm. The planner at the highest level will also tend to favor big projects as well as minimal inventories in the hands of individual plants in order to increase his control, even if it is purchased at the cost of a loss in efficiency. Moreover, big centralized inventories seem like a good way to save on material.

That things have not worked out that way is another matter. Here I wish only to suggest what the rationale for the behavior of the system might have been. Plans appear to have been drawn up in such a way that they might have been feasible under optimal conditions. *If* a worker had a continuous flow of high-quality materials to work with, he could perhaps fulfill his norm; *if* all raw materials were available at the proper time, the plans could be fulfilled. Yet we know from statements in the communist press that the plans were not fulfilled, and one asks why the planning system has not become more realistic.

To some extent it has. Constant revisions of plans may be signs of failures, but they may also be signs of increasing realism. Still a problem remains. The planner has certain priorities, and, in any case, he wants to maximize output, which is, as we shall see, defined in a somewhat peculiar manner in communist countries. To the extent that output is tied up in inventories it must appear as waste. To maximize output, goals are set beyond what is feasible on the theory that what will be achieved may fall short of the announced goal but will exceed what would have been achieved had a more modest goal been announced. One way of inducing managers to obey the plan would of course be to give them proper incentives in the form of appropriate prices, the method that is now being followed to an increasing extent but certainly was not followed before the formulation of the Second Five Year Plan for the years 1956–1960. During the First Five Year Plan a system of so-called *Messwerte,* or shadow prices (discussed in detail in Chapter 3), which made no sense even in its own terms, was used. Since 1956, factory prices actually received, which have themselves been reformed, have been used for planning and control.

If prices do not do the job, direct controls are needed, the chief mechanism of which, aside from direct allocation, is the banking system employed by every firm for its accounts and for all payments except those to the workers themselves. (A very interesting account of money in Socialism by an iron curtain economist, but in Western terms, appeared recently.[6]) Every undertaking receives a basic fund for wage payments, investments, and so on, the control problem being to assure that any money issued will flow back to the issuing authority promptly. Thus the only way in which an undertaking can get more money to purchase inventories or pay wages is to sell its output; keeping the manager short of cash *and* short of inventories forces him to produce fast and sell fast. If he were allowed more inventory to start with he might be more efficient, but the pressure to make him fulfill his sales plan would be removed; if he had more freedom for individual decision he might be more efficient, but control over what he did with the increased efficiency would be lessened. The conflict between control and efficiency is real as long as planning is primarily in physical terms and as long as there is no price system that expresses the values of the planner *and* is internally consistent.

So far as East Germany is concerned, it may be that particular planning methods were used simply because there were no appropriate precedents, and the simplest solution was to take over lock, stock, and barrel the methods developed in the Soviet Union. Thus the early failures may be interpreted as *Lehrgeld,* the tuition the economy had to pay for learning to adapt Soviet methods to East German conditions.

In a sense the old question of whether economic planning can work has already been answered in the affirmative by history. The Soviet Union has not yet collapsed because of any failure in its planning. But there can be no doubt that although projects dear to the planner can be achieved, they are often achieved at unnecessary cost; nor is there any doubt that planning becomes more efficient to the extent that it gets away from its original dream of doing away with money. That dream certainly has not been realized.

On the other hand, we are now learning that the use of a market mechanism does not inevitably make a free market, and that perhaps a free market does not inevitably make a free society. I cannot pretend to understand how the Communist Party keeps its power, but if, as history has shown, it can control its own monstrous secret police, for a while it can probably even control a market mechanism for its own ends. But these are political questions. From an economic standpoint there is at present a conflict between efficiency and control that could be reconciled in the planned economy by creating an internally consistent price system reflecting the values of the planner.

Were it not for the fact that the planned economy is a scarcity economy par excellence, even such a system might eventually create difficulties. There is a tremendous and almost mystical communist emphasis on investment and growth and on keeping consumption down. In terms of control, once more, consumers should not have too much cash on hand; they should immediately deposit what cash they have left in savings accounts so that there is a reflux of all money to the planner; and, preferably, they should spend their money on the goods that are in plentiful supply. There should be at all times an equilibrium between the money receipts and the money payments of the population. If consumers have too much cash, either because there are not enough goods to sell at the fixed prices or because they just do not like what has been produced, trouble ensues, and planning has gone wrong. Currency reforms are the externally visible sign of this trouble, which can be prevented by keeping the consumer short of funds.

Perhaps this statement is somewhat unfair. Although it was much below that of West Germany, the standard of living in East Germany has now improved and in 1957 may have been almost as high per capita as in 1936 (when it was still a depression standard that the Nazis had not permitted to rise very much). Nevertheless, there is currently an emphasis on investment and heavy industry that must be explained. Immediately after the war the need for investment and rebuilding was too obvious to need explanation. But why should the emphasis on investment now have the status of a *Weltanschauung*?

Marx analyzed capital formation in interesting ways, and all Marxist economists stress today that, if an economy is to grow, *Abteilung* I, that is, producer goods, must grow faster than *Abteilung* II, consumer goods. Some East German economists tried to prove that this was not necessarily the case and their contentions were quickly disputed by men of affairs, such as the then chief ideologist and theorist of the party, Fred Oelssner (who was himself dismissed from the Politbureau early in 1958). Whatever the current economic reason for the stress on investment, it has a clear ideological basis in Marxist theory; and the communist emphasis on growth undoubtedly derives from the fact that communism first came to power in a backward country.

Leaving Marxist economic theory aside, the reasons Soviet practice should be so slavishly imitated in East Germany are mainly political. The development of the East German economy is planned for communist political and economic ends — not for the benefit of the East German population, but to strengthen the military and political power of the Soviet Union and the bloc directly, or indirectly, by using the output of East Germany for the development of China, say, or of uncommitted areas.

This brings me to the final and startling fact that East German planning, not only for obvious reasons of control but also for other reasons to be discussed, has a strong autarkic bias. It has been directed toward eliminating disproportionalities caused by partition, communist planning being obsessed by the "law of the proportionate development of the economy."

West Germany moved decisively to integrate its economy with that of the free world, and its growth cannot be understood except as part of the growth of the free world. Moreover, the free world contains not only fast-growing economies — as does the communist world — but also the richest countries in the world. The East German economy has been only imperfectly — one might say crudely — integrated with that of a larger world; and the larger world for East Germany has been one which, although it has grown rapidly, has remained poor. Thus East Germany is almost a textbook case for the importance of being part of a larger area, of planning one nation's development in the context of a larger world, and for the desirability of being a member of a rich rather than a poor society.

Since this study does not deal anywhere in detail with the foreign trade of East Germany, a few facts may be appropriate here. According to official data, the area now East Germany had an export surplus in 1936, in 1951, and from 1954 to 1958; and it had import surpluses in the intervening years. But intra-German trade between East Germany and West Germany is only about 10 per cent of its prewar value despite the fact that prices are now much higher. These data are expressed in reichsmarks (RM) for the prewar year and in either East German Deutschemarks (DM-Ost) or rubles for the postwar years and refer, of course, only to commercial transactions excluding reparations. At this time no data on the postwar terms of trade are available.

In 1955, 73 per cent of East German exports went to the Soviet bloc, 16 per cent to capitalist countries (including India), and 11 per cent to West Germany; imports were distributed in the ratio of 71 per cent, 18 per cent, and 11 per cent, respectively. All these figures are based on official data expressed in rubles at unknown prices f.o.b. shipping country for both imports and exports. In 1956, of the total exports valued at 5.013 billion rubles (excluding intra-German trade), 2.277 billion went to the Soviet Union, 556 million to Poland, 439 million to Czechoslovakia, and 380 million to Communist China. West Germany received 616 million rubles' worth of goods; the next most important capitalist country, Holland, received only 85 million. Of total imports of 4.750 billion rubles in the same year from the non-German world, the Soviet Union supplied 2.228 billion, Poland 419 million, Czechoslovakia 421 million, and China 344 million. West Germany exported 585 million rubles and Holland sent 108 million.[7]

These figures are not easy to interpret in detail, and their incompatibility with Soviet trade statistics points out the extent of our ignorance of the prices used to value foreign trade. Thus in 1957 the East Germans reported an export surplus to the Soviet Union of 295 million rubles, while in the same year the Soviet Union claimed to have an export surplus to East Germany of 390.8 million rubles. Since both sets of figures refer to rubles and f.o.b. prices for both exports and imports, the only rational explanation is that each country values its shipments at different prices. For the present purpose we need not go into these still unsolved problems. Suffice it to say that the percentage distribution of imports and exports for 1956 is also characteristic for other years.

What makes East German trade particularly significant is not only that it is with a poor world but also that it is essentially on a bilateral basis at prices that are only partly known. Trade between a communist country and the "capitalist" world takes place at world market prices, we are told,[8] while intra-bloc trade is all settled by haggling — Ausfeilschen — a rather opprobrious term. The prices used do not necessarily have anything to do with world market prices or domestic costs of production or with comparative costs. If domestic prices are higher than export prices, subsidies are given, and any export profits are taxed away. So far as possible the domestic and foreign price structures are kept separate.

The bilateralism is evidenced by the fact that in any one year the exports to a particular country and from it do not differ very much. More important, any excess or shortage must be settled by special agreement. Although the ruble may be based on gold and be as sound as gold, it is not an international currency even within the bloc; it may be used as a unit of account, but no bloc member can, without special arrangements, transfer ruble balances acquired in Moscow to another country or use them for triangular offsets. This restriction has apparently been modified but not abolished by recent agreements.[9]

The failure to treat international trade, even theoretically, on a respectable level is startling, but it undoubtedly has historic origins. Until ten or fifteen years ago the problem of trade among socialist countries simply did not arise — there was only the Soviet Union. Communist literature before 1957 abounded with statements that trade should be "naturally" balanced bilaterally because it is only fair to exchange equals for equals (whatever this is supposed to mean), but there is now an awareness of the wastefulness of such bilateral procedures.

The fact remains that planning during the period of the First Five Year Plan of East Germany and of all the other satellites proceeded essentially on a national scale. Although the Second Five Year Plan, which started in 1956, was supposed to be internationally coordinated, there is no evidence that the problems of multilateralism have been solved within the Soviet bloc, and there is some evidence to the contrary. The international coordination of the Second Five Year Plans appears to have been essentially a partial coordination of trading plans, which, however, was not intended to affect the planning of production. The problem of permitting the operation of some spontaneous elements, which foreign trade necessarily represents, must certainly offer difficulties to centrally planned economies. Control of deliveries lies outside the borders; and to permit transfers of balances even within the bloc would lead to changes not so much in the aggregate demand — which to the planned economy would hardly matter much — as in the demand for individual goods, which would matter very much.

Only in the preparation of the Third Five Year Plan for the years 1961–1965 will international coordination reach down to the actual formulation of production plans. I shall have something to say on this matter in the estimation of future developments below.

Clearly, the failure to plan internationally during the decade of the fifties forced even small areas to plan "balanced" growth, as this term might be understood in East Germany. Although the inherited industrial structure and the natural resource endowments made some trade inevitable, in the absence of a pricing mechanism or an effective international planning substitute, trade undoubtedly remained less than it should have been and it certainly shifted from more to less efficiently produced goods. The changes planned for 1961–1965 indicate that the planners have become conscious of these weaknesses.

The wastefulness can be illustrated by the following example. East Germany was a fertile agricultural area. Although not the breadbasket of the Reich, it had an exportable surplus of grains and was a major sugar beet and potato producer and exporter. In 1956 East Germany imported one million tons of bread grains, and its agricultural production was down — for two reasons, insufficient investment in farms and not enough fertilizer. Some fertilizers, such as phosphates, must be imported; others of which farmers do not have enough, such as potash, are produced in sufficient amounts, but in 1955 about 1 million tons of a total production of 1.5 million tons of potash were exported to pay for imports of food and raw materials. Export demands determined in such a bilateral and arbitrary manner also explain why agricultural investment is not higher. In fact, I have calculated (see Chapter XX) that total investment in equipment between 1950 and 1954 was 40 per cent or less of production of investment goods (defined as the output of the engineering-construction industries, of road vehicles, except bicycles and motorcycles, electrical machinery production, and fine mechanics and optics) and rose in 1956 to about 50 per cent.

Thus the conclusion is almost inevitable that in East Germany the structure of foreign trade has been inefficient, that it has shifted exports and imports from more to less efficient lines, has interfered with investments and consumption, and has depressed the possible output. No wonder that the East German planners would like increased trade with the "capitalist world" market and less with the "democratic world" market.

The reader may at this point say: Well, all this is in the past. What about the future? Is it not likely that the East German economy will perform much better in the future than in the past? After all, you have told us that reparations (but not occupation costs) were abolished by 1954. We have read in the papers that beginning in 1959 East Germany will save another 600 million rubles because the Soviet Union has agreed to forego payments for occupation costs, and this adds to the resources available for economic development in East Germany. The price system was reformed and rationing was abolished in 1958. And the international planning of the bloc also has made progress.

The questions are well taken. Undoubtedly the economy will perform better in the future. In 1958, for the first time, there was evidence that West German growth was rather small, about 2.8 per cent in real terms, and there is a likelihood that East German growth during that year was bigger, although, as this chapter is written, sufficient data on East German production have not yet been published to make possible even a rough calculation.

There are, however, several other factors involved. In the first place, there is no reason to suppose that the decline in the rate of growth of the West German economy is permanent. The West German problem has become the "Keynesian" problem of insufficient demand; the East German problem continues to be the "classical" problem of insufficient productivity, and the difference is great. Second, East Germany still loses several hundred thousand people every year, which must be a drain and is certainly a sign of the performance of the economy as well as of the state. Third, although the East Germans are learning how to plan and although the price system has been improved, there remains the unresolved question of how far this process can go under centralized political control.

Finally, the improvement in international planning is far from perfect. There is evidence that the structure of the East German economy is being shifted back toward the production of the traditional labor-intensive goods, such as fine mechanics, but there is no evidence that East Germany will be exploited any less on behalf of the development of the Soviet bloc. Nor is there evidence that the problem of pricing in international trade or the problem of multilateralism has been solved satisfactorily.

The problems of the efficient international integration of East Germany into the Soviet bloc receives increasing attention from East German writers, and the Warsaw Pact countries have in fact decided to coordinate production plans beginning with 1961. On the theoretical level, discussions deal with measuring the effectiveness of international trade and establishing the prices to be used. Imre Vajda, writing on pricing on the socialist world market has all but suggested that the "socialist law of proportionate development of the economy" be applied not as in the past to a single country but to the Soviet bloc as a whole.[10]

Existing information on communist international planning relates mostly, however, to production plans rather than to prices. The construction of a pipeline from the Soviet Union to start a major petrochemical industry has received wide attention. More interesting for our present purpose is the projected specialization in machine construction, which indicates that the expansion of metallurgy and heavy machine building requiring large imports is to be halted. Walter Mostertz, in an article on specialization and coordination in machine building among the socialist countries, comments:

In principle, the profile of machine construction of a country with a weak metallurgical base will always tend toward wage-intensive production.[11]

And, although some industrialization is necessary everywhere, he continues:

[It] is not necessary that all industries be equally developed everywhere. Considering the economic strength *of the whole socialist camp,* one should concentrate on those branches which correspond to the peculiarities of the particular country. . . . Basically, specialization in machine building must be diverted to ensure that all countries [of the socialist camp] are supplied with such machines as are not yet produced or are imported from the capitalist world.

The measures of international division of labor must increase the ability of each country and therefore of the whole socialist camp to defend itself. But this results only within limits in the production of the same goods in all countries.[12]

The application of the law of comparative advantage has certain specific results. Whereas in the past East Germany built ships of many sizes although only in small numbers, now only the Soviet Union will produce ships of all sizes up to 25,000 BRT (gross registered tons), particularly tankers and specialized ocean-going fishing vessels, and East Germany will specialize in ocean-going freighters of 3000 and 10,000 BRT. East Germany will produce machinery for the production of synthetic fibers and products made of lignite, leaving the production of machinery for soft coal mining and coking to Poland and that for bauxite to Hungary. Potato harvesting machines will now be produced only in East Germany and Poland, those for corn in Rumania and Hungary, and sugar beet combines will be made in East Germany and Czechoslovakia.

Because the bloc as a whole already has enough spindles and looms, planned investments in their manufacture in East Germany were cut by 24 million East marks. The quantities and types of other machinery to be manufactured in East Germany have also been reduced as the result of international planning: 27 types of industrial diesel locomotives instead of 40, and 56 types of machine tools instead of 64. Furthermore it appears that since trucks everywhere in the bloc are too heavy relative to their capacity, engineering research must be coordinated.[13] (Further details on the results of the conference of May 20 to 23, 1958 of the members of the Council for Mutual Economic Aid can be found in an article by Georg Henke and Lothar Rouscik on a new phase of economic cooperation in the socialist camp, which also describes some of the deliveries of entire factories made by East Germany to other bloc countries.[14])

Thus the international coordination of the bloc seems to be progressing and East Germany apparently is going to produce more of the goods in which she has a comparative advantage. This cannot help but improve the performance of the economy. Yet it is clear that there are limits to this kind of physical planning on an international scale. Unless the organization of international trade itself is improved, unless reasonable prices are used and multilateral clearing is established as a matter of course, the international integration will be substantially less efficient than it might be. Possibly these problems will be solved in due time. At present, the published discussion shows only an awareness of the problem; the proposed solutions themselves are still primitive.

Before proceeding to a detailed analysis of the East German economy, it seems worth while to summarize here some of our conclusions with regard to the imposition of the communist planned economy on East Germany. First, in East Germany all problems have been complicated by inefficient planning and inefficient and insufficient integration into a poor world. During the last few years planning has been improved, and one cannot rule out the possibility that East German planners will continue to learn how to use prices efficiently, how to decentralize, and how to deal with international problems; but when they do, the mechanism of planning will become increasingly similar to that of free societies.

Second, planning in East Germany — it may be different in the Soviet Union, but it seems to be true of all the satellites — has not made optimal use of the available resources, including resources for capital formation, nor has it used them as efficiently as they have been used in West Germany. Some of these inefficiencies become evident in the comparisons with West Germany; others can be established beyond doubt without such comparison.

Third — a conclusion which needs no East-West statistics — is the fact that the political costs of the communist system *do* matter, and in East Germany they have resulted directly in a population loss. Between 1950 and 1956, in spite of the fact that in each of these years there were more births than deaths, the net decline in the East German population was 672,000 persons. The westward migration in Germany has a long history, the West-East gradient of wages being a well-known and well-studied phenomenon in Germany. The significant fact is that all the deliberate policies for the development of East Germany have been unable to reverse the century-old tendency.

Fourth, if one compares the economic development of West Germany with that of East Germany, it is obvious that, compared with the prewar period, West Germany has done much better both in the aggregate and on a per capita basis in all sectors but mining. Compared with 1936, the East German gross national product has increased only about 10 to 20 per cent in the aggregate; compared with 1950, when the First Five Year Plan was inaugurated, the over-all growth is about 60 per cent. However, agricultural output in 1956 was no greater than in 1950 and was much below the 1936 level; industrial output was about 80 per cent above 1950, but only 30 per cent above 1936. Although the rates of economic growth in East and West Germany have been similar since 1950, the actual levels of production are much lower in East Germany than in West Germany. The relative positions of East and West Germany will undoubtedly continue.

Finally, a somewhat chastening comment. In spite of the undeniable shortcomings of the communist East German system, it does show growth. The labor inputs are high, and people work longer hours than in West Germany and get less for their work; but, even where the communist system is less rational and less efficient than the market economy, it seems that human effort, however extracted, can overcome the irrationality and inefficiency to a remarkable extent.

PART ONE

POPULATION MOVEMENTS
AND THE LABOR FORCE
IN EAST GERMANY

CHAPTER I

POPULATION AND THE LABOR FORCE

Aℒᴛʜᴏᴜɢʜ the division of Germany in 1945 left the Eastern and Western Zones with the same over-all proportions of various types of economic activity, the gross aggregative figures hide important differences that indicate that the Eastern Zone has in fact suffered more than the Western Zone by the division. In addition to similar cultural, economic, and natural resource endowments, both areas at the end of the war were left with a distorted population pyramid. The mere passage of time since the end of the war has tended to normalize the population pyramid, but the substantial East-West movement of population has been only in small part offset by a return flow from the West. The populations of the two areas have, for a number of years, developed in opposite directions. The East-West movement has been going on for a hundred years, but in recent years it has been primarily among persons of working age and among men. Thus the age and sex distribution of West Germany had tended to become more normal at the expense of an offsetting deterioration in East Germany.

Economic planning has had to cope with this difficulty. Even if planning had been ideally efficient and the regime popular with its own people, the problem would have arisen. Under ideal conditions East Germany might have lost fewer people; it would nevertheless have lost some. There are some indications that it is not merely the lack of political popularity of the communist regime but also the economic opportunities in the West that have increasingly attracted migrants, two factors that are not independent of each other. For the economic planner the migration and resulting structure of the population have had serious effects, since the fulfillment of the Plans requires the successful mobilization of all available manpower.

The development of manpower in East Germany, which sets serious limits on any plans for economic development is encountering many difficulties: although still larger than in 1939, the total population has been declining since 1949; the ratio of women to men is unusually large and increasing; and the number of men and women of working age is not increasing and will probably decline.

POPULATION STRUCTURE

Compared with 1939, the areas of both the Federal Republic and East Germany contain many more inhabitants, mainly because of the influx of expellees. In fact, Germany with its 1937 borders had 67.3 million inhabitants in 1936, 69.3 million in 1939, and a maximum of 70.8 million in 1942. Table 2 shows the estimated population for both the

Table 2

Population of areas of the Federal Republic and East Germany,
1936, 1939, and 1946–1958 (millions)

| Year | Federal Republic[a] | | East Germany[b] | Federal Republic (including West Berlin) plus East Germany |
	Excluding West Berlin	Including West Berlin		
1936	38.2	40.950	16.160	57.110
1939[c]	39.3	42.1	16.745[c]	58.845
1946[d]	43.694	45.707	18.057	61.751
1947	44.6	46.651	18.892	65.543
1948	45.9	48.002	19.066	67.068
1949	46.8	48.905	18.892	67.797
1950[d]	47.519	49.658	18.388[d]	68.046
1951	48.079	50.241	18.351	68.592
1952	48.478	50.642	18.328	68.970
1953	48.994	51.227	18.178	69.405
1954	49.516	51.708	18.059	69.767
1955	49.995	52.190	17.944	70.134
1955 (31 Dec.)	50.318	52.521	17.832	70.353
1956	50.595	52.900	17.716	70.616
1956 (31 Dec.)	50.111[e]	52.335[e]	17.604	69.939[e]
1957	50.473[e]	52.698[e]	17.517	70.215[e]
1957 (31 Dec.)	50.813[e]	53.042[e]	17.411	70.453[e]
1958 (31 Dec.)	51.452[e]	53.678[e]	17.312	70.990[e]

Sources: Federal Republic: *SJBR*, 1956, p. 30; 1957, p. 32; 1958, p. 28. East Germany: *SJDDR*, 1956, p. 7; 1958, p. 7. West Berlin: Figures for the years 1946 through 1949 are from *SJBR*, 1955, p. 14; for other years, *SJBR*, 1955 p. 30; 1956, p. 32; 1957, p. 28.
a Figures refer to the middle of the year except when they refer to census dates. They exclude the Saar.
b Figures refer to the average annual population, except when they refer to census dates.
c Census results as of 17 May 1939.
d Census data.
e The apparent decline is spurious. *SJBR*, 1958, p. 28, contains revised estimates for 1952 through 1957 that are slightly below previous estimates.

Federal Republic and East Germany since 1936. From these figures it is apparent that about as many people lived in the two parts of postwar Germany in 1948 as in the old Reich of 1936, and that by 1954 the population level of 1939 had again been reached. For the labor force and future prospects for economic growth, however, the considerably changed age and sex structure is decisive.

At the end of 1955 East Germany had over a million more inhabitants than in 1939, but the number of men had decreased. In 1939, 8.1 million men were counted in the area comprising East Germany;[1] by 29 October 1946 (that is, before the return of prisoners of war and the great influx of expellees) the number of men counted was 7.792 million; by 31 August 1950 it had risen to 8.161 million; but by the end of 1955 it had fallen to 7.969 million. By the end of 1957, the number of men had fallen further to 7.795 million.[2] The population increase of East Germany since 1939, about 6.5 per cent, was entirely due to an increase of about 15 per cent in the female population. Compared with 1946, East Germany by the end of 1957 had lost 943,400 women and 1,000 men, but compared with 1950, it had lost 331,800 women and 366,000 men. The losses may be attributed mainly to a migration to the West and, at least until 1948, to an excess of deaths over births.[3] From 1946 to 1948, inclusive, the excess of deaths amounted to 381,757. For the years 1949 through 1955 the excess of births over deaths is claimed to be 529,975; for the years 1950 through 1957, it is 627,416. Since the total population declined by 1.375 million people from 1950 through 1957 (average population 1957 less average population 1949), there must have been a net migration of 2.002 million persons in those eight years, surely a substantial number by any standard and probably the most serious indictment of the regime.

The migration from East to West is estimated at 130,000 for 1947, and 150,000 for 1948.[4] For the years since 1949 the Federal Republic has published figures on the number of persons presenting themselves in emergency camps as refugees. These figures do not include the substantial number of other people who come, nor do they allow for the much smaller stream of persons returning to the East. The figures are given in Table

Table 3

East-West migration: persons presenting themselves in emergency camps, 1949–1958

Year	Refugees
1949–1951	492,681
1952	182,393
1953	331,390
1954	184,198
1955	252,870
1956	279,189
1957	261,622
1958	204,092
Total	2,188,435

Source: Kurt Spormann, "Der permanente Flüchtlingsstrom," *Bulletin des Presse- und Informationsdienstes der Bundesregierung,* 17 January 1959, No. 11, p. 99.

3. The stream of refugees continues at the rate of 2,500 to 5,000 a week.

Thus from 1949 through 1958, 2.188 million refugees officially asked to be admitted to the Federal Republic and to receive assistance, a figure which is consistent with the population loss implied in the East German statistics.

The net decrease in the population of East Germany during the nine years 1950 through 1958 amounted to over two million, about 11 per cent of the entire 1950 population, and more than three times the natural population increase during those years. Although the number of persons fleeing East Germany decreased after 1953, the year of the June uprising, the loss is truly staggering. Unlike the probable pattern of the earlier period, the migration after 1950 undoubtedly affected the most productive age groups, and men more than women. The official figures for the population structure by sex of the Eastern Zone, exclusive of East Berlin, are given in Table 4.

Table 4

Population structure by sex, East Germany, selected years, 1939–1958 (thousands)

	Male	Female	Total	Percentage female
May 1939,	8.1	8.6	16,745.0	51.4
of which East Berlin	0.7	0.9	1,588.0	56.7
October 1946,	7,796.2	10,558.8	18,355.0	57.5
of which East Berlin	480.0	694.6	1,174.6	59.1
August 1950,	8,161.2	10,227.0	18,388.2	55.6
of which East Berlin	506.4	682.7	1,189.1	57.4
December 1955,	7,968.7	9,863.5	17,832.2	55.3
of which East Berlin	486.7	653.2	1,139.9	57.3
December 31, 1956,	7,876.3	9,727.3	17,603.6	55.3
of which East Berlin	478.5	643.4	1,121.9	57.3
December 31, 1957,	7,795.2	9,615.4	17,410.7	55.2
of which East Berlin	473.1	636.9	1,110.0	57.4
December 31, 1958,	7,769.8	9,541.9	17,311.7	55.1
of which East Berlin	464.3	626.0	1,090.4	57.4

Sources: *SJDDR*, 1955, pp. 8, 9 except for figures for males and females for 1939, which are from *SJBR*, 1956, p. 13; *SJDDR*, 1956, pp. 24, 25; 1957, pp. 24–26; 1958, pp. 8, 9. Percentages calculated.

Migration accounts for the fact that in the immediate postwar years, as prisoners of war returned, the ratio of women to men tended to improve in both parts of Germany, and that it later deteriorated again in the Eastern Zone and improved in West Germany. Before the war there were 103.4 women per 100 men in the area of the Eastern Zone (excluding East

Berlin) and 103.5 per 100 in the area of the Federal Republic (excluding West Berlin). In 1946 the figures were 135.4 and 121.9 for East Germany and the Federal Republic, respectively, and by 1950 the ratios had improved in both parts of Germany — to 125.3 and 113.4, respectively. By 1955 they had improved slightly for both areas — to 123.8 in the German Democratic Republic and 112.5 in West Germany. The ratio of women to men is the same in East and West Berlin, about 135.5:100.[5] (See Table 5.)

Table 5

Ratio of women to men, East Germany, Federal Republic,
and Berlin, selected years 1939–1958 (per cent)

	East Germany		Federal Republic	
	Including East Berlin	East Berlin only	Excluding West Berlin	West Berlin only
May 1939	106.2	128.6	103.6	125.0
October 1946	135.4	144.7	122.9	147.5
August 1950	125.3	134.8	n.a.	n.a.
September 1950	n.a.	n.a.	113.4	135.5
December 1955	123.8	134.2	n.a.	n.a.
June 1955	n.a.	n.a.	112.5	135.3
December 1957	123.0	135.0	n.a.	n.a.
June 1958	n.a.	n.a.	112.4	135.7
December 1958	122.8	134.8	n.a.	n.a.

Sources: *SJDDR*, 1955, p. 9; 1957, p. 26; 1958, pp. 8, 9; *SJBR*, 1956, pp. 13, 31, 37; 1959, p. 35.

Although the sex structure of a new generation is, of course, likely to be the same in both parts of Germany, the slower normalization in East Germany indicates that the population must be expected either to continue to fall there or at least to rise less than in West Germany. This fact alone must create difficulties for production in East Germany, which suffers even more than West Germany from labor shortages.

Two attempts to account for the population change, 1948–1955, are presented in Table 6. The first is an estimate from the Deutsches Institut für Wirtschaftsforschung; the second — using in part the same figures — is based on official East German figures.

The balance sheet leaves no doubt as to the correctness of the figures for persons migrating westward, which in fact may even be slightly greater than assumed by the Institute. The implications for the labor force are very serious. In East Germany, persons of working age are defined as all men aged 15–64, and women age 15–59 years inclusive. In 1939 East Germany, inclusive of East Berlin, had 11.310 million persons of both sexes in these age groups, or 67.5 per cent of the population. The ratio of men to women was 102.4 to 100. By October 29, 1946 the number had

Table 6

Analysis of population change, East Germany,
31 December 1948–31 December 1955 (millions)

	DIW data	Official data
	(1)	(2)
Population, 31 December 1948	19.068	18.989
Migration, 1948–1955	−1.828	−1.828
Excess of deaths over births, 1949–1950	−.035	——— 17.161
Excess of births over deaths, 1951–1955	+.500	+.530
Return migration	+.180	+.180
Immigration from countries of Soviet bloc	+.015	+.015
		——— 17.896
Population as of 31 December 1955	17.900	17.832

Sources: Col. 1: *DIW, Wochenbericht*, 24 February 1956, No. 8, p. 33. Col. 2: *SJDDR*, 1955. Estimate of 31 December 1948 population is arithmetic mean of average populations of 1948 and 1949.

increased slightly to 11.552 million, of which over 6.8 million were women. By August 31, 1950 the total had again increased, to 11.646 million. The male labor force increased sharply with returning prisoners of war and the influx of expellees and other immigrants while the number of women declined. By the end of 1955 all figures had declined, but those of the male labor force the least. Table 7 shows the official figures for East Germany and the Federal Republic.

The figures clearly show that in East Germany (1) the potential labor force (that is, persons of working age)* is a smaller percentage of the total population, and the percentage of both the young *and* the old is greater than before the war; (2) the ratio of women to men in the potential labor force is unusually unfavorable, with obvious implications for the efficiency of an industrialization program that relies strongly on heavy industries; (3) since the older age groups are relatively more numerous than they used to be, even such improvement in the structure of the population as has taken place has been accompanied by a decline in the potential labor force.

By contrast, in 1939 the proportion of the population of working age as well as the proportion of males in the potential labor force was more favorable in the area now East Germany than in that of the Federal Republic. Since the war the proportions have been consistently and substantially more favorable in the Western area. Moreover, although the proportion of men in the potential labor force has improved sharply in both parts of Germany, it is still substantially below the prewar norm. The potential labor force has been a declining proportion of the total

* Actually, persons above the retirement age are undoubtedly working. Figures in the Statistical Yearbook of the German Democratic Republic, 1958, pp. 266 ff. indicate that as many as 3 per cent of all production workers may be 65 years of age and over.

Table 7

Persons of working age, East Germany and Federal Republic, selected years, 1939–1958

A. *East Germany*

	Total (thousands)	Per cent of popu- lation	Men, aged 15–64 (thousands)	Women, aged 15–59 (thousands)	Per cent of men in potential labor force
	(1)[a]	(2)	(3)	(4)	(5)[a]
17 May 1939	11,309.7	67.5	5,721.3	5,588.4	50.6
29 Oct. 1946	11,552.4	62.5	4,736.5	6,815.8	41.0
31 Aug. 1950	11,646.1	63.3	5,185.0	6,461.1	44.5
31 Dec. 1955	11,269.4	63.2	5,153.1	6,116.2	45.7
31 Dec. 1957	10,899.3	62.6	5,037.9	5,861.4	46.2
31 Dec. 1958	10,781.5	62.3	5,019.4	5,762.1	46.6

B. *Federal Republic*

Excluding West Berlin

17 May 1939	26,206	66.6	13,215	12,991	50.4
29 Oct. 1946	27,901	63.8	12,300	15,601	44.1
13 Sept. 1950	30,825	64.6	14,620	16,204	47.4
31 Dec. 1954	32,647	65.6	15,721	16,925	48.2
31 Dec. 1956	33,140	66.1	16,021	17,119	48.3
31 Dec. 1957	33,312	65.6	16,145	17,167	48.5

Including West Berlin

31 Dec. 1954	34,069	65.5	16,356	17,713	48.0
31 Dec. 1956	34,590	66.1	16,675	17,915	48.2

Sources: East Germany: *SJDDR*, 1955, pp. 24, 25; 1957, p. 26, 1958, p. 24. Federal Republic: *SJBR*, 1953, pp. 44, 45; 1956, p. 42; 1959, p. 40.
 [a] Col. 1: Col. 3 + col. 4. Col. 5: Col. 3 ÷ col. 1.

population in East Germany, but an increasing one in West Germany.

Besides the changed sex and age distribution, the fact that numerous persons suffer from the effects of the war has affected the efficiency of the labor force. Günther Ipsen has made an attempt to recalculate the labor force in terms of a standard, defined as the physical working ability of a man between the ages of 20 and 24 (VAK = *Vollarbeitskraft*). To quote his findings:

In the area of the later German Democratic Republic (i.e., the Zone plus East Berlin), there were in 1939 8.6 million VAK. The labor value index (i.e., the ratio of VAK to labor force) of 0.719 surpassed the German and West German average of 0.709 substantially, thanks to a favorable age distribution. By 1946 population increased by 1.8 million, but the labor potential of 8.61 million VAK remained unchanged. The increase was a burden, not a benefit. Even at its most favorable moment at the end of 1948 it was only 8.9 million VAK, which is just slightly higher. Since 1949 the labor potential has declined: by 1951 it had fallen below the prewar level; at the beginning of 1953 it was 8.22; and at the beginning of 1955 it was 8 million VAK.[6]

Ipsen does not give the details of his calculations. However, with all the skepticism one naturally must have, it seems legitimate to conclude that increases in numbers do not necessarily mean an increase in labor availability when efficiency is taken into account, and that population developments eventually set serious limits to attempts at increasing output. But, as will be shown in the following section, there must have been some hidden unemployment, and it is unlikely that the labor force was the actual limiting factor prior to 1955.

LABOR FORCE

If the population figures are correct, it follows that any increase in output can come about only if the actual (as distinguished from the potential) labor force is increased by absorbing unemployed workers, working longer hours, using a higher percentage of women, young persons, and other persons not normally in the active labor force or by increasing the productivity of labor. Productivity could be increased by technological progress, improved capital equipment, or better organization of the production process. A final possibility consists in an improved organization of the labor market so that even frictional unemployment is minimized.

All methods are used in East Germany. In his talk on the First Five Year Plan, Walter Ulbricht stated that the aim of the plan was to increase the proportion of women in the labor force to 42 per cent by 1955,

Table 8

Percentage of women in the employed labor force and among
employees only, East Germany, selected years, 1939–1958

Year	Employed labor force[a]	Year	Total employees only
	(1)		(2)
1939	36.7	1950	38.4
1946	44.9	1951	38.8
1948	41.0	1952	40.2
1950	37.0	1953	40.6
1952	42.3	1954	41.9
1953	42.8	1955	41.7
1954	43.8	1956	42.0
1955	42.0 Plan	1957	42.0[b]
1955	43.7 Actual	1958	42.8[b]
1956	46.6		
1957	44.0		
1958	43.5[b]		

Sources: Col. 1: For 1939, 1946, and 1948, see Bruno Gleitze, "Das Problem der gespaltenen Wirtschaft Deutschlands," *Mitteilungen des Wirtschaftswissenschaftlichen Instituts der Gewerkschaften*, February–March 1954, Vol. VII, No. 2/3, p. 29, based in part on the estimates of the Deutsches Institut für Wirtschaftsforschung, West Berlin; for 1950 and 1955 (Plan), W. Ulbricht, *Der Fünfjahrplan und die Perspektiven der Volkswirtschaft* (East Berlin, Dietz, 1950), p. 51; and for 1952–1958, *SJDDR*, 1957, p. 182; 1958, pp. 194, 197. Col. 2: *SP*, July 1956, p. 90; and *SJDDR*, 1956, p. 168; 1957, p. 179.
    [a] Includes self-employed.   [b] Preliminary.

the last year of the First Five Year Plan, compared with 37 per cent in 1950. The percentage of women in the labor force is given in Table 8.

Ulbricht's statement implies that in 1950 the total working population must have been about 6,692,000, of which about 2,476,000 were women, but this figure is almost certainly too low. To quote Ulbricht at length:

> The total working population* in 1955 must rise to 113.3 per cent of 1950, i.e., 890,000 more persons must be active in the economy [implies total employment of 6.692 million]; of these, 448,000 will be in industry, 230,000 in construction, and 25,000 in transport. The share of technical personnel must, however, rise faster than the number of production workers, namely, by 26.5 per cent.
>
> Compared with 1950, the percentage of female labor in the economy as a whole must rise from 37 per cent to 42 per cent, and in nationalized industry from 33.3 to 42 per cent. It is therefore necessary to overcome the reactionary view that a few factory directors hold against the employment of female labor. This is particularly true in the Reichsbahn, where the share of female labor is only 6 per cent. In order to increase the number of skilled female workers, the number of women apprentices will be increased to 48 per cent.[7]

Employment in 1955 was originally planned to be about 7.781 million, of which 3.268 million were to be women. This means that of the planned increase of 880,000, about 792,000 (almost 88 per cent) were expected to be women. A revision of the Five Year Plan, however, reduced the planned employment by 1955 to 7.1 million and the proportion of women to 39 per cent.[8] Even this more modest proposal envisaged an increase in employment of 410,000 persons, of which 293,000, or about three-fourths, were to be women.

It must be pointed out that it is quite unclear precisely to what category of labor the figures refer. Although the term *Beschäftigte* clearly can refer to anyone in the economy, it is possible that the figures refer only to persons working in "material production." By the end of 1955 the total number of persons working in "material production" was 7.167 million, or roughly the number planned. This explanation is, however, only a supposition unsupported by any official (or unofficial) statement.

The figures indicate that the chief increase in employment to produce the planned increase in production was to come from the thus far unexploited reservoir of female labor. This obviously requires a much greater increase of female labor in manufacturing industry, as indicated by the figures quoted for nationalized industry, which includes all heavy industries as well as most other manufacturing industries. The absorption of so many additional women into the labor force is a revolution in age-old habits that cannot be expected to come off smoothly. In the communist system everyone physically able to work is obviously to be integrated into the planned production process, even if he would not voluntarily go on the labor market if a Western context prevailed. Thus an increase in the

---

* The term used is *"Beschäftigte,"* or occupied, without reference to whether they are self-employed, employees, etc.

labor force requires "social" measures such as the cutting of social security payments to force women, older people, and the disabled onto the labor market. It also requires the organization of collective kitchens, factory kindergartens, and so on. These conditions must be kept in mind in interpreting the unemployment figures to be given presently.

Detailed official figures for all persons in the productive process by social category as well as by industrial classification are now available for the years 1952 through 1957. For the years 1950 through 1955 we also have figures for workers and employees only and for apprentices. No figures appear to be available for other groups in the working population prior to 1952,* and there are none for any groups before 1950. The data are presented in Table 9.

Table 9

Working population, all economic sectors, East Germany, 1950–1958 (thousands)

	1950	1951	1952	1953	1954	1955	1956	1957	1958a
			A. *End of year*						
1. Workers and employees			6,004.6	6,215.2	6,510.2	6,459.8	6,482.2	6,576.7	6,513.1
2. Members of cooperatives			39.6	123.5	159.4	192.8	219.3	236.8	419.1
3. Self-employed persons			1,025.1	948.2	919.0	928.3	889.0	847.4	746.5
4. Working family members			783.8	668.4	657.4	650.0	587.9	575.0	497.5
5. Totalb			7,853.2	7,955.1	8,246.1	8,231.8	8,178.3	8,235.9	8,176.3
			B. *Annual averages, workers and employees only*						
6. Workers and employees	5,268.4	5,603.0	5,815.7	5,991.7	6,362.9	6,411.0	6,366.8	6,491.9	6,416.0
7. Apprentices	372.4	486.5	507.8	492.4	472.2	453.8	439.8	427.0	388.0
8. Persons looking for employment	325.4	243.4	107.2	90.9	54.3	43.6	40.8	negl.	negl.
9. Total labor force (employed plus unemployed)c			7,960.4	8,046.0	8,300.4	8,275.4	8,219.1	8,235.9	8,176.3

Sources: Year-end figures: *SJDDR*, 1955, p. 106. Annual averages: for workers and employees, *ibid.*, p. 111; for apprentices, *ibid.*, p. 116. Apprentices are included among workers and employees, *ibid.*, p. 104, introductory note. For unemployed: *ibid.*, p. 119, and *SJDDR*, 1956, pp. 166, 182; 1957, pp. 176, 178; 1958, pp. 194, 210.
    a Preliminary.   b Totals do not add up because of rounding.   c Sum of lines 5 and 8.

It is not clear whether persons registered as looking for employment are included in the official figures. In the following discussion it will be assumed that they are not. It is explicitly stated that the figures do *not* include, among others, the following working persons: employees of the Ministry of Interior, including those in plants run by the Ministry, the people's police, members of the armed forces, persons employed in uranium mining, and employees of offices abroad. That is, the armed forces, the secret police, concentration camp labor, and the possibly forced labor in uranium mining are excluded.

At the same time it is just as explicitly stated that everyone who works more than six weeks is counted, whether working full time or part

* But see Chapter II, particularly Tables 12 and 13, for a reconstruction of the employment picture in 1950 and 1951.

time, on vacation, or sick.[9] No attempt is made to convert part-time work into full-time equivalents.

The figures indicate that total employment had hit a peak by the end of 1954 and then declined slightly. Even in 1957, when there was an increase again, total employment was less than in 1954. The declining population, and particularly the declining number in the potential labor force (and perhaps also increased rearmament), appears to have caught up with actual employment only in 1954 or 1955. Until then it clearly was not the limiting factor in the development of increased employment.

A rough calculation, taking the number of actually employed as a percentage of the potential labor force for 1939 and 1955, indicates that the increase in the working labor force recruited from among the unemployed must have been larger than was admitted. In 1939 this percentage was 74.4 per cent,[10] but by 31 December 1955 it was 73 per cent. Since we do not have official figures for the potential or actual labor force for other years, these percentages could be calculated only for 1939 and 1955. Calculations of the proportion of employment to population or of total working population to total population show the same picture: in 1939, 50.3 per cent of the total population was working. The percentages at year-end for 1952 through 1955 are 42.9 per cent in 1952, 43.9 per cent in 1953, 45.8 per cent in 1954, and 46.2 per cent in 1955. Similarly, figures for the proportion of workers and employees only to total population show an increase from 28.6 per cent in 1950 to 36.2 per cent in 1955. The last two figures refer to annual averages.*

If 46.2 per cent of the population is assumed to be the normal full employment for the postwar period, that is, if it is assumed that the unfavorable shift in the age and sex distribution makes a return to the prewar figure of 50 per cent impossible, we can calculate an approximate unemployment of about 602,000 for 1952, or about 7.1 per cent of the total population. It is clear that such calculations (which are not included here) have to be considered very rough approximations; they can only indicate orders of magnitude. It is also clear, however, that the absorption of the potential into the actual labor force proceeded in East Germany no faster than in the much criticized Federal Republic in spite of the fact that the population of East Germany was declining. The reasons are to be found, of course, in the planning that emphasized heavy industries where there was no experienced labor force. They are found also in insufficient capital formation which, as far as one is able to determine, fell substantially short of that achieved and consistently maintained in the Federal Republic.† However understandable the causes and however one

* Prewar and postwar data are not strictly comparable, but they are undoubtedly sufficiently comparable for our purposes. Prewar data also do not include the armed forces, labor service, or concentration camp labor.

† These problems will be discussed in connection with the index of industrial production and in the final section on the East German GNP.

appreciates the difficulties that had to be overcome in East Germany, there is no doubt that, insofar as efficient use of the labor force and absorption of unemployment resources into productive uses are concerned, this particular planned economy did no better than the free market economy, even though the absence of unemployment is one of the "talking points" of central planning.

Since they obviously do not have the same meaning that they would in the West, such unemployment figures as have been published must be treated with caution. For example, according to *Die Arbeit*,[11] there were on 30 September 1949 altogether 768,857 unemployed of both sexes, of whom, however, 445,922 did not look for work. Moreover, of those 445,922 persons, only 348,034 were completely able to work and 344,676 of those were women. Only 3,358 men able to work were not looking for jobs! An additional 97,886 were partially disabled, again most of them women — 84,961. In addition to the figures mentioned, there were on the same date 2,892,556 persons classified as temporarily freed from the obligation to work. Again, almost 2.5 million were women. Even among those listed as able to work and looking for work 80 per cent were women. Only among the partially disabled unemployed looking for work were men in the majority. The possibility that they were veterans suggests itself.

The high percentage of women in the largest category of unemployed persons, fully able to but not looking for work, suggests that they were primarily housewives or, in general, persons receiving social security payments and pensions of various types. Therefore, while high unemployment figures may in part reflect other causes, the fact that plans were constantly shifted indicates that to some extent planning must have gone wrong. Seasonal factors may have affected the published figures and so may frictional factors. But the figures may also evidence success in driving people on to the labor market, for example, by cutting their social

Table 10

Persons registered as looking for employment, March 1953,
Soviet Occupation Zone (excluding East Berlin)

	Thousands	Per cent
Fully able to work	302.4	36
Partially able to work	187.6	22
Youths up to 18 years	60.8	7
Persons working less than 24 hours per week	161.5 ⎫	35
Other unemployed	130.0 ⎭	
Total	842.3	100

Source: B. Gleitze, "Das Problem der gespaltenen Wirtschaft Deutschlands," *Mitteilungen des Wirtschaftswissenschaftlichen Instituts der Gewerkschaften*, February–March 1954, Vol. VII, No. 2/3, p. 31.

security payments, which in itself may reflect the need for saving male labor and the pressure resulting from the lack of an adequate supply of male labor. At the same time it is clear that this kind of labor is apt to be unskilled and therefore more difficult to absorb quickly.

Dr. Bruno Gleitze gives the figures presented in Table 10 for the number of persons looking for employment in March 1953, but he names no official East German source. (See also Table 11.)

Table 11

Persons looking for work, annual average,
East Germany, 1950–1958 (thousands)

Year	Number of persons
1950	325.4[a]
1951	243.4
1952	107.2
1953	90.9
1954	54.3
1955	43.6[b]
1956	40.8[c]
1957	negl.
1958	negl.

Sources: SP, July 1956, p. 91; SJDDR, 1956, p. 182; 1957, p. 196; 1958, p. 210.
[a] Equals 4.9 per cent of total employed persons, or 6.2 per cent of employees.
[b] 79 per cent female. [c] 83 per cent female.

On the basis of the 1949 figure quoted by Gleitze it is likely that about 80 per cent of those fully able to work and about 40 per cent of those partially able to work are women. Gleitze therefore counts only 550,000 of the 842.3 thousands given in Table 10 as truly unemployed by Western standards. Allowance for seasonal factors would reduce this figure somewhat.[12] If it is assumed that the ratio of workers and employees to total population of 46.2:100, which was achieved in 1954 and 1955, is "normal," it is possible to calculate average figures for unemployed workers: 341,500 for 1953, about 619,600 for 1952, 1.040 million for 1951, and 1.388 million for 1950. The figures for 1950 and 1951 are almost certainly too high, but the 1953 figure is of about the same order of magnitude as Gleitze's and is plausible. This would give for 1953 an average ratio of unemployed to employed workers and employees of 5.2:100. This ratio is the equivalent of Gleitze's figure for the unemployed fully able to work plus the youths below 18 years of age coming onto the labor market, which add up to 361,200, or a little over 5 per cent. Gleitze states that the simultaneous unemployment of youthful labor and obvious need for more was due to the pressure that was put on high output in early 1953 — a pressure that erupted on the 17th of June — which induced work managers to attempt to get more experienced, older workers.

There is some official evidence for the existence of unemployment among young workers. Statistical Practice* mentions "shortcomings of the training system," [13] and further states that, although the required labor during the First Five Year Plan could be found within the available resources, there were nevertheless difficulties in getting sufficient labor into construction, agriculture, and some branches of basic industry. "In these branches there were fluctuations in the numbers employed, which rose in the years 1951 to 1955." [14] This suggests that the unemployment of young workers was peculiar to the period for which the data are given. It also confirms the existence of hidden unemployment during the first few years of the First Five Year Plan.

The absorption of the unemployed into production is a matter of time. In the West, the need for additional labor would have raised wages substantially and induced the flow of labor into the jobs waiting for them. In East Germany, wages cannot easily be raised beyond what is planned. The method of enlarging the labor market is to push, not to pull; a person enters the labor market before a job is apparently there. Nevertheless, there is no reason to doubt that the new laborers (and some old) were eventually absorbed into industry. In the meantime they were apparently "induced to find work in the agricultural production cooperatives as harvest workers. Such short-term labor does not give rise to unemployment compensation. Thus the right to a higher social security payment is changed into a lower welfare payment after a means test" [15]; i.e., the "social" cost is cut by transferring labor from rent receivers to workers. (Statistical Practice suggests a similar process for later years, explaining that after 1953 most persons looking for work were either women who could work only locally and seasonally or war invalids.[16])

In spite of the large differences between the unemployment figures estimated in the West and the number of recipients of unemployment insurance officially given in the East, there is at least one common tendency of the figures. With few exceptions, the number of female unemployed is higher, frequently at least twice as high, than the number of male unemployed. The latest available figure for female unemployed and looking for work is more than three times the number of male unemployed. This alone suggests that in East Germany the term "unemployment" is not used as it is in the West.

It does not seem worth while to pursue this line of statistical investigation further. The following conclusions seem to be permissible. There has been some increase in the working part of the labor force in spite of the failure of the potential labor force to increase. Unemployment must have existed to a much greater extent than officially admitted although it might be accounted for by the friction of a not too efficient system,

* A list of abbreviated titles of books and journals faces page 1.

suffering, among many handicaps, from the division of Germany and, specifically, from a low rate of capital formation. The number of women, old people, and invalids forced into the production process must have increased — in part by draconic measures. Such a situation must be reflected in productivity and must be a drag on the fulfillment of the Plans.

CHAPTER II

EMPLOYMENT BY ECONOMIC SECTORS AND INDUSTRIES

In the following pages I shall try to build up a statistical picture of the labor force by industrial groups in order to trace changes in the structure of the economy, and to see later to what extent the picture derived from the labor force is consistent with that to be derived from production statistics.

Tables 12 and 13 give the existing employment statistics for the major sectors of the economy. For the years 1947 through 1949 the available data are so inadequate that it did not seem worth while to reproduce them.

From 1950 on, official data are available in some detail. The first Statistical Yearbook for the German Democratic Republic,* which appeared late in 1956, gives figures for December 31, 1952 through 1955 for the total working force by type of employment, whether as worker or employee or independent, whether as a member of a cooperative or a working family member. For the years 1950 through 1955 official indices are available that enable us to complete the series for workers and employees, independents, and working family members back to 1950. Membership in cooperatives was small at all times, negligible in 1952, and probably nonexistent before. For the years 1952 through 1955 the total number of workers shown in the tables is somewhat greater than the sum of the subgroups. The difference is accounted for by members of cooperatives, virtually all of whom are to be found in agriculture, with about 1,500 among producing artisans, and less than 1,000 each in construction and in "areas outside of material production." (These figures refer to 31 December 1955.[1]) This means that the figures for 1950 and 1951 must refer to substantially the whole working labor force even though each is the sum of only the two most important categories.

For a meaningful analysis, comparison with prewar years is extremely useful. Because of differences in concepts and changes in classification, no exact comparison can be made. However, it is still possible to make a meaningful though rough comparison and some estimates which permit

* A list of German titles of the various yearbooks faces p. 1.

Table 12

Employment by economic sectors, East Germany, 1939 and 1950–1958[a] (millions)

	1939	1950	1951	1952	1953	1954	1955	1956	1956[b]	1957	1958[c]
	(1)	(2)	(3)	(4)	(5)	(6)	(7)	(8)	(9)	(10)	(11)
Industry (excluding construction)	3.550 [d]	2.146	2.388	2.621	2.723	2.841	2.750	2.719	2.797	2.884	2.940
Producing artisans and small industry (excluding construction)		.699	.638	.603	.565	.575	.590	.575	.575	.563	.525
Subtotal	3.550	2.845	3.026	3.224	3.298	3.416	3.340	3.294	3.372	3.447	3.465
Construction (industry and artisans)	.481	.391	.482	.485	.508	.478	.488	.485	.485	.494	.498
Agriculture, forestry, water supply	1.704	1.983	1.802	1.702	1.673	1.697	1.775	1.684	1.678	1.622	1.567
Transportation	.583 [e]	.454	.486	.422	.424	.448	.437	.454	.383	.394	.404
Communications				.120	.113	.125	.123	.125	.125	.130	.130
Trade	.940 [e]	.636	.716	.836	.865	.890	.904	.930	.930	.932	.926
"Areas outside of material production": Private and public services, including domestic services	1.159	1.136	1.119	1.066	1.083	1.193	1.165	1.206	1.206	1.217	1.187
Total	8.417	7.445	7.611	7.853	7.955	8.246	8.232	8.178	8.178	8.235	8.176
Per cent of total											
Industry and artisans	42.17	38.21	39.76	41.05	41.46	41.43	40.57	40.28	41.23	41.88	42.38
Construction	5.71	5.25	6.33	6.18	6.39	5.60	5.93	5.93	5.93	5.97	6.09
Agriculture	20.24	26.64	23.68	21.67	21.03	20.58	21.56	20.59	20.52	19.72	19.17
Transportation and communications	6.93	6.10	6.39	6.90	6.75	6.95	6.80	7.08	6.21	6.34	6.53
Trade	11.17	8.54	9.41	10.65	10.87	10.79	10.98	11.37	11.37	11.31	11.33
Areas outside of material production	13.77	15.26	14.70	13.57	13.61	14.47	14.15	14.75	14.75	14.79	14.52

Sources: Col. 1: *SJBR*, 1955, p. 15. Date refers to the census of May 17, 1939. Cols. 2 and 3: Indices in *SP*, July 1956, pp. 89, 90, were used. Cols. 4–7: *SJDDR*, 1955 ed., p. 106. Col. 8: *Ibid.*, 1956 ed., pp. 169 ff. Cols. 9–11: *Ibid.*, 1957; 1958, p. 189.

[a] Detailed calculations are found in Table 13. Data for 1950 and 1952 probably are annual averages. Data for 1952 through 1955 refer to December 31 of each year.
[b] Reclassified figures. The reclassifications are described in *SJDDR*, 1957, p. 161. In general, railroad repair shops, ship repair yards, and machine tractor stations (MTS) are now classified with industry.
[c] Preliminary.   [d] Refers to "industry and producing artisans." Construction is shown separately.   [e] The given figure of 1.523 million working in transport, communications, and trade together has been split up in the ratio of 5.4:8.7. See *SHD*.

Table 13

Total working force by major economic sectors, East Germany, 1939 and 1950–1958

	1939	1950	1951	1952	1953	1954	1955	1956	1957[a]	1958[b]
	(1)	(2)	(3)	(4)	(5)	(6)	(7)	(8)	(9)	(10)
Industry:										
Workers and employees		2,126,294	2,368,691	2,601,780	2,706,787	2,823,438	2,734,414	2,601,691	2,869,237	2,925,761
Self-employed and working family-members		19,318	19,318	19,209	16,163	17,522	15,918	14,719	14,688	13,871
Total[c]	3,550,000	2,145,612	2,387,909	2,620,989	2,722,950	2,840,960	2,750,332	2,718,595	2,883,925	2,939,632
Artisans and small industry:										
Workers and employees		379,852	356,301	336,474	320,306	329,963	343,766	329,407	324,250	283,649
Self-employed and working family members		318,645	281,363	265,707	243,549	244,222	245,038	242,030	233,780	208,625
Total[c]		698,497	637,664	602,731	565,314	575,338	590,325	575,124	562,786	525,028
Construction:										
Workers and employees		340,317	421,653	441,542	465,505	435,126	442,753	442,910	451,638	436,697
Self-employed and working family members		50,831	50,831	43,326	42,602	42,669	44,223	39,768	39,405	32,812
Total[c]	481,000	391,148	482,484	484,885	508,366	477,745	487,601	484,911	494,120	497,948
Agriculture, forestry, water supply:										
Workers and employees		627,089	516,721	447,116	479,944	506,716	555,601	527,938	485,573	431,515
Self-employed and working family members		1,355,680	1,285,185	1,215,496	1,071,584	1,032,194	1,028,961	943,939	909,227	782,177
Total[c]	1,704,000	1,982,769	1,801,906	1,701,673	1,673,180	1,696,689	1,774,747	1,684,333	1,622,491	1,566,929
Transport, post, telegraph:										
Workers and employees		422,164	458,892	521,726	522,813	555,480	539,848	558,048	503,718	514,874
Self-employed and working family members		31,816	26,725	19,627	14,922	17,481	20,012	21,422	20,148	19,130
Total[c]	583,000	453,980	485,617	541,354	537,735	572,961	559,860	579,470	523,866	534,004
Trade:										
Workers and employees		406,249	505,780	661,162	705,737	739,335	755,623	789,385	798,186	805,457
Self-employed and working family members		229,854	210,546	174,846	159,068	150,417	148,256	140,166	133,749	120,060
Total[c]	940,000	636,103	716,326	836,008	864,803	889,752	903,879	929,551	931,935	925,517
Nonmaterial production:										
Workers and employees		1,031,072	1,020,761	994,831	1,013,992	1,120,121	1,087,781	1,130,591	1,141,017	1,115,146
Self-employed and working family members		105,387	88,314	70,744	68,670	72,574	76,827	74,863	74,630	67,392
Total[c]	1,159,000	1,136,459	1,119,075	1,065,575	1,082,756	1,192,820	1,165,084	1,206,359	1,216,726	1,187,252
Total:										
Workers and employees		5,331,037	5,647,668	6,004,631	6,215,084	6,510,179	6,459,786	6,482,631	6,573,619	6,513,099
Self-employed and working family members		2,111,531	1,963,488	1,808,955	1,616,566	1,576,379	1,579,235	1,476,907	1,425,627	1,244,067
Members of cooperatives		n.a.	n.a.	39,628	123,454	159,407	192,787	219,281	236,603	419,144
Total	8,417,000	7,442,568	7,611,156	7,853,214	7,955,104	8,246,065	8,231,808	8,178,343	8,235,849	8,176,310

Sources: *SJDDR*, 1955, p. 106; 1956, p. 180; and *SP*, July 1956, pp. 89, 90.
[a] Reclassified — certain repair shops of the transport sector and machine tractor stations (MTS) are now included with industry. See *SJDDR*, 1957, p. 180, note 1; 1958, p. 189.
[b] Preliminary.   [c] Members of cooperatives included in total but not separately shown.

an approximate breakdown of prewar classifications into fairly comparable groups.

The prewar classification of "industry" contains not only artisans but also construction workers. It is possible to separate out construction figures in an unequivocal way; it is not possible to separate out from the total of "industry and artisans" those groups classified after the war as "producing artisans and small industry." * In fact, it is not possible to separate out those artisans who are considered to be producing from those who are not. Thus it is possible that the 1939 figures for "industry" contain persons who in the postwar classifications would be placed in the "areas outside material production." In fact, however, of the "persons employed in technical units by major industry classification in 1939," only the following groups might possibly be considered "unproductive": No. 1212, Laundries, Ironing, Chemical Cleaning, employing 22,310 persons; No. 1404, Typing Bureaus, employing 583 persons; No. 2008, Shoe Repairs, employing at most 43,974 persons; No. 2101, Architects, Construction Engineers, 5,578; and No. 2105, Chimney Sweeps, Building Cleaning, 4,289. The figures for these groups add up to a maximum of 76,734 persons, or, if only laundries and typing bureaus are considered "unproductive," to a maximum of 22,893.

The smallness of the necessary reclassifications involved in making prewar data comparable to postwar usage of terms may seem surprising until one notices that the definitions of what is material production and what is not are not vastly different in capitalist and communist terminology. In particular, the dichotomy of material and nonmaterial production is not to be equated with the dichotomy of goods and services.

Thus the official Russian text on "Political Economy" states that:

> The social product is created by the labor of workers in material production, i.e., industry, agriculture, and transportation, insofar as it serves production, and by the labor of trade personnel insofar as it performs work which is a continuation of the production process in the sphere of circulation (inventories, final working, transportation, packaging of goods, etc.). . . . However, the labor of the workers in nonproducing branches is necessary for socialist society, for material production; it is socially useful labor. . . . It is therefore of the greatest economic importance to raise the proportion of workers in material production through reduction of the share of labor in the various nonproducing branches.[2]

And in Marxist usage, as practiced in Poland:

* The difference between industry and handicraft seems partly legal — registration as industry or in the *Handwerksrolle,* belonging to an industry or a *Handwerkskammer* — partly sociological, that is, taking pride in workmanship, rules about the manner in which apprentices are taught, etc. The difference is not one of size. There are very small industrial plants employing a handful of people, and artisan shops (particularly in construction) that employ more than 100 people and even under communist rules up to 20 people. And the product may be the same: buildings, machinery, paints, etc. Certainly there is no "arts and crafts" connotation with "artisans" or "handicraft," although there is a connotation of medieval guilds or of specially high-quality goods.

Material production is currently interpreted in a very broad sense. It includes not only those outside services to commodity-production enterprises which are, as is said, crystallized in real (i.e., material) products . . . and a number of services which can by no stretching of language be brought under this heading — passenger transportation, communications serving final consumers, laundries, and other services "within the scope of commercial economy."

The only services excluded, therefore, are personal services "outside the scope of commercial economy" — and the services of the government administration itself. . . . In practice, the coverage of the excluded classes would seem to differ somewhat from country to country: thus photographers do not contribute to national income in Yugoslavia but do, as material production, in the USSR and probably also in other Eastern European countries. [Footnote: In Poland, in recent years, urban passenger transport has been included in national income, and rural transport excluded.][3] Those certainly excluded everywhere are doctors, teachers, lawyers, artists and domestic servants. . . .

I have found no specific German definition of who is and who is not unequivocally engaged in "material production." However, from the notes to the various published national income data and the discussions of the procedures for the calculation of the national accounts, it appears that since the Second Five Year Plan passenger transportation services are included with material production, and that the whole difference between the income and cost of trade is considered the "production of trade," essentially because joint costs make it as impossible to allocate railroad income between "productive" and "unproductive" services as to separate in trade the selling act itself (which is "nonproductive") from the "productive" functions of trade.[4] Although for the transportation and communication sector some theoretical reasons are adduced for considering passenger transportation and the delivery of love letters "productive" (after all, the physical location of a good is changed!), the author states explicitly that practical considerations were primarily responsible for the decision to consider the whole transportation and communications sector productive.[5]

These considerations mainly affect the evaluation of the output of labor, however. It is almost certain that, because of joint costs, all railroad labor was included with productive labor during the years 1950–1955, when the "total product of society" did not yet include passenger traffic or private communications.*

The impression is very strong that in fact only personal services including banking and insurance and governmental services including social services, are considered areas of nonmaterial production, that is, the categories that used to be classified as "public and private services" and

* For a further discussion see Part II. "Corrections" made by the Deutsche Wirtschaftsinstitut of East Berlin in the American national income of 1955 to make it comparable with Soviet terminology, which give clues as to the comparability of prewar and postwar data, are given in the appendix to this chapter.

as "domestic services." For purposes of comparison I have assumed this to be the case.

Mail, telegraph, communications, transportation, trade — all are definitely areas of "material production." For prewar years no separate figures for trade and for communications are available. The combined figure for trade and communications (including transportation) has been divided in the ratio 8.7:5.4 between the two categories. These are the proportions of these two classifications in the total German employment of 1939.[6] It has been assumed that they hold also in the area of East Germany.

If these corrections and interpretations are accepted — and they are both reasonable and apparently the best that can be made — a meaningful comparison with prewar years becomes feasible. It shows, first, that even in 1954, the year with the highest postwar employment, total employment fell somewhat short of 1939; 170,000 to 185,000 persons fewer were gainfully employed by the end of the First Five Year Plan than in 1939.

Second, between 1950 and 1955 total employment increased by 813,000 persons (the increase at the end of 1954 was 827,000), of whom 495,000 went to industry (both big and small, including producing artisans). Construction absorbed 97,000 more; transportation and communications 106,000; trade showed an increase of 168,000; and agriculture lost 208,000. The areas outside of material production also gained, but only the small number of 29,000.

A comparison with 1939 is rather startling, but not in the way expected. As shown in Table 12, 20.24 per cent of the active population of the area of East Germany was engaged in agriculture in 1939. The immediate postwar figures (which are not reproduced here) are probably not wholly reliable, although they indicate a large increase, which is plausible. By 1950 the percentage was 26.73, and by the end of 1955 it had once more declined to 21.56 per cent, which was still higher than before the war. Moreover, the number of persons engaged in agriculture was undoubtedly higher at the end of 1955 than it had been in 1939, though by the end of 1956 there was a big drop in agricultural employment which incidentally is reflected in a big drop in agricultural output. (See below, Part IV.) And even during the years 1952, 1953, 1954, and 1956, when the absolute numbers were smaller than in 1939, agriculture still absorbed a higher proportion of the labor force.

This development, which is the reverse of what one might have expected, must be unique. It sheds some light on the effectiveness (or lack thereof) of the mechanization program in agriculture, on the strong autarkic tendencies apparently present in communist planning, and on the effects of the division of Germany. While this development undoubtedly also reflects land reform, with its emphasis on relatively small units, it still does not explain why the communist system did not succeed in making its agriculture more efficient. That it undoubtedly tried to do so is shown by the decline in the absolute numbers of persons working in agriculture in the period 1952–1954.

In 1939, 42.17 per cent of the working population were classified as being engaged in industry and as (producing) artisans. Again the low percentage of persons engaged in industry in the immediate postwar years (which are not the figures reproduced here) are not surprising in view of the chaotic conditions then prevailing. But between the end of 1950 and the end of 1955 the percentage rose only slightly — from 38.21 per cent to 40.57 per cent and thus was still considerably below the prewar figure. Moreover, this percentage (given in Table 12) has been declining ever since the end of 1953, even though in that year it was still below the prewar ratio. No reasonable reclassification of the category "industry" (such as was suggested above) would substantially change the result. It undoubtedly remains true that in percentage as well as in absolute numbers, agriculture is a more important user of men than it was in 1939 and industry a less important one. The development during the period of the First Five Year Plan essentially succeeded in "normalizing" the situation. But it has definitely not succeeded in changing the prewar pattern of employment very much, and such changes as took place were obviously in the "wrong" direction.

Only in 1957 did the percentage of the labor force in agriculture fall below its 1939 level; and although the percentage of industrial workers rose in 1957, partly because of a reclassification of those considered employed in industry, it was still short of the 1939 level.

Of the other sectors, the areas outside material production also absorbed a higher percentage of manpower in 1955 than in 1939, but it, too, declined between 1950 and 1957. Since the end of 1952, however, this percentage too has once more increased. Trade absorbs relatively more and transportation and communications relatively less labor than before the war although their shares are almost "normal" by prewar standards.

In general, the study of the changes in employment statistics leaves one with the strong impression that the result of the First Five Year Plan was to bring the distribution of manpower almost, but not quite, back to where it was before the war. One feels, however, that this result was reached in spite of rather than because of the Plan. It can hardly be said that the growth of "nonmaterial" production has high priority in East German planning (although this need not be so elsewhere in the communist orbit). The quotation from the official text, *Politische Ökonomie*, given above indicates that in the orbit as a whole attempts are made to minimize employment in "nonmaterial" production and even in the transportation and trade sectors. It is stated that, since during the Second Five Year Plan the needed labor cannot come to the same extent from "immediately available manpower in the economy," it will be necessary not only to raise productivity substantially but also

> to interest housewives, youths under 18 years of age who are not being trained, persons looking for work, persons working only part time, and persons of retirement age able to work in accepting work. Mainly, however, it will be necessary to change by planned measures the uneven distribution of labor among the different sectors. . . . A further reserve . . . consists in the increase of the proportion of those directly engaged in material production to the total number of employees and workers.[7]

This statement does not refer, of course, to a diminution of technical personnel. It goes on to explain that:

> The reduction in the proportion of production workers during the years 1951 to 1955 in the nationalized plants of material production is, among others, the result of an inflation of the administrative apparatus by the creation or enlargement of sections for planning, labor sales, and accounting. Because of insufficient mechanization of transport, inventory, cleaning, and repair works, auxiliary labor increased substantially.[8]

The interpretation of the development of the labor force requires, first, that one accept as true that the dismantling and the reparations in kind were fully as great as Rupp's careful study indicates,[9] and that the heroic exertions of the First Five Year Plan have only barely succeeded in restoring the damage done. This does not mean that individual sectors within the aggregate did not develop very well. Nor does it prejudge anything that might be said on the efficiency of planning. Second, however, it is worth while to point out that the increase in the working labor force from 7.4 million in 1950 to 8.2 million in 1955, which was accomplished in the face of an aging and declining population with an abnormally high percentage of women, took place in all major sectors of the economy. A friendly critic might call this a sign of balanced growth. Whether it is or not depends on the evaluation of this kind of balance in a small area that would presumably do better with a more "unbalanced" development of some sectors or a greater integration into a world economy, or both. A less friendly critic might point out that employment in 1939 was still higher, and might interpret the higher percentage of employment in agriculture (which here also means greater numbers) not so much as the success of land reform — which it is also — but the price for attempted self-sufficiency as the crutch for the bones broken by partition and by diminished contact with the world. It should also be remembered that, as was shown above, there was more unemployment than officially admitted, and the fact that the age and sex distribution was unfavorable and the population was declining was probably not a real limitation on growth until 1955 or even later.

Third, one should remember that some increases in output would inevitably have occurred. In East Germany as elsewhere there have been increases in productivity, and the statistics give only the number of workers, not the hours worked.*

We may summarize as follows. Although the population has decreased substantially since 1946, the number of persons who earn a living — to put it in such a round-about way — has certainly not decreased and may have substantially increased. Total employment, as well as employment in material production, decreased between 1939 and 1955. But between 1950 and 1955 there was a substantial increase in the total working labor force and in all its major subclassifications except agriculture.

Table 14 shows these changes in summary form. It is assumed that all

Table 14

Changes of employment by major sectors, East Germany, 1939, 1950, 1955, 1958[a] (millions)

| Employment in — | 1939 | 1950 | 1955 | 1957 | Changes | | | |
					1955/39	1955/50	1957/55	1958/55
Industry and artisan shops	3.550	2.845	3.340	3.449	−.210	+.495	+.109[b]	+.124
Agriculture, forestry and water supply	1.704	1.983	1.775	1.624	+.071	−.208	−.151[b]	−.208
Construction (industry and artisan shops)	0.481	0.391	0.488	0.492	+.007	+.097	+.004	+.011
Trade	0.940	0.636	0.904	0.932	−.036	+.168	+.028	+.022
Transportation and communication	0.583	0.454	0.560	0.522	−.023	+.106	−.038[c]	−.026
Subtotal	7.258	6.309	7.067	7.019	−.191	−.784	−.058	−.077
(Per cent of total employment)	(86.23)		(85.84)					
Nonmaterial production	1.159	1.136	1.165	1.218	+.006	+.029	+.052	+.022
Total	8.417	7.443	8.232	8.236	−.185	+.813	+.004	−.055

Sources: Tables 12 and 13.
   [a] Discrepancies between these figures and Table 13 due to rounding.
   [b] Of which about 70,000 due to statistical reclassification.
   [c] Probably mostly due to statistical reclassification.

the persons classified in 1939 under "public and private services" and as domestic servants should be counted as employed in areas outside of material production, and that the figure of 1.523 million persons employed in "trade and communications" in 1939 should be divided between trade and communications in the ratio of 940,000 : 583,000.

As the figures in Table 14 show, "nonproductive" employment has increased slightly while "productive" employment in the economy has decreased by more. The figures seem to imply, further, that the increased "productive" employment has mainly come from an absorption of (postwar) unemployment both open and hidden. As about 85.8 per cent of total

* Moreover, they give only the number of workers classified as belonging to a certain classification. In addition, there was some more or less voluntary work of persons in one category working off and on in others, e.g., school teachers in rolling mills (one of whom I met at Cambridge), school children and industrial workers or the army helping to bring in the harvest.

employment, the "productive" labor force in 1955 was slightly below the percentage of about 86.23 per cent in 1939. The decline is very small. The surprising fact is that the productive labor force has not increased.

EMPLOYMENT BY INDIVIDUAL INDUSTRIES

Since the publication of the first Statistical Yearbook of the German Democratic Republic there have been available official breakdowns of employment by major industrial classifications from 1950 through 1955, which make possible a rough comparison between 1955 and 1939. It is first necessary, however, to describe the available data and to explain the estimating procedure that was used to make employment at the end of 1955 comparable with the data for 1939. It has not proven feasible to make the data for the years 1950 through 1954 also comparable with the data for 1939.

As was discussed in the preceding section, the first Statistical Yearbook of the German Democratic Republic gives a breakdown of total employment from 31 December 1952 through 1955 by economic sectors and by type of employment, whether worker, employee, self-employed, member of a cooperative, or working family member. Three of the major sectors which are now our concern are: (1) industry exclusive of construction, (2) producing artisan shops and small industry exclusive of building trades, and (3) construction (both industry and trades). A later section of the Yearbook gives a further breakdown of the category "industry exclusive of construction" by major industries. These figures are reproduced in Table 15 for the ends of the years 1950 through 1955.

The first difficulty arises in the fact that the figures for the ends of the years 1952 through 1955 for the total numbers working given on page 106, or in connection with a discussion of "work force and productivity," and those given on page 126, in connection with a detailed discussion of "industry," differ by about 60,000 to 70,000 persons without any explanation of the discrepancy. It is conceivable that the difference is accounted for by cottage workers and working family members, whose exact numbers are given on page 106; but even when these two groups are — quite arbitrarily — eliminated, there still remains a discrepancy of several thousand.

The second difficulty lies in the fact that "producing artisans and small industry" are included in the 1939 figures. On the other hand, no figures for 1950 to 1955 for the working persons so classified have been found.

The dividing line between "industry" and "small industry" lies as a rule at 10 employees. However, in certain trades, particularly in the construction trades, up to 20 workers may be employed by an artisan or in a small industry. In all cases apprentices and disabled persons employed are not counted within the limits of 10 or 20 employees, re-

Table 15

Employment in industry, by major classification,[a] East Germany, 1939, 1950–1955, and 1958 (thousands)

Industry classifications	1939 (1)	1950 (2)	1951 (3)	1952 (4)	1953 (5)	1954 (6)	1955 (7)	Artisans and small industry 1955 (8)	Industry and artisans 1955 (thousands) (9)	Percentage increase from 1939 to 1955 (10)	1957 (thousands) (11)	1958[a] (12)
Energy (electricity and gas)	58.8	50.7	56.4	57.3	58.1	61.6	62.7	0.0	62.7	106.6	63.1	63.9
Mining	104.5	168.0	179.7	185.1	192.6	208.5	211.4	0.226	211.6	202.7	212.9	216.6
Metallurgy	62.2[b]	67.1	79.1	90.3	76.4	81.5	80.9	0.0	80.9	130.3	86.5	90.5
Chemical industry	197.2[c]	195.8	205.2	215.2	227.3	236.0	238.1	9.058	247.2	125.4	247.9	251.0
Building materials	194.1[d]	137.4	144.2	146.5	144.4	150.7	154.6	14.880	169.5	87.3	90.5	92.7
Engineering construction	942.3[e]	534.8	578.0	626.1	648.2	655.4	647.6	121.753	769.4	81.7	719.0	732.8
Electrical equipment and supplies	188.2	144.3	169.2	182.4	205.1	203.6	201.2	31.107	232.3	123.4	201.2	210.5
Fine mechanics and optics	84.9	71.6	77.7	81.1	84.6	88.6	89.5	19.374	108.9	128.3	94.3	97.5
Woodworking	245.6	144.3	145.7	142.6	143.8	141.7	140.6	102.873	243.5	99.1	148.4	150.9
Textile industry	509.5	325.4	353.3	347.0	354.8	359.7	363.4	20.793	384.2	75.4	359.0	357.3
Clothing, leather and shoes, and furs (combined)	363.7	137.8	153.1	157.7	164.3	170.0	170.4				183.8	191.1
Clothing	242.4				97.6	101.8	104.6	78.873	183.5	75.7	115.9	121.4
Leather and shoes, and furs	121.3				66.7	68.2	65.8	58.251	124.1	102.3	67.9	69.7
Pulp and paper	109.6	53.7	56.8	58.1	58.8	57.1	56.8	6.320	63.1	57.6	60.9	61.9
Printing	73.9	51.2	50.1	50.6	45.0	44.6	41.3	12.818	54.1	73.2	41.5	41.3
Food, drink, and tobacco	383.1	170.2	195.0	216.7	230.6	230.6	224.4	13.668	238.1	62.2	201.1	207.7
Subtotal	3,517.6	2,255.9	2,443.4	2,556.7	2,634.1	2,679.4	2,683.0	489.994	3,173.0	90.2	2,776.5	2,833.5
Construction	498.5			484.9	508.4	477.5	487.6		487.6	97.8	491.6	497.9
Total	4,015.9											

Sources: Col. 1: SHD, 1949, pp. 258 ff. One-third of Berlin allocated to East Berlin. Includes artisans and small industry. Cols. 2–7: SJDDR, 1955, pp. 126 ff; 1957, pp. 176, 254 ff; 1958, pp. 278 ff. Cols. 8–10: SJDDR, 1955 ed., p. 190. For estimating method, see text and Table 16.

[a] One-third of Berlin allocated to East Berlin. Includes artisans and small industry.   [b] Excluding artisan shops and small industry.   [c] Including rubber and asbestos, synthetic fibers.   [d] Stones and earths.   [e] Without castings.   [e] Including machinery, steel construction, vehicle construction, castings and iron, steel and metal goods.

spectively. Persons on vacation and sick persons (even when sick for more than 6 weeks) are counted as employed.

The difference between "producing" and "service" artisan shops is defined as follows:

Producing artisan shops consist of producing units which manufacture goods out of their own materials or out of materials furnished by the customer; process material or products of customers or do repair and assembly work. *Service artisan shops* consist of units active, for example, in the areas of hygiene or public health which do not create new values, such as exterminator, barber, or masseur shops.[10]

The distinction corresponds closely to the prewar division of those artisans included among industry and those included among personal services, although there may be differences in detail.

The numbers of those working in "producing artisan shops and small industry" by major industries are not available. For 1955, however, there exists a breakdown of the number of shops by the numbers working in them (except for working family members). Thus there were on 31 December 1955, four mining enterprises that did not employ any hired labor, eleven with 1, eight with 2, eight with 3, one with 4, three with 5, nine with 6–10, and none with 11 or more hired workers. This kind of information enables us to estimate the total number of working persons classified as artisans or working in small industries. If we assume an average hired employment of 8 for class 6–10, and of 15 for the class 11 and more, the total number of owners and hired workers is estimated to be 465,813.

Since there were 590,325 persons working in the category "producing artisan shops and small industry," of whom 50,959 were working family members[11] there were still 73,553 hired workers unaccounted for. The final allocation was made as follows: the calculated employment in each industry group was first recalculated as a percentage of the total calculated number (that is, 465,813), and these percentages were then applied to the total number of 539,366.

The 50,959 working family members were allocated in a similar manner among different industries, except that the number of units was used to calculate the percentage distribution, since this procedure seemed to make better sense. The figures are reproduced in Table 16.

The third difficulty has to do with the reclassification of industries which has occurred. Metallurgy no longer includes castings, which are now included with machinery production. Machinery production now also includes metal products. Woodworking appears to be the sum of the categories "woodworking" and "musical instruments and toys." The textile industry no longer includes the production of synthetic fibers, which are now included in the chemical industry. Rubber and asbestos products, which were a separate category in 1939, are also included in the chemical industry now. All these adjustments have been made. A minor adjustment,

Table 16

Estimation of proprietors and nonfamily employees and of working family-members
for artisans and small industry, by industry group, East Germany, 31 December 1955[a]

	Per cent of employment	Per cent of number of units	Proprietors and outside help	Working family-members	Total working force
Mining	0.4	.02	216	10	226
Machine Construction	20.8	18.77	112,188	9,565	121,753
Electrical equipment and supplies	5.4	3.89	29,125	1,982	31,107
Fine mechanics and optics	3.3	3.09	17,799	1,572	19,374
Chemicals	1.6	.84	8,630	428	9,058
Building materials	2.6	1.68	14,024	856	14,880
Woodworking	17.6	15.59	94,928	7,945	102,873
Textiles	3.6	2.70	19,417	1,376	20,793
Clothing	12.9	18.24	69,578	9,295	78,873
Leather, shoes, furs	9.6	12.70	51,779	6,472	58,251
Paper and pulp	1.1	.76	5,933	387	6,320
Printing	2.2	1.87	11,866	952	12,818
Food, drink, and tobacco	19.2	19.84	103,558	10,110	113,668
Total	100.0	100.00	539,041	51,493	589,994

[a] Total working force: 590,325, of which working family members = 50,959. (*SJDDR*, 1955, p. 106.) Because of rounding, the sum of the detailed breakdowns may not equal the figures in the total column.

which consists in the change of office machinery from "machinery production" to "fine mechanics and optics" has not been made.

The final difficulty arises from the absence of separate figures for East
and West Berlin in 1939. I have therefore arbitrarily, but reasonably,
allocated one-third of Berlin's employment to East Berlin. Without
question, this solution results in some errors, but there appears to be no
better way of estimating.

The adjusted figure for employment for 1939 in industry and artisan
shops outside of construction is 3.518 million; by the end of 1955 the
working force in comparable industry was 3.273 million, or 93 per cent of
1939. The industry-by-industry comparison shows decreases not only in
light- and consumer-goods industries (which is to be expected) but also
in the production of building materials and, most surprisingly, machinery
construction. There are, however, explanations for the latter: airplane
construction in 1939 in the area which after the war became the Soviet
Occupation Zone and which excluded East Berlin employed 110,748
persons, and 63,922 persons were employed in motor vehicle and bicycle
construction. An additional 47,857 persons were employed in repair shops
for machinery and vehicles. The last two production categories have not
recovered to anywhere near their prewar output — in 1955 the production
of passenger cars had reached only one-third of the 1936 level, sub-

stantially less than the 1939 level, and even truck production was at only three-fourths the 1936 level — and aircraft production had probably not yet started on a large scale in 1955 or 1956. Allowing for these facts, there seems to be a slight increase in employment between 1939 and 1955 in machinery production other than cars, trucks, and planes.

The drop in the labor force working in construction materials can probably be explained in part by the substitution of cement for labor-intensive brick manufacture, which is now substantially below the prewar level.

Although inferences as to productivity will be postponed until after the calculation of the index of industrial production has been described, it should be noted here that where output has increased sharply, labor input has too. Thus mining employment has just about doubled, and so has the output of raw lignite. The expanding industries, in terms of labor force, are metallurgy, chemicals, fine mechanics and optics, and electrical equipment and supplies. The industries that have increased their labor force slightly or maintained it at roughly the prewar (1939) level are energy production (that is, electricity and gas), leather, shoes and furs, and woodworking and related industries. The industries that have been starved of manpower to make these increases possible, in addition to engineering construction and building material production, are textiles, clothing, pulp and paper, printing, and food, drink, and tobacco. By 1955, employment in construction too had recovered to only 97.8 per cent of the prewar level.

These changes are as expected (except for the decrease in employment in machinery production); all is in line with the known objectives of a planned society, and all is reflected in the output figures, as will be seen later. In terms of the reallocation of the labor force, the First Five Year Plan has certainly succeeded in making a radical change in the industrial structure.

APPENDIX TO CHAPTER II
WHO IS EXCLUDED FROM THE "PRODUCTIVE" LABOR FORCE?

Some notion of what is or is not counted as "productive" labor can possibly be gained from an East German publication dealing with the second postwar economic downturn in the United States.[12]

In this article, published by the Deutsches Wirtschaftsinstitut, adjustments are made so that American national income statistics for 1953 * will be comparable with East German usage. The following deductions were made on the production side: From the category "finance, insurance, and real estate": (p. 177, line 44) consumption expenditures were deducted (p. 207, lines 52–57), except, strangely enough, "legal business" (line 56) and "other" (line 58), as well as "car insurance" (line 66). Also deducted from this category are rents. "Communications and public utilities" (line 61) is included as a whole; that is, no attempt is made to exclude personal travel by rail or personal telephone calls. Of all services, only "miscellaneous repair services and hand trades" are allowed. Finally, of the total category "government and government enterprises" only the latter (federal, state, and local) are included.

On the use side of national income, the following deductions were made: personal consumption expenditures were taken from Table 3. Then the following personal consumption expenditures were deducted. (All numbers refer to Table 30, pp. 206, 207.)

Line	Category	Line	Deduction
1–6	I. Food and tobacco		None.
7–17	II. Clothing, accessories and jewelry	15	Laundering.
		17	Other (watch repairs, jewelry repair, clothing services, seamstresses).
18–20	III. Personal care	20	Barbershops, beauty parlors, baths, 50 per cent. The rest is supposed to be expenditure on physical goods.
21–25	IV. Housing		
26–41	V. Household operations	40	Domestic service.
		41	Other (i.e., maintenance for household equipment, moving, postage, fire and theft insurance, etc.).
42–50	VI. Medical care and death expenses	45	Physicians.
		46	Dentists.
		47	Other professional services (all medical).
		48	Private hospitals and sanatoriums.
		49	Medical care and hospitalization insurance.
		50	Funeral and burial expenses.
51–58	VII. Personal business		No deduction — probably because it has been deducted from the production side.
59–75	VIII. Transportation	65	Bridge and other tolls.
		66	Automobile insurance premiums.
76–91	IX. Recreation	84	Movie, theater admissions, etc.
		88–91	Clubs, parimutuel betting, etc.
92–95	X. Private education and research	92–95	All deducted.
97–101	XII. Foreign travel and remittances		Nothing apparently deducted.

Five per cent of the deducted service items is restored in order to allow for implied expenditures on goods, such as soap for laundries.

Domestic net investment and net foreign investment remain as given in the American publication. The "material consumption of the government" is found

* Refers to U.S. Department of Commerce, Office of Business Economics, *National Income, 1954 Edition,* A Supplement to the Survey of Current Business, (Washington, Government Printing Office, 1954). Page numbers in parentheses refer to this Supplement.

by deducting from government purchases of goods and services the amount of "income originating in general government" (Table 12, line 36, p. 175).

No critical examination of some strange reasoning is here intended, but merely an attempt to find out what is or is not considered "productive" labor. The detailed calculations are specified in the East German publication (p. 34, Appendix, Table II, footnotes).

PART TWO

EAST GERMAN METHODOLOGY

CHAPTER III

NATIONAL ACCOUNTING AND THE EAST GERMAN INDEX OF GROSS PRODUCTION

THE AVAILABLE DATA

Before 1956 the only index of production published in East Germany was one of industrial gross production, broken down into three subgroups: Investment Goods Industries, Production Goods Industries, and Consumer Goods Industries.* That index purports to be methodologically comparable with 1936; it was used, for example, by Sanderson to calculate that part of the GNP which is attributable to industry by multiplying the 1936 GNP of the industrial sector by the later index of industrial gross production.[1]

With the publication of the first Statistical Yearbook of the German Democratic Republic in 1956,[2] substantially more detail became available. The Yearbook gives not only the gross product by major economic sectors in constant 1950 prices for 1950 through 1955 but also the value of the means of production used up and the net product, which is, ideally, comparable to the Western concept of net value.†

Moreover, all this information is further broken down by types of ownership: nationalized, cooperative, and private. For the years 1950 through 1955 a percentage breakdown of the social product in current prices (communist definition, of course) has been published by major categories, including means of production used; accumulation, consisting of plant and equipment (*Erweiterung der Produktion*) and social capital (*Erweiterung der Anlagen der gesellschaftlichen Konsumtion*) and formation of public reserves; and consumption, consisting of individual and "societal" consumption.[3] These data with explanatory notes are reproduced in Table 17.

* Since then, there has also been published a breakdown by four subgroups.
,† It has been necessary to give prices used in the text and tables in three currencies, for which the following abbreviations are used:
RM — Prewar reichsmark
DM — Deutsche mark, issued by the Central Bank of the Federal Republic (Deutsche Bundesbank)
DM-O — Deutsche mark-Ost, the Deutsche mark issued by the East Berlin (communist) Deutsche Notenbank.

East German Methodology

Table 17

Economic balance sheet: total product of society and national income[a]

1. Origin of the total product of society by ownership and economic sector, 1950–1955, in 1950 prices (million DM-O in 1950 prices)

	Total product of society					
	1950	1951	1952	1953	1954	1955
By ownership						
Gross product						
Total	52,316	63,775	70,391	75,982	83,536	89,085
Socialized	27,616	35,561	40,876	47,671	51,826	55,713
Cooperative	1,895	2,280	2,917	3,929	4,465	5,146
Private	22,805	25,934	26,598	24,382	27,245	28,226
Means of production used up						
Total	21,654	27,262	30,646	34,461	37,171	39,266
Socialized	12,878	16,113	18,895	23,294	25,068	26,234
Cooperative	415	561	837	1,376	1,523	1,933
Private	8,361	10,588	10,914	9,791	10,580	11,099
Net product						
Total	30,662	36,513	39,745	41,521	46,365	49,819
Socialized	14,738	19,448	21,981	24,377	26,758	29,479
Cooperative	1,480	1,719	2,080	2,553	2,942	3,213
Private	14,444	15,346	15,684	14,591	16,665	17,127
By economic sector						
Gross product						
Economy as a whole	52,316	63,775	70,391	75,982	83,536	89,085
Industry without construction	27,223	33,405	38,699	43,066	48,098	51,795
Construction (industry and artisans)	2,389	3,411	3,791	4,145	4,330	4,632
Artisans and small industry (without construction artisans)	3,514	4,433	4,603	4,650	5,366	5,922
Agriculture and forestry	8,653	10,371	10,357	10,310	11,253	11,390
Water	135	145	156	167	138	187
Transportation and communication	1,847	2,148	2,425	2,706	2,923	3,123
Trade	8,555	9,862	10,360	10,938	11,428	12,036
Means of production used up						
Economy as a whole	21,654	27,262	30,646	34,461	37,171	39,266
Industry without construction	14,849	17,685	20,346	23,760	25,761	27,123
Construction (industry and artisans)	810	1,232	1,389	1,537	1,606	1,707
Artisans and small industry (without construction artisans)	1,285	1,716	1,764	1,773	2,108	2,353
Agriculture and forestry	3,316	4,988	5,118	5,092	5,377	5,435
Water	63	67	72	77	64	87
Transport and communication	644	727	838	854	1,135	1,294
Trade	687	847	1,119	1,368	1,180	1,267
Net product						
Economy as a whole	30,662	36,513	39,745	41,521	46,365	49,819
Industry without construction	12,374	15,720	18,353	19,306	22,337	24,672
Construction (industry and artisans)	1,579	2,179	2,402	2,608	2,724	2,925
Artisans and small industry (without construction artisans)	2,229	2,717	2,839	2,877	3,258	3,569
Agriculture and forestry	5,337	5,383	5,239	5,218	5,936	5,955
Water	72	78	84	90	74	100
Transportation and communication	1,203	1,421	1,587	1,852	1,788	1,829
Trade	7,868	9,015	9,241	9,570	10,248	10,769

[a] This table is reproduced from, and its heading literally translated from, the official account in *SJDDR*, 1955, pp. 90, 93.

Table 17 (Continued)

3. Uses of total product of society, 1950–1955 [b]

	1950	1951	1952	1953	1954	1955
	Per cent of annual total					
Total product of society	100.0	100.0	100.0	100.0	100.0	100.0
Of which used as:						
Replacement for means of production	41.4	42.0	42.3	43.8	45.1	45.3
Accumulation	8.6	8.5	8.5	7.8	8.1	8.1
Expansion of production	4.0	4.3	4.5	4.7	4.7	4.5
Expansion of institutions of societal consumption and formation of state reserves	4.4	4.2	4.0	3.2	3.5	3.6
Consumption	50.0	49.6	49.2	48.3	46.8	46.6
Societal consumption	9.7	10.5	10.1	9.4	7.8	7.4
Individual consumption	40.3	39.1	39.1	38.9	38.9	39.2
	Per cent of 1950					
Total product of society	100	122	139	152	164	173
Of which used as:						
Replacement for means of production	100	124	142	161	179	190
Accumulation	100	120	138	139	156	164
Expansion of production	100	124	150	169	182	188
Expansion of institutions of societal consumption and formation of state reserves	100	117	127	110	130	142
Consumption	100	121	137	147	153	162
Societal consumption	100	131	144	147	132	132
Individual consumption	100	118	135	147	163	169

[b] Stated to be derived from data in current prices. These data are not given.

Explanations

Total product of society (gross product)

Gross product of material production at final sales prices. Included are sales taxes and excises. Subsidies are deducted. The total product of society is found as the sum of the gross production values of the plants of the following economic sectors:

1. Industry and artisans. (Production reports of plants in delivery prices.)
2. Agriculture, forestry. (Production. Market production and own consumption, respectively.)
3. Water economy.
4. Transportation and communications. (Value of transport services of freight transportation and services of post and telegraph unless for administration and population [presumably, consumers].)
5. Trade (only markups including sales taxes and consumption levies, except when they have been included in the delivery price of plants).

Replacements of means of production

Value of means of production used up, including, however, cost of maintaining installations of societal sector and of institutions outside of material production if financed by the plants themselves.

Expansion of production

Value of the increase in the means of production, i.e., increase in plants and circulating capital (*Umlaufsmittel*), including increase in value of stock of animals).

Expansion of institutions of societal consumption

Value of the increase of societal institutions outside of material production plus value of the increase in societal [state?] reserves.

Table 17 (Continued)

Societal consumption

Value of maintaining societal installations and institutions unless financed by plants themselves plus current consumption of goods for societal purposes outside of material production, plus imports minus exports.

Individual consumption

Individual consumption has been derived from:

1. Sales of goods to the population by retail trade (including artisans and restaurants), farmers markets and farm sales.
2. Deliveries to the population of electricity, gas, and water.
3. Own consumption by farmers.
4. Working of materials supplied by customers, repairs and assemblies, and construction services to the population insofar as they were paid for by the population.
5. Material services of social insurance.
6. Food deliveries to the population (all kinds of community kitchens including factory canteens and school lunches).

The section entitled "Industry excluding Construction" in the Statistical Yearbook of the German Democratic Republic[4] gives a further breakdown of gross production from 1950 through 1955 by major industries, for example, power, metals, chemicals, but gross product is valued in *Messwerte** and no information is given as to the means of production used up in the process of production.

The 1956 edition contained rather meager information on the social accounts, but in 1958 more detailed data on gross product, means of production used up, depreciation allowances, and net product by economic sectors were published in current prices,[5] and calculations in constant prices are apparently in preparation.[6]

The industrial gross and net products for the years 1956 and 1957 are also available in constant plan prices. But, alas, since the statistical definition of the individual sector differs when measured in constant and in current prices, the calculations in different prices can be compared only within limits. This is also true for comparisons between different years. Thus when we deal with industry in the national accounts, gross production also includes any construction by plants classified with industry. But when we deal with gross production in constant plan prices as reported in the industrial statistics, industrial gross production does not include construction.

The official published data are summarized most quickly in tabular form (see Fig. 1). It is clear that even the rapidly increasing official information is not sufficient to analyze the performance of the East German economy. There is, moreover, a substantial amount of discussion in the East German journals which indicates that, even from the standpoint of

---

* *Messwerte* ("measure values") is a system of artificial prices used exclusively for the calculation of this index. For a further description, see below.

the East German economy itself, not all is well with the concepts used and the calculations made.

Over the years, the East German concepts of what should and what should not be counted have changed considerably. The concepts of gross production itself, which is now calculated in several sets of prices (at least one of which is completely fictitious), includes a great deal of what Western economists would consider multiple counting. Moreover, although only material goods are supposed to be included, the range of so-called material goods has broadened considerably since 1955.

For a Western analyst, the concept of gross production itself is puzzling and useless; and even the more familiar concept of net production cannot be interpreted unless something more is known about the coverage and the prices used. In this chapter I shall present as detailed a description as possible of East German methodology, going into great detail for the index of industrial production and the calculations of the national accounts.

Obviously, the statistics are published for the use of a planned economy. Gross production is used to measure the performance of the economy, to measure productivity, to allocate investment funds or bonuses, to measure plan fulfillments, and to prepare future plans. A concept of such operational importance, which is used both to measure performance and to formulate plans, ought to be eminently suited to the tasks it is to perform; and the prices used to value outputs should not lead to distortions which would seriously hamper the planning process. The East German discussions show that neither was the case. Naturally, ideology determines what the content of the output is that is supposed to be measured, but this ideology will certainly meet practical exigencies tending to modify it.

This chapter considers the special problems of the gross production index for industry and then discusses details of the calculations of the national accounts.

THE GROSS PRODUCTION OF INDUSTRY

Industry is the largest economic sector in East Germany. Even if it were not, it would still have a special role in value judgments of communist ideology (and by no means only there). It is therefore natural that most attention should be given to measuring the performance of the industrial sector. This has been done by calculating gross production. Both the concept of gross production itself and the methods of calculating it have changed over the years.

Purpose

The first question which arises is, What do East German statisticians wish to measure? The answer to this question is largely ideological. What

Figure 1

Officially available data

	Prices	Period	Breakdown	How available	Comments	Source

Social accounts	1950 prices	1950–1955	1) By economic sector
			2) By property form
			3) a. By total gross product
			   b. By means of production used up
			   c. By net product
			4) By use
				In DM–O
				In DM–O
				In DM–O
				
				Percentage distribution
					Final sales prices, including all indirect taxes, less subsidies	*SJDDR*, 1955, pp. 90–93.

Social accounts	Current prices	1950–1957	1) By economic sector
			2) By property form
			3) a. By total gross product
			   b. By material means used up
			   c. By depreciation
			   d. By net product
				In DM–O
				In DM–O
				In DM–O
					Precise definition of industry sector not stated. Prices used supposedly actual industry received prices. Classification on basis of plants	*Ibid.*, 1957, pp. 152–160.

	Current prices	1950–1957	4) By use	Percentage distribution	Refers only to domestically available national income	
Industrial production	*Messwerte*	1950–1955	1) By property form 2) By major industry groups 3) By major industries	In DM–O and indices	Excludes output of construction firms, uranium mines, and 237 food plants run by the state trading organization. Includes industrial output of nonindustrial plants. Apparently includes construction if undertaken by plants classified as industrial	*Ibid.*, 1955, pp. 120 ff.

	Prices	Years	Classification	Currency	Definition	Source
Industrial production	Unchanged plan prices (1955 prices)	1956–1957	By major industry groups and by major industries	In DM-O	Output of plants classified as industry. Excluded are construction performed by industrial plants and industrial output by nonindustrial plants. Prices exclude turnover taxes, etc.	*Ibid.*, 1956, pp. 219 f.;1957, pp. 221 f.
Construction industry	Unclear, probably current	1950–1955 1953–1955	1) By property form 2) By type	In DM-O In DM-O	Without construction artisans and architects, bureaus	*Ibid.*, 1955, pp. 171 f.
	Unclear, probably current	1950–1957	1) By property form 2) By type	In DM-O In DM-O	Without artisans but includes construction performed by units in other economic sectors. Figures for 1950–1955 differ therefore from previously published data	*Ibid.*, 1957, pp. 319 f.
Construction artisans	Unclear, probably current	1952–1955	Only for selected groups	In DM-O	No definition	*Ibid.*, 1955, p. 189.
	Current prices received by plant	1953–1957	All artisans	In DM-O	As construction industry, 1950–1957	*Ibid.*, 1957, pp. 339 f.
Other sectors	No information given aside from the social accounts					

is supposed to be measured is the total product of labor. In Marxist theory, labor has a double character as a producer. As live (abstract) labor it produces values that differ from what it produces as concrete (productive) labor. The former produces what we call net value added, the latter what Marxists call gross production.

> Concrete and live labor are, however, by no means . . . identical categories. Concrete (productive) labor belongs to the work process and as such it contains also the value of the means of production which enters into the new product. Economically, this appears as the fact that . . . concrete labor creates also the use values which can replace the means of production used up. Abstract labor, however, belongs to the process of value formation, and as such it does not create a useful production result but only value.[7]

Marx, we are told, proved Adam Smith wrong in identifying the "value product of output" with the results of productive labor. Since the calculation of the total product should measure everything that is produced, including all intermediate goods, an analysis, along Marxist lines, of the processes of simple and expanded reproduction may be made.

A non-Marxist specialist might think that the differences between Marx and Smith relate to GNP *versus* national income or net national product as proper measures of the output of labor, and that, for the analysis of simple and expanded reproduction, GNP, broken down into gross investment and depreciation allowances on the one hand and consumption expenditures on the other, might be desirable.

The only explanation I can envisage for insisting on measuring a more "gross" concept than our GNP derives from the fact that Marxist theory is interested not only in capital formation and growth — to translate "expanded reproduction" freely into a more familiar idiom — but also in sociology and the class structure of society. Growth of output, advanced industrial methods, the growth of an industrial proletariat, and the increasing division of labor are associated; and the degree of the division of labor becomes a measure of the degree of social and economic development. A Western economist is interested in the division of labor only if he is a specialist in industrial organization. If he is interested in the performance of the economy, he is indifferent to the division of labor except insofar as the output of final goods is affected by increased productivity.

If my interpretation of Marxist doctrine is correct, it becomes understandable that a Marxist economist would want a measure that varies with the amount of intermediate goods produced because this will reflect the "societal division of labor."

There is nothing to stop East German economists and statisticians from employing a concept they feel to be meaningful and useful for their purposes. A Western analyst, however, must ask specifically how the gross product is calculated and what the methods of calculation do to the index;

what biases are involved in the changing amount of intermediate products counted or the price system used; and what effects the use of the concept may have on the planned economy. As will be seen, these very questions are asked increasingly also by East German statisticians who are wondering just how suitable "gross production" is for operational purposes — with results that come close to the criticisms Western economists have made of communist procedures for years.

Coverage

Granted that "gross production" is a meaningful concept to a Marxist economist, the second major question arises: What is actually counted as gross production of industry?

The problem to be solved by the communist ideology is: When is a product a product? The answer on principle is that "The extent of gross production depends on the existing system of the division of labor in society." [8] On principle, unfinished products within a plant are not part of gross production, "since the result of the intra-plant partial labor [Teilarbeit] is not a product; only the contribution of all the partial work performed within a plant leads to the product." [9] In practice this principle does not help very much in deciding when labor produces only part of a product and when it produces a whole product. It is, however, worth noting that a change in the division of labor which is considered to be "objective" will change the gross product, although by Western standards nothing whatever happened. The following remarkable quotation is therefore produced in extenso.

Discussions have shown that the historical character of the division of labor of society and its importance for the size of the gross product is frequently not recognized. For example, it is known that the construction industry in the Soviet Union is being increasingly industrialized. Whole parts of buildings, like stairs, ceilings, parts of façades, etc., are now prefabricated. Thereby house construction increasingly takes the form of an assembly.

The application of these new construction methods in society means a change in the system of the division of labor of society in the Soviet Union. . . . [Translator's note: Here follows a lengthy footnote from Marx, Vol. I, on the production of umbrellas in New York and Philadelphia.]

The prefabrication of building parts in the Soviet Union has led to a new stage of production in society and with it to an increase in gross production. The products of this new stage of production become part of the formation of gross product since they are the expression of a new need of society.

It may be objected that in this example the increase in gross product is only apparent, not real; for sand, cement, and steel, of which the new product "concrete stairs" consists, enter into the gross production value already as the products of the production stages sand, cement, and steel.

Followers of this wrong idea do not see that the formulation of new production stages in society within the production process of a product (in our example the house) always leads to an increase in gross production. We shall here disregard the fact that the formation of new production stages always results in increases in labor productivity. This wrong opinion is due to the fact that its representatives are not clear as to the connection between the historic character of the state of the division of labor within society and gross production. [Footnote: In this connection we want to point out that it is not irrelevant, as some of our economic functionaries believe, whether to start the calculation of total industrial production, with the division of labor in society as such (*schlechthin*) or with that of the Soviet Union. Even though the system of social division of labor in the Soviet Union and with us is approximately the same, this does not mean that they are identical. It would therefore not be correct to use the system of social division of labor of the Soviet Union to calculate total industrial production in the German Democratic Republic, because this would not show our total production correctly.][10]

This quotation is interesting in that it throws light on the socialist law of a continuously increasing industrial production. Whatever else it may mean, it *also* means that under socialism the "societal" division of labor increases steadily. Hence the production index increases steadily simply because more and more things are produced in factories; because, in "Austrian" terms, the "societal" roundaboutness of production increases steadily. If it is objected that nothing really happened to increase output, the answer is, "So what?" It is not the aim of the gross production index to measure the total output by Western standards. There is no doubt that by Western standards the industrialization of processes formerly performed in craftsman shops inflates the index, and that the index is seriously and admittedly affected simply by different methods of organizing the same processes. (The increased efficiency of factory production over craftsman production is, of course, a different matter.) The Western observer simply must rid himself of any idea that the East German index intends to measure output as it is understood in the West.

So much for generalities. I turn now to such details of the calculation of the index as I have been able to find.

The period of the First Five Year Plan. The gross production of industry during the First Five Year Plan was specified to consist of the following items:

Value of products intended for sale made of the producer's own materials or of materials supplied by the customer;

Value of work done to materials or products of customers, if no new products result; repairs and assembly for other accounts;

Value of products and material services for investment in one's own plant and general overhauling [*Generalreparaturen*];

Value of work in process of specified products with long-term periods of production;

In order to eliminate as far as possible the influence of structural changes within industry upon the level of the value of gross production, the value of industry's own consumption of certain specific products is included in gross production.[11]

Thus the definitions make it clear that no inter-industry or inter-plant flows are excluded, and that even intra-plant flows ("own consumption") are not excluded in the most important cases. Moreover, from 1950 through 1955 unusable goods appear to have been counted as part of output.

But this still leaves open the questions of when a product is a product and what is an objective division of labor. The theoretical criteria given are completely formal, such as "The result of *societal* division of labor is a product which satisfies a societal need and enters circulation as a good . . . the result of intra-plant partial work as distinguished from societal partial work is not a product but incomplete production." [12] On the basis of this sort of statement only three things can be said. First, it is abundantly clear that inter-firm flows are *not* excluded. Second, on principle, goods produced and consumed within a plant must be counted as part of gross production if they are a "product," but not if they are only "partial production." Thus "lignite does not lose its character as a good if it is used up in lignite briquet production within the same combine." [13] Also, gross production and commodity production (*Warenproduktion*) are not identical; the gross production consists of both the goods destined for the market and those products that could be "goods" but are instead used up within the plant. The treatment of inventory accumulation is yet another problem.* [14] Third, it is clear that all this "objectivity" still is so vague that one must know what the specific instructions are.

The specific instructions changed during the period of the First Five Year Plan. In 1950 gross production was defined as total production of the plant. In 1951 producers' own consumption had to be reported as part of the total production for about 220 plan positions (that is, groups of commodities), and in 1952 for about 290 plan positions. In 1952, however, numerous plants in fact reported their own consumption as gross production as part of commodity production, while in 1950 all producers' own consumption in all plan positions was (supposedly) counted.[15] The actual instructions were the same for the economic plans for 1952 as for the preceding two years but not for the plans for the individual plants. Thus it is clear from East German criticisms themselves that the content of what is to be reported has changed and, moreover, that instructions in any particular year are contradictory. The backsliding from the true Marxist way of doing things to include only part of the producers' own consumption can perhaps be explained by the desire to make the later gross production index comparable to that of 1936, an impossible undertaking, but it has had the result that "the central planning authorities are not in a position to state the extent of total own consumption of

---

* Unlike practice in the USSR or Bulgaria, inventory accumulation even if involuntary is counted as part of gross production in East Germany. See below, p. 67, for a further discussion.

nationalized industry," [16] which, it is admitted later, has led to mistakes in planning.

The principle that all producers' own consumption is to be counted as part of gross production leads to obvious difficulties with machine production and chemicals. Dr. Schmidt is at great pains to explain why yarn and cloth are both to be counted while parts of a machine are not to be counted, only the finished machine being counted even though parts of the machine can be individually purchased as goods. The reason she gives is that yarn and cloth reflect true stages in the division of labor whereas the sale–purchase of machine parts is linked to the *consumption process* of the machine.[17] Therefore in East German practice producers' own consumption of machine parts is not to be included in gross production; only the final machine is to be considered. On the other hand, parts for sale and in trade are to be included in gross production.

In chemical production difficulties arise because its peculiar nature makes it impossible to state "in general what the producers' own consumption is. The determination of the producers' own consumption and gross production of the chemical industry must be made by the individual chemical plant according to the method of production used."[18] This means that if two processes of production produce the same end-product, in one case intermediate products are counted and in the other they are not; that is, if technical progress does not eliminate an intermediate product but simply makes for a necessarily continuous production process, the intermediate product is *not* to be counted.

If the foregoing account is confusing, it is because the calculation of gross production during the First Five Year Plan was confused. It is clear that the coverage was intended to include anything produced that was recognizably a "product," whether it was consumed within the same plant or not; that, in fact, reporting varied because instructions (a) changed over the years, (b) were contradictory, and (c) were not obeyed; and, finally, that in the two major areas of machine production and chemicals the treatment of the producers' own consumption differed from that in other industries. In addition, the coverage was intended to change if it was felt that the "objective system of division of labor of society" changed.

Changes for the Second Five Year Plan. For the Second Five Year Plan some order was brought into the confusion. First, defective output is no longer counted as the product of "concrete labor." Second, the producers' own consumption of products is reported only for coal, ores, pig iron, and ingot steel. This means that instead of the old concept of "gross production" the concept of "commodity production" (*Warenproduktion*) has been substituted for the industrial sector only, except for the four basic sectors specifically mentioned.

But some confusion has been added, since the treatment of industrial gross production differed in the national accounts and in the sectoral accounts. In the national accounts the gross product of industry has been defined to include construction and other services performed by industry and inventory changes of unfinished production, both of which are excluded from industrial gross production in the sectoral accounts (except, of course, for projects planned to take more than a year to finish). In other words, the gross product of industry in the national accounts has been defined as the output of *plants* classified as industry, and the gross product of industry in the sectoral accounts as the gross value of *products* defined as industrial. On the other hand, the industrial sector in the national accounts excluded all producers' own consumption, even that of coal, ores, pig iron, and ingot steel, and is therefore equivalent to commodity production.[19]

Valuation

Not only the coverage but also the prices used to value whatever was being measured made the East German gross production figures almost meaningless. During the period of the First Five Year Plan a system of artificial, constant prices was established to measure production. These so-called *Messwerte*, however, were not in fact as constant as they were supposed to be. Moreover, unlike practice in the Soviet Union or Bulgaria, gross production included changes in inventories even if unplanned — a practice discontinued with the Second Five Year Plan — but these changes were *not* valued in constant *Messwerte* at all, but at the actual cost of production. In addition, prices were not uniform for the same product.[20]

Thus the valuation practice differed before and after 1950, and during and after the First Five Year Plan.

The system of Messwerte. The first Statistical Yearbook of the German Democratic Republic states that in 1948 about 1,200 plan positions were formed, with prices (that is, the *Messwerte*) based in part on the 1944 price ceilings and in part on the actual producer prices of 1947–1948.[21] However, Dr. Schmidt gives the number of original plan positions as about 1,500. "In 1951, *Messwerte* were calculated for about 40,000 commodity groups in 1950 prices. With few exceptions, these were adapted to the plan prices in such a manner that the average of the *Messwerte* of a plan position, weighted according to the composition of production in 1950, became equal to the plan price of the plan position." [22] It appears that gross production in 1950 and 1951 was planned by means of the 1,200–1,500 odd positions which received arbitrary and constant plan prices.

It was not possible to ascertain what points of view formed the basis for the formation of these plan prices. No worksheets [*Unterlagen*] exist any more . . . the 1936 prices or the factory prices of 1944 were supposedly used. . . . A comparison of the 1936 prices with the 1948 plan prices shows, however, that the plan prices lie considerably above the 1936 level. [Footnote: This calculation was undertaken by the Staatliche Zentralverwaltung für Statistik at the State Planning Commission.] Comparing the actual 1950 prices with the 1948 plan prices, we find that the 1950 prices also are on the average higher than the 1948 prices. [Footnote: Implied in a comparison of the sum of all prices of 1950 with the sum of all plan values.] This means that our plan values are based neither on 1936 nor on post-1945 prices.[23]

The more than 40,000 positions of 1950–1951 supplement the original 1,500 in the planning process, that is, detailed planning refers to 1,500 positions "because central planning for 40,000 positions is difficult."[24] Each of the 40,000 subpositions is given a fixed *Messwert,* which supposedly makes the plan values variable.[25] Furthermore, it appears not only that the control figures for 1951 of the State Planning Commission were based on the old plan values rather than the new *Messwerte* but also that gross production valued in *Messwerte* was higher than the sum of all plan values with approximately the same quantities.[26] However, Dr. Schmidt states that:

> The decree that all *Messwerte* are to be set in such a manner that their weighted average was the old plan position value was not obeyed in many cases. . . . The plan value of plan position 22–12–120 "special presses" was DM 600; the *Messwerte,* however, are between DM 5,300 and DM 45,000. Of the approximately 375 plan positions in machine construction, about 360 show deviations of more than ±10 per cent, where the highest deviation of the sum of the new *Messwerte* from the old plan value is 8,450:100, and the lowest 1.1:100.[27]

Furthermore, "the relations of the *Messwerte* to each other do not correspond to the relation of the actual prices to each other and . . . a large number of the *Messwerte* deviate too much from the actual prices."[28]

How meaningless the *Messwerte* are is shown by a quotation from Oelssner, who is showing the necessity for a change, since the present system is a "hindrance to the development of production."

> Of the innumerable examples of nonsensical *Messwerte* . . . I shall give one of the worst. Of the nationalized copper rolling mill Hettstedt, Director Bandel reports: "We receive, e.g., for a copper ingot, DM 4.25 per kg. If we roll it to copper wire we get 1.48 DM/kg . . . if we draw it further to finest wires of 1/200 mm, the same *Messwert* applies. But if we work the copper wires into a cable, its value falls to 1.26 DM/kg. The heavier and more complicated the cable, the lower the *Messwert.* For a very complicated cable we receive only 0.88 DM/kg, i.e., one-fifth of the *Messwert* for the copper ingot." . . . Furthermore, the existing *Messwerte* are too little differentiated so that simple changes in the composition of output have a serious effect on the fulfillment of the gross production plan. It is obvious that the existing *Messwerte* have ceased to be useful as instruments of planning. . . . I am aware of the difficulties in solving this problem since most actual prices, particularly for means of production, do not correspond to the expenditure of labor.[29]

All of this amounts to saying that "the present *Messwerte* [not only] are of little use in our planning. We are not in a position to express by means of the *Messwerte* the structure and development of our industrial gross production in a realistic manner." [30] Oelssner further stated:

> In the first place, the concept of gross production is by no means clear . . . second, it has already been proved that the existing *Messwerte* are anything but trustworthy values. It thus follows that the figures about the development of labor productivity in socialist industry with which we operate do not have a very persuasive power of proof.[31]

It is thus somewhat of an understatement to say that the published figures cannot be used to show the development of industrial production as the West understands this term.

Not only are the valuations arbitrary, but the so-called constant prices used to calculate the gross production index in fact varied over the period of the First Five Year Plan. The Statistical Yearbook of the German Democratic Republic itself states that repairs and assemblies for the accounts of others are calculated at actual cost.[32] New products clearly present a problem and give the prices used an upward bias. In addition, as Professor Janakieff has pointed out, since different prices are used for the same product even in the calculation of an index in supposedly constant prices, "production" can increase simply because a good is produced by an inefficient firm instead of an efficient one and hence is counted at a higher price! [33]

The special problem of multiple pricing. Normally, with a Western pricing system, one would have to worry merely about double counting (from our standpoint, of course). *If,* as appears generally to be assumed and partly to be true for the Soviet Union, the gross production index were simply a calculation of all the outputs and all the producers' own consumptions of plants valued at a consistent set of fixed prices (for example, the price of a good at a later stage would contain the full cost of the good entering it from a preceding state), such an index might tend to understate the rate of growth compared with an index based on value added. This might be so both because the value added at earlier stages is apt to be lower than at later stages and because goods produced at earlier stages of production enter the index more often than goods produced at later stages. Thus they would receive a greater weight and therefore hold the index back.

But the actual determination of the factory received prices did not proceed this way in East Germany. There is a problem of multiple pricing which is quite distinct from what is usually meant by the term. In agriculture there is basically a double pricing system, with a third price of very small importance thrown in: a low price is paid for forced deliveries; a higher but still official price is paid for so-called *freie Spitzen,* that is, sales to the government above the obligatory amounts; and for small quantities of unimportant commodities there exists an apparently really free price — as this term is understood in the West. However, both the price for the obligatory deliveries and the *freie Spitzen* are uniform for all sellers.

This is not the case in industrial pricing. I quote from a speech by Ulbricht:

> The area in which we are most backward in the application of economic laws is that of price policy. We do not use price sufficiently as an economic lever in the socialist economy. . . . It is known that since February 1953 we have had a decision of the Ministerial Council about the principles of price policy in which it is . . . determined that for each product and each quality uniform fixed prices have to be determined. This extremely important decision has remained to this day on paper. The basis we use for price formation in the overwhelming majority of cases is the calculated cost of plants, that is, individual costs of plants, but not the socially necessary cost of the industrial branch as a whole . . . to give one example. . . . Six different plants produce the wheel N–13 262a at different calculated prices. . . . For twenty such wheels the works price, including material, basic cost, and overhead is as follows:

at the VEB*	"8 Mai"	338.31 DM
VEB	"W. Friedel"	443.00 DM
VEB	"F. Heckert"	492.37 DM
VEB	"Modul"	675.43 DM
VEB	"Kratos"	472.41 DM
VEB	"Schleifmaschine"	771.79 DM.[34]

The only thing that is hard to understand is how, in the face of a 100 per cent variation in the price permitted to individual plants and calculated on cost, it is possible that anyone has unplanned losses. Yet in the same speech Ulbricht reported that in machine construction there were 133 plants operating at a loss instead of the 85 plants planned; and that in the food industries the number of enterprises showing losses had increased from 65 in 1954 to 73 in 1955, "that is, 30.6 per cent of all plants in the food industry." [35]

All of this means that even such figures for industrial production in terms of factory received prices or any other set of prices which are available in the West must be treated with extreme caution. They should be used only as supplementary information to statistics given in physical units.

Bruttoproduktion *and Industrial Output*

It should by now be clear that the index of gross production as calculated in East Germany would only accidentally move parallel to an index of gross production as calculated in the West to show either total industrial output — which is what the 1936 German calculation of gross production was intended to be — or that part of social product attributable to industry.

If we imagine a super Leontief input-output table in which each plant

* VEB = *Volkseigener Betrieb* (nationalized plant).

appears on both the horizontal and the vertical axis, and in which each plant is supposed to produce only one commodity, then the gross production as calculated in East Germany would be the sum of all the columns, that is, the sum of what each firm sells to every other firm and what it sells to itself. Each entry in each box would be *not* a value added but the *total* value (arbitrary to be sure, but total nevertheless) of the good without any deductions for cost of raw materials and other inputs. This would imply that the whole Leontief table would have to be added twice. In fact, each commodity sold by a firm would appear as often as there are recognized stages between it and the final consumer.

Now if all the stages were invariant, the multiple counting would not matter. Using Western concepts, we would start with a lower base, and the increases would be absolutely lower, but percentagewise the two indices would move exactly the same way. But this condition is precisely what is not given. The index of gross production does not move parallel to any index of production that we would recognize as such by Western standards for the following reasons:

1. The number of plan positions for which the producers' own consumption has to be reported changed from 1,200–1,500 in 1950 to about 220 in 1951 and to about 290 in 1952. Other things being equal, this would tend to lessen the inflation of the index between 1950 and 1951, then increase it again with no real change having occurred. (Attempts to find out the precise number of plan positions involved or any list of goods they represent have been without success.)

2. The inclusion of previously private industry in the nationalized sector would tend to increase the index without bringing about any real change. This would not seem to be the case since private firms also have to report their own consumption, except that the reporting procedure does not apply to "simple commodity production." Furthermore, as smaller private production and previously artisan production become industrialized, the "societal division of labor increases" and with it the gross product.

3. It might be thought that the counting of producers' own consumption introduces a factor that would make the gross production invariant with respect to such factors as the existing degree of vertical integration, but, as has been shown, this is not so. What takes the place of the capitalist "degree of vertical integration" is the pseudo-scientific distinction between "production stage" and "production phase." What is classified as the producers' own consumption with a more industrialized method of production is not classified that way with a less industrialized method. The increase in the roundaboutness of production changes the gross product independent of any changes in productivity.

4. Shifts in the composition of industrial output might cause changes in gross production that are quite different from those that would occur

in a Western economy. If the number of recognized production stages in good A is greater than in good B, a shift from A to B would increase the number of double countings, and vice versa. There is no corresponding effect of change of composition of a Western index.

5. The arbitrary system of *Messwerte* could increase gross product when calculations based on a reasonable system of prices or a Western calculation based on value added would show a decrease in output. It may be worth while to calculate a hypothetical example based on the actual prices — admittedly extreme — quoted above. Suppose that a kilogram of copper ingot is valued at DM 4.25, 1 kg of wire at DM 1.48, and two different cables at DM 1.26 and DM 0.88 per kg, respectively. Suppose we assume that copper products belong to the list of products for which the producers' own consumption has to be counted. In the following example an integrated Firm A is assumed which sells 1,000 kg each of ingot, wire, and the two kinds of cable. Firm B, purchasing the ingot, makes wire. Firm C buys wire from A and B to make the simple cable. Gross production is in this case DM 27,580 if Firm A's own consumption is counted, DM 11,870 if it is not. (See Fig. 2, p. 75.)

By abandoning production of the complex cable and doubling production of the simple cable, the gross product can immediately be increased by DM 380. Furthermore, if copper does not belong to the plan position in which the producers' own consumption is to be reported, the degree of vertical integration would make a difference.

6. Thus it follows that the emphasis on heavy industries and primary production in East Germany raises the gross product by increasing the number of stages and the roundaboutness of production. Hence it is clear that gross production measured in *Messwerte* or, for that matter, in actual factory received prices does not move in the same way as gross production measured by value added. It is apt to have a substantial upward bias. For our purposes it is therefore necessary to build up an independent industrial production index.

7. The upward bias of the gross production index appears to be particularly strong when production is inefficient. If production is for any reason inefficient, the value added of a particular sector might be negative when calculated by Western standards. This could never be the case when inter-industry or inter-firm flows are not excluded, for as long as there is any output whatsoever at a later stage, gross production must increase, although it might increase by less than it would with efficient production. This problem is compounded by the fact that until 1955 rejects were included in the index. Hence the index can show great increases with no products going to their final users. The emphasis on this and other aspects of physical planning and the gross production index in Poland has been severely criticized by Oskar Lange, a criticism that is as valid for the other satellites and possibly for the Soviet Union itself.[36]

East German criticisms

We now have clear-cut evidence that statisticians in East Germany are quite aware of the difficulties mentioned here and of the bias involved in the index. Although the concept of gross production is defended as meaningful in the Marxist system of thought, it is admitted that for many purposes net production is the more useful concept. In other words, according to communist logic, although it would be wrong to correct the calculation of gross production, one should not expect from it the information that it is not intended to convey.[37]

Forbrig distinguishes three methods of measuring gross production: (1) the "plant method," which counts only goods intended for sale, that is, where intra-firm flows are excluded but inter-firm flows are not; (2) the "gross turnover method," in which nothing is excluded; (3) the "economic method," "which was introduced in the Soviet Union" and which "is related to the bourgeois concept of adjusted gross production," [38] in which "the economy is treated as if it were one plant" and which measures in fact what in Western usage is called gross value added. He goes on to say that in East Germany the "gross turnover method" was used during the First Five Year Plan and that the "plant method" is now used, modified for coal, ores, pig iron, and ingot steel, for which "gross turnover" is still employed.

If the economy shows no structural changes as production expands, the turnover method and the economic method will show the same percentage changes, although their levels will be different. But, with changing structure (or, in Marxist terminology, with changing cooperative relations), the two methods will show different increases. If "the organic composition" increases, that is, if the productive process consists of more stages than before, "gross turnover shows a greater development of production than the economic method" and vice versa for a falling "organic composition." [39] "Although the economic method abstracts from the process of value creation [whatever that means], it has the advantage that all changes in cooperative relationships can be isolated, which is only conditionally possible with the method of gross turnover." [40]

Some of the estimating procedures used in Part III of this book involve the application of the 1936 relation of value added to sales value. Forbrig's discussion implies that as an industry becomes organized in an increasing number of stages the ratio of value added to total turnover (or sales value) should decrease. This in turn seems to imply that even the estimating method I have used overestimates the production of East Germany. The degree of this upward bias cannot be established. With a reasonable pricing system, which is assumed in Forbrig's article, net production should increase substantially slower than gross turnover. (For the years 1953 through 1955 for the metalworking industry, Statistical

Practice has published estimates of the degree to which changes in cooperative relationships bias the value of gross production. Although in these branches gross production has not been essentially affected by changes in cooperative relationships, the author concludes that this is due to substantial offsetting changes in individual industry groups.)[41]

Shortcomings of gross production as a planning device

While Forbrig is concerned mainly with gross production as measuring output, Janakieff,[42] in his outspoken criticism, worries about the shortcomings of gross production as an operational planning device, since the gross production index is actually used in planning industrial production and in controlling its fulfillment, in evaluating the dynamics of industrial production, in planning and controlling labor productivity, and in determining the amount of the wage funds, which depends on the degree of plan fulfillment as measured by gross production. Thus the figure is extremely important in a planned economy.

But, as Janakieff points out (and we have been at great pains to stress), this figure does not show the real production.[43] He finds that the concept of gross production has seven operational defects, of which the following are relevant here:[44]

1. Because there are more and less profitable commodities (see Fig. 2), plants deliberately violate the assortment plan in order to fulfill the gross production and labor productivity plans. Plant managers violently criticize the gross production figure for this reason. Since the use of expensive materials is preferred to that of cheaper materials, "gross production clearly does not move parallel with real output." Hence the index has the effect of inducing the waste of inputs. "The size of gross production depends on the value of the raw materials and intermediate goods used, while real production is independent of them." Second, the deviation of actual prices from the theoretically correct ones distorts the index.

2. The use of the gross production index leads to a complete lack of interest in reducing the weight of machinery and other products.

3. The indices of labor productivity are completely fictitious.

4. "Changes in the inventory of unfinished production are to be counted at their full value. . . . Only in special cases, however, is unfinished production evaluated according to the extent to which it is finished. . . . [There exists] the possibility of including the whole value of raw materials and intermediate goods which have been received artificially into the gross production value without expending any live labor whatsoever." *

7. Because of the double counting, and the other shortcomings, it is

---

* Fault 5, that gross production does not correctly reflect changes in organizational structure, and Fault 6, that it does not correctly reflect changes in cooperative relationships, are not relevant here.

Figure 2

FIRM A

Product	Kilograms Production	Used in next stage	Sold to other firms or public	Price per kg in DM–O	Value of gross production in DM–O if the firm's own consumption Is counted	Is not counted
Ingot	4,000	3,000	1,000	4.25	17,000	4,250
Wire	3,000	2,000	1,000	1.48	4,440	1,480
Simple rope	1,000		1,000	1.26	1,260	1,260
Complex rope	1,000		1,000	0.88	880	880
					23,580	7,870

FIRM B

	Purchases	Produces	Sells to C	Price per kg in DM–O	Value of gross production in DM–O
Ingot	1,000				
Wire		1,000	1,000	1.48	1,480

FIRM C

	Purchases	Produces	Sells to public	Price per kg in DM–O	Value of gross production in DM–O
Wire	2,000				
Simple rope		2,000	2,000	1.26	2,520

Gross production of firms A, B, C
(a) if the firms' own consumption is reported 23,580 + 1,480 + 2,520 = DM–O 27,580
(b) if their own consumption is not counted 7,870 + 1,480 + 2,520 = DM–O 11,870

impossible to compare the rate of development of various branches of the economy.

In view of these shortcomings — which, ironically, Western economists have been trying to point out to their communist colleagues for years — why does the gross production figure continue to be used? It is obviously meaningless. Indeed, Professor Janakieff sings the praises of value added — known in communist idiom as the economic method as distinct from the plant method — but he cannot quite bring himself to accept it, first, because value added "depends on the structure of prices and the *peculiarities of price formation under socialism at the present time*" [45] and, second, because it makes no allowance for depreciation. However, since he expressly enumerates as advantages of value added all the things which are wrong with gross production, it seems likely that value added will eventually be used even east of the iron curtain, particularly as Janakieff does not agree with the criticism that value added understates true output.

Perhaps East German economists who see the present study will there-fore feel that it has done some of their work for them, even though the results are rather different from their published statements.

Changes for the Second Five Year Plan

I have described the changes in coverage above. Some progress has also been made in the reform of prices. During the Second Five Year Plan industrial production is to be reported in terms of either "unchang-ing plan prices" or current prices received by industry; the latter is used in the national accounts, the former in the sectoral accounts. The "un-changing plan prices" are "factory received prices as of 1 January 1955. However, for particular products or product groups they are fixed prices confirmed by finance authorities or determined by the Central Statistical Office in conjunction with the relevant ministries." [46] These prices do not include turnover taxes and excises.

Thus prices do not reflect necessarily any real prices received, nor do they reflect expenditures of socially necessary labor. Moreover, it is not clear to what extent the problem of multiple pricing has been solved. East German literature is silent on this problem.

THE SOCIAL ACCOUNTS

Coverage of social product by sectoral origin

The gross or total product of society is intended to be the measure of everything that is produced during a given period in a given area. I have already dealt with the ideology behind the desire to construct such a measure. In spite of all general discussions, the questions of what "everything" means and of what "produced" means remain unanswered until the specific methods of calculation are known. In fact, the Marxist concept of social product must be operationally defined; it cannot be derived from Marxist theory.

While a Western economist has great difficulties in understanding why anyone would wish to spend time and energy to construct what is essentially a turnover measure, the quest for the definition of "product" can be translated into Western language; it is essentially the Marxist attempt to find an answer to what is and what is not a transfer income. All transfer incomes are obviously to be excluded. Unlike his Western colleagues, the communist economist has a magic word to decide what is not a transfer income. It is "material." If it is "material" it is "pro-duced," otherwise it is "redistributed." Unfortunately, the magic word is no sure guide, and the communist practitioner no less than his Western counterpart must make decisions in individual instances.

During the First Five Year Plan only industry and artisan shops, agriculture and forestry, the water supply, transportation and communications (except for the government and population), and trade were counted as productive sectors.[47] During the Second Five Year Plan not only do we get changes in what is specifically meant by gross production, but also whole new sectors are now declared "productive."

During the First Five Year Plan *agricultural gross production* included fodder and other plants consumed in further agricultural production. During the Second Five Year Plan only production for the market (forced deliveries and sales) and the peasants' own consumption of their products (which includes seeds) are counted. No such change has been made for animal products. Eggs used to maintain the stock of laying hens continue to be part of reported gross production. In addition, since 1956, the increase in the value of the stock of animals is also part of production. The performance of the Machine Tractor Stations (MTS) — which in Western usage is clearly an intermediate good — is also included. The reason is ideological: the MTS produce material goods, and, unlike the fodder produced and used at the farm, they represent a separate stage of the societal division of labor.[48] Thus the communist concept has come slightly closer to Western ideas.

Perhaps the greatest change in coverage has occurred in the *transportation and communications sector*. During the First Five Year Plan only freight traffic and the delivery of business letters or telegrams were considered part of gross production. Now passenger traffic and all communications are included. Two reasons are given for this change. It is wrong to suppose that the function of transportation and communications is to move material goods. Its function is movement in itself. If so, the logical basis for distinguishing between freight and passenger traffic, between business and private or government letters or telegrams, disappears.

Moreover, practically speaking, the calculations are needed for other investigations, for example, for an analysis of employment or investments. But joint costs make any allocation of investments between investments for "productive" and "unproductive" transportation arbitrary. Hence it is better not to distinguish in the first place.[49]

The gross product of *domestic trade* is equivalent to the total difference between selling price and cost even though selling *per se* is apparently not productive — only storage and packaging are. The contribution of foreign trade enterprises is considered to be zero.

During the First Five Year Plan the *water economy* was the only other sector considered productive in part (that is, the supply of water for household, industrial, and other uses). During the Second Five Year Plan gross production also includes removal of damage to water installations and various other services performed, for example, in landscaping!

The Second Five Year Plan now recognizes also a production of "culture, public hygiene, and social services," which is quite inadequately described, and "other economic sectors," which include among others the total sales of publishing houses.

Thus the changes that have occurred in the methods of East German statisticians during the Second Five Year Plan have considerably broadened the concept of social product by including as productive many services previously excluded. At the same time, we observe that the double counting has diminished. Although it is still present in agriculture (and industry, which has been separately discussed), there is virtually no double counting in the trade or transportation sector, all turnover taxes being allocated to the trading sector.

The social product by use

East German economists recognize a double classification of the social product by use. Ideally, the allocation of a product is made in the best Böhm-Bawerkian manner according to the way product is actually used. In practice, however, this is not always feasible, and the allocation is made either by allocating a *product* to one or the other *"Abteilung,"* or, in the case of industry, by allocating the *production of a whole plant*. The second, and more interesting for us, is the division by consumption and what we would call investments. Here, too, methodology has changed substantially between the two Five Year Plans. The concept of investments does not exist in the national accounts; instead, a distinction is made between accumulation and consumption. In other communist economies accumulation is broken down into productive and unproductive accumulation, and such a distinction is also found in the East German literature. But in the official statistics the distinction is relegated to a footnote.

Before 1956 "accumulation" included (1) the increase in the means of production, both fixed means and inventories, and increases in the stock of animals and (2) increases both in institutions and plants of social consumption and in the state reserve. Consumption consisted of individual consumption and social consumption, the latter consisting of the maintenance of social plant and equipment and the foreign trade balance.

Everything has now been reshuffled. Individual consumption now includes housing, previously with nonproductive accumulation, and also expenditures on passenger traffic.

Pricing

The crucial difficulties for the interpretation of the East German statistics arise with respect to pricing. During the First Five Year Plan *agricultural production* in current prices was valued at double prices: forced deliveries and sales to the government at higher prices were valued at actually realized prices, which differed substantially for the two categories, while the valuation of the production which remained at the farm was valued at the prices for forced deliveries, the lowest of the permissible prices. Since 1956 the consumption on the farm (which includes, it will be remembered, a substantial quantity of intermediate goods) has been valued at an average of the prices received for "market" production. This is true both for animal and for crop production. The effect is, of course, to raise the value of gross production substantially because the double counting now enters with an increased weight into the final result.

The calculation of agricultural gross production in 1950 prices was made by multiplying physical output by the average of the prices for forced deliveries and for government purchases. However, inland fishing, horticulture, and forestry were not recalculated but entered gross production in supposedly constant, but actually current prices.[50] While fishing and horticulture are relatively insignificant, forestry is not. Hence the calculations in supposedly constant 1950 prices have an upward bias even from the standpoint of the East German accounts themselves.

The calculation in 1955 prices (which has not been published) proceeds in the same manner. The actual amounts produced — and the reader is reminded that "production" here is a more inclusive term than in the West — are valued at the average prices for the base year. However, the multiple price system raises its ugly head once more: socialized farms and private farms have different impositions of forced deliveries and government sales at higher prices. Hence, even where the prices for each category of sales are the same for each kind of property, the average price varies with the change in the relative size of the type of property. The calculations are made separately for private, socialized, and cooperative productions, but the average prices for the base year 1955 are automatically transferred to later years. Since private farms are penalized by relatively higher impositions at lower prices, the changing structure of agriculture toward more socialization raises the average prices in the economy without raising the prices paid to the various types of farms. Hence the method of calculation also imparts a bias to the calculations of the agriculture sector in constant 1955 prices, which is then corrected in the trade sector.

Construction is a very important sector. Its valuation in current prices proceeded at actual prices, including all costs that must legally be paid, such as payments for work interruptions and idle time! Contrary to Koziolek's statements, no recalculations were made during the First Five Year Plan "because there exist no data suitable for a calculation of price developments," [51] and even in 1959 no calculations in constant 1955 prices were made because price developments were still unclear and because "fixed prices are not unchanging for they are continuously corrected." [52]

For the *transportation and communications* sector, no deflation to

1950 prices was made during the First Five Year Plan. The figures for the construction and the transportation sectors, reproduced in Table 17, are therefore mislabeled. Koziolek[53] states that the reason for the failure to deflate the product of the transportation sector was that tariffs did not change very much. But the real reason seems to have been that it was too difficult to get the data necessary for such a deflation.[54] The problem of deflating has not yet been solved even for the Second Five Year Plan,[55] but ideally the sector is to be valued in 1955 prices.

What was done in the trade sector is not clear from the descriptions given. It is impossible to understand Koziolek's account of the recalculation of the gross product of trade in 1950 prices.[56] Nor is the account of the procedures that are being followed for the Second Five Year Plan much clearer. It is stated that the trade sector's gross product must be deflated in a special manner, that price indices cannot be used because the greatest change in the receipts is due not to prices but to changes in turnover taxes, and that turnover taxes may change either because the rates themselves have been changed or because their imposition has been transferred to other sectors. Hence only changes in "actually realized excises and taxes" are allowed for.[57] Just what all this amounts to is quite unclear to me.

The other economic sectors are not to be calculated in 1955 prices at all. As of 1958, calculations in constant 1955 prices have been published only for the important industrial sector. The discussions in East German journals suggest that the reason for the failure to publish calculations for the other sectors is that the methods of deflation used thus far have been found unsatisfactory.

National income in constant prices

The problems of finding suitable deflators seem to be especially intractable for the calculation of national income in constant prices. The calculations of the First Five Year Plan are admitted to have been essentially arbitrary; no data by economic sector existed on the structure of the means of production used up and on their price changes.

> Such data did not exist and we are still unable to procure them. Proper methods to find these data by sampling are yet to be developed. The previously published figures on the structure of the total product of society in constant prices by value components [i.e., means of production used up, net product] were found simply by apportioning the share of each sector in the total product at current (effective) prices to each value component. Such a procedure has, however, no economic meaning. *Until proper methods are developed no further data about the value structure of the total social product in constant prices by economic sector and property form will be published.*[58]

This is an admission of total defeat. To be sure, aggregate national income in constant prices is still being calculated (though the results are not yet published) by deflating the total of all means of production used up with a price index (also not published) of all domestically produced means of production (*Arbeitsgegenstände*), and by deducting this value from the total social product in constant prices.

The admission of defeat is even more significant than it first appears. For, as I have repeatedly pointed out, the multiple counting in the gross product has the peculiar result of changing the end result simply because the division of labor is changing even if output is not changed at all. But

It has thus far been impossible to eliminate the change in the total product due to structural changes in the societal division of labor. Even now no methods exist to eliminate these changes and to make calculations according to the structure of the base year. The only possibility of eliminating these changes consists in abstracting from all societal division of labor and simply calculating the total social product according to the economic method; or calculating the real product as this measure is called by some economists.[59]

However, this "real product" or "total product of society according to the economic method" is none other than our net value added. This calculation, too, seems at present beyond the ability of the East German Central Statistical Office. This is equally true for the calculations of the domestically available national income by use in constant prices for which "methods are yet to be developed to determine price indices for the individual uses." [60]

Concluding remarks

What follows from this account is rather discouraging. The concepts used by East German practitioners, although *in abstracto* more similar to ours than one would expect, are nevertheless much broader and contain double countings which are also felt to be double countings on the other side of the iron curtain. But a discussion *in abstracto* will go only a very short way. The actual description of the steps taken to calculate given results reveals that the figures do not measure what they pretend to measure. Not only is the gross product dependent on the degree of the recognized division of labor (so that it will change with each division even when there is no change in actual output), but also "constant" prices are not constant when the producer's kind of property changes as in agriculture, and in fact prices are frequently not even constant over time. If the interpretation of the social accounts presents so many difficulties even for the economy that calculates them for its own purposes, surely the difficulties are even greater for a Western observer.

The conclusion of this discussion is that either a meaningful interpretation of the officially published social accounts is impossible or it is possible only after independent calculations with consistent prices and a consistent methodology have been made. The rest of this book is devoted to providing such independent calculations.

PART THREE

INDUSTRIAL PRODUCTION

EVALUATION PROCEDURES

In the literature on Soviet production indices the problem of valuing the various outputs in standard units receives major attention, and all solutions are presented as tentative. For example, if American prices are used, the practice is subject to the strictures (clearly recognized by the various authors) that it imposes a set of scarcity relations on circumstances in which they are not applicable. It may, however, be defensible to value East German outputs by West German prices whenever feasible.

The following considerations are intended to justify such a procedure. First, not enough information on East German prices was available for the purposes of this study. Furthermore, the trouble with the East German price system, whether that of *Messwerte* or of prices received by producers, is that it is inconsistent, that it makes no sense even in its own terms. Awareness of the inconsistencies is of course shown by the fact that the pricing methods in East Germany were revised in 1956 in favor of uniform prices based on "technically determined norms." Even these prices, however, do not have the same function in the Soviet system as they have in the West; nor would the price structure necessarily be the same, except perhaps in some long-range equilibrium. Such prices would not necessarily reflect relative scarcities of commodities, but at least they would be consistent in the sense that the copper-wire-cable example given in Chapter III could not occur and that some process of imputing factory received prices for a product at a later stage of production to products at preceding stages would be possible. Moreover, they could be used to sort out efficient from inefficient plants. It remains to be seen whether the reforms of the pricing system begun in 1956 will lead to an internally more consistent system. For the reasons discussed in Chapter III, calculations of East German output in East German prices is not feasible, nor would such a calculation be meaningful even if it could be made.

The trouble with applying to one economy the prices developed in the context of another economy is usually that they reflect different demand and supply conditions. In the case of East Germany this otherwise almost unsurmountable difficulty is somewhat mitigated by historical circumstances. It is, of course, true that even within an area that is politically unified there are substantial price differentials due to transportation costs (or, where transportation costs are absorbed, there are differences in profits); and within such areas there are also differentials in factor prices, which are much greater than those of commodity prices and which, in a market economy, apparently have no tendency to disappear completely. Yet before the war East and West Germany were a well-integrated whole and a cultural unit with consumers' tastes that were not substantially different, with a pricing system that internal mobility kept reasonably uniform, and with a known and fairly regular West-East wage gradient.

Consumers' tastes are not likely to have changed very radically in the few years since 1945. Although consumers' choices are quite a different matter, it seems permissible to rule out the possibility that prices in East and West Germany differ greatly because consumers' tastes have grown apart. There are, however, great differences in supply and in the demands, which do not come from final consumers.

So long as the two parts of Germany were one, the supply of different factors could vary only within the cost of moving them. With division, the mobility of factors was reduced substantially. What mobility of labor does exist is (as it has always been) overwhelmingly in the East-West direction; the intra-German mobility of basic inputs such as coal, steel, and steel products is regulated by interzonal trade. Since the frontier between the two parts of Germany has not been and still is not airtight, black market transactions are likely to exist. Furthermore, initially the basic factor endowments (used in a wide sense to include capacities of industries) were not very different, with the important exception of soft coal concentrated in the West and lignite in the East and heavy industries concentrated in the West against lighter industries in the East. (Admittedly this is a very simplified picture.)

A few modifications of this rough picture are necessary. Before the war the area that is now East Germany imported substantial amounts of soft coal, steel, and steel products. Since 1945 the structure of the East German industry (as will be shown in detail) has expanded precisely in the direction of heavy industries, which, with the exception of synthetic chemicals, require more soft coal and iron and steel at the very time when imports of these materials, at least from the West, have been severely curtailed. In a market economy the prices of these basic inputs would have risen substantially. As it is, however, it is precisely these prices that are kept low by controls in the planned economy, and that are either higher in the West or not very different. On the whole, the use of West German prices paradoxically understates the relative scarcity of basic materials in the East, but, at the same time, reflects it better than the controlled East German prices would.*

Considering these facts, it is not clear just how the use of West German prices — which are the prices used in interzonal trade — would bias the evaluation of East German output, but any distortions introduced by using prices appropriate to West German relative scarcities to the East German situation would necessarily be much smaller than those introduced by similar procedures for any other set of countries, for example, using dollar prices for Soviet output. The initial economic situation at the time of partition was fairly similar in the two parts of Germany. They were part of a closely integrated economy; dismantling was heavier in the East, but the reconstruction of the East German economy was intended to reduce the differences in the structures of the East and West German economies by emphasizing heavy industry.

The use of West German prices to evaluate East German output therefore appears to be a defensible procedure, somewhat less vulnerable to the objections that are usually made to using a price system appropriate to one set of circumstances in an alien context. Moreover, the West German price system has the invaluable advantage of being internally consistent, while the East German price system is not.

The use of West German prices, however, does not end our troubles. For example, the index of Soviet machinery production calculated by Gerschenkron dealt primarily with final goods. Hence the basic problem in computing the index was to find appropriate prices. Most commodities for which we have data in standard units are, however, clearly intermediate goods, and it is completely impossible to calculate an index on a value added basis, for example, by using wages and "profits" (that is, indirect taxes) in the East German economy. No such figures exist by industries. Furthermore, only very few official input-output data exist. Nevertheless, procedures have been followed that can be justified as giving a rough approximation to an index of industrial production on a gross value added basis.

In equilibrium, the price of each commodity should cover its total cost, including the cost of commodities purchased and used in production. By breaking down the available material into subgroups it ought to be possible to find values that at a later date must be deducted, which is, of course, impossible without some estimates of where materials go. Some rough information is available to aid in making such estimates. Wherever feasible, we shall attempt to make some rough input-output

---

* Although West German prices may be more appropriate to an economy with a fairly easy supply situation, they are in fact frequently higher than the producer prices in East Germany. By the time products reach the consumer the relation is quite the opposite.

calculations; where this is not possible, other methods will be used. Basically, these other methods involve calculating some sort of index of sectoral output and applying it to a 1936 figure for value added of each particular sector. The specific method will be described in detail as each case arises.

The basic statistical information is given in the Production Statistics of 1936, which divided all German industry into 30 major subgroups. Group 30 includes construction and apparently also the airplane industry and will not be considered in this part of the study. For the rest, wherever possible, the 1936 classifications will be followed. Whenever changes are made — for example, synthetic yarns were classified in 1936 among textiles and are now classified among chemicals — they will be specifically described and justified. Crosschecks will be applied to ensure that the results found are at least possible.

All calculations were made in terms of 1936 and 1950 West German prices. It did not prove feasible to recalculate all series in current West German prices in order to arrive at price indices in comparable terms. The year 1936 was chosen because of the availability of the production census; the year 1950 was chosen as a postwar year because the new calculation of West German industrial production is based on 1950 prices.

It is clear that all calculations can claim only very approximate validity. When input-output relations are estimated, only the major inputs can be considered. When the 1936 relation of value added to gross production or sales value is used to estimate later value added figures, the implication is not only that technology has remained roughly the same but also that efficiency has remained roughly the same. Changed technology seems to be important only in the latest years of our calculations, beginning in 1954 at the earliest. Until 1954, efficiency appears to have been low; since then it probably has increased substantially. In such important areas as machinery production, castings, and car production, it is known not only that East German output as late as 1955 was qualitatively much below current world standards but also that the technology differed little from that of 1936. In particular, it is known that machinery was until very recently built as heavy as before the war. Hence, using the 1936 value added in the manner described involves probably only a small error in the calculations for East Germany. In any case, it is not quite self-evident how increased efficiency will affect the ratio of value added to sales value — the greater the efficiency of production, the lower this ratio is likely to be. The immediate effect of inefficiency would be to lower total output with the same inputs. It was not usually possible to allow for changes in efficiency or technology — an omission that probably gives the benefit of the doubt to the East German economy.

CHAPTER V

MINING AND GAS

FUELS

T HE first index to be calculated is for solid fuel production, consist-ing of lignite, lignite briquets, lignite coke (including so-called BHT coke*), soft coal, soft coal coke, and peat. In many respects, this is not only the most fundamental index to calculate but also one of the easier ones and one that is likely to be reasonably reliable. The importance of the sector requires and justifies the detail with which the calculations are described.†

Lignite and lignite products

Lignite is the most important East German product. In fact, East Germany, with its very highly developed lignite technology, is probably the largest producer of lignite in the world. Lignite is used primarily for briquets and as a base for power and synthetic gasoline production, only about 17 per cent being used in the production of lignite itself. Other fuels and water power are of subordinate importance for power and heat-ing. Lignite is *the* basic raw material of East Germany. The whole de-velopment of the East German economy depends to an unusual degree on the development of its lignite output.

For our calculations, the problem consists of finding where the lignite goes and of valuing at this stage, in West German prices (which are also controlled and relatively low and virtually identical with East German prices), that portion of the lignite that is not used in the production of lignite briquets and lignite coke. The basic estimating schema is as follows:

---

* *Braunkohlen Hochtemperatur Koks,* i.e., coke of metallurigical quality made from lignite. Ordinary coke made from lignite cannot be used in metallurgy.

† The very considerable details of the calculations are given in a Supplement, which interested persons may purchase from the Publications Office, Center for International Studies, Massachusetts Institute of Technology. The main results will be summarized in the text. Because of the importance of the lignite sector to the whole economy, more detail is given in the text tables for this than for other sectors.

Raw lignite distribution
{
1. Exports
2. Used to produce lignite
3. Used as fuel in homes
4. Used as a base for chemicals
5. Used as a base of electric power production
6. Used to produce briquets
7. Used to produce ordinary lignite coke and BHT coke
8. Inventories, including State Reserve
}

Since the index of fuel production should be limited to lignite going to final consumers, items 2, 6, and 7 are not included. Fortunately, virtually no lignite is imported.

For 1936 and for 1952 the *Materialien** contain an attempt to account for the use of lignite and lignite briquet production.[1] The 1952 input-output relations are applied to the period from 1950 through 1954. The basic problem here was to find the best data for the output of lignite by weight and the price of lignite in 1950.

The 1936 price for lignite used was the average value of gross production after deducting the lignite consumption by the lignite sector. Other prices are based on information given by Thimm[2] and the German Yearbook.†

The information on output comes entirely from official East German sources.‡ The gross value added of the lignite sector was calculated by making estimates of the approximate input-output relations. So far as possible, intermediate products of the whole lignite sector, that is, of either lignite or its products, were eliminated. The amounts of raw lignite going into briquet and coke production were found by using the known 1936 relations for briquets and estimates based on caloric content and checked against information from the East German *Neue Hütte* for coke (February 1956, a special issue on low-shaft furnaces).

Inputs were derived as follows: (1) From the total production of raw lignite, only 17 per cent was deducted to allow for consumption within the lignite sector§ in conformity with Production Statistics of 1936, where gross production refers to 83 per cent of total production. (2) For briquets, only raw lignite inputs were allowed for, on the basis of information given in *Materialien*. (3) Lignite used as fuel and lignite used as raw material were calculated separately, the latter on the basis of the known water content of raw lignite. (4) For ordinary lignite coke, it was assumed that briquets were the major input for production and raw lig-

---

* A list of short titles of German books and journals faces p. 1.

† Note that this is not an official year book.

‡ The precise methods of calculation and estimation are described in the notes to Table A.1 of the Supplement.

§ It is impossible to say precisely how this input is used, e.g., whether it is used to heat boilers or to generate electricity for use within the sector, etc.

nite for heating purposes. (5) For BHT coke, raw lignite inputs were based on detailed information in *Neue Hütte*. In addition to these inputs, 40 per cent of the total electricity used in the mining sector as a whole was allocated to lignite mining and the production of lignite products.*

The values and the indices calculated correspond very roughly to the prewar concept of *Nettoproduktion*, that is, the gross value added (of the output of the lignite and lignite products sector) with the major intra-sector and inter-sector (electricity) flows excluded.

The major output figures and results of the calculations are given in Table 18 for the period 1936–1958. Output of the lignite sector was almost the same in 1945–1946 as in 1936. By 1956 the expansion was substantial. In 1936 prices, the output was 93.8 per cent greater than 1936; in 1950 prices, it was slightly less. Compared with 1950, when the First Five Year Plan was started, it was only about 45 per cent, and 1950 was the first year in which the peak production of 1943 was surpassed. Since lignite is *the* important fuel and power source, this last increase provides a useful check on the official claim of a 100 per cent increase in gross production between 1950 and 1955.

In order to have a check on whether there were sufficient supplies of lignite and its products for the reported uses, an attempt must now be made to allocate the available supplies of raw lignite, briquets, and coke to the various uses in the next stages of production.

It is known that ordinary lignite coke cannot be used for producing metal. There has been substantial technological progress in the use of lignite coke for smelting, and an expansion of facilities for iron ore smelting. Usable BHT coke has been produced only since 1954, however, and even at the end of 1955 there was only one major producing unit using the new process by means of which low-grade native iron ores of about 20 to 25 per cent iron content could be reduced. The maximum capacity of these iron works is given as 900 tons of pig iron per day, or 329,500 tons per year, working full time every day. Native iron-ore production in 1955 was 1,664,000 tons[3] with a probable iron content of about 472,000 tons, which appears to be the maximum feasible at the present time. The relative rise of iron ore mining reported and the capacity of the low-shaft furnaces provide a reliable check on the mining of iron ore as well as on the production of iron from native ore. Only the new Calbe Works produce iron from native ores — probably the only smelter in the world using low grade ores with BHT coke.†

In allocating the raw lignite and briquets to the production of synthetic gasoline and synthetic diesel fuel,‡ it is assumed that the input is

---

* For details, see notes to Table A.1 of the Supplement.

† The estimates of the value added of BHT coke are given in Table A.2, of the Supplement.

‡ See Table A.3 of the Supplement.

roughly the same per unit for both. According to one West German source,[4] which considers the estimate too low, in the opinion of East German experts 6 to 8 million tons of lignite briquets are required to produce 1,230,000 tons of gas and oil. Such optimistic figures imply that for each ton of raw lignite, 7.7 per cent would be gas or diesel fuel, and, if briquets are the input, twice as much gas or diesel fuel would result.

It is very probable that at least some of the 17 per cent of lignite used within the raw lignite sector is used for power generation at the mines. (Otherwise, as a rough check showed, not enough lignite would be available for all the reported uses.) Of the total installed capacity, so-called industrial generating stations (as distinct from public generating stations) account for about 50 per cent. A substantial number of these are generating stations connected with lignite mining. It is therefore possible that the 17 per cent of raw lignite stated to have been used within the lignite sector is used not only to produce lignite (for heating, running locomotives, and so on), but also to produce electric power. Of the 23 industrial generating stations with an installed capacity of more than 10 mw, having a total installed capacity of 1,287.1 mw, those that were definitely associated with mines accounted for 27 per cent.[5] For the end of 1951 the

Table 18

Production and value added, lignite sector, East Germany, 1936, 1938, 1943, and 1946–1958

Year	Lignite production (million tons)[a]	Index (1936 = 100)	Lignite leaving fuel sector, including fuel used to produce power at the mines (million tons)[a]	Production of briquets (million tons)[a]	Briquets available for use outside the fuel sector (million tons)[a]
	(1)	(2)	(3)	(4)	(5)
1936	101.1	100.0	40.44	23.5	16.45
1938	119.6	118.3	43.70	30.0	22.06
1943	165.1	163.3	55.91	43.8	33.95
1946	108.4	107.5	32.22	29.0	18.28
1947	102.2	101.1	30.83	27.0	17.13
1948	108.4	108.6	31.33	29.9	19.07
1949	127.2	125.8	35.98	34.8	24.33
1950	137.1	135.5	38.31	37.7	22.42
1951	151.3	149.6	42.58	41.1	24.85
1952	158.5	156.7	44.35	43.6	26.58
1953	172.8	170.9	52.02	45.7	27.47
1954	181.9	179.9	56.38	46.9	28.40
1955	200.6	197.8	61.77	51.0	31.71
1956	205.9	204.2	64.30	51.6	32.13
1957	212.6	210.3	64.81	53.4	33.29
1958	215.0	212.7	63.96	54.0	33.91

Table 18 (Continued)

Year	Production of coke (million tons)[a]	Production of BHT coke (million tons)[a]	Value added of lignite sector (million RM/DM)[b]		Index of value added of lignite sector (million RM/DM)	
			1936 Prices	1950 Prices	1936 Prices	1950 Prices
	(6)	(7)	(8)	(9)	(10)	(11)
1936	1.90	0.000	317.374	576.016	100.0	100.0
1938	1.90		395.065	695.330	124.5	120.7
1943	1.90		571.398	981.109	180.0	170.3
1946	3.50		338.684	582.748	106.7	101.2
1947	3.20		317.851	548.667	100.2	95.3
1948	3.50		346.601	591.027	109.2	102.6
1949	3.00		416.906	703.532	131.4	122.1
1950	5.22	0.000	423.163	723.349	133.3	125.6
1951	5.66	0.000	467.833	800.250	147.4	138.9
1952	5.71	0.021	493.958	842.558	155.6	146.3
1953	6.18	0.235	527.178	914.282	166.1	158.7
1954	6.24	0.424	550.984	963.643	173.6	167.3
1955	6.37	0.458	609.183	1066.319	191.9	185.1
1956	6.418	0.732	621.896	1094.294	196.0	190.0
1957	6.625	0.782	609.445[c]	1109.457	192.0[c]	192.6
1958	6.581	0.995	618.664	1123.545	194.9	195.1

Sources: Cols. 1, 4, 6, and 7: For 1936, 1946, 1948, and 1950–1955, see *SJDDR*, 1955, pp. 162–163; for 1956 and 1957, *ibid.*, 1957, p. 294; for 1938 and 1943, Gleitze, *Ostdeutsche Wirtschaft*, p. 192. 1947 and 1949 are calculated with index in *SP*, October 1956. Col. 2: Calculated from col. 1. Col. 3: For derivation see text and Supplement Table A.1. Lignite used to produce lignite, lignite briquets, and lignite coke has been deducted. Other "outside" use are exports (including interzonal trade), households, state reserves, industries, public utilities, and transportation. Col. 5: Col. 4 less estimated inputs of briquets into the making of coke and briquets. See Supplement Table A.1. Cols. 8 and 9: Defined as the sum of the sales values of lignite and briquets leaving the lignite or briquet sector plus the sales values of coke and BHT coke, less the cost of electricity inputs and of the lignite used as fuel for coke production. For prices and other details, see Supplement Tables A.1 and A.2. Cols. 10 and 11: Derived from cols. 8 and 9.
    [a] All ton figures refer to metric tons of 1,000 kg.
    [b] Calculations in 1936 prices are in reichsmark (RM) of 1936 purchasing power; calculations in 1950 prices are in Deutsche mark (DM) of 1950 purchasing power.
    [c] The decrease in the value added, measured in 1936 prices, from 1956 to 1957 is probably spurious. For 1957, *SJDDR*, 1957, p. 314, states that the lignite sector used 2,899.864 million kwhr of power, of which 1,022.184 million were purchased from outside the lignite sector. Previous estimates may overestimate the value of electricity consumed by the lignite sector.

installed capacity of generating stations associated with mining is given as 570 mw, compared with 1,424 mw for Sowjetische Aktiengesellschaften (SAG)* stations and 795 mw for the other (German) industrial stations. Since the SAG's were later returned to German ownership, this means that at the end of 1951 about 20 per cent of the installed capacity was in generating stations associated with mining.[6]

Soft coal, soft coal coke, and gas

Very little soft coal is found in the Soviet Zone, and what there is is not particularly good. The existing deposits are being exhausted; the 1913

* Production units taken over by the occupation forces and incorporated in Moscow, working for the Russians. By 1955 all of them had been returned to German ownership.

output[7] of 5½ million tons has never again been even approximated nor has the 1936 output of 3½ million tons been reached again.* Of the soft coal found in the Zone only about 9 per cent is suitable for coking, and the resulting coke is of inferior quality, at least for producing metal.[8] In general, the coke derived from imported coal is said to be of variable quality. Domestic coal apparently yields coke which is very acid and has a high water and high sulfur content.[9] In the following calculation it was assumed that all cokeable East German soft coal is actually used as coke.

The value added of soft coal production was estimated by valuing the total output in 1936 and 1950 prices and applying the 77.11 per cent ratio of value added to gross production in 1936 for all of Germany.[10] In 1956, output was still about 20 per cent below 1936 and had not quite reached the 1950 level.

The scanty information available on coke production is largely from various West German sources. Since there is a fairly fixed technical relation between gas and coke and coal, for many years it was possible to approximate the amount of coke produced from the amount of gas produced. A plan figure for coke production was found for 1954 that seemed reasonable in size and consistent with both the figures for the preceding years and the actual and planned imports. It was accepted. The plan figure for 1954 was assumed unchanged for 1955. These estimates cannot be very far from the actual outputs, but it should be stressed that they are essentially calculated guesses.†

In order to calculate the value added of coke production, the coal inputs at least must be deducted from the sales value of coke. For domestic coal this was done on the assumption that 9 per cent of Saxonian coal is cokeable and that 67 kg of coke and 31 cu m of gas are produced from each 100 kg of coal.‡ However, since most coke is produced from imported coal, the value of these imports must similarly be deducted. In 1946–1947 most of the coal was from West Germany; in 1949 about 60 per cent was Polish (Upper Silesian) coal.

Since gas and tar are produced as joint products in the process of making coke, the coal input should be deducted from the joint value of the three products. Hence it became necessary to include gas in the discussion of the mining sector. The value added of coke alone (exclusive of gas) is certainly negative. However, including gas and other products jointly produced, it is positive. It was impossible to allow for other inputs.

The price series chosen for coke refers to the so-called blast-furnace coke of the Ruhr and Aachen districts. If the lump-coke price of the lower Saxony district had been chosen, the index of the value of coke produced would not have been substantially different. However, if the price of

---

* Except for the estimates for 1947 and 1949, all figures are based on East German sources.

† In November 1957 a series for coke production was published for the first time.

‡ The sources for most of the technical data are given in the footnotes to the tables.

foundry coke had been chosen, the values for the index in constant 1950 prices would have been higher. By 1950 a noticeable gap had developed between the prices of foundry and blast-furnace coke. In 1936 blast-furnace coke was only 5 per cent cheaper than foundry coke, but in 1950 it was about 16 per cent cheaper. The coke actually produced in East Germany is of lower quality than either West German blast-furnace or foundry coke.

It should be mentioned that, although some gas is produced from lignite* and some as a by-product of hydrogenation, no lignite or lignite briquet inputs were deducted. Deduction was implicitly made by allocating all such inputs to lignite coke. On the other hand, although some lignite tar is produced, it is almost certainly also used in hydrogenation and is therefore allowed for in synthetic fuel production. (Water-free Central German lignite, the coking of which is worth while, yields on the average 20–25 per cent tar, 50–55 per cent coke, 15–20 per cent gas, and 8–10 per cent combined water.[11]) There are actually only two gas works based on lignite, but both are said to be efficient.[12]

Most figures for gas production are official and substantially higher than the estimates made by the Deutsche Institut für Wirtschaftsforschung. However, since it is known that the caloric content of gas in East Germany is only 3,200–3,800 cal per cu m compared with 4,200–4,500 in West Germany, the official figures are consistent with the lower estimates. For purposes of evaluation, the official gas series was adjusted to the higher caloric content.

Only the amount needed within gas works was deducted from the total production of gas. The coal used was allowed for in coke production, and it was assumed that no other fuels are used in gasworks. The low average consumption of gas within the gas sector is the result of a high consumption of gas in works primarily producing coke — about 50 per cent — and a low one in gasworks primarily producing gas — about 12.5 per cent. Although the former figure corresponds to West German usage, the latter figure is about half of that usual in West Germany. This low use of gas within the gas sector suggests either that there are fewer other by-products or that the quality of the coke produced in East German gasworks is relatively low. Gas produced in works based on lignite apparently does not require gas for its own production, and the same is true for gas produced as a by-product of hydrogenation.

The presumably low quality of coke produced in gasworks also explains why there are additional substantial imports of coke. Of necessity, all this is speculation, but it is consistent with the known facts. (In 1955,

* Of the total gas capacities in 1956 of 2.2–2.4 billion cu m about 1.7–1.8 billion cu m are based on imported Polish or West German soft coal, about 0.1 billion cu m on Saxonian soft coal, and about 0.4–0.6 on lignite. The latter figure is valid only for 1956 and had increased somewhat in 1957–1958. There are about 1 million cu m of natural gas in Thuringia.

2.6 million tons of coke were imported, and in 1956, 2.3 million tons.[13])

In the process of producing coke and gas a number of additional products are almost automatically produced, the most important being soft coal tar and benzol. Since it may have been impossible to make use of these important by-products, particularly in the early postwar years, the qualification "almost" has to be inserted. For each 100 kg of coal, 6 kg of tar are produced from Silesian coal, but only 5 kg from domestic Saxonian coal and 4.5 kg from Ruhr coal.[14] At present, however, there are insurmountable difficulties in estimating the value or the amount of raw tar and raw benzol that are actually produced with the coke.

Both raw tar and raw benzol are scarce products in the Zone, but it is possible to calculate the maximum amount of raw tar that could be produced with the known or calculated amounts of coal used in coking, based on the technical coefficients referred to above. (See Table 19.) For

Table 19

Maximum amount of raw soft coal tar that could be produced
in East Germany, 1936 and 1946–1953

Year	Thousand tons	Year	Thousand tons
1936	75 (actual, 74)[a]	1950	158
1946	48	1951	149
1947	69 (actual, 34.2)[a]	1952	150
1948	109	1953	204
1949	115		

[a] Actual figures are from *Die Gaswirtschaft in der Sowjetischen Besatzungszone Deutschlands* ("*Mitteilungen aus dem Institut für Raumforschung*," No. 3), Bad Godesberg, 1950, p. 7.

1947 the Institut für Raumforschung reports a production of raw benzol of 5,639 tons.[15] It was not possible, however, to calculate figures for other years, and the value of such outputs is negligible in any case. Even though these by-products are scarce in the Zone, the total value of their output cannot be large enough to make a difference in the final calculations. Furthermore, no price was found that could be used as a weight. This case illustrates once more the difficulties of using West German scarcity relations in East German facts.

The most important information on the soft coal sector is summarized in Table 20.* Valued in 1936 or 1950 prices, the soft coal produced in 1955 or 1956 was only about 75 to 80 per cent of 1936. The sales value of coke production increased by 80 per cent between 1936 and 1956, whether measured in 1936 or 1950 prices. For the whole period the value of the coal needed to produce this coke was slightly higher than the value of the coke produced from it. The amount of gas produced and available for other uses increased substantially — almost 270 per cent of 1936 in

* For detailed calculations see Tables A.4–A.6 in the Supplement.

1956. The value of the whole soft coal-coke-gas sector increased from 100 in 1936 to 194.5 in 1956 if measured in 1936 prices, but to only 167.8 if measured in 1950 prices. This difference is entirely attributable to the higher valuation of the coal imports in 1950 prices.

The known errors involved in this calculation are twofold. Since the value of the by-products, tar and benzol, could not be ascertained, the true value added of the sector is greater than that shown in Table 20. However, the true value added ought to be smaller because no allowance was made for inputs other than the coal used to produce coke and the

Table 20

Production of soft coal, soft coal coke, and gas, and value added of soft coal sector, East Germany, 1936, 1938, 1943, 1946–1958, and 1960 plan

Year	Soft coal production (thousand tons)	Value added[a] (million RM/DM)		Soft coal coke produced (thousand tons)	Production of gas (million cu m)	Adjusted amounts with 4,200 kcal/cu m (million cu m)
		1936 Prices	1950 Prices			
	(1)	(2)	(3)	(4)	(5)	(6)
1936	3,523	49.578	100.514	1,942	944	944
1938	3,513	49.437	100.227	1,899	1,078	1,078
1943	2,919	41.077	83.279	2,362	1,401	1,068
1946	2,509	35.309	71.584	976	695	562
1947	2,800	39.403	79.886	857	604	488
1948	2,848	40.079	81.255	1,132	796	644
1949	3,000	42.218	85.592	1,181	851	688
1950	2,805	39.473	80.029	1,528	1,498	1,212
1951	3,204	45.089	91.412	1,719	1,714	1,387
1952	2,745	38.755	78.574	1,992	1,774	1,435
1953	2,638	37.124	75.264	2,327	1,935	1,565
1954	2,648	37.264	75.549	2,581	2,217	1,793
1955	2,667	37.532	76.091	2,705	2,459	1,989
1956	2,743	38.601	78.260	2,795	2,710	2,202
1957	2,753	38.742	78.545	2,818	2,766	2,338
1958	2,903	40.853	82.825	2,996	3,074	2,488
1960 (Plan)	2,900					

Sources: Col. 1: For 1936–1943, see Gleitze, *Ostdeutsche Wirtschaft*, p. 191; for 1946, 1948, 1950–1956, *SJDDR*, 1956, p. 278, and 1957, p. 294; for 1947 and 1949, DIW, "Statistisches Kompendium über die sowjetische Besatzungszone," unpublished, Section 4, Table 7; and for 1960 Plan, Karl C. Thalheim and Peter D. Propp, *Die Entwicklungsziele für die gewerbliche Wirtschaft der sowjetischen Besatzungszone in der zweiten Fünfjahrplan-Periode*, Bonn, Bundesministerium für Gesamtdeutsche Fragen, 1957, p. 78. Cols. 2 and 3: Prices refer to lump coal. 1936 price = RM 18.25 per ton; 1950 price = DM 37.00 per ton. *SJBR*, 1956, p. 458. Col. 4: For 1936–1943, see Gleitze, *op. cit.*, p. 210, for coke produced in gas works (exclusive of East Berlin), and p. 191 for coke produced in cokeries (none in East Berlin); for 1950–1956, see *SJDDR*, 1956, pp. 278–279; for 1957, see *ibid.*, 1957, p. 294. Cols. 5 and 6: For 1936–1943, see Gleitze, *op. cit.*, p. 210, gas works gas + *Kokereigas* (gas produced in coke plants); for 1946, 1948, and 1950–1955, see *SJDDR*, 1955, p. 162; 1947 and 1949 interpolated; for 1956 and 1957, see *ibid.*, 1957, p. 294. Postwar gas has a caloric content of about 3,400 kcal per cu m; prewar gas had a caloric content of 4,200–4,500 kcal per cu m.

[a] 77.11 per cent of gross production.

gas used to produce gas. To the extent to which lignite or some of its products are used within the mining sector, these inputs have been allowed for. No estimate can be made for the electricity inputs into coal mining alone but only for the mining sector as a whole. Other inputs probably cannot be ascertained.

Total coal mining, including gas

The development of the total coal mining sector, including gas, is shown in Table 21. Measured in 1936 prices, production in the coal mining sector increased about 94 per cent between 1936 and 1956; measured

Table 21

Value added, coal mining, including gas, East Germany, and indices, West and East Germany, 1936 and 1950–1958

A. *Value added, East Germany*
(million RM/DM)

	1936 Prices			1950 Prices		
Year	Lignite sector	Soft coal sector	Total	Lignite sector	Soft coal sector	Total
1936	317.374	117.666	435.040	576.016	178.260	752.462
1950	423.163	145.206	568.369	723.349	200.045	925.232
1951	467.833	166.214	634.047	800.250	231.172	1031.322
1952	493.958	163.502	657.460	842.558	223.642	1064.409
1953	527.178	172.727	699.905	914.282	230.676	1144.863
1954	550.984	193.005	743.989	963.643	254.033	1218.023
1955	609.183	210.922	820.005	1066.319	276.099	1341.746
1956	615.117	231.288	846.405	1088.172	299.038	1388.495
1957	609.445	234.713	844.158	1109.457	304.462	1413.919
1958	618.664	259.289	877.953	1123.545	335.030	1458.575

B. *Indices*

	East Germany		West Germany	
Year	Total 1936 prices	Total 1950 prices	Coal mining[a] (1936 = 100)	Gas production (1936 = 100)
1936	100.0	100.0	100.0	100.0
1950	130.7	123.0	97.8	122.5
1951	145.8	137.1	107.0	142.4
1952	151.0	141.5	111.3	156.9
1953	160.9	152.2	112.5	155.9
1954	171.0	161.9	114.6	168.7
1955	188.5	178.3	118.8	191.4
1956	194.6	184.5	123.0	211.4
1957	194.0	187.9	124.0	212.0
1958	201.8	193.8	122.0	207.0

Sources: For East Germany, see Tables 18 and 20. For West Germany, coal mining, see *SJBR*, 1955, p. 228; 1957, p. 235; and 1958, p. 187. For gas production, see *ibid.*, 1955, p. 230; 1957, p. 234; and 1958, p. 187.
[a] Average daily production.

in 1950 prices, the increase was only about 84 per cent. When compared with both 1943 and 1950, the growth is smaller but still substantial.

To facilitate comparison, the index of coal production of the Federal Republic is included in Table 21, together with the index of gas production. Since the bulk of West German mining is soft coal mining, however, the comparison must not be taken too seriously. West German soft coal output rose from about 117 million tons in 1936 to about 128 million tons during 1954, an increase of only about 9 per cent; lignite increased by about 50 per cent, from about 58.5 million tons to 87.8 million tons; and lignite briquets increased 60 per cent, from about 10 million tons to about 16 million tons. When compared with the indices of production, the figures indicate that the calculated East German index must be approximately correct.[16]

ORES

Iron ore

The Soviet Zone produces low-grade iron ores with an Fe content ranging from about 18 to 28 per cent.[17] Before the war the ores used had a slightly higher Fe content, about 23 per cent. The quantities of iron ore produced (regardless of Fe content) are given by Statistical Yearbook of the German Democratic Republic. In sheer tonnage, production increased about fourfold between 1936 and 1955. The actual Fe content was apparently somewhat higher in the early 1950's than was originally thought. The figure given for iron production for 1956 suggests an Fe content of over 28 per cent. Although this figure seems high, it was accepted as possible. The present ore reserves are estimated at around 400 million tons, of which 350 million tons have an Fe content of less than 25 per cent. There are, however, a few higher-grade ores.

The price to be applied to this series raised some problems.* For 1936 the price of RM 9.43 per ton referred to ore with a 34 per cent Fe content, the cheapest West German iron ore at the time. In 1948 the lowest-grade West German ore with an Fe content of about 34 per cent cost DM 20.43. It is assumed that the ore price is roughly proportional to the Fe content. Although the other components of the ore must also affect the price, proportional prices seem to be the best approximation possible. For an Fe content of 28.4 per cent, the estimated price for 1936 is RM 10.04 per ton. An Fe content of 28.4 per cent seems to be the absolute maximum allowable for Eastern Zone ores, and it is bound to fall rapidly in the near future. The average iron content even of West German ore is given as 26.5 per cent,[18] and it is known that West German ores are better than Eastern Zone ores. It is necessary to mention the West German figure because the Fe content of the ores mined, as given by Gleitze,[19]

* See note on currency on p. 55.

amounts to about 30 per cent for the prewar years. If anything, the 28 per cent implied by the East German statistics overstates the Fe content of the ore, and, when applied to the output of ore measured in tons, places too high a value on the ore. In addition, it should be remembered that the East German ores not only have a low Fe content but also contain much unwanted matter. Hence the adjustment of the ore price by means of the Fe content gives too high a value for the ore.

The value added of iron ore production was estimated by applying to the sales value of iron ore production the ratio of value added to gross production of iron ore mining in 1936. Table 22 (and Table A.8

Table 22

Value added, iron ore sector, East Germany, and indices,
West and East Germany, 1936 and 1950–1958

			East Germany			Index, West Germany, 1936 = 100	
	Ore production (thousand tons)	Fe content (thousand tons)	Value added (million RM/DM)		Index 1936 = 100 1936 prices and 1950 prices		
Year			1936 Prices	1950 Prices		1936 prices	1950 prices
	(1)	(2)	(3)	(4)	(5)	(6)	(7)
1936	362	131.0	2.832	5.316	100.0	100.0	100.0
1950	401	113.9	3.138	5.888	110.8	134.8	141.4
1951	487	138.3	3.810	7.151	134.6	165.8	167.2
1952	772	219.2	6.241	11.335	213.3	195.5	196.6
1953	1359	386.0	10.634	19.956	375.5	185.8	187.3
1954	1470	417.5	11.503	21.585	406.1	169.4	170.7
1955	1664	472.0	13.027	24.433	459.7	n.a.	203.0
1956	1757	498.3	13.749	25.800	485.4	n.a.	217.1
1957	1478	419.2	11.566	21.703	408.3	n.a.	234.0
1958	1506	427.1	11.785	22.114	416.1	n.a.	229.0

Sources: Col. 1: See *SJDDR*, 1955, p. 162; 1956, pp. 278–279; 1957, p. 294; 1958, p. 344; Gleitze, *Ostdeutsche Wirtschaft*, p. 191; and index, *SP*, 1955, No. 10. Col. 2: Figure for 1936 calculated from Gleitze, *Ostdeutsche Wirtschaft*, p. 191; calculations for other years based on ore content of 28.36 per cent for 1955 given in *Neues Deutschland* (East Berlin), 14 February 1957. Cols. 3 and 4: For prices and method of calculation, see text. Col. 5: Derived from preceding columns. Col. 6: Monthly averages. Refers to the old index based on 1936 prices. See *SJBR*, 1955, p. 228. Col. 7: Average daily production. Refers to the new index based on 1950 prices. See *ibid.*, 1957, p. 235; 1958, p.187; 1959, p. 181.

in the Supplement), which gives the relevant detail, indicates that iron ore mining (regardless of Fe content) had already risen above the 1936 level when the First Five Year Plan was launched in 1950 but did not rise above the prewar high of 1938 until 1952. Since then the expansion has been rapid, with the 1956 output rising to 443 per cent of the 1936 level.

A comparison with the West German index of iron ore mining is instructive. West German iron ore mining reached the 1936 level earlier — between 1948 and 1949 — and rose faster until 1951. By 1952 the growth was about the same in the two parts of Germany, but after that date East German production rose rapidly while West German production declined substantially although it remained about 70 per cent above the prewar level during 1954. By 1956, however, West German output was double the prewar output.

The interpretation of these movements in opposite directions is fairly obvious. As native ores decline in quality and foreign exchange conditions improve, West Germany relies more on imports of high-grade ores. However, since imports of iron ore also declined from 1953 to 1954, the temporary peak of 1952 appears to be connected with the Korean war. The increased production of a poor grade of iron in East Germany reflects both the autarkic mythology that seems to be characteristic of Soviet-type economies (at least in the fifties) and the urgent need to make the best use of what is available. Nevertheless, the achievement should not be minimized, particularly when seen in the light of the technical progress achieved in reducing these low-grade ores with BHT coke in the Calbe low-shaft furnaces.

Copper ore

Copper ore is the most important nonferrous ore found in East Germany. It proved impossible to obtain a copper ore price. Therefore, the method of estimating the value added consisted of taking the value added for 1936 and multiplying it by an index of the copper contained in the ore mined. Since virtually 100 per cent of the copper mined in Germany before the war was mined in the Harz region of East Germany,* this method was feasible.

The index was not based on the quantity of copper ore mined because of the variations in copper content; for example, the 1936 ores had an average copper content of 2.4 per cent, and by 1938 the content had fallen to about 2.07 per cent. It is stated in *Materialien* that the copper content of the mined ores steadily declined from 1946 to 1952, but increased thereafter as the Sangershausen fields (in the southern part of the Harz) were increasingly exploited. In 1952 the copper content was 0.97 per cent. The official *Direktive* states that the copper content in 1955 was 1.5 per cent, and that by 1960 the copper content of the ores is to be raised to 1.63 per cent. The 1950 figure used for the copper content of the ores mined is the Plan figure which, in light of the *Direktive* figure for the actual content in 1955, seems plausible. For the early years interpolations were used.[20] The summary of these calculations is presented in Table 23.†

It is likely that the 1936 value added also contains other metals recovered as by-products of copper. This is not certain, however, and East German copper ore apparently contains only small amounts of other metals. It might be added that the Statistisches Reichsamt apparently

* Of the total 1,124,000 tons of copper ore mined in 1936 within the 1936 German borders, all but 1,000 tons were mined in the Soviet area. The rest was mined in what became the British Zone.

† The calculations themselves are given in Table A.9 of the Supplement.

Table 23

Production and value added, copper ore and pyrites mining,
East Germany, 1936 and 1950–1958

Year	Copper production (thousand tons)	Value added copper production (million RM/DM)		Amount of pyrites produced (thousand tons)	Value added pyrites production (million RM/DM)		Pyrites (thousand tons sulfur content)
		1936 Prices	1950 Prices		1936 Prices	1950 Prices	
	(1)	(2)	(3)	(4)	(5)	(6)	(7)
1936	1123.0	8.641	33.674	8.4	0.109	0.190	...
1950	804.0	2.650	10.327	92.0	1.193	2.261	41
1951	1013.0	3.242	12.634	101.8	1.320	2.301	...
1952	1048.0	3.264	12.720	108.7	1.409	2.457	...
1953	1292.0	4.634	18.059	119.3	1.547	2.696	...
1954	1302.0	5.417	21.110	130.1	1.687	2.941	...
1955	1333.0	6.400	24.941	142.8	1.851	3.229	...
1956	1350.0	6.481	25.256	159.5	2.067	3.605	49
1957	1393.0	6.687	26.026	159.5	2.067	3.605	54
1958	1457.0	6.994	27.257	153.6	1.990	3.471	52

Sources: Col. 1: For 1936, see Gleitze, *Ostdeutsche Wirtschaft*, p. 191; for 1950–1955, see *SJDDR*, 1956, pp. 278–279; 1958, p. 344. Col. 2: For 1936 price, see *Die Deutsche Industrie: Gesamtergebnisse der amtlichen Produktionsstatistik*, Monographs of the Reich Office for Economic Planning of Defense, No. 1, 1936 (hereinafter referred to in tables and reference notes as *Produktionsstatistik, 1936*, p. 44. It has been assumed that value added increased after 1956 in proportion to production. Col. 3: 1950 value added calculated by multiplying 1936 value added by ratio of price for *Elektrolytkupfer* (copper by electrolysis). For 1936, see *SHD*, p. 466, RM 54.73 per 100 kg; for 1950, see *SJBR*, 1955, p. 454, which gives DM 213.31 per 100 kg. Price ratio = 3.897. Col. 4: For 1936 and 1950–1955, see *SJDDR*, 1955, p. 102; for 1956 to 1958, see *ibid.*, 1958, p. 344, which gives production only in terms of sulfur content. It is assumed that total production increased in proportion to the sulfur content. Cols. 5 and 6: Value added is 81.06 per cent of the sales value. *Produktionsstatistik, 1936*, p. 44. Col. 7: See *SJDDR*, 1958, p. 344.

ran into the same difficulty as I have in evaluating the gross production. Their solution was to approximate the prewar value on the basis of the amount of ore produced.[21]

The value added in 1950 prices was estimated by raising the value added in 1936 prices by the price increase of refined copper. No other estimating method seemed feasible.

Although the production of ore increased as late as 1956 the copper content of the increased amount was still substantially below 1936. Since the quality of the ore deteriorated so much, the value added of copper ore production must be presumed to have fallen. The figures indicate a fall by 1946 to about 13 per cent of 1936, thereafter a steady rise to 30.5 per cent in 1950, and a substantial increase during the First Five Year Plan; but by 1955 the value added of copper ore was only 74 per cent of 1936. In any case the total value added is very small.

In the Federal Republic, copper production increased from a negligible amount in 1936 to 2,230 tons in 1954. With West German production still only about one-eighth of East German production, the calculation of an index would be purposeless.

Other ores and summary

The small amounts of other ores, such as lead, zinc, tin, antimony, nickel, and pyrites, produced in the Zone may be important for East

Germany, but they are unlikely to make a great difference in the value added of the mined ores. Only pyrites can be accounted for separately, and their value added was calculated from their sales value. If an allowance for the other ores is made equivalent to about 15 per cent of the combined value of iron ore and copper, the East German output of these ores undoubtedly receives much more than its due.* The figure of 15 per cent was arrived at by comparing the gross value of the iron and copper contained in the native ores with the value of all the other ores.

The value per ton of pure metal of some of the rare metals is quite high, but so is the cost of refining them. The total quantities involved are small, and there is a possibility of double counting. Since many ores contain more than one metal, any inference from the metal content to the ore is hazardous. Before the war there was probably no production of nickel, antimony, or wolframite, the production of arsenic was negligible, and tin ore probably was either not mined at all or mined only in negligible amounts within the present area of East Germany.

Depending on whether the 1936 or the 1950 price is chosen, there are substantial differences in the increase between 1936 and 1955, which are, of course, due to the much sharper rise in the price of copper than of iron ore.† The other nonferrous metals have been included, as stated, by allowing a flat 15 per cent of the value added of iron and copper ores and of pyrites.

POTASH AND ROCK SALT

Potash and rock salt are two of the major resources of East Germany. In 1936 about 60 per cent of German potash and well over 50 per cent of rock salt was mined in the Zone. The technology of the potash industry appears to be so organized that most of the raw potash salt is further refined at the mine to a commercial grade of salt, although a substantial part is used in raw form as fertilizer. Furthermore, the pricing of the raw salts in the past appears to have varied consistently with the K_2O (potassium oxide) content. Although this information is based on a description of the American industry,[22] it is probably also true for the German industry.

It is necessary to describe the organization of the potash industry at the outset in order to explain the estimating procedure followed. The only current production series published refers to potash measured in terms of its K_2O content; figures for the actual amounts mined regardless of K_2O content are available only for the prewar years; and no price could

---

* The production figures are given in Table A.11 in the Supplement, which also includes figures for the small peat output.

† Table A.12 in the Supplement summarizes the value added of the iron ore and nonferrous ore sector. The figures certainly give too large a value added for 1946 and the immediate postwar years, but because of the forcing of the production of such ores as tin and zinc, they are likely to be roughly correct toward the end of the period.

be found for raw potash salts. However, the average sales value of potash salts in 1936 can be found by dividing the 1936 sales value* by the K_2O content of the salts produced in all of Germany. This permits the evaluation of the sales value of the K_2O content of the mined salts in a consistent manner. The value added in 1936 prices can then be found by applying to the sales value the percentage of value added to sales value in 1936 (79.3 per cent).

The sales value of potash in later years was found by applying to the 1936 average value the index of the wholesale price of 40 per cent K_2O fertilizer. Since, as stated earlier, there is good reason to assume that the raw salt price varies with the K_2O content, this procedure seems defensible.

The calculations of East German output of potash, measured in K_2O content, are based entirely on information published by the East Germans. It was impossible to make any separate calculation for rock salt production. Since the values given in the Production Statistics of 1936 are for the combined output of potash and rock salt mining, however, the procedure followed makes an implicit allowance for the production of rock salt. So far as the outputs in tons are concerned, the production of rock salt and production of potash salts are likely to vary in the same way, partly because rock salt and potash salt may be mined jointly. The probable course of rock salt production may also be inferred from the expansion of chlorine production.† It is impossible to say whether rock salt prices and potash salt prices moved differently over time. Therefore the value added calculated in terms of 1936 prices may be more reliable than that measured in 1950 prices. The data are summarized in Table 24.‡

By 1949 the output of potash had surpassed its 1936 level, but it should be observed that in 1952 and 1953 it was below the level reached in 1951. (I do not know the reasons for this decrease in production.) By 1956 the output was again substantially higher — about 63 per cent above the 1936 level. The same increase is implicitly assumed for rock salt. Although rock salt production increased less than potash production in West Germany, West Germany production figures for potash and rock salts indicate that the parallel movement assumed is justifiable. The percentage increase of raw potash salt production (measured in K_2O content) from 1949 to 1954 was 217.3 per cent; from 1951 to 1954, 141.2 per cent. Over the same

* The Production Statistics of 1936 (p. 44) uses sales value as an approximation to gross production. The value refers actually to the combined output of potash and rock salt. It has proved impossible to make an allowance for rock salt, but its value cannot have been sufficiently large to affect the result seriously. (For example, the average value of American salt sold or used by producers in 1947 was $3.25 per short ton. The average value of the fertilizer material "potash" in the same year was $32.97 — ten times as high. *Statistical Abstract of the United States: 1950*, p. 930.)

† These figures are given in Table A.41 of the Supplement.

‡ Detailed data are given in Table A.13 of the Supplement.

Table 24

Production and value added, potash and rock salt mining, East Germany,
and indices, West and East Germany, 1936 and 1950–1958

Year	Production of K$_2$O (thousand tons)	Gross value added (million RM/DM)		Index, East Germany (1936 = 100)	Index, West Germany (1936 = 100)
		1936 Prices	1950 Prices		
	(1)	(2)	(3)	(4)	(5)
1936	953	87.491	117.236	100.0	100.0
1950	1336	122.653	164.352	140.2	147.3
1951	1409	129.354	173.332	147.9	176.6
1952	1346	123.570	165.610	141.3	200.4
1953	1378	126.508	169.518	144.6	206.7
1954	1463	134.312	179.975	153.5	247.2
1955	1552	142.482	190.924	162.9	260.1
1956	1556	142.849	191.416	163.3	256.4
1957	1604	147.256	197.321	168.3	263.0
1958	1650	151.480	202.980	173.1	265.0

Sources: Col. 1: *SJDDR*, 1956, pp. 278–279, and 1958, pp. 344–345.

Cols. 2 and 3: Sales value × $\dfrac{\text{value added in 1936 for all of Germany}}{\text{sales value in 1936 for all of Germany}} = \dfrac{149.041}{187.901} = 79.3\%$.

Produktionsstatistik, 1936, p. 44. 1936 price: RM 115.77 per ton; 1950 price: DM 155.13 per ton. Col. 4: Derived from col. 1. Col. 5: Refers to potash and rock salt combined, average daily production, *SJBR*, 1957, p. 235, and 1959, p. 18.

periods, rock salt production increased by 183.9 per cent and 115 per cent, respectively.[23]

Comparison with the Federal Republic shows that until 1949 East German production was ahead of West German production. From 1950 on, however, West German production increased substantially faster than East German production; in 1954 it was more than twice as high as in 1936, and production in East Germany was only 52 per cent greater. Ironically, West German production began to overtake the growth rate of East German production in the year in which the First Five Year Plan was launched.

It is known that uranium was and certainly still is produced in East Germany; in fact, the *Direktive* gives plans for the automation of uranium mining.[24] This sector has grown from nothing in 1936 to substantial proportions since the war, employing probably between 130,000 and 150,000 persons. Since no data are available for evaluating the output, no allowance for uranium mining will be made in the calculations.

THE MINING SECTOR AS A WHOLE, INCLUDING GAS PRODUCTION

Before calculating the value of the mining sector as a whole, it should be stressed that the electricity produced by generating stations associated with lignite mines is attributed to the electric power sector.

The lignite used to produce the electric power was treated as having left the lignite sector, and the electricity used by the mining sector was considered to have been purchased by it. The mining sector actually produces much more power than it consumes, and in general the industrial sector produces about one-half of all the power produced. In approximating the gross value added of the mining sector, the procedure previously outlined seemed to be the only logical one to follow.

Since it is not certain whether or not the lignite used to generate electricity at the mine is part of the 17 per cent of lignite consumed in the mines themselves, two alternative estimates are presented. One employs the value added estimate for the lignite sector as a whole given in Table 18, which implies that these 17 per cent do not include the lignite used for power generation at the mine. The alternative estimate adds the estimated value added of lignite used for power production, valued in the manner described above, which actually gives too high a figure for the value added because the 1936 gross production value given in the Production Statistics of 1936 has already made an allowance for lignite consumed within the sector.[25] The two estimates differ by only about 8 per cent.

In calculating the value added for the mining sector as a whole, gas production had to be included. Although unfortunate from some standpoints, this procedure had to be followed for two statistical reasons. First, it was not possible to distinguish between coke plants and gasworks with respect to gas or coke production. Although each produces a different type of coke, no allowance could be made for this fact. Second, in calculating the value added of coke and gas, it was impossible to allocate the coal inputs separately. Thus all coal has been deducted from the figures for coke production, which is therefore undervalued, and nothing has been deducted from the value of gas production, which is therefore overvalued by the same amount. The calculations are given in Table 25.

The Federal Republic publishes an index for mining as a whole and a separate index for gas production. These two indices were combined into an index comparable with the calculated East German index, using the weights that mining (7.56) and gas production (1.37) have in the 1936 index of production.[26] The West German index rises much less than the East German index, reflecting in part the higher base, particularly for iron ore and soft coal, but, so far as East Germany is concerned, reflecting the tremendous expansion of lignite production. The differences in the growth rates are somewhat smaller when the East German output is valued in 1950 prices.

For comparison, it should be stated that in 1950 the gross value added of West German coal production, iron ore and other mining, and potash and rock salt mining, excluding gas production, was DM 3.261 billion (in 1950 prices); the East German figure for the same categories, but in-

Table 25

Value added, total mining sector, including gas, East Germany,
and indices, West and East Germany, 1936 and 1950–1958

A. *1936 Prices, million RM*

| | | | East Germany | | | | |
Year	Coal mining and gas	Total ore sector	Potash	Total value added including gas, first alternative[a]	Index 1936 = 100	Total value added including gas, second alternative[b]	Index 1936 = 100	West Germany old index,
	(1)	(2)	(3)	(4)	(5)	(6)	(7)	(8)
1936	435.040	13.319	87.491	552.669	100.0	535.850	100.0	100.0
1950	568.367	8.028	122.653	730.535	131.2	699.048	130.5	105.0
1951	634.047	9.628	129.354	807.744	146.2	773.029	144.3	117.8
1952	657.460	12.321	123.570	830.848	150.3	793.351	148.1	126.8
1953	699.905	19.337	126.508	884.969	160.1	845.750	157.8	130.2
1954	743.989	21.389	134.312	941.814	170.4	899.690	167.9	133.6
1955	820.005	24.463	142.482	1033.360	187.0	986.950	184.2	146.4
1956	846.465	25.645	142.849	1064.962	192.7	1014.959	189.4	n.a.
1957	844.158	23.368	147.256	1072.333	194.0	1014.782	189.4	n.a.
1958	877.953	23.890	151.480	1114.633	201.7	1053.323	196.6	n.a.

B. *1950 Prices, million DM*

| | | | East Germany | | | | |
Year	Coal mining and gas	Total ore sector	Potash	Total value added including gas, first alternative[a]	Index 1936 = 100	Total value added including gas, second alternative[b]	Index 1936 = 100	West Germany, new index
	(9)	(10)	(11)	(12)	(13)	(14)	(15)	(16)
1936	752.462	45.055	117.236	957.312	100.0	914.753	100.0	100.0
1950	925.232	21.247	164.352	1190.409	124.3	1110.831	121.4	105.0
1951	1031.322	25.399	173.332	1317.793	137.7	1230.053	134.5	119.0
1952	1064.409	30.512	165.610	1355.313	141.6	1260.522	137.8	127.7
1953	1144.863	46.818	169.518	1460.324	152.5	1361.199	148.8	130.8
1954	1218.023	52.481	179.975	1556.946	162.6	1450.479	158.6	136.2
1955	1341.746	60.493	190.924	1710.463	178.7	1593.163	173.2	146.4
1956	1388.495	62.860	191.416	1769.303	184.8	1642.771	179.6	154.2
1957	1413.919	59.073	197.321	1815.772	189.7	1670.313	182.6	158.0
1958	1458.575	60.768	202.980	1877.290	196.1	1722.323	188.3	157.5

Sources: Cols. 1, 2, and 3: See Tables 21–24 and Supplement Tables A.1-A.14 for details. Col. 4: See Supplement Table A.15, where the value of lignite assumed to be used at mining stations is given. (It is the difference between col. 4 and col. 6.) Col. 5: Derived from col. 4. Col. 6: Sum of cols. 1, 2, and 3. Col. 7: Derived from col. 6. Col. 8: Calculated by using the weights of mining and of gas production in the old index. *SJBR*, 1956, p. 217. Cols. 9–15: Same as cols. 1–7. Col. 16: Calculated by using weights of mining and of gas production in the new index. *SJBR*, 1957, p. 234, and 1959, p. 180.
a First alternative: Assumes that the 17 per cent of own consumption of lignite mines includes lignite used for power generation at the mine. See text and Supplement Table A.15.
b Second alternative: Assumes that the 17 per cent of own consumption of lignite mines *does not* include lignite used for power generation.

cluding gas production, was at most DM 1.2 billion (in the same 1950 prices).

Using the official figures, it is unfortunately impossible to trace output per man for each of the major subsectors of mining. For the group of industries as a whole, however, a rough comparison is feasible (see

Table 26

Output per man in mining, East Germany, 1936 and 1950–1958

Year	Index of mining and gas production	Employment (thousands)	Index of employment	Index of output per man 1936 = 100	Index of output per man 1950 = 100	Official indices of productivity Per production worker	Official indices of productivity Per person employed
	(1)	(2)	(3)	(4)	(5)	(6)	(7)
1936	100.0	109.7	100.0	100.0	116.1	...	...
1950	132.2	168.0	153.1	86.1	100.0	100.0	100.0
1951	146.2	179.7	163.7	89.1	103.5	110.7	105.9
1952	150.3	185.1	168.7	89.1	103.5	114.1	104.6
1953	160.1	192.6	175.5	91.1	105.8	114.7	102.3
1954	170.4	208.5	190.0	89.6	104.4	119.7	104.4
1955	187.0	211.4	192.6	96.9	112.5	129.4	n.a.
1956	192.7	206.9	188.6	102.0	118.5	132.0	n.a.
1957	194.0	212.9	194.1	100.0	116.1	134.0	n.a.
1958	201.8	216.6	197.4	102.3	118.8	136.0	n.a.

Sources: Col. 1: See Supplement Table A.14, index in 1936 prices. This index assumes that part of own consumption of lignite in mines is used for power generation. Col. 2: For 1936, see Gleitze, *Ostdeutsche Wirtschaft*, p. 174. For 1950–1956, see *SJDDR*, 1955, p. 126; 1956, p. 11; 1957, p. 225; and 1958, p. 317. In 1936, mining proper employed 92,873 persons; *Kraftstoffindustrie* employed an additional 16,871. (Lignite and lignite briquets alone employed 54,869 persons; potash and rock salt mining, 9,524. Among the *Kraftstoffindustrie* the most important subgroup was mineral oil derivatives, employing 11,530 persons.) Col. 3: Derived from Col. 2. Col. 4: Col. 1 ÷ Col. 3. Col. 5: Col. 4 ÷ 861. Col. 6: Production in *Messwerte* per production worker. For 1950–1955, see *SJDDR*, 1955, p. 119; for 1956, 1957, *ibid.*, 1957, p. 269; 1958, p. 264. Col. 7: Gross production in *Messwerte* per employed person. See *ibid.*, 1955, p. 119.

Table 26). For the year 1936, detailed figures on employment are available; for the years 1950 through 1955, the figures for mining probably include the categories that before the war were listed separately as fuel industries, that is, petroleum-derivative production, carbonization, and soft coal tar distillation.

Although the employment figures are probably comparable for the different years, they are compared with an index which includes both mining and gas. Since the war the employment figures for gas production are included with those for electric power generation and cannot be isolated. But the general picture would not be changed essentially even if they were.

By the end of 1956, productivity (defined as output per man) had probably reached or slightly surpassed the prewar level. In other words, the substantial expansion of output was achieved primarily by additional labor. Investments during the First Five Year Plan increased productivity substantially, yet barely succeeded in making good the war damage and immediate postwar damage.

The official index of productivity per production worker increases about twice as fast as the calculated index, chiefly because it is based on gross production (turnover) rather than value added. However, the equally official index of productivity per industrial employee alone shows virtually no increase since 1950. (The category "industrial personnel" includes only persons engaged in producing the main output of a plant, for example, production workers, technical and administrative personnel, apprentices, and plant police; nonindustrial personnel consist of others employed in plants, such as workers engaged in construction and employees in canteens or plant stores.[27]) Together, the figures suggest strongly that the considerable expansion of output is almost entirely attributable to increased labor input.

A comparison with the Federal Republic indicates that there, too, productivity in coal mining presented problems. It must, however, be remembered that coal mining in West Germany is largely soft coal, deep-pit mining, whereas it is open-pit lignite mining in East Germany. Since the rapid increases in the mining sector as a whole since 1950 are mostly due to improvements in petroleum production, which hardly exists in East Germany, separate categories are given in Table 27.

Table 27

Indices of output per man in mining, West Germany, 1936 and 1950–1958

Year	Coal mining (1936 = 100)	Coal mining (1950 = 100)	Iron ore mining (1936 = 100)	Iron ore mining (1950 = 100)	Other ore mining (1950 = 100)	Potash and rock salt (1936 = 100)	Potash and rock salt (1950 = 100)	Petroleum and natural gas (1950 = 100)	All mining (1936 = 100)	All mining (1950 = 100)
1936	100		100			100			100	
1950	63	100.0	91	100.0	100.0	85	100.0	100.0	69	100.0
1951	67	106.7	103	108.4	96.7	90	105.6	117.6	73	108.1
1952	67	107.5	111	116.1	99.2	92	112.3	138.0	75	111.5
1953	66	105.3	102	106.3	122.1	93	112.4	157.2	76	111.5
1954	67	107.2	104	108.1	137.2	103	125.6	184.4	80	115.8
1955	69	111.3	120	124.8	146.4	102	123.0	214.0	84	123.0
1956	n.a.	113.5	n.a.	127.3	154.0	n.a.	120.8	236.7	n.a.	126.9
1957	n.a.	112.0	n.a.	129.0	n.a.	n.a.	124.0	252.0	n.a.	128.0
1958	n.a.	111.0	n.a.	129.0	n.a.	n.a.	127.0	284.0	n.a.	129.0

Sources: For figures based on 1936 relations, see *SJBR*, 1956, p. 215. For recalculated figures (1950 relationships) for 1950–1956, see *Wirtschaft und Statistik*, May 1957, p. 238; for 1957 figures, see *SJBR*, 1958, p. 190; for 1958, *SJBR*, 1959, p. 184.

Unfortunately, figures based on 1936 relations are not available for all categories. With respect to methodology the 1936-based figures for the Federal Republic are directly comparable with the calculated figures for East Germany. They too are based on 1936 relations and are frequently calculated by a similar method, that is, by projecting the 1936 figures with a series of typical outputs, whereas the figures based on 1950 are based on 1950 relations. A comparison of the two indices gives some idea of the possible bias involved in the procedure used in this book. On the whole, the 1950 relations appear to yield lower figures.

CHAPTER VI

ELECTRIC POWER

The evaluation of the value added of the electric power sector presents numerous problems, the attempted solution of which must be discussed first and, unfortunately, at length. Figures on the number of kilowatthours produced are based on official East German publications. The problems to be solved are, first, the evaluation of the inputs and, second, the average price that must necessarily be substituted for the complicated tariff schedules characteristic of power production.

Certain structural changes have occurred in power generation, which have previously been discussed in connection with the calculation of the amount of lignite needed to produce electric power. Before the war about 12 per cent of electric power was based on soft coal, compared with about 7 per cent after the war. By 1955, 88.2 per cent was based on lignite, 5.9 per cent on soft coal, and 3.1 per cent on gas, which, in the calculations made, is included with lignite.[1] The rest is based on water power, with a very small amount based on diesel fuel. These sources have been neglected.

In the process of changing from soft coal to lignite the efficiency of the operations undoubtedly suffered, as is frequently stated; and it is also true that the Soviet Zone was bedeviled by antiquated equipment and dismantling. Nevertheless, it should be realized that even before the war 85 per cent of East German power was generated from lignite. Some efficiencies reached are rather impressive. Thus, considering the caloric content of lignite, the ratio of 2.8 tons lignite used per 1,000 kwhr, while substantially below that reached in the best plants and with advanced technology, is not a bad input-output ratio.*

Lignite has been used for electric power production for a long time; it is economically efficient, even though the conversion of its caloric content to energy is about 22 per cent less efficient than the conversion of the caloric content of soft coal. Except for 1955, for which year official data

---

* Table A.15 of the Supplement presents the calculations. The value of electricity produced by water power and diesel fuel is included, but no inputs are deducted.

are available, the values for the inputs used are based on the following consideration. No German data have as yet been found for any prewar years. In the United States in 1937, 0.63 to 0.65 kg of soft coal were needed to produce 1 kwhr of electricity.[2] In 1952 West Germany needed 0.556 kg per kwhr of soft coal of over 4,500 kcal[3] and 2.51 kg per kwhr of lignite of the West German type.[4] In 1953, these relations had improved to 0.541 kg per kwhr of soft coal and 2.32 kg per kwhr of lignite.[5] In 1954 the soft coal input-output ratio remained at 0.541 kwhr while the lignite ratio had improved further to 2.15 kg per kwhr.

The actual caloric content of West German lignite in 1935 was 2,050 kcal per kg, that of East German lignite much higher, with 2,700 kcal per kg.[6] The best Saxonian soft coal had 7,200 kcal per kg,[7] about equal to the worst Ruhr soft coal and much below the 7,665 kcal per kg for Virginia soft coal.[8] By 1952 West German coal had deteriorated somewhat. Soft coal was down to 7,000 kcal per kg and lignite to 1,900 kcal per kg.[9]

On the basis of these figures, 2,048 kg of lignite would have been needed in 1935 for each kilowatthour of electricity produced if caloric content had been the sole determinant of efficiency. Actually, the amount needed was 2.51 kg per kwhr, that is, for each kilowatthour generated, 22 per cent more lignite (in terms of caloric content) was needed than soft coal. This relation between the relative efficiency of lignite and soft coal will be applied throughout. It is the only figure we have been able to find.

Similarly, no figure for the actual soft coal input in Germany before the war could be located. It is assumed, however, that the technical know-how of German plants at the time cannot have been very different from that of American plants using Virginia soft coal, for which we do have a figure. Since German soft coal has a lower caloric content, however, the input must be increased proportionately. The American input was 0.65 kg per kwhr of coal with a content of 7,665 kcal per kg. Therefore, German coal with a content of 7,200 kcal per kg would require an input of 0.6919 kg per kwhr. This figure is used for the 1936 input-output ratio of electric power based on soft coal.

If caloric content alone were relevant, 1.85 kg per kwhr of East German lignite of 2,700 kcal per kg caloric content would be used. Since lignite is 22 per cent less efficient, however, the actual requirement for 1936 would be 2.257 kg per kwhr. This is the figure used for that year for the input-output ratio of electricity based on lignite.

Since 1936 the quality of the lignite mined has gone down. Thus the Deutsche Institut für Wirtschaftsforschung gives lower values for the soft coal equivalents of lignite.[10] *Neue Hütte* gives a value of 2,200 kcal per kg of raw lignite for an unspecified year in the 1950's.[11] These lower values have to be allowed for in the postwar years. In *Materialien*[12] it is stated that the Finkenheerd power station uses 2.2 kg per kwhr of lignite and that this is an exceptionally good value; the Lauta power station uses 2.8 kg per kwhr, which is considered more normal.

When the 1936 input of 2.257 kg per kwhr, based on lignite of 2,700 kcal per kg caloric content, is adjusted for lignite of only 2,200 kcal per kg, the input used is 2.769 kg per kwhr. In our calculations the ratio of 2.8 kg per kwhr has been used.* This implies that there has been no further technical progress since 1936 and that generating plants have been efficiently maintained and are run at prewar rates. In view of the known fact that much of the machinery is badly run down, that some of it was not designed for lignite heating but for soft coal, and that all of it is run at more than the optimal technical rate, the figure of 2.8 kg per kwhr appears more than generous.[13]

It should be noted, however, that a new lignite field near Senftenberg has been developed and that new investments will substantially increase the efficiency of electric power generation.

The soft coal input after the war probably increased because of a deterioration of the machinery, the quality of coal, and so on. Since there was no problem of conversion, as with power stations built for soft coal and now converted to lignite, we assume that the deterioration in input was only about half that of the deterioration in lignite and arrive at a figure of 0.7735 kg of soft coal per kilowatthour generated. The deterioration may be more or less, depending on whether Saxonian or Silesian coal is used.

The above considerations lend support to the figures given in *Materialien* and explain in detail our procedure. For quick reference, they are summarized in Table 28.

Table 28

Caloric content and conversion figures for different types of coal

Year	Type of coal	Kcal/kg	Kg/kwhr
1937	Virginia soft coal	7,665	0.63–0.65
1935	West German soft coal	7,250	0.69
1935	East German soft coal	7,200	0.69
1935	East German lignite	2,700	2.57
1935	West German lignite	2,050	2.51
1952	West German soft coal	7,000	0.556
1952	West German lignite	1,900	2.51
1953 1954	West German soft coal	7,000	0.541
1953	West German lignite	1,900	2.32
1954	West German lignite	1,900	2.15
Postwar	East German lignite	2,200	2.8
Postwar	East German soft coal	?	0.774

* See Table A.15 in the Supplement.

In calculating the net output of electricity, we must deduct consumption of power in generating plants and the loss in transmission. In 1955 an official publication gave the loss figure as 10 per cent,[14] and this figure has been applied throughout; comparable American figures for losses and consumption of electricity in generating plants are about 14 per cent higher, possibly because of the longer distances involved.

The largest source of possible error lies not in the technical input-output relations just described but in the price used to evaluate the sales value of electricity. It is exceedingly arbitrary to use a single value for a commodity that characteristically is sold according to a schedule. Even a very small difference in the assumed price per kilowatthour makes a tremendous difference in the end results.

The cost of electricity in 1936 ranged from about 4.5 pfennig per kilowatthour for the largest users to about 40 pfennig for the smallest users, while ordinary consumers using at least 23 kwhr per month paid 19 pfennig. A personal inquiry at a small North German power station elicited the response that the 1936 wholesale price for large users was 4.7 to 5.0 pfennig. The choice of the proper price for electric current depends somewhat on what it is intended to measure. In 1936, industry and other businesses consumed 82 per cent of the power produced; railroads used 4.3 per cent; agriculture 1.2 per cent; street lighting 0.5 per cent; power stations themselves 3.3 per cent; and households and very small businesses together used only 8.7 per cent.[15] Hence the proper price must be near the low end of the scale. The average sales value of the 38.026 billion kilowatthours generated in 1936 (after allowing 10.5 per cent for losses) was 4.347 pfennig.[16] The price used in the calculations is 4.5 pfennig per kilowatthour. The later prices were estimated by using the price index for electricity as a whole given in the Statistical Yearbook of the Federal Republic.[17] This source gives separate indices for different consumers — households, agricultural consumers, industrial consumers, and special users of high- and low-voltage current. In the average for the sector as a whole, the special users evidently have a much heavier weight.

In 1936, total electricity production *and* distribution had a ratio of value added to sales value of electricity of almost 90 per cent.[18] Of the value added, only 19.5 per cent[19] was wages and salaries, which is more what one would expect. The remaining 89 per cent of the value added is evidently mostly depreciation allowances.

The calculations summarized in Table 29,* using the kilowatthour price of 4.5 pfennig and the prices for lignite used before, yield a ratio of value added to sales value of about 80 per cent. By raising the assumed price of current to about 9 pfennig it would have been easy to reach a ratio of 90 per cent to conform to the actual experience of 1936.

I have, however, refrained from making this adjustment. The reasons

* For details see Table A.15 of the Supplement.

Table 29

Production and value added of electricity sector, East Germany, and indices of electric power production, East and West Germany, 1936, 1938, 1943, 1946–1958, and 1960 plan

A. *East Germany: production and value added*

Year	Electricity generated (billion kwhr)	Electricity generated less 10% losses (billion kwhr)	Sales value of electricity (million RM/DM)	
			1936 Prices	1950 Prices
	(1)	(2)	(3)	(4)
1936	14.000	12.600	567.000	602.280
1938	17.120	15.408	693.360	736.502
1943	25.233	22.700	1,021.500	1,085.060
1946	11.356	10.220	459.900	488.516
1947	12.580	11.322	509.490	541.192
1948	14.599	13.139	591.255	628.044
1949	16.610	14.949	672.705	714.562
1950	19.466	17.519	788.355	837.408
1951	21.463	19.317	869.265	923.353
1952	23.183	20.865	938.925	997.347
1953	24.247	21.822	981.990	1,043.092
1954	26.044	23.440	1,054.800	1,120.432
1955	28.695	25.825	1,162.170	1,234.483
1956	31.182	28.064	1,263.105	1,341.698
1957	32.735	29.462	1,325.789	1,408.184
1958	34.874	31.387	1,412.419	1,500.302
1960 Plan	44.000			

Value added of electricity sector (million RM/DM)

Year	Assumption 1		Assumption 2	
	1936 Prices	1950 Prices	1936 Prices	1950 Prices
	(5)	(6)	(7)	(8)
1936	464.090	399.366	447.251	356.807
1938	567.524	488.390	546.932	436.343
1943	836.060	719.429	805.722	642.749
1946	359.535	291.279	341.170	244.863
1947	398.300	322.694	377.951	271.261
1948	462.210	374.456	438.595	314.771
1949	525.889	426.013	499.026	358.117
1950	616.299	499.293	584.814	419.716
1951	679.571	550.574	644.856	462.834
1952	734.035	594.709	696.539	499.938
1953	767.705	621.937	728.486	522.812
1954	824.622	668.095	782.498	561.628
1955	909.768	736.816	863.710	620.406
1956	990.051	803.948	939.988	677.416
1957	1,039.184	843.846	986.637	711.034
1958	1,101.086	898.985	1,051.106	757.494

Table 29 (Continued)

B. *Indices of electric power production: East and West Germany*

East Germany

Year	1936 Prices		1950 Prices	
	Assumption 1	Assumption 2	Assumption 1	Assumption 2
	(9)	(10)	(11)	(12)
1936	100.0	100.0	100.0	100.0
1938	122.3	122.3	122.3	122.3
1943	180.2	180.1	180.2	180.1
1946	77.5	76.3	72.9	68.6
1947	85.8	84.5	80.8	76.0
1948	99.6	98.1	93.8	88.2
1949	113.3	111.6	106.7	100.4
1950	132.8	130.8	125.0	117.6
1951	146.4	144.2	137.9	129.7
1952	158.2	155.7	148.9	140.1
1953	165.4	162.9	155.7	146.5
1954	177.7	175.0	167.3	157.4
1955	196.0	193.1	184.5	173.9
1956	213.3	210.2	201.3	189.9
1957	223.9	220.6	211.3	199.3
1958	237.3	235.0	225.1	212.3

West Germany

Year	Electricity generated (billion kwhr)	Index of production	
		Old index	New index
	(13)	(14)	(15)
1936	25.802	100.0	100.0
1938			137.0
1948		122.9	157.0
1949	39.103	151.2	183.1
1950	44.466	171.7	205.8
1951	52.848	200.8	241.8
1952	56.781	219.7	263.6
1953	61.026	236.4	279.6
1954	68.521	265.4	318.3
1955	76.542		358.2
1956	85.054		401.0
1957	90.912		436.0
1958	94.211		446.0

Sources: Col. 1: For 1936, 1938, and 1943 data, see Gleitze, *Ostdeutsche Wirtschaft*, p. 210: 1946–1949 figures calculated from *Karteiblatt* (unnumbered statistical sheet) in *SP*, 1955, No. 10; for 1950–1956 data, see *SJDDR*, 1956, p. 278; for 1957, see 1957, p. 294; and for 1960 Plan, see *Protokoll der dritten Parteikonferenz*, East Berlin, Dietz, p. 1032. Col. 2: See DIW, *Zahlen zur Energiewirtschaft in der sowjetischen Besatzungszone Deutschlands vor und nach 1945, Mitteilungen*, Special Issue, 25 June 1953, Pt. IV, p. 26; see also *SP*, No. 8, 1956, p. 108, where losses of 8–10 per cent are indicated; *SJDDR*, 1957, p. 313, gives losses as 6.6 per cent. Cols. 3 and 4: For input calculations, see text. Cols. 5–12: 1936 price: RM 45.00 per 1,000 kwhr. 1950 price: DM 47.80 per 1,000 kwhr. See text for discussion of the price. Assumption 1: fuel used by mining generating stations is here *excluded*, and included in the mining sector. Assumption 2: fuel used by mining generating stations is here *included*, and excluded in the mining sector. Col. 13: For 1936, see Gleitze, *op. cit.*, p. 210; for 1949–1954, see *SJBR*, 1955 ed., p. 235; for 1955, 1956, see *ibid.*, 1958, p. 208; and for 1957, see *ibid.*, p. 54*. Cols. 14 and 15: For old index, see *SJBR*, 1955, p. 230. For new index, 1950–1955, see Neuberechnung, p. 79, and for 1956, 1957, see *SJBR*, 1958, p. 186.

for the discrepancy between the actual and the calculated ratio may be threefold. First, it is possible, and likely, that power stations can purchase lignite at a special lower price than the already low price used in the calculations of Table 18. This is especially likely for the evaluation of the lignite used by generating stations affiliated with mines. In order that the figures be consistent with Table 18, in which a single price was substituted for a schedule, I did not use a lower price here. Second, the 1936 statistics include both producer and distributer stations; our calculations refer only to producing stations. Third, it is possible that in general the efficiency of lignite-based power generation is below the average for Germany as a whole. The second and third reasons would lead one to expect a smaller ratio of value added to sales value in East Germany than the average for all of Germany, and they are sufficiently important to make any adjustment of the assumed price inadvisable.

Table 29 presents the results of the calculations of the gross value added of the electricity sector. It will be noted that electric power production measured in kilowatthours slightly more than doubled between 1936 and 1955, but in terms of value added the growth is somewhat smaller. The differences are an indication of the conversion difficulties mentioned above. The indices of power production for East Germany and, for comparison, for the Federal Republic are also given in Table 29.

It is necessary to make two alternative estimates for East German power production to allow for the possibility that the lignite used by generating stations affiliated with mines was already allowed for in the amount of lignite deducted for the use of the mines themselves. It should be observed, however, that in adding the estimates for both lignite and power generation to arrive at the index of industrial production, it does not make any difference which estimate is used.

In terms of value added, if measured in 1936 prices, power production rose by 1955 to 193.1 or 196.1 per cent, depending on which assumption is made about the lignite input of generating stations affiliated with mines. In terms of 1950 prices, the level of output reached in 1955 was between 174 and 185 per cent of 1936.

To put this substantial growth into proper perspective two comparisons are useful: by 1938, East Germany generated 18.385 billion kwhr; in 1943 it generated 25.233 billion kwhr, almost as much as was claimed in 1955! The fact that it took until 1954 to exceed the highest electricity generation during 1943 indicates the substantial difficulties caused by the dismantling and wearing out of equipment. It also reconciles the substantial growth figures with the constant and justifiable complaints about severe power shortages.

The comparison with the development in the Federal Republic shows that East Germany was substantially outstripped through all the years, in spite of the fact that it used its equipment for substantially more hours during the year than the Federal Republic (5,600–5,700 hours compared with 4,500 hours). In the Federal Republic the official index of power production lies below any index one might wish to calculate from the kilowatthours generated, although by 1954 this difference was very small. There, too, the development between 1936 and 1943 was substantial. Power generation was 32.894 billion kwhr in 1938 and 42.932 billion kwhr in 1943, but the 1943 achievement was surpassed in 1950 by the Federal Republic and not until 1954 by East Germany.

The relative lag in electric power generation in East Germany behind that in the Federal Republic sheds light on the credibility of the official East German index of production; and it makes it virtually certain that neither productivity nor production can have increased as much in East Germany as in the Federal Republic. East German literature frequently stresses the need for electric power to increase faster than total output if productivity is to increase.

Since the consumption of power during the Second Five Year Plan will increase through the application of the newest techniques, the increase in gross production to 155% must be accompanied by a corresponding increase in power generation. However, if the [projected] rates of increase are compared with those provided for in the Sixth Five Year Plan of the Soviet Union the increase in power generation in the German Democratic Republic appears too small.[20]

The East German lag is undoubtedly due to the insufficient capacity of installations, which makes necessary unusually long hours of running but cannot be increased quickly enough because of shortages in the machinery sector. The change-over from soft coal to lignite was apparently finished by 1950.[21] No important new generating plants were installed until 1953, and only during 1954 did capacities increase substantially.[22] This lag is more serious for East Germany because the area has always emphasized — and still emphasizes — industries that are heavy power consumers — and therefore always produced more power per capita than the West. (Chemical production alone used 34 per cent of the power generated in 1953 and 35.1 per cent in 1955, and the five biggest chemical plants alone used a third of all power used in industry in 1955.) Yet the

Table 30

Per capita power generation in East Germany, West Germany, the United States, and United Kingdom, 1936 and 1952–1955 (kwhr)

	1936	1952	1953	1954	1955
East Germany	866	1264	1322	1445	1595
West Germany	631	1171	1245	1371	1520
United States	1062	2948	3221	3415	3782
United Kingdom	460	1294	1361	1467	1707

Source: *SP*, 1956, No. 8, p. 108.

gap in per capita production between the two areas has virtually closed, and England, for example, which in 1936 produced only slightly more than half as many kilowatt-hours per capita as East Germany, now produces substantially more. Moreover, all of the Western countries listed in Table 30 could easily surpass East Germany if they chose to run their equipment as many hours as the East Germans are forced to do.

The index of power generation undoubtedly exaggerates the true gross value added of this sector. Since, in order to run the equipment as intensively as is done, "quick repairs" are constantly needed, current maintenance must be substantially higher than in West Germany. However, none of these extra inputs, as it were, have been deducted.

CHAPTER VII

METALLURGY

THE present section will deal with the production of pig iron, steel, cast iron and cast steel, and aluminum and other nonferrous metals.

IRON AND STEELMAKING (EXCLUDING ROLLED STEEL)

Since the estimating procedures used for the iron and steel production sector of the economy were complicated, their description makes the present section unavoidably complex. It would have been desirable to estimate the value added of pig iron and then treat it as an input of the next stage, but the paucity of data, official and otherwise, made this straightforward approach impracticable. It was impossible even to guess from the available data where the pig iron goes. A method was therefore devised that bypassed the whole intermediate stage of pig-iron making, even though the data on pig iron production were utilized in the estimating procedures.

In 1936, iron and steel production comprised one industrial subclassification (No. II), and the casting industry comprised another (No. V); in East German methodology, cast iron and cast steel are apparently treated as part of machine construction — a perfectly reasonable procedure. It was impracticable to follow the procedures used in 1936 by the old Statistische Reichsamt or that currently employed in the Eastern Zone. Instead, castings and iron and steel production were consolidated into one group,* a procedure that permitted the elimination of the pig-iron subsector.

Figure 3 schematizes the procedure followed. The inputs go into blast furnaces, steelworks, and foundries; the final products are ingot steel, cast steel, cast and malleable iron, and slag. Since, so far as is known, no pig iron is exported, all of it must go into one or another of these products; and, since steel production requires more inputs than are domestically produced, the difference must be imported. These facts made it possible both to use the data on domestic pig-iron production and to avoid a

---

* In order to preserve as much detail as possible, the production of hot rolled steel was evaluated separately. See the next section.

separate evaluation of pig-iron production. Furthermore, if the outputs are defined according to Figure 3, the inputs become iron ore, coke, imported pig iron, and imported as well as domestic scrap. The calculation of the joint amounts of pig iron and scrap needed, together with the information on the domestic supplies, made it possible to estimate imports where these were not separately known.

Figure 3

Schematic outline of input-output relations in iron and steelmaking
(excluding hot and cold rolled steel)

Inputs	Intermediate products (Inputs in next stage cancel out. See text.)	Final products
I. *Blast Furnace*		
Soft coal coke		
Lignite BHT hard coke		
Domestic iron ore		
Limestone		
Scrap*	Domestic pig iron*	Slag
Imported ore*	Blast furnace gas	
II. *Steelworks*		
Imported pig iron		Ingot steel
Limestone		Electric-furnace steel
Scrap*		
Spiegeleisen*		
Imported ore*		
Fuel to melt pig iron and scrap		
Electricity for electric furnaces		
III. *Foundries*		
Electricity for melting steel		
Coke needed for melting cast iron ⟶		Cast steel
Scrap used (foundry scrap)		Cast and malleable iron
Ingot steel used to make cast steel		

Note: Items marked (*) were evaluated as indicated. No breakdown into the individual components was possible and substitutions among them are technically possible.

A number of inputs and outputs could not be treated separately. In the process of making pig iron, a considerable quantity of gas is generated. It was assumed that this gas is used for heating and other, minor, needs in the making of pig iron, so that the blast-furnace gas would affect both gross value and inputs to the same extent and would thus be canceled out. Some of the considerable amount of slag produced is now used to make roman cement. Although its quantity might be calculated, it could not be evaluated, and this may possibly lead to a very slight undervaluing of industrial production; but it is probably offset by the omission of other inputs, such as refractories, for which the data available were insufficient.

It is now necessary to describe the available series and the methods used to fill in the gaps in the data. When the first calculations were made, the only official East German figures available were for total pig iron and total ingot steel production, and the combined quantities of gray, malleable, and steel castings since 1946. Later official figures and details on different types of castings, the amount of steel made in electric furnaces, and so on, have been used to correct the original estimates.

There is a problem concerning the intermediate product *Spiegeleisen*. For some years the sum of the subgroups of iron is greater than the total pig iron output claimed. It is known, however, that scrap has become increasingly scarce and that the use of scrap in the Eisenkombinat Ost was forbidden.[1] Soviet Russia was supposed to supply so called steel iron (*Stahleisen*), and it is assumed — probably correctly — that *Stahleisen* is used instead of scrap as an input in steelmaking.

The other inputs were calculated as follows: All calculations started with the known gross output of ingot steel (which includes the amount of steel to be used for steel castings) and worked backward to the needed inputs. The amount of ingot steel used in castings was treated as an input in the steel casting process.

The amounts of cast iron and cast steel produced are known from East German sources. Thus the end-products are considered the final output of blast furnaces and foundries. The outputs were valued in West German prices as follows: for cast iron and cast steel, average West German prices for foundries were used; for steel, the West German Siemens-Martin steel prices were used.

From the gross sales values thus found the necessary inputs were deducted as follows: Pig iron and scrap are used to produce steel; as scrap becomes scarcer, imported or domestic *Stahleisen* is substituted.[2] We estimate that steel is produced with equal amounts of pig iron and scrap. This guess is based on the following information which was also used to calculate the other inputs.

In 1933, 18.86 tons of scrap, 11.27 tons of pig iron, 0.6 tons of *Spiegeleisen*, 0.2 tons of ferromanganese, 0.65 tons of iron ore (Fe content unknown), and 0.8 tons of limestone were used to produce 29.38 tons of Siemens-Martin steel. There was a loss through remelting of 4 per cent. In addition to 29.38 tons of Siemens-Martin steel, 0.31 tons of slag were produced.[3] Because of the diminished supply of scrap, it is assumed that the supply of pig iron relative to scrap has increased. It is unlikely that the low-grade native East German iron ores are used as an input. These ores contain too much silicon, which produces too much slag, which in turn should be avoided in the Siemens-Martin process. This assumption does not exclude the possibility that higher-grade imported ores may be used, although nothing is known about this.

This 50–50 estimate for pig iron and scrap inputs led in turn to an estimate of the amount of pig iron and scrap needed to produce the known amount of steel. Since the amount of cast iron was also known (after allowing for a 4 per cent loss), it was possible to estimate the amount of pig iron needed for this output; and the fact that all pig iron goes to produce either steel or cast iron led to an estimate of the total amount of pig iron that must have been available for the final outputs claimed.*

Knowing the available amount of pig iron made it possible to determine the needed imports (with domestic production known) and also to calculate the needed inputs to be deducted eventually from the sales value of the final products of this sector. First, the approximate domestic ore output and average Fe content are known; and it is further known that, since 1954, domestic ore has been increasingly reduced with lignite BHT coke, a process that is still being improved. The remaining pig iron must be produced from imported ores or scrap. (See Figure 3.)

To find the proper prices for the approximate mixtures was the major problem to be solved. For certain years the amount of ore imports is known. For the years for which no information on ore imports could be found, the input mixture was valued at average scrap prices, a method that probably overstates the cost of the inputs slightly. From the amount of pig iron produced, the amount of coke input needed could be estimated, which (until 1954) was all soft coal coke, both imported and domestic.

To complete the calculation of the inputs for blast furnaces, the limestone input was estimated according to the 0.8 figure given for 1933. The price used, which is probably too high,[4] refers to lump limestone.

The inputs of the steelworks were calculated as follows.[5] The 50–50 ratio of pig iron and scrap used allowed a calculation of the required inputs. It is likely that the imported pig iron goes into steel production because of its higher quality and that most domestic pig iron goes to steel mills in a solid state and must be reheated. The fuel input for melting down pig iron and scrap — which probably takes place in cupola furnaces — is soft coal coke.

The amount of steel made in electric furnaces is known. This steel is normally produced in a cold charge and requires about 500 kwhr per ton. The metal input is assumed to be ingot steel. Finally, we know the pig iron and ingot steel inputs for foundries. The ingots have to be remelted to produce cast steel, while cast-iron foundries use pig iron and cast-iron scrap.[6]

All these inputs were deducted from the sales value of the final product to arrive at an approximate value added of the iron and steel subsector of the metallurgy sector. The estimates of the amounts of inputs used

* Thus far the amount of ingot steel needed to produce cast steel has not been deducted. Cast steel is normally produced by melting ingots and scrap in a so-called cold charge process which uses no additional pig iron.

depend on the input-output relations assumed, which for the earlier years probably overestimate the efficiency of East German iron and steel production.*

Finally, an estimate for the products of iron foundries was made. It is unlikely that much pig iron was imported before 1949, the first year for which a figure is available; and it is likely that scrap was sufficiently plentiful even for exports at least until 1949. The total amount of gray and malleable iron castings is not known for the years 1950 through 1956. In general, the amount of malleable iron produced was small. In order to calculate the inputs that go into the making of castings, the actual output was raised by 14 per cent to allow for a 4 per cent loss and for the 10 per cent of the material that is assumed to stay permanently within the foundries as a circulating fund for scrap.

The 1936 prices applied to inputs and outputs were assumed to have prevailed until 1948.[7] The basic output data and the results found by the methods just described are given in Tables 31 and 32.†

Since all the inputs assumed are based on prewar relations in efficient plants suffering from neither supply nor personnel difficulties, it should be added that they are likely to be minimum figures. On the other hand, except for the inclusion of BHT coke inputs after 1954 in reducing domestic iron ores, no allowance has been made for technological progress. For a good number of years after the war — probably for all the years considered here — these assumptions are not likely to be far from the truth. Complaints about the low quality of castings have been particularly numerous and there has been a great percentage of unusable production in this category. The poor performance in the past should, however, probably not be extrapolated into the future.

The value added of the iron and steel sector has increased substantially between 1936 and 1957, but, depending on whether the outputs and inputs are valued in 1936 or in 1950 prices, there are important differences in the increase. The figures indicate that, whether measured in 1936 or in 1950 prices, by 1950, the output of the sector had about recovered to the prewar level. Valuation in 1950 prices indicates that the 1957 output was about 80 per cent above 1936; measured in 1936 prices the increase above 1936 was only 72 per cent. This difference is due primarily to the fact that the increase in inputs if measured in 1936 prices was substantially greater

* Official data are now available for the amount of pig iron that went into cast iron and the amount of ingot steel that went into rolled steel (treated as a final product of this sector) and that went into further production for steel castings.

† The details of the input calculations are given in Supplement Tables A.16 through A.18, Table A.19 for the sales value, and Table A.20 for the value added of iron and steel production. The output figures for pig iron, ingot steel, castings, etc., by weight, which form the basis of the calculations, are given in Table A.21. Tables A.19a and A.21a give the later official data used to correct the earlier calculations. The actual calculations of the inputs have not been reproduced. The major methodological problems that had to be faced and the solutions adopted have been discussed in the text.

Table 31

Production of iron and steel sector,[a] by major product,
East Germany, 1936 and 1950–1958 (thousand tons)

Year	Pig iron	Ingot steel	Total castings[b]	Gray castings[b]	Malleable castings[b]	Steel castings[b]	Electric-furnace steel[c]
1936	201.8	1198.6	646.0	567.0[d]	16.0[e]	63.0[d]	14.0[f]
1950	337.2	998.7	556.8	409.7	11.3	135.8	75.5
1951	341.6	1551.8	577.1	462.3	11.5	103.3	97.4
1952	659.5	1885.9	765.2	559.8	14.4	191.0	138.3
1953	1078.3	2163.2	832.5	598.0	18.6	215.9	198.2
1954	1317.8	2330.5	841.7	627.3	19.3	195.1	203.1
1955	1516.6	2507.5	840.0	651.1	24.0	164.9	207.2
1956	1573.7	2739.9	904.5	693.3	26.2	185.0	224.5
1957	1662.9	2894.5	982.7	754.2	23.8	204.7	252.4
1958	1774.9	3043.0	1019.7	784.8	26.7	208.0	298.5

[a] Except for the 1936 figures noted, all figures are from *SJDDR*, 1956, pp. 278, 284; 1957, pp. 294, 300; 1958, pp. 344, 350.

[b] Late in 1959, the following information was published on the rate of rejects:

	1951	1952	1955	1956	1957	1958
gray castings	10.4	10.3	8.8	8.7	8.0	7.5
steel castings	8.0	6.3	6.5	6.0	4.3	3.8
malleable castings	8.9	12.0	10.6	9.9	10.7	8.2
light metals	9.0	8.0	5.4	6.7	5.9	5.3
heavy metals	5.8	6.1	5.4	4.2	4.2	3.3

Source: *Presse-Informationen*, 21 October 1959, No. 117 (1800), p. 3.
[c] Included with ingot steel.   [d] *SJBR*, 1954, p. 545.   [e] Found as remainder.   [f] *SJBR*, 1955, p. 533.

Table 32

Value added of the iron and steel sector (excluding hot rolled steel), East Germany,
1936, 1938, 1943, and 1950–1958[a]

Year	1936 Prices		1950 Prices	
	Value (million RM)	Index	Value (million DM)	Index
1936	187.446	100.0	313.690	100.0
1938	211.349	112.8	350.690	111.8
1943	186.796	99.7	311.165	99.2
1950	177.194	94.5	304.562	97.1
1951	189.806	101.3	323.472	103.1
1952	255.969	136.6	442.809	141.2
1953	283.563	151.3	498.554	158.9
1954	289.196	154.3	514.237	163.9
1955	285.680	152.4	510.579	162.8
1956	303.667	162.0	542.030	172.8
1957	317.358	169.3	562.014	179.2
1958	330.891	176.5	586.108	186.8

[a] 1957 and 1958 were estimated to increase as sales value of ingot steel and castings. The inputs for 1957 and 1958 were not evaluated, but the error is not likely to be great.

than if measured in 1950 prices. The difference in the increase of the sales value is comparatively minor. That the increase was not greater in spite of the very substantial expansion in pig iron and ingot steel output is probably due to a large extent to the failure of the output of castings to expand more vigorously, a failure which is also reflected in machinery production. Since the necessary data are completely lacking, it is unfortunately not possible to make productivity calculations. For example, there can be little doubt that the industries considered employed more people in 1955 than in 1936, but it is impossible to indicate how many more. The creation of even so small an iron and steel industry is a tour de force and undoubtedly should be considered a success of the regime.

HOT ROLLED STEEL

In the calculations of the value added of rolled steel,* the basic problem consisted of finding the proper prices to be used for a large variety of products. The output of hot rolled steel as a whole is given officially in tons for 1936 and for 1946 through 1957. Official data for cold rolled steel became available after the calculations were finished. Differences are negligible and have not been evaluated. Previously published West German estimates grossly overestimated the now officially given output.[8]

It was first necessary to subdivide the total production of hot rolled steel into subgroups that could be legitimately priced by a single price. The Statistical Yearbook of the German Democratic Republic gives figures for the output of steel sheets (*Walzbleche*), so-called *Walzsorteneisen*, that is, rolled sections, rolled rods, strips and bands (*Bandagen*). West German sources also give data for seamless tubes. When the subgroups are added, a small remainder is still unaccounted for, which in 1950 amounted to 5.2 per cent of the total hot rolled steel produced and in 1955 to 8.2 per cent. The remainder that was not accounted for was distributed among the various categories according to their relative importance in total hot rolled steel production.

Although the detailed distribution is undoubtedly subject to error, its general order of magnitude makes sense, as does the direction of the development. Since seamless tubes are extremely difficult to make and a shortage of them causes bottlenecks in other industries, it is likely that they form a small but increasing part of total production as compared with 1936. It is similarly probable that structural shapes become relatively less important and sheets relatively more important with further development of the rolled steel industry.

Thus total rolled steel output was divided into three major classes, sheets, structural shapes, and seamless tubes, according to the official data

---

* The details are presented in Table A.22 of the Supplement.

available since 1950. For the years before 1949 and for 1950 through 1952, the 1952 percentage was applied.

It is not likely that any tubes were produced in the years 1946 through 1948. Output will therefore be split evenly between sheets and structural shapes. For the years 1954 and later, it was assumed that the output of seamless tubes was the same percentage of total rolled steel production as in 1953.

In determining the appropriate prices for the individual subgroups, the following considerations were applied. It would have been useful to break down sheet production into more homogeneous subgroups, such as thick and thin sheets, and even sheets for special uses such as shipbuilding, but no information of this kind is available. It is known, however, that sheets were imported in larger amounts than structural shapes, and it is probable that much of the imported sheet steel was of special types needed for shipbuilding. In the *Direktive* it is stated that by 1960 rolled steel production is to be increased to more than double that of 1955. "Because of the development of our own production it should be limited essentially to low carbon steel." [9] It is certain that heat- and corrosion-resistant steels, particularly steels suitable for ship screws, were not then produced, since the *Direktive* states that their production was to be started in 1958 at the latest.[10] Furthermore, the *Direktive* calls for increased production of standard sizes of medium and very thick sheets and for the start of production of structural shapes to save weight.[11] In general, the equipment of the rolled steel industry must be in poor condition. The *Direktive* states as a Plan aim for 1960 that the ratio of rolled steel output to ingot input is to be reduced to 1:1.29,[12] a figure reached at present in West Germany, although only in the more efficient rolling mills. It therefore seemed appropriate to use the price for thick and for thin sheets and evaluate half of the sheet output with each, or, what amounts to the same thing, to evaluate the output of sheets with the arithmetic mean of the two average prices.*

For rolled sections two price series of approximately the same level are available, one referring to structural steel and a slightly higher one referring to bar steel (*Stabstahl*), Thomas quality. Bar steel of Siemens-Martin quality is more expensive than Thomas quality steel which in turn costs about the same amount more than structural steel. The bar steel, Thomas quality price, was adopted as a reasonable average.

The greatest difficulty consisted in evaluating seamless tubes. No series was found. However, Thimm gives prices for the Federal Republic in 1954 and 1955 for 21 types of seamless tubes by diameter and thickness of tubing, varying from DM 831.49 per ton for a tube of 146 mm diameter

---

* Actually, the two prices moved mostly in the same direction between 1953 and 1954. In 1953 the standard of "thin sheets" in West Germany was reduced from 3 mm to 2.75 mm, and that for thick sheets correspondingly increased.

and 4.25 mm thickness to DM 1,635.97 for a tube of 14 mm diameter and 2 mm thickness — the smallest as well as the most expensive tube made.[13] The distribution of prices as a function of thickness and diameter is shaped like a reversed J, with the righthand branch rising to a much lower level than the lefthand branch.

Seamless tubes are difficult to make and require good equipment. They are also an essential and scarce item. It is reasonable to assume that at this stage of its development the Soviet Zone has trouble making the more specialized types. All but four pipes listed by Thimm cost less than DM 1,200, and 9 cost less than DM 1,000. It seems reasonable to allow for seamless tubes in each year three times the price allowed for structural shapes, which in 1954 was DM 386.75. This would allow DM 1,160.25 for tubes, which corresponds to the price of a 38 mm tube of 5 mm thickness (DM 1,162.35). If anything, this price is slightly high.

To calculate the approximate value added, the only input taken into consideration was steel. In other words, it was assumed that the rolling mill is integrated with the steel plant and no reheating is necessary. Since the data refer to *ingot* steel, this is probably not true, but no more reasonable figure could be found. If we allow for the reheating of the inputs, the already poor showing of this sector would be even worse. The assumed input-output ratio of steel to rolled steel products is 1.5 tons of steel per ton of product for 1946 through 1953; 1.45:1 for 1954; and 1.35:1 for 1955 and 1956. For 1936 the ratio of 1.3:1, which is probably more nearly normal, was applied.* The waste steel must go back into the steelmaking process as scrap (if it is not lost altogether) and cannot be reused within the rolling mill. Since scrap was deducted in making ingot steel, the scrap "produced" in the course of making hot rolled steel is allowed for as a "product" of the rolling mill, with 4 per cent of the steel lost in the process. Comparison with the calculations made for the ingot steel sector shows that domestic production was not quite sufficient in the later years to provide the necessary input of steel.† The production figures and the major results are given in Table 33.

* The ratios for West Germany were suggested by a rolling mill expert. He stated that even in 1955 a ratio of 1.34:1 in West Germany was considered normal, and his own plant was doing unusually well with a ratio of 1.29:1.

† For 1953 and 1954 the following check using the tables above and *Aussenhandel 1953 und 1954 Plan* (Foreign Trade 1953 and 1954 Plan), *Materialien,* p. 13, can be made:

	1953 (Thousand Tons)	1954 (Thousand Tons)
Ingot steel production	2,163.2	2,330.5
Imports	118.4 Actual	240.0 Plan
Total available	2,281.6	2,570.5
Needed for rolled steel	2,270.3	2,481.1
Needed for cast steel	291.3	294.4
Total	2,561.6	2,775.5
Deficit	280.0	205.0

By 1956 the output of hot rolled steel products, measured in tons and by sales value in constant prices had risen to 226 per cent of its 1936 level. When allowance for inputs is made, however, the picture looks rather different. Measured in 1936 prices, the value added was 164.7 per cent of 1936; measured in 1950 prices the increase above 1936 was 75 per cent; but even this result was derived only by assuming an efficiency of operations close to West German performance, which is certainly not the case. The difference in the results is due mainly to the fact that ingot steel prices rose only 90.5 per cent between 1936 and 1950, while prices of various rolled steel products doubled or more than doubled. The actual performance is undoubtedly worse, and the final output is known to be of poor quality.

In 1936 the value added was about 26.4 per cent of sales value. By

Table 33

Production and value added, hot rolled steel, East Germany, 1936, 1950–1958, and 1960 plan

A. *Production, thousand tons*			
Year	Total[a]	Sheets	Structural shapes, including bands	Tubes
	(1)	(2)	(3)	(4)
1936	898.0	434.0	393.0	43.0
1950	780.7	286.8	440.6	26.9
1951	1113.1	398.2	623.8	36.5
1952	1330.6	524.7	687.3	40.4
1953	1513.5	588.9	790.9	46.0
1954	1711.1	666.8	875.7	77.7
1955	1906.7	710.7	994.5	103.0
1956	2035.4	709.3	1351.4[b]	102.3
1957	2115.4[b]	711.6	1250.1	129.2
1958	2264.8	754.6	1328.8	134.8
1960	2600.0 Plan			

B. *Value added, 1936 prices*				
Year	Total value (million RM)	Value of scrap produced (million RM)	Value of steel input (million RM)	Value added (million RM)	Index
	(5)	(6)	(7)	(8)	(9)
1936	118.906	9.807	97.361	31.352	100.0
1950	95.878	15.082	97.661	13.299	42.4
1951	136.531	21.504	139.253	18.782	59.9
1952	165.561	25.708	166.458	24.811	79.1
1953	189.295	29.240	189.343	29.192	93.0
1954	214.311	29.467	206.924	36.854	117.5
1955	238.184	24.826	214.671	48.339	154.2
1956	254.398	26.515	229.275	51.638	164.7
1957	281.061	27.947	241.660	67.348[c]	214.8[c]
1958	297.532	29.488	254.996	72.024[c]	229.7[c]

Table 33 (Continued)

C. *Value added, 1950 prices*

Year	Total value (million DM)	Value of scrap produced (million DM)	Value of steel input (million DM)	Value added (million DM)	Index
	(10)	(11)	(12)	(13)	(14)
1936	243.218	17.550	185.477	75.291	100.0
1950	195.450	36.990	186.048	36.392	48.3
1951	279.770	38.482	265.282	52.970	70.4
1952	338.987	46.005	317.108	67.884	90.2
1953	387.681	52.326	360.705	79.302	105.3
1954	438.855	52.732	394.197	97.390	129.4
1955	487.895	44.427	408.957	123.365	163.9
1956	521.106	47.448	436.777	131.777	175.0
1957	575.315	50.011	451.678	173.648[c]	230.6[c]
1958	610.395	52.770	476.603	186.562[c]	247.8[c]

Sources: Col. 1: For 1936 and 1950–1955, see *SJDDR*, 1955, pp. 162–163; for 1956 and 1957, see 1957, p. 294; for 1960 Plan, see *Direktive*, p. 13. Cols. 2, 3, 4: For 1936, see Gleitze, *Ostdeutsche Wirtschaft*, pp. 193–194; for 1950–1955, see *SJDDR*, 1955, pp. 162–163; for 1956 and 1957, see 1957, *ibid.*, 1957, p. 294. Col. 5: Average prices. See text. Cols. 6 and 7: 1936: input-output, 1.3:1. Until 1953: input-output, 1.5:1. 1955: input-output, 1.35:1.

Year	Production coefficient	Loss through oxidation	Scrap
1936	1.30	0.04	0.26
1950	1.50	0.04	0.46
1951	1.50	0.04	0.46
1952	1.50	0.04	0.46
1953	1.50	0.04	0.46
1954	1.45	0.04	0.41
1955	1.35	0.04	0.31

Col. 7: 1936 price of scrap, RM 42.00 per ton; 1950 price, DM 75.16 per ton. *SJBR*, 1956, p. 462. Col. 8: For 1936, 1950–1956, col. 5 + col. 6 − col. 7. For 1957, assumed to increase as output of hot rolled steel: 105.453 per cent of 1956. Col. 9: Calculated from col. 8. Cols. 10, 11, 12, 13, 14: Derived as cols. 5–9.

ᵃ Total includes some minor production of other types of structural shapes not separately shown.

ᵇ Revised.

ᶜ The jump from 1956 to 1957 is probably spurious and due to an undervaluation of tube output in preceding years.

1956, measured in 1936 prices, value added had declined to 20.3 per cent of sales value, and, in 1950 prices, to 25.3 per cent, which of course reflects the slightly greater wastefulness of steel inputs.

It should be added that in 1950 the ratio of value added to sales value (*Nettoquota*) of the category blast furnaces, steel furnaces, and hot steel rolling mills is given as 50 per cent for West Germany. This category includes output of forging presses, but in the calculations of the sales value (*Bruttoproduktionswert*), deliveries within the industry group are excluded. If these deliveries were added both to the sales value and to the materials used, the value added as a percentage of gross output would decline substantially, since the gross value added (*Nettoproduktionswert*) would obviously remain unchanged, but the denominator by which it would have to be divided would increase substantially.[14]

The whole iron and steel production sector (including castings and hot rolled steel) increased by 60.8 per cent between 1936 and 1955 if measured in 1936 prices, but by 71 per cent when measured in 1950 prices (see Table 34). The West German increase was 43.7 per cent. This is rather surprising. One would expect a much more vigorous increase in East Germany where the base was so much lower. In 1954, ingot steel output

Table 34

Value added, iron and steelmaking and foundries, East Germany, and indices, West and East Germany, 1936 and 1950–1958

	East Germany				West Germany			
	Value added		Index		Old index			
	1936 Prices (million RM)	1950 Prices (million DM)	1936 Prices 1936 = 100	1950 Prices 1936 = 100		Castings		New index combined
Year					Iron	Steel	Combined	
	(1)	(2)	(3)	(4)	(5)	(6)	(7)	(8)
1936	218.798	388.981	100.0	100.0	100.0	100.0	100.0	100.0
1950	194.343	347.754	88.8	89.4	81.7	87.4	83.3	82.7
1951	216.738	390.692	99.1	100.4	92.9	112.1	98.4	98.7
1952	289.030	525.143	132.1	135.0	107.3	118.5	110.5	112.2
1953	324.655	598.706	148.4	153.9	102.2	105.7	103.2	86.6
1954	340.600	637.577	155.7	163.9	114.5	122.1	116.7	115.5
1955	351.819	665.194	160.8	171.0	142.0	148.0	143.7	143.7
1956	362.305	686.097	165.6	176.4	n.a.	n.a.	n.a.	154.3
1957	384.706	735.662	175.8	189.1	n.a.	n.a.	n.a.	158.9
1958	402.915	772.670	184.1	198.6	n.a.	n.a.	n.a.	145.0

Sources: Cols. 1 and 2: The methods of calculation are described in the text. The detailed calculations are given in Supplement Tables A.17–A.22. Cols. 3 and 4: Derived from cols. 1 and 2. Cols. 5 and 6: For 1936–1954, see *SJBR*, 1955, p. 228; for 1955, *Monthly Report of the Bank Deutscher Laender* (BDL; Frankfurt/Main), March 1956, p. 92 (English edition). The *SJBR* figures refer to average monthly production, the BDL figures to production per working day. However, except for rounding, the two indices agree. Col. 7: Combined in the ratios 5.34 and 2.15. These are the weights given to the two series in the West German production index. See *SJBR*, 1955, p. 228. Col. 8: *Ibid.*, 1959, p. 181. Combined in the ratios 3.88 and 1.28 corresponding to the weights in the new West German index.

in tons was more than seven times larger in West Germany than in East Germany, and rolled steel production in West Germany was about 6½ times the East German output in tons.

ALUMINUM, COPPER, AND MAGNESIUM

The value added of aluminum could not be found by the same method used for iron and steelmaking. It was impossible to evaluate the cost of one major input — the carbon electrode input, which is about one-half ton per ton of aluminum. The bauxite inputs, although large in quantity, probably do not amount to more than about 15 per cent of the sales value of the aluminum. According to information obtained at the Massachusetts Institute of Technology, at present about 22,000 kwhr of electricity are used in producing one ton of aluminum. An ECE publication states that before the war 25,000 kwhr per ton of aluminum were usually required, but that this figure has been reduced to below 20,000 kwhr.[15]

The method used was to calculate the output of aluminum in the prices for aluminum given in the Statistical Yearbook of the Federal Republic[16] and apply it to the ratio of value added to sales value found in the United States *Census of Manufactures* for 1947—40.5 per cent. Unfortunately, the German Production Statistics of 1936 gives the necessary figures only for the combined production of aluminum and alumina. In 1936 the corresponding German ratio would have been 48.64 per cent.

Even in 1955, for which year an official German figure was available,

Table 35

Production of aluminum, copper, and semi-finished nonferrous metal products, and value added of nonferrous metal sector, East Germany, and indices, West and East Germany, 1936 and 1950–1958

A. *Production, thousand tons*

Year	Aluminum East Germany	Aluminum West Germany	Copper, East Germany	Semi-manufactured nonferrous metal products, East Germany
	(1)	(2)	(3)	(4)
1936	48.84	48.341	68.530	192.705
1950	0.8	27.838	26.000	64.933
1951	7.0	74.134	26.600	65.332
1952	13.5	100.474	28.000	72.384
1953	20.0	106.940	31.000	75.899
1954	26.6	129.219	28.700	86.224
1955	26.8	137.066	28.700	84.391
1956	28.0	147.362	31.000	84.391
1957	29.0	153.838	31.000	84.391
1958	29.0	136.766	n.a.	n.a.

B. *Value added*

Year	East Germany Value added 1936 prices (million RM)	East Germany Index 1936 = 100	West Germany, old index, semi-manufactured products
	(5)	(6)	(7)
1936	175.431	100.00	100.0
1950	43.595	24.85	85.9
1951	48.875	27.86	105.1
1952	58.647	33.43	97.1
1953	66.313	37.80	113.0
1954	77.926	44.42	149.0
1955	76.786	43.67	n.a.
1956	77.769	44.33	n.a.
1957	77.769	44.33	n.a.
1958	77.769	44.33	n.a.

Table 35 (Continued)

| Year | East Germany | | West Germany, new index | |
	Value added 1950 prices (million DM)	Index 1950 prices 1936 = 100	Semi-manufactured nonferrous metal products	Nonferrous metal castings
	(8)	(9)	(10)	(11)
1936	478.927	100.00	100.0	100.0
1950	137.021	28.61	99.9	120.0
1951	145.546	30.39	120.3	156.0
1952	167.864	35.15	113.7	147.0
1953	183.716	38.36	130.0	161.0
1954	211.255	44.11	161.1	210.0
1955	207.950	43.42	178.2	266.0
1956	210.201	43.89	181.0	278.0
1957	210.201	43.89	189.0	285.0
1958	210.201	43.89	194.0	299.0

Sources: Col. 1: For 1936–1946, see Gleitze, *Ostdeutsche Wirtschaft*, p. 194; for 1955, see *Direktive*, p. 15; figures for other years are estimates of Western experts. Col. 2: For 1936, Gleitze, *op. cit.*, p. 194; for 1950-1955, *SJBR*, 1955, p. 251; 1956, p. 207. Col. 3: For 1936 see Gleitze, *op. cit.*, p. 194; for 1951–1954, *Die Nicht-Eisen Metallindustrie in der Sowjetischen Besatzungszone*, *Materialien*, p. 27. 1955–1957 estimates based on advice of Western experts. Figures refer only to refined copper. Since no figures for the postwar years could be found, so-called black copper is not included. Col. 4: For 1936 see Gleitze, *op. cit.*, p. 195. The 1936 figure coincides with that given in *SJDDR*, 1955 ed., p. 162. For 1950–1955, see *ibid*. No values are given in 1956, 1957, or 1958 eds. Hence, values for 1956, 1957, and 1958 have been assumed to be the same as in 1955. Col. 5: For 1936 value added, see Table 37 below. Other years calculated from index, Col. 6. Cols. 6 and 8: Derived from Supplement Table A.25b, where detailed calculations are presented. 1957 and 1958 assumed to be same as 1956. Col. 7: *SJBR*, 1955, p. 228. Col. 9: From Col. 8. Col. 10: *Neuberechnung; SJBR*, 1959, p. 181. Col. 11: *Ibid*.

aluminum production was still only about 55 per cent of 1936, and it has remained substantially below the planned level.*

In contrast, West German production, which in 1936 had been slightly below that in East Germany, zoomed after the limitations of the Potsdam Agreement were removed. In 1954 it was 267 per cent of 1936, almost five times the amount claimed by East Germany for 1955.

A similar procedure had to be followed to calculate the value added of copper, except that the 1936 German ratio of gross value added to gross production for the classification "copper refineries and copper electrolysis" was applied. Because of the availability of copper scrap, copper production is throughout higher than the Cu content of domestically mined ores. It is likely, however, that no copper ores were imported although quite a bit of refined copper was imported. (See Table 35.)

Since no magnesium was produced in the Soviet Zone even as late as 1956, a single value had to be calculated for 1936.[17] Before the war 11,643 tons of Germany's total production of 12,800 tons were produced

* Figures for the production of various nonferrous metals and for the estimated value added of the nonferrous metal sector are found in Table A.33 of the Supplement, and the supporting detail is in Tables A.24 through A.25b.

in the present Soviet Zone. (The additional 1,157 tons were produced in the area of the United States Zone.) No value added could be found either in German or in American statistics; in fact, it is stated in the United States *Census of Manufactures* for 1947 that this information cannot be given out. Therefore, *faute de mieux*, the ratio of value added to sales value for aluminum was assumed here.

Similar difficulties arose concerning prices. No German price is available, nor any American price before 1940. The 1940 price is the price calculated by the *Statistical Abstract of the United States: 1950* — 27.0 cents per pound.[18] The 1950 price, found in *The Minerals Yearbook,* for primary magnesium is 24.5 cents per pound.[19] These prices were translated into marks at the obtaining official exchange rates — RM per dollar, 2.48 for 1940 and DM per dollar, 4.20 for 1950, although there is no doubt that the prewar official rate is highly artificial. The results are given in Table 36.

Table 36

Value added of magnesium, East Germany, 1936, at 1936 and 1950 prices

Year	Quantity (tons)	Price per ton (RM/DM)	Sales value (million RM/DM)	Value added (million RM/DM)
1936	11,643	1344.16	RM 15.67	RM 6.35
1950	0	2276.40	DM 26.50	DM 10.73

Sources: The quantity produced is from Gleitze, *Ostdeutsche Wirtschaft*, p. 195. For prices and value added, see text.

NONFERROUS METAL PRODUCTS

The Statistical Yearbook of the German Democratic Republic gives a series in tons for rolling mill products of nonferrous metals that combines the two categories of nonferrous metal smelting and nonferrous metal semi-manufactures given in 1936. The total tonnage in 1936 was 192,700, and by 1955 it had fallen to 84,391 tons, or 42.8 per cent. In terms of sales value, this series accounted in 1936 for RM 229.291 million of a total German sales value of RM 1,641.496 million, or 14 per cent. However, the two types of manufactures accounted for 45.4 per cent of the total sales of the nonferrous metal industry in the area which became East Germany. Thus the representation of the series adds substantially to the coverage of the nonferrous industry of the preceding section.

In 1936 the value added of the industries covered by series for nonferrous metals and semi-finished products in Germany as a whole was RM 309.289 million, but the representation of different industries in the area now East Germany varied considerably before the war. On the basis of sales values, the value added attributable to the area of East Germany may be estimated as in Table 37. The value added in 1950 prices,

Table 37

Value added of nonferrous metal products, East Germany, 1936

	Value added in all Germany (million RM)	Per cent of sales in East Germany	Value added attributable to East Germany (million RM)
	(1)	(2)	(3)
Semi-manufactures	298.687	26.88	80.287
Smelting	10.602	11.48	1.217
Total	309.289		81.504

Sources: Col. 1: *Produktionsstatistik, 1936*, p. 45. Col. 2: Gleitze, *Ostdeutsche Wirtschaft*, p. 175. Col. 3: Col. 1 × col. 2.

estimated by means of the producer price index for nonferrous semi-finished products (1938 = 100, 1950 = 273), is RM 222.517 million.[20]

VALUE ADDED OF NONFERROUS METALS

The value added of nonferrous metals can be estimated by an index constructed from the sum of the values added of copper, aluminum, and magnesium production, and nonferrous metal semi-manufactures. In 1936 these four categories accounted for RM 117.848 million (in 1936 prices). The value added of the whole industry in 1936 may be estimated as in Table 38.

Table 38

Value added of the nonferrous metal industry, East Germany, 1936

	Value added in all Germany (million RM)	Per cent of sales in East Germany	Value added attributable to East Germany (million RM)
	(1)	(2)	(3)
Copper, lead, silver	55.283	27.61	15.264
Other metals	133.020	47.07	62.613
Ferrous alloys	38.739	41.43	16.050
Nonferrous semi-manufactures	298.687	26.88	80.287
Metal smelting	10.602	11.48	1.217
Total	536.331		175.431

Sources: Col. 1: *Produktionsstatistik, 1936*, p. 45. Col. 2: Gleitze, *Ostdeutsche Wirtschaft*, p. 175. Col. 3: Col. 1 × col. 2.

The 1936 value added in 1950 prices was found to be, using the price index for nonferrous metals (273 per cent), RM 478.927 million. The subindustries separately calculated thus account for 67.2 per cent of the value added attributable to the area of East Germany, a very good representation.* By 1955 their output had fallen to 43.77 per cent of 1936, measured in 1936 prices, and to 43.42 per cent, measured in 1950 prices. By chance this almost exactly equals the decline of semi-finished products alone.

By contrast with this dismal development, the nonferrous metal industry in the Federal Republic reached its 1936 level in 1950 and its 1938 level in 1951. By 1955 it had surpassed its 1936 level by 78.2 per cent. In the (new) total West German index[21] nonferrous metal has a weight of 1.14, almost as great as iron and steel castings (1.24). The development of this industry, so important for the manufacture of electrical machinery, should be kept in mind in the later discussion of machinery output.

Table 39

Output per man, metallurgy, East Germany, 1936 and 1950–1958

Year	Employ-ment	Index of employment		Index of production, total metal sector		Index calculated output per man	Index, claimed output	
							Per production worker[a]	Per industrial employee[b]
		1936 = 100	1950 = 100	1936 = 100	1950 = 100	1950 = 100		
	(1)	(2)	(3)	(4)	(5)	(6)	(7)	(8)
1936	36,587	100.0	54.5	100.0	112.6	206.6	100.0	100.0
1950	67,100	183.4	100.0	88.8	100.0	100.0	100.0	100.0
1951	79,100	216.2	117.9	99.1	111.6	94.7	117.2	109.4
1952	90,300	246.8	134.6	132.1	148.8	105.5	136.7	124.0
1953	76,400	208.8	113.9	148.4	167.1	146.7	169.8	154.4
1954	81,500	222.8	121.5	155.7	175.3	144.3	183.7	165.5
1955	82,544	225.6	123.0	160.8	181.1	147.2	200.0	n.a.
1956	82,862	226.5	123.5	165.6	186.4	150.9	212.0	n.a.
1957	86,457	236.3	128.9	175.8	198.0	153.6	218.0	n.a.
1958	90,467	247.3	134.8	184.1	207.3	153.8	228.0	n.a.

Sources: Col. 1: For 1936, see Gleitze, *Ostdeutsche Wirtschaft*, p. 174; for 1950–1954, *SJDDR*, 1955 ed., p. 126; for 1955–1958, *ibid.*, 1958 ed., p. 278. Gleitze refers to iron making and all nonferrous metals; *SJDDR* to *Metallurgie*, i.e., metalmaking only. Cols. 2 and 3: Derived from col. 1. Cols 4 and 5: Table 34, col. 3. Col. 6: Col. 5 ÷ col. 3. Cols. 7 and 8: *SJDDR*, 1955, p. 119, 1957, p. 269 and 1958, p. 264. Refers to socialized industry only.

[a] Production workers are defined as "employed, directly active in production processes or aiding them by auxiliary services, repairs, intraplant transports, etc. Technical personnel are not included with production workers." (*SJDDR*, 1955, p. 104.)

[b] Industrial personnel are defined as "production workers, technical personnel, economists, and administrative personnel, auxiliary labor, plant police, social workers [*Betreuungspersonal*], and apprentices." (*Ibid.*)

Since castings could not be separated in our calculations, it was not possible to make calculations of output per man. However, a rough idea can be obtained from the following figures: In 1936 the area that is now East Germany employed 36,587 persons in the production of iron and nonferrous metals, including ferrous alloys and nonferrous semi-finished products. In 1955, 80,900 persons were employed in metallurgy in East Germany, a high of 90,300 having been during 1952.

* Detailed figures are found in Tables A.25a and A.25b of the Supplement.

Thus there was undoubtedly a substantial improvement in output per man during the period of the First Five Year Plan, as the data — both calculated and official — of Table 39 shows. There can be little doubt, however, that by 1955 the 1936 level of productivity had certainly not yet been reached.

CHAPTER VIII

ENGINEERING-CONSTRUCTION

I n communist usage, machine construction includes a number of industries that are treated separately in West German methodology — for
example, not only machine construction proper but also steel construction, construction of vehicles, shipbuilding, and iron and steel
products (including nuts, bolts, and wire) and other metal products
(ferrous and nonferrous).

In this section the estimating procedures differed for various subgroups
according to the amount of information available. Road vehicles could be
estimated directly. Machine construction in the narrow sense (excluding
electrical equipment and supplies and fine mechanics and optics) combined
with steel construction and shipbuilding, was estimated by two methods,
which are described in detail. These depend essentially on the assumption
that the chief inputs of such construction are steel.

The output of iron and steel products and of metal products was subdivided according to contents — so far as these could be ascertained.
Nuts, bolts, wire, nails, and so on, are, in the narrow sense, obviously
closely linked to machinery and require steel as chief input. Their output
was assumed to vary with machinery output. On the other hand, the output
of vehicle parts is more likely to vary with vehicle production. In the
absence of a better method of estimating, miscellaneous metal products
were assumed to vary with the combined calculated index for machinery
and road vehicles.

The output of electrical machinery was separately estimated by two
methods. For one calculation, East German data in East marks were
used; for the other, output data in numbers of units produced were used,
from which an index could be constructed which in turn could be linked
to the 1936 value added. The same methods were used for fine mechanics
and optics.

ENGINEERING-CONSTRUCTION, INCLUDING STEEL CONSTRUCTION
AND SHIPBUILDING

Under the best of circumstances, the calculation of the value added of
the engineering-construction portion of any nation's industry is tricky

business. The difficulties are compounded many times for Communist Germany for a number of reasons. Although information does exist on the number of some types of important machinery, such as turret lathes and hydraulic presses, and for the weight in tons of the equipment for rolling mills, it is insufficient for the calculation of an index. Official figures in East marks refer to machine construction of various types — power-generating equipment, machine tools, machines for metallurgy and mining, equipment for the fuel industry, equipment for the casting industry, equipment for transportation, agricultural machinery, steel construction, and new construction of rail vehicles. In addition, there is some information on the number of passenger cars and of trucks, truck trailers, and, presumably, wheeled, non-agricultural tractors, motorcycles and bicycles (including *"Mopeds"**), and a few value figures referring to shipbuilding and electrical equipment and supplies.

Since this information was inadequate for constructing an index of output, the best that could be hoped for was some approximation to the gross value added of the engineering-construction sector by indirection. Such a rough approximation procedure is, for example, employed in Gerschenkron's attempt to calculate a pre-World War I index of industrial production in Italy.[1] His method consists essentially in applying the American value added per worker for subgroups of machinery production to the number of workers in each of these subgroups.

Two methods have been employed here.† Although they are not much more subtle, they differ from Gerschenkron's method.

First method. Basically, it was assumed that engineering-construction output varies, in ways to be specified, with the total amount of steel and iron available, which implies that virtually all steel and iron goes into some phase of machine or iron-and-steel construction. Since such relatively minor industries as pots and pans manufacture, minor agricultural implements, and so on, use relatively little steel, this assumption seems warranted.

It should be noted that this method is not applicable to electrical equipment and supplies, and fine mechanics and optics (a category which in East German practice also includes office machinery), in which the amount of steel or iron used is relatively small — except perhaps for electric motors. Too many other materials are used — glass for radio tubes, wiring, wood, copper, and so on — which do not vary directly with the amount of iron and steel consumed. For this reason it was decided to treat the electrical industry and fine mechanics and optics separately. Fortunately, in the industries treated in this section, materials other than iron and steel play only a minor role — estimated to be about 5 per cent

---

* Bicycles with auxiliary motors.

† The second method is described in the appendix to this chapter.

of the value of iron and steel used for engineering products and negligible for iron-and-steel construction and for shipbuilding.[2] (This point will be discussed in more detail below.)

Before describing the methods of estimating in detail, a word is needed about the sources of information and the categories of machinery for which information in value terms is available. For 1936 the available figures are from the official Production Statistics of 1936 (given in detail also by Gleitze, *Ostdeutsche Wirtschaft,* and in somewhat less detail by the Statistical Yearbook of the Federal Republic. For the postwar years, some figures are from *Materialien,* the sources being specified in detail in the footnotes to the tables, and others are from the recently published Statistical Yearbooks of the German Democratic Republic.

The term "Power-generating equipment" probably includes turbines and steam engines; "Machine tools" obviously includes machine tools but may also include precision instruments; "Equipment for metallurgy and mining" is interpreted to include smelters and rolling mills as well as cranes, machinery for mining, bulldozers, and so on; and the category "Equipment for the fuel industry" probably includes boilers and various other kinds of apparatus. It is not clear how "Transportation equipment" differs from construction of new rail vehicles, which themselves probably include regular and narrow-gauge locomotives, while railroad cars and cars for industrial and mining railroads are included with iron-and-steel construction (or at least were so included in 1936). Transportation equipment probably includes signals, switches, and masts. "Shipbuilding" includes both ocean-going and inland ships. There are serious gaps in the available information.* In particular, except for power-generating machinery, machine tools, and equipment for the metallurgy, mining, and fuel industries, most of the data start with 1950. The paucity of official East German information is unfortunate.

Although such East German figures as exist have to be used with care, there is no reason to disbelieve their general tenor, which is consistent with official statements and general knowledge.† It is known that the first attempts at reconstruction consisted in putting machine tools back into production, that early shipbuilding used mostly wood and was

---

* See Supplement Table A.26.

† It is of course possible that West German sources have an interest in painting the situation in East Germany blacker than it is — although this is not self-evident. It is even more possible that the persons who risk their lives to bring figures to the West are biased. Yet when East German official information has become available it has borne out the West German claims surprisingly well. For example, *Materialien* claimed a loss of 16 per cent in recovering copper from the ore, which seemed high. A telephone call to the Department of Engineering at M.I.T. elicited the response that even 10 per cent was a high loss. Yet the *Direktive* admits 18 per cent! Examples could be multiplied.

limited to fishing trawlers of about 30 tons, that no regular-gauge locomotives were built before 1950, and that dismantling losses were extremely heavy. The absence of figures before 1950 probably is an indication that production was small.

The figures for the production values are given in East marks but it is by no means certain whether they are measured in *Messwerte,* current prices, or what. However, this uncertainty is probably not very serious, since I did not intend to derive a price index or to deflate these value figures to arrive at a quantity estimate of output. The method used to derive an index of engineering-construction output avoids the problem of year-to-year price changes completely, although it still assumes that within a given year the price system implied in the value figures is not more distorted for one kind of machinery or construction than for another. This is probably a safe assumption to make, even though, for example, the price of *identical* wheels could vary several hundred per cent.* There is, however, no reason to believe that the cheaper wheels go, say, to power-generating equipment while the more expensive wheels systematically go to machine tools.

The estimating procedure was as follows:

1. It was assumed that all of the rolled steel, steel castings, and iron castings available (that is, domestically produced plus imported) goes into the production of items considered in this section, including road vehicles. This assumption has been justified. The amounts going into electrical equipment, fine mechanics and optics, or household goods are of minor importance or negligible. The estimated amount used to produce automobiles, trucks, motorcycles, and so on, was deducted from the amount of iron and steel available. The production of road vehicles was evaluated separately.†

2. The next problem was to find some sort of index of the volume of output for each category. It was assumed that the amount of iron and steel going into each category of machine building is a reasonable approximation to its physical volume. Since $(100\% - \dfrac{\text{value added}}{\text{total value}}\%)$ is the percentage of sales value spent on inputs, and since inputs other than iron and steel for the categories considered are small, negligible, or vary more or less with the iron and steel inputs, multiplying the total value

---

* See page 70.

† The figures, the sources, and the specific estimating procedures are given in tables A.27a and b in the Supplement. An attempt to evaluate ship construction separately was defeated by the paucity of the data. By the end of 1958, the East German ocean-going merchant marine consisted of 29 ships totaling about 100,000 tons. The increase during 1958 alone was about 80,000 tons, including tankers imported from Russia. East Germany produces various types of ships which are exported. (*Der Aussenhandel und der Innerdeutsche Handel,* East Berlin, Verlag Die Wirtschaft, no. 23, 1958, p. 824.)

of each category by the approximate index would give the value of inputs for the year. The calculations are not reproduced.*

3. Next, the total amount of steel and iron available was distributed among the various subgroups in the proportions that the value of inputs in each category (as found by the method just described) has to the total value of inputs for all categories combined. Applied to successive years, this gives an index of the way the volumes of inputs of each category have been changing.† As we have observed, the correctness of this index depends on three major assumptions:

a. Most inputs are iron and steel. This is substantially correct.

b. The distortions of the price system are not systematic between the different subcategories. This is probably true. However, year-to-year price changes have been eliminated, except insofar as there are again systematic differences in the change in the prices of one subcategory with respect to another.

c. The degree of efficiency of operations is the same after the war as before. This is certainly wrong for the early postwar years, but it is likely to have been more or less correct by 1955. This problem will be raised again when the total index of the sector is considered.

4. The amounts of iron and steel so used were then multiplied by the fraction, per cent of value/per cent of value of inputs, in order to derive a quantity of iron and steel that moves parallel to the value added of each subcategory. Since the value added for the various categories is different and their relative importance changes over time, the two series for each subcategory differ only by a constant multiplicative factor, but, when combined, they of course behave differently.‡

5. The amounts of steel and iron calculated by the procedure in paragraph 4 were then combined and recalculated on the basis of 1936 equal to 100.§ This gives the index of the output of this sector, defined as gross

---

* The factors $(100\% - \dfrac{\text{value added}}{\text{total value}}\%)$ applied to the various categories were as follows:

Power-generating equipment	.419
Machine tools	.319
Equipment for: metallurgy	.419
fuel industry	.419
casting industry	.419
transport	.466
Agricultural machinery	.447
New rail vehicles	.466
New ships	.457
Steel construction	.465

For the years 1950–1955, steel construction in tons is given directly in the Statistical Yearbook of the German Democratic Republic, 1955, p. 164. Hence the figure was applied only to prewar data.

† See Supplement Table A.28.

‡ The calculations are given in Supplement Table A.29.

§ See Table A.29 in the Supplement.

value added and (implicitly) measured in 1936 prices. Since the efficiency of production in the early postwar years was certainly below that for the prewar years, this index overstates the amount of output (measured by value added); but by 1954 or 1955 the shortcoming in efficiency had probably diminished or vanished. In any case, in the absence of direct information about input-output relations the procedure adopted seems to have been the only one possible.

6. This index was then applied to the value added of the same categories for 1936, which was found to be RM 719.771 million when valued in 1936 prices.*

The major results are reproduced in Table 40. The calculations show

Table 40

Value added, engineering-construction, East Germany, 1936, 1938, and 1950–1958

Year	Index 1936 = 100	Value added, 1936 prices (million RM)	Value added, 1950 prices (million DM)
	(1)	(2)	(3)
1936	100.00	719.771	1903.792
1938	124.35	895.035	2367.368
1950	73.01	525.505	1389.959
1951	79.53	572.434	1514.086
1952	89.22	642.180	1698.563
1953	117.35	844.651	2234.100
1954	129.77	934.047	2470.551
1955[a]	133.86	963.485	2548.416
1956[a]	146.04	1051.154	2780.298
1957[a]	159.31	1146.667	3032.931
1958[a]	175.86	1265.789	3348.009

Sources: Col. 1: Index from Supplement Table A.29. The methods of calculation are described in the text. The calculations are found in Supplement Tables A.26–A.34. Col. 2: 1936 value added calculated from Gleitze, *Ostdeutsche Wirtschaft*, p. 177, and *Produktionsstatistik, 1936*, p. 46; other years found by applying index in col. 1. Col. 3: 1936 value added in 1950 prices found by multiplying value added in col. 2 by 2.645. For other years, index in col. 1 was applied.

[a] Value added after 1954 is assumed to increase as the available iron and steel.

that between 1936 and 1955 engineering output (as defined in this section) increased by about 34 per cent, and that by 1956 it had apparently risen to 146 per cent of 1936. Compared with 1946, the increase by 1956 is, of course, much larger; compared with 1950, the expansion by 1955 was 83 per cent and by 1956 about 100 per cent.

Table 41 presents West German indices that are roughly comparable to the calculated East German indices. The East German index, based on official figures, is not entirely comparable because it also contains the output of castings and some double counting. There seems no question

* See Tables A.30 and A.31 in the Supplement.

Table 41

Indices of value added, engineering-construction, East and West Germany, 1936, 1950–1958

| | East Germany | | | | West Germany | | | | | | | |
| | Calculated | | Official | | Old indices | | | | New indices | | | |
Year	(1) 1936 Prices	(2) 1950 Prices	(3) (1950 = 100)	(4) Rebased (1936 = 100)	(5) Machinery	(6) Steel construction	(7) Shipbuilding	(8) Combined	(9) Machinery	(10) Steel construction	(11) Shipbuilding	(12) Combined
1936	100.0	100.0	100.0	100.0	100.0	100.0	100.0	100.0	100	100	100	100.0
1950	73.0	84.6	100.0	84.6	123.7	57.9	53.3	105.3	116	58	54	102.7
1951	79.5	94.2	123.1	104.1	164.5	67.5	71.2	138.7	155	64	70	134.7
1952	89.2	102.8	150.7	127.5	188.7	87.9	91.5	161.8	180	70	99	156.5
1953	117.4	121.0	174.4	147.5	184.5	116.5	107.5	165.0	177	81	130	157.6
1954	129.8	140.5	193.0	163.3	208.1	114.8	121.7	183.7	198	84	164	176.0
1955	133.9	146.0	208.8	176.6					243	96	194	214.4
1956	146.0	159.1	227.0	192.0					265	107	202	233.7
1957	159.3	172.6	239.0	202.2					274	109	211	241.5
1958	175.9	190.2	275.0	232.7					277	108	212	243.7

Sources: Col. 1: From Supplement Table A.38. "Value added" method. Col. 2: From Supplement Table A.34. "Input" method. Cols. 3 and 4: *SJDDR*, 1955, p. 128, 1958, p. 262. Index not strictly comparable to West German index since it includes iron and steel products and metal goods, as well as castings, which are excluded in Western methodology. Cols. 5, 6, 7: *SJBR*, 1955, p. 229. Col. 8: Index calculated by combining subindices in proportion to the weights given in the West German index of industrial production (*SJBR*, 1955, p. 229: machinery = 8.05; steel construction = 1.66; and shipbuilding = 1.33 for the old index). Cols. 9, 10, 11: *SJBR*, 1958, p. 188; 1959, p. 182. Col. 12: Index calculated by combining subindices: machinery = 7.47; steel construction = 1.73; shipbuilding = 0.45.

that East Germany has lagged behind West Germany, but perhaps less than might have been expected.

ROAD VEHICLES

Road vehicles are discussed separately because information as to the numbers produced is available. In 1936 the area of what is now East Germany accounted for only about 4 per cent of tractor production, but it accounted for about 25 per cent of passenger car production and about 28 per cent of truck production.

The procedure employed to calculate the value added for road vehicles consisted in evaluating the output of motor vehicles with average prices and applying to the figure thus found the ratio of value added to gross production value for 1936 for all of Germany. A similar procedure was used for bicycles. East Germany produced a great variety of motor cars — Horch, Adler, Wanderer, DKW, BMW, Brennabor — some of which were medium and heavy cars, but then as now heavy cars were produced only in small numbers. In 1955, East Germany built only the DKW (Deutsche Kraftwagen Werke), essentially still the prewar model except that steel rather than wood was used for its upper structure, and the slightly larger BMW (Bayrische Motoren Werke) in small numbers. A new medium car, the Wartburg, appears to be a development of the DKW. For the postwar period, the appropriate price seems to be that of the Volkswagen less dealer markup (which should be allocated to the value added of distribution), but, qualitatively, even this price substantially overestimates the value of East German output. For the prewar period the price of the Ford Eiffel is taken as appropriate.*

As for trucks, a 3-ton truck is taken as average, although this is, at least for the early postwar years, probably slightly high. It is certain that trucks of 7 to 10 tons hardly exist in East Germany, and even 5-ton trucks are relatively scarce.[3] Beginning with the Second Five Year Plan, no trucks heavier than 6 tons were to be produced, but, like all plans, this too is subject to change. For the prewar period the price of a 3-ton German-built Ford truck is assumed to be typical; for the postwar period, the price of a German-built Ford truck for 1950 is used, and for the other years the index of vehicle prices found in the Statistical Yearbook of the Federal Republic was applied to the 1950 price.[4]

* In 1936 the Ford Eiffel cost RM 2,650.00, which, allowing for a 15 per cent markup, gives a factory price of RM 2,250.00. In 1954 the Volkswagen cost DM 4,000.00, and in 1955, DM 3,890. Allowing for a 15 per cent markup, this gives DM 3,400.00 and DM 3,306.00, respectively. If the price of the Volkswagen were reduced to the prewar level by means of the index of vehicle prices, it would be RM 1,511.00, or about 60 per cent of the Ford Eiffel price. There were much cheaper cars produced in 1936, but they were of inferior quality. (When the VW was announced, it was to cost RM 1,000.00, and it was to be a better car.) Since the Ford Eiffel is without question a better approximation to the average German car produced before the war, this price was used in preference to the lower price obtained by using the price index.

With tractors there is some ambiguity. Gleitze lists two categories for 1936 — agricultural machinery (which includes agricultural tractors) and non-agricultural tractors. After the war, however, the official figure for the number of tractors produced almost certainly refers to agricultural tractors, although perhaps some nonagricultural tractors are also being built in East Germany.

The statistics are frequently given in standard 30-hp tractors. It is certain that the tractors are fairly small and that the very heavy road freight tractors (*Zugmaschinen*) are not being built in the Soviet Zone. The price was estimated as follows: For 1951 the Statistical Yearbook of the Federal Republic gives value and tonnage figures for agricultural tractors, and for one-axle tractors and other one-axle motor implements,[5] which are relatively light. This gives an average price per ton of DM 4,255.

The closest American approximation is a 33 hp McCormick tractor, which has a shipping weight of 4,800 pounds,[6] or 2.018 tons. We assumed a weight of over 2 tons. It was impossible to allow for the weight or the price relative to the weight of the more expensive smaller implements, but the over-all error is small. This procedure gives a 1951 price for tractors of DM 8,500.00. In 1954 a 30-hp tractor cost about DM 8,000, which would mean a factory price of about DM 6,800. In Germany tractors were considerably more expensive relative to cars before than after the war, since their production was not developed.

Motorcycles vary in size and price from about DM 750 for a small motorbike to about DM 1,900 for a heavy BMW. Since the series for motorcycles also includes the so-called *Mopeds*, which are essentially bicycles with auxiliary motors, costing between DM 300 and DM 350, for the 1950 price it seemed best to use an average sales price of DM 750. Allowing for a 20 per cent markup, this gives a factory price of DM 600. For the other years the same index of vehicle prices was applied.

For bicycles, a prewar price of RM 60.00 has been assumed (more or less from memory), and the price index of the Statistical Yearbook of the Federal Republic has been applied to it. Thus, for 1950 the price becomes RM 174.00. The major results are reproduced in Table 42.* There is no doubt that motor-vehicle construction has substantially increased since 1950, but there is equally no doubt that, in real terms, motor-vehicle output as a whole in 1955 was still about 30 per cent below 1936, even if quality deterioration is not taken into consideration. This statement is particularly true for passenger cars, which as consumer goods naturally would take second place. For 1955 their production had recovered to only 37 per cent of 1936, and even in 1956 the level reached was well below half the 1936 output. It is also true for trucks, the production of which in 1955 was still about 25 per cent below 1936. The output of

* The calculations and their results are given in detail in Supplement Table A.35.

Table 42

Production and value added, road vehicles, East Germany, and indices,
West and East Germany, 1936 and 1950–1958

A. *Production*

Year	Cars	Trucks	Road freight wheeled tractors	Motorcycles	Bicycles (thousands)
	(1)	(2)	(3)	(4)	(5)
1936	60,849	19,061	n.a.	54,196	398.6
1950	7,165	1,003	5,170	9,607	338.3
1951	11,092	5,137	5,946	23,896	460.0
1952	12,161	6,687	5,526	36,727	568.5
1953	13,490	11,144	5,729	47,146	767.6
1954	19,677	12,222	7,041	50,270	728.4
1955	22,247	14,191	6,459	88,155	723.8
1956	28,145	17,201	5,345	181,608	694.4
1957	35,597	15,481	3,146	223,381	581.7
1958	38,422	15,741	4,139	254,396	591.5

B. *Value added*

	East Germany						West Germany	
Year	Index, all road vehicles, 1936 prices (1936 = 100)	Value added, all road vehicles, 1936 prices (million RM)	Index, all road vehicles, 1950 prices (1936 = 100)	Value added, all road vehicles, 1950 prices (million DM)	Index of motor vehicles only 1936 Prices (1936 = 100)	Index of motor vehicles only 1950 Prices (1936 = 100)	Old index, all road vehicles	New index, all road vehicles
	(6)	(7)	(8)	(9)	(10)	(11)	(12)	(13)
1936	100.0	210.010	100.0	366.971	100.0	100.0	100.0	100
1950	24.0	50.402	26.5	97.247	17.6	17.8	125.7	143
1951	39.7	83.374	43.7	160.366	31.8	33.1	164.1	183
1952	42.8	89.884	51.9	190.458	32.4	38.5	193.6	215
1953	61.2	128.526	69.0	253.210	47.5	50.7	201.8	231
1954	69.4	145.747	76.4	280.366	57.6	66.6	267.6	301
1955	77.9	163.596	86.1	315.962	67.1	72.0	n.a.	396
1956	95.4	200.350	106.3	390.090	87.3	96.2	n.a.	430
1957	97.3	204.340	107.8	420.517	92.5	102.2	n.a.	454
1958	105.0	220.605	116.3	426.787	100.5	111.6	n.a.	543

Sources: Cols. 1–5: For 1936, 1950–1955, see *SJDDR*, 1955, p. 164; for 1956 to 1958, *ibid.*, 1958, pp. 350–351. Cols. 6–10: See text for method of calculation. Details of calculations are given in Supplement Table A.35. Col. 12: Refers to *Fahrzeugbau* (vehicle construction). *SJBR*, 1955, p. 229. Col. 13: *Neuberechnung*, p. 67, *SJBR*, 1959, p. 182.

tractors, on the other hand, almost quadrupled and that of motorcycles (including *"Mopeds"*) increased by over 60 per cent.

The road-vehicle sector as a whole did somewhat better, reaching between 78 and 86 per cent of the 1936 level in 1955, depending on which prices are used. This increase is entirely due to the production of bicycles, which in 1955 reached a level 80 per cent above that of 1936.

A word should be said about the value added that was applied to the gross value of output. The value added as a percentage of gross production value for motor vehicles alone (44.32%) was applied to the sales value of motor vehicles; the ratio of value added to gross production value for trailers or bicycles (47.35%) was applied to bicycles.

The calculated sales value of motor vehicles is RM 246.69 million for 1936, or 77.4 per cent of the RM 318.614 million shown in Gleitze.[7] The total sales value of the vehicle industry, which includes the construction of bodies and so on, is given by Gleitze as RM 463.914 million. The calculated sales value of bicycles in 1936 prices amounted to 16.5 per cent of the remainder of the vehicle industry.

The estimated value added for 1936 is therefore RM 210.010 million in 1936 prices* and DM 366.971 million in 1950 prices.† The indices derived from the combined calculated value added of motor vehicles and of bicycles were applied to these basic values on the assumption that the production of the items not covered varies with that of the items covered. This is almost certainly not the case but, with the limited information available, it seems the best procedure.

By comparison, the West German value added for vehicle construction in 1950 was 47 per cent.[8] In 1937 the American value added for motorcycles was 45.08 per cent and for other motor vehicles 22.64 per cent.[9] The latter low figure is obviously chiefly for assembling. For bodies and parts the percentage in 1937 was 38.7 per cent.

As Table 42 shows, in this branch of production East Germany has lagged far behind West Germany. Attempts have been made to remedy the situation, which, at least so far as trucks and road freight tractors are concerned, is undoubtedly serious. For 1956 the average age of the stock of about 100,000 passenger cars and about 80,000 trucks was estimated at 18 years.[10] The program for agricultural machinery also leaves something to be desired.[11]

IRON AND STEEL PRODUCTS AND METAL PRODUCTS

Iron and steel products and metal products, two industry groups that were listed separately in 1936, are now included with machinery production in East German classifications.

Iron and steel products. The value added of this industry group in the area now East Germany can be estimated to have been RM 314.907 million in 1936. The major component of this group is a miscellaneous collection of unspecified industries. The next most important group consists of producers of sheet metal (like tin cans), of which East Germany sold 27.53 per cent in 1936. Next in importance are vehicle parts, of which

---

*Sales value		Value added
Of motor vehicles:	RM 318.614 million	44.32% = RM 141.210 million
Of other vehicles:	RM 145.300 million	47.35% = RM 68.800 million
Of all vehicles:	RM 463.914 million	RM 210.010 million

† Calculated by multiplying 210.010 by the ratio of the calculated value added in 1950 and 1936 prices.

East Germany sold 23.5 per cent. Other industries are wire manufacture, tools, locks, knives and scissors, and stoves and ovens — locks and knives being of very minor importance.

Sales of metal products made of sheet iron or steel and vehicle parts together accounted for 37.03 per cent of all sales in 1936. It may be assumed that the output of vehicle parts varies with the number of vehicles produced, even though this may overestimate the output, since spare parts, even for newly produced goods, were notoriously scarce. For the rest it is clearly impossible to assume a movement parallel to the available rolled steel, say, because to a large extent the industry produces for the consumer goods sector, which is known to have been slighted in the allocation of scarce steel. The output in the wire industry (which includes nails) was low. For all these reasons, it is assumed that vehicle production as a whole is typical for this group of industries, excluding those that are not separately specified.

In 1928 the unspecified industries produced machine parts, materials made of wire, screws, nuts and bolts, and so on,[12] and used large amounts of wire, sections, and so on. These industries are clearly more closely related to the investment industries and may be presumed to move parallel to engineering-construction output. This assumption is probably also reasonable for the output of tools.

In 1936 the value added for the miscellaneous group, in 1936 prices, which was attributable to East Germany was RM 120.460 million, and for tools it was RM 24.475 million. The value added to which the engineering-construction index is applied is therefore RM 144.935 million. The remainder, RM 169.972 million, is presumed to move parallel to the index of vehicle production. To find the 1936 value in 1950 prices, the former was multiplied by an index of produced prices of tools (140 per cent of 1938) and the latter by an index of products made from sheet metal (186 per cent of 1938).[13]

The calculations made by this method indicate that by 1955 this group of industries had surpassed its 1936 output by about 6 per cent if measured in 1936 prices and by less than 1 per cent when measured in 1950 prices.*

Metal products and related industries. This group of industries includes manufacturers of jewelry, fountain pens, toys, phonographs and records, rubber stamps, cast types, and so on. By far the most important subgroup is the metal-products industry — not further specified, which appears to include the manufacture of nonferrous hardware, plumbing equipment, installation of gas lines, and so on. In 1936 it accounted for 72.5 per cent of the value added of the group as a whole and 42.13 per cent of its value added is attributable to East Germany. An equal percentage is attributable to toys and musical instruments, which are, how-

* See Table A.36 in the Supplement.

ever, of minor importance. The value added in 1936 prices for the industry as a whole may be estimated at 37.96 per cent of the total, or RM 292.693 million, of which RM 231.777 million may be attributed to the miscellaneous group.[14] *Faute de mieux*, the output of this group of industries is estimated to vary directly with the combined output of engineering and vehicles.

By 1955 the combined output of these miscellaneous metal products industries was probably between 12 and 13 per cent above 1936. Considering the nature of the products — consumer goods like pots and pans, spare parts, nails, wire, and other minor and unspectacular producer goods, this appears to be a plausible estimate. By comparison, West German output had increased to almost 80 per cent above the 1936 level. (See Table 43.)

Table 43

Value added, iron and steel products, and metal products, East Germany, and indices, West and East Germany, 1936 and 1950–1958

	East Germany				West Germany	
	Value added		Index		Index	
Year	1936 Prices (million RM)	1950 Prices (million DM)	1936 Prices 1936 = 100	1950 Prices 1936 = 100	Old index	New index
	(1)	(2)	(3)	(4)	(5)	(6)
1936	607.600	1086.881	100.0	100.0	100.0	100
1950	327.787	603.848	53.9	55.6	94.0	95
1951	389.094	718.017	64.0	66.1	121.0	122
1952	432.701	817.546	71.2	75.2	123.5	125
1953	580.554	1078.591	95.5	99.2	127.3	129
1954	646.445	1193.055	106.4	109.8	149.1	150
1955	681.162	1222.935	112.1	112.5	177.8	180
1956	767.781	1395.413	126.4	128.3	n.a.	193
1957	821.562	1481.161	135.2	136.3	n.a.	196
1958	901.515	1622.245	148.4	149.3	n.a.	195

Sources: Cols. 1 and 2: The method of calculation is described in the text. The detailed calculations are given in Supplement Table A.36. Cols. 3 and 4: Derived from cols. 1 and 2. Col. 5: Average daily production, *Eisen, Blech, und Metallwaren Industrie* in *SJBR*, 1956, p. 221. Col. 6: *Neuberechnung*, p. 43 and *SJBR*, 1959, p. 18.

One further point on the reliability of our own estimate needs to be made. Professors Bergson, Gerschenkron, and Granik have informed me that there is evidence that engineering-construction increases faster than the amount of steel input. This is certainly true in many countries. In the particular case of East Germany, however, such a difference in rates of growth is not likely to be significant. For example, West German observers point out that construction in East Germany tends to be heavy because of deficiencies in the quality of metal; that unusually large amounts of cast iron or iron and steel are used to make up for flaws in the metal (while the designs themselves are said to be good) ; and that, at best, technology and execution are back to their 1936 level.*

There is now direct evidence from East German sources that the system favors heavy construction and wasteful use of materials. The nonsensical gross production index and the fact that it is used to control the plan fulfillment of the individual plant, the inconsistent price system, and the habit of counting work in progress as part of gross production — all combine to induce a plant to use as much metal and as little of its own labor as possible. In this manner its plan is more easily fulfilled. Professor Janakieff has observed that in East Germany one frequently hesitates to increase the production of machines of lighter construction even though such machines are technically superior because, since they contain a smaller amount of metal, they are "disadvantageous" from the standpoint of the plant as its direct cost (*Selbstkosten*) and the corresponding producer prices for the lighter machines are lower.[15] The same author states explicitly that one virtue of the concept of value added is that, "Greater interest is created in reducing the weight of the machines produced. . . ."[16]

COMPARISON WITH OFFICIAL DATA

It may be worth while to compare our findings with the official data for machine construction, which includes all the industries whose output has been estimated in this chapter. The official data are given in *Messwerte* which, it will be recalled, are based on the 1936 or 1944 stop prices. However, since they have been revised upward several times, they probably lie somewhere between 1936 and 1950 prices. Although sales values for the engineering-construction sector, in the narrower sense, and for motor vehicles were calculated separately, the iron and steel products and metal products group was calculated only on the basis of value added. However, the sales value may be estimated by allowing for the fact that in 1936 the ratio of value added to gross production was 57 per cent for iron and steel products and 60 per cent for other metal products. The figures are given in Table 44.†

In 1936 the value of gross production in *Messwerte* was only 138.5 per cent of the calculated sales value for that year in 1936 prices and 63.2 per cent of the sales value in 1950 prices. It must be presumed that the term "gross production" in 1936 was akin to the Western concept and that it has changed (in the sense of increased double counting) from 1950 on; that is, in 1936 inter-industry flows are not excluded, but inter-plant flows are excluded, and in 1950 and subsequent years neither flow

* *Aussenhandel,* 1957, no. 9, p. 312, reports, for example, that a railroad passenger car with 100 seats manufactured in East Germany weighs 50 tons, manufactured in Czechoslovakia 43.7 tons, and manufactured in the Federal Republic 41.8 tons. Other examples could be given.

† Details are presented in Supplement Table A.37.

Table 44

Comparison of official and calculated output of "machine construction,"
East Germany, 1936 and 1950–1955

A. *Sales value and gross production*

Year	Sales values, calculated		Gross production in *Messwerte*[a] (million DM–O)	Index from sales values		Official index	
	1936 Prices (million RM)	1950 Prices (million DM)		(1950 = 100)	Year-to-year change	(1950 = 100)	Year-to-year change
	(1)	(2)	(3)	(4)	(5)	(6)	(7)
1936	2524.4	5532.6	3497.3				
1950	1742.4	4054.1	3879.8	100.0		100.0	
1951	1891.7	4347.6	4775.1	108.6	108.6	123.1	123.1
1952	2171.0	5062.9	5846.5	124.6	114.7	150.7	122.4
1953	2711.8	6249.1	6767.8	155.7	125.0	174.4	115.7
1954	2845.4	6519.2	7489.3	163.3	104.9	193.0	110.7
1955	3051.2	7005.8	8099.7	175.1	107.2	208.8	108.2

B. *Total value added, calculated*

Year	1936 Prices (million RM)	Index (1936 = 100)	Index (1950 = 100)	1950 Prices (million DM)	Index (1936 = 100)	Index (1950 = 100)
	(8)	(9)	(10)	(11)	(12)	(13)
1936	1537.4	100.0		3357.7	100.0	
1950	1058.7	68.9	100.0	2457.7	73.2	100.0
1951	1149.9	74.8	108.6	2636.7	78.5	107.3
1952	1319.5	85.8	124.6	3070.7	91.5	124.9
1953	1648.6	107.2	155.7	3790.0	112.9	154.2
1954	1729.9	112.5	163.4	3954.2	117.8	160.9
1955	1855.3	120.7	175.2	4249.5	126.6	172.9

Sources: Cols. 1, 2, 8, 11: Calculated from Supplement Tables A.33, A.35, and A.36. Cols. 3 and 6: *SJDDR*, 1955, p. 128. Col. 4: Calculated from col. 2. Col. 5: Calculated from col. 4. Col. 7: Calculated from col. 6. Cols. 9 and 10: Calculated from col. 8. Cols. 12 and 13: Calculated from col. 11.
  [a] East German definition. For explanation of *Messwerte*, see Chapter III.

is excluded. The fact that the 1936 *Messwerte* value lies halfway between our two estimates confirms what is known, namely, that the value of *Messwerte* lies between the 1936 or 1944 stop prices and the 1950 level.

From 1950 on, there is a substantial amount of additional double counting. Vehicle parts are counted several times, as are wire, bolts, nuts, castings, and so on. Hence the higher level and faster growth of the official index is to be expected and is quite consistent with our calculations.

An indirect confirmation of our calculations is found in the fact that the year-to-year changes of the official index decline, and by the end of the period investigated they agree fairly closely with the calculated increases. Therefore we may attribute the faster growth of the official index compared with the calculated index in the period 1950 through 1955 — 208.8 per cent compared with about 175 per cent — to its peculiar nature. In addition, the substantially larger growth of the official index than that of the calculated index compared with 1936 — 231.6 per cent and 120.7

to 126.6 per cent, depending on whether we measure output in 1936 or in 1950 prices — may be attributed to the fact that the concept of gross production in 1936 was different from that in 1950 and later.

Within machine construction there have been substantial changes. Before the war the area now East Germany chiefly produced machine tools, machinery for the textile industry and other light machinery, and a good share of boilers and other apparatus, apparently including equipment for the synthetic fuel industry, which was concentrated in that area. There is now much more emphasis on heavy construction particularly shipbuilding, which hardly existed before the war.

ELECTRICAL EQUIPMENT AND SUPPLIES

The estimation of the value added of the production of the electrical industry by any of the methods used thus far was impossible. However, official East German figures in *Messwerte* exist for gross production (as this term is defined in East Germany) for 1950 through 1955 of electrical equipment and supplies, fine mechanical and optical goods and of machinery production. A comparable 1936 figure can be computed from percentages given in Statistical Practice.

The estimating procedure used was as follows. It was assumed that the ratio of the output of electrical equipment and supplies (and of fine mechanics and optics) to machine output, as measured in *Messwerte* and officially given, is a correct measure of the movements of various metal-using industries *relative to each other*. In spite of the distortion of the system of *Messwerte,* this seems to be fairly correct at least for the output of electrical products. The percentages found were then applied to the sales value of "machine construction," including road vehicles, iron and steel products, and metal products, found in the preceding section.

In the process of calculation the following fact appeared. It is officially stated that the value of electrical products output, expressed in *Messwerte,* in 1955 was DM 3,016.3 million,[17] which in turn was 367.6 per cent of 1936.[18] This gives a figure of DM 820.538 million for 1936. The 1936 sales value of electrical equipment and supplies in 1936 prices is given by Gleitze as RM 514 million.[19] If this figure is recalculated in 1950 prices by multiplying it by the West German price index for this subgroup, the 1955 sales value becomes RM 812.120 million.

In 1936 the gross production value of electrical equipment and supplies was 23.5 per cent that of machinery output. If this percentage is applied to the sales value of machinery output in 1936 prices given in the preceding section, we arrive at a 1936 sales value (in 1936 prices) of RM 593.469 million, which is reasonably close to the RM 514 million given by Gleitze. Moreover, when this value is raised by the same West

German price index, the 1936 sales value in 1950 prices becomes DM 859.818 million, which is very close to the official figure of DM 820.538 million.

Unless these similarities are sheer coincidence (which is unlikely), they suggest that for this industry the *Messwerte* are very close to the 1950 West German prices. The estimated value added, derived by applying the ratio of value added to the gross production value of 69.7 per cent* to the calculated sales value of RM 593.469 million, would be RM 413.648 million. This agrees well with Böttcher's estimate[20] of RM 350.2 million, derived by the entirely different method of multiplying the number of employees by the value added per worker for 1936. The fairly close agreement of these independent estimates permits us to place considerable confidence at least in the 1936 value arrived at by the method described.

However, the similarities of these various estimates do not end the difficulties. It may be taken for granted that the gross production value for 1936 corresponds more or less to the sales value (that is, with intra-industry flows eliminated, but revalued in *Messwerte*) and that for the later years the use of the concept in the Communist sense includes more of what we would consider double counting. Hence it seemed best first to calculate an index from the estimated value added in *Messwerte,* which can here be equated to 1950 prices, by computing the ratio of electrical equipment and supplies to "machine construction" output, and then applying this index to the value added in 1936 prices found by deflation, which agrees fairly well with the figure found directly.

This procedure was also dictated by the fact that the ratio of the value of electrical products output to "machine construction" output is correct only if both are measured in 1950 prices (*Messwerte*). Since "machine construction" prices rose much more than prices in the electrical industry, these ratios would be quite different if the value were measured in 1936 prices.

The official East German figures for "machine construction," electrical equipment and supplies, and fine mechanics and optics are given in Table 45.† The results are presented in Table 46.

The derived values added and the index of electrical products output can be checked by constructing an index from four products whose output is given in numbers of units — light bulbs, radios, a-c motors, and

---

* 69.7 per cent is the ratio of value added to the sum of the gross production values of the individual subgroups of the electrical industry. (Production Statistics of 1936, pp. 46–47.) Because of the interindustry flows within an industrial group, the official statistics of 1936 never make this kind of calculation, and it has not been possible here to eliminate these interindustry flows. In any case, the ratio was applied to a sales value which also includes some double counting. The two errors are likely, therefore, to offset each other.

† Detailed calculations are given in Supplement Table A.38.

transformers.* The method consisted essentially of calculating the sales values of each of the four products and converting the sum to an index that could be applied to the 1936 figure of value added. Since the four products together accounted for only about 17 per cent of the sales value of the whole industry in 1936, and presumably are favored compared with products not shown, the result of the calculation is used only as a corroboration of the first estimating procedure.†

Table 45

"Gross production value," "machine construction," electrical equipment and supplies, and fine mechanics and optics, East Germany, 1936 and 1950–1955

Year	Machine construction[a] *Messwerte* value (million DM-O)	Electrical products *Messwerte* value (million DM-O)	Per cent of machine construction (2):(1)	Fine mechanics and optics *Messwerte* value (million DM-O)	Per cent of machine construction (4):(1)
	(1)	(2)	(3)	(4)	(5)
1936	3497.3	820.539	23.5	265.925	7.6
1950	3879.8	1242.200	32.0	488.500	12.6
1951	4775.1	1628.000	34.1	582.000	12.2
1952	5846.5	1993.100	34.1	648.000	11.1
1953	6767.8	2475.700	36.6	719.900	10.6
1954	7489.3	2830.500	37.8	816.000	10.9
1955	8099.7	3016.300	37.2	933.400	11.5

Source: *SJDDR*, 1955, p. 128.
  [a] Excluding electrical machinery.

The two methods yield similar results. The East German claim that electrical products output increased by 367.6 per cent between 1936 and 1955 is credible when we remember that the calculation refers to a gross production concept of a peculiar nature. Even by Western standards, production more than doubled from 1936 to 1956. West German output, however, has grown almost twice as fast and by 1954 was almost four times and by 1955 almost five times the 1936 level. Even between 1950 and 1955 the growth was faster in West Germany. Incidentally, this faster growth is admitted by an East German source.[21] It should also be stated that between 1936 and 1943 or 1944, the capacity of the electrical industry in the area now East Germany increased substantially for military reasons; on the other hand, it is estimated that after dismantling and war

* For electric motors, a sales value is available only for 1936, but this is quite sufficient for the present purpose so long as the postwar output can be evaluated at prewar prices. For transformers we acknowledge gratefully the expert advice of the W. M. Horlick Corporation of Boston, which is familiar with German production. Details are given in the footnotes to Table A.39 in the Supplement.
  † See Supplement Table A.39.

damage only about 20 per cent of the 1936 capacity remained.[22] This makes the expansion a considerable achievement, one which is put into proper perspective only when we remember that mechanical and electrical industries all over the world seem to have burst into bloom in the postwar period.

Table 46

Value added, output of electrical equipment and supplies, East Germany, and indices, West and East Germany, 1936 and 1950-1958[a]

	East Germany			West Germany	
Year	Value added, 1936 prices (million RM)	Value added, 1950 prices (million DM)	Index 1936 = 100	Old index	New index
	(1)	(2)	(3)	(4)	(5)
1936	358.258	566.048	100.0	100.0	100
1950	296.638	468.688	82.8	197.9	200
1951	364.707	576.237	101.8	272.0	274
1952	413.071	652.653	115.3	287.6	291
1953	584.319	923.224	163.1	319.1	319
1954	667.435	1054.547	186.3	391.8	396
1955	682.123	1058.715	190.4	n.a.	493
1956	764.164	1186.050	213.3	n.a.	543
1957	877.732	1362.318	245.0	n.a.	581
1958	801.781	1244.435	223.8	n.a.	667

Sources: Col. 1: Value added for 1936 calculated from Gleitze, *Ostdeutsche Wirtschaft*, p. 181. Col. 2: 1936 value added calculated from producer price, electrical equipment: 1938 = 100, 1950 = 158. See *SJBR*, 1955, p. 437. 1950–1957: calculated with index in col. 3. Col. 3: For derivation see text and Supplement Table A.38. Col. 4: *SJBR*, 1955, p. 229. Col. 5: *Ibid.*, 1959, p. 182.
[a] The extended calculations are given in Supplement Table A.38. An alternative calculation by evaluating the individual products is given in Supplement Table A.38.

There has also undoubtedly been an improvement in productivity. Between 1950 and 1953, employment rose 42.1 per cent and output rose about 100 per cent. Since then there has been a further improvement. By the end of 1955, employment had fallen to 139.4 per cent of 1950 while output had risen to 230 per cent.[23] Between 1950 and 1954, West German employment rose 52 per cent; the number of hours worked — information not available for East Germany — increased almost 50 per cent; and output rose 98 per cent. For East Germany between 1950 and 1954 employment increased to 141.1 per cent and output to 225 per cent. Thus output per man rose about 32 per cent in West Germany, and 59 per cent in East Germany between 1950 and 1954.[24]

FINE MECHANICS AND OPTICS

As stated earlier, the method used to estimate the output of fine mechanics and optics was essentially the same as that developed for electrical equipment and supplies. A check reveals that the level of the

Messwerte for fine mechanics and optics also must have been between the levels of 1936 and 1950 prices. On the basis of East German figures, we find that the value of the output in 1936 *Messwerte* was DM 265.925 million. The sales value of fine mechanics and optics, which includes office machinery (classified here rather than with machinery, and omitted in the machinery calculations above) given by Gleitze is RM 240.351 million, which is very close to the official East German figure. The sales value found by taking the ratio of the value of fine mechanics and optics to "machine construction" output and applying it to the sales value of "machine construction" output found above gives a value of RM 191.930 million in 1936 prices and of DM 440.478 million in 1950 prices.

The 1936 value added in *Messwerte,* found by taking 77.66 per cent* of the sales value, is RM 206.517 million. The actual value added, calculated separately for fine mechanics and optics and for office machinery (121.854 and 69.597) is RM 191.45 million. Böttcher[25] gives a value of RM 129.1 million, which evidently refers to the old classification exclusive of office machinery.

These facts justify the following procedure for deriving the value added. First, the sales value of output in 1950 prices was calculated by the method used above for electrical equipment and supplies; this series was then reduced to an index that was applied to the value added of RM 191.45 million as a base, for 1936. The value added in 1950 prices is the 1936 value in 1936 prices multiplied by the price index for fine mechanics and optics — reported to be 163 per cent of 1938, and presumably also of 1936.[26] (As before, we did not apply the percentages to the 1936 value of "machine construction." If we had, the growth from 1936 to 1955 would be only 83 per cent instead of about 92 per cent.)

Once more there is no reason to disbelieve the East German figures, which show an increase of 350 per cent between 1936 and 1955, provided that one bears in mind the peculiar nature of East German "gross production." Even when the double counting is eliminated by our roundabout estimation, an increase of more than 80 per cent over 1936 remains.

Since there are no raw material bottlenecks that could prevent an expansion, this increase is quite possible. Before 1936, optical goods and office machinery were manufactured in the area now East Germany. Capacities increased substantially in that area after 1936,[27] but war losses and dismantling are estimated at 70 to 75 per cent. However, it is stated that the desire for reparations led to a quick rehabilitation of these industries. The quality of these goods is known to be excellent — particularly in optics, and also, apparently, in fine mechanics and office machinery.

In spite of these facts, our estimates are likely to be on the high side.

* The *Nettoquota* for fine mechanics and optics. The *Nettoquota* for office machinery is 88.43.

Table 47

Value added, fine mechanics and optics, East Germany, and indices, West and East Germany, 1936 and 1950–1958 (estimation by *Messwerte* method)[a]

| Year | East Germany | | | West Germany | | East Germany | |
	Index (1936 = 100)	Value added, 1936 prices (million RM)	Value added, 1950 prices (million DM)	Old index	New index	Calculated index	Official index
	(1)	(2)	(3)	(4)	(5)	(6)	(7)
1936	100.0	191.454	312.070	100.0	100		
1950	100.8	192.986	314.567	121.9	123	100.0	100.0
1951	112.6	215.577	351.391	162.5	161	111.7	119.1
1952	116.0	222.087	362.001	182.6	184	115.1	132.7
1953	146.0	279.523	455.622	195.4	205	144.8	147.4
1954	161.6	309.390	504.305	222.2	235	160.3	167.0
1955	182.0	348.446	567.967	266.4	275	180.6	191.1
1956	203.9	390.375	636.311		293	202.3	201.2
1957	168.8	323.174	526.774		298	167.5	
1958	202.6	387.886	632.254		294		

Sources: Col. 1: Index calculated by method described in text. Since the series in *Messwerte* was discontinued,   t-put in 1956 to 1958 is calculated with a ratio based on East German gross production in constant plan prices. See *SJDDR*, 1958, pp. 272–273. Col. 2: The 1936 figure refers to the actual value added. For its calculation, see text. The index has been applied to this base. Col. 3: To find the base, the 1936 value added in 1936 prices has been multiplied by 163 per cent, corresponding to the price rise of *Feinmechanik und Optik*, *SJBR*, 1955, p. 438. For other years this base has been multiplied by the index in col. 1. Col. 4: *SJBR*, 1955 ed., p. 229. The 1955 figure is also given in *SP*, 1956, No. 12, p. 61. Col. 5: *SJBR*, 1959, p. 182. Col. 6: Rebased from col. 1. Col. 7: *SJDDR*, 1956, p. 273.
[a] Detailed calculations are given in Supplement Table A.40.

From 1936 to 1955 the total output of cameras rose by only 62.7 per cent,[28] and this is an important output. It is difficult to link other outputs, such as watches, alarm clocks, and bookkeeping machinery, for which output figures in numerical units are now officially available, to any prewar figures, but even a generous allowance would seem to make our estimate high.

As the figures given in Table 47 indicate, the growth since 1950 shown

Table 48

Indices of production, selected articles of fine mechanics and optics, East Germany, 1950–1958

Year	Total, calculated	Total, official	Portable typewriters	Bookkeeping machinery	Wrist watches	Pocket watches	Cameras (all kinds)
	(1)	(2)	(3)	(4)	(5)	(6)	(7)
1950	100.0	100.0	100.0	100.0	100.0	100.0	100.0
1951	111.7	119.1	107.1	143.4	143.0	47.0	153.6
1952	115.1	132.7	118.5	162.6	171.5	82.9	202.1
1953	144.8	147.4	152.2	190.7	170.2	75.1	312.4
1954	160.3	167.0	149.8	219.7	208.1	78.8	564.0
1955	182.0	191.1	149.8	227.4	219.7	80.0	643.6
1956	203.9	201.2	163.2	223.5	218.2	75.2	667.2
1957	168.8		163.0	232.0	261.0	61.0	443.0
1958	202.6		187.2	281.5	278.3	60.2	356.4

Sources: Col. 1: Table 47. Col. 2: *SJDDR*, 1955, p. 128. Col. 3: *SJDDR*, 1955, pp. 166–167; 1956, p. 287; 1957, p. 303; and 1958, pp. 352–353.

by our index is reasonable. By 1955, East German output stood at 182 per cent of 1936 and West German output had reached the level of 275 per cent of 1936[29] (see Table 48). The West German index is not strictly comparable with the calculated East German index because the coverage is narrower.

<h2 style="text-align:center">APPENDIX TO CHAPTER VIII</h2>

A SECOND METHOD OF CALCULATION

Second method. It is possible to make a rough check on the calculations made thus far by an independent estimating method. According to Professor Milton C. Shaw of the Massachusetts Institute of Technology, the input of materials other than steel — copper, bronze, and so on — averages not more than 5 per cent for most of the machine categories considered here and is negligible for steel construction and shipbuilding.

However, it should be noted that electricity input amounts to about 2 kwhr per man-hour worked in the United States, and this would be as true for shipbuilding as for other engineering-construction. Unfortunately, no figures for man-hours worked or for electricity consumed are available for East Germany. For 1936, total employment was found for comparable categories in both Gleitze and the Statistical Yearbook of the Federal Republic. Taking 48 hours as the work week and 50 as the number of weeks worked per year, an estimate of man-hours worked was derived, one which is almost certainly on the high side.

For 1936, the price of rolled steel was assumed to be that of bar steel, which is roughly the average for all rolled-steel products; the prices of gray and malleable iron castings and of steel castings are from Supplement Table A.19; and the average price for the available iron and steel was derived by dividing the total amount into the sum of the values of the subgroups.

The iron and steel going into the individual sectors (as given in Supplement Table A.28) was evaluated at this average price, and 5 per cent of this value was added for other materials. The American figure for electricity consumption, however, is certainly much too high, judging from the West German figures for 1949 through 1954 (given in Supplement Table A.32). Although no figure for electricity consumption per man-hour worked in Germany in 1936 has been found, it can be estimated at around 0.8 kwhr for engineering construction, which is somewhat lower than the 0.93 kwhr per man-hour for machine construction in West Germany in 1950. The West German estimate is probably a reasonable value to be applied to East German output since machine construction dominates the output of this sector and electric power input has been increasing. For the rough calculation made in Supplement Table A.33, it was assumed that the electricity used was 0.8 kwhr per man-hour in 1936, but that from 1946 to 1949 it fell to about 80 per cent of 1936; that it reached the 1936 level in 1950 and 1951, and that it then rose to 110 per cent and 120 per cent of 1936 in 1952 and 1954, respectively. These percentages vary roughly with those for West Germany. Considering that power is a bottleneck in East Germany, this estimated increase is probably high; however, the main sufferers from bottlenecks are not apt to be the crucial engineering sectors. In any case, it should be remembered that this calculation was made only as a check. Since no employment figures are available for later years, it was necessary to recalculate electricity as a percentage of the materials input, on the basis of the 1936 figures, and correct these percentages by the increasing use of power in the 1950's.

The result of this independent check for 1936 gives a gross value (sales value) of RM 1,149.355 million, compared with the actual value of RM 1,166.071 million found in Supplement Table A.30; that is, the independent evaluation comes within less than 2 per cent of the actual value, which, considering the scantiness of the information, is almost suspiciously close.

The result of the independent calculations is given in detail in Supplement Tables A.33 and A.34. The index in constant 1936 prices reaches a higher level than the series given in Supplement Table A.29, and it rises slightly less until 1950, but then pulls ahead. This probably reflects the increase in the amount of electricity used after 1951, which will correspondingly affect the value added, which is assumed to be a constant multiple of the value of inputs.

CHAPTER IX

CHEMICALS

It was not possible to make input-output calculations for the chemicals sector. It was possible to estimate the amount of lignite going into the sector, but it was impossible to evaluate either the electricity or the other raw materials (for example, salt) used.

ESTIMATING PROCEDURE

The definition of the chemical industry has changed in East and West Germany. Before the war, the Production Statistics of 1936 distinguished between the chemical, "chemotechnical," * synthetic fuels, and rubber products industries. Synthetic fibers were treated as a part of the textile industry.

Since the war, the chemotechnical industry has been included with chemicals in both East and West Germany. In West Germany, however, synthetic fibers are part of chemicals (though separately shown), and rubber products and synthetic fuels are treated separately; whereas in East Germany synthetic fibers are still included with textiles, and both rubber products and synthetic fuels are part of chemicals.

In order to make data for the two industries comparable, the following procedure was employed for the calculation. The value of the output of the following major groups was separately calculated and linked to the appropriate figures for 1936:

    a. Inorganic (heavy) chemicals
    b. Organic chemicals, including synthetic rubber
    c. Fertilizers
    d. Plastics and other chemical products
    e. Synthetic fibers
    f. Synthetic fuels
    g. Chemotechnical products
    h. Rubber products

* Includes soaps, paints, cosmetics, and so on.

Groups a, b, c, and d make up the chemical industry by the prewar definition. Groups a, b, c, d, e, and h make up the chemical industry as now defined in West Germany although, to repeat, a separate index for synthetic fibers production is published. Groups a, b, c, d, f, g, and h make up the chemical industry as now defined in East Germany, and e is still part of textiles.

The sales value of each sector was separately calculated in 1936 and 1950 prices. Next, the *Nettoquota*, that is, the ratio of value added to gross production value as given in the Production Statistics of 1936, was applied to these sales values, and the series thus found was converted to an index on the basis of 1936 = 100.

This index was then applied to the actual value added for 1936, derived by taking the sales value for each subgroup for the area now East Germany, as given by Gleitze, and applying to it the appropriate *Nettoquota*. The 1936 value added in 1950 prices was found by multiplying the 1936 value added in 1936 prices by the ratio of the calculated sales value in 1950 prices to the calculated sales value in 1936 prices.

The evaluation of the individual commodities necessitated some recalculation. For example, the output of sulfuric acid is measured in tons of SO_3, while the price refers to tons of H_2SO_4. Consequently, the given outputs had to be recalculated on the basis of their atomic weights. It was not possible to make detailed allowances for the innumerable forms in which this and other chemicals are sold, but care was taken to make all price and quantity data comparable and to compute the correct weight equivalent for whatever form was chosen in which to express the output of the chemical. (Figures for diesel oil had to be recalculated for some years from liters to tons, and so on. The details are given in the footnotes to the tables.)

The prices chosen are for sulfuric acid (technical) 66° Bé. strength, purchased in quantities of between 100 and 500 tons, as given in the Statistical Yearbook of the Federal Republic.[1] For several commodities the Statistische Bundesamt in Wiesbaden was kind enough to supply the 1950 price; for still others only 1954 prices in Thimm[2] were available; and for a few others, prices were taken from the 1950 wholesale catalog of Merck and Company. In these cases, prices were calculated for other years on the assumption that the price movement over time was parallel to that of sulfuric acid. (The detail of the prices used are described in the footnotes to the tables.)

Finding the appropriate prices of the chemicals involved often presented major difficulties. They were resolved as follows. For important forms of various chemicals prices in the United States were found for one year (ending December 1953). Whenever no direct price quotations were available, the prices were computed on the assumption that the prices of other chemicals always bear the same relation to the price of sulfuric acid as in the United States in December 1953. This assumption is apt to be quite reasonable.*

It should be noted that for the chemical sector correct prices for inorganic chemicals are important. The output of most chemicals for which there are official East German data has expanded very rapidly, but their prices are relatively low. Since ammonia is more expensive than other alkalizers, small differences in price can affect our index of the production of inorganic chemicals greatly. Even if a higher price for ammonia had been assumed, however, the output of inorganic chemicals as a whole would have risen less than that of sulfuric acid or sodium hydroxide. Although every caution has been exercised, the possibility of a large error remains.

INORGANIC (HEAVY) CHEMICALS

Inorganic chemicals are well represented in the available data. An indirect check of the calculations is possible for 1936. Gleitze gives the total value of sales of the chemical industry (after deducting chemicals used within the sector) for Germany as a whole in 1936 as RM 2,220.879 million, of which RM 674.173 million were in Central Germany and RM 94.237 million in Berlin. Allowing about one-third of Berlin sales for East Berlin, in 1936 the area now East Germany accounted for RM 705.585 million in chemical sales,[3] or 31.8 per cent of total German prewar output.

No further breakdown is available in Gleitze. The Production Statistics of 1936 gives a further breakdown. The "heavy inorganic chemicals" industry accounted for RM 424.043 million of the total for all Germany, or about 19.1 per cent. The production of heavy chemicals was concentrated in the present area of East Germany, which produced about 21 per cent of the sulfuric acid and nitric acid, about 47 per cent of the sodium hydroxide and sodium carbonate, 48 per cent of the chlorine, and 55 per cent of the synthetic ammonia of prewar Germany. According to the Statistical Handbook of Germany, the Soviet Zone (exclusive of Berlin) employed 24,164 of the total 51,835 persons working in basic chemicals, which includes 5,982 of the 8,342 in the nitrogen industry.[4]

---

* For sulfuric acid there are generally accessible German and American wholesale prices which move in close accord at the official exchange rate (Statistical Yearbook of the Federal Republic and U. S. Department of Commerce *Business Statistics*). The relative 1953 prices are based on prices supplied by Professor Walter C. Schumb of the Massachusetts Institute of Technology, whose help was essential in this section. These prices apply to small lots for use in universities and research laboratories. In our procedure we therefore had to assume that the wholesale rebates are about the same for the different basic chemicals. Professor Schumb also supplied us with the atomic weight relation between the pure product and the form in which it is commonly traded, transported, and stored, and in which it is priced. The details and conversion factors are found in the notes to the tables.

If it is assumed that the total output of heavy inorganic chemicals was roughly proportional to employment in these branches, 50 per cent of the output of heavy chemicals was in the area now East Germany.[5] (The Berlin output in these fields was very small.) This would give a gross production value for East Germany for 1936 in 1936 prices of RM 212.025 million, almost exactly 30 per cent of the total "adjusted" chemical sales (output). The sales value of the output of the six major chemicals for which data were assembled was RM 136.61 million, a quite substantial representation of about 64.4 per cent of the total sales value of chemicals.

The proportion of the value added of this subsector to the value of its output in 1936 was 56.19 per cent.[6] This percentage has been applied throughout to the sales value as found. Thus the value added for 1936 is RM 119.137 million. The 1936 value added in 1950 prices (to which the appropriate index was applied) was estimated by multiplying the 1936 value added in 1936 prices by the ratio: 1936 output valued in 1950 prices/1936 output valued in 1936 prices = 161.6 per cent.

Undoubtedly the inorganic chemical sector has expanded very substantially. In 1950 it had reached the 1936 level, and in 1955 the index of output measured in 1936 prices was 192.86 per cent; measured in 1950 prices it was 191.93 per cent. A summary of the calculations is reproduced in Table 49.*

FERTILIZERS

Fertilizers, including calcium carbide, are represented by four series: calcium carbide, nitrogen fertilizer, phosphate fertilizer, and potash fertilizer. Calcium carbide is included because the 1936 classification of the Production Statistics reads "Fertilizer industry, including production of carbide, and technical nitrogen and phosphorous combinations."

The series for nitrogen fertilizer is expressed in tons of N, and so is the price, even though it refers to "Ammonium sulfate, 21 per cent." The prices given in Thimm,[7] recalculated to a 100 per cent content, agree with the prices used, which come from the Statistical Yearbook of the Federal Republic.

The figure of 32,200 tons for phosphate production in 1936 in the area now East Germany is low but reasonable. Total German production of phosphates during 1936–1937 was 508,500 tons.[8] Phosphates were imported from French North Africa and the Soviet Union. Domestic phosphates (Thomas phosphates) were a by-product of steel production. "Sixty-two per cent of the phosphates used by agriculture were Thomas phosphates (*Thomasmehl*) derived from Swedish ores or imported from the Saar, Luxembourg, or Belgium."[9] In other words, phosphate produc-

---

* The details of the calculations are presented in Tables A.41 and A.42 of the Supplement.

Table 49

Production, value added, and indices, inorganic heavy chemicals,
East Germany, 1936, 1950–1958, and 1960 plan

A. *Production, thousand tons*

Year	Sulfuric acid, in SO_3	Sodium hydroxide, NaOH	Sodium carbonate, 100% Na_2CO_3	Ammonia, NH_3	Chlorine,[a] Cl	Nitric acid, HNO_3
	(1)	(2)	(3)	(4)	(5)	(6)
1936	301.2	124.0	378.1	283.0	93.3	106.0
1950	245.3	149.8	103.3	293.8	106.0	194.0
1951	289.0	184.0	122.0	325.0	126.0	258.0
1952	302.0	209.0	191.0	340.7	145.0	328.0
1953	364.0	221.0	297.0	362.0	180.0	342.0
1954	434.0	228.0	372.0	381.7	200.0	387.0 Plan
1955	483.2	256.9	458.5	407.6	230.0 Plan	485.0 Plan
1956	499.0	274.8	500.6	417.1	230.0 Est.	485.0 Est.
1957	522.4	276.8	530.7	420.9	230.0 Est.	485.0 Est.
1958	530.9	296.4	553.0	444.3		
1960 Plan	725.0	350.0	730.0			

B. *Value added*

Year	1936 Prices		1950 Prices	
	Value added (million RM)	Index, 1936 = 100	Value added (million DM)	Index, 1936 = 100
	(7)	(8)	(9)	(10)
1936	119.137	100.0	192.254	100.0
1950	116.921	98.1	190.754	99.2
1951	139.247	116.9	226.956	118.1
1952	160.239	134.5	260.024	135.3
1953	181.005	151.9	292.188	151.0
1954	199.947	167.8	321.852	167.4
1955	229.780	192.8	368.993	191.9
1956	245.720	206.3	382.547	199.0
1957	250.283	210.1	388.738	202.2
1958	260.874	219.0	403.234	209.7

Sources: Cols. 1–4: For 1936, 1950–1956, see *SJDDR*, 1956, pp. 278, 279; for 1957 and 1958, *ibid.*, 1958, pp. 344–345; for 1960 Plan, *Protokoll der dritten Parteikonferenz*, East Berlin, Dietz, p. 1032. Col. 5: For 1936; see Gleitze, *Ostdeutsche Wirtschaft*, p. 203; for 1950–1953, *SJBR*, 1955, p. 533; for 1954, output estimated by Bodo Böttcher, *Industrielle Strukturwandlungen im sowjetisch besetzten Gebiete Deutschlands*, West Berlin, Duncker and Humblot, 1956, p. 59. Col. 6: For 1936, see Gleitze, *Ostdeutsche Wirtschaft*, p. 203; for 1950–1953 and 1955 Plan, *Die Chemische Industrie in der sowjetischen Besatzungszone, Bonner Berichte*, Bonn, n.d., pp. 41, 76, and *SJBR*, 1954, p. 546; 1954 Plan, *Industrieproduktion, Materialien*, Bonn, Bundesministerium für Gesamtdeutsche Fragen, 1953/1954, p. 25. Professor Schumb of the Chemistry Department, Massachusetts Institute of Technology, has told me that when production is quoted in terms of HNO_3, it usually refers to a 69.5 per cent solution. Therefore no further recalculation has been done. Col. 7: 56.19 per cent of the sales value of this sector (*Produktionsstatistik, 1936*, p. 50). See text. Col. 8: Derived from sales value of calculated output. Col. 9: 161.6 per cent of value added in 1936 prices for 1936. Col. 10: Derived from sales value of calculated output. The detailed calculations are given in Supplement Tables A.41 and A.42.
[a] A new series of the production of hydrochloric acid (HCl) indicates that output has fallen since 1955.

tion was closely linked to steel, of which the Soviet Zone had very little.*

* The price used to evaluate phosphates refers to Thomas phosphates with a 16 per cent P_2O_5 content. In the Statistical Yearbook of the Federal Republic superphosphates are reported to have an 18 per cent P_2O_5 content; Thimm says they contain 16 per cent P_2O_5 and Thomas phosphates 14 per cent P_2O_5. Thimm's prices refer to a mixture, and those in the Statistical Yearbook refer to tons of P_2O_5 content.

The output of calcium carbide is now officially given in tons. The price of calcium carbide has been based on information supplied by the Statistische Bundesamt, Wiesbaden, and on the price index of sulfuric acid.

Complete official figures are available for the preceding three groups. Potash fertilizer, however, presents a special problem because the only figures available refer to the raw salts or the K_2O content and we had to deal with the product of the next stage. The problem of how to determine the amount of the raw potash salts which are further treated as fertilizers was solved as follows:

In 1936, 34.1 per cent of total potash (plus rock salt) was exported in raw form,[10] and about 25 per cent of the remainder was used in raw form as fertilizer.[11] This latter percentage fell substantially between 1937 and 1941.[12] It is assumed that this figure, which is an average for all of Germany, applies equally to West and East German production in 1936. Kramer gives an index of potash consumption per hectare in terms of K_2O.[13] He states that 30 per cent was in the form of raw salts.[14] For the postwar years we assume, for want of better information, that the supplies of potash fertilizer to agriculture were all in the form of a 40 per cent K_2O concentrate, while exports and the remaining domestic consumption were in raw form. For 1936, the known percentages for all Germany were applied to East Germany.

A rough check on the assumptions and calculations is possible for 1936. The gross production value of the fertilizer group (including potash fertilizers) in 1936 in all Germany was RM 567.375 million. The area now East Germany produced 63 per cent of the nitrogen fertilizers (except calcium cyanamide), 29–30 per cent of the carbides, 65 per cent of the potash, and virtually none of the phosphates in Germany as a whole. Using these percentages and the known production of Thomas phosphates in West Germany, and evaluating them at 1936 West German prices, gives the rough results shown in Table 50. Of the total RM 567.375 million we account for RM 485.66 million, leaving RM 81.720 million for

Table 50

Value of fertilizer output by major subgroups,
West and East Germany, 1936 (million RM)

Fertilizer	West Germany	East Germany
Phosphates	108.50	6.868
Nitrogen fertilizers	61.40	104.580
Carbides	56.80	23.887
Potash	44.25	79.370
Total accounted for:	270.95	214.705

Sources: Calculated from Gleitze, *Ostdeutsche Wirtschaft*, p. 203, and *Produktionsstatistik, 1936*, p. 50.

all other products in this sector. These figures appear to be reasonable, or at least plausible and possible.

The calculations of the four main components of the fertilizer group are given in Supplement Tables A.43 and A.44. The value added was calculated by assuming that the 1936 ratio of value added to sales value of the fertilizer group as a whole held throughout the period. The figures thus found were then computed on the basis of 1936 = 100 as an index

Table 51

Production and value added, fertilizers and calcium carbide, and combined value added of fertilizers and inorganic chemicals, East Germany, 1936, 1950–1958, and 1960 plan[a]

A. *Production, thousand tons*

Year	Nitrogen fertilizer	Phosphates	Potash fertilizer (40% K_2O)	Calcium carbide
	(1)	(2)	(3)	(4)
1936	254.5	32.20	1190	209.3
1950	231.4	24.74	975	619.8
1951	252.0	33.48	892	678.3
1952	257.0	38.10	1081	690.8
1953	265.0	72.31	1024	702.4
1954	277.0	79.20	1120	735.4
1955	293.3	84.55	1164	813.2
1956	299.9	111.70	1113	801.7
1957	305.4	128.77	1158	799.1
1958	300.0	136.32	1296	830.7
1960 (Plan)	335.0	200.00		

B. *Value added*

Fertilizers and calcium carbide combined

Year	1936 Prices		1950 Prices	
	Value added (million RM)	Index 1936 = 100	Value added (million DM)	Index 1936 = 100
	(5)	(6)	(7)	(8)
1936	114.816	100.0	186.930	100.0
1950	142.690	124.3	238.905	127.8
1951	150.518	131.1	253.962	135.9
1952	109.057	95.0	267.230	143.0
1953	164.394	143.2	275.078	147.2
1954	174.011	151.6	290.520	155.4
1955	183.147	159.5	307.388	164.4
1956	188.252	164.0	314.769	168.4
1957	192.729	167.9	321.477	172.0
1958	204.329	178.0	339.834	181.4

Table 51 (Continued)

| | Fertilizers and inorganic chemicals combined | | | |
| | 1936 Prices | | 1950 Prices | |
Year	Value added (million RM)	Index 1936 = 100	Value added (million DM)	Index 1936 = 100
	(9)	(10)	(11)	(12)
1936	233.953	100.0	378.523	100.0
1950	259.611	111.0	429.659	113.5
1951	289.765	123.9	480.918	127.1
1952	269.196	115.1	527.254	139.3
1953	345.399	147.6	567.266	149.9
1954	373.958	159.8	612.372	161.8
1955	412.927	176.5	676.381	178.7
1956	433.972	185.5	697.316	184.2
1957	443.012	189.4	710.215	187.6
1958	465.203	198.8	743.068	196.3

Sources: Cols. 1, 2, 4: See *SJDDR*, 1955, p. 162, and 1958, pp. 344–345; and Gleitze, *Ostdeutsche Wirtschaft*, p. 203. Col. 3: No figure for the production of potash fertilizer in concentrated form has been found. For 1936, 34.1 per cent of potash production is known to have been exported in raw form, and 25 per cent of the rest was used by agriculture in raw form. For the years 1950 through 1957, exports of potash salts are known, which are about two-thirds of production. The figures used for the production of potash fertilizer are the supplies of K_2O to agriculture as given in *SJDDR*, 1958, p. 476. It is assumed that all was in the concentration of 40 per cent K_2O, which is certainly not true. On the other hand, some 40 per cent K_2O fertilizer may have been exported. Cols. 5 and 6: Index derived from sales value of fertilizers and calcium carbide and applied to the 1936 value added in 1936 prices, the derivation of which is described in the text. Cols. 7 and 8: 1936 value added in 1950 prices was found by multiplying the 1936 value added in 1936 prices by 1.61, i.e., the ratio of sales value of the fertilizer group in 1950 and 1936 prices. For other years the index derived from the sales values in 1950 prices of the fertilizer group has been applied.
  [a] For detailed calculations, see Supplement Tables A.43 and A.44.

of fertilizer production. The actual value added of sales of this subgroup, or, rather, its 1936 gross production value of RM 567 million for Germany as a whole was allocated to East and West Germany in the ratio of 214.705:270.95; that is, it was assumed that the products that were not covered were produced in East and West Germany in the same proportion as the four main subgroups. In the absence of any specific information, this is the best assumption that could be made.*

This gives as a base for 1936 a sales value of RM 250.836 million in 1936 prices, of which our calculations account for 90 per cent. The 1936 gross production in 1950 prices was found by multiplying this figure by the ratio of the calculated sales value in 1936 and 1950 prices given in Table 51. The value added thus derived was RM 114.816 million in 1936 prices.

By 1955 the fertilizer sector increased to between 160 and 164 per cent of 1936, depending on whether 1936 or 1950 prices are used in the evaluation, and by 1957 to 168 and 172 per cent, respectively. According

* That is, 44.21 per cent of gross sales are assumed to originate in East Germany.

to this calculation, inorganic chemicals and the fertilizer group account for RM 462.351 million in 1936, or about 65.7 per cent of the RM 705.585 million sales value probably produced in the Soviet Zone (including East Berlin) in 1936. Their combined output rose by about three quarters between 1936 and 1955. Tables 49 and 51 give the relevant figures.

ORGANIC CHEMICALS

Of the RM 705.585 million sales value of chemicals presumably originating in East Germany in 1936, we have thus far accounted for RM 212.025 million for inorganic (heavy) chemicals and RM 251.572 million for the fertilizer group,* leaving RM 241.988 million to be accounted for by organic chemicals and other chemical subgroups. Synthetic fibers, however, were classified with textiles in 1936 and are not included in these RM 242 million.

It is certain that East Germany was not well represented in the remaining branches of the chemical industry. According to the figures given in the Production Statistics of 1936, two-thirds of the value added and slightly less of the sales value of the total chemical industry as defined in 1936 is yet to be accounted for. Except for buna (the production of which started only in 1938) and methanol, the Soviet Zone was substantially underrepresented. This is true not only for coal tar dyes but also for pharmaceuticals and photographic paper (though not for film). In other synthetic materials, the Soviet Zone was apparently represented roughly in proportion to its size.[15] The data are insufficient, however, for more than a rough estimate of the sales value in 1936 by the method chosen above. It was impossible to estimate an actual value added for this group.

The group of organic chemicals is represented by the production of buna (which, since it was not produced in 1936 and was produced only in small quantity in 1938, shows an exceedingly large and atypical rate of growth), coal tar dyes, acetic acid, synthetic tannins and solvents. In 1936 the combined calculated sales value of these products in 1936 prices was RM 152.03 million, or 62.8 per cent of the RM 241.988 million still to be accounted for. The scanty information on methanol and formaldehyde reproduced in Table 52 was not used in the calculations.

---

* The figure for inorganic chemicals was estimated as follows: For 1936, the estimated value added of inorganic chemicals was RM 119.137 million. The value added of the chemicals actually accounted for was only RM 71.260 million, and their sales value was RM 126.820 million. The estimated sales value of all inorganic chemicals, whether accounted for or not, is assumed to bear the same relation to the sales value of the chemicals actually accounted for as the values added. Accordingly, RM 126.820 million was multiplied by the ratio 119.137/71.260 = 167.186%. See Supplement Table A.42.

The figure for the fertilizer group was derived by the same method used for inorganic chemicals. The figures are: sales value of fertilizers accounted for, RM 214.705 million; ratio of estimated value added to calculated value added, 114.816/97.99 = 117.171%. See Supplement Table A.44.

Table 52

Production of methanol and formaldehyde, East Germany,
1936 and 1950–1958 (thousand tons)

Year	Methanol	Formaldehyde
1936	104	...
1950	38	16.8
1951	41	20.7
1952	45	27.5
1953	49	31
1954	55	35
1955	60	n.a.
1956	62	n.a.
1957	63	n.a.
1958	64	

Sources: Methanol: For 1936, see Bodo Böttcher, *Industrielle Strukturwandlungen im sowjetisch besetzten Gebiet Deutschlands*, West Berlin, Duncker and Humblot, 1956, p. 61; for 1950–1957, see *SJDDR*, 1956, p. 280; 1957, p. 296; 1958, p. 346. Formaldehyde: For 1950–1952, see Böttcher, *op. cit.*, p. 61; 1953–1954, estimated; 1936, 1955–1957, not available.

By 1955 the production of this important sector had increased substantially, rising to about 250 per cent of its 1936 level. The overwhelming portion of this increase was due to buna, but the output of acetic acid increased more than thirteen-fold and that of solvents about doubled. Coal-tar dyes did not quite reach the low 1936 level. The data are given in Table 53.

PLASTICS AND SIMILAR PRODUCTS, AND CHEMICAL PRODUCTS
NOT OTHERWISE ACCOUNTED FOR

This group of products, the importance of which has been growing, is only poorly represented by the output of raw film and photographic paper. Fortunately, however, the ratios of value added to sales value are at least not very dissimilar for the various chemical subgroups other than pharmaceuticals. Figures given in the Production Statistics of 1936 allow the calculation of the following ratios: organic chemicals and coal tar dyes, 61.53 per cent; pharmaceuticals and drugs, 73.06 per cent; synthetic materials, 51.97 per cent; mineral dyes, 50.24 per cent; and others, 55.85 per cent. According to the *U. S. Census of Manufactures: 1937*, the ratio of plastics was only 41.44 per cent; of buna, 41.39 per cent; of organic chemicals 49.4 per cent; and of pharmaceuticals, 51.46 per cent. For films and paper the ratio of 51.97 per cent for synthetic materials was applied.

Although in 1936 the production of pharmaceuticals was apparently substantially underrepresented in East Germany, production of the category "chemical products not otherwise accounted for" was not. The two series, film and photographic paper, may therefore be quite typical of the output for this group. Between 1936 and 1955 film output (in square

Table 53

Production and value added, organic chemicals, East Germany, 1936 and 1950–1958[a]

A. Production, thousand tons

Year	Synthetic rubber (buna)	Coal tar dyes	Acetic acid	Synthetic tannins	Solvents
	(1)	(2)	(3)	(4)	(5)
1936	4.738	8.476	2.354	0.093	120.636
1950	39.804	4.869	23.942	1.640	106.561
1951	50.327	6.583	24.858	2.744	122.775
1952	57.277	8.028	24.007	2.810	129.987
1953	64.097	6.726	26.025	3.766	145.666
1954	67.707	8.219	28.196	3.925	164.205
1955	72.226	7.894	31.861	3.694	198.934
1956	73.435	8.353	34.645	3.694 (Est.)	213.549
1957	75.369	8.547	40.313	3.694 (Est.)	224.710
1958	84.969	9.627	47.110	3.694 (Est.)	226.246

B. Value added

	1936 Prices		1950 Prices	
Year	Value added (million RM)	Index (1936 = 100)	Value added (million DM)	Index (1936 = 100)
	(6)	(7)	(8)	(9)
1936	93.54	100.00	159.95	100.00
1950	133.30	142.50	222.92	139.38
1951	161.46	172.61	269.29	168.36
1952	178.26	190.57	296.69	185.50
1953	193.34	206.68	321.99	201.32
1954	212.94	227.63	354.98	221.94
1955	237.80	254.22	397.64	248.61
1956	247.30	264.38	414.11	258.90
1957	260.76	278.77	436.94	273.17
1958	280.27	299.62	468.75	293.06

Sources: Col. 1: Figure for 1936 given in Gleitze, *Ostdeutsche Wirtschaft*, p. 205. (For 1943 he gives 69,000 tons as the production in the Zone and 115,716 tons as that in all Germany.) For postwar years see *SJDDR*, 1955, p. 162; 1956, p. 281; and 1958, p. 346. Col. 2: For 1936, see Gleitze, *op. cit.*, p. 204, and *Die Chemische Industrie in der sowjetischen Besatzungszone* ("*Bonner Berichte*"), Bonn, n.d., p. 45. For 1950–1957, see *SJDDR*, 1955, p. 162; 1956, p. 281; and 1958, p. 346. *SJDDR*, 1955 ed., gives as production in 1951 a figure of 16,583, which is obviously a misprint. Since only 6,000 tons were planned for that year, it should read 6,585 tons. The figure given for 1951 in *Die Chemische* . . . ("*Bonner Berichte*"), p. 45, refers to Farbenfabrik Wolfen, the only firm in East Germany that produces these dyes. Col. 3: For 1936, see Gleitze, *op. cit.*, p. 204, which specifies 100 per cent acetic acid. For 1950–1958, see *SJDDR*, 1955, 1956, and 1958, as in col. 1. Cols. 4 and 5: See *ibid.* Cols. 6 and 8: Derived as follows: the sales values of the five major products were evaluated in 1936 and 1950 prices, respectively, and then added. The value added was estimated at 61.53 per cent of sales value. *Produktionsstatistik, 1936*, p. 50. Cols. 7 and 9: Derived from cols. 6 and 8.

[a] For further details see Supplement Table A.45.

meters) increased almost 2.5 times, but the output of photographic paper hardly increased at all.*

On the basis of these figures, by 1955 the synthetics industry appears to have grown to 221 per cent of 1936—a reasonable result (see Table 54).

Table 54

Production and value added, synthetics, East Germany, 1936 and 1950–1958

| | Production | | Value added, raw film and photographic paper | | | |
| | | | 1936 Prices | | 1950 Prices | |
Year	Raw film (million sq m)	Photo- graphic paper (million sq m)	(million RM)	Index 1936 = 100	(million DM)	Index 1936 = 100
	(1)	(2)	(3)	(4)	(5)	(6)
1936	7.052	8.348	32.306	100.00	56.536	100.00
1950	13.822	3.845	55.150	170.71	96.824	171.26
1951	14.126	4.423	56.875	176.05	99.509	176.01
1952	14.013	4.728	56.636	175.31	99.091	175.27
1953	13.034	5.832	53.592	165.89	93.776	165.87
1954	14.958	7.724	62.163	192.42	108.764	192.38
1955	17.229	8.589	71.403	221.02	124.928	220.97
1956	18.272	8.973	75.641	234.14	132.345	234.09
1957	19.187	9.072	79.205	245.17	138.508	244.99
1958	21.788	9.965	89.727	277.74	156.995	277.69

Sources: Cols. 1 and 2: For 1936, see Gleitze, *Ostdeutsche Wirtschaft*, p. 204, SBZ and East Berlin; for 1950–1958, see *SJDDR*, 1956, p. 280, and 1958, pp. 346–347. Col. 3: The 1936 value added is estimated at 27.08 per cent of the value added for the Reich. For details see Supplement Table A.47, note j. Indices for 1950–1957 calculated by applying index in col. 4. Cols. 4 and 6: Calculation of the index is explained in the text. See Supplement Table A.47 for details. Col. 5: The 1936 value added in 1950 prices has been found by multiplying the 1936 value added in 1936 prices by the price index of *Chemische Gebrauchsgueter* which stood at 175. *SJBR*, 1956, p. 433. For 1950–1957, index in col. 6 has been applied.

The index calculated for these two important products was applied to a value added in 1936 and in 1936 prices of RM 32.306 million. Thus the calculated value added of films and of photographic paper accounts for about one-third of the presumed actual value added.†

* Since prices are given "per ton," it was necessary to change the square meters to tons. This involved considerable measurements. For photographic paper, a ratio of 65.61 kg per 1,000 sq m was found experimentally, and for film, 183.22 kg per 1,000 sq m. Thus the production of film in 1955 was 3,156 tons and that of paper 563.5 tons. To judge the reasonableness of these results, one can compare the exports of the Federal Republic in 1956 of "photographic papers, etc." of 3,794.8 tons and of film, 959 tons.

† The figure of RM 32.306 million was derived in the following way. According to the Production Statistics of 1936 (p. 50), total gross production of the synthetic industry in 1936 was RM 229.541 million, and the gross value added was RM 119.300 million. The tonnage of synthetics produced in 1936 in East Germany (including East Berlin) is given by Gleitze as 27.08 per cent of the German total. This percentage was applied to the value added for Germany as a whole. The 1950 value added was found by applying the index of chemical consumption goods of 175 per cent to the value added in 1936. The data are presented in Supplement Table A.47.

In 1936 the chemical industry did not include synthetic fibers (listed as textiles) or synthetic fuels, which was a separate industry group. The chemotechnical industry was also separately shown.

We have now accounted for the major part of the chemical industry by the 1936 definition:

Industry group	1936 Sales value (million RM)
Inorganic chemicals	212.015
Fertilizers	251.608
Organic chemicals	152.030
Plastics	62.126
	677.779

This amounts to 96 per cent of the estimated sales value of RM 705.585 million. Of the remaining RM 27.814 million, RM 11.359 million are accounted for by pharmaceuticals (or about 5 per cent of total pharmaceutical production in the Reich). The other products not separately shown were evaluated with an index of the combined output of inorganic chemicals and fertilizers. The value added was assumed to be 55 per cent, or RM 15.298 million for 1936 in 1936 prices, and, after allowing for a price increase of 175 per cent, DM 26.772 million in 1950 prices.*

By 1955 the output of the chemical industries thus far discussed had increased to about 215 per cent of its 1936 level. In 1950 it was already about 35 to 37 per cent above 1936, and between 1950 and 1955 it expanded another 57 per cent. It should be noted that the chemical industry is a collection of industries which, in many cases, have had a natural favorable basis (with the primary exceptions of soft coal tars and soft coal tar dyes) and which have been essential to the planner as well as to the occupying force.

The items calculated thus far make up the chemical industry as it was defined in Germany in 1936. Since, as we noted earlier, the definitions of the industry in East and West Germany differ, comparisons must be postponed until the calculations of synthetic fibers and fuels are presented.

SYNTHETIC FIBERS

The index of this sector was calculated on the basis of continuous-filament rayon, staple rayon, and perlon (a type of nylon). All output figures are based on official East German data.

The price for continuous-filament rayon is a West German price. For staple rayon, however, only one West German price, that for 1954, is given by Thimm. This price was extrapolated to the other years by an English index given in the Statistical Yearbook of the Federal Republic. The English price in 1954 was virtually identical with the price given by

* For calculations, see Supplement Table A.48.

Thimm. An American nylon price, also given in the Statistical Yearbook of the Federal Republic had to be used for perlon.

The index of this branch of the industry was applied to the 1936 value added as follows. Gleitze gives total sales of the "continuous-filament and staple rayon industry" for 1936 as RM 93.723 million for the Zone proper, and RM 10.399 million for East Berlin.[16] (No perlon was produced in 1936.) As a total sales value for Germany as a whole, he gives RM 303.061 million, while the Production Statistics of 1936 gives a gross production value of only RM 275.492 million, the difference of RM 27.569 million consisting of intra-industry flows. To allow for these, the sales value for East Germany of RM 104.122 million was reduced in the proportion of the 1936 gross production value to the 1936 sales value, that is, to 90.9 per cent, which yields a value of output for 1936 in 1936 prices of RM 94.647 million. The 1936 ratio of value added to value of output for Germany as a whole, 60.40 per cent,[17] was applied to this figure to arrive at a value added of RM 57.167 million. The 1936 value in 1950 prices was found by raising the 1936 value in 1936 prices by the average price increase of continuous-filament and staple rayon to 187.5 per cent.[18] These calculations are summarized in Table 55.* They indicate that in 1936 prices the output of this sector increased almost 4.5 times between 1936 and 1955, compared with an increase of 492.8 per cent in the Federal Republic.[19] The East German increase is, however, largely due to the high perlon price in 1936. Measured in 1950 prices — which here seem the more reasonable measure — the increase was still substantial, but only 339.3 per cent.

Not only was the East German increase less than that in the Federal Republic but also it must be understood in the context of a serious lag in the production of materials made from cotton and wool. In 1955, according to official figures, only 32.3 million sq m of woolen cloth were produced,[20] that is, about 2 sq m per person, and only about 266.8 million sq m of cotton cloth, or about 15 sq m per person. About 4.5 to 5 sq m of woolen cloth are required to make a man's winter coat, about 3.5 sq m of cotton cloth for a woman's summer dress, and about half as much for a man's shirt.

SYNTHETIC FUELS

The production of synthetic gasoline and diesel oil used to be classified as a major component of the fuel industry. It is now apparently classified under chemicals. In 1936 the gross value added of the production of petroleum derivatives and montan wax was RM 173.373 million, about 71 per cent of the total value added of this industry group in all of Germany.[21] In general, 38.3 per cent of the output of this group (plus a small amount in Berlin, which is not further subdivided between East

* Details are given in Supplement Table A.48.

Table 55

Production and value added, synthetic fibers, East Germany, and indices,
West and East Germany, 1936 and 1950–1958

A. *Production and value added, East Germany*

	Production			Value added	
Year	Continuous-filament rayon (thousand tons)	Staple rayon, all types (thousand tons)	Perlon (thousand tons)	1936 Prices (million RM)	1950 Prices (million DM)
	(1)	(2)	(3)	(4)	(5)
1936	12.446	17.127	0	57.167	107.188
1950	9.019	78.044	311	113.248	199.048
1951	14.478	82.581	899	153.665	252.213
1952	16.977	87.140	1295	178.361	283.298
1953	19.030	93.091	1375	193.167	307.951
1954	20.897	96.948	2038	223.351	339.036
1955	22.301	96.857	2875	253.593	363.689
1956	22.765	98.280	3603	278.832	385.019
1957	23.067	109.108	3968	301.556	411.173
1958	25.081	111.210	4736	333.512	441.936

B. *Indices, West and East Germany*

	West Germany		East Germany	
Year	Old	New	1936 Prices 1936 = 100	1950 Prices 1936 = 100
	(6)	(7)	(8)	(9)
1936	100.0	100.0	100.0	100.0
1950	265.6	267.4	198.1	185.7
1951	308.2	318.7	268.8	235.3
1952	239.1	262.6	312.0	264.3
1953	298.8	333.7	337.9	287.3
1954	326.8	377.5	390.7	316.3
1955	n.a.	492.8	443.6	339.3
1956	n.a.	538.0	487.7	357.4
1957	n.a.	613.0	527.5	383.6
1958	n.a.	628.0	583.4	412.3

Sources: Cols. 1 and 2: See Gleitze, *Ostdeutsche Wirtschaft*, p. 208; *SJDDR*, 1955, p. 162, and 1958, p. 354. Col. 3: *Ibid.*, 1956, p. 288, and 1958, p. 354. Cols. 4 and 5: For estimation of value added for 1936, see text. For the years 1950–1957, the index in cols. 8 and 9 has been applied. Col. 6: Average monthly production. *SJBR*, 1955, p. 229. Col. 7: For 1950–1955, average monthly production, given in *Neuberechnung*, p. 67; for 1956–1957, average daily production, given in *SJBR*, 1959, p. 181. Cols. 8 and 9: The method of calculation is described in the text. Details of calculations are given in Supplement Table A.48.

and West Berlin) and 80.9 per cent of carbonization plants, producing an earlier product for hydrogenation, were located in the Soviet Zone. The industries based on soft coal (benzol and soft coal distillation) were as overwhelmingly concentrated in the area of West Germany. The out-

Table 56

Estimated production of synthetic fuels, East Germany, and indices,
West and East Germany, 1936 and 1950–1958

A. *Production and value added, East Germany*

	Production		Value added, fuel industry	
Year	Gasoline (thousand tons)	Diesel fuel (thousand tons)	1936 Prices (million RM)	1950 Prices (million DM)
	(1)	(2)	(3)	(4)
1936	482.3	42.9	76.185	117.142
1950	470.3	432.1	101.722	166.353
1951	603.0	522.0	128.174	209.016
1952	665.0	560.0	140.249	228.415
1953	801.2	627.2	165.634	268.853
1954	784.0 Plan	628.0 Plan	163.081	264.987
1955	830.4	697.4	174.997	284.971
1956	882.7	830.0	192.253	314.772
1957	882.7 Est.	830.0 Est.	192.253	314.772
1958	n.a.	n.a.	n.a.	n.a.

B. *Indices, West and East Germany*

	West Germany, petroleum refining		East Germany, fuel industry	
Year	Old	New	1936 Prices 1936 = 100	1950 Prices 1936 = 100
	(5)	(6)	(7)	(8)
1936	100.0	100.0	100.00	100.00
1950	155.0	139.5	133.52	142.01
1951	200.7	190.2	168.24	178.43
1952	223.6	214.9	184.09	194.99
1953	264.9	251.2	217.41	229.51
1954	319.8	315.9	214.06	226.21
1955		367.5	229.70	243.27
1956		398.0	252.35	268.71
1957		404.0	n.a.	n.a.
1958		492.0	n.a.	n.a.

Sources: Cols. 1 and 2: For 1936, see Gleitze, *Ostdeutsche Wirtschaft*, p. 192; for 1951 and 1952, see *DIW, Zahlen zur Energiewirtschaft in der sowjetischen Besatzungszone Deutschlands vor und nach 1945, Mitteilungen*, Special Issue, 25 June 1953, Pt. III, p. 15; for 1950, 1953, and 1955, *DIW, Wochenbericht*, 1957, No. 24, p. 96; 1956, estimated from *ibid.;* 1957 estimated to be unchanged from 1956. Cols. 3 and 4: For estimation of 1936 value added, see text. For other years, indices given in cols. 7 and 8 were applied. Col. 5: *SJBR*, 1955, p. 229. Col. 6: For 1950–1955, see *Neuberechnung*, p. 67; for 1956–1958, *SJBR*, 1959, p. 182. Cols. 7 and 8: Indices calculated from combined sales value of gasoline and diesel fuel. For details, see Supplement Table A.49.

put of synthetic gasoline and diesel fuel is therefore a good index of the way this sector as a whole has fared (see Table 56).*

* A few scattered estimates for heating oil and for benzol are available, but they are insufficient to be included in the calculation of an index.

Except for a figure for 1955 giving the total tonnage of all fuels as 1,575,000 tons,[22] all figures are from West German sources. In their general tenor, however, they fit this officially reported figure remarkably well. The 1955 figure for gasoline and diesel fuel combined is 1,527, 800 tons, which is very close indeed. The difference between the two figures may be benzol output, estimated at 52,000 tons in 1955.[23] The prices are taken from the Statistical Yearbook of the Federal Republic and from Thimm. Recalculations from liters to tons were based on data from Dubbel.[24]

The index calculated for the two fuels was then applied to the 1936 value added of the fuel industry, which was estimated as follows. Gleitze gives for the sales value of this industry in 1936 RM 796.695 million, of which 31.1 per cent was produced in the Soviet Zone proper and a very small amount in Berlin as a whole.[25] No further breakdown was given for the output of Berlin, which is neglected here. Assuming that production in the area of East Germany was 31.1 per cent of the Reich, the value added in 1936 prices for 1936 is RM 76.185 million. In order to state the 1936 gross value added in 1950 prices, the 1936 value added in 1936 prices was raised by the combined sales value in 1950 prices/combined sales value in 1936 prices = 153.76 per cent.

The calculations are presented in Table 54. The figures indicate an increase of 252 or 268 per cent (depending on the prices used), which is not only very substantial but also probably a slight overstatement of the true increase, since the production of coal tar carbonization plants lagged and benzol output almost certainly was not above the 1936 level. But these are relatively small amounts. To put this increase in the proper perspective, a further statement should be made. In 1938 the production of synthetic gasoline had already increased to 769,088 tons, and by 1943 it had further increased to 821,000 tons (exclusive of aviation gasoline).[26] Compared with 1938, the increase in gasoline production was 86 per cent; compared with 1943 it was about 70 per cent. By 1938 the production of diesel fuel had also increased — to 60,225 tons.

No production figures are available for 1943 for the Soviet Zone, but the production of diesel fuel in Germany as a whole increased. By 1955 the output of this industry in the Federal Republic had increased to 367.5 per cent of 1936.*

---

* Based on a similar calculation for West Germany, a comparison with the East German production of diesel fuel may be tabulated as follows.

Year	West Germany		East Germany	
	Tons	Per Cent	Tons	Per Cent
1936	101,381	100	42,911	100
1938	204,267	201	60,225	140
1954	2,318,098	2,287	628,000	1,464

Sources: Gleitze, p. 192 (including West Berlin; there was apparently no production in East Berlin); Statistical Yearbook of the Federal Republic, 1955, p. 220.

CHEMOTECHNICAL INDUSTRY

The chemotechnical industry is represented by three series — soaps, washing powders, and paints and varnishes — which together accounted for about 63 per cent of the total value added of the industry in all of Germany in 1936, RM 742 million, of which RM 223 million or almost exactly 30 per cent were accounted for by soaps and similar products. The remainder consisted of cosmetics (RM 83 million), candles and wax products (RM 64 million), paints and varnishes (RM 116 million), matches and incandescent mantles (RM 36 million), and artificial leather (RM 83 million). It is assumed that the output of the industry as a whole varies more or less with the outputs of the representative series.

It is likely that the cosmetics output has not regained its prewar importance. Paints and varnishes, on the other hand, appear to have expanded vigorously although nothing is known about their quality. On the whole, basing the expansion of the group on the three industries probably overstates their growth. Although the production of artificial leather has increased substantially, at least since 1950, none of these industries has any strategic value, and many of the industries in this sector are based on fats, an input in very short supply.

The production of artificial leather is now listed under leather and shoe production. It accounted for only RM 54.384 million of value added in all of Germany in 1936, or about 7.3 per cent of the total value added of this industry group. With 2,320 tons, East Germany accounted for about half of the 4,719 tons produced in all of Germany.[27] Since the postwar figures for artificial leather are in value terms and no price could be found to convert these prices to tons, the value added of this sector cannot be separately calculated. Because this sector is of so little importance, the damage resulting from this omission is not likely to be great.*

For the entire sector, the 1936 value added in 1936 prices was found by prorating the value added figures found in the Production Statistics of 1936 with the percentages for the individual subclassifications for sales values given by Gleitze.[28] (See Table 57.) The error resulting from the use of this procedure is likely to be very minor. The data are summarized in Table 58.†

---

* A rough calculation can be made as follows: If the RM 54.384 million value added are apportioned between the area of East Germany and the rest of Germany in the ratio of the tonnage produced, i.e., in the ratio of $2320/4719 = 49.1629$ per cent, we can estimate the value added as RM 26.737 million. The ratio of value added to sales value of leather in 1936 was about 33 per cent. This gives an estimated sales value of RM 81 million. Allowing for a doubling in price between 1936 and 1955, this would give a value added of about RM 160 million. The claimed production of artificial leather in 1955 was DM–O 169.834 million. (Statistical Yearbook of the German Democratic Republic, pp. 166–167.) Even juggling the figures some other way does not suggest a very great increase.

† Details of sources and calculations are given in Supplement Table A.50.

Table 57

Value added, chemotechnical industry, East Germany,[a] 1936

Subgroups	Percentage produced in East Germany	Value added (million RM)
(1)	(2)	(3)
Matches, etc.	26.3	13.198
Resins, linoleum, artificial leather	24.0	19.855
Paints and varnishes	29.7	48.456
Pencils	0.0	0.000
Candles and wax industry	20.4	14.842
Soaps, etc.	26.6	69.462
Cosmetics	27.5	22.837
Total		188.650

Sources: Percentages: Gleitze, *Ostdeutsche Wirtschaft*, p. 183. Value added: *Produktionsstatistik, 1936*, p. 25. See text.
 [a] One-third of Berlin production is allocated to East Berlin.

According to official data, in 1955 the production of soaps had reached 71 per cent of the 1936 level, a trend that is quite universal. On the other hand, according to our calculations, washing powders, which may include detergents had reached only about half the prewar level. Officially paints and varnishes are said to have expanded to almost 2.5 times the prewar level. According to our calculations this sector was at most 25 per cent above its 1936 level. The results are given in Table 58.

RUBBER PRODUCTS (RUBBER AND ASBESTOS)

The estimation of the output of the rubber products industries presents problems for which only very rough solutions can be offered. For the years from 1948 on, the number of car and bicycle tires and tubes produced is given, but one can only guess at their distribution by size.

In 1936 the largest subgroup consisted of rubber products (not further specified), with tire production an important second industry, and asbestos products a weak third. It is obvious that the industry as a whole cannot move parallel to the rapidly expanding buna industry for a number of reasons: East Germany has imported big tires, does not produce many vehicles, has not had the facilities for making large tires until recently, and buna is both exported and used as a substitute for natural rubber. On the other hand, the output of this industry group is likely to move parallel with the domestically available, rather than the domestically produced, rubber. (The asbestos industry must be neglected for lack of information.)

The procedure adopted was as follows. In 1936 no synthetic rubber was produced. The available natural rubber (imports less exports) is given as 72,945 tons.[29] No consumption figure is given for all rubber. It

Table 58

Production and value added, chemotechnical industry,
East Germany, 1936 and 1950–1958

A. *Production, thousand tons*

Year	Soap (40% fat content)	Washing powder	Paint and lacquer
	(1)	(2)	(3)
1936	57.291	142.283	43.356
1950	34.365	72.278	55.093
1951	40.784	65.315	61.489
1952	40.718	83.478	66.729
1953	40.068	79.487	72.957
1954	45.476	67.813	95.096
1955	40.650	78.626	102.645
1956	48.322	78.754	110.115
1957	50.798	72.360	122.378
1958	53.282	101.012	134.672

B. *Value added*

Year	1936 Prices		1950 Prices	
	Value added (million RM)	Index 1936 = 100	Value added (million DM)	Index 1936 = 100
	(4)	(5)	(6)	(7)
1936	188.650	100.00	328.251	100.00
1950	150.826	79.95	265.325	80.83
1951	159.296	84.44	286.169	87.18
1952	179.444	95.12	316.007	96.27
1953	186.556	98.89	329.104	100.26
1954	216.514	114.77	387.599	118.08
1955	233.473	123.76	410.740	125.13
1956	248.905	131.94	442.646	134.85
1957	264.318	140.11	474.356	144.51
1958	304.896	161.62	536.953	163.58

Sources: Cols. 1 and 3: For 1936 and 1950–1955, see *SJDDR*, 1955; for 1956 to 1958, *ibid.*, 1958, pp. 346–347. Col. 2: 1936 figure calculated from Gleitze, *Ostdeutsche Wirtschaft*, p. 205. (Combined sales of soap and washing powders in East Berlin and the Soviet Zone are given as 193,845 tons. To make washing powders comparable with soap, the tonnage had to be reduced by about 10 per cent to allow for additional water absorption. Hence the Gleitze figure was multiplied by 0.9, and the soap tonnage was then deducted from this figure.) For 1950–1955, see *SJDDR*, 1955, p. 162; for 1956 to 1958, *ibid.*, 1958 ed., pp. 346–347. Col. 4: For calculation of 1936 figure, see text. For other years, index in col. 5 has been applied. Cols. 5 and 7: The indices were calculated from the value added of the three series given in cols. 1–3. The precise method, prices used, and actual calculations are given in Supplement Table A.50. Col. 6: 1936: 1936 value added multiplied by index prices given for *Chemische Verbrauchsgüter* in *SJBR*, 1956, p. 433. 1950: 174 per cent of 1938, which was assumed to be unchanged from 1936. For other years indices given in col. 7 have been applied.

is stated, however, that 40,250 tons of rubber were used in the production of tires, 1,810 tons in the production of rubber footwear and 25,696 tons of rubber and other materials in the production of other "rubber, balata, and gutta percha" products.[30] In addition, these industries used 8,593 tons and 17,777 tons of reclaimed rubber and scrap rubber, respectively. These figures add up to a minimum use of 67,756 tons of new rubber or 94,643 tons of new and scrap rubber. Prorating this amount to East Germany according to the percentage of German sales of the rubber industry originating in East Germany (that is, 16.54 per cent[31]) gives an estimated availability of 11,207 tons or 15,654 tons, depending on whether scrap rubber is excluded or included. If net imports are used as a base, the East German share would be 12,065 tons. This figure has therefore been adopted as a base.

For the postwar years, imports of natural rubber and exports of synthetic rubber are given in the 1956 and 1957 editions of the Statistical

Table 59

Production of rubber and rubber goods, value added, rubber and asbestos sector,
East Germany, and indices, West and East Germany, 1936 and 1950–1958

A. *Production and value added, East Germany*						
Year	Tires (thousands)	Tubes (thousands)	Bicycle tires (thousands)	Bicycle tubes (thousands)	Buna (thousand tons)	Buna exports (thousand tons)
	(1)	(2)	(3)	(4)	(5)	(6)
1936	176.0	148.0	. . .ᵃ	. . .ᵃ	4.738	
1950	467.5	514.0	240.0	330.0	39.804	18.521
1951	610.4	614.4	1005.3	1321.6	50.327	24.129
1952	786.4	797.8	3267.3	3196.2	57.277	26.932
1953	915.9	875.1	3913.3	4306.8	64.097	22.752
1954	1139.7	1128.0	4951.9	5005.0	67.707	37.166
1955	1438.9	1344.9	4844.2	4180.3	72.226	38.729
1956	1743.4	1714.8	4455.0	4597.6	73.435	39.723
1957	1739.1	1496.0	4504.5	4193.5	75.369	42.973
1958	1979.8	1749.6	4755.2	5385.9	84.969	48.019

			Value added, rubber and asbestos	
Year	Natural rubber imports (thousand tons)	Total rubber available (thousand tons)	1936 Prices (million RM)	1950 Prices (million DM)
	(7)	(8)	(9)	(10)
1936		12.065	44.723	71.110
1950	1.969	23.252	82.614	131.357
1951	1.904	28.102	97.596	155.179
1952	2.322	32.667	108.137	171.940
1953	3.663	45.008	153.736	244.442
1954	5.682	36.223	111.582	177.416
1955	9.548	43.045	133.060	211.566
1956	9.677	42.242	123.250	195.966
1957	16.482	48.478	149.107	237.081
1958	16.996	53.946	164.888	262.888

Table 59 (Continued)

B. *Indices, West and East Germany*

| Year | West Germany | | East Germany, 1936 and 1950 prices, 1936 = 100 | | |
	Old	New	Tires and tubes	Others	Total
1936	(11) 100.0	(12) 100.0	(13) 100.0	(14) 100.0	(15) 100.0
1950	116.9	117.8	285.9	173.8	184.7
1951	129.7	130.6	369.4	198.2	218.2
1952	143.7	143.5	607.6	202.3	241.8
1953	166.0	164.5	713.8	303.8	343.8
1954	194.5	191.9	890.4	180.3	249.5
1955		231.1	1046.1	216.7	297.5
1956		229.0	1216.5	174.0	275.4
1957		238.0	1197.6	240.1	333.4
1958		246.0	1358.7	261.8	368.7

Sources: Cols. 1–5: For 1936, see Gleitze, *Ostdeutsche Wirtschaft*, p. 206; for 1950–1957, *SJDDR*, 1956, p. 280; 1958, p. 346. Col. 6: *SJDDR*, 1956, p. 521, and 1958 ed., p. 571. Col. 7: *Ibid.*, 1956, p. 523, and 1958 ed., p. 575. Col. 8: Col. 5 + col. 7 − col. 6. Cols. 9 and 10: For 1936 value added, see text for other years the indices in cols. 13 and 14 were applied to separate estimates for "tires and tubes" and "all other" and then added. For details, see Supplement Table A.51. Col. 11: Figures given for *Gummiverarbeitung* in *SJBR*, 1955, p. 229. Col. 12: Figures given for *Kautschuckverarbeitende Industrie* in *Neuberechnung*, p. 37, and *SJBR*, 1959, p. 182. Cols. 13–15: For method of calculation, see text. Details of calculations, prices used, etc. are given in Supplement Table A.51. Since the indices were calculated from the rubber available as inputs, separate indices in 1936 and 1950 prices were not calculated.
ᵃ Negligible.

Yearbook GDR.[32] It is virtually certain, however, that a very large part of the buna produced was exported to the Soviet Union as reparations, and that these exports are not included with the figures for commercial exports.

Since tire production was only the second most important industry in this group in 1936, an attempt has been made to calculate separately the value added of tires and of rubber products not further specified. It has been assumed that no large tires are produced in East Germany. The weight of the tires and tubes was estimated from the numbers of tires given.[33] The value added of the tire and tube industry in East Germany can be assumed to have been around 5 per cent of that of all Germany,[34] or RM 4.458 million. An index of the rubber used for tires and tubes was applied to this figure to estimate the output for the postwar years.

The index of available rubber for all other rubber products was calculated by deducting from the domestically available rubber the amount used for tires and tubes, and this index was applied to the value added of the "rubber industry not further specified," RM 40.365 million.[35]

Tire and tube production increased more than tenfold between 1936 and 1955, which, considering both the small production in 1936 and the likelihood of some exports, is reasonable even in the face of the lagging

car and truck production. The output of all other rubber products probably increased about 375 per cent between 1936 and 1955. Altogether the
output of rubber products (including asbestos) increased about 440 per
cent in this span of time. By comparison, the output of rubber products
increased to 231 per cent of 1936 in the Federal Republic, where the base
had been much bigger (see Table 59).

VARIOUS COMPARISONS

The first comparison to be made is between the development of the
chemical industry in the Federal Republic and in East Germany, using
the old definition, which includes the chemotechnical industry but excludes synthetic fibers, fuels, and rubber products. By this definition, the
industry had recovered to exactly the same extent in East and West Germany by 1950, when both were about 25 per cent above 1936. By 1955
the West German industry had reached 237.0 per cent of 1936, measured
by the old index, and the East German industry had just about doubled
its output.

The postwar definition of the chemical industry in the Federal Republic includes synthetic fibers but continues to exclude fuels and rubber
products. Thus defined, the industry in East Germany had reached about
117.5 per cent of its 1936 level in 1950 and had risen to 210.1 or 222 per
cent in 1957, depending on whether we use 1950 or 1936 prices. Since the
new index of the Federal Republic is based on 1950 relations, the 1950
prices are preferable for comparison. By this definition, the industry in
the Federal Republic, measured by the new index, had already risen to
222.6 per cent by 1955. The indices are, unfortunately, still not quite
comparable, since coal tar derivatives are part of the coal mining industry in West Germany but are included in the chemical industry in our
calculations.

In the East German definition, the chemical industry includes synthetic fuels, rubber and asbestos products, and the chemotechnical industries but excludes synthetic fibers, which continue to be a part of the
textile industry. Measured in either 1936 or 1950 prices, the industry had
recovered to about 117 per cent of its 1936 level by 1950, and has continued to rise, reaching 207 per cent in 1957. Between 1950 and 1956 the
increase in the calculated indices is about 68 per cent, while the official
gross production index shows the expected faster increase to 208 per cent
in 1956. Expressed in *Messwerte,* the "gross production" rose from DM
4.126 billion in 1950 to DM 7.924 billion in 1955. The corresponding figures for the calculated value added are RM 800 million and RM 1.291
billion in 1936 prices and DM 1.341 billion and DM 2.151 billion in 1950
prices. The wider range of the figures should be expected from the differences between the East and West German concepts of the makeup of
the chemical industry. The data are given in Table 60.

Table 60

Summary: chemical output, East Germany, East and West German production indices, and East German official index of gross production, 1936 and 1950–1958

A. *Value added, subgroups, East Germany, 1936 prices* (million RM)

Year	Inorganic chemicals	Ferti-lizers	Organic chemicals	Syn-thetics	Other chemical products	Synthetic fibers	Fuels	Chemo-technical industries	Rubber and asbestos industries
	(1)	(2)	(3)	(4)	(5)	(6)	(7)	(8)	(9)
1936	119.137	114.816	93.540	32.306	15.298	57.167	76.185	188.650	44.723
1950	116.921	142.690	133.300	55.150	16.936	113.248	101.722	150.826	82.614
1951	139.247	150.518	161.460	56.875	18.905	153.665	128.174	159.296	97.596
1952	160.239	109.057	178.260	56.636	17.562	178.361	140.249	179.444	108.137
1953	181.005	164.394	178.260	53.392	22.521	193.167	165.634	186.556	153.736
1954	199.947	174.011	212.940	62.163	24.382	223.351	163.081	216.514	111.582
1955	229.780	183.147	237.800	71.403	26.930	253.593	174.997	233.473	133.660
1956	245.720	188.252	247.300	75.641	28.304	278.832	192.253	248.905	123.250
1957	250.283	192.729	260.761	79.205	28.899	301.556	192.253	264.318	149.107
1958	260.874	204.329	280.265	89.727	30.412	333.512	192.253	304.896	164.888

B. *Value added, subgroups, East Germany, 1950 prices* (*million DM*)

Year	Inorganic chemicals	Ferti-lizers	Organic chemicals	Syn-thetics	Other chemical products	Synthetic fibers	Fuels	Chemo-technical industries	Rubber and asbestos industries
	(10)	(11)	(12)	(13)	(14)	(15)	(16)	(17)	(18)
1936	192.254	186.920	159.950	56.536	24.837	107.188	117.142	328.251	71.110
1950	190.754	238.905	222.920	96.824	28.190	199.048	166.353	265.325	131.357
1951	226.956	253.962	269.290	99.509	31.568	252.213	209.016	286.169	155.179
1952	260.024	267.230	296.690	99.091	34.598	283.298	228.415	316.007	171.940
1953	292.188	275.078	321.990	93.776	37.231	307.951	268.853	329.104	244.442
1954	321.852	290.520	354.980	108.764	40.186	339.036	264.987	387.599	177.416
1955	368.993	307.388	397.640	124.928	44.384	363.689	284.971	410.740	211.566
1956	382.547	314.769	414.110	132.345	45.750	385.019	314.772	442.646	195.966
1957	388.738	321.477	436.935	138.508	46.594	411.173	314.772	474.356	237.081
1958	403.234	339.834	468.749	156.995	48.755	441.936	314.772	536.953	262.888

C. *Value added, total, East Germany, three definitions* (*million RM/DM*)

	Old definition[a]		West German definition[b]		East German definition [c]	
Year	1936 Prices (1) through (5)	1950 Prices (10) through (14)	1936 Prices (19 + 6 + 8)	1950 Prices (20 + 15 + 17)	1936 Prices (19 + 7 + 8 + 9)	1950 Prices (20 + 16 + 17 + 18)
	(19)	(20)	(21)	(22)	(23)	(24)
1936	375.097	620.497	620.914	1055.936	684.655	1137.000
1950	464.997	777.593	729.071	1241.966	800.159	1340.628
1951	527.005	881.285	839.966	1419.667	912.071	1531.649
1952	521.754	957.633	879.559	1556.938	949.584	1673.995
1953	614.652	1020.263	994.375	1657.318	1120.578	1862.662
1954	673.443	1116.302	1113.308	1842.937	1164.620	1946.304
1955	748.560	1243.333	1235.626	2017.762	1290.690	2150.610
1956	785.217	1289.521	1312.954	2117.186	1349.625	2242.905
1957	811.877	1332.252	1377.510	2217.781	1417.555	2358.461
1958	865.607	1417.567	1504.015	2396.456	1527.644	2532.180

Table 60 (Continued)

D. *Indices, West and East Germany*

| | West Germany | | East Germany | | | | East Germany | | |
| | | | West German definition[b] | | East German definition[c] | | Calculated index | | Official gross production 1950 = 100 |
Year	Old 1936 prices[d] 1936 = 100	New 1950 prices[e] 1936 = 100	1936 Prices 1936 = 100	1950 Prices 1936 = 100	1936 Prices 1936 = 100	1950 Prices 1936 = 100	1936 Prices 1950 = 100	1950 Prices 1950 = 100	
	(25)	(26)	(27)	(28)	(29)	(30)	(31)	(32)	(33)
1936	100.0	100.0	100.0	100.0	100.0	100.0			
1950	125.3	124.1	117.4	117.6	116.9	117.9	100.0	100.0	100.0
1951	150.1	147.0	135.3	134.4	133.2	134.7	113.9	114.2	117.1
1952	154.7	146.3	157.8	147.4	138.7	147.2	118.6	124.9	137.1
1953	182.0	173.4	160.1	157.0	163.7	163.8	140.0	138.9	161.8
1954	210.4	197.0	179.3	174.5	170.1	171.2	145.5	145.2	176.3
1955	237.0	222.6	199.0	191.1	188.5	189.1	161.2	160.4	192.0
1956	n.a.	243.0	211.5	200.5	197.1	197.3	168.6	167.3	207.6
1957	n.a.	272.0	221.9	210.0	207.0	207.4	177.1	175.9	224.0
1958	n.a.	292.0	242.2	227.0	223.1	222.7	190.8	188.9	247.5

Sources: Cols. 1–24: Figures from Tables 49–59, added as indicated. Col. 25: *SJBR*, 1955 ed., p. 228; *Monthly Report of the Bank Deutscher Laender*, March 1956. Col. 26: *Neuberechnung*, p. 67, and *SJBR*, 1959 ed., p. 181. Col. 27: Calculated from col. 21. Col. 28: Calculated from col. 22. Col. 29: Calculated from col. 23. Col. 30: Calculated from col. 24. Cols. 31 and 32: Indices, cols. 29 and 30, rebased. Col. 33: *SJDDR*, 1956, p. 273, and 1957, p. 281. 1958 calculated from monthly data in *ibid.*, 1958, p. 268, and linked to 1955.

    [a] Excludes synthetic fibers, fuel, and rubber.

    [b] West German definition: chemical industry (old definition) + synthetic fibers + chemotechnical industry. (It excludes fuel industry and rubber and asbestos industry.)

    [c] East German definition: chemical industry (old definition) + fuel industry + chemotechnical industry + rubber and asbestos industry. (It excludes synthetic fibers.)

    [d] Old index, based on 1936 prices and old definition.

    [e] New index, based on 1950 prices and new West German definition.

CHAPTER X

BUILDING MATERIALS, WOOD, PAPER AND PRINTING

BUILDING MATERIALS*

OUR index of the building materials industry is based on the output of cement, bricks and roofing tile, and burnt lime which in 1936 accounted for 39 per cent of the gross value added of the whole industry. Within this classification, the only other industry with an output of major importance was "quarrying and the working of natural stones," but no figures are available for the postwar years. A few figures are available for fire brick, but they are also insufficient to be included in the calculation of the index. We therefore had to base our index on a 39 per cent representation of the total.

Of total German production in 1936 the Soviet Zone produced 14.4 per cent of the cement, 32 per cent of the brick, and 18 per cent of the roofing tile.[1] (East Berlin produced none of these products.) Gleitze states that in 1936 East Germany (including East Berlin) accounted for RM 383,935 million, or 23 per cent, of all sales of the building materials industry and for an equal percentage of employment.[2] The only way to estimate the 1936 value added attributable to the Soviet Zone was by using the 23 per cent figures for the value of all sales to calculate the value added for Germany as a whole.† In 1936 the reported value added for all of Germany was RM 1,231.106 million.[3] Thus we can estimate that the 1936 value added in 1936 prices for the area of East Germany was RM 283.154 million. The 1936 value added in 1950 prices is found by multiplying the 1936 value added by value added in 1936 in 1950 prices as calculated/value added in 1936 in 1936 prices as calculated = 215.1 per cent.

Although cement output in 1955 was much above prewar, the produc-

---

* The German industry classification is "Stones and Earths," which covers all mining other than ores and fuels. It includes, for instance, the mining of kaolin.

† Except for omitting the production of asphalt and barite — in which East Germany was substantially underrepresented, but which accounted for only a negligible amount of total sales — the allocation is likely to be a reasonably average.

Table 61

Production and value added, building materials industry, East Germany,
and indices, West and East Germany, 1936 and 1950–1958

A. *Production and value added, East Germany*

| | Production | | | | Value added | |
Year	Bricks (millions)	Roofing tiles (millions)	Burnt lime (thousand tons)	Cement (thousand tons)	1936 Prices (million RM)	1950 Prices (million DM)
	(1)	(2)	(3)	(4)	(5)	(6)
1936	3668	306.0	1139	1687.0	283.154	609.060
1950	1356	165.8	1497	1412.0	173.375	335.836
1951	1678	202.0	1708	1656.0	206.249	402.528
1952	1759	209.4	1782	2023.0	226.268	437.427
1953	1920	186.9	2045	2448.0	254.754	485.604
1954	1907	181.4	2303	2635.0	268.770	506.068
1955	1963	185.5	2453	2971.0	288.676	539.505
1956	1954	191.0	2560	3268.8	300.908	558.630
1957	2148	207.8	2678	3460.0	323.872	603.213
1958	2187	215.6	2769	3558.0	332.791	619.231
1960 Plan				5200.0		

B. *Indices, West and East Germany*

| | West Germany, 1950 prices 1936 = 100 | East Germany | |
Year		1936 Prices 1936 = 100	1950 Prices 1936 = 100
	(7)	(8)	(9)
1936	100.0	100.00	100.00
1950	100.3	61.23	55.14
1951	114.1	72.84	66.09
1952	122.8	79.91	71.82
1953	136.7	89.97	79.73
1954	147.6	94.92	83.09
1955	168.0	101.95	88.58
1956	177.0	106.27	91.72
1957	177.0	114.38	99.04
1958	180.0	117.53	101.67

Sources: Cols. 1 and 2: For 1936 and 1950–1955, see *SJDDR*, 1955, p. 162; for 1956 to 1958, *ibid.*, 1958, p. 346. (For 1936, Gleitze, in *Ostdeutsche Wirtschaft*, p. 202, gives 2,622 million *Hintermauerungsziegel* [bricks for main walls of second quality, i.e., not a face brick]; for 1938, 2,557 million; for 1943, 604 million.) In the 1957 edition of *SJDDR* (p. 280) the series for roofing tiles was changed to a new unit. It is assumed that the increase in roofing tiles in the old units was equal to that of the new units. Thus 1957 is 112 per cent of 1955, and 1958 is 116.25 per cent. Col. 3: For 1936 and 1950–1955, see *SJDDR*, 1955, p. 162; for 1956 to 1957, *ibid.*, 1958 ed., p. 346 (Gleitze, *op. cit.*, p. 202, as the sales of the same product in 1936 gives 994,000 tons, of which 283,000 tons were for building purposes.) Col. 4: For 1936 and 1950–1955, see *SJDDR*, 1955, pp. 162–163; for 1956 to 1958, *ibid.*, 1958, p. 346, for 1960 Plan, *Protokoll der dritten Parteikonferenz*, East Berlin, Dietz, 1956, Vol. II, p. 1032. Cols. 5, 6, 8, and 9: For 1936 value added and method of calculation, see text and Supplement Table A.53. Col. 7: *SJBR*, 1959, p. 181, average daily production.

tion of brick and tile was still substantially short of 1936. The failure to increase production reflects not only the lag in construction but also a real shortage of building materials and, in part, the fact that in 1936 brick production was more than proportionately represented in East Germany.

The ratio of value added to value of sales varies greatly for the three groups (81.37 per cent for brick and tile, 57.50 per cent for cement, and 70.0 per cent for burnt lime). The index of value added was, therefore, calculated separately for each group.

The figures and calculations are presented in Table 61. By 1955 the industry had barely reached the 1936 level. Measured in 1936 prices, the value added in 1955 was only 2 per cent higher than in 1936; measured in 1950 prices it was less than 90 per cent of 1936. Compared with this stagnation, in 1955 the index of the building materials industry for the Federal Republic stood at 167 or 168 per cent of 1936, depending on whether it was measured by average monthly or average daily production.

The calculated index of value added increases to 166.5 per cent between 1950 and 1955 when measured in 1936 prices and to 160.6 per cent when measured in 1950 prices, compared with the official gross production value of 117.5 per cent. This indicates that our calculation is at least consistent with the facts known to East German authorities, and our results cannot be far different from the actual situation. Furthermore, although the percentage changes in East Germany and in the Federal Republic between 1950 and 1955 are of the same order of magnitude, it should be observed that in 1950 the output of the industry had reached the 1936 level in West Germany while it was still about 40 to 45 per cent below that level in East Germany. Neither the same rate of growth since 1950 nor the greater population increase in West Germany modify the meaning of these developments.

WOOD PRODUCTS

Although in West German and prewar German practice, sawmill and woodworking products are treated separately — the former belonging to production goods industries and the latter to consumer goods industries — the Statistical Yearbook of the German Democratic Republic treats both as one industry group and includes both among light industries.

Sawmill products, veneers, and wood impregnation

The area of East Germany is not heavily endowed with forests. Of the total value of sales of sawmill products in Germany in 1936, 24.4 per cent is attributable to the Soviet Zone and 25.2 per cent to East Germany, if East Berlin is included; the area east of the Oder-Neisse line accounted for 15.8 per cent. The area of East Germany produced gross sales of RM 194.810 million. Of the three subgroups making up this industry by far the most important is sawmill products, with veneer production and wood impregnation being a poor second and negligible third. In 1936 there were also imports of wood into the area, amounting, in physical terms, to about 20 per cent of domestic production, even though there was already substantial overcutting in 1936.

The information relating to this industry group consists of a series in cubic meters for sawed timber, railroad ties, and similar products. Only the information relating to these products can be linked to 1936. The postwar series on veneers and pressed wood (also in cubic meters) cannot be traced back to prewar years.

According to official claims, the output of sawmills in 1950 and 1951 was about one-fifth above 1936, but by 1955 it had fallen to the prewar level. The figures are found in Table 62. The decline between 1950–1951

Table 62

Production and value added of sawmill industry, East Germany, and indices, East and West Germany, 1936 and 1950–1958

| | East Germany | | | | West Germany, index sawmills and woodworking | |
| | | Value added | | | | |
Year	Wood sawed (thousand cu m)	1936 Prices (million RM)	1950 Prices (million DM)	Index 1936 = 100	Old	New
	(1)	(2)	(3)	(4)	(5)	(6)
1936	3210.0	79.74	156.29	100.00	100.0	100.0
1950	3924.0	97.72	191.53	122.55	105.6	101.0
1951	3979.0	98.85	193.74	123.96	113.4	121.0
1952	3430.3	85.21	167.01	106.86	100.7	109.0
1953	3489.0	86.67	169.87	108.69	98.2	105.0
1954	3446.3	85.61	167.79	107.36	108.8	115.0
1955	3270.3	81.24	159.23	101.88	n.a.	126.0
1956	3154.3	78.35	153.57	98.26	n.a.	133.0
1957	3049.0	75.74	148.44	94.98	n.a.	126.0
1958	3065.0	76.11	149.18	95.45	n.a.	120.0

Sources: Col. 1: For 1936, see Gleitze, *Ostdeutsche Wirtschaft*, p. 202; includes small amounts of plywood. (*SJDDR*, 1957, p. 304, gives 3,461,400 cu m for 1936.) For later years, see *Schnittholz und Schwellen* in *SJDDR*, 1955, pp. 166–167, and 1958, p. 354. Cols. 2 and 3: Value added for 1936 derived as follows: Sales of sawmill industry in East Germany were 25.21 per cent of all German sales (Gleitze, *op. cit.*, p. 181), which yields a sales value of RM 194.810 million. The value added of sawmills was 40.93 per cent of sales, or RM 79.74 million (*Produktionsstatistik, 1936*, p. 49). The value added in 1950 prices was derived by applying the price index of sawmills (*Schnittholz*) to the 1936 value added in 1936 prices (*SJBR*, 1955, p. 440). The index in 1950 was 196 per cent of 1938, which is assumed to have been equal to 1936. Col. 4: Derived from col. 1. Col. 5: See *SJBR*, 1955, p. 229. Col. 6: *SJBR*, 1959, p. 182, average daily production.

and 1955 suggests that before 1950 some of the timber had been used for firewood, so that the decline in output might indicate a favorable development.

Woodworking products

In 1936 the woodworking industries in Germany had a value added of RM 720.830 million.[4] By far the largest subgroup of this classification was the furniture and building parts (doors and window frames, for example) industry, which accounted for RM 385.860 million, or 53.5 per cent. Next in importance was the wood products (for example, kitchen spoons) industry, which had a net production of RM 106.867 million, or 14.8 per cent. Other parts of the industry produced plywood, brushes, boxes and barrels, caned chairs and baskets, and so on, but no one subindustry amounted to more than 7.5 per cent. In all subindustries, except plywood, barrels, cane furniture and baskets, and preparation of bristles and hairs, the area of East Germany was well represented.

The value of total sales of the whole industry in East Germany (including East Berlin) was RM 361.195 million, or 28.3 per cent that for all Germany.[5] Of this total, RM 203.999 million, or 56.5 per cent, were attributable to furniture, building parts, and a small number of musical instruments.

The only usable information relating to this sector refers to furniture. Official figures in East marks* are available which can be linked with the prewar figures. Since no reference is made to *Messwerte,* it is likely that the figures refer to actual East marks, but whether they are given in constant 1950 prices, current prices, or whatever else is not stated. If the prices are producer prices, or possibly *Messwerte,* they can be deflated and made comparable with the 1936 figure by the following roundabout method.

First, it is known that producer prices of furniture were more or less constant after 1950, and that retail prices fell substantially during the years after 1950.† [6] Second, however, it is known that the *Messwerte* lie 20 per cent and 30 per cent below the producer prices, as shown in Table 63.

Third, for May 1950, the Deutsches Institut für Wirtschaftsforschung compares the East and the West German retail prices in East and West Berlin of two comparable kitchen sets. In East Berlin the price was DM–O 980 and in West Berlin it was DM 220.[7] If it is assumed that the producer price of the East German set was DM–O 391.40 and if a combined retail and wholesale markup of 35 per cent is deducted from the West German price, this would give an East-West price relation of 273.71 per cent. If the official figure is given in terms of 1950 prices, the figure of 273.71 per

---

* See note on currency, p. 55.

† "For the majority of goods, the HAP [*Hersteller Abgabepreis,* producer price] has remained essentially constant since 1950. The HOP [*HO-Preis,* Government store price], on the other hand, shows a constantly falling tendency since 1948" (Thimm, *Preis und Kostenstruktur,* p. 329).

Table 63

Producer prices and *Messwerte* for furniture, East Germany, 1950

Classification (1)		Producer price (HAP)[a] (DM–O) (2)	Messwerte (3)	Messwerte as percentage of HAP[a] (4)
54 31 10 00	Bedroom, veneer	1042.00	820	78.69
54 31 15 00	Bedroom, without veneer	n.a.	365	
54 31 20 00	Living room, veneer	796.00	640	80.40
54 31 25 00	Living room, without veneer	n.a.	275	
54 31 30 00	Study, veneer	796.00	910	114.32
54 31 35 00	Study, without veneer	n.a.	545	
54 31 40 00	Dining room, veneer	796.00	590	74.12
54 31 45 00	Dining room, without veneer	n.a.	365	
54 31 50 00	Kitchen-dinette, veneer	n.a.	410	
54 31 55 00	Kitchen-dinette, without veneer	n.a.	255	
54 31 60 00	Kitchen	391.40	285	72.81

Source: Data given the author.
   [a] HAP = *Hersteller Abgabepreis*, producer price.

cent could be used to deflate the East mark figure to the comparable West German 1950 price level, which in turn is known to have been 170 per cent that of 1938.[8] (Prices were roughly constant after 1936.) Thus, by a double deflation, the East mark figures for 1950 through 1955 could be adjusted to a mark value that is comparable with the 1936 value given by Gleitze.[9] Among the many assumptions employed in this procedure is the assumption that the same ratio of East and West German prices holds for all types of furniture. Although this is not true, any error is apt to overestimate rather than underestimate the East German output of furniture, since other types of furniture are more complicated and contain more of the scarcer materials (for example, metals and textiles) than the simple kitchen sets.

However, if the official figure is in terms of *Messwerte* (which is possible), the deflation by 273.71 per cent would understate the output of furniture by about 25 per cent. In the few known figures given in Table 63, *Messwerte* are on the average about 25 per cent below producer prices, which would indicate that a deflation by 205.28 per cent would reduce the official figures to comparable West German prices of 1950. The deflation to 1936 prices was made as for other industries.

The 1936 figure given by Gleitze includes doors, windows, and other building parts made of wood. Although he gives no further breakdowns, and no such breakdown is included in the Production Statistics of 1936, the Statistical Yearbook of the Federal Republic indicates that in West Germany in the period from 1951 through 1954 furniture comprised about 82 per cent of the value of the whole woodworking industry — 82.89 per cent in 1951, 82.81 per cent in 1952, 83.35 per cent in 1953, and 83.22 per cent in 1954. Undoubtedly, people bought more furniture after the war, but there was also more construction. Thus the proportion of furniture in the total may have been constant, and it may be reasonable to estimate furniture output before the war by reducing the figure given by Gleitze by 18 per cent.

In the absence of any other information, it is assumed that the development of the whole woodworking industry parallels that of furniture. Since furniture, together with building parts, accounts for 56 per cent of the value of all sales in 1936 in the area of East Germany, and, since even an allowance for building parts would reduce the share only about 10 percentage points, the representation is not bad. Furthermore, since the output of other items such as boxes and brushes is not likely to have been pushed by the planning authorities, this assumption is likely, if anything, to overstate the growth of this sector. Thus the value added of the woodworking industry was estimated by the following procedure: First, the official mark figures were deflated to constant 1936 and 1950 prices, respectively, as indicated. Next, an index was constructed for furniture output alone. Finally, this index was applied to the estimated value added for the woodworking industries in 1936.

The value added of furniture and building parts for 1936 in the area of East Germany was estimated as follows. Gleitze gives as the value of total sales RM 203.999 million. Allowing 18 per cent for building parts and the small number of pianos, organs, and so on, included by Gleitze, yields and adjusted sales value for furniture alone of RM 167.279 million. The ratio of value added to sales value in 1936 was 56.712 per cent. This gives an estimated value added for furniture in 1936 in 1936 prices of RM 94.867 million. To obtain the value added in 1950 prices, this value was multiplied by 170 per cent, giving a value of RM 161.274 million. The 1936 sales value in 1950 prices was found in a similar manner. The index to be applied to the whole woodworking sector was then applied to these figures.

The value added of the woodworking industries as a whole for 1936 in 1936 prices was estimated by applying the ratios of value added to values of sales for each subgroup, as given in the Production Statistics of 1936 to the corresponding values of sales given by Gleitze (see Table 64). The 1936 value added in 1950 prices was arrived at by applying the price index for the woodworking industry as a whole, which was 178 per cent of 1938. The values added thus derived are RM 204.086 million and DM 363.273 million, respectively.

The calculations under alternative assumptions are presented in Table 65. Even on the assumption that the index and the absolute mark value of furniture production were given in *Messwerte,* the industry was about 1 per cent below the 1936 level; if the absolute mark value of furniture production was given in 1950 prices, there was a fall of about 25 per cent

Table 64

Value added, woodworking industry, East Germany, 1936
(1936 prices)

Commodity	Sales value (million RM)	Value added as per cent of sales value	Value added (million RM)
	(1)	(2)	(3)
Plywood	4.303	49.560	2.133
Furniture and building parts[a]	203.999	56.712	115.692
Wooden products, sawdust	62.669	61.110	38.297
Barrels	3.691	53.630	1.979
Boxes, etc.	27.966	46.010	12.867
Baskets, etc.	1.942	70.300	1.365
Straw weaving, etc.	1.289	50.420	0.650
Bristles, etc.	1.362	40.300	0.549
Brushes	10.690	52.770	9.863
Others	35.284	58.640	20.691
Total	361.195		204.086

Sources: Col. 1, see Gleitze, *Ostdeutsche Wirtschaft*, p. 183; col. 2, see *Produktionsstatistik, 1936*, p. 49; col. 3 = col. 1 × col. 2.

   [a] Includes pianos, organs, and harmoniums.

between 1936 and 1955. This compares with an increase to 168 per cent of the 1936 level [10] in the Federal Republic for woodworking proper, and to 140.5 per cent for toys and musical instruments. This poor showing is startling but, on reflection, quite plausible. Except for plywood and

Table 65

Value added, furniture and woodworking industries, East Germany, and indices, West and East Germany, 1936 and 1950–1958

A. *Value added, East Germany*
1. On assumption that official figures are in *Messwerte*

Year	Production, furniture only			Value added, furniture only		Value added, total woodworking	
	(million RM/DM–O)	1936 Prices (million RM)	1950 Prices (million DM)	1936 Prices (million RM)	1950 Prices (million DM)	1936 Prices (million RM)	1950 Prices (million DM)
	(1)	(2)	(3)	(4)	(5)	(6)	(7)
1936	167.279	167.279	284.374	94.867	161.274	204.086	363.273
1950	258.600	74.102	125.974	42.025	71.442	90.410	160.930
1951	316.100	90.580	153.985	51.370	87.328	110.513	196.712
1952	390.300	111.945	190.307	63.486	107.927	136.574	243.102
1953	448.800	128.605	218.628	72.934	123.988	156.901	279.284
1954	523.600	150.040	255.067	85.091	144.654	183.065	325.856
1955	577.500	165.484	281.323	93.849	159.544	201.902	359.386
1956	612.150	175.413	298.202	99.459	169.081	213.964	380.855
1957	658.350	188.694	320.708	106.989	181.841	230.168	409.699
1958	747.094	209.172	355.592	118.625	201.664	255.204	454.264
1960 Plan	810.000						

Table 65 (Continued)

2. On assumption that official figures are in current prices

	Production, furniture only		Value added, furniture only		Value added, total woodworking	
Year	1936 Prices (million RM)	1950 Prices (million DM)	1936 Prices (million RM)	1950 Prices (million DM)	1936 Prices (million RM)	1950 Prices (million DM)
	(8)	(9)	(10)	(11)	(12)	(13)
1936	167.279	284.374	94.867	161.274	204.086	363.273
1950	55.577	94.480	31.519	53.581	67.797	120.679
1951	67.934	115.487	38.527	65.495	82.880	147.525
1952	83.880	142.596	47.570	80.869	102.330	182.145
1953	96.452	163.969	54.699	92.990	117.680	209.463
1954	112.528	191.298	63.817	108.489	137.290	244.374
1955	124.112	210.990	70.386	119.647	151.410	269.512
1956	131.645	223.797	74.659	126.920	160.620	285.896
1957	n.a.	n.a.	n.a.	n.a.	172.616	307.256
1958	n.a.	n.a.	n.a.	n.a.	191.382	340.663

B. *Indices, West and East Germany*

	West Germany				East Germany	
Year	Woodworking 1936 = 100	Musical instruments and toys 1936 = 100	Woodworking, musical instruments and toys combined 1936 = 100	Assumption 1, total woodworking 1936 or 1950 prices 1936 = 100	Assumption 2, total woodworking 1936 or 1950 prices 1936 = 100	
	(14)	(15)	(16)	(17)	(18)	
1936	100.0	100.0	100.0	100.00	100.00	
1950	111.1	55.9	101.8	44.30	33.22	
1951	129.3	75.5	120.3	54.15	40.61	
1952	120.6	80.2	113.8	66.92	50.14	
1953	138.3	99.6	131.7	76.88	57.66	
1954	156.9	123.5	151.3	89.70	67.27	
1955	168.0	140.5	163.4	98.93	74.19	
1956	187.0	n.a.		104.84	78.70	
1957	196.0	n.a.		112.78	84.58	
1958	204.0	n.a.		125.05	93.78	

Sources: Col. 1: For 1936, see Gleitze, *Ostdeutsche Wirtschaft*, p. 183. Estimate for furniture alone is 82 per cent of Gleitze's figure (see text). For 1950–1955, see *SJDDR*, 1955, pp. 166–167; 1956 to 1958 are calculated from an index, *ibid.*, 1958, p. 373 which gives for 1956, 106 per cent, for 1957, 114 per cent, and for 1958, 126.4 per cent of 1955; for 1960 Plan, see *Protokoll der dritten Parteikonferenz*, East Berlin, Dietz, 1956, Vol. II, p. 1032. Cols. 2 and 3: For deflation procedure, see text. Cols. 4 and 5: Ratio of value added to sales value in 1936: 56.7 per cent. *Produktionsstatistik, 1936*, p. 43. Col. 6: See Table 64 for 1936 estimate. For other years, index in col. 17 has been applied. Col. 7: Price index, woodworking industry as a whole, 1950: 178 per cent of 1938, assumed to be the same as 1936. *SJBR*, 1955, p. 440. Cols. 8 and 9: The deflation to 1936 prices proceeded in two steps: (1) Divide by 273.71 to arrive at West German 1950 prices (col. 9). (2) Divide again by 170 to arrive at 1936 prices (col. 8). Cols. 10 and 11: See cols. 4 and 5. Col. 12: For 1936, see col. 6; for 1950–1955, index, col. 18, has been applied. For sources see col. 1. Col. 13: See cols. 6, 7, and 12. Cols. 14 and 15: For 1936, 1950–1955, see *Neuberechnung*, p. 73; for 1956, 1957, *SJBR*, 1959, p. 182. Col. 16: Combined in ratio 2.04 for woodworking and 0.41 for toys and musical instruments, as given in *Neuberechnung*, p. 73. Col. 17: Derived from cols. 4 and 5. Col. 18: Derived from cols. 10 and 11.

furniture, industries grouped under woodworking are of minor importance in the eyes of the planner. Production of pianos, organs, kitchen utensils (an industry concentrated rather heavily in the Soviet Zone), brushes, caned chairs, and so on, is not likely to receive much official encouragement.

The increase in the gross production of woodworking, valued in

Messwerte, between 1950 and 1955 was 158.4 per cent.[11] The increase in the calculated index of woodworking alone between these years is 223.3 per cent. However, the East German index of woodworking includes sawmills, which did not increase their output between 1936 and 1950. When we calculate a combined index of sawmills and woodworking, one that is to be comparable in coverage with the East German "gross production" index, we find that the East German index rises faster than the index calculated by Western methods, as it should (see Table 66).

Table 66

Indices, gross production and value added, sawmills and woodworking combined, East Germany, and value added, West Germany, 1950–1955

	East Germany			
		Calculated index		West Germany official index 1950 = 100
Year	Official index 1950 = 100	1936 Prices 1950 = 100	1950 Prices 1950 = 100	
	(1)	(2)	(3)	(4)
1950	100.0	100.0	100.0	100.0
1951	114.4	111.3	110.8	114.8
1952	123.2	117.9	116.4	106.8
1953	135.0	129.5	127.4	115.8
1954	148.3	142.8	140.1	131.1
1955	158.4	150.5	147.1	142.3

Sources: Col. 1: *Holzbearbeitung und Holzverarbeitung.* See *SJDDR*, 1956, p. 129. Col. 2: Value added in 1936 prices only. Calculated from Supplement Tables A.54 and A.55. Col. 3: Value added in 1950 prices. Calculated from *ibid.* Col. 4: Calculated by combining indices of sawmills, woodworking, and musical instruments in ratio 1.51:2.04:0.41. See *Neuberechnung*, pp. 41, 43.

The evidence suggests that using furniture as an indicator of what happened to the entire woodworking sector cannot involve any substantial errors. Production figures are available for some other subgroups, which, however, could not be linked to 1936.* Neither the percentage increases nor the absolute amounts involved suggest that major corrections are required. (The figures in the Statistical Yearbook of the German Democratic Republic are, except for pianos and accordions, and so on, in East marks. The value of musical instruments [gross production in *Messwerte*] is about one-sixth that of furniture, that of toys about one-fourth, that of brooms and brushes about one-eighth. All figures refer to 1955.[12])

There is also some indication that the production of plywood increased after 1936, when it was heavily concentrated in West Germany. An estimate for the value added of the East German share of the plywood

* The value of their output increased between 1950 and 1955 as follows: musical instruments, to 254 per cent of 1950; toys, to 181 per cent; and brooms and brushes, to 381 per cent.

industry in 1936 is RM 1.968 million,[13] with an estimated production of 13,537 cubic meters. The plan for 1954 was 27,500 cubic meters.[14] Even if this goal was reached, the doubling of plywood production would hardly make a dent in the value added of the industry as a whole.

PULP, PAPER, AND PRINTING

In the Production Statistics of 1936, pulp and paper are listed separately. In the West German statistics, pulp is counted among producer goods, while industries using paper as a raw material, as well as printing, are listed among consumer goods. In East German statistics all categories are included in the light-industry group.

Pulp and paper

Of the total value added in 1936 of the pulp and paper industry in Germany as a whole, almost exactly three-quarters was produced by the first subindustry listed, the paper and cardboard industry; the rest was produced in the earlier stages of production. The total gross production value of paper and cardboard for all of Germany in 1936 was RM 819.204 million, of which 37.5 per cent or RM 307.202 million (measured by sales value) was in the area of East Germany.[15] In 1936, the value added was 38.4 per cent of gross production value, which gives as a basic value added for paper and cardboard RM 118.211 million.

The cellulose (*Zellstoff*) industry, the second subindustry, which accounted for another quarter of the total value added in 1936, had a total gross production value for all Germany of RM 249.307 million. No regional breakdown appears feasible for the third subgroup, pulping (*Holzschleifereien*), which had a gross production value for all of Germany of RM 87.875 million. Within the area of East Germany, the combined share of these two groups was 29.2 per cent. The ratio of value added to gross production value of the two subgroups is substantially different. Even if it is assumed that East Germany's share of both was 29.2 per cent, it appears preferable to calculate separately the value added for cellulose and for pulpwood.

The gross production value of cellulose attributable to East Germany can thus be estimated as RM 72.598 million, and that of pulpwood as RM 25.660 million. With a ratio of value added to value of gross production of 46.10 per cent and 35.71 per cent, respectively, we arrive at estimated values added for 1936 of RM 33.468 million and RM 9.163 million. The East German total value added of the pulp and paper industry as a whole can thus be estimated as RM 160.842 million.

For the interpretation of the later developments it should be noted that in 1936 the area east of the Oder-Neisse produced 30.4 per cent of the cellulose but only 15.5 per cent of the paper and cardboard. This suggests both that the area of East Germany imported cellulose and exported paper and that expansion of cellulose output and contraction of papermaking are consistent and to be expected.

All production figures are from official East German sources. Since the official East German figures for cellulose were insufficient for calculating an index of production, it was assumed that the combined output of pulp

Table 67

Production and value added, cellulose, paper, and cardboard, East Germany, and indices, West and East Germany, 1936 and 1950–1958[a]

A. Production and value added, East Germany

Year	Cellulose (thousand tons)	Paper and cardboard (thousand tons)	Value added, cellulose		Value added, paper and cardboard		Value added, cellulose, paper and cardboard combined	
			1936 Prices (million RM)	1950 Prices (million DM)	1936 Prices (million RM)	1950 Prices (million DM)	1936 Prices (million RM)	1950 Prices (million DM)
	(1)	(2)	(3)	(4)	(5)	(6)	(7)	(8)
1936	205.4	1195.0	42.631	103.593	118.211	291.981	160.842	395.574
1950	226.1	491.7	46.928	114.035	48.643	120.150	95.571	234.185
1951	258.7	549.0	53.694	130.475	54.306	134.136	108.005	264.611
1952	273.3	583.9	56.725	137.841	57.758	142.662	114.483	280.503
1953	289.1	591.5	60.003	145.807	58.514	144.531	118.517	290.338
1954	302.2	607.6	62.744	152.468	60.110	148.472	122.854	300.940
1955	303.0	647.1	62.889	152.820	64.011	158.108	126.900	310.928
1956	313.0	671.1	65.004	157.959	66.387	163.977	131.392	321.936
1957	315.1	705.0	65.400	158.922	69.744	172.269	135.144	331.191
1958	325.0	733.5	67.450	163.905	72.558	179.218	140.008	343.123

B. Indices, West and East Germany

Year	West Germany		East Germany			
			Cellulose 1936 = 100	Paper and cardboard 1936 = 100	Cellulose, paper and cardboard combined	
	Old	New			1936 Prices 1936 = 100	1950 Prices 1936 = 100
	(9)	(10)	(11)	(12)	(13)	(14)
1936	100.0	100	100.00	100.00	100.00	100.00
1950	97.3	95	110.08	41.15	59.42	59.20
1951	111.9	109	125.95	45.94	67.15	66.89
1952	103.8	100	133.06	48.86	71.18	70.91
1953	120.3	116	140.75	49.50	73.69	73.40
1954	139.9	135	147.18	50.85	76.38	76.08
1955	151.0	146	147.52	54.15	78.90	78.60
1956	n.a.	154	152.48	56.16	81.69	81.38
1957	n.a.	163	153.41	59.00	84.02	83.72
1958	n.a.	165	158.22	61.38	87.05	86.74

Sources: Col. 1: For 1936 and 1950–1955, see *SJDDR*, 1955, pp. 166–167; for 1956 to 1958, *ibid.*, 1958, p. 356. Col. 2: For 1936, see Gleitze, *Ostdeutsche Wirtschaft*, p. 207; for 1950–1955, *SJDDR*, 1955, pp. 166–167; and for 1956–1958, *ibid.*, 1958, p. 356. Cols. 3–6: For 1936 value added see text; for 1950–1957, indices in cols. 11 and 12 have been applied. The 1936 value added in 1950 prices was derived by multiplying the 1936 value added by the price index of cellulose, 243 per cent of 1938 (*SJBR*, 1955, p. 446), and of paper and cardboard, 247 per cent of 1938 (*ibid.*, p. 440). Col. 7: Col. 3 + col. 5. Col. 8: Col. 4 + col. 6. Col. 9: *SJBR*, 1955, p. 229. Col. 10: *SJBR*, 1959, p. 182, average daily production. Col. 11: Calculated from col. 1. Col. 12: Calculated from col. 2. Col. 13: Calculated from col. 7. Col. 14: Calculated from col. 8.

[a] For detailed calculations, see Supplement Table A.56.

and cellulose moves parallel to the cellulose series. This procedure implies that the ratio of pulp and cellulose production remained constant, which is almost certainly not the case.

The estimating procedure consisted of calculating one index for cellulose and another for paper and cardboard. The former was applied to the 1936 value added for both cellulose and pulping, the latter was applied to the figure for value added of paper and cardboard. The sum of the two values added thus derived completely covers the whole industry. The evaluation in 1950 prices consisted of applying the proper West German price indices as indicated in Table 67.

By 1955 the value of output of paper of all kinds had declined to 51.5 per cent of 1936 and that of cardboard to only 69.4 per cent. Compared with this development, the value of West German output of pulp and paper had expanded by 1955 to 151 per cent of 1936 according to the old index and to 144.3 per cent of 1936 according to the new index.

Printing and paper products

In 1936 about 65 per cent of the printing and paper products industries was accounted for by the printing industry, which was heavily concentrated in the area of East Germany, Leipzig being the German book-publishing center. The second most important subgroup, the industries using cardboard as an input, accounted for another 16 per cent, and the production of paper goods for 10.3 per cent. All the paper products industries, except for the manufacture of wallpaper, were well represented in the area of East Germany (see Table 68).

Table 68

Value added, paper and printing, East Germany, 1936

Industry	Value added all Germany 1936 prices (million RM)	Per cent attribut- able to East Germany	Value added attributable to East Germany	
			1936 Prices (million RM)	1950 Prices (million DM)
	(1)	(2)	(3)	(4)
Paper finishing	44.866	38.87	17.439	33.832
Printing and plano-graphic reproduction	666.411	31.19	207.854	351.273
Bookbinding	55.064	30.39	16.734	32.464
Paper products	117.394	25.90	30.405	58.986
Cardboard products industry	102.438	46.15	47.275	91.714
Wallpaper industry	15.308	10.50	1.607	3.118
Total	1,101.476		321.314	571.387

Sources: Col. 1: *Produktionsstatistik, 1936*, pp. 51–52. Col. 2: Calculated from Gleitze, *Ostdeutsche Wirtschaft*, p. 179. Col. 3: Col. 1 × col. 2. Col. 4: See text.

Table 69

Production and value added, paper and printing, East Germany, and indices,
West and East Germany, 1936 and 1950–1958

A. Production and value added

	Production (thousand tons)			Value added of paper and printing industries	
Year	Paper (including printing and writing papers)	Printing and writing papers only	Cardboard	1936 Prices (million RM)	1950 Prices (million DM)
	(1)	(2)	(3)	(4)	(5)
1936	918.0	767.00	330.2	321.314	571.387
1950	320.8	170.15	170.9	88.875	161.702
1951	369.5	196.00	179.5	99.253	190.044
1952	378.2	235.00	196.7	115.673	209.299
1953	388.8	248.00	202.7	119.240	219.127
1954	391.4	306.00	216.2	143.435	258.210
1955	417.8	326.64	229.3	152.849	275.180
1956	438.7	342.98	232.4	158.954	282.665
1957	465.3	363.77	239.7	167.340	300.720
1958	487.3	n.a.	246.2	174.409	313.234

B. Indices, West and East Germany

	West Germany, new index		East Germany			
			Printing and	Cardboard	Printing and cardboard products industries combined	
Year	Paper-using industry 1936 = 100	Printing and reproduction 1936 = 100	planographic reproduction industry 1936 = 100	products industry 1936 = 100	1936 Prices 1936 = 100	1950 Prices 1936 = 100
	(6)	(7)	(8)	(9)	(10)	(11)
1936	100.0	100.0	100.00	100.00	100.00	100.00
1950	100.9	111.4	22.18	51.76	27.66	28.30
1951	107.2	116.6	25.55	54.36	30.89	31.51
1952	114.2	124.9	30.64	59.57	36.00	36.63
1953	129.2	147.1	32.33	61.39	37.71	38.35
1954	144.3	161.8	39.90	65.47	44.64	45.19
1955	159.4	173.3	42.60	69.44	47.57	48.16
1956	179.0	186.0	44.72	70.38	49.47	50.03
1957	191.0	202.0	47.42	72.59	52.08	52.63
1958	192.0	221.0	49.67	74.56	54.28	54.82

Sources: Col. 1: For 1936, see Gleitze, *Ostdeutsche Wirtschaft*, p. 207; for 1950–1955, *SJDDR*, 1955, p. 166; for 1956–1958, *ibid.*, 1958, p. 356. Col. 2: For derivation see Supplement Table A.56a. Col. 3: For 1936, see Gleitze, *op. cit.*, p. 206; for 1950–1957, same sources as col. 1. Col. 4: For 1936 value added in 1936 prices, see Table 68; for other years the index in col. 10 was applied. Col. 5: For 1936 value added in 1950 prices, see text; for other years the index in col. 11 was applied. Col. 6: *Neuberechnung*, p. 73, average monthly production; *SJBR*, 1958, p. 183, average daily production. Col. 7: Ibid., p. 79. Col. 8: Derived from col. 2. Col. 9: Derived from col. 3. Cols. 10 and 11: For method of calculation see text. For details, see Supplement Table A.56a.

Postwar data in tons are available for such items as paper bags, wall-paper, and corrugated cardboard, but none of these series could be linked to prewar data. Furthermore, neither employment data nor the number of titles published seemed adequate for constructing an index which could be applied to the 1936 value added as a base for printing.

The procedure adopted was to assume that the value of printing and planographic reproduction moved parallel to the available amount of paper. The availability of cardboard was, reasonably, assumed to indicate how the cardboard products industry had developed.

Total paper production is given in the Statistical Yearbook of the German Democratic Republic. However, since the 1936 figure appears too low, the Gleitze figure was adopted. The amount of writing and printing papers is given in the various sources listed in Table 69. When no official figure was available, an estimate was interpolated by assuming that the percentage of writing and printing papers, as well as of newsprint, was the same as in the nearest year for which data are available — a hazardous but unavoidable procedure. From the series thus derived, an index was constructed which was then applied to the value added of printing and planographic reproduction. The value added in 1950 prices was estimated by multiplying the 1936 value added by 169 per cent, the producer price index for printing (base year, 1938; see Table 69).[16]

A similar procedure was used to estimate the output of the cardboard products industry except that it was assumed that in 1948 and 1949 the increase in cardboard output was parallel to that of paper output. All other data are officially given. The 1936 value added in 1950 prices was estimated by multiplying the 1936 value added in 1936 prices given in Table 68 by 194 per cent, the producer price index of paper products (base year, 1938).[17]

The value added of the whole printing and paper products industry was found by first constructing an index of the two major industries and then applying this to the value added in 1936. The value added in 1950 prices was estimated by multiplying the value added of the printing part by 169 per cent and the rest of the industry by 194 per cent.

While paper production as a whole had declined to 45.5 per cent of its 1936 level by 1955,* the amount of paper available for printing had fallen to 42.6 per cent. In spite of the great amount of paper work in a planned economy, these percentages are reasonable, since exports of books clearly diminished radically and paper is scarce. Cardboard output fell to only 69.5 per cent of its 1936 level, and the industry as a whole probably reached a level only 47 per cent or 48 per cent of the 1936 level.

By contrast with this rather dismal development, by 1955 the paper products industries (excluding printing) in the Federal Republic had increased to 159.4 per cent of their 1936 level, and printing and plano-

* Or to "only" 51.5 per cent if the official East German figures are used for 1936.

graphic reproduction had reached a level of 173.1 per cent of 1936, according to *Neuberechnung*.[18]

Since the East German index of gross production rose only 9.2 per cent between 1950 and 1955, it is likely that the output, at least of the printing and planographic reproduction industry, is still seriously overestimated. The value added of the industries discussed in this section is of unusual uncertainty even by the generous standards one must in any case apply to communist statistics.

CHAPTER XI

TEXTILES, CLOTHING, LEATHER, AND SHOES

TEXTILES (EXCLUSIVE OF RAYON AND OTHER SYNTHETIC YARNS)

BEFORE the war textiles were the most important single industry in the area now the Soviet Zone. Moreover, textile production was largely concentrated in East Germany. In Germany as a whole, as well as in East Germany in particular, the following four major subgroups had sales values of more than RM 100 million: spinning (both cotton and wool), weaving (cotton and wool), knitting (hosiery and knitwear), and finishing (*Textilveredelungsindustrie*). In 1936 the first three amounted to 86.12 per cent of the value of the German textile industry (exclusive of synthetic yarns) and to 83.96 per cent of East German textiles.

The other industries were smaller, and at least some of them, such as flax spinning, hemp spinning, silk weaving, and horsehair spinning, have almost certainly become insignificant since the war. Even lacemaking and embroidery, which were heavily concentrated in East Germany, are only minor industries.

The three following major groups are well represented by official data: all yarns (except synthetic yarns); wool and cotton cloth of all kinds (but without bagging materials, duck, and so on), hosiery and knit underwear (*Trikotagen*).

Yarn

For yarn we have an official series in tons going back to 1936.[1] The East German figure for total yarn production in 1936 is actually slightly higher than the Gleitze figure (213,000 tons and 210,000 tons, respectively). The difference may possibly be due to an allowance for East Berlin. An index of yarn production was applied to the value added for 1936 of RM 155.530 million. This value was estimated by finding the ratio of the sales value originating in East Germany to the total German sales value[2] and applying it to the value added for all of Germany. The 1936 value in 1950 prices was found by applying the West German index of *Gespinste* (literally, the spinning output). In tonnage, 1955 production was about 18.5 per cent above 1936, but only barely above 1938.

This is rather surprising, considering the great concentration of spinning in East Germany. One would have expected output to have declined to proportions more in keeping with domestic needs and the loss of the West German market. The expansion strongly suggests that inferior synthetic yarns probably made from rayon were substituted for better ones. To this extent, the calculation based on tonnage overstates the increase in output since it assumed the product mix to be unchanged.

Cloth

Separate series were calculated for cloth made of wool, of cotton, and of rayon and other materials. For the first series, there exists an official index and an absolute figure for 1955 which can be calculated from the *Direktive*. The series for cotton cloth and for rayon cloth are given directly by the Statistical Yearbook of the German Democratic Republic.

For cloth, an initial difficulty arises because some prewar figures are given in tons while postwar figures are given in square meters. For cotton cloth, official East German information on the number of square meters produced is available back to 1936. Gleitze's figures in tons suggest that 5.1417 sq m weighed 1 kilogram, which in turn appears to be slightly more than half the number of square meters of British cotton exports per kilogram. The latter can be calculated as 5 sq yds per pound, or, converted to metric measures, 9.1723 sq m per kg.[3] German cottons were thus much heavier than British cotton exports. Whether the increase in the number of square meters produced conceals a reduction in weight is not clear, but it is likely. For woolen cloth the prewar American average for apparel cloth was taken.[4] A square meter of rayon was assumed to weigh about the same as a square meter of cotton. It is probably somewhat heavier.

A second difficulty arises in finding comparable prewar data. We made separate calculations for cotton, woolens, and silk, rayon, and linen. For cotton products, Gleitze and Statistical Practice give the same tonnage although Gleitze adds that this figure includes cloth made with staple rayon. In 1936, however, staple rayon production was still very small. For woolen cloth, the Gleitze figure is 83,500 tons, substantially below the figure of 106,200 tons given by Statistical Practice.[5] Similarly, the figure for all Germany given by Statistical Practice is substantially above that given by Gleitze for woolen cloth although there is only a slight difference in the total weight of all cloth given by the two sources. This problem is important because of the necessity of allocating the remainder to other fibers.

The discrepancy between the figures given by East and West German sources is clearly one of definition. Gleitze apparently includes among woolens only cloth made entirely or substantially of wool. In East Germany, however, "wool is generally not worked into pure wool-fiber cloth but is used mainly in admixture to improve the quality of staple rayon yarns and cloth." [6] In fact, the percentage of wool in woolen cloth increased from 1950 to 1955 from 5.5 per cent to 19.3 per cent for worsted-spun fabric (*Kammgarngewebe*), and from 26.6 per cent to 44.5 per cent for woolen-spun fabric (*Streichgarngewebe*).[7] Similarly, cotton cloth contains only an admixture of the natural fiber. It seemed best to use the East German figures for woolens and also to include the 2,300 tons produced by "silk" weaving (primarily continuous-filament rayon). The postwar figures are then presumably directly comparable with these three figures: woolen cloth, cotton, and the difference between these two and the total output of "fine" cloth. The Eastern Zone authorities state explicitly that weaves made of rough yarns are excluded; Statistical Practice indicates that most of the remainder was made of bast fiber, which is hard and rough.[8] Gleitze states that the total weight of all cloth produced in the area of East Germany was 162,000 tons, while Statistical Practice gives a figure of only 157,900 tons.[9] (According to the information given by Gleitze, no cloth was produced in East Berlin.) Table 70 compares the figure given by Gleitze with those from Statistical Practice.

Table 70

Production of woven cloth, East Germany, 1936

	All Germany (thousand tons)		Soviet Zone (thousand tons)		Soviet Zone as per cent of all Germany	
	(1)	(2)	(3)	(4)	(5)	(6)
Woolens	139.3	177.2	83.5	106.2	59.9	59.9
Cotton cloth	233.3	233.3	32.0	32.0	13.7	13.7
Bast cloth	...[a]	137.0	...[a]	17.4	...[a]	12.7
"Silk" cloth	...[a]	23.7	...[a]	2.3	...[a]	9.7
Total	571.1	571.1	162.0	157.9		

Sources: Cols. 1 and 3: Figures given by Gleitze, *Ostdeutsche Wirtschaft*, p. 208. Cols. 2 and 4: *Karteiblatt* (unnumbered statistical sheet) and article on "Standort und Struktur der Textilindustrie in der sowjetischen Besatzungszone (Nach dem Stande von 1936)," *SP*, 1947, No. 12.
[a] Not separately shown.

Although before the war almost all rayon seems to have gone into hosiery production, for the postwar years it can be reasonably assumed that the cloth for which we have not yet accounted was made of rayon and various other synthetic fibers. The quantities of rayon are converted from tons to square meters on the assumption that it weighs as much as cotton.[10] The series for cloth other than wool and cotton was compared with the prewar "silk" (natural and artificial) production.[11] The value added of the remaining cloth was RM 107.710 million, which was distributed between cotton cloth and rayon and other cloth in the ratio of the tonnage of cloth produced.*

The value added of woolens in 1936 was found by taking the production in the Eastern Zone as a percentage of total German production in 1936 and applying this percentage (that is, 59.9 per cent) to the value added given in the Production Statistics of 1936. (Suiting is assumed to be mainly wool.) This gives a 1936 value added in 1936 prices for woolens of RM 177.400 million.

The calculations are given in Table 71. The results are not unexpected. Between 1936 and 1955 the production of woolen cloth declined to less than 10 per cent of its former level, and even by 1960 it is planned to be only 18 per cent of its prewar level. This decline in production is the result of three facts: first, the woolen industry was overwhelmingly concentrated in East Germany, exported to the rest of Germany and even abroad, and its production was much above local needs; second, there was and continues to be a severe shortage of wool, which has to be imported; third, there was in Germany as elsewhere a substitution of synthetic for natural fibers, which in East Germany, because of the shortage of imported wool, probably went much further than elsewhere. The substitution also involved fewer of the superior synthetics than elsewhere.

By 1955, production of cotton yardgoods had recovered to about 22 per cent above its prewar level, and by 1957 to about 25 per cent above it. Here, only the second and third reasons given for the decline of woolen production apply. Before the war the concentration of cotton cloth production was not beyond local needs. The production of yardgoods from synthetic fibers more than doubled compared with 1936, but the increase would be much smaller if a later prewar year had been taken as a base, just as the decrease in woolen production[12] would have been relatively smaller, particularly since staple rayon of various types apparently came into its own, about 1936.

It should be noted that the total development indicates an output of the three subgroups combined of RM 193.068 million in 1955, still quite substantially below the RM 284.510 million produced in 1936 (both in 1936 prices). Expressed in 1950 prices, the fall is still more substantial: from DM 1,032.209 million in 1936 to DM 441.875 million in 1955. This is, of course, due to the relative difference in the price variations of wool, cotton, and synthetic fibers.

---

* According to Gleitze, 162,000 tons of cloth were produced, of which 106,200 tons were woolens and 32,000 tons were cotton. This leaves 23,800 tons for all others. Allocating the RM 107.710 million to cotton and rayon in the ratio of 32:23.8 gives a value added of RM 61.172 million for cotton and of RM 45.938 million for rayons.

Hosiery and knitwear

The production of hosiery and knitwear is represented by two series, one of which raises major difficulties. For socks and stockings there is a more or less comparable official East German series of the number of pairs produced in 1936 and from 1950 on. For knitwear and other hosiery, however, the prewar German figures refer only to outer garments and are in marks,[13] and the postwar figures refer to the numbers of outer garments and undergarments produced.

The two major problems which arise have been handled as follows: In 1936 the hosiery and knitwear industry produced goods valued at RM 840 million,[14] of which RM 525.2 million were goods other than stockings and gloves. Of this figure, 42.3 per cent was for outer garments* (for which Gleitze gives a mark figure for East German production), 49.1 per cent was for undergarments, and the rest was for cloth. The 1936 figures for the values of sales of outer and undergarments produced were found by multiplying the Gleitze figure by 49.1/42.3, assuming thereby that the East German production of the various types of garments corresponded to that of the Reich as a whole. Since figures are not available for the production of gloves, we have assumed it to be proportional to the production of knitwear.

Second, the question arises as to how to value the postwar production. This really quite impossible problem was "solved" as follows. The only prewar figures which could be found refer to rayon underwear for women and to pullovers for men. Before the war there was a substantial woolen production, but there can be no doubt that since the war most of the knitwear has been made of rayon and other synthetic fibers. In 1950 the textile industry as a whole worked up only 5,200 tons of pure wool, 22,300 tons of reclaimed wool which includes both reclaimed natural wool and synthetic yarns of woolen-type staple rayon, and 82,200 tons of other synthetic fibers.[15]

We have taken as typical the price of women's underwear made of continuous filament rayon and of average quality, for which the Statistical Yearbook of the Federal Republic gives a 1938 retail price of RM 1.99.[16] This is the only applicable price found. Forty per cent was deducted for retail and wholesale markups to obtain the producer price.

Valuing the whole output of knitwear with this one price is obviously a risky business. However, the following considerations are in its favor. First, there has been a wide substitution of the cheaper and poorer synthetics for the woolen yarns used in 1936. Second, there must have

---

* The actual title of the classification given in the Statistical Handbook of Germany (p. 326) is "Other Hosiery and Knitwear (outer garments, caps, etc.)." Most of it must be outer garments.

been many children's goods which were much cheaper and which, therefore, can be assumed to offset the more expensive men's garments. Third, it is known from newspaper complaints that for many years the Eastern Zone produced too many garments which were both too small and of too poor quality. Much of the output could not be sold even at reduced prices. In spite of these justifications, the figures derived for this sector must be used with unusual caution.

For stockings and socks, there is an official East German series for 1936 and for 1950 through 1957. The 1936 figure adopted here is slightly higher than the one given by Gleitze.[17] (According to Gleitze, there was apparently no production in East Berlin.) The value of output was estimated by pricing it with the average value of all types of stockings and socks in 1936, when all of Germany produced 358.884 million pairs, worth RM 267,500,000.[18] (The Eastern Zone produced 322 million pairs in 1936, or about 90 per cent of the total.)[19]

From a map in Gleitze showing the locational distribution of production it appears that stocking production was indeed heavily concentrated in the Eastern Zone, while the production of knitwear (except for fancy items) was much less concentrated.[20] The combined 1936 value in 1936 prices for both stockings and knitwear found by the method described is RM 418.982 million. Gleitze gives as total sales value of the industry RM 524.144 million for the area of East Germany.[21] We have thus accounted for about 78.03 per cent of the total known production of hosiery and knitwear, which possibly suggests some undervaluation of the knitwear sector. However, it is just as likely that the very substantial knit production of decorative materials (or "fancy goods," as it is called on Gleitze's map)[22] makes up the difference.

From the sum of the two values of sales the two indices were constructed which were then applied to the estimated value added of hosiery and knitwear in 1936 and 1950 prices.[23]

The calculations indicate that the 1955 output of hosiery and knitwear was between 60 and 61 per cent of the 1936 level. This is entirely plausible (in spite of the noted difficulties with the pricing of knitwear) since the official East German figures indicate a fall in the production of stockings and socks to about 43 per cent of 1936. In view of the prewar concentration of this production in East Germany this decline is perhaps no more than should be expected.

The textile industry as a whole (excluding synthetic fibers)

Finally, from all the subgroups calculated in Table 71 an index of textile production as a whole was calculated and applied to the value added of textile production (exclusive of synthetic yarns) of East Germany in 1936. This value added was estimated by applying the percentage of sales in East Germany (including East Berlin) to sales in all Germany to

Table 71

Production and value added, textile industry, East Germany, and indices,
West and East Germany, 1936, and 1950–1958[a]

A. *Production*

Year	Yarns (thousand tons)	Cottons (million sq m)	Silk (natural and artificial) and linen weaves (million sq m)	Woolens (million sq m)	Stockings and socks (million pairs)	Knit goods (million pieces)
	(1)	(2)	(3)	(4)	(5)	(6)
1936	212.630	164.534	122.372	325.545	312.300	n.a.
1950	170.950	74.402	199.860	14.837	145.899	57.954
1951	200.739	121.976	216.593	23.442	179.365	80.698
1952	208.482	152.987	216.022	22.450	166.544	101.743
1953	228.871	169.136	236.292	28.101	141.430	117.040
1954	243.275	197.133	243.462	42.715	146.586	132.595
1955	251.985	200.508	268.853	32.300	142.108	119.403
1956	246.281	207.704	269.655	26.525	128.008	118.532
1957	245.805	204.515	285.678	28.748	130.692	129.061
1958	251.228	217.112	297.599	34.463	140.034	136.723
1960 Plan		395.000		58.800		

B. *Value added, 1936 prices (million RM)*

Year	Yarns	Cottons	Silk (natural and artificial) and linen weaves	Woolens	Hosiery and knit goods	Calculated value added	Actual value added
	(7)	(8)	(9)	(10)	(11)	(12)	(13)
1936	155.530	61.172	45.938	177.400	273.789	713.829	982.277
1950	125.046	27.662	75.017	8.089	119.093	354.912	488.388
1951	146.836	45.347	81.310	12.773	153.951	440.217	605.770
1952	152.497	56.878	81.081	12.241	164.383	467.080	642.704
1953	167.412	62.885	88.706	15.310	164.082	498.395	685.826
1954	177.942	73.290	91.417	23.275	179.085	545.009	749.968
1955	184.319	74.544	100.926	17.598	166.327	543.714	748.200
1956	180.135	77.224	101.247	14.458	158.597	531.661	731.600
1957	179.793	76.037	107.265	15.664	168.353	547.112	752.817
1958	183.759	80.723	111.721	18.787	179.113	574.103	790.045

C. *Value added, 1950 prices (million DM)*

Year	Yarns	Cottons	Silk (natural and artificial) and linen weaves	Woolens	Hosiery and knit goods	Calculated value added	Actual value added
	(14)	(15)	(16)	(17)	(18)	(19)	(20)
1936	522.381	143.142	85.445	803.622	603.458	2158.048	2986.515
1950	419.994	64.729	139.532	36.645	263.228	924.128	1278.826
1951	493.180	106.111	151.238	57.861	339.626	1148.016	1588.826
1952	512.195	133.093	150.810	55.450	360.808	1212.356	1677.824
1953	562.291	147.150	164.994	69.353	358.333	1302.121	1802.063
1954	597.656	171.498	170.036	105.435	390.558	1435.183	1986.032
1955	619.074	174.433	187.723	79.719	363.161	1424.110	1970.801
1956	605.022	180.702	188.321	65.495	345.742	1385.282	1917.044
1957	603.872	177.926	199.514	70.960	366.353	1418.625	1963.335
1958	617.193	188.890	207.802	85.104	390.136	1489.125	2060.695

Table 71 (Continued)

D. *Indices, West and East Germany*

| | West Germany | | East Germany | |
| | Old | New | 1936 Prices | 1950 Prices |
Year	1936 = 100	1936 = 100	1936 = 100	1936 = 100
	(21)	(22)	(23)	(24)
1936	100.0	100.0	100.0	100.0
1950	118.6	120	49.7	42.8
1951	130.2	136	61.7	53.2
1952	125.2	132	65.4	56.2
1953	145.2	157	69.8	60.3
1954	150.8	168	76.4	66.5
1955	160.0	182	76.2	66.0
1956	n.a.	193	74.5	64.2
1957	n.a.	202	76.6	65.7
1958	n.a.	190	80.4	69.0

Sources: Col. 1: For 1936, see Gleitze, *Ostdeutsche Wirtschaft*, p. 208; for 1950–1955, *SJDDR*, 1955, pp. 166–167; for 1956–1958, *ibid.*, 1958, pp. 354–355. Col. 2: For 1936 and 1950–1957, same as col. 1; for 1960 Plan, *Direktive*, p. 14. Col. 3: 1936 figure calculated as follows:

Total production of weaves	162,000 tons (*Gleitze, op. cit.*, p. 208)
Of which:	
Cotton	32,000 tons
Woolens	106,200 tons (*SP*, 1947, No. 12)
All others	28,800 tons

Conversion ratio: the same as for cotton, i.e., 23.8/32.0 = 74.375% = 164.534/122.372. 1950–1957: Difference between total *Gewebe* (woven goods) and sum of cottons and woolens (without *Grobgewebe* [rough cloth, such as canvas]). Total *Gewebe* for 1950–1955 given in *SJDDR*, 1955, pp. 166–167; for 1956–1958, *ibid.*, 1958, pp. 354–355. Col. 4: For 1950–1955, see index in *SP*, 1956, No. 4, p. 44, and absolute value of 32.3 million sq m for 1955 calculated from *Direktive*, p. 14; and for 1956 to 1958, *SJDDR*, 1958, p. 354. The figures given in the 1956 and 1957 eds. of *ibid.* differ slightly from the calculated figures. Cols. 5 and 6: Same as col. 1. Cols. 7–11: For details see text and Supplement Table A.57. Col. 12: Sum of cols. 7–11. Col. 13: For 1936 value added, see Table 72 below; for other years, index in col. 23 was applied. Cols. 14–18: For details see text and Supplement Table A.57. Col. 19: Sum of cols. 14–18. Col. 20: 1936 value added in 1950 prices derived by multiplying the 1936 value added in 1936 prices by the following ratio: calculated value added for 1936 in 1936 prices/calculated value added for 1936 in 1950 prices = 3.03. Col. 21: *SJBR*, 1955 ed., p. 231; *Monthly Report of the Bank Deutscher Laender*, March 1956, p. 1952. Col. 22: *SJBR*, 1959 ed., p. 183, average daily production. Col. 23: Index calculated from col. 12. Col. 24: Index calculated from col. 19. (No production figure in physical units was found for 1936. But a figure in reichsmark was available and was substituted into the value.) For method of calculation see text.

ᵃ For detailed calculations see Supplement Table A.57.

the corresponding value added figures given by the Production Statistics of 1936. This calculation is presented in Table 72.

If the average percentage of East German sales had been used instead of calculating the value added of the individual subgroups, the estimated value added would have been slightly less, RM 932.184 million rather than RM 982.277 million. The 1936 value added in 1950 prices for the whole textile industry was estimated in the same manner as that for the individual subgroups.

The procedures assume implicitly that the value of nonrepresented sectors varied in the same manner as the represented sectors. Measured by value added, the sectors for which calculations were made comprise 72.7 per cent of the whole industry. The figures in Gleitze indicate that yarns, woven cloth and hosiery and knitwear accounted for 86.12 per cent of total sales of textiles (exclusive of synthetic yarns) in all Germany,

Table 72

Value added, textile industry, East Germany, 1936 (1936 prices)

	Value added all Germany (million RM)	East German sales as per cent of all German sales	Estimated value added, East Germany (million RM)
	(1)	(2)	(3)
Preparation of yarns	50.732	30.85	15.651
Spinning	604.943	30.00	181.483
Weaving	1123.565	27.96	314.149
Hosiery, knitwear	428.733	63.86	273.789
Textile finishing	353.587	39.82	140.798
Embroidery, lace	43.137	83.80	36.149
Duck, bagging, etc.	28.480	26.61	7.579
Bandages	19.627	33.02	6.481
Other textiles	20.538	30.18	6.198
Total		34.87 (Average)	982.277

Sources: Col. 1: Calculated from *Produktionsstatistik, 1936*, pp. 52–53. Col. 2: Calculated from Gleitze, *Ostdeutsche Wirtschaft*, p. 179. Col. 3: Col. 1 × col. 2.

and for 83.96 per cent in East Germany (including East Berlin).[24] Any error involved in the assumption of parallel movement can only be minor.

By 1955, total textile output in 1936 prices was about one-fourth below that for 1936; in 1950 prices it was still about one-third below 1936, and there was no improvement to 1957. This reflects, in part, the fact that using earlier prices frequently gives an upward bias to later developments. Here, however, it reflects primarily the unfavorable development of woolens, the price of which rose substantially between 1936 and 1950 while the price of the rapidly expanding sectors (rayon and other synthetics) rose much less steeply. It should also be pointed out that 1950 saw the highest prices for most goods, but price declines for woolens thereafter were only slightly greater than for synthetics.

By contrast, West German textile output in 1955 was 60 per cent above 1936 by the old index and almost 80 per cent above 1936 by the new index. The contrasting developments are due to the following circumstances: Where East Germany had excess capacities, the Federal Republic had shortages. Substitution of cheaper for more expensive material went much further in East Germany than in the Federal Republic and, in addition, involved inferior synthetics. This is not a fanciful and spiteful capitalist assertion but one which is stated clearly in an extraordinarily frank article by Fred Oelssner, then the chief theorist of the communist East German regime.*

It is known that our textile industry depends to a large extent on imports of foreign raw materials, particularly wool. The foreign trade situation does not permit

* As noted earlier Oelssner fell into disgrace in 1958 because of "revisionist" tendencies.

us to satisfy the need for these important raw materials entirely, particularly not for wool. Hence we are forced to add to our cloths more synthetics, particularly staple rayon, than other countries. In this respect we are probably the world leaders. While in the world as a whole there is an admixture of perhaps 9 per cent staple rayon in textiles, in the German Democratic Republic the admixture is 41.6 per cent. . . . An investigation of the Ministry for Foreign and Intra-German Trade during the last Leipzig Fair has, however, shown that 80 per cent of our staple rayon is below world qualities.[25]

Finally, a check of the development between 1950 and 1955 shows our calculations to be consistent with East German claims. Our calculations show an increase of 53.2 per cent in total textile production between 1950 and 1955 if calculated in 1936 prices and of 54.1 per cent if calculated in 1950 prices. The gross production of the textile industry, which in communist terminology appears to include synthetic fibers, had increased by 1955 to 178.8 per cent of its 1950 level.[26] Measured by value added, the combined increase in textile (Western definition) and synthetic fiber production was 54.3 per cent or 54.8 per cent, depending on whether 1936 or 1950 prices are used to measure it. (The similarity in the increases between 1950 and 1955 measured in 1936 or in 1950 prices is due to the fact that the substitution of material occurred between 1936 and 1950 and was complete by that date.) Considering the differences in the concepts of value added and of gross production the two percentage changes appear to be quite compatible.

CLOTHING

In 1936 the clothing and fur industries produced a value added of RM 753.968 million, of which RM 725.200 million was attributable to clothing. How much of this total can be attributed to the area of East Germany is not entirely clear. Table 73 gives a derivation based on the percentages of sales.[27]

Table 73

Value added, clothing industry, East Germany, 1936

	Value added all Germany (million RM)	Per cent attributable to East Germany	Value added, East Germany	
			1936 Prices (million RM)	1950 Prices (million DM)
	(1)	(2)	(3)	(4)
Clothing	725.200	36.81	266.946	
Fur finishing and dressing	11.590	96.63	11.199	
Fur working	17.178	41.56	7.139	
Total	753.968		285.284	533.481

Sources: Col. 1: *Produktionsstatistik, 1936*, p. 53. Col. 2: Calculated from Gleitze, *Ostdeutsche Wirtschaft*, p. 179: Col. 3: Col. 1 × col. 2. Col. 4: Total of col. 3 multiplied by producer price index of clothing industry in 1950. 187 per cent of 1938, which is assumed to be equal to 1936. *SJBR*, 1955, p. 442.

The output of the industry as a whole may reasonably be assumed to move parallel to the value of inputs. Much the most important inputs are various kinds of cloth. In 1936, cloth accounted for RM 590.2 million out of total inputs valued at RM 767.3 million (i.e., 76.9 per cent).[28] It therefore seemed best to estimate the value added of the clothing industry by applying to the 1936 base the index of output of various kinds of woven cloth rather than the index for textiles as a whole, since textiles include yarns (which are an earlier stage of both clothing and knitwear), hosiery, and knitwear, which is a final stage of production by itself and has been separately estimated above.

Using the index of woven goods indicates a fall to 67.8 per cent of the 1936 level in 1936 prices, and to only 42.8 per cent of the 1936 level if measured in 1950 prices. As stated before, this reflects the shift from wool to synthetics and the fact that the price of wool increased much more than that of synthetics. The shift in the composition of textiles is, of course, reflected in the calculations of the value added of cloth. It seems proper that it be also reflected in the calculation of the value added of the clothing industry. In addition, the sharp reduction in the output of the industry is reflected in the more than proportionate representation of clothing in the area before the war (furs also were heavily concentrated there) and the second-fiddle role of consumer goods in a planned economy.

The clothing industry in West Germany reached its prewar level some time between 1949 and 1950, and by 1955 it was more than three times the prewar level (336.3 per cent of 1936).[29] This fact reflects not only the obvious truth that a market economy caters more to consumers' wishes than a planned economy but also the fact that the West German clothing industry before the war was less than proportionately developed and received imports from the Eastern area, primarily East Berlin. Materials in West Germany are superior, the proportion of synthetics used is much smaller than in East Germany, and what is used is of superior quality. The value added figures are reproduced in Table 74.

LEATHER AND SHOES

The leather industry is represented by two series on leather and two series on shoes. Almost all data are based on official East German information. In 1936 the manufacturing of leather (including tanning) and the shoe industry together accounted for RM 510.709 million of the RM 647.416 million value added for the industry as a whole in all of Germany, or about 78.9 per cent. The remaining value creation was chiefly due to leather goods (RM 106.325 million), leather gloves, and leather conveyor belts. Shoe production apparently included not only leather shoes but also shoes made of other materials. As before, the procedure adopted here was to calculate an index of production from the available

Table 74

Value added, clothing industry, East Germany, and indices,
West and East Germany, 1936 and 1950–1958

| | East Germany | | | | |
| | 1936 Prices | | 1950 Prices | | |
Year	Index of value added, woven cloth 1936 = 100	Value added, clothing (million RM)	Index of value added, woven cloth 1936 = 100	Value added, clothing (million DM)	West Germany, new index
	(1)	(2)	(3)	(4)	(5)
1936	100.00	285.284	100.00	533.481	100
1950	38.93	111.061	23.34	124.514	172
1951	49.01	139.818	30.54	162.925	206
1952	52.79	150.601	32.88	175.409	226
1953	58.66	167.348	36.96	197.175	266
1954	66.07	188.487	43.30	230.997	281
1955	67.86	193.594	42.81	228.383	340
1956	67.81	193.451	42.10	224.596	382
1957	69.93	199.499	43.44	231.744	413
1958	74.24	211.795	46.67	248.976	393

Sources: Col. 1: Index derived from sums of value added of woolens, cotton, and silk, rayon, and linen weaves given in Table 71, cols. 8–10. Col. 2: For 1936, see Table 73; for 1950–1958, index in col. 1 applied. Col. 3: Index derived from Table 71, sum of cols. 15–17. Col. 4: For 1936, see Table 73; for 1950–1958, index in col. 3 applied. Col. 5: *SJBR*, 1959, p. 183, average daily production.

data and to apply it to the estimated value added of the leather industry as a whole for the area of East Germany in 1936.

Leather

In calculating the index we departed from the usual procedure of accepting all official East German figures given in units. In this particular case the change made is in favor of East Germany. The Statistical Yearbook of the German Democratic Republic gives the 1936 production of soft leather as 25.587 million sq m and proceeds to state that production had fallen to 7.601 million sq m by 1955, or 29.7 per cent of 1936.[30] The 1936 base appears impossibly high and quite inconsistent with other sources.

Gleitze gives the production of "upper leather," which is here equated with soft leather, as 4,765 tons.[31] During the years 1951 to 1955 the average weight of 1,000 sq m of soft leather in the Federal Republic varied from 1.081 tons to 1.140 tons.[32] Assuming a conversion ratio of 1.1 tons per 1,000 sq m, 1936 production would be around 4.332 million sq m, or less than one-fifth the production assumed by the East German Central Statistical Office. This figure was adopted even though it implies an increase in that particular branch of production between 1936 and 1955 rather than the decrease of 70 per cent shown by the official East German source.*

In 1936 the wholesale price of stiff leather was RM 3,560 per ton, that of soft leather RM 11.300 per sq m.[33] By 1950 the price had risen to 244 per cent and 289 per cent for stiff and soft leather, respectively. Since the quality of the soft leather undoubtedly deteriorated after the war, the use of these prices — and there seems to be no alternative — is bound to be misleading.

In 1936 the area of East Germany produced 20.77 per cent of all leather, but only 17.5 per cent of soft and 18.87 per cent of stiff leather. To estimate the value added for 1936, 20.77 per cent of the value added for all of Germany was taken — RM 47.559 million. The index applied to it was calculated on the sum of the two estimated sales values. To weigh the sales values by the relative importance of soft and hard leather would reduce the index somewhat, but the reduction would be so small as to be well within ordinary limits of error.† The value added in 1950 prices was found by multiplying the 1936 value added measured in 1936 prices with the price index for leather production.[34]

Between 1936 and 1955 the production of the leather sector is reported to have increased by about 15 to 20 per cent, which is almost certainly an overestimate. Since the rapidly expanding production of soft leather probably involved production of a much inferior quality than before the war, it is overpriced in the index. Furthermore, the fact that official figures indicate a fall in all leather output should make one suspicious of the result. The data are given in Table 75. In 1955, West German production of leather was still 15 per cent below that of 1936.

Shoes

The information for shoes consists of an East German series for shoes of all kinds and one for leather shoes. The quality of the leather shoes is known to be substantially below prewar and below that of West German shoes.‡ Moreover, it is stated that a shoe which contains any leather at all is classified as a leather shoe. For 1936 the Gleitze figure was chosen,

---

* The following control calculation shows that this figure must be much closer to the real facts. The total value added of leather production attributable to the area of East Germany in 1936 is RM 47.559 million, or 40 per cent of sales value. The latter is therefore RM 118.898 million. The calculated sales value of hard leather is RM 60.680 million and of soft leather RM 48.952 million. The calculated combined sales value is RM 109.632 million, which is 92 per cent of the actual sales value calculated from the Production Statistics of 1936.

† The value added in 1936 was 39.75 per cent of the approximate gross production value. Since it is assumed to be the same for both types of leather, it was unnecessary to calculate it for the index needed.

‡ It is known that pigskin is used frequently, and that East Germans will come from great distances to buy West German shoes in West Berlin even when they risk having the shoes confiscated or going to jail, and even when they will not buy other goods.

Table 75

Production and value added, leather industry, East Germany,
and indices, West and East Germany, 1936 and 1950–1958

A. *Production and value added, East Germany*

| | Production | | Value added, stiff and soft leather combined | |
| | | | | |
Year	Stiff leather (thousand tons)	Soft leather (million sq m)	1936 Prices (million RM)	1950 Prices (million DM)
	(1)	(2)	(3)	(4)
1936	17.045	4.332	47.559	126.031
1950	5.774	3.960	28.331	78.127
1951	8.010	4.713	35.474	97.283
1952	9.322	5.955	43.588	119.906
1953	12.419	7.233	54.636	149.775
1954	12.827	7.898	58.526	160.778
1955	11.634	7.601	55.226	152.044
1956	11.691	7.454	54.593	150.166
1957	11.091	7.657	54.664	150.783
1958	11.871	8.560	60.295	166.575

B. *Indices, West and East Germany*

| | West Germany | | East Germany | |
| | | | 1936 Prices 1936 = 100 | 1950 Prices 1936 = 100 |
Year	Old	New		
	(5)	(6)	(7)	(8)
1936	100.0	100.0	100.00	100.00
1950	72.7	69.8	59.57	61.99
1951	70.9	70.4	74.59	77.19
1952	73.5	74.2	91.65	95.14
1953	76.1	78.0	114.88	118.84
1954	75.0	77.6	123.06	127.57
1955	82.0	84.9	116.12	120.64
1956	n.a.	87.0	114.79	119.15
1957	n.a.	95.0	114.94	119.64
1958	n.a.	91.0	126.78	132.17

Sources: Col. 1: For 1936 and 1950–1955, see *SJDDR*, 1955, pp. 166–167; for 1956 to 1958, *ibid.*, 1958, p. 356.
Col. 2: For 1950–1958, same as col. 1; for 1936, *ibid.*, 1955, p. 166, gives a production of 25.587 million sq m, which
is impossible. For calculation of adopted figure, see text. Col. 3: For 1936 value, see text; postwar years calculated
from index, col. 7. Col. 4: For 1936 value, see text; postwar years calculated from index, col. 8. Col. 5: *SJBR*,
1955, p. 230. Col. 6: For 1936, 1950–1955, see *Neuberechnung*, p. 79, average monthly production; for 1956–1957,
SJBR, 1959 ed., p. 183, average daily production. Cols. 7 and 8: Indices calculated from sales value of soft and stiff
leather combined. For details of calculations, see Supplement Table A.58.

which is higher than the East German figure but appears to be more
reliable.

There is evidently considerable ambiguity as to what a leather shoe
is, and what shoes are in general. Gleitze states that production of shoes

of all kinds in the area of East Germany in 1936 was 44.3 million pairs and that of leather shoes 17.5 million pairs.[35] The Statistical Yearbook of the German Democratic Republic on the other hand, claims a total production of 38.497 million pairs of shoes and 15.341 million pairs of leather shoes.* [36]

The 1936 definition may possibly include shoes with rubber soles. The 1955 definition certainly includes shoes which are only in part leather. It is conceivable that Statistical Practice counts for 1936 only shoes made wholly of leather. If so, to make our figures comparable we must adopt Gleitze's figure. It should be stressed, however, that adopting Gleitze's figure makes the base for 1936 sufficiently higher; that the output of the industry as a whole would be seen to decline between 1936 and 1955 while if we used the 1936 figure from Statistical Practice, the output would be seen to rise.

Leather shoes and other shoes (found by subtracting leather shoes from all shoes) are valued separately. For leather shoes, the retail price of men's street shoes (size 42, simple quality, with leather sole) was taken, allowing 40 per cent for retail and wholesale markup.[37] Calculation of the average value of West German leather shoe production for 1950 indicates an average value of DM 19.48 per pair.[38] The retail price of a low-quality men's shoe in 1950 was only DM 24.50, which would give an estimated producer price of only DM 14.70 after allowing 40 per cent for retail and wholesale markup.[39] Since the quality of East German shoes is known to be very low, the low shoe price for the postwar years was used. On the other hand, the 1936 quality was higher. The 1936 price was therefore calculated by using the 1950 average production value and calculating back by means of an index of postwar shoe prices.[40] This gives a 1936–1938 price of RM 8.77 instead of RM 7.04 for the lower-quality pair of shoes. However, since it is the average price of all shoes, leather and otherwise, even this price is likely to underestimate the value of leather shoes in 1936.

The valuation of the other shoes is rather complicated. The category includes anything from the cheapest kind of beach shoes made of a piece of wood and a strap to sports sneakers and house slippers and even rubber

* The figures given by Statistical Practice and the Statistical Yearbook of the Federal Republic are actually very close to the 1933 figures given by Gleitze — 38.2 million pairs for all shoes and 13.9 million pairs for leather shoes. Other sources make it reasonably certain that the figures for 1936 given in Statistical Practice and the Statistical Yearbook of the German Democratic Republic are too low, and that Gleitze is correct. Thus the Statistical Handbook of Germany (p. 319) gives as the total production of leather shoes in the Soviet Zone, Berlin, and areas east of the Oder-Neisse 24.7 million pairs of a total 85.1 million pairs. The number of persons employed in the shoe industry east of the Oder-Neisse was 15.38 per cent of the number employed in the Eastern Zone proper, all of Berlin, and the areas east of the Oder-Neisse; the Zone proper (that is, without East Berlin) employed 77.02 per cent. On the basis of the number employed, the Zone alone (without East Berlin) would account for 19 million pairs.

boots. The average value is undoubtedly low. For 1950 we know that the average production value of shoes other than leather street shoes* was only DM 5.86 per pair,[41] or only about 29.5 per cent of the average producer price of leather shoes. The 1936 price of "other" shoes was found by assuming that their price was also 29.5 per cent of the leather shoe price. This gives a 1936 price of DM 2.59.

The value added for 1936 was estimated as follows. The total value added of the shoe industry in Germany as a whole was RM 281.732 million.[42] East Germany (including East Berlin) originated 23.28 per cent of total sales.[43] Assuming that East Germany originated an equal percentage of value added gives an estimated gross value added for 1936 prices of RM 65.591 million. The 1936 value in 1950 prices was then found by multiplying the 1936 value in 1936 prices by the price index for all shoes.

The calculations presented in Table 76 indicate that by 1955 shoe production was about 5 per cent below 1936, although in 1954 it had been above it and in 1950 equal to it. The calculations almost certainly overestimate the actual development of output even though an attempt was made to allow for the lower quality of leather shoes by using the price of lower-quality shoes as typical.

The output of the West German shoe industry in 1955 was almost 8 per cent above 1936. In order to interpret these developments it should be realized that the East German production of 17.564 million pairs of leather shoes in 1955 amounted to less than one pair a year per man, woman, and child, while the 66.938 million pairs of leather street shoes produced in the Federal Republic (not including work boots and shoes, or skiboots, etc. which are also made of leather, or light street shoes with uppers not made of leather, which would be classified as leather shoes in East Germany) amounted to about 1.28 pairs per capita.†

Shoe and leather industries combined

To estimate the output of the leather and shoe industry as a whole, a combined index of shoe and leather production was constructed, and this was applied to the estimated value added for the leather industry as a whole for East Germany, the unavoidable implication being that other nonrepresented industries moved as shoes did. Since the conveyor belt and glove industries were relatively small in all of Germany, the error introduced with respect to them cannot be great; the leather goods industry (women's bags, saddles, and so on) was of major importance but

---

* This refers to "light street shoes, house slippers, and *Hilfsschuhe*." It is not clear what is meant by *Hilfsschuhe*, literally, "auxiliary" shoes.

† It is amusing to note that, despite this fact given in Statistical Practice, the author of the article nevertheless boasts that leather shoe production had increased faster in East Germany than in the Federal Republic, an increase based on too small a base in 1936!

Table 76

Production and value added, shoe industry, East Germany,
and indices, West and East Germany, 1936 and 1950–1958

A. *Production and value added, East Germany*

	Production		Value added, Leather and "other" shoes	
Year	Leather shoes (million pairs)	"Other" shoes (million pairs)	1936 Prices (million RM)	1950 Prices (million DM)
	(1)	(2)	(3)	(4)
1936	17.500	26.800	65.591	145.612
1950	7.958	24.345	39.086	89.595
1951	10.889	27.811	49.292	112.019
1952	14.145	27.826	57.714	129.551
1953	17.573	26.943	65.886	146.282
1954	19.374	25.211	69.218	152.630
1955	17.564	23.131	62.961	138.899
1956	17.166	19.837	59.425	130.425
1957	17.635	21.325	61.767	135.812
1958	19.774	24.904	70.018	154.189

B. *Indices, West and East Germany*

	West Germany		East Germany	
Year	Old	New	1936 Prices 1936 = 100	1950 Prices 1936 = 100
	(5)	(6)	(7)	(8)
1936	100.00	100.00	100.00	100.00
1950	77.7	78.4	59.59	61.53
1951	80.4	80.8	75.15	76.93
1952	88.0	88.5	87.99	88.97
1953	93.5	93.6	100.45	100.46
1954	96.2	96.2	105.53	104.82
1955	n.a.	107.8	95.99	95.39
1956	n.a.	117.0	90.60	89.57
1957	n.a.	128.0	94.17	93.27
1958	n.a.	125.0	106.75	105.89

Sources: Col. 1: For 1936, see Gleitze, *Ostdeutsche Wirtschaft*, p. 207; for 1950–1955, *SJDDR*, 1955, pp. 166–167; for 1956 to 1958, *ibid.*, 1958, p. 356. Col. 2: Difference between production of all shoes and production of leather shoes. Sources same as col. 1. Col. 3: For 1936, see text; for 1950–1957, index from col. 7 applied. Col. 4: For 1936, 1936 value added in 1936 prices multiplied by price rise of 222 per cent between 1938 and 1950 given in *SJBR*, 1955, p. 441; for 1950–1957, index from col. 8 applied. Col. 5: *SJBR*, 1954, p. 230. Col. 6: For 1936, 1950–1955, see *Neuberechnung*, p. 79, average monthly production; for 1956–1957, *SJBR*, 1959 ed., p. 183, average daily production. Cols. 7 and 8: Indices derived from sales value of all shoes. For details of calculation, see Supplement Table A.59.

is not likely to have developed very much. This means that the value added thus calculated probably overstates the real output.

The estimated value added in 1936 in 1936 prices for East Germany as a whole is found by the calculations given in Table 77 to have been RM

Table 77

Value added, shoe and leather industry, East Germany, 1936 (in 1936 prices)

	Value added all Germany (million RM)	East German sales as per cent of all German sales	Estimated value added, East Germany (million RM)
	(1)	(2)	(3)
Leather manufacturing and tanning	228.977	23.12	52.939
Shoe industry	281.732	23.40	65.845
Conveyor-belt industry	14.028	27.87	3.910
Leather goods	106.325	24.28	25.816
Leather gloves	16.354	57.22	9.358
Total	647.416		157.868

Sources: Col. 1: See *Produktionsstatistik, 1936*, p. 52. Col. 2: Calculated from Gleitze, *Ostdeutsche Wirtschaft*, p. 179. Col. 3: Col. 1 × col. 2.

157.868 million. The 1936 value added in 1950 prices is found by multiplying this figure by an average of the price increases of leather production and of leather products. Since one price rose to 265 per cent and the other to 226 per cent of 1936, 246 per cent was accepted as the average increase.[44] This gives a 1936 value added in 1950 prices of RM 388.355 million.

The calculations presented in Table 77 indicate that the shoe and leather industry just about reached its 1936 level in 1953, was slightly above it in 1954, and fell to or slightly below it in 1955.

Measured in 1936 prices in East Germany and by the old index in West Germany, the development in the two parts of Germany between 1936 and 1955 is about the same, the big difference being, of course, that West Germany produced shoes for export to other sections of the country and to the world before the war, while East Germany probably was a net importer. The new index of the Federal Republic, which can be constructed from the indices for leather production, shoes, and leather-working industries (such as luggage and gloves) indicates that production in 1955 was more than 10 per cent above 1936. This development is largely due to the great expansion of leather-goods industries other than the shoe industry.

The gross production leather, shoes, and furs (for which the major production center was Leipzig) increased by 82.2 per cent between 1950 and 1955 if measured in *Messwerte*.[45] The calculated index shows an increase of 74.6 per cent when measured in 1936 prices and of 71.4 per cent when measured in 1950 prices (see Table 78). Considering the difference in definition of gross production and value added, the two rates of increase suggest that the calculated increase is somewhat above the real increase of this industry.

Table 78

Value added, shoe and leather industry, East Germany,
and indices, West and East Germany, 1936 and 1950–1958

A. *1936 Prices*

| Year | East Germany | | West Germany, old index |
	Index applied 1936 = 100	Value added (million RM)	
	(1)	(2)	(3)
1936	100.00	157.868	100.0
1950	57.63	90.979	75.5
1951	72.47	114.407	76.2
1952	86.53	136.603	81.5
1953	102.75	162.209	85.7
1954	108.87	171.871	86.7
1955	100.65	158.894	96.4
1956	100.82	159.163	n.a.
1957	102.90	162.446	n.a.
1958	115.17	181.817	n.a.

B. *1950 Prices*

| Year | East Germany | | West Germany, new index |
	Index applied 1936 = 100	Value added (million DM)	
	(4)	(5)	(6)
1936	100.00	388.355	100.0
1950	56.27	218.527	76.3
1951	70.03	271.965	78.4
1952	83.34	323.655	86.2
1953	98.23	381.481	93.0
1954	103.96	403.734	97.2
1955	96.45	374.568	110.5
1956	93.50	363.112	119.3
1957	105.50	409.715	130.6
1958	118.08	458.570	125.1

Sources: Cols. 1 and 4: Calculated from combined value added of leather and shoes, Tables 75 and 76. Cols. 2 and 5: See text for estimating procedure. Col. 3: See *SJBR*, 1955, and *Monthly Report of the Bank Deutscher Laender*, March 1956, p. 92. Combined in proportion of leather:shoes = 0.89:1.10. Col. 6: Indices of leather production, leather working, and shoes combined in proportion 0.66:0.39:1.02. For 1936 and 1950–1955, see *Neuberechnung*, p. 79; for 1956 to 1958, *SJBR*, 1959, p. 183.

CHAPTER XII

FATS AND OILS, AND FOOD, DRINK, AND TOBACCO

FATS AND OILS

In 1936 the fats and oils industry in Germany produced RM 402.782 million gross value added. Of this total, RM 165.939 million, or 41.2 per cent, were accounted for by margarine and similar vegetable fats. The only other subindustries of major importance were the outputs of oil mills and of oil refineries (*Oelveredlung*) but neither reached a value added of RM 100 million. Most of the production was in the western areas of Germany. The area now East Germany accounted for only about 36,400 tons of the total 422,500 tons of margarine produced.*

Estimates of the 1936 value added in 1936 prices are given in Table 79. The 1936 value added in 1950 prices was derived by multiplying the 1936 value added in 1936 prices by the average of the price rise of the products of the "feed stuff industries" and the "oil mill and margarine industries," that is, by 145 per cent.[1]

In order to estimate the movements of production of oils and fats, three series were used. First, there is now an official series of margarine production. In 1955 East Germany produced about 182,258 tons of margarine, about 10 kg per capita per year, or about ½ lb per person per week, compared with about 12 kg per capita in the Federal Republic, which had a production of 611,985 tons.[2] In 1936, per capita production was about 2.3 kg per capita, while per capita consumption within the 1937 borders of Germany was 6.28 kg. Clearly, the expansion of margarine production in part makes up for the quantity once imported but also goes beyond it. Butter production in 1955 was claimed to be 126,400 tons,[3] or about 7 kg per person. In 1936 the per capita butter consumption was 8.5 per person.[4]

---

* The Statistical Handbook of Germany (p. 322) gives 33,000 tons as the Soviet Zone production and 10,100 tons as the production of all of Berlin. One-third of the Berlin production was allocated to East Berlin. Except for the relatively small industry of animal glues and gelatin, in which the share of the Zone in total German sales was 23.1 per cent (with Berlin being negligible), the shares of the Zone varied in 1936 between 8.5 per cent of sales for margarine and 13.8 per cent for feed stuffs (Gleitze, *Ostdeutsche Wirtschaft*, p. 179).

Table 79

Value added, oils and fats, East Germany, 1936

	Value added all Germany (million RM)	East German sales as per cent of all German sales	Value added East Germany (million RM)
	(1)	(2)	(3)
Oil mills	144.779	9.01	13.045
Margarine and other fats	175.359[a]	10.63	18.640
Fish meal and fish liver oil	12.297[b]	12.89	1.585
Animal glues and gelatin	31.420[c]	23.55	7.399
Feed stuff industry	38.827	15.42	5.987
Total			46.656

Sources: Col. 1: See *Produktionsstatistik, 1936*, p. 54. Col. 2: See Gleitze, *Ostdeutsche Wirtschaft*, p. 179. Col. 3: Col. 1 × col. 2.
   [a] Includes talc making and lard boiling.   [b] Includes slaughter houses.   [c] Includes factories using bones.

In 1936, 9 kg of lard per person were also consumed, but no postwar figures for lard have been found. (The 1936 population figure used to calculate per capita production is 67.3 million; the 1955 figure is 18 million.) The margarine consumption of a four-person working-class family in the Federal Republic in 1954 is given as 3.982 kg per month.[5] This too comes to about ½ lb of margarine per week per person. Butter consumption is given as 1.390 kg per month for a family of four, or about 4.17 kg per year per person.[6] Thus in East Germany margarine production increased almost sixfold between 1936 and 1955.

The index of margarine production was applied to the value added of margarine production alone (that is, without other butter substitutes) in 1936. Since the Production Statistics of 1936 gives only the combined value added for margarine and other fats, this value had to be reduced in proportion to the sales value of margarine to the total group as given by Gleitze.

Second, there now exists an official series on animal fats. An index derived from this series was applied to the value added of all industries, except margarine and the products of oil mills, but with the addition of the estimated value added of "other fats," which were excluded from the margarine category. This industry increased by about 76 per cent between 1936 and 1955.

Finally, a series on the production of edible oils was applied to the value added of the output of oil mills. There may be a difficulty in that the 1936 figure refers to "raw oils" while the postwar figures refer to refined oil, but no adjustment — if such an adjustment is necessary — seemed feasible. This industry increased about 3.5 times over 1936.

Altogether, the output of the fats and oils industry increased about fourfold between 1936 and 1955. No separate index for fats and oils was found either for the Federal Republic or for East Germany. In both parts of Germany the fats and oil industry is included with food industries, which in the East but not the West also include tobacco products. The relevant figures are presented in Table 80.

Table 80

Production and value added, oils and fats, East Germany, 1936 and 1950–1958

Year	Production (thousand tons)			Value added		Indices	
	Margarine	Animal fats	Edible oils, refined	1936 Prices (million RM)	1950 Prices (million DM)	1936 Prices 1936 = 100	1950 Prices 1936 = 100
	(1)	(2)	(3)	(4)	(5)	(6)	(7)
1936	38.6	20.335	46.200	46.656	66.718	100.00	100.00
1950	46.3	11.331	43.198	48.093	67.118	103.08	100.60
1951	78.5	22.356	83.388	86.500	122.681	185.40	183.88
1952	99.5	41.845	100.667	110.281	154.679	236.37	231.84
1953	108.4	39.875	106.642	117.685	164.727	252.24	246.90
1954	144.3	39.270	128.362	148.049	205.091	317.32	307.40
1955	183.3	35.855	167.483	187.063	260.761	400.94	390.84
1956	193.5	43.271	179.938	199.912	279.075	428.48	418.29
1957	178.4	46.264	175.489	189.727	266.552	406.65	399.52
1958	181.4	45.629	190.002	197.360	279.686	423.33	419.33

Sources: Cols. 1 and 3: For 1936, see *SHD*, p. 329; for 1950–1955, *SJDDR*, 1955, pp. 168–169; for 1956–1958 *ibid.*, 1958 ed., p. 356. Col. 2: For 1936, see Gleitze, *Ostdeutsche Wirtschaft*, p. 209; other years, same as col. 1. Col. 4: For 1936, see Table 79; for other years, index in col. 6 applied. Col. 5: For 1936, 1936 value in 1936 prices multiplied by producer price index for oil mills and the margarine industry given in *SJBR*, 1956, p. 437; for other years, index in col. 7 applied. Cols. 6 and 7: Indices derived from sum of separately calculated sales values of the three products listed. For details of calculations, see Supplement Table A.61.

FOOD, DRINK, AND TOBACCO

The food, drink and tobacco industry is the largest single industry group in Germany. The value added in 1936 attributable to the area of East Germany is estimated once more by the percentage of East German area sales in total German sales in 1936. The calculation is presented in detail in Table 81. Of the industries forming this major group, sugar and sweets production, vegetable canning, starch products, malt, and tobacco were rather more heavily represented in the area than would correspond to the population, and most other industries (except canned milk, macaroni products, and, perhaps, vinegar and spices) were represented roughly in proportion to the population.

The output of the industry group is estimated on the basis of seven major subdivisions.

Grain products

Flour mills and bread baking. In 1936 flour mills and bread baking accounted for a value added of RM 76.914 million. The industry must have moved parallel to the output of flour of all kinds, which is officially given. On the basis of this estimating procedure, the output of flour mills and

Table 81

Value added, food, drink, and tobacco, East Germany, 1936 (in 1936 prices)

	Value added all Germany (million RM)	East German sales as per cent of all German sales	Value added attributable to East Germany (million RM)
	(1)	(2)	(3)
Flour mills	228.646	23.58	53.915
Bread	87.450	26.30	22.999
Meat and fish	187.529	23.00	43.132
Sugar and sweets	607.592[a]	43.50	246.303 = 30.39%
Fruit and vegetable canning	73.786	34.50	25.460
Juices, wines, champagnes	34.429	18.00	6.197
Canned milk, cheese	44.247	8.70	3.849
Macaroni products (*Nährmittel*)	133.639	7.90	10.557
Coffee substitutes, starch	98.662	43.50	42.918
Malt	25.800	39.40	10.165
Breweries	705.302	21.90	154.461 = 17.76%
Vinegar, mustard, spices	31.703	19.10	6.055
Tobacco	702.717	32.10	225.572 = 25.94%
Total	2,961.512		869.583 = 100.00%

Sources: Col. 1: *Produktionsstatistik, 1936*, pp. 54–55. Col. 2: Calculated from Gleitze, *Ostdeutsche Wirtschaft*, p. 185. Col. 3: Col. 1 × col. 2.
[a] Of which, sugar = 315.658; sweets = 291.934.

bread together had increased by 1955 to 107.33 per cent of 1936. Considering that the population had increased by about 11 per cent, this is consistent with the known supplies.

Macaroni, cereal products, and starches. The two industries are related. Starch is an input into some cereal products (*Nährmittel*), which in 1936 accounted for a value added of RM 10.165 million. Starches and coffee substitutes accounted for another RM 42.918 million. The output of these industries probably varies with the tonnage of cereal products. By 1955 the industry seems to have reached a level of 70.2 per cent of the 1936 level and by 1956 it had risen to 83.2 per cent of 1936. The postwar figures are official. They are linked to the tonnage of food made from starch in 1936.

Malt. The value added attributable to malt production estimated on the basis of sales was RM 10.165 million in 1936. For the postwar years, production figures are available in tons, but for 1936 only a sales value of RM 45.960 million is given. This was deflated by a price of RM 211.9 per ton, derived by dividing the quantity of malt exported in 1936 into the value of exports.[7] The 1950 price was found by assuming that the (unknown) price rise for malt was the same as the (known) price rise for beer. It was probably larger. On this basis it appears that malt production in 1955 was only 70.79 per cent of 1936 — which reflects somewhat on the quality of the beer. Since barley output in 1955 was only about 80 per cent of the prewar 1935–1938 average and brewing barley is in part imported, this development is plausible.

Beer production. Breweries in 1936 produced a value added of RM 154.461 million. Their value added must move parallel to beer production which, in volume, had risen steadily by 1955 to 156.4 per cent of 1936. Nothing is known about the quality, but the consumption of cereals in the brewing of beer is small. The increase in production is quite believable, particularly as Munich beer is presumably less available than formerly.

Meat and fish

The value added of meat and fish production in 1936 can be estimated at RM 43.132 million. The development of the industry must move parallel with the meat output and the fish catch. In using the official statistics, however, we encounter difficulties which can be only partially overcome. First, for 1936, meat and fish (with their products) should be split into separate components. This can be done roughly by valuing the meat output in 1936 and the fish catch separately. At most, the fish catch was about 15 per cent of the meat output.

Second, the official figures are not trustworthy. According to the figures, the quantity of meat from domestically slaughtered animals increased almost five times between 1950 and 1955. This increase is not consistent with the equally official figures, which show that the live weight of slaughtered animals increased 187.1 per cent between 1950 and 1955. The latter figure includes consumption by farmers of farm-slaughtered animals, while the former series presumably includes only the meat from commercially slaughtered animals. Nevertheless, it is highly unlikely that farmers ate so much better than their brothers in the city in 1950.

Also, it is not likely that the occupying power received all the available meat in 1950. It is most likely that the phenomenal growth of the statistics — not that of the available amount of meat — is due to some statistical trick, such as the increasing "industrialization" of commercial slaughtering; that is, the growth must be spurious and due to an increase in statistical coverage.

The procedure chosen here was to start with the official postwar figures for the live weight of slaughtered animals and convert these to marketable meat on the basis of the technical conversion ratios available for West Germany. The details are given in the tables with the calculations.

For the prewar years, data are directly available for 1938. The Soviet Zone alone produced 741,748 tons of meat (of which 449,388 tons were pork). If one-third of total Berlin output (or 39,285 tons) is allocated to East Berlin, the presumed output of East Germany in 1938 was 781,033 tons.[8] The 1936 tonnage can be estimated from per capita consumption (including imports less exports), which in 1936 was 45 kg per person if the greater weight of farm slaughtered pigs is considered.[9] This gives an estimated 1936 tonnage of 727,200 tons. Since the area exported pigs, this base is undoubtedly on the low side, but no allowance can be made for this fact.

On this basis, which seems quite reliable, by 1955 total meat production (including animals slaughtered on the farms) had reached a level of about 98.6 per cent, which is probably too high. Meat production, however, was estimated by means of the tonnage of meat available from domestic slaughterings.

The estimation of fish and fish products was not possible. We have information on the fish catch, which increased substantially from an estimated 11,000 tons in 1936 [10] to an officially claimed 62,200 tons in 1955. However, this development, which is quite natural, would violently overstate the production of fish products. The latter cannot, unfortunately, be estimated for 1936. We have a figure of 11.8 kg as the average per capita consumption of fish in 1936, but a large quantity of fish was — and still is — imported. For 1950, per capita fish consumption is stated as 4 kg,[11] and for 1955 it can be calculated at 9.1 kg — although Statistical Practice states that it was 11.9 kg, 3.5 kg from domestic catches and 8.4 kg from imports.[12] If an index of consumption were applied, the value added in 1936 prices would have declined between 1936 and 1955.

Because the difficulties could not be resolved, it was assumed that the output of fish and fish products varies with meat and meat products. This in turn implies that while there was rapid (but still very small) increase in the fish catch, the output of fish products must have fallen, which seems likely. In any case, the amounts involved are very small — perhaps RM 5.5 million in 1936 prices in 1936 — and any error introduced must be small.

Sugar and sweets

Sugar and sweets in 1936 accounted for RM 264.303 million, or 30.39 per cent of the total value added of food, drink, and tobacco attributable to East Germany. The output of this industry must move more or less parallel to the output of refined sugar available. Owing to the poor crop in 1955, the industry cannot have reached a level of much more than 90 per cent, although in some earlier years the level may have been about the same as prewar.

Tobacco

The last group to be calculated separately relates to tobacco products, which in 1936, with a value added of RM 225.572 million, accounted for almost 26 per cent of the whole group. There are two official series linking prewar and postwar output: a series on *Papyrosse* and cigarettes, the former being a Russian type of cigarette which was not produced in

Table 82

Production and value added, food, drink, and tobacco, East Germany, and indices, West and East Germany, 1936 and 1950–1958

A. *Production and value added, East Germany*

| | Production | | | | | | | | | Value added | |
Year	Flour, all kinds (thousand tons)	Macaroni products (thousand tons)	Refined sugar (thousand tons)	Meat (thousand tons)	Meat products (thousand tons)	Malt (thousand tons)	Beer (thousand hectoliters)	Cigarettes (billions)	Pipe tobacco (tons)	1936 Prices (million RM)	1950 Prices (million DM)
	(1)	(2)	(3)	(4)	(5)	(6)	(7)	(8)	(9)	(10)	(11)
1936	1274.7	206.19	705.47	727.200	43.0	216.895	7.527	16.982	2700	869.583	1608.729
1950	1252.0	98.50	605.00	374.890	45.2	70.910	3.800	9.877	2267	550.533	929.363
1951	1326.0	110.60	739.00	511.480	88.4	107.640	5.739	11.753	2995	682.710	1160.859
1952	1335.0	129.60	688.90	664.060	137.5	119.270	6.992	14.141	2511	727.058	1267.196
1953	1404.2	141.80	724.80	714.990	196.5	118.370	8.391	17.289	3315	813.060	1442.226
1954	1308.2	134.10	733.20	687.440	193.8	137.450	10.617	16.999	2865	851.496	1519.284
1955	1368.1	144.70	641.50	717.160	189.1	153.550	11.772	17.811	3064	857.757	1553.067
1956	1369.6	171.60	549.60	717.870	206.9	117.640	11.073	17.473	3368	809.756	1472.952
1957	1275.4	168.30	647.70	751.670	202.8	165.530	12.954	18.096	3668	893.149	1620.473
1958	1273.1[a]	145.10[b]	785.90	766.287	251.6	154.915	12.885	17.091	3317	929.671	1657.473

B. *Indices, West and East Germany*

| | West Germany | | | | East Germany | |
| | Old | | New | | | |
Year	Food, drink, and tobacco	Food only	Food, drink, and tobacco	Food and drink only	1936 Prices 1936 = 100	1950 Prices 1936 = 100
	(12)	(13)	(14)	(15)	(16)	(17)
1936	100.0	100.0	100	100	100.00	100.00
1950	108.2	120.9	108	121	63.31	57.77
1951	122.2	135.6	122	136	78.51	72.16
1952	131.5	144.6	132	145	83.61	78.77
1953	153.8	173.4	154	173	93.50	89.65
1954	162.4	183.2	162	183	97.92	94.44
1955	178.4	200.8	178	201	98.64	96.54
1956	n.a.	n.a.	191	216	93.12	91.56
1957	n.a.	n.a.	210	242	102.71	100.73
1958	n.a.	n.a.	219	252	106.91	103.03

Sources: Cols. 1, 7, 8, and 9: For 1936 and 1950–1955, see *SJDDR*, 1955, p. 168; for 1956 to 1958, *ibid*, 1958, p. 356. Col. 2: For 1936, see Gleitze, *Ostdeutsche Wirtschaft*, p. 209; other years same as col. 1. Col. 3: For 1936, see text; other years same as col. 1. Col. 4: For 1936, see text; for other years, see Supplement Table A.64. Col. 5: Same as col. 1. This information has not been used to calculate the value added of the industry. Col. 6: Value attributable to East Germany, RM 45.960 million (Gleitze, *op. cit.*, p. 185), divided by average price of malt exported in 1936, RM 211.9 per ton. (For price, see text.) Col. 10: For 1936, see Table 81; for other years, index in col. 16 applied. Col. 11: For 1936, 1936 value added in 1936 prices multiplied by producer price index for food, drink, and tobacco, 1950 = 185 per cent of 1938, given in *SJBR*, 1956, p. 428; for other years, index in col. 17 applied. Cols. 12 and 13: *SJBR*, 1956, pp. 217, 223. Col. 14: *SJBR*, 1959, p. 180. Col. 15: *Ibid.*, p. 183. Food and drink, but not tobacco. Cols. 16 and 17: Index calculated from the sum of the separately calculated values added of the products listed in cols. 1–9. For detailed calculations, see Supplement Table A.63.
    ᵃ Including farina made from wheat.   ᵇ Without farina.

quantity in Germany before the war; and a series on pipe tobacco. As before, the procedure consisted of evaluating cigarettes and pipe tobacco separately and using their combined estimated sales value to construct an index which was then applied to the value added for 1936.

In evaluating the postwar output, a slightly different price was used from that used in evaluating the prewar output. According to a West German tobacco expert, the typical German cigarette in 1936 cost about 3⅓ pfennig, and in 1950, 10 pfennig. After allowing for various markups, this gives a price of RM 16 per 1,000 for 1936 and of DM 30 per 1,000 for 1950, both for West German quality. However, at present, according to the same source, in West Germany the typical East German quality would cost at most 70 per cent of the cost of typical West German cigarettes, and even this estimate is likely to be slightly high. Consequently, the postwar East German output has been evaluated at 70 per cent of the West German price.[13]

When the allowance for quality deterioration is made, the output of cigarettes — which in numbers produced rose by 5 per cent between 1936 and 1955 — decreased during the same period by 27 per cent of 1936.

On the advice of the same West German tobacco expert, the problem of evaluating pipe tobacco was similarly solved. The 1950 price of East German quality pipe tobacco was DM 4,000 per ton compared with 10,850 DM per ton for West German quality. Consequently, the 1936 price at which postwar qualities were evaluated was reduced by about 60 per cent to RM 3,060 per ton. Thus, while in mere tonnage pipe tobacco production increased by 13.5 per cent between 1936 and 1955, its value in constant prices (which were adjusted for quality differences in the postwar period) fell by 32 per cent. The combined sales value, and presumably also the value added, fell from 1936 to 1955 by 27 per cent. An attempt to separate the cigarette industry and the pipe tobacco industry from the tobacco industry as a whole in order to evaluate their value added separately was unsuccessful. American figures obviously cannot be used because of the substantially different structure of the industry. The ratio of value added to sales in the United States in 1933 was 27.4 per cent; in 1935, 26 per cent; and in 1937, 25.6 per cent.[14]

Food, drink, and tobacco combined

Food, drink, and tobacco separately calculated account for RM 828.022 million of the total RM 869.583 million value added found in Table 81 above. To calculate the 1936 value added in 1950 prices, the index for the whole group of food, drink, and tobacco was used.

On the other hand, the individual industries comprising the food group were recalculated in 1950 prices by means of indices appropriate to each of them. This accounts for the fact that the sum of the values added of the individual industries in 1950 prices is slightly larger than the total value added of 1936 revaluated at 1950 prices. The sum reflects the changed commodity composition, while the direct revaluation of the sum does not, but, rather, continues to reflect the 1936 product mix.

In 1936 prices, the industry had recovered by 1950 to 63.31 per cent of its prewar level and by 1955 to 98.64 per cent. In 1950 prices, the recovery in the first year of the First Five Year Plan was only 60.35 per cent, but by 1955 the level reached was 100.84 per cent. An inspection of the components of the group shows that this result is due primarily to the sharp increase in beer brewing and, secondarily, to the fact that flour and bread baking were above the 1936 level. All other industries were below, and some substantially below, the prewar level.

The contrast with the Federal Republic is very sharp. Whether measured by the old or the new index, food production in the Federal Republic about doubled between 1936 and 1955, and the composition of the diet is much richer than that of the East German diet (although the meager East German diet may be more healthful). According to the old index, the tobacco industry in the Federal Republic had increased to 178.4 per cent of its 1936 level; according to the new index, production had increased to 141.9 per cent of the 1936 level. Even after allowing for a 25 per cent population increase, this is a superior showing.

The relevant figures in the food, drink, and tobacco industries in East Germany are given in Table 82.

CHAPTER XIII

ALL OTHER INDUSTRIES

In the 1936 German methodology, construction is a part of industrial production. However, in the postwar classification, construction has been treated separately. It is not included here.*

Of the 29 other major industry groups identified in 1936, we have dealt thus far with all but three — ceramics, glass, and alcohol. Data on these industries are scanty. In 1936 their combined value added was only RM 721.490 million. This figure may be broken down as follows:

Industry	Value added (million RM)
Ceramics	255.342
Glass	237.548
Alcohol	228.600

CERAMICS

The only series on ceramics output which could be linked to 1936 relates to household china, which for the postwar period is given in tons and for the prewar period (1939) both in tons and in marks. This allows the calculation of an average price for 1939 of RM 1,347.46 per ton. Assuming that prices of household china did not change between 1936 and 1939, the total tonnage of sales in Germany in 1936 can be found by deflation to be 61.057 tons.[1]

The share of East Germany can be estimated by a rather roundabout method. The area of East Germany in 1936 produced 39.44 per cent of Germany's industrial porcelain.[2] If it is assumed that this percentage also holds for household china, the area of East Germany produced 24,081 tons in 1936. In the absence of better information, this is the basis on which the index of ceramics was constructed, which in turn was applied to the estimated gross value added in 1936.

This estimate in turn proceeded as follows. The total ceramics industry had a value added of RM 255.342 million in all Germany in 1936,

* According to Gleitze (p. 184, note 4), the value added for construction given in the Production Statistics of 1936 also included the aircraft industry.

of which the overwhelming part, RM 212.916 million, was accounted for by fine ceramics, the rest by other related industries. The sales of fine ceramics attributable to the area of East Germany were 39.44 per cent, those of other ceramics 21.95 per cent. Allocating the value added on this basis gives RM 83.974 million for fine ceramics and RM 312 million to the rest, or RM 93.286 million altogether. This is the base to which the index of household porcelain was applied. The value added in 1950 prices was found by means of the producer price index of fine ceramics (base 1938 = 100; 1950 = 185).[3]

Since the East German area was famous for fine chinas — Meissen and Dresden, and Royal Porcelain Manufacture, Berlin — the share of almost 40 per cent in value added seems reasonable.

The calculations indicate that by 1955 the industry had recovered to about 75 per cent of its prewar level. As a consumer goods industry (moreover, one which needs coal for firing), it would naturally be starved, but as an export industry, one might have expected a better showing. The values derived are given in Table 83.

Table 83

Value added, ceramics industry, East Germany, and indices,
West and East Germany, 1936 and 1950–1958

| Year | Production of household ceramics (tons) | East German index 1936 = 100 | Value added | | West German index |
			1936 Prices (million RM)	1950 Prices (million DM)	
	(1)	(2)	(3)	(4)	(5)
1936	24.081	100.00	93.286	172.579	100
1950	11.738	48.74	45.468	84.115	97
1951	13.526	56.17	52.399	96.938	124
1952	15.775	65.51	61.111	113.057	125
1953	16.324	67.79	63.239	116.991	131
1954	17.511	72.72	67.838	125.499	160
1955	18.204	75.60	70.524	130.470	183
1956	17.288	71.79	66.970	123.894	190
1957	16.391	68.07	63.500	117.475	192
1958	17.930	74.46	69.461	128.502	193

Sources: Col. 1: For derivation of 1936 figure, see text; for 1950–1955, see *Haushalt Porzellan einschliesslich Hotelgeschirr* in *SJDDR*, 1955, pp. 162–163; for 1956 to 1958, *ibid.*, 1958, p. 356. Col. 2: Calculated from col. 1. Col. 3: For derivation of 1936 values, see text; other years calculated with index, col. 2. Col. 4: Calculated with index for *Feinkeramik:* 1938 = 100; 1950 = 185. See *SJBR*, 1956, p. 434. Col. 5: Fine ceramics, *SJBR*, 1959, p. 183.

The reasons for the poor showing may lie, in part, in faulty planning. In 1957 Oelssner frankly stated that planning was not based to a sufficient degree on the actual conditions in a country, and he gave the ceramics industry as a particular example, stating:

Although we have almost all the necessary raw materials, we are unable to satisfy either our own or the export needs for household china and other ceramic products. The reason is to be found in the fact that we have badly neglected the development of the ceramics industry during the past years. Here, too, relatively small means will bring quick and big results. Hence we must make all efforts to make the necessary means available.[4]

GLASS

The glass industry must be considered in two parts. Flat or window glass was poorly represented in the area of East Germany in 1936, but production has apparently expanded vigorously. Data on hollow glass and glass products are virtually nonexistent.

According to official sources, flat (window) glass production expanded from 2.153 million sq m in 1936 to 14.281 million sq m in 1955, or 663 per cent. As only 8.7 per cent of the value added of flat glass production in all Germany in 1936 is attributable to East Germany, this increase is quite believable.

The probable development of hollow glass production is quite another matter. The value added of hollow glass and glass products industries may be estimated as about 40 per cent of the value added for the industry in all of Germany.

The part of the industry that makes products for home use is not likely to have fared better than household china. Other parts produce lenses for cameras or Christmas tree ornaments for export. The various products cannot be allocated. Hence it has seemed best not to calculate

Table 84

Production and value added, flat glass industry, East Germany, 1936 and 1950–1958

			Value added	
Year	Production (million sq m)	Index 1936 = 100	1936 Prices (million RM)	1950 Prices (million DM)
	(1)	(2)	(3)	(4)
1936	2.153	100.00	16.521	21.973
1950	13.213	613.70	101.389	134.848
1951	13.531	628.47	103.830	138.094
1952	11.697	543.29	89.756	119.377
1953	9.981	463.59	76.590	101.865
1954	12.032	558.85	92.328	122.796
1955	14.281	663.31	109.585	145.749
1956	14.304	664.38	109.762	145.984
1957	14.885	691.36	114.220	151.913
1958	14.702	682.86	112.815	150.045

Sources: Col. 1: For 1936 and 1950–1955, see *SJDDR*, 1955, pp. 162–163; for 1956 to 1958, *ibid.*, 1958, p. 356. Col. 2: Calculated from col. 1. Col. 3: Value added in all Germany = RM 189.896 million; 8.7 per cent assumed attributable to the area of East Germany. Col. 4: Price index of flat glass industry: base 1938 = 100; 1950 = 131. See *SJBR*, 1955, p. 440.

this subindustry separately but to assume, in the end and by implication, that it has varied with the industry as a whole. The values can be found in Tables 84 and 85.

Table 85

Value added, hollow glass industry,[a] East Germany, and indices,
West and East Germany, 1936 and 1950–1958

Year	Index of all industries separately calculated		Value added		West Germany, index, hollow glass
	1936 Prices 1936 = 100	1950 Prices 1936 = 100	1936 Prices (million RM)	1950 Prices (million DM)	
	(1)	(2)	(3)	(4)	(5)
1936	100.0	100.0	19.061	26.114	100
1950	75.3	66.8	14.353	17.444	185
1951	87.8	78.1	16.735	20.395	232
1952	95.3	85.6	18.165	22.354	221
1953	110.2	99.4	21.005	25.957	246
1954	119.7	108.1	22.816	28.229	276
1955	127.1	113.4	24.221	29.604	303
1956	133.8	118.9	25.499	31.058	346
1957	140.6	125.6	26.800	32.796	354
1958	147.8	132.6	28.180	34.637	

Sources: Cols. 1 and 2: See below, Table 87. Col. 3: Estimated as 40 per cent of the total value added of the German hollow glass industry. Col. 4: 1936 value in 1950 prices calculated from index for *Hohlglasindustrie*, 1938 = 100 and 1950 = 137, given in *SJBR*, 1956, p. 434. Col. 5: *SJBR*, 1959, p. 183.
 [a] *Hohlglas und Flachglas veredelnde Industrie.*

ALCOHOL

The production of alcohol, both for human consumption and as an industrial raw material, was disproportionately small in the area of East Germany in the prewar period. Of a total value added of RM 228.600 million in the Reich in 1936, only 19.1 per cent, or RM 43.663 million, originated in the Eastern Zone.[5] There must have been substantial imports from the areas east of the Oder-Neisse line, which produced a disproportionately large share. Although the production of drinking alcohol in all Germany, measured by sales (and also by value added), was almost half of the total alcohol production, this branch of the industry was not well represented in the Eastern Zone (about 13 per cent), while that of industrial alcohol was well represented with about 23 per cent of all German sales.

Available data include an official index for alcohol production from 1946 through 1952 [6] and two absolute figures for the production of crude alcohol.[7] However, there is no way to link these scanty data to 1936, and no attempt was made to calculate the value added of this industry.

Procedure for estimating alcohol output

It was assumed that this last industry, for which no estimates of any kind could be made, moved as the average of all industries. The estimated value added of this industry in 1936 was RM 43.663 million, a negligible amount. The industries for which it was possible to account in some detail produced in 1936, and in 1936 prices, a value added of RM 7,656.632 million of a total RM 7,786.399 million. The industry for which no calculations whatever were possible, is thus only 0.6 per cent of the total estimated value added produced in 1936 in the area of East Germany.

The 1936 value added in constant 1950 prices was found by applying the official price index for spirits, which was 245 per cent of 1938.[8]

CHAPTER XIV

THE DEVELOPMENT OF INDUSTRIAL
PRODUCTION IN EAST GERMANY

In the foregoing pages an attempt has been made to calculate the value added of industrial production industry by industry for the area of East Germany in 1936 and to estimate the development of the whole industrial sector as well as the various subsectors through 1958. It now remains to add up the results and to make various comparisons in order to put the findings in perspective.

According to the calculation presented above, production, defined as gross value added, amounted in 1936 in 1936 prices to RM 7,786.399 million.

Sanderson estimated the comparable figure at $7.4 billion,[1] a very close approximation to our calculation. Dr. Abeken's estimate was RM 8.755 billion — substantially higher than our estimate.[2] In the Statistical Yearbook of the Federal Republic the *net* social product of industry and artisans combined was estimated at RM 6.4 billion, a figure which, however, excludes not only depreciation but also the important production of East Berlin.[3]

According to our calculations, the gross value added in 1955 measured in 1936 West German prices was DM 9,898.350 million, an increase of about 30 per cent over 1936. Measured in 1950 West German prices, the absolute values are of course much higher, but the increase from 1936 to 1955 is only about 15 per cent, in many cases reflecting the substitution of cheaper for more expensive goods. In order to evaluate the plausibility of these findings, a number of comparisons with both West German and official East German data have to be made. However, before entering on this task, a few points regarding methodology should be made in order to clarify the meaning of our figures.

A FEW COMMENTS ON METHODOLOGY

So far as possible the index calculations have been based on officially published East German data which, since 1956, have been reasonably plentiful. These data have been taken at their face value unless there were compelling reasons for doing something else; for example, in at least one case the 1936 base was set below the figure given by the Statistical Yearbook of the German Democratic Republic, thus increasing the gains achieved by East Germany beyond the claims made. In general, in this study we have leaned over backwards to give East Germany its due. Nevertheless, the results of the present calculations are about three percentage points *below* the results of a preliminary study which frequently had to be based on West German guesses.[4]

German statistics distinguish between industry and artisans. On the whole, the distinction has to do with the number of employees and such sociological criteria as attitudes toward work. Unfortunately, the line of demarcation between industry and artisans is neither sharply drawn nor unchangeable. In the Production Statistics of 1936, which was compiled for military purposes, it is quite clear that "industry" simply means all the plants covered by the census, which does not coincide with any theoretical concept of "industry" or with any membership in a particular organization (*Reichsgruppe Industrie*).[5] Wherever small plants were important with respect to raw materials, they were included. Usually, the omitted plants had fewer than five workers. In other words, the 1936 base covered more than industry and included substantial numbers of what are frequently classified as artisan shops. The Production Statistics of 1936 gives detailed accounts of the omitted plants in the comments on the calculations. For example, in machinery construction, only firms made up of five workers or fewer (including the owner) were excluded; in furniture manufacture the firms with ten or fewer workers (including the owner) were excluded; in the basket-making industry, plants with a turnover of less than RM 15,000 in annual production were excluded. As a generalization it can be asserted that only in textiles and in the food, drink, and tobacco industries were artisan shops of any importance at all. Overall it seems doubtful that their output in 1936 amounted to more than 5 per cent of the output covered or, at most, 10 per cent.*

Since 1945, artisans certainly have not had an easy time in East Germany. More important in the present context, as a result of increasing socialization and "industrialization" a part of the output which in 1936 was classified as produced by artisans is undoubtedly now attributed to industry. This is especially true for the clothing industry and for the food, drink, and tobacco industries. In our estimation of the output of these industries, all the available inputs (for example, woven cloth, slaughter weight of animals) were allocated to the industrial part. This means that the growth shown by official data (which, to repeat, were accepted at their face value) is in part purely statistical since it coincides with the increasing coverage of the industry.

* This figure does not include the artisans in pure service trades or the building trades.

Thus, even if the 1936 base is raised only by 5 per cent, the figures for the later years would not have to be raised to adjust for production by artisans, and the growth shown by the index would be that much smaller.*

Throughout we shall make comparisons (wherever feasible) with both the old and the new index of production of the Federal Republic. The old index is compared with the calculations in 1936 prices, and the new index with the calculations in 1950 prices. Ideally, the difference between the two indices corresponds to the difference in calculations in 1936 and in 1950 prices. The old index of the Federal Republic, in fact, used the same methodology as this study: it started with the figures given in the Production Statistics of 1936 as a base and then estimated later values by a number of series typical for industry. That the Statistische Bundesamt in Wiesbaden, with its superior resources and undoubtedly also with its very competent director, Dr. Fürst, and deputy, Dr. H. Bartels, could reach more satisfactory results than this study is another matter. However, had the author started with West German figures from the Production Statistics of 1936 and the output of a limited number of industries, he would have arrived at substantially the same results as those published by the Statistische Bundesamt in the Statistical Yearbooks for the Federal Republic.

The similarity in methodology also permits a tentative answer to another question: What difference would it have made if the assumed 1936 relations of value added to sales value or gross production value (in the Western sense) had been replaced by true input-output ratios? What is the possible bias involved?

For many industries, particularly the basic industries, approximations to input-output calculations were in fact made. But for others the method of assuming that the industry moved as a set of subseries was used, which means that the 1936 valuations are maintained throughout.

There is no question in my mind that this method imparts an upward bias to the calculations made in 1936 prices. To the extent to which increasing productivity requires increased division of productive processes, "gross production" tends to increase faster than net production. Vertical integration may offset this tendency, but technological progress also tends toward better use of inputs. Hence the ratio of value added to inputs should decrease in many cases (although certainly not necessarily).

Whatever the situation is in theory,† Table 86 indicates that at least

---

* Dr. Abeken of the Deutsche Institut für Wirtschaftsforschung has shown me calculations based on the value of capital and capital-output ratios which indicate that the gross value added of industry in 1936 was substantially above the figure given by the Production Statistics of 1936.

† I am not proposing as an immutable law that, with progress from the monkey to superman, value added as a percentage of turnover declines. But I am stating that this is likely to have happened during the past 20 or 30 years.

Table 86

Ratio of value added to "gross production value," Western definition,
West Germany, 1936, 1950, 1954, and East German ratios of net
product plus depreciation allowance to gross production, 1956

| | West Germany | | | | | |
Industry	1936	1950	1954	Increase or decrease 1936–1950	Increase or decrease 1950–1954	East Germany 1956
(1)	(2)	(3)	(4)	(5)	(6)	(7)
Coal mining:						
Soft coal	⎰77.11	74	74	− ...	0	⎱
Lignite	⎱87.60					⎰ 77.5
Potash and rock salt	79.33	72	75	−7.33	+3	
Iron ores	77.97	71	63	−6.97	−8	
Iron making	49.48		38			
Blast furnaces, steel, and hot rolled steel		50				⎰ 30.2
Nonferrous metal semi-manufactures	37.07	38	42	−1.07	+4	
Iron, steel castings	67.39	60	51	−7.39	−9	
Nonferrous metal castings	51.98	48	47	−3.98	−1	64.5
Stones and earths	73.83	65	62	−8.83	−3	
Rubber and asbestos	56.26	50	50	−6.26	0	
Pulp and paper	39.91	46	45	+6.09	−1	
Sawmills	40.93	42	38	+1.07	−4	
Chemical	⎰57.01	48	49	− ...	+1	⎱ 60.0a
Chemicotechnical	⎱55.26					
Steel construction	53.50	54	48	+0.50	−6	
Machine construction	65.40	60	54	−5.40	−6	49.4–55.7b
Vehicles	45.76	47	42	+1.24	−1	47.5
Shipbuilding	54.31	45	38	−9.31	−7	44.7
Electrical engineering	69.71	57	55	−12.71	−2	54.8
Fine mechanics and optics	74.97	65	61	−9.97	−4	71.7
Fine ceramics	76.83	71	69	−5.83	−2	⎱ 69.8
Glass	68.90	62	61	−6.90	−1	
Woodworking	56.36	54	52	−2.36	−2	54.2
Paper using	49.76	48	47	−1.76	−1	46.3e
Printing	63.76	66	62	+2.24	−4	58.3
Leather	39.88	37	34	−2.88	−3	⎱ 58.7
Shoes	43.52	39	45	−4.52	+6	
Textiles	43.15	46	41	+2.85	−5	57.0
Clothing	47.50	40	40	−7.50	0	51.9
Food, drink, and tobacco	41.16	32	32d	−9.16		54.5

Sources: West Germany: For 1936, see *Produktionsstatistik, 1936, passim.*; for 1950, *SJBR*, 1955, p. 232; 1954 *ibid.*, 1958, p. 201. East Germany: *SJDDR*, 1957, p. 311; 1958, p. 331.
[a] Includes also rubber and asbestos.   [b] Heavy machinery: 49.4; general machinery: 55.7.
[e] Refers to paper using industry, including pulp and paper.   [d] Excludes tobacco.

in the Federal Republic, and for a roughly comparable industry classification, the *Nettoquota*, as it is called in West German terminology, has in fact decreased for many important industries, and precisely for those industries which have expanded vigorously in East Germany, such as lignite, potash mining, chemicals, fine mechanics and optics, and shipbuilding.*

The implications are twofold. First, since the 1950 price structure differs from the 1936 price structure, the much smaller growth of industrial output in East Germany in 1950 prices compared with the growth shown in 1936 prices is to be expected. Second, using the 1936 *Nettoquotas,* if anything, gives an upward bias to the calculations that is modified only because in some instances it was possible to approximate the true input-output relations of the postwar years. It will be observed that the new index of production of the Federal Republic also grows less rapidly than the old one, although the differences in growth are not as spectacular as for East Germany. Ironically, to state that there was any substantial technological progress in East Germany compared with 1936 would imply that we have overstated the true growth in the calculations. The one sure result of technological progress, increased output, has been valued at the old prices, and the percentage of sales value assigned to value added was higher than it should have been.

OVER-ALL COMPARISONS

By 1955, industrial production as a whole in East Germany had increased to 127.1 per cent of 1936, and by 1957 to 140.7 per cent (both computed in 1936 prices). Production in the Federal Republic rose to 197.8 per cent. In 1950 prices, industrial production in East Germany rose to only 113.4 per cent by 1955 and to 125.6 per cent by 1957. The 1950-base index of the Federal Republic shows that by 1955 there was already an increase to 198 per cent. The aggregate showing of the Federal Republic was undoubtedly and spectacularly better.

Two comments should be made on the interpretation of these figures. First, the population increase between 1936 and 1955 was much greater in the Federal Republic than in East Germany. For this reason alone, the tremendous increase in industrial production officially claimed in East Germany as compared with the Federal Republic is not credible. Even adjusted to a per capita basis, by 1955 the 1936 index of East Germany had risen to only 114.1 per cent of 1936, compared with the rise for the

---

* Since this was written, new data for West Germany have become available, and East German data have for the first time been published which make the calculation of similar ratios possible. These figures have been included in Table 86. It will be noticed that for most West German industries the *Nettoquota* has declined further between 1950 and 1954. The East German figures for 1956 are not immediately comparable with the West German figures because of the peculiarities of the East German price system discussed above in Part II. It is striking, however, that in the mining sectors where East and West German prices did not differ very much, the East German *Nettoquota* in 1956 was comparable to the German *Nettoquota* of 1936. In the various metallurgical and metal products industries the East German *Nettoquota* is so much smaller that one wonders how it has been calculated. In the building materials industries, it is about the same as in West Germany in 1950. In the various consumer goods industries, it is much above any of the West German quota, a fact which can only be explained by the nature of the prices used.

Federal Republic's 1936-base index to 155.1 per cent. In 1950 prices there is virtually no growth at all in per capita production of East Germany between 1936 and 1955, while the growth of the Federal Republic's new index compared with the old one is hardly smaller than when calculated in 1936 prices.

It may be objected that West German growth reflects basically the fact that West German industry blossomed out following the currency reform of 1948 and by 1950 had already reached a level 10 to 13 per cent above 1936 while East German industry did not really start to grow until 1950, when the First Five Year Plan was inaugurated. True, the level of production of East Germany in 1950 was only two-thirds to three-fourths of the 1936 level, an admission which is not, of course, officially made. (The index of industrial gross production of the Zone [that is, without East Berlin] given in the Statistical Yearbook of the Federal Republic shows for 1950 a level of 85 per cent of 1936.[6]) However, the planned economy has developed vigorously since 1950. Thus it might be argued that the most relevant comparison is the rates of growth since 1950.

Before making such a comparison, it should be pointed out that it is by no means clear just what such growth comparisons are supposed to prove. Usually growth rates of the United States and the Soviet Union are compared — to give the most frequently used example — in order to prove either that the Soviets will or will not catch up with the United States or to show that the failure of consumers to be better off in the planned economy was a necessary sacrifice to achieve high growth rates in the economy, to lift a backward country out of stagnation, to break the chains of feudalism, and to release the productive powers of a sleeping economy.

‧ Whatever may be said about such comparisons for underdeveloped countries, the reasons usually given to justify an interest in growth rates rather than in absolute levels do not apply to East Germany. It was not a feudal country in any sense; and culturally, sociologically, and historically it did not differ significantly from the area of the Federal Republic. If anything, it was more radical in politics, had more Socialists and Protestants, and about the same number of "feudal" barons and backward peasants. Certainly the cure of communism was not needed to establish the conditions for growth.

Economically, the East German area was not backward either (as we were at pains to establish in the Foreword). Backward areas do not pioneer in the production of synthetic gasoline or synthetic rubber, or establish world leadership in optical goods or national leadership in electrical goods.

Hence even a growth rate no different from that in West Germany would prove at best that with sufficient labor inputs the planned economy can produce something which after all was denied only by a diehard minority of self-appointed guardians of free-market economy purity.

Between 1950 and 1955 the growth of East German industrial output was about 70 per cent compared with a growth in the Federal Republic of 75 per cent (1936 prices and old index, respectively). In terms of 1950 prices and the new index the growth was slightly larger for both areas.*

On an aggregate level, the gap between East and West Germany continued to widen between 1950 and 1955. The aggregate growth rates of the West were undoubtedly better, but on a per capita basis, the picture is substantially modified. Per capita output in East Germany (the population of which had declined by 1955 to 97.6 per cent of its 1950 level) rose to about 173 per cent by 1955. Per capita production of the Federal Republic (the population of which had increased by about 5 per cent between 1950 and 1955) rose to 166.5 per cent. (Both figures refer to the old index for the Federal Republic and the index in 1936 prices for East Germany (see Tables 87 and 88).

This rise could be considered an achievement for East Germany. But its true meaning cannot be discussed without reference to the fact that the base with which East Germany started was substantially lower (both in the aggregate and on a per capita basis) than that of the Federal Republic. Furthermore, the substantial increase in the industrial labor force, the composition of the growth, and the development of other sectors should all be considered. To anticipate the findings of Part IV, it may be stated that agricultural output undoubtedly increased in the Federal Republic between 1950 and 1955 and between 1936 and 1955. In East Germany there was a decrease between 1936 and 1955, although no marked change occurred between 1950 and 1955. Construction particularly of housing undoubtedly lagged catastrophically in East Germany. There is evidence that the growth of industrial production in East Germany is limited by unsatisfied import needs for raw materials and, possibly, insufficient investments; in the West any possible stagnation comes only from the demand side and can therefore more easily be remedied.

BREAKDOWN BY WEST GERMAN SCHEMA
OF CLASSIFICATION — 1936 PRICES

The comparison by major industry groups is our next task. The first comparison to be made follows West German statistical usage, the major groupings of which are mining; basic and production goods industries;

---

* The reason growth since 1950 is larger when measured in 1950 prices, while compared with 1936 it is larger when measured in 1936 prices, is that the important price changes occurred before 1950 and were largely completed by that year. For example, comparing 1955 with 1936, wool prices rose much more than rayon prices, but the total increase was before the Korean war.

Table 87

Value added, East German industry, indices of industrial production, West and East Germany, and East German index of gross production, 1936 and 1950–1958

Year	East Germany, 1936 prices			West Germany, old index	
	Value added (million RM)	Index 1936 = 100	Index 1950 = 100	1936 = 100	1950 = 100
	(1)	(2)	(3)	(4)	(5)
1936	7,786.399	100.0	132.8	100.0	
1950	5,863.832	75.3	100.0	113.0	100.0
1951	6,838.070	85.3	113.3	134.4	118.9
1952	7,417.964	95.3	126.6	144.2	127.6
1953	8,517.292	109.5	145.4	157.2	139.1
1954	9,323.925	119.7	159.0	176.3	156.0
1955	9,298.350	127.1	168.9	197.8	175.0
1956	10,426.787	133.8	177.8	n.a.	n.a.
1957	10,952.291	140.7	186.9	n.a.	n.a.
1958	11,585.552	148.8	197.6	n.a.	n.a.

Year	East Germany, 1950 prices			West Germany, new index	
	Value added (million DM)	Index 1936 = 100	Index 1950 = 100	1936 = 100	1950 = 100
	(6)	(7)	(8)	(9)	(10)
1936	15,668.999	100.0		100.0	
1950	10,472.226	66.7	100.0	111	100
1951	12,241.240	78.1	116.9	131	119
1952	13,406.815	85.5	128.2	140	126
1953	15,573.300	99.3	148.9	154	139
1954	16,944.316	108.0	161.9	172	155
1955	17,770.079	113.4	170.0	198	178
1956	18,634.433	118.9	178.3	213	192
1957	19,685.176	125.6	188.3	225	203
1958	20,797.187	132.7	199.0	232	209

Year	East Germany, 1950 East German prices	
	Official gross production index	Official net production index
	(11)	(12)
1936		
1950	100.0	100.0
1951	122.7	127.0
1952	142.2	148.3
1953	158.2	156.0
1954	176.7	180.5
1955	190.3	199.4
1956	202.0	
1957	217.0	

Sources: Cols. 1 and 6: Figures from totals in preceding tables. Cols. 2, 3, 7, and 8: Derived from cols. 1 and 6. Cols. 4 and 5: Refers to total industry without construction. *SJBR*, 1956, p. 217. Cols. 9 and 10: *SJBR*, 1959. p. 180, average daily production. Cols. 11 and 12: 1950–1955 calculated from *SJDDR*, 1955, p. 90; 1956–1957 are given in *ibid.*, 1957, p. 280 (prices not specified).

Table 88

Indices of per capita industrial production, West and East Germany, 1936 and 1950–1958

Year	West Germany, old index 1936 = 100	East Germany, 1936 prices 1936 = 100	West Germany, new index 1936 = 100	East Germany, 1950 prices 1936 = 100	West Germany, old index 1950 = 100	East Germany, 1936 prices 1950 = 100	West Germany, new index 1950 = 100	East Germany, 1950 prices 1950 = 100	East Germany Official gross index 1950 = 100	East Germany Official net index 1950 = 100
	(1)	(2)	(3)	(4)	(5)	(6)	(7)	(8)	(9)	(10)
1936	100.0	100.0	100.0	100.0						
1950	93.1	66.2	89.2	58.6	100.0	100.0	100.0	100.0	100.0	100.0
1951	109.5	75.1	104.1	68.8	117.6	113.4	116.7	117.4	108.0	111.8
1952	116.5	84.0	110.3	75.4	125.1	126.9	123.7	128.7	125.4	130.8
1953	125.7	97.3	120.0	88.3	135.0	147.0	134.5	150.7	140.6	138.7
1954	139.5	107.1	132.7	96.6	149.8	161.8	148.8	164.8	158.1	161.5
1955	155.1	114.1	151.3	102.1	166.5	172.4	169.6	174.2	171.4	179.6
1956		122.0	160.9	108.5		184.3	180.4	185.2		
1957		129.8	171.1	115.9		196.1	191.8	197.8		
1958		138.6	172.2	123.6		209.4	193.0	210.9		

Sources: All figures calculated from Table 87 and population figures given in Table 2.

investment goods industries; food, drink, and tobacco; electricity; and gas. In our comparison, gas has been included with mining because it was impossible to separate it satisfactorily in the calculations for East Germany. For the comparisons in 1936 prices, the old index of the Federal Republic was used; for the comparison in 1950 prices the new index was used.

The index of all mining and gas increased by 87 per cent in East Germany between 1936 and 1955, compared with a 47 per cent increase in the Federal Republic. However, for the subgroups that can be compared there are substantial differences. Coal mining as a whole (including gas) increased by 88.5 per cent in East Germany, compared with an increase of only a third in the Federal Republic. Potash mining, on the other hand, increased by 63 per cent in East Germany and by 160 per cent in the Federal Republic.

These figures reflect what can be observed again and again: the two economies tend to approach each other structurally. Or, statistically speaking, if the base in East Germany was relatively small, the increase is big, and vice versa. For coal mining in East Germany, however, and for potash mining in the Federal Republic this is only a partial explanation, since lignite, particularly, was always important in the former and potash in the latter.

Similarly, the output of electric power increased by 260 per cent in the Federal Republic compared with 93 per cent in East Germany. The severe lag which this nevertheless substantial increase in power production represents has many causes which cannot be discussed here. However, they make the lag of the general index in East Germany behind that in the Federal Republic quite plausible. The shortages of metals, of engineering construction, of skilled manpower, all of which keep the increase of power production in East Germany at about one-third that in the Federal Republic, go a long way to explain why the increase in the total index in East Germany remained at one-third the increase shown in the Federal Republic.

Under the heading "basic and production goods industries," West German statistics include the following classifications: building materials; iron-making; iron, steel, and malleable castings; wire industries and related products and cold rolled steel; nonferrous metals, including castings; chemical industry, including fibers; petroleum, rubber manufacturing; flat glass; sawmills; some woodworking; and cellulose and paper production. The figures for the corresponding East German industries have been added, including the estimate for the flat glass industry. Unfortunately it was necessary to include all of woodworking here, although some of it — perhaps even the major portion — should have been included with the consumer goods industries. In East Germany the output of this group of basic industries increased by 52.7 per cent between 1936 and 1955, compared with 80.7 per cent in the Federal Republic.

The third group of industries consists of the so-called investment-goods industries. In West Germany this term covers steel construction, machine construction, vehicle construction, shipbuilding, electrical equipment and supplies, fine mechanics and optics, and iron and metal goods. The East German industries which were grouped together to arrive at figures roughly comparable with those for the West German classification are engineering construction (which includes steel construction and shipbuilding), road vehicle construction, electrical equipment and supplies, fine mechanics and optics, iron and steel products, and metal goods.

By 1955 these industries had increased their output to 136.0 per cent of their 1936 level in East Germany, compared with 251.9 per cent in the Federal Republic. Since the increase in the Federal Republic is astonishingly far ahead of that in East Germany, even the per capita increase in the Federal Republic is substantially greater than in East Germany. In the Federal Republic the 1955 level was 223 per cent of the 1950 level; in East Germany it was 203.6 per cent of the 1950 level. Since this group of industries uses metals which are extremely scarce and since there is no question that in East Germany vehicle manufacture lagged badly behind West Germany, this result is quite believable. The growth in East Germany since 1950 is of course much more substantial than the growth since 1936. This is also true for other industries or industry groups.

The calculations for the years before 1950 are seriously handicapped by large gaps in information. They have therefore not been reproduced. But from 1950 on, the information becomes quite full (and official). There is no reason to doubt that the development since 1950 occurred as shown by our calculated index. The crucial question appears to be whether the 1936 level was reached by 1950 or not. It certainly was surpassed in mining and electric-power production, and it was reached in basic and production goods. But the investment goods industry was certainly below the 1936 level, although the particular values are, of course, subject to error. Yet a 1950 level of about two-thirds of the 1936 level seems plausible in the light of the East German information.*

The fourth group of industries, consumer goods industries, comprises fine ceramics, glass (excluding flat glass), part of woodworking, paper and printing, leather and shoes, and textiles and clothing. Except for the

---

* An index of industrial *Bruttoproduktion* for East Germany was published in the 1954 edition of the Statistical Yearbook of the Federal Republic, p. 544. This index reads as follows: for 1936, 100; for 1946, 42; for 1949, 70; for 1950, 85; for 1951, 97; or 1952, 109. Professor Bruno Gleitze, who was responsible for the index for the early years, told me that until 1950 the concept of *Bruttoproduktion* corresponded to the western concept of gross production, which would be the sales value of industries with all intra-industry flows eliminated. Our index was calculated independently. The near-agreement is reassuring.

part of woodworking which does not belong here but could not be separated from the part listed among the investment-goods industries, the groups are identical with the East German categories.

According to our calculations, by 1950 this industry had recovered to only 44 per cent of its 1936 level, and even by 1955 the index stood at only 72.7 per cent of 1936, compared with 184.1 per cent in the Federal Republic. Compared with 1950, however, the improvement in East Germany was about the same as in the Federal Republic: 65 per cent above 1950, compared with 62 per cent in the Federal Republic. Again, there can be little doubt that the result is substantially correct. The figures for the per capita availability of woolen and cotton cloth and of leather shoes make it quite plausible. Synthetic yarns are not included here, but rayon woven goods are, which, while relatively plentiful, are inferior to both the natural and the newer synthetic materials. The general shortage of manufactured consumer goods (except such items as cameras) is well known. In addition it should be remembered that a *slight* fall from the 1936 level of production for such goods as textiles, clothing, and some cheaper chinas could still leave the population better off than in 1936, since those industries were heavily concentrated in the area of East Germany and their products were exported to the rest of the Reich.

The final group is food, drink, and tobacco, which here also includes fats and oils and alcohol. By 1955 the output of this group of industries was only between 14 and 15 per cent above 1936; this is hardly more per capita than in 1936. By comparison, in 1955 the index in the Federal Republic reached 178.4 per cent of 1936, a smaller increase than that of any other group except mining, but one which indicates a substantially higher level of living in West Germany in 1955 than in 1936.

The results of the comparison between East and West Germany are found in Table 89.

BREAKDOWN BY EAST GERMAN CLASSIFICATION — 1936 PRICES

The official data on gross production (East German definition) are available in 1950 prices and in *Messwerte*. The subgroups defined by the East German Central Statistical Office are basic industries; metalworking industries; light industries; and food, drink, and tobacco. The last category is apparently identical with the West German classification, and metalworking appears to be very similar to the West German investment goods industries.

Basic industries include energy, mining, metallurgy, chemicals, and building materials (including glass and ceramics). Metalworking includes machine construction, electrical equipment and supplies, fine mechanics and optics, castings and forgings, and iron and metal goods. Light industries include everything else except food industries. They also include the products of saw mills, which in the West German classification are part

Table 89

Industrial production of East Germany, major industry groups, West German classification, and indices, West and East Germany, 1936 and 1950–1958, in 1936 prices

A. *Total industrial production*

Year	East Germany, calculated value added (million RM)	Indices			
		East Germany 1936 = 100	West Germany 1936 = 100	East Germany 1950 = 100	West Germany 1950 = 100
	(1)	(2)	(3)	(4)	(5)
1936	7,786.399	100.0	100.0	131.7	90.17
1950	5,863.832	75.3	110.9	100.0	100.0
1951	6,838.070	85.3	131.4	113.3	118.5
1952	7,417.964	95.3	139.8	126.6	126.1
1953	8,577.292	109.5	153.9	145.4	138.8
1954	9,323.925	119.7	171.8	159.0	154.9
1955	9,898.350	127.1	197.8	168.9	178.4
1956	10,426.787	133.8		177.8	
1957	10,952.291	140.7		186.9	
1958	11,585.552	148.8		197.6	

B. *Coal mining including gas*

Year	East Germany, calculated value added (million RM)	Indices			
		East Germany 1936 = 100	West Germany[a] 1936 = 100	East Germany 1950 = 100	West Germany 1950 = 100
	(6)	(7)	(8)	(9)	(10)
1936	435.040	100.0	100.0	76.5	98.1
1950	568.369	130.7	101.9	100.0	100.0
1951	634.097	145.8	113.9	111.6	111.8
1952	657.460	151.1	120.7	115.6	118.5
1953	699.905	160.9	122.6	123.1	120.4
1954	743.989	171.0	125.8	130.8	123.5
1955	820.005	188.5	134.3	144.2	131.8
1956	846.405	194.6		148.9	
1957	844.158	194.0		148.4	
1958	877.953	201.8		154.4	

Table 89 (Continued)

C. *Potash mining*

Year	East Germany, calculated value added[b] (million RM)	Indices			
		East Germany 1936 = 100	West Germany[b] 1936 = 100	East Germany 1950 = 100	West Germany 1950 = 100
	(11)	(12)	(13)	(14)	(15)
1936	87.491	100.0	100.0	71.3	67.0
1950	122.653	140.2	149.3	100.0	100.0
1951	129.354	147.9	176.6	105.5	118.3
1952	123.570	141.3	200.4	100.8	134.2
1953	126.508	144.6	206.7	103.1	138.4
1954	134.312	153.5	247.2	109.5	165.6
1955	142.482	162.9	260.1	116.2	174.2
1956	142.849	163.3		116.5	
1957	147.256	168.3		120.0	
1958	151.480	173.1		123.5	

D. *Total mining and gas*

Year	East Germany, calculated value added (million RM)	Indices			
		East Germany 1936 = 100	West Germany[c] 1936 = 100	East Germany 1950 = 100	West Germany 1950 = 100
	(16)	(17)	(18)	(19)	(20)
1936	552.669	100.0	100.0	75.6	94.7
1950	730.535	132.2	105.6	100.0	100.0
1951	807.744	146.2	119.0	109.7	112.7
1952	830.848	150.3	127.7	113.7	120.9
1953	884.969	160.1	130.8	121.1	123.9
1954	941.814	170.4	136.2	128.9	129.0
1955	1,033.360	187.0	146.6	141.5	138.8
1956	1,064.762	192.7		145.8	
1957	1,072.333	194.0		146.7	
1958	1,114.633	201.7		152.6	

Table 89 (Continued)

E. *Electricity*

Year	East Germany, calculated value added (million RM)	Indices			
		East Germany 1936 = 100	West Germany 1936 = 100	East Germany 1936 = 100	West Germany 1936 = 100
	(21)	(22)	(23)	(24)	(25)
1936	447.251	100.0	100.0	76.5	48.3
1950	584.814	130.8	207.0	100.0	100.0
1951	644.856	144.2	242.9	110.3	117.3
1952	696.539	155.7	264.4	119.1	127.7
1953	728.486	162.9	281.4	124.6	135.9
1954	782.498	175.0	319.9	133.8	154.5
1955	863.710	193.1	359.8	147.7	173.0
1956	939.988	210.2		160.7	
1957	986.637	220.6		168.7	
1958	1,051.106	235.0		179.7	

F. *Production goods*

Year	East Germany, calculated value added (million RM)	Indices			
		East Germany 1936 = 100	West Germany 1936 = 100	East Germany 1950 = 100	West Germany 1950 = 100
	(26)	(27)	(28)	(29)	(30)
1936	1,676.308	100.0	100.0	100.8	96.7
1950	1,616.740	96.3	103.4	100.0	100.0
1951	1,841.476	109.7	121.8	113.9	117.8
1952	1,984.517	118.2	126.7	122.7	122.5
1953	2,230.855	132.9	137.0	138.0	132.5
1954	2,363,034	140.8	156.2	146.2	151.1
1955	2,562.471	152.7	180.7	158.6	174.8
1956	2,683.577	159.9		166.0	
1957	2,830.562	168.9		175.4	
1958	3,003.564	179.2		186.1	

Table 89 (Continued)

G. *Investment goods*

Year	East Germany, calculated value added (million RM)	Indices			
		East Germany 1936 = 100	West Germany 1936 = 100	East Germany 1950 = 100	West Germany 1950 = 100
	(31)	(32)	(33)	(34)	(35)
1936	2,087.093	100.0	100.0	149.8	88.6
1950	1,393.318	66.8	112.9	100.0	100.0
1951	1,625.186	77.9	147.3	116.6	130.5
1952	1,799.923	86.2	164.3	129.2	145.5
1953	2,417.593	115.8	173.4	173.5	153.6
1954	2,703.064	129.5	204.6	194.0	181.2
1955	2,838.812	136.0	251.9	203.6	223.1
1956	3,173.824	152.1		227.7	
1957	3,373.475	161.6		241.9	
1958	3,577.576	171.4		256.6	

H. *Manufactured consumer goods*

Year	East Germany, calculated value added (million RM)	Indices			
		East Germany 1936 = 100	West Germany 1936 = 100	East Germany 1950 = 100	West Germany 1950 = 100
	(36)	(37)	(38)	(39)	(40)
1936	2,063.176	100.0	100.0	227.5	88.2
1950	906.921	44.0	113.4	100.0	100.0
1951	1,111.262	53.9	128.8	122.5	113.6
1952	1,227.187	59.5	130.2	135.3	114.8
1953	1,336.547	64.8	151.9	147.4	134.0
1954	1,481.705	71.8	165.6	163.4	146.0
1955	1,499.692	72.7	184.1	165.4	162.3
1956	1,496.257	72.5		164.8	
1957	1,545.018	74.9		170.2	
1958	1,647.089	79.8		181.4	

Table 89 (Continued)

I. *Food industries*

Year	East Germany, calculated value added (million RM)	Indices			
		East Germany 1936 = 100	West Germany 1936 = 100	East Germany 1950 = 100	West Germany 1950 = 100
	(41)	(42)	(43)	(44)	(45)
1936	959.902	100.0	100.0	151.9	92.4
1950	631.504	65.8	108.2	100.0	100.0
1951	807.546	84.1	122.2	127.9	112.9
1952	878.950	91.6	131.5	139.2	121.5
1953	979.862	102.0	153.8	155.0	142.1
1954	1,051.810	109.6	162.4	166.5	150.1
1955	1,100.305	114.6	178.4	174.2	164.9
1956	1,068.079	111.3		169.1	
1957	1,144.266	119.2		181.2	
1958	1,191.584	124.1		188.6	

Sources: East German figures are the values added totaled from columns in the preceding tables. West German figures are from *SJBR*, 1956, pp. 217 ff.

ᵃ Index of coal mining and gas production combined in proportion of 6.93 and 0.91, corresponding to weight in West German index. *SJBR*, 1956, p. 217.

ᵇ Including rock salt mining.   ᶜ Includes gas. Weight of total mining: 8.15; weight of gas: 0.91. *Ibid.*, p. 217.

of basic industries. Even though the *Messwerte* are not 1936 prices but lie somewhere between 1936 and 1950 prices, the results will be compared with the official gross production index. A comparison with our calculations in 1950 prices is given below. The figures and calculations are found in Table 90.

The basic industries started in 1946 at a rather high level and had already reached their 1936 level at the end of the Two Year Plan. By 1955 the level had increased to 351 per cent of the 1946 level, but only to 155.3 per cent of the 1950 level.

When allowance is made for the peculiar nature of the East German concept of gross production, the calculated figures are consistent with East German claims. Thus the increase between 1950 and 1955 is claimed to have been 78.8 per cent; the increase from 1946 to 1955 is claimed to have been 457.7 per cent. By the nature of the "value added" concept used, the calculated increase ought to be substantially smaller than the increase in gross production with its multiple counting. The value of gross production in *Messwerte* is between 2.9 and 3.3 times the values added in 1936 prices. This, too, seems reasonable, since *Messwerte* were certainly substantially higher than 1936 prices. All in all, our findings appear plausible. (The more significant comparison of our calculations with the official gross production will be made below.)

The metalworking group coincides substantially with what in West

Table 90

Industrial production of East Germany, major industry groups, East German classification, 1936 and 1950–1958, and corresponding East German gross production figures, 1950–1955, in 1936 prices

A. *Basic industries*

| Year | Value added (million RM) | Index of value added | | Gross production in *Messwerte* (million DM–O) | Index of gross production | Ratio of gross production to value added |
		1936 = 100	1950 = 100			
	(1)	(2)	(3)	(4)	(5)	(6)
1936	2,547.993	100.0				
1950	2,797.429	109.8	100.0	7,964.5	100.0	2.85
1951	3,155.012	123.8	112.8	9,321.1	117.0	2.95
1952	3,390.059	133.0	121.1	10,662.9	133.9	3.15
1953	3,721.856	146.1	133.1	11,909.3	149.5	3.20
1954	3,968.011	155.7	141.8	13,063.1	164.0	3.29
1955	4,344.564	170.5	155.3	14,238.5	178.8	3.28
1956	4,569.620	179.4	163.4			
1957	4,768.948	187.2	170.5			
1958	5,050.826	198.2	180.5			

B. *Metalworking*

| Year | Value added (million RM) | Index of value added | | Gross production in *Messwerte* (million DM–O) | Index of gross production | Ratio of gross production to value added |
		1936 = 100	1950 = 100			
	(7)	(8)	(9)	(10	(11)	(12)
1936	2,087.093	100.0				
1950	1,393.318	66.8	100.0	5,610.5	100.0	4.03
1951	1,625.186	77.9	116.6	6,985.1	124.5	4.30
1952	1,799.923	86.2	129.2	8,487.6	151.3	4.72
1953	2,417.573	115.8	173.5	9,913.4	177.6	4.10
1954	2,703.064	129.5	194.0	11,135.9	198.5	4.12
1955	2,838.812	136.0	203.6	12,049.2	214.8	4.24
1956	3,173.824	152.1	227.7			
1957	3,373.475	161.6	241.9			
1958	3,577.576	171.4	256.6			

C. *Light industries*

| Year | Value added (million RM) | Index of value added | | Gross production in *Messwerte* (million DM–O) | Index of gross production | Ratio of gross production to value added |
		1936 = 100	1950 = 100			
	(13)	(14)	(15)	(16)	(17)	(18)
1936	2,191.411	100.0	210.5			
1950	1,041.581	47.5	100.0	6,305.9	100.0	6.05
1951	1,250.326	57.1	120.2	7,567.7	120.0	6.05
1952	1,349.032	61.6	129.7	8,304.9	131.7	6.16
1953	1,459.001	66.6	140.2	8,941.0	141.8	6.13
1954	1,601.040	73.1	153.9	9,951.9	157.8	6.22
1955	1,614.669	73.7	155.2	10,484.1	166.3	6.49
1956	1,615.164	73.7	155.2			
1957	1,665.602	76.0	160.0			
1958	1,765.566	80.6	169.7			

Table 90 (Continued)

D. *Food industries*

Year	Value added (million RM)	Index of value added 1936 = 100	Index of value added 1950 = 100	Gross production in *Messwerte* (million OM–O)	Index of gross production	Ratio of gross production to value added
	(19)	(20)	(21)	(22)	(23)	(24)
1936	959.902	100.0	152.0			
1950	631.504	65.8	100.0	3,456.1	100.0	5.47
1951	807.546	84.1	127.9	4,739.9	137.1	5.87
1952	878.950	91.6	139.2	5,763.1	166.8	6.56
1953	978.862	102.0	155.0	6,441.8	186.4	6.58
1954	1,051.810	109.6	166.6	6,919.0	200.2	6.58
1955	1,100.305	114.6	174.2	7,470.1	216.1	6.79
1956	1,068.079	111.3	169.2			
1957	1,144.266	119.2	181.2			
1958	1,191.584	124.1	188.6			

Sources: The calculated figures are totals from the preceding tables. The gross production figures are from *SJDDR* 1955, p. 125. This series was discontinued in 1955. Col. 6: Ratio of col. 4 to col. 1. Col. 12: Ratio of col. 10 to col. 7, Col. 18: Ratio of col. 16 to col. 13. Col. 24: Ratio of col. 22 to col. 19.

German terminology is called "investment goods." The data for 1946 through 1949 are too inadequate to be taken seriously, but for the years 1950 through 1955 the representation is good. Between 1950 and 1955 our index rose to 210.7 per cent compared with 203.6 per cent for gross production. In 1950, production was about two-thirds of the 1936 level. The gross production values in *Messwerte* are between 4 and 5 times the "value added" values in 1936 prices. On the whole, therefore, the movements of the calculated and the official indices are consistent.

The light industries (which to a considerable extent produce manufactured consumer goods but also include some investment goods) had not recovered to their 1936 level even in 1955. For the years 1946 through 1949 the figures are too scanty for meaningful analysis; from 1950 through 1955 the calculated index and the official index move in an appropriate fashion. Here, too, the results seem plausible. The gross production value is about 6 to 6.5 times the calculated "value added" value, which, considering the different price levels employed and the nature of the industries, is equally reasonable.

For the food industries, the official index also increases about as much as might be expected. The gross production value is between 5.5 and 7 times the value added figure, which is also reasonable because of the increasing number of stages involved with increasing industrialization.

The comparison of the calculated values added to the appropriate gross production values in *Messwerte* was made as a check on the reliability of the calculation. The fact that these ratios increase as we move from the basic industries through investment goods to light industries and finally to food, drink, and tobacco strengthens the plausibility of our calculations. For as we move along to higher stages of production their number increases and with them the extent of double counting.

BREAKDOWN BY EAST AND WEST GERMAN CLASSIFICATION — 1950 PRICES

Measured in 1950 prices, East German industrial production, defined as value added, increased only from 100 in 1936 to 113.4 in 1955 and to 125.6 in 1957. That is, the increase was substantially smaller, as is frequently the case when later prices are used. The increase between 1950 and 1955 was slightly larger when measured in 1950 prices than when measured in 1936 prices. This index is probably more nearly comparable with the index of gross production, since the "1950 constant plan prices," or *Messwerte,* are closer to 1950 prices than to 1936 prices. For industrial production as a whole we now also have official figures in constant 1950 prices which are about 117 per cent those of the *Messwerte* (see Table 91).

The relation of the calculated index to the gross production index is exactly what should be expected. The latter increases from 100 in 1950 to 189.6 in 1955. It is consistently higher than the calculated index — about as much as one might expect from the differences in concepts.

The reasons for comparing the calculated index with that of gross production can be appreciated when it is borne in mind that the latter is essentially the sales value of total output in fictitious *Messwerte* which, however, are closely related to actual East German 1950 prices. Somewhat more precisely, the gross production is the value in constant 1950 prices or in *Messwerte* of total output. Not only have interindustry or interplant flows not been excluded, but even some intra-plant flows are included.

In absolute values, gross production in *Messwerte* is 223 per cent of the calculated value added in 1950, and the value increases unsteadily to 249 per cent in 1955. In 1936 the ratio of total sales value of all industries except construction and airplanes (as given by Gleitze) to the net production (that is, the gross value added) was 179 per cent. But in 1936 all intra-plant flows and all intra-industry flows were eliminated from total sales. Thus the differences in coverage and in concept explain the different ratios and confirm the calculations made. The inverse of these percentages, which in West German terminology is called the *Nettoquota,* is sufficiently close to the 1936 figure to make it reasonable to attribute the differences between the 1936 and the higher postwar figures to what from a Western standpoint is clearly double counting.

Table 91 also includes the official net industrial product in constant 1950 East German prices. It is incredible that the net industrial product could have doubled in any meaningful sense between 1950 and 1955. This good showing is entirely due to the practice of valuing final outputs at

Table 91

Industrial production of East Germany, gross production[a] and the new index
of the Federal Republic, 1936 and 1950–1958, in 1950 prices

A. *Value added and West and East German indices*

Year	East Germany			West Germany, index of industrial production	
		Index			
	Value added (million DM)	1936 = 100	1950 = 100	1936 = 100	1950 = 100
	(1)	(2)	(3)	(4)	(5)
1936	15,668.999	100.0	149.7	100.0	93
1950	10,472,226	66.8	100.0	111	100
1951	12,241.240	78.1	116.9	131	119
1952	13,406.815	85.6	128.1	140	126
1953	15,573.300	99.4	148.8	154	139
1954	16,944.315	108.1	161.8	172	155
1955	17,770.079	113.4	169.8	198	179
1956	18,634.433	118.9	178.0	213	193
1957	19,685.176	125.6	188.0	226	204
1958	20,797.187	132.7	198.7	233	210

B. *Official East German figures*

Year	Gross production		Index of gross production in *Messwerte* 1950 = 100	Net production, 1950 East German prices (million DM–O)
	Messwerte (million DM–O)	1950 East German prices (million DM–O)		
	(6)	(7)	(8)	(9)
1936				
1950	23,337.0	27,223	100.0	12,374
1951	28,613.9	33,403	122.6	15,720
1952	33,218.4	38,699	142.3	18,353
1953	37,255.6	43,066	159.6	19,306
1954	41,069.8	48,098	176.0	22,337
1955	44,241.9	51,795	189.6	24,672
1956			201.5	
1957			216.6	

Table 91 (Continued)

C. *Various comparisons*

Gross production

Years	In *Messwerte* as per cent of value added	In 1950 East German prices as per cent of value added	In 1950 East German prices as per cent of gross production in *Messwerte*	Value added as per cent of net production
	(10)	(11)	(12)	(13)
1936				
1950	223	260	117	84.6
1951	234	273	117	77.9
1952	248	289	110	73.0
1953	239	277	116	80.7
1954	242	284	117	75.9
1955	249	291	117	72.0
1956				
1957				

Sources: Col. 1: Added from preceding tables. Cols. 2 and 3: Derived from col. 1. Cols. 4 and 5: Refers to total industry without construction; *SJBR*, 1959, p. 180, average daily production. Col. 5: *Ibid.*, p. 54. Col. 6 *SJDDR*, 1955, p. 125. Cols. 7 and 9: *Ibid.*, p. 90. Col. 8: The identical index is given in *SJDDR*, 1957, p. 280, on the basis 1956 = 100 for the years 1946–1957, and on the basis of 1950 = 100 for the years 1950–1957. The explanatory note on p. 223 does not say whether or not the series in 1950 prices has been continued. Figures in some tables are stated to be in *Messwerte*, others in 1955 prices. Cols. 10–13: Calculated.
ᵃ Rejects have not been included in gross production since 1956. *SJDDR*, 1956, p. 208, and 1957, p. 222.

high prices which include fantastically high excises, while raw materials and intermediate goods are kept low in price.*

Finally, it may be worth while to check the calculations against the published figures of net national product in constant (East German) 1950 prices. Using the East German concept of net product, the value of the means of production used up, apparently valued at sales prices which usually do not, however, include turnover taxes, is deducted from the gross production, valued at final prices, including taxes but excluding subsidies. Depreciation is probably also deducted, but this is not expressly stated. In addition, any expenditures made by a plant to maintain social installations (such as recreational facilities) are also deducted. Thus the East German concept of national product is basically the same as the Western concept except that it includes less goods and services.†

The comparison of our calculated index and the movement of national income shows an almost exact parallelism (see Table 92).

The big difference is not in the movement of the index since 1950 ‡

* The detailed discussion of the price system and its effects on the measure of output is found in Chapter III.
† For a detailed discussion the reader is referred to Chapter III.
‡ I am confident that the index is correct, and I am sure that the pre-1950 data cannot be taken very seriously.

Table 92

East German net national product in 1950 East German prices,
and industrial production, 1950–1955

Year	East German net national product (billion DM–O)	Index of national product	Calculated index of industrial production
	(1)	(2)	(3)
1950	30.662	100.0	100.0
1951	36.513	119.1	116.9
1952	39.745	129.6	128.2
1953	41.521	135.4	148.9
1954	46.365	151.2	161.9
1955	49.819	162.5	170.0

Sources: Col. 1: *SJDDR*, 1955, p. 90 (East German definition). Col. 2: Calculated from col. 1. Col. 3: See Table 87, col. 8.

but in the absolute level of the value added as calculated. In 1950 West German prices for the year 1950, the calculations give a gross value added of industrial output of DM 10.472 billion. The East German national income in that year was officially DM-O 30.662 billion. Our value added of industry was thus about one-third of national income. The 1957 edition of the Statistical Yearbook of the German Democratic Republic, appeared in July 1958, gives gross and net product in current prices. The total industrial net product for 1950 in 1950 prices is given as DM-O 14.626 billion, or 47.4 per cent of the net social product.[7]

The identical calculation cannot be made for West Germany for 1950. In the West German "value creation of industry," depreciation has been allowed for, while in our calculation of value added no depreciation has been deducted. But the following calculations show the general reasonableness of our findings. The net addition of West German industry to national income at factor cost was DM 29.079 billion in 1950. National income at factor cost was then DM 71.521 billion. Thus the share of industry was 40.66 per cent. (Our calculations were based on market prices.) The West German national product in market prices was DM 83.401 billion. Thus the share of industry was 34.87 per cent. The gross national product of the Federal Republic was DM 89.765 billion. The share of industry (calculated on a net-of-depreciation basis) was 32.39 per cent.[8]

In the light of these figures, one-third, which is our calculated percentage of gross value added of the official national income, appears reasonable, particularly in light of the fact that East German market prices for all goods except basic industrial commodities and foodstuffs sold on rations (that is, excluding those sold outside of rations in HO-stores*) were very high, that the industrial sector was favored at the expense of other

* HO = *Handelsorganisation*, i.e., state stores.

economic sectors, and that the differences in the concept of national income between East and West Germany are surprisingly small. Our calculated ratio of one-third appears more plausible than 40.35 per cent which is the ratio of (official) net industrial product to the (official) net national product in 1950. For 1955 our calculated ratio of value added to the net national product is still 36.3 per cent, which also seems more plausible than the officially claimed 49.5 per cent.*

The comparison of the individual industry groups yields the following results (see Table 93):

Mining and gas (which, it will be remembered, cannot be separated statistically) rose by 1955 to 178.7 per cent of 1936, compared with 187 per cent expressed in 1936 prices. The index of mining of the Federal Republic rose to 140.4 per cent and that of gas to 191 per cent of 1936; and the combined index (calculated by multiplying each index by its weight in the total index) rose to 145.5 per cent. This is again the one area in which the development in East Germany surpassed that of the Federal Republic. While undoubtedly an East German achievement, the price is high in terms of labor inputs and of other goods foregone. That price is essentially the cost of autarky.

The electricity index of East Germany rose to 173.9 per cent of 1936, compared with 358.2 per cent for the Federal Republic. Both indices lie below those calculated in 1936 prices, but the difference is negligible for the Federal Republic and substantial for East Germany. Perhaps it reflects mainly the increased shift to lignite as an input to which East Germany has been forced.

When all "basic and production goods" are considered together, however, again the aggregate development in the Federal Republic has been substantially faster than in East Germany. (Per capita developments, interesting for some purposes, will be discussed below.) Again, the East German index in 1950 prices is substantially below the index calculated in 1936 prices, reflecting the shift to the more expensive inputs necessitated by autarky, while the difference between the old and new indices of the Federal Republic is negligible.

Table 93 also gives figures for the development of the industries by East German classifications and comparisons with the official gross production figures. Suffice it to say that the calculated indices consistently increase less rapidly than the "gross production" indices — as they should — and that the ratio of value added to "gross production" steadily declines from 1950 through 1955, as must be expected.

By 1955 engineering construction in East Germany increased to 135.3 per cent of 1936, and to 249.3 per cent of 1936 in West Germany. In this

---

* These ratios can be calculated from figures given in the 1955 edition of Statistical Yearbook GDR. For current prices as given in the 1957 edition (p. 156), the share of the industrial net product in social net product rose from 47.4 per cent in 1950 to 57.5 per cent in 1956, and it fell slightly in 1957 to 56.8 per cent.

Table 93

Industrial production of East Germany, major industry groups,[a] West and East German
classifications, and production indices, West and East Germany,
1936 and 1950–1958, in 1950 prices

A. *Mining and gas*

			Indices		
				West Germany	
Year	East Germany, value added (million DM)	East Germany 1936 = 100	Mining only	Gas only	Mining and gas combined
	(1)	(2)	(3)	(4)	(5)
1936	957.312	100.0	100.0	100.0	100.0
1950	1,190.409	124.3	103.0	122.2	104.9
1951	1,317.793	137.7	115.2	142.1	117.9
1952	1,355.303	141.6	123.6	156.2	126.8
1953	1,460.324	152.5	126.9	155.5	129.8
1954	1,556.946	162.6	131.5	168.3	135.2
1955	1,710.463	178.7	140.4	191.0	145.5
1956	1,769.303	184.8	148.0	211.0	154.3
1957	1,815.772	189.7	152.0	212.0	158.0
1958	1,877.290	196.1	152.0	207.0	158.0

B. *Electricity*

	East Germany, value added (million DM)	Indices	
Year		East Germany	West Germany
	(6)	(7)	(8)
1936	356.807	100.0	100.0
1950	419.716	117.6	205.8
1951	462.834	129.7	241.8
1952	498.938	140.1	263.6
1953	522.812	146.5	297.6
1954	561.628	157.4	318.3
1955	620.406	173.9	358.2
1956	677.416	189.9	401.0
1957	711.034	199.3	436.0
1958	757.494	212.3	446.0

C. *Basic industries*

Year	Value added, West German classification (million DM)	Indices East German	Indices West German	Value added, East German classification (millionDM)	Index 1936 = 100	Gross production (million *Messewerte*)	East German indices Official	East German indices Calculated	Value added as per cent of gross production
	(9)	(10)	(11)	(12)	(13)	(14)	(15)	(16)	(17)
1936	3,294.993	100.0	100.0	4,225.941	100.0			99.8	
1950	2,914.045	88.4	102.8	4,200.019	98.7	7,964.5	100.0	100.0	52.7
1951	3,304.811	100.3	121.0	4,744.432	111.5	9,321.1	117.0	113.0	50.9
1952	3,640.165	110.5	125.9	5,183.306	121.8	10,662.9	133.9	123.0	48.6
1953	3,979.875	120.8	136.0	5,645.738	132.7	11,969.3	149.5	133.9	48.3
1954	4,205.829	127.6	154.9	6,009.388	141.2	13,063.1	164.0	142.5	46.0
1955	4,511.598	136.9	179.4	6,532.390	153.5	14,238.5	178.8	155.1	45.9
1956	4,692.034	142.4	193.0	6,818.217	160.2			161.7	
1957	4,950.254	150.2	204.0	7,147.700	167.9			169.9	
1958	5,218.566	158.4	210.0	7,524.186	176.8			179.2	

Table 93 (Continued)

D. *Metalworking — investment goods*

| | | | Value added as per cent of gross production | Indices | | | West Germany, new index, investment goods |
| | | | | East Germany | | | |
Year	Value added (million DM)	Gross production (million *Messwerte*)		Value added	Gross production	Value added	
	(18)	(19)	(20)	(21)	(22)	(23)	(24)
1936	4,235.762			100.0		147.4	100.0
1950	2,874.309	5,610.5	52.2	67.9	100.0	100.0	112.0
1951	3,320.097	6,985.1	47.5	78.4	124.5	115.5	146.0
1952	3,694.221	8,487.6	43.5	87.2	151.3	128.5	163.0
1953	4,944.747	9,963.4	49.6	116.7	177.6	172.0	171.7
1954	5,502.824	11,135.9	49.4	129.9	198.5	191.3	203.0
1955	5,713.995	12,049.2	49.5	135.3	214.8	199.3	249.3
1956	6,388.162			150.8		222.1	274.0
1957	6,823.701			161.1		237.3	285.0
1958	7,273.730			171.7		252.9	306.0

E. *Manufactured consumer goods — light industry*

Manufactured consumer goods, West German classification

| | | Indices | |
| | | East Germany, value added | West Germany, consumer goods industries |
Year	Value added (million DM)		
	(25)	(26)	(27)
1936	5,041.704	100.0	100.0
1950	2,005.807	39.8	112.5
1951	2,468.618	49.0	127.6
1952	2,703.743	53.6	129.2
1953	2,952.257	58.6	150.6
1954	3,277.075	65.0	164.2
1955	3,278.518	65.0	182.3
1956	3,228.265	64.0	199.0
1957	3,363.041	66.7	211.0
1958	3,585.277	71.1	209.0

Light industry, East German classification

| | | | Gross production (million *Messwerte*) | Indices | | Value added as per cent of gross production |
Year	Value added (million DM)	Index 1936 = 100		Official	Calculated	
	(28)	(29)	(30)	(31)	(32)	(33)
1936	5,394.875	100.0			231.54	
1950	2,329.958	43.2	6,305.9	100.0	100.00	31.8
1951	2,809.624	52.1	7,567.7	120.0	120.58	33.9
1952	3,015.843	55.9	8,304.9	131.7	129.43	32.8
1953	3,269.530	60.6	8,941.0	141.8	140.31	33.0
1954	3,592.090	66.6	9,951.9	157.8	154.16	32.9
1955	3,588.595	66.5	10,484.1	166.3	154.02	31.3
1956	3,548,801	65.8			152.30	
1957	3,692.401	68.4			158.33	
1958	3,914,441	72.6			168.06	

Table 93 (Continued)

F. *Food industries*

			Indices				
			East Germany			West Germany, food, drink, and tobacco 1936 = 100	Value added as per cent of gross production
		Gross production (million *Messwerte*)	Value added		Gross production		
Year	Value added (million DM)		1936 = 100	1950 = 100			
	(34)	(35)	(36)	(37)	(38)	(39)	(40)
1936	1,782.421		100.0	169.5		100.0	
1950	1,067.940	3,456.1	59.9	100.0	100.0	107.3	30.9
1951	1,367.087	4,739.9	76.7	130.0	137.1	121.1	28.8
1952	1,513.445	5,763.1	84.9	143.9	166.8	130.5	26.3
1953	1,713.285	6,441.8	96.1	162.9	186.4	152.3	26.6
1954	1,840.014	6,919.0	103.2	174.9	200.2	161.1	26.6
1955	1,935.099	7,470.1	108.6	184.1	216.1	176.9	25.9
1956	1,879.253		105.4	178.6		191.0	
1957	2,021.374		113.4	192.2		210.0	
1958	2,084.830		117.0	198.3		219.0	

Sources: For derivation of East German values added, see preceding tables. Indices for 1950–1955 are taken from *Neuberechnung*, pp. 55 ff., average monthly production; for 1956 and 1957, from *SJBR*, 1959, p. 180, average daily production. All East German data are from *SJDDR*, 1955, p. 125. Col. 5: combined in ratio 8.15:0.91, corresponding to the weight of mining and gas in the total index, *Neuberechnung*, pp. 55 ff.
ᵃ For definition of industry classifications, see text and notes to Table 94.

particular instance the difference between the indices calculated in 1936 and 1950 prices is minor. This is also true of the indices of consumer goods and of food, drink, and tobacco.

STRUCTURAL CHANGES, 1936–1957

The structural changes shown by the calculations conform to expectations (see Table 94).

Measured in 1936 prices, basic industries (as defined in East Germany) increased in relative importance from 33 per cent in 1936 to 48 per cent in 1950. Thereafter, their relative importance declined somewhat to 43.9 per cent in 1955 and to 43.5 per cent in 1957, but still remained substantially above 1936. The picture is the same when the output is measured in 1950 prices except that the change in the relative importance of basic industries was from 27 per cent in 1936 to 40.1 per cent in 1950 and then to about 36.8 per cent in 1955 and 36.3 per cent in 1957.

The relative importance of metalworking industries increased from about 27 per cent in 1936 (whether measured in 1936 or in 1950 prices) to between 29 and 33 per cent in 1955 and to between 31 and 35 per cent in 1957, depending on which prices are used. Unlike basic industries, however, the relative importance of these industries (which correspond to "investment goods" in West German terminology) increased from 1950 to 1957.

The importance of light industries declined substantially, from about

Table 94

Percentage share of major industry groups, East German classification,
in industrial production, 1936 and 1950–1958, in 1936 and 1950 prices

A. *1936 Prices*

	1936	1950	1951	1952	1953	1954	1955	1956	1957	1958
Basic industries[a]	32.7	47.7	46.1	45.7	43.4	42.6	43.9	43.8	43.5	43.6
Metalworking industries[b]	26.8	23.8	23 8	24.3	28.2	29.0	28.7	30.4	30.8	30.9
Light industries[c]	28.1	17.8	18.3	18.2	17.0	17.2	16.3	15.5	15.2	15.2
Food industries[d]	12.3	10.8	11.8	11.8	11.4	11.3	11.1	10.2	10.4	10.3
Total	99.9	100.1	100.0	100.0	100.0	100.1	100.0	99.9	99.9	100.0

B. *1950 Prices*

	1936	1950	1951	1952	1953	1954	1955	1956	1957	1958
Basic industries[a]	27.2	40.1	38.8	38.7	36.3	35.5	36.8	36.6	36.3	36.2
Metalworking industries[b]	27.0	27.4	27.1	27.6	31.8	32.5	32.2	34.3	34.7	35.0
Light industries[c]	34.4	22.2	23.0	22.5	21.0	21.2	10.2	19.0	18.8	18.8
Food industries[d]	11.4	10.2	11.2	11.3	11.0	10.9	10.9	10.1	10.3	10.0
Total	100.0	99.9	100.1	100.1	100.1	100.1	100.1	100.0	100.1	100.0

Sources: Calculated from preceding tables.
    a Basic industries are defined as energy, mining, gas, metallurgy, chemicals (including fuels and fibers), and building materials.
    b Metalworking industries are defined as machine industries, electrical engineering, and fine mechanics and optics.
    c Light industries are defined as woodworking, textiles, leather and shoes, clothing, cellulose and paper, and printing.
    d Food industries are defined as food, drink, and tobacco, fats and oils, and alcohol.

28.1 per cent in 1936 to 16.3 per cent in 1955 and 15.2 per cent in 1957, when measured in 1936 prices, and from 34.4 per cent in 1936 to about 22 per cent in 1955 and 19 per cent in 1957 when measured in 1950 prices. On the other hand, the relative importance of the food industries did not change very much over the years, falling from 12.5 per cent to 11 per cent.

Clearly, food industries and light industries were successfully held down while basic industries and engineering were emphatically developed, especially engineering, as the First Five Year Plan unfolded. In 1936 the industries producing for the needs of consumers accounted in 1936 prices for over 40 per cent of total industrial production, and measured in 1950 prices for more than 45 per cent. By 1950, when the First Five Year Plan was inaugurated, their combined share was down to 28 per cent and 32 per cent, respectively; it remained at that level in 1955 and fell even lower in 1957.

Some of the structural change reflects the substitution of domestic production in the nonconsumer goods industries, some reflects the shift from exports of light goods to exports of machinery of heavier types, and some reflects the communist preoccupation with the conviction that the output of the means of production, must grow faster than the output of final consumer goods. The fact that this belief is fallacious — as some East German theorists have unsuccessfully tried to explain — and that policies based upon it did not have the desired growth effect is perhaps beside the point in explaining what happened.

PER CAPITA GROWTH IN EAST AND WEST GERMANY

That industry has in the aggregate grown substantially faster in West Germany than in East Germany compared both to 1936 and to 1950 has been established beyond reasonable doubt,* the one exception being coal mining. If the East German regime were not so entirely absorbed in its own propaganda, it could of course point out that this should be expected. After all, it could be argued, the population of the Federal Republic increased about 27 per cent between 1936 and 1955 while that of East Germany increased only 11 per cent; and the Federal Republic has absorbed increasing numbers of emigrants from East Germany since 1949, thus reducing the East German population. Hence, it might be argued, per capita changes are more significant.

Because the old and new index of the Federal Republic differ only insignificantly, only the new one, which is less favorable to the Federal Republic, will be presented. But for East Germany, calculations in both 1936 and 1950 prices must be shown. Only the West German classification will be discussed in this section.

In West Germany, per capita production was substantially restored to the 1936 level in all industries by 1951. Only the mining (and gas) sector was still 3 per cent below prewar. By 1955 all per capita production was substantially above prewar, the least increase being shown by mining, the most by electricity and investment goods. The average per capita increase was 55.5 per cent above 1936, with mining, basic materials, consumer goods, and food, drink, and tobacco being below and electricity and investment goods (which, however, also includes passenger cars) being above the average. Per capita production, which in 1950 was still 9 per cent below 1936, was 7 per cent above it in 1951.

The story in East Germany is quite different. In 1936 prices, aggregate per capita production exceeded the 1936 level only in 1954, and in 1950 prices only in 1955. But in 1950, mining was already 9 to 16 per cent above 1936. In 1950 prices, basic and production goods and investment goods passed the 1936 level in 1953. Neither consumption goods nor the

---

* The comparison with 1950 is made because adequate East German data became available with this year and because in 1950 the First Five Year Plan was started. But this comparison date is not as meaningful in the Federal Republic. The logical starting date in the Federal Republic is 1948; and what corresponds to the Five Year Plan in East Germany is the currency reform of 1948 and the whole range of policies from derationing to (at a later date) increasing use of monetary policy — policies usually associated with Ludwig Erhard.

output of food, drink, and tobacco had reached the 1936 per capita level by 1955, or, for that matter, by 1957; and in 1955 manufactured consumer goods were still more than 40 per cent below the 1936 level.

In 1936 prices the story is somewhat more favorable to East Germany. Basic and production goods definitely reached their 1936 level in 1951. But the only other significant change is that food, drink, and tobacco were about 3 per cent above 1936 in 1955. Aggregate per capita production reached the 1936 level between 1953 and 1954.

Since 1950, per capita developments in the two parts of Germany are almost the same, although in aggregate development East Germany lags slightly. But as recovery started earlier in the Federal Republic and was much more vigorous, a comparison of the growth since 1950 is of only limited significance. It is particularly interesting, however, that only in mining (including gas), and, *mirabile dictu,* consumer goods and food, drink, and tobacco was the per capita development in East Germany faster than in the Federal Republic. I need not labor the point that the comparatively fast growth in consumer goods industries was, to vary a classic phrase of Winston Churchill's, primarily due to the fact that East Germany had so little to grow from. In addition, we are dealing here with per capita production of manufactured consumer goods and not per capita consumption. It is known that East Germany exports a substantial portion of its manufactured consumer goods output. Even at the end of rapid growth the East German consumer is still worse off than before the war. The comparison of per capita growth in East Germany and the Federal Republic for 1955 compared with 1936 is, except in mining and basic and production goods, unfavorable to East Germany, to say the least. All figures are found in Tables 95 and 96.*

OUTPUT PER WORKER — EAST AND WEST GERMANY

Finally, a comparison of output per man in the Federal Republic and in East Germany will serve to put developments in perspective. The comparability is unfortunately far from perfect, but the data are sufficient to furnish a good idea both of developments since 1950 and of the absolute magnitudes involved. In 1955, output per worker in all industries (including electricity and gas) was DM 6,687 in East Germany. In the Federal Republic, total output per worker in 1955 (excluding electricity and gas) was DM 13,125. These figures are comparable to the extent that they are both based on West German prices. But our calculations do not include indirect taxes, and West German figures do. Hence industry-by-industry figures would be somewhat more relevant. In basic industries output per worker in East Germany in 1955 was DM 9,750; in West Germany (where the coverage is narrower and the electricity output with its high output per worker, as well as mining, is omitted) it was DM

* Details are given in the Appendix to Part III, Table A and B.

Table 95

Indices, aggregate and per capita production, major industry groups, West German classification, West and East Germany, 1936 and 1950–1958

A. East Germany, 1936 and 1950–1958

	1936	1950	1951	1952	1953	1954	1955	1956	1957	1958
1. Aggregate production, 1936 prices										
Mining	100.0	132.2	146.2	150.3	160.1	170.4	187.7	192.7	194.0	201.7
Electricity production	100.0	130.8	144.2	155.7	162.9	175.0	193.1	210.2	220.6	235.0
Basic materials and production goods	100.0	96.3	109.7	118.2	132.9	140.8	152.7	159.9	168.9	179.2
Investment goods	100.0	66.8	77.9	86.2	115.8	129.5	136.0	152.1	161.6	171.4
Consumer goods	100.0	44.0	53.9	59.5	64.8	71.8	72.7	72.5	74.9	79.8
Food, drink, and tobacco	100.0	65.8	84.1	91.6	102.0	109.6	114.6	111.3	119.2	124.1
All industry	100.0	75.3	85.3	95.3	109.5	119.7	127.1	133.8	140.7	148.8
2. Aggregate production, 1950 prices										
Mining	100.0	124.3	137.7	141.6	152.5	162.6	178.7	184.8	189.7	196.1
Electricity production	100.0	117.6	129.7	140.1	146.5	157.4	173.9	189.9	199.3	212.3
Basic materials and production goods	100.0	88.4	100.3	110.5	120.8	127.6	136.9	142.4	150.2	158.4
Investment goods	100.0	67.9	78.4	87.2	116.7	129.9	135.3	150.8	161.1	171.7
Consumer goods	100.0	39.8	49.0	53.6	58.6	65.0	65.0	64.0	66.7	71.1
Food, drink, and tobacco	100.0	59.9	76.7	84.9	96.1	103.2	108.6	105.4	113.4	117.0
All industry	100.0	66.8	78.1	85.6	99.4	108.1	113.4	118.9	125.6	132.7
3. Population index	100.0	113.79	113.56	113.42	112.49	111.75	111.04	109.63	108.40	107.3
4. Per capita production, 1936 prices										
Mining	100.0	116.2	128.7	132.5	142.3	152.5	169.0	175.8	179.0	188.0
Electricity production	100.0	114.9	127.0	137.3	144.8	156.6	173.9	191.7	203.5	219.
Basic materials and production goods	100.0	84.6	96.6	104.2	118.1	126.0	137.5	145.9	155.8	167.0
Investment goods	100.0	58.7	68.6	76.0	102.9	115.9	122.5	138.7	149.1	159.7
Consumer goods	100.0	38.7	47.5	52.5	57.6	64.3	65.5	66.1	69.1	74.4
Food, drink, and tobacco	100.0	57.8	74.1	80.8	90.7	98.1	103.2	101.5	110.0	115.7
All industry	100.0	66.2	75.1	84.0	97.3	107.1	114.5	122.0	129.8	138.7
5. Per capita production, 1950 prices										
Mining	100.0	109.2	121.3	124.8	135.6	145.5	160.9	168.6	175.0	182.8
Electricity production	100.0	103.3	114.2	123.5	130.2	140.9	156.6	173.2	183.9	197.9
Basic materials and production goods	100.0	77.7	88.3	97.4	107.4	114.2	123.3	129.9	138.6	147.6
Investment goods	100.0	59.7	69.0	76.9	103.7	116.2	121.8	137.6	148.6	160.0
Consumer goods	100.0	35.0	43.1	47.3	52.1	58.2	58.5	58.4	61.5	66.3
Food, drink, and tobacco	100.0	52.6	67.5	74.9	85.4	92.3	97.8	96.1	104.6	109.0
All industry	100.0	58.7	68.8	75.5	88.4	96.8	102.1	108.5	115.9	123.7

B. West Germany, 1936, 1948, and 1950–1955

	1936	1948	1950	1951	1952	1953	1954	1955
1. Aggregate production, old index								
Mining	100.0	79.4	105.6	119.0	127.7	130.8	136.2	146.6
Electricity production	100.0	157.3	207.0	242.9	264.4	281.4	319.9	359.8
Basic materials and production goods	100.0	54.5	103.4	121.8	126.7	137.0	156.2	180.7
Investment goods	100.0	56.4	112.9	147.3	164.3	173.4	204.6	251.9
Consumer goods	100.0	51.8	113.4	128.8	130.2	151.9	165.6	184.1
Food, drink, and tobacco	100.0	60.9	108.2	122.2	131.5	153.8	162.4	178.4
All industry	100.0	60.0	110.9	131.4	139.8	153.9	171.8	197.8
2. Population index	100.0	117.54	121.35	122.76	123.79	125.09	126.37	127.57
3. Per capita production, old index								
Mining	100.0	67.5	87.00	96.90	103.10	104.60	107.80	114.90
Electricity production	100.0	133.8	170.58	197.87	213.59	224.96	253.15	282.04
Basic materials and production goods	100.0	46.4	85.21	99.22	102.35	109.52	123.61	141.65
Investment goods	100.0	48.0	93.04	119.99	132.72	138.62	161.91	197.46
Consumer goods	100.0	44.1	93.45	104.92	105.18	121.43	131.04	144.31
Food, drink, and tobacco	100.0	51.8	89.16	99.54	106.23	122.95	128.51	130.84
All industry	100.0	51.0	91.39	107.04	112.93	123.03	135.95	155.05

Sources: Cols. A.1 and A.2: From preceding tables. Cols. A.3 and B.2: For population figures, see Table 2. Cols. A.4 and A.5: From sections A.1, A.2, and A.3. Col. B.1: *SJBR*, 1956, 217. Col. B.3: *Ibid.*

Table 96

Increases in per capita production between selected years, 1948–1955, major industry groups,
West German classification, West and East Germany

	West Germany (1936 prices)			East Germany 1950–1955		East Germany compared with West Germany, 1950–1955, 1950 = 100	
	1948– 1955	1950– 1955	1948– 1953	1936 Prices	1950 Prices	1936 Prices	1950 Prices
	(1)	(2)	(3)	(4)	(5)	(6)	(7)
Mining and gas	170.2	132.0	154.9	145.4	147.3	110.2	111.6
Electricity	210.8	165.3	168.1	151.3	151.6	91.5	91.7
Basic and production goods	305.2	166.2	236.0	162.5	158.7	97.8	95.9
Investment goods	411.3	212.2	288.7	215.8	212.6	101.7	100.2
Consumer goods	327.2	154.4	275.3	169.3	167.1	109.7	108.2
Food, drink, and tobacco	269.9	156.8	237.3	178.7	186.1	114.0	118.7
Total	304.0	169.6	241.2	174.5	176.5	102.9	104.1

13,812. Since indirect taxes are not significant at that level, it is fair to say that productivity in West Germany in 1955 was almost certainly one and a half times the level in East Germany. Western output in mining alone was DM 9,323.

In investment goods (which so far as coverage is concerned, are completely comparable), output per man in 1955 was DM 11,253 in West Germany and DM 6,241 in East Germany. Here, too, indirect taxes are probably insignificant. It is fair to estimate West German productivity in 1955 as about three-fourths higher than in East Germany. For consumer goods industries and food, drink, and tobacco, indirect taxes play a larger role; hence the figures must be taken with caution, particularly as the coverage, too, is not identical. Nevertheless, whatever adjustments

Table 97

Output per employed person in 1955, West and East Germany,
major industry groups, in 1950 prices (DM)

	West Germany	East Germany
Total production	13,125	6,687
Basic industries	13,812	9,750
Mining	9,323	. . . [a]
Investment goods — metalworking	11,253	6,241
Consumer goods — light industries	9,775	4,109
Food, drink, and tobacco	33,734	9,875

Sources: For East German calculations, employment figures from *SJDDR*, 1956, p. 245, were used. The 1956 figures differ from the same data given in the *SJDDR*, 1955, p. 121. No details are given about the extent to which industries have been reclassified. West German figures are derived from *Neuberechnung* and indices of productivity per employed person, *SJBR*, 1957, p. 233.
   [a] Impossible to calculate mining without including gas.

are necessary, there can be little doubt that output per man is substantially higher in West Germany than in East Germany.

For West Germany, data for output per hour worked and per production worker employed are available. But no comparison with East Germany is possible. The official East German data on output per production worker and output per person employed in industry refer only to socialized industry; and they are vitiated by the fact that they are based on gross production in *Messwerte*. Since it is now even officially admitted that this is a meaningless and even harmful figure, it has not been considered. The data are summarized in Table 97.*

* Details are given in the Appendix to Part III, Tables C and D.

APPENDIX TO PART THREE

TABLES A—D

Table A

Indices of individual industries, in 1950 prices, East Germany, 1950–1958, 1936 = 100

Branch of industry	1950	1950ª	1951	1951ª	1952	1952ª	1953	1953ª	1954	1954ª	1955	1955ª	1956	1956ª	1957	1957ª	1958
Lignite sector	125.6	110.4	138.9	122.3	146.3	129.0	158.7	141.1	167.3	149.7	185.1	166.7	190.0	173.3	192.6	177.7	195.1
Soft coal, including gas	112.2	98.6	129.7	114.2	125.5	110.7	129.4	115.0	142.5	127.5	154.9	139.5	167.8	153.1	172.6	159.2	189.9
Total coal mining, including gas	123.0	107.6	137.1	120.7	141.5	124.8	152.2	135.3	161.9	144.9	178.3	160.6	184.5	168.3	187.9	173.3	193.8
Iron ore sector	110.8	97.4	134.6	118.5	213.3	188.1	375.5	333.8	406.1	363.4	459.7	414.0	485.4	442.8	408.3	376.7	416.1
Total ore sector	47.2	41.5	56.4	49.7	67.7	59.7	103.9	92.4	116.5	104.3	134.3	120.9	139.5	127.2	131.1	120.9	134.9
Potash and rock salt	140.2	123.2	147.9	130.2	141.3	124.6	144.6	128.5	153.5	137.4	162.9	146.7	163.3	149.0	168.3	155.3	173.1
Iron and steel making	97.1	85.3	103.1	90.8	141.2	124.5	158.9	141.3	163.9	146.7	162.8	146.6	172.8	157.6	179.2	165.3	186.8
Rolled steel	48.3	42.4	70.4	62.0	90.2	79.5	105.3	93.6	129.4	115.8	163.9	147.6	175.0	159.6	230.8	212.7	247.8
Non-ferrous metal industry	28.6	25.1	30.4	26.8	35.2	31.0	38.4	34.1	44.1	39.5	43.4	39.1	43.9	40.9	43.9	40.9	43.9
Engineering construction except road vehicles	73.0	64.2	79.5	70.0	89.2	78.6	117.4	104.4	129.8	116.2	133.9	120.6	146.0	133.2	159.3	147.0	175.9
Road vehicles	26.5	23.3	43.7	38.5	51.9	45.8	69.0	61.3	76.4	68.4	86.1	77.5	106.3	97.0	107.8	99.4	116.3
Electrical equipment and supplies	82.8	72.8	101.8	89.6	115.3	101.6	163.1	145.0	186.3	162.2	190.4	171.5	213.3	194.6	245.0	226.0	223.8
Fine mechanics and optics	100.8	88.6	112.6	99.2	116.0	102.3	146.0	129.8	161.6	144.6	182.0	163.9	203.9	186.0	168.8	155.7	202.6
Chemical industry (West German definition)	117.6	103.3	134.4	118.4	147.4	130.0	157.0	139.6	174.5	156.2	191.1	172.1	200.5	182.9	210.0	193.7	227.0
Fuel production	142.0	124.8	178.4	157.1	195.0	171.9	229.5	204.0	226.2	202.4	243.3	219.1	268.7	245.1	268.7	247.9	268.7
Fiber production	185.7	163.2	235.3	207.2	264.3	233.0	287.3	255.4	316.3	283.0	339.3	305.6	357.4	326.0	383.6	353.9	412.3
Chemotechnical	80.8	71.0	87.2	76.8	96.3	84.9	100.3	98.2	118.1	105.7	125.1	112.7	134.9	123.1	144.5	133.3	163.6
Stones and earths	55.1	48.4	66.1	58.2	71.8	63.3	79.7	70.9	83.1	74.4	88.6	79.8	91.7	83.6	99.0	91.3	101.7
Woodworking	33.2	29.2	40.6	35.8	50.1	44.2	57.7	51.3	67.3	60.2	74.2	66.8	78.7	71.8	84.6	78.0	93.8
Sawmills	122.6	107.7	124.0	109.2	106.9	94.3	108.7	96.6	107.4	96.1	101.9	91.8	98.3	89.7	95.0	87.6	95.5
Cellulose, paper, and cardboard	59.2	52.0	66.9	58.9	70.9	62.5	73.4	65.3	76.1	68.1	78.6	70.8	81.4	74.2	83.7	77.2	86.7
Textile industry	42.8	37.6	53.2	46.8	56.2	49.6	60.3	53.6	66.5	59.5	66.0	59.4	64.2	58.6	65.7	60.6	69.0
Shoe and leather industry	56.3	49.5	70.0	61.6	83.3	73.4	98.2	87.3	104.0	93.1	96.5	86.9	93.5	85.3	105.5	97.3	118.1
Fats and oils	100.6	88.4	183.9	161.9	231.8	204.4	246.9	219.5	307.4	275.1	390.8	351.9	418.3	381.6	399.5	368.5	419.3
Food, drink, and tobacco	57.8	50.8	72.2	63.3	78.8	69.5	89.7	79.7	94.4	84.5	96.5	86.9	91.6	83.6	100.7	92.9	103.0
Clothing industry	23.3	20.5	30.5	26.9	32.9	29.0	37.0	32.9	43.3	38.7	42.8	38.5	42.1	38.4	43.4	40.0	46.7
Iron and steel ware/metal goods	55.6	48.9	66.1	58.2	75.2	66.3	99.2	88.2	109.8	98.3	112.5	101.3	128.3	117.0	136.3	125.7	149.3
Paper and printing	28.3	24.9	31.5	27.7	36.6	32.3	38.4	34.1	45.2	40.4	48.2	43.4	50.0	45.6	52.6	48.5	54.8
Rubber and asbestos	184.7	162.3	218.2	192.1	241.8	213.2	343.8	305.6	249.5	223.3	297.5	267.9	275.4	251.2	333.4	307.6	368.7
Flat glass	613.7	539.3	628.5	553.4	543.3	479.0	463.6	412.1	558.9	500.1	663.3	597.4	664.4	606.0	691.4	637.8	682.9
Ceramics	48.7	42.8	56.2	49.5	65.5	57.7	67.8	60.3	72.7	65.1	75.6	68.1	71.8	65.5	68.1	62.8	74.5
Spirits	66.8	58.7	78.1	68.8	85.6	75.5	99.4	88.4	108.1	96.7	113.4	102.1	118.9	108.5	125.6	115.9	132.6
Glass, excluding flat glass	66.8	58.7	78.1	68.8	85.6	75.5	99.4	88.4	108.1	96.7	113.4	102.1	118.9	108.5	125.6	115.9	132.6
Population index	113.79		113.56		113.42		112.49		111.75		111.04		109.63		108.40		107.39

Sources: Tables in Part III.

ª Index of per capita production.

Table B

Indices of various (selected) industries, West Germany, 1950–1955

Branch of industry	1950	1950[a]	1951	1951[a]	1952	1952[a]	1953	1953[a]	1954	1954[a]	1955	1955[a]
Total coal mining	99.2	81.7	110.2	89.8	116.1	93.8	118.3	94.6	120.2	95.1	126.9	99.5
Iron ore sector	141.4	116.5	167.2	136.2	196.6	158.8	187.3	149.7	170.7	135.1	203.0	159.1
Potash and rock salt mining	149.3	123.0	176.6	143.9	200.4	161.9	206.7	165.2	247.2	195.6	260.1	203.9
Iron and steel making }												
Rolled steel	80.1	66.0	94.0	76.6	109.9	88.8	101.0	80.7	113.4	89.7	142.1	111.4
Nonferrous metal industry	100.5	82.8	121.1	98.6	114.4	92.4	130.9	104.6	162.2	128.4	179.5	140.7
Engineering (steel construction)	58.4	48.1	64.1	52.2	69.9	56.5	81.0	64.8	84.4	66.8	95.7	75.0
Engineering (machine construction)	115.7	95.3	154.5	125.9	179.5	145.0	177.3	141.7	197.9	156.6	243.3	190.7
Engineering (shipbuilding)	53.7	44.3	70.2	57.2	99.4	80.3	130.0	103.9	163.8	129.6	194.1	152.2
Road vehicles	143.5	118.3	182.8	148.9	215.4	174.0	231.1	184.7	301.0	238.2	395.7	310.2
Electrical equipment and supplies	199.6	164.5	274.3	223.4	290.6	234.8	319.2	255.2	396.2	313.5	492.6	386.1
Fine mechanics and optics	123.0	101.4	160.8	131.0	183.9	148.6	205.2	164.0	234.7	185.7	274.5	215.2
Chemical industry (new definition)	125.0	103.0	148.3	120.8	147.1	118.8	175.1	140.0	198.5	157.1	224.5	176.0
Fuel production	…	…	…	…	…	…	…	…	…	…	…	…
Fiber production	268.1	220.9	319.6	260.3	262.7	212.2	334.6	267.5	378.6	299.6	494.1	387.3
Chemotechnical	…	…	…	…	…	…	…	…	…	…	…	…
Stones and earths	100.3	82.7	114.1	92.9	122.8	99.2	136.7	109.3	147.6	116.8	168.0	131.7
Woodworking	112.0	92.3	130.3	106.1	121.6	98.2	139.6	111.6	158.1	125.1	169.5	132.9
Sawmills	110.0	90.6	120.8	98.4	109.0	88.1	105.0	83.9	115.1	91.1	126.4	99.1
Cellulose, paper, and cardboard	94.6	78.0	109.0	88.8	100.3	81.0	116.1	92.8	134.8	106.7	145.8	114.3
Textile industry	120.5	99.3	136.0	110.8	131.8	106.5	156.9	125.4	168.0	132.9	181.7	142.4
Leather industry	70.4	56.0	70.9	57.8	74.6	60.3	78.7	62.9	78.1	61.8	85.7	67.2
Shoe industry	79.1	65.2	81.6	66.5	89.2	72.1	94.5	75.5	97.2	76.9	109.0	85.4
Fats and oils	…	…	…	…	…	…	…	…	…	…	…	…
Food industry	120.9	99.6	135.6	110.5	144.6	116.8	173.4	138.6	183.2	145.0	200.8	157.4
Tobacco industry	88.3	72.8	101.3	82.5	110.8	89.5	122.7	98.1	129.7	102.6	143.1	112.2
Clothing industry	171.8	141.6	206.0	167.8	225.6	182.2	266.5	213.0	281.3	222.6	339.9	266.4
Iron and steel wares/metal goods including steel forming	94.8	78.1	122.3	99.6	124.7	100.7	128.6	102.8	150.4	119.0	179.6	140.8
Paper products	101.7	83.8	108.2	88.1	115.3	93.1	130.4	104.2	145.5	115.1	161.0	126.2
Printing industry	112.2	92.5	117.5	95.7	126.0	101.8	148.5	118.7	163.1	129.1	174.7	136.9
Rubber and asbestos	117.8	97.1	130.6	106.4	143.5	115.9	164.5	131.5	191.9	151.9	231.1	181.2
Flat glass industry	132.5	109.2	165.8	135.1	157.1	126.9	162.0	129.5	196.6	155.6	234.3	183.7
Ceramics	97.4	80.3	123.7	100.8	124.6	100.7	130.9	104.6	159.6	126.3	183.2	143.6
Spirits	…	…	…	…	…	…	…	…	…	…	…	…
Glass (except flat glass)	185.2	152.6	231.9	188.9	220.6	178.2	246.1	196.7	275.6	218.1	303.3	237.8
Population index	121.35		122.76		123.79		125.09		126.37		127.57	

Sources: *SJBR*, 1956, pp. 219–223.
[a] Index of per capita production.

Table C

Production per employed person in industry, East Germany, 1950–1957

Year	Index of production (1950 prices)	Index of employment		Index of productivity per person employed	
		Without producing artisans	With producing artisans	Without producing artisans	With producing artisans
	(1)	(2)	(3)	(4)	(5)
1950	100.0	100.0	100.0	100.0	100.0
1951	116.9	111.3	106.4	105.0	109.9
1952	128.2	122.2	113.3	104.9	113.2
1953	148.9	126.9	115.6	117.3	128.8
1954	161.9	132.4	120.1	122.3	134.8
1955	170.0	128.2	117.5	132.6	144.7
1956	178.3	126.7	115.8	140.7	154.0
1957	188.3	134.4	121.2	140.4	155.4
1958	199.0	137.0	121.8	145.3	163.4

Year	Gross value added 1950 prices (million DM)	Number of employed persons in industry, without producing artisans (millions)	Output per worker 1950 prices (DM)
	(6)	(7)	(8)
1950	10,472.2	2.2559	4,642
1951	12,241.2	2.4434	5,009
1952	13,406.8	2.6209	5,115
1953	15,573.3	2.7230	5,719
1954	16,944.3	2.8410	5,964
1955	17,770.1	2.7503	6,461
1956	18,639.4	2.7186	6,854
1957	19,685.2	2.8839	6,826
1958	20,797.2	2.9396	7,075

Sources: Cols. 1 and 6: From Table 91. Cols. 2, 3, and 7: Calculated from Table 13. Col. 4: Col. 1 ÷ col. 2. Col. 5: Col. 1 ÷ col. 3.

Table D

Index of production per person employed, and output per worker
in the Federal Republic (without West Berlin), 1950–1958

Year	Index of production per person employed	Output per worker (1950 prices; DM)
	(1)	(2)
1950	100.0	9,921
1951	107.9	10,705
1952	111.1	11,022
1953	117.6	11,667
1954	124.9	12,391
1955	132.3	13,125
1956	134.2	13,314
1957	137.0	13,592
1958	141.0	13,989

Sources: Col. 1: *SJBR*, 1959, p. 184. Col. 2: Calculated as follows: The value added of West German industry in 1950 prices in 1950 was DM 47,591.7 million, produced by 4.7969 million persons (*Neuberechnung*, p. 9, and *SJBR*, 1954, p. 218). This means that a worker produced on the average DM 9,921. Other years were calculated with the index in col. 1.

PART FOUR

AGRICULTURE AND FORESTRY

CHAPTER XV

THE CROP SECTOR

T HE gross value added of agriculture was estimated in the following manner. First, an estimate was made of the sales value of all major crops. The amounts evaluated should in principle be net amounts in the sense that a correction is made for the fact that in communist ideology biological yields* are used rather than barn yields. Furthermore, the amount of feed needed, the amount of seed put back into agriculture, and the losses that occur both before and after moving out of the barn to final use ought to be deducted.

It is possible to determine at least approximately the amounts going into human consumption. Fodder grown and used on the farm was not evaluated, and only those amounts of feed used which were imported or otherwise came from outside the agricultural sector were later deducted from livestock and animal products sector. From the combined total sales value thus found, the value of the fertilizer input was deducted. The total amounts supplied are known, but these cannot, of course, be allocated among the various crops. An over-all estimate was also made for the electricity used and for other current inputs such as gasoline for tractors.

Fortunately, the special problem of machine tractor stations (MTS) can be sidestepped — although information concerning them will be supplied. If their value added were to be shown separately, the wages and "profits" would have to be found by estimating the value of all their services and then deducting the various inputs such as machinery and gasoline. As it is, their services are included in agricultural output. By not evaluating them separately in the first place, they need not be deducted in the second. On the other hand, the value of the gasoline used by them and other current inputs have to be deducted. The tractors purchased were not deducted, even though the tractors and other implements produced were originally counted among industrial output. Rather, they were treated as investments. Fortunately, imports of agricultural implements, which might have to be treated differently, appear to be small.

* That is, yields in the field before harvesting and other handling, as distinguished from barn yields, which are net crops after harvesting and other losses have been deducted.

The livestock and animal products sector was treated in an analogous manner.

AGRICULTURAL AREAS

East Germany (including East Berlin) has an area of 107,862 sq km, which is about 30.6 per cent of postwar Germany.[1] In 1938, 61.7 per cent of the land in all Germany was used in agriculture. Of agricultural land in East Germany 76.5 per cent was crop land, compared with 58.2 per cent in the area of the Federal Republic; 14.6 per cent was meadows, compared with 25.2 per cent in the Federal Republic; and 5.9 per cent in pasture, compared with 13.1 per cent in the Federal Republic.[2] In proportion to the population, therefore, the area of East Germany had relatively more grains or feed (except hay), more pigs (which are fed potatoes), sheep, and goats than the Federal Republic; the latter had a relative surplus of cattle, milk, and chicken and eggs.[3] Besides being affected by the division of the agricultural land into crop land and pastures and meadows, the animal density and the utilization of crop land depend of course also on the size of the farms, which in the area of East Germany was relatively greater. Hence postwar changes are not only the result of attempts to overcome "disproportionalities," as in industry, but also of land reform, which, although politically determined, leads to increases in the numbers of pigs and sheep as typical small-farm animals. For the comparative distribution of farms by size in the Federal Republic and in East Germany, see Table 98.

Table 98

Percentage distribution of farms by size of agricultural area,
West and East Germany, prewar

Size (hectares)	Number of farms		Acreage	
	West Germany	East Germany	West Germany	East Germany
(1)	(2)	(3)	(4)	(5)
Less than 5	61.1	57.7	18.5	9.2
5– 20	32.4	31.7	46.3	31.8
20– 50	5.6	8.2	24.0	22.4
50–100	0.7	1.4	6.3	8.4
More than 100	0.2	1.0	4.9	28.2
	100.0	100.0	100.0	100.0

Source: Dr. Matthias Kramer, *Die Landwirtschaft in der sowjetischen Besatzungszone* ("*Bonner Berichte*"), Bonn, Federal Ministry for All German Questions, 1953 (hereinafter referred to in the tables as Kramer, *Die Landwirtschaft*), p. 11.

Since it is not our major purpose to discuss the changes brought about by land reform, no further analysis will be made here. Where such changes are relevant, however, comments will be made. Here, the development of land utilization is of major interest.

Table 99

Agricultural and forest land, East Germany, 1938, 1950, 1955, and 1957 (thousand hectares)

	1938		1950		1955[a]		1957	
	Hectares	Per cent	Hectares	Per cent	Hectares	Per cent	Hectares	Per cent
	(1)	(2)	(3)	(4)	(5)	(6)	(7)	(8)
Total agricultural land	6,656.5	100.0	6,528.4	98.1	6,482.0	97.4	6,465.5	97.1
Of which:								
Crop land[b]	5,093.0	76.5	5,017.0	76.9	4,991.6	77.0	4,949.6	76.6
Meadows	970.7	14.6	894.2	13.7	872.0	13.5	878.1	13.6
Pastures	390.9	5.9	396.9	6.1	389.7	6.0	403.8	6.2
Forests	2,945.8		2,898.6		2,942.3		2,935.1	

Source: *SJDDR*, 1957, pp. 374–375. [a] Refers to December 31, 1955. [b] Includes commercial gardens but excludes other garden land.

From Table 99, it may be seen that total acreage has declined steadily since 1938, as have the major utilizations except pastures. By 1957 the amount of crop land had returned to its prewar level, while the combined acreage devoted to meadows and pastures had increased slightly. There was less forest land than in 1938 also, although more than in 1950.

The acreage devoted to the major crops has also changed. As may be seen from Table 100, by 1957, in comparison with 1938, the acreage of

Table 100

Acreage in major crops, East Germany, 1938, 1950, 1955, 1957, and 1958 (thousand hectares)

	1934–1938	1938	1950	1955	1957	1955 as per cent of 1938	1957 as per cent of 1938	1958	1958 as per cent of 1938
	(1)	(2)	(3)	(4)	(5)	(6)	(7)	(8)	(9)
Wheat and spelt	632.2	615.6	478.9	400.5	420.1	65.1	68.2	441.1	71.7
Rye	1,208.6	1,159.5	1,294.3	1,074.0	1,099.0	92.6	94.8	109.6	94.6
Barley	438.8	446.7	261.0	336.6	321.8	76.7	72.0	337.3	75.5
Oats	739.1	709.8	531.5	535.5	456.4	72.5	64.3	428.3	60.3
Rapeseed and other oilseed crops	17.6	23.8	152.8	154.0	151.2	647.0	635.2	148.6	624.4
All fiber plants	12.9	14.8	30.3	41.6	32.7	322.5	220.9	34.2	231.1
Sugar beets	185.6	224.6	223.7	223.9	230.2	99.7	102.5	236.1	105.1
Potatoes	790.7	808.9	811.6	842.9	810.2	102.0	100.2	775.7	95.1
Beets, etc. for feed	229.7	229.4	262.8	336.9	286.5	146.5	124.9	248.4	108.3

Sources: *SHD*, pp. 146 ff.; *SJDDR*, 1957, pp. 328 f.; 1958, pp. 444, 445. (Some of these figures differ from data given in the earlier editions.)

grain (except rye) had decreased sharply; that of oilseed, fiber plants, and feed had increased sharply; rye has decreased somewhat; and sugar beets and potatoes — the major crops — roughly held their own. A comparison with the acreage of 1934–1938 rather than 1938 alone, however, shows sharp increases also in sugar beet and potato acreage and a sharp decrease in rye.

THE MAJOR CROPS

Although acreages are directly comparable, a communist hectare being the same as a capitalist hectare, this is not true for yields. Until 1957, communist yields were biological yields rather than barn yields. Before proceeding to our estimates for the crop sector, it might be well to describe the estimating procedures used in East Germany. The easiest, as well as the shortest and most impressive, method is to give an extensive translation from *Statistical Practice*:

Estimates of yields per acre until 1950 were based on reports of honorary reporters from among the agricultural population. Since their estimates were, however, well known to be subject to substantial subjective influences, it became necessary to introduce a method which was suitable to the needs of our society. At first, the making of estimates of crop yields was given over to the agronomists of the then MAS* (MTS). But this did not have the expected success. The agronomists lacked the necessary technical and political prerequisites to estimate yields on their own responsibility. Only with the formation of county [*Kreis*] estimating commissions with politically and technically qualified personnel chosen from the Administration, and with the aid of the agronomists of the MTS, the directors of the nationalized farms and of cooperatives, as well as individual peasants, have estimates become more realistic.

In order to make the work of the commissions easier, the counties [*Kreise*] were originally grouped into five growth regions, depending on their soil quality and climate. This turned out to be too crude. It depended more or less on the commission as to which soil group the individual areas were to be included in. Hence seven yield areas were determined for our republic based on the soil estimates of 1952 (raw yield index [*Rohertragsverhältniszahl*] and a distribution by soil qualities) which make it possible to get definite relations to individual yields. The results can then be compared with each other and corrected by sample harvestings or sample threshings. Individual communities are allocated to the individual yield areas. Since only particular important villages [*Schwerpunktgemeinden*] now have to be estimated, this eases the estimating work considerably. . . .

In considering the hectare yields for individual years, the 1951 yields for grains and oilseeds are very high compared with other years. Undoubtedly the weather in 1951 led to high yields of all crops. But beyond this, the insufficient technical qualifications of the estimating commission at the time have certainly also led in a few cases to an overestimation of grains and oilseeds.[4]

This quotation indicates that at least for some time, probably until 1954, the technical incompetence of the estimators made the yield data of doubtful value. Other articles indicate furthermore that, by accident or deliberately, the communities chosen in the sample were not typical. For example, it is stated that "in 1952 the extreme yield areas has a higher representation than was consistent with their importance,"[5] and the same article proposes new sampling procedures for the future, that is, for the

---

* MAS: *Maschinen Ausleihstationen,* or Machine Lending Station, the original name of the MTS or Machine Tractor Station.

period of the Second Five Year Plan. The following statement appeared in *Statistical Practice* in July 1955:

The county estimating commissions will estimate crop yields as raw [biological] yields in representative selected communities which are specially important [*Schwerpunktsgemeinden*]. Raw yields are the yields which may be expected from a hectare at harvest time considering the stand at the time of estimation. For planning and guidance of the supply of food to the population, of fodder for animals, and of raw materials for industry, net [barn] yields [or harvesting or threshing yields] are estimated.[6]

For 1957 the biological yields were abandoned altogether, and only net yields (barn yields) were to be estimated.[7] These yields were published in 1958, but corrected series go back at most to 1953 and in many cases only to 1956.

The extensive quotation, a study of East German estimating procedures, and the 1957 changeover to Western concepts of net yields indicate, however, that the proposed corrections in the crop data suggested by Western experts are the absolute minimum adjustments that must be made.

According to figures given in Professor Kramer's unpublished manuscript, an allowance of 10–15 per cent has to be made for grain yields, and larger allowances must be made for potatoes (25 per cent), sugar beets (20 per cent), and feed beets (25 per cent), while oilseeds are closer to grains (13 per cent).* This corrected yield is the starting point for the following calculation of the available amounts.[8] From the barn yield we have to deduct waste, which runs 3 to 5 per cent in the case of grains and over 15 per cent in the case of potatoes in 1949 in East Germany (according to the Food and Agriculture Organization) and probably more normally around 10 per cent. After these corrections we arrive at the domestic crop that is available for all uses. With imports or exports allowed for, we have total available supplies. The part remaining in agriculture consists of seed requirements, feed, and the peasants' own consumption. The rest goes directly to the market or to factories for processing.

It seems best first to evaluate the total production available for the market, including the peasants' own consumption after an allowance for losses, waste, and seed has been made, and then to deduct inputs from the market value of all crops combined. This enables one to make an estimate of the gross value added of field crops.

* These figures were confirmed in talks with other experts. The adjustments are necessary to compensate on the one hand for overoptimistic estimates in the estimation procedures, which were constantly changed because they evidently were felt to be unsatisfactory, and on the other hand to allow for the fact that even in the best of circumstances there are inevitable losses between the crop in the field — the raw yield — and what can be got into the barn after threshing, leaving crops in the field in the rain, having inadequate storing facilities, and so on. Considering the inadequate supplies of commercial fertilizers (about which more will be said below), only after such allowances are made are the yields believable.

Wheat and rye

Wheat. Wheat acreage in the area of East Germany before the war was slightly more than half the acreage devoted to rye. By 1955 it had fallen to less than two-thirds of the prewar acreage, but "raw" yields were supposed to have increased to prewar levels. This is hardly believable. In the opinion of experts, prewar data are underestimated by at least 10 per cent, and this adjustment is made by the Ministry of Agriculture of the Federal Republic when making postwar comparisons with prewar yields.[9] The postwar difference between biological and barn yields is estimated at between 10 and 15 per cent. In the calculations below, 13 per cent has been assumed. The wastage in the barns before the war was assumed to be 3 per cent of the barn yield; experts believe that 5 per cent is a closer approximation, which allows for deteriorated storage conditions after the war. Seed requirements are given as 180 kg per hectare. The Rules of Thumb for Agriculture give a requirement of between 100 and 200 kg per hectare. East Germany is not especially suitable for wheat production. Since the prewar average for all of Germany was 162 kg per hectare, the estimate of 180 kg per hectare seems reasonable. Finally, there are market losses of about 2.5 per cent which occur after the grain leaves the barn.

The remaining crop is the total output of wheat, evaluated as the sales value at a 1936 price of RM 210.9 per ton.[10] The prewar price is the wholesale price of wheat of Mark Brandenburg delivered in Berlin. The 1950 price of DM 299.0 per ton[11] refers to the wholesale price, f.o.b. producer station, Cologne. The Cologne price was chosen because in 1938 it was closest to the Berlin price — 210.2 and 208.2, respectively. By 1955 total wheat output, as defined, had decreased to 65 per cent of its 1934–1938 average level. If 1938 is taken as the base year, the decline is to 52.6 per cent, but 1938 was an unusually good year. The decline is largely due to a reduction in acreage of 63.4 per cent compared with the 1934–1938 average, and of 64.7 per cent compared with 1938. Between 1950 and 1955, wheat acreage fell by 16.4 per cent, while output (as defined) apparently increased by 9.3 per cent.

Rye. Except for 1955 and later years, the postwar acreage was *above* both the 1934–1938 average and the 1938 level. Only in 1955 was there a reduction — to 91.6 per cent of the 1934–1938 average and to 92.6 per cent of the 1938 level.

The various deductions are assumed to be identical with those for wheat, except that seed requirements are put at 152 kg per hectare. The prices at which the output is evaluated are RM 172.4 per ton for 1936 (refers to the wholesale price, Berlin, rye of Mark Brandenburg[12]) and DM 265.9 per ton for 1950.*

---

* F.o.b. producer station, price of Munich market, which was chosen because its price in 1938 was identical with the Berlin price.

The total output of rye (as defined) had reached 90 per cent of the 1934–1938 average by 1950, then rose substantially above it, but by 1955 it was 7.5 per cent below it. Rye output has never reached the level of the record year 1938 even though total acreage has been higher in every year except 1955.

Wheat and rye combined. Except for the years 1951 and 1952, the combined output of the two major bread grains has not risen above 90 per cent of the 1934–1938 average level, and in 1955 it was about 20 per cent below it. Compared with the record year 1938, the lag was much more substantial — almost 35 per cent in 1955. It makes little difference whether output is measured in 1936 or 1950 prices (see Tables 101 and 102).

In interpreting the figures it should be kept in mind not only that total acreage diminished but also that a prewar export surplus gave way to a postwar import surplus of substantial proportions. At the same time, however, the feed needs have increased because before the war feed imports came from the other areas into the East German area, and in particular because East Germany now produces milk, which used to be imported. Furthermore, the inadequate imports of oil cake have put a heavy strain on cereals (apparently including bread grains) as a feed basis.

The use of wheat and rye and imports. Total domestic production plus imports are used to feed the human and animal populations. The amounts going to human consumption could be equated with the combined amounts of forced deliveries (*Erfassung*) and government purchases (*Aufkauf*). Such figures are now officially given back to 1953. However, Kramer gives such over-all figures for the years 1951 through 1955 for all grains and legumes.[13] Although legumes are a negligible tonnage, cereals other than wheat and rye are included.

It is possible to make an approximate calculation of the amount of wheat and rye used for human consumption on the basis of flour consumed per capita. These figures, which are now given officially, are divided between wheat and rye in proportion to the total amount of each available, after adding imports. The prewar consumption of rye and wheat flour in all Germany is known directly, and it is assumed to have been the same in all parts of the Reich. The amount of flour can be converted to rye and wheat grains on the basis of 1 kg rye flour = 1.225 kg rye grain, and 1 kg wheat flour = 1.250 kg wheat grain.

On the basis of these assumptions, it appears that the human consumption of rye rose from an average of 1.091 million tons for 1934–1938, or 1.076 million tons in 1938, to a high of 1.778 million tons in 1951. By 1955 it had decreased to 1.470 million tons, a level still 34.8 per cent above the prewar average. Wheat consumption on the other hand increased from an average of 958,100 tons for 1934–1938 to a high of 967,400 in 1938, decreased sharply until 1953, but rose by 1955 to the 1938 level. In 1955 the combined bread grain consumption of the population was 25

Table 101

Acreage, production, imports, and government purchases and forced deliveries of wheat and rye, East Germany, 1934–1938 average, 1938, and 1950–1958

A. *Wheat*

Year	Acreage (thousand hectares)	Biological yield (thousand tons)	Barn yield (87 per cent of biological yield) (thousand tons)	Net yield[a] (thousand tons)	Imports (thousand tons)
1934–1938 (av.)	632.2		1,708.1		
1938	618.8		2,079.0		
1950	478.8	1,213.9	1,056.1		250.8
1951	464.4	1,493.9	1,299.7		364.0
1952	475.7	1,442.4	1,254.9		334.0
1953	419.8	1,187.5	1,033.1	1,152.1	349.2
1954	424.1	1,140.4	992.1	1,080.8	327.9
1955	400.5	1,272.9	1,107.4	1,211.5	554.9
1956	391.3	1,151.2	1,001.5	1,086.2	606.1
1957	420.1			1,259.2	1,078.0
1958	441.4			1,363.3	1,292.0

B. *Rye, and purchases and forced deliveries of wheat and rye combined*

Year	Acreage (thousand hectares)	Biological yield (thousand tons)	Barn yield (87 per cent of biological yield) (thousand tons)	Net yield[a] (thousand tons)	Imports (thousand tons)	Purchases and deliveries of wheat and rye (thousand tons)[b]
1934–1938	1,209.6		2,277.2			
1938	1,159.5		2,682.5			
1950	1,294.3	2,418.0	2,103.7			2,758.5
1951	1,276.9	2,991.9	2,603.0			2,784.8
1952	1,291.4	2,864.1	2,491.8		49.0	2,839.0
1953	1,223.2	2,362.3	2,055.2	2,292.2	65.0	2,249.9
1954	1,215.3	2,581.5	2,245.9	2,393.8	610.0	2,125.7
1955	1,074.0	2,463.7	2,143.4	2,336.8	187.3	2,056.7
1956	1,121.8	2,434.1	2,117.7	2,298.9	481.5	1,932.7
1957	1,099.4			2,230.5	342.0	2,032.2
1958	1,096.6			2,367.8	207.0	1,945.6

Sources: *SHD*, p. 146; *SJDDR*, 1955, p. 206; 1956, pp. 439 and 452; 1957, pp. 444 and 520; 1958, pp. 452 f., 502, and 576. The calculation of the market value of grain crops is based on the calculated barn yield rather than the claimed "net" yields, which seem unrealistic. For details see Supplement Tables B.1 and B.2.

[a] The "net" yield is defined as "actual yield after threshing, but without allowance for deterioration in storage and losses," *SJDDR*, 1957, p. 353.

[b] Includes some legumes for human consumption.

Table 102

Sales value of output of wheat and rye, East Germany,
1934–1938 average, 1938, and 1950–1958

A. *1936 Prices*

Year	Rye (million RM)	Wheat (million RM)	Rye and wheat combined (million RM)	Index 1934–1938 av. = 100	Index 1938 = 100
	(1)	(2)	(3)	(4)	(5)
1934–1938 (av.)	188.054	224.503	412.557	100.0	100.1
1938	185.416	226.696	412.112	99.8	100.0
1950	302.820	188.608	491.428	119.0	119.3
1951	306.475	201.346	507.821	122.9	123.2
1952	305.592	200.756	506.348	122.6	122.9
1953	279.443	186.267	465.710	112.7	113.0
1954	267.237	178.105	445.342	107.8	108.1
1955	253.445	201.494	454.939	110.1	110.4
1956	250.221	181.163	431.384	104.4	104.7
1957			453.730[a]	109.8	110.1
1958			434.401[a]	105.3	105.4

B. *1950 Prices*

Year	Rye (million DM)	Wheat (million DM)	Rye and wheat combined (million DM)	Index 1934–1938 av. = 100	Index 1938 = 100
	(6)	(7)	(8)	(9)	(10)
1934–1938 (av.)	290.044	318.286	608.330	100.0	100.2
1938	285.975	321.395	607.370	99.8	100.0
1950	467.053	267.396	734.449	120.7	120.9
1951	472.690	285.455	758.145	124.6	124.8
1952	471.334	284.618	755.952	124.3	124.5
1953	430.997	264.077	695.074	114.3	114.4
1954	412.172	252.506	664.678	109.3	109.4
1955	390.900	285.665	676.565	111.2	111.4
1956	385.927	256.841	642.768	105.7	105.8
1957			676.063[a]	111.2	111.3
1958			647.263[a]	106.4	106.6

Sources: Only amounts leaving the agricultural sector were evaluated. The 1936 price of what was RM 210.9 per ton and of rye RM 172.4 per ton. The 1950 price of wheat was DM 299 per ton and of rye DM 265.9 per ton. For methods of calculation, see text. Details are given in Supplement Tables B.1 and B.2.

[a] Assumed to increase as government purchases and forced deliveries of wheat and rye; 1957 = 105.18 per cent of 1956; 1958 = 95.74 per cent of 1957.

per cent above the 1934–1938 average even though the population was only about 10 per cent bigger, and it was as much as 35 per cent above the prewar average during 1950 and 1951.

These figures refer to the whole population. A check against the availability of domestic production alone reveals that they are quite reasonable. The calculations reveal a small deficit of 21,500 tons for rye in 1950, but in this year negligible amounts of rye were imported, wheat had a sufficient surplus, and imports of wheat were 151,000 tons. For wheat there is an apparent deficit of 72,800 tons in 1954, but imports were 328,000 tons. Imports of wheat were 349.2 million tons in 1953, 554.9 million tons in 1955, rising to 606.1 million tons in 1956, and over 1 million tons in 1957.[14] Imports of rye have also been rising. In an area with an exportable surplus of bread grains before the war, the rising import figures themselves indicate that our calculations are reasonable.

There is another check. The calculated figures refer to all human consumption, including consumption on the farms. If about 15 per cent is allowed for consumption at the farm level — almost certainly too little — the resulting figures ought to come quite close to the combined amount of forced deliveries and government purchases. The available figures for all grains and legumes also indicate that the consumption figures are possible though perhaps slightly on the high side. Thus for 1955, total grain deliveries were 2.057 million tons. The calculated value of the amount of wheat and rye leaving the farm sector during the calendar year 1955 was 2.072 million tons.

If the farm sector is allowed 20 per cent of total food consumption, which is approximately its share in total employment (including the self-employed), the figures are well within the possible limits (see Table 103).[15]

Actually, for the years for which data are available, farm employment

Table 103

Presumed consumption outside of agriculture, and government purchases
and forced deliveries of wheat and rye, East Germany, 1950–1958

Year	Human consumption of wheat and rye		Government purchases and forced deliveries	Agricultural employment as per cent of total employment
	80 per cent of total (thousand tons)	85 per cent of total (thousand tons)		
	(1)	(2)	(3)	(4)
1950	2108.6	2240.0	2758.5	26.6
1951	2109.5	2241.4	2784.8	27.7
1952	2103.4	2234.9	2839.0	21.7
1953	1994.5	2119.1	2249.9	21.0
1954	1983.3	2107.3	2125.7	20.6
1955	1950.0	2072.1	2056.7	21.6
1956			1932.7	20.6
1957			2032.2	20.5
1958			1945.6	19.2

Sources: Cols. 1 and 2: See text and Supplement Tables B.1 and B.2. Col. 3: *SJDDR*, 1957, p. 450; 1958, p. 502. Includes some legumes for human consumption. Col. 4: See Table 12.

was always more than 20 per cent of total employment; and not only do farmers probably have larger families on the whole but also they almost certainly eat better than most of their fellow citizens in the cities. All in all, therefore, the estimates appear reasonable.

They imply that the amount of wheat and rye together available for other purposes inside the agricultural sector and for exports fell from the 1.287 million-ton 1934–1938 average, or 1.771 million tons in 1938, to about 1.108 million tons in 1955; and they make it clear that, while in the prewar years there must have been substantial amounts available for exports, in 1955 the high availability was achieved only by imports of 747,200 tons, or about two thirds of the total supply available inside the agricultural sector.

Coarse grains

The information on coarse grains is included only as a background for the animal sector. Thus coarse grains are not included as an output of agriculture or later deducted as an input into the animal sector, as explained above.

Detailed postwar information is available for oats, barley, mixed grains, and corn (maize). No prewar output could be found for corn. It is likely that only very little or no corn was produced. Even as of 1955 the total acreage of corn was only 4,594 hectares, and the output was 11,414 tons — both negligible amounts. No comparable price could be found. Corn therefore was not included in the calculations.

In East German statistics mixed grains are included with feed grains, which indicates that they are a barley-oats mixture. In addition, the series of mixed grains also includes buckwheat and millet.

As with bread grains, in order to allow for the underestimation of prewar yields and outputs, both were increased 10 per cent above the figures given. As before, a postwar allowance of 13 per cent was made to derive barn yield from biological yield, and 3 per cent was allowed for further losses after harvesting for the prewar years and 5 per cent for the postwar years. And, as before, seed requirements were deducted before the remaining output was valued as the domestically produced output available for all purposes.

Although a small amount of oats may go to human consumption and a small amount of barley to beer brewing, these quantities must be negligible. This is undoubtedly true because, even though brewing barley is a more expensive kind, it appears to be mainly imported. On the whole, all the domestic output of coarse grains must go into the feeding of animals.

The acreage devoted to feed grains fell from an average 1.279 million hectares in 1934–1938 or 1.273 million hectares in 1938 to 1.009 in 1955, a decline of about 21 per cent. In sheer tonnage, however, the change was bigger: the available tonnage fell from an average 2.803 million tons in 1934–1938 or 3.556 million in 1938 to 2.147 million in 1955, or about 76.6 per cent compared with the 1934–1938 average and 60.4 per cent compared with the record year 1938. Even the *biological* yield figures given in the Statistical Yearbook of the German Democratic Republic, which also include the small tonnage of corn, claim an output of only 2.812 million tons of feed grains.[16] The prewar *barn* crops (after an allowance for 10 per cent underestimation) were 3.080 million tons and 3.864 million tons in 1934–1938 and 1938, respectively, that is, at least 15 to 25 per cent higher. The acreage reduction was limited to oats and barley; mixed grains and presumably corn acreage was expanded.

Except for mixed grains, yields (as understood in the West) by 1955 had not quite reached their prewar level. With mixed grains they had surpassed it, but this may be due to a changed product mix.

By 1955 the sales value of feed grains available for all purposes had fallen from the 1934–1938 average by almost 24 per cent, while acreage had declined only about 21 per cent. Compared with the record year 1938, the drop by 1955 was 40 per cent.

Potatoes

Total output. Potatoes are a main staple of the region. They are used for food, for animal feed, and as an industrial raw material in the production of starch and alcohol. In 1955 the acreage was indeed larger than before the war, reaching 106.6 per cent of the 1934–1938 average and 102.0 per cent of 1938. Yet, except in 1954, even the biological yield has lagged seriously behind the prewar crop; when an allowance is made for the losses which occur between the field and the barn, the shortage must be catastrophic.

The prewar data were raised by 10 per cent according to the instructions of the Federal Ministry of Agriculture to allow for underestimation of the crop. For the postwar years, on the advice of the Institut für Landwirtschaftliche Betriebslehre (Institute for Farm Management) in West Berlin, a minimum of 25 per cent was deducted to estimate barn yields.

Lest the reader think that the results are excessively pessimistic, I quote *in extenso* from Fred Oelssner, at that time chief theorist of the Socialist Unity Party, who, in discussing the problems of East Germany in the transition period to socialism, points to serious shortages which are not necessary:

Although [potato] starch is an important raw material for foodstuffs and an excellent export article, the Plan has not been fulfilled for years. We are increasingly producing starch from grains, in particular, from corn. This year, too, we had to change our production over to grains again because we did not have enough potatoes.[17]

And before giving this example he stated:

> We have a critical situation with precisely those [agricultural] products which we can produce ourselves. We must unfortunately state the fact that the commodity production* of our agriculture lags in several areas. This is frequently felt in the supplies to the population.[18]

Potatoes are difficult to store. Losses in storage before the war averaged 8 to 12 per cent, and in the years forming the basis of our calculations they are known to have been 8 per cent. Inferior storage facilities since the war make it certain that spoilage must have increased to at least 10 per cent. After deducting the required amount of seed potatoes, the amounts available for all other purposes can be estimated at an average 12.110 million tons for 1934–1938 and at 6.551 million tons in the apparently catastrophic year 1955.† But even in the best year, 1954, after adjusting for barn yield, waste, and seed, the available amount was only 9.504 million tons. No wonder Mr. Oelssner was worried. For estimated figures on potato output, see Table 104.

The reasons official sources give for this remarkably poor showing are as follows: The yield depends essentially on the care of the fields; the shortage of labor and insufficient mechanization have led to insufficient plowing and to an excessive growth of weeds in the fields; supplies of fertilizer were not on time and were not adequate; and the machine tractor stations do not like to deal with potato and sugar beet fields "because in cultivation work they can barely fulfill their hectare norms for plowing." Hence even in 1954, when the weather was good, the MTS fulfilled only 82 per cent of their plan; in other years the percentage of fulfillment was much less.[19] With potatoes, in particular, the quality of the seeds has deteriorated seriously:

> The low potato yields in 1952 and 1953 were basically due to insufficient cultivation. In 1953 there was also a drought period in July and August. During 1955 a short growing season, lacking cultivation, and phytophthora sickness led to yield reductions up to 50 per cent.[20]

Thus the fall by 1955 in the available amount of potatoes to 54 per cent of the average 1934–1938 level is quite believable. Even the 22 per cent reduction in available supplies between 1934–1938 and the good year 1954 is plausible.

Uses of potatoes. The nonagricultural uses of potatoes are probably equivalent to the amounts of forced deliveries and government purchases at higher prices. For 1951–1952, the Institut für Landwirtschaftliche Betriebslehre in West Berlin kindly supplied the figures. The figures

---

* Commodity production, it will be recalled, essentially refers to output of goods for final use.

† Biological yields of late potatoes in 1955 were 14.59 tons per ha, compared to 20.6 tons per ha in 1954, and compared to a *barn* yield in 1938 of 18.21 tons and an average yield of 17.64 tons per ha in the 1934–1938 period.

Table 104

Production, sales value, and government purchases and forced deliveries of potatoes, East Germany, 1934–1938 average, 1938, and 1950–1958[a]

Year	Biological yield (million tons) (1)	Barn yield (75 per cent of biological yield) (million tons) (2)	Net yield (million tons) (3)	Sales value of available crop 1936 Prices (million RM) (4)	Sales value of available crop 1950 Prices (million DM) (5)	Forced deliveries and government purchases (million tons) (6)	Remaining within agriculture (million tons) (7)	Of which, for animal feeding (million tons) (8)
1934–1938 (av.)		15.023		542.528	1,259.440	5.583	6.527	5.931
1938		16.016		581.594	1,350.128	5.985	6.997	
1950	14.706	11.030		366.061	849.784	4.804	3.799	2.964
1951	14.872	11.154		369.152	856.960	4.441	3.095	2.372
1952	13.935	10.451		341.018	791.648	4.338	3.533	2.813
1953	13.971	10.478	13.273	341.690	793.208	3.721	5.457	4.169
1954	16.754	12.566	15.520	425.779	988.416	4.011	3.223	2.566
1955	12.108	9.081	11.194	284.435	660.296	3.430		
1956	14.841	11.131	13.565	372.960	865.800	3.554		
1957			14.529	401.081[b]	931.081[b]	3.822		
1958			11.498	317.407[b]	736.839[b]	3.297		

Sources: Col. 1: *SJDDR*, 1956, p. 397. Series discontinued in 1957. Col. 2: Figures from *SHD*, pp. 150–151, raised by 10 per cent to allow for underestimation. See *Statistisches Handbuch fuer Landwirtschaft und Ernaehrung*, Hamburg and Berlin, Paul Parey, 1956, Table 91, note 5, p. 53. Postwar adjustment based on information supplied by the Institut fuer Landwirtschaftliche Betriebslehre, West Berlin. Col. 3: *SJDDR*, 1957, p. 403; 1958, p. 464. Col. 4: RM 44.8 per ton. *SHD*, p. 463. Col. 5: DM 104 per ton. *SHD*, p. 463. Col. 6: Forced deliveries (*Erfassung*) and government purchases at a higher price (*Aufkauf*), *SJDDR*, 1957, p. 450; 1958, p. 502. Col. 7: See text. Col. 8: Remaining within agriculture less estimated farmers' own consumption.

a Further details as to prices, allowance for seed, etc. are given in Appendix Table B.8.

b Assumed to increase as government purchases and forced deliveries: 1957 = 107.5 per cent of 1956; 1958 = 79.14 per cent of 1957.

for 1953 through 1957, now officially published, agree with the Western figures previously available. The prewar figures were calculated as follows.

The Agriculture and Food Handbook states that before the war 21.5 per cent of potatoes were sold, 45.3 per cent were used for feed, 13.7 per cent were used as seed, and 11.5 per cent were consumed by farmers. The remaining 8 per cent were lost through deterioration.[21] On this basis, an annual average of about 3.230 million tons in the 1934–1938 period and 3.443 million tons in 1938 would be the equivalent of the government purchases and forced deliveries in the postwar period. These figures, which refer to the total crop of 19 million tons in the area of the Federal Republic, appear too low for the area of East Germany, which is a major potato producer.

The Statistical Handbook of Germany states that in 1939–1940 the following amounts of potatoes were consumed (million tons): [22]

Seed	6.900
Deterioration	6.600
Feed	23.632
Total within agriculture	37.132
Total consumption	57.347

We have deducted seed and deterioration from total use of potatoes, leaving a "net" crop of 43.847 million tons. It is assumed that the proportion of feed to net crop (23.632/43.847 = 53.8965%) is a ratio that held in other prewar years. This method of calculation more than doubles the amounts of potatoes staying within agriculture in East Germany, and it still leaves substantial surpluses for industrial uses and exports to other regions. Hence these figures were used.

On that basis, forced deliveries and government purchases never reached the large amounts of potatoes made available by East German agriculture before the war. Clearly this would be true even if we had not deducted a single potato as lost between the field and the barn.

The amount going to human consumption can be estimated as follows. The Statistical Yearbook of the German Democratic Republic gives the per capita consumption of potatoes. It is assumed that this figure refers to the whole population (including farmers, who are not supplied through the market). Per capita consumption, which in 1936 was 170.8 kg per person per year, increased to 219.3 kg during 1950, but it was stated to be again at the prewar level in 1955 — probably owing to the shortage of potatoes rather than the abundance of other more suitable food. This information permits calculation of the amount of potatoes consumed (see Table 105).

The amount consumed on the farms is assumed to be 21.6 per cent of the total, which is the proportion of the agricultural labor force to the

Table 105

Consumption of potatoes, East Germany, 1936 and 1950–1958

Year	Per capita consumption (kilograms)		Population (millions)	Total consumption (million tons)	Consumption within agriculture (million tons)	Consumption outside agriculture (million tons)	Available for industrial uses (million tons)
	(1)	(1a)	(2)	(3)	(4)	(5)	(6)
1936	170.8		16.160	2.760	0.596	2.164	3.419
1950	219.3		18.388	4.032	0.871	3.161	1.643
1951	210.6		18.351	3.865	0.835	3.030	1.411
1952	182.6		18.328	3.347	0.723	2.624	1.714
1953	197.3		18.178	3.332	0.720	2.612	1.482
1954	176.5		18.059	3.187	0.688	2.499	1.512
1955	169.6	179	17.944	3.043	0.657	2.386	1.044
1956	170.3	180	17.716	3.017	0.652	2.365	1.189
1957	173.1	179	17.517	3.032	0.655	2.377	1.445
1958		171.7					

Sources: Col. 1: *SJDDR*, 1957, p. 218. Col. 1a: Revised figures from *SJDDR*, 1958; not comparable with earlier figures. Col. 2: Annual averages. *Ibid.*, p. 7. Col. 3: Col. 1 × col. 2. Col. 4: Assumed to be proportional to the ratio of agricultural to nonagricultural labor force (21.6 per cent) in 1955. See text. Col. 5: Col. 3 − col. 4. Col. 6: Government purchases and forced deliveries less nonagricultural consumption.

total labor force in 1955. Although this figure is slightly above the 1936 level, the amounts thus found for the farmers' own consumption still understates their use because farmers typically eat more of their own produce than other consumers when food is scarce.

If the amounts consumed by the nonagricultural population found in this manner are deducted from forced deliveries, we arrive at the amounts going into industrial uses, some of which themselves flow back to the population as food. The tonnage in 1936 is estimated to have been 3.419 million tons; in 1952 it reached its postwar peak of 1.893 million tons; but in 1955 it was below 1 million tons, which accounts for Mr. Oelssner's worries.

The amount of potatoes going to animal feed can similarly be estimated by deducting consumption by farmers from the amounts remaining within agriculture. This amount, too, never reached its prewar level, and in 1955 (a bad year) it was less than half the quantity available.

It should be stressed once more that the results would be essentially the same if the biological yield data had been accepted without any deductions. The total crop in 1955 is given officially as 12.408 million tons against an average of 15.023 million tons for 1934–1938, even though the acreage had increased from 790,746 hectares to 842,930 hectares. Only in 1954 was the biological crop greater than the average barn crop of the years 1934–1938, and this took an extra 44,000 hectares to produce. All figures and calculations are presented in Table 105.

Sugar beets

Sugar beets, like potatoes, were heavily represented in the Soviet Zone, for the area of East Germany has world-famous sugar beet seed farms and is well represented in sugar refineries. About 43 per cent of the total crop land was devoted to sugar beets in 1938 as well as in 1955, when the acreage devoted to sugar beets was slightly below 1938. The sugar beet acreage in 1938 was itself about 12 per cent above the average for the years 1934–1938. On the whole, the acreage used for sugar beets has remained very close to the record 1938 level.

Nevertheless, as with potatoes, the results have been highly unsatisfactory. In order to make crop data comparable, we have deducted 20 per cent from the biological yield data. Deterioration both before and after the war is estimated at 3 per cent. Use of sugar beets for feed is estimated at 3 per cent for the postwar years. The remaining crop can be assumed to have been available for sugar production. The calculations are presented in Table 106.

The calculations indicate that the 1938 level was not reached even in the good year 1954, and that except in 1954 the crop fell short of even the much lower 1934–1938 average. In addition to the reasons also given to "explain" the poor output of potatoes (for example, poor weather and a labor shortage) the reduction in yield as well as sugar content, particularly in the years 1953 and 1955, is attributed to "insufficient supplies of fertilizers, particularly the substantial shortages of potash, and insufficient cultivation work." [23]

The result is that East Germany has become a sugar-importing area! Once more I quote from the highest official source, *in extenso,* in order to make quite clear that the poor results are not the result of the spiteful assumptions of a Western observer.

The sugar beet flourishes with us and we have a developed sugar industry. In earlier years we exported larger amounts of sugar and had in addition substantial reserves. In two years we have changed into a sugar-importing country, and this year [1956? 1957?] our situation with respect to sugar supplies is so serious, as Bruno Leuschner has already pointed out, that we will not be able to do without economy measures. This need not be so! Admittedly, the weather has been unusually unfavorable during the past two years. Many peasants have made great efforts to bring in the beets; the soldiers of our people's army stood knee-deep in water in order to bring the beets out of the field in small baskets. But the weather alone does not explain the serious reduction in sugar production.[24]

Undoubtedly, part of the need for sugar imports must have been due to previous exports. Nevertheless, East German sugar beet production has not flourished. A check on the production figures, which Mr. Oelssner's statement has made quite plausible, can be made by calculating the possible sugar production from beets and comparing it with the prewar output. Normal sugar content in a beet is about 16 per cent. In a modern sugar refinery, 13 to 13.4 per cent of the 16 per cent sugar content of the beets becomes refined sugar, and most of the rest molasses.[25] Assuming a 14 per cent refined sugar relationship — which is almost certainly too high for

Table 106

Production, sales value, government purchases and forced deliveries of sugar beets, East Germany, 1934–1938 average, 1938, and 1950–1958[a]

Year	Biological yield (million tons)	Barn yield (80 per cent of biological yield) (million tons)	Net yield (million tons)	Sugar content 12 per cent (thousand tons)	Possible sugar production (14 per cent sugar) (thousand tons)
	(1)	(2)	(3)	(4)	(5)
1934–1938 (av.)		5.461		616.6	719.3
1938		6.375		719.8	839.7
1950	5.754	4.603		519.7	606.3
1951	6.047	4.838		546.2	637.3
1952	6.336	5.069		572.3	667.7
1953	6.186	4.949	6.062	558.8	652.0
1954	7.334	5.867	6.952	662.4	772.8
1955	6.145	4.916	5.712	555.1	647.6
1956	4.864	3.891	4.324	439.3	512.5
1957			6.465		
1958			6.976		

Year	Claimed sugar production from beets (thousand tons)	Claimed sugar production from raw sugar (thousand tons)	Total claimed (thousand tons)	Surplus or shortage to 14 per cent yield (thousand tons)	Surplus or shortage to 12 per cent yield (thousand tons)
	(6)	(7)	(8)	(9)	(10)
1934–1938 (av.)					
1938					
1950	327	278	605	−1.3	+65.3
1951	364	375	739	+101.7	+192.8
1952	295	394	689	+21.3	+116.7
1953	375	350	725	+73.0	+166.2
1954	330	403	733	−39.8	+70.6
1955	308	333	642	−6.6	+85.9
1956			550	+37.5	+110.7
1957			648		
1958			786		

Year	Sales value of available crop — 1936 Prices (million RM)	Sales value of available crop — 1950 Prices (million DM)	Government purchases and forced deliveries — Million tons	Government purchases and forced deliveries — As per cent of biological yield
	(11)	(12)	(13)	(14)
1934–1938 (av.)	179.830	256.900		
1938	209.930	299.900		
1950	151.585	216.550	5.430	94.4
1951	159.320	227.600	5.186	85.8
1952	166.915	238.250	5.097	80.4
1953	162.995	232.850	5.250	84.9
1954	193.200	276.000	5.763	78.6
1955	161.910	231.300	4.914	80.0
1956	128.135	183.050	4.034	82.9
1957	194.679	278.113	6.129	
1958	214.497	300.916	6.753	

Sources: Col. 1: *SJDDR*, 1956, p. 398. Series discontinued in 1957. Col. 2: For prewar, see *SHD*, p. 152. Postwar adjustments based on the advice of West German experts. Col. 3: *SJDDR*, 1957, p. 404. Col. 4: 12 per cent of col. 2. Col. 5: 14 per cent of col. 2. Cols. 6–8: *SJDDR*, 1955, pp. 168–169; 1957, p. 306; 1958, 357. Col. 9: Col. 5 less col. 8. Col. 10: Col. 4 less col. 8. Cols. 11 and 12: Prewar price = RM 35 per ton; postwar price = DM 50 per ton. *SHLE*, p. 109. For details see text and Supplement Table B.9; 1957 figures assumed to increase as in col. 13 (1957 = 151.9 per cent of 1956); 1958 = 110.18% of 1957. Col. 13: *SJDDR*, 1956, p. 439; 1957, p. 446; 1958, p. 504. Col. 14: Col. 13 ÷ col. 1.

   [a] Further details (e.g., on seed requirements, sugar beets as feed) are given in Supplement Table B.9. Note that since these calculations were made, the actual sugar content of the beets has been given as follows (percentages):

1950: 14.39	1953: 14.28	1956: 11.58
1951: 14.28	1954: 12.13	1957: 12.58
1952: 12.68	1955: 11.68	

VHS, 1958, No. 4, 131.

the postwar years — gives an average figure for 1934–1938 of 719,300 tons, which agrees well with the 705,000 tons assumed in Part III. The ECE figure (based on official information received from the East German Central Statistical Office) mentioned above, 618,000 tons,[26] agrees with the average sugar production of 1934–1938 if the average sugar content is lowered to 12 per cent — a figure more likely to obtain in postwar years.

Even with a 14 per cent sugar content, the amounts produced (or claimed to have been produced) are greater than the sugar content of the beets during the years 1951 through 1953, and substantially so in 1951 and 1953. In 1950, 1954, and 1955 there is a possible surplus, but this is so small in 1950 and 1955 that a small variation in the sugar content would change the sugar surplus to a deficit — as, indeed, Mr. Oelssner stated to have been the case in 1955 and 1956. With a 12 per cent sugar content, there would be substantial deficits in all years.

There can be no doubt that, except for 1954 and probably also 1957, total sugar beet production has remained below the 1934–1938 average, and that it has never reached the 1938 level. Output in 1955 was only 90 per cent of the 1934–1938 average, and in 1954 about 7.5 per cent above it.

An indirect check can be made by comparing the biological yield data and the corrected barn yield data with the forced deliveries and government purchases. In 1951, forced deliveries are said to have been 4.940 million tons, while our barn yield calculation shows 4.838 million tons. A comparison of the two series follows (million tons):

Year	Forced deliveries and government purchases	Calculated barn yield	Difference
1951	4.940	4.838	−.102
1953	4.914	4.949	+.035
1954	5.360	5.867	+.507
1955	4.891	4.916	+.025
1956	4.034	3.891	−.143

Except for 1951 and 1956, the calculated barn yields are above the reported forced deliveries. Only in 1954 are they substantially above it, but there is reason to assume an unusually high spoilage for that year. Only in 1951 and 1956 are the calculated barn yields slightly below the forced deliveries. On the whole, the procedure followed is confirmed by this comparison.*

Oilseeds and fibers

Before the advent of the Nazis, oilseeds and fibers were a very minor crop. Even when they were favored by the Nazis, the acreage was still only a fraction of what it has become in the postwar period, when an acreage hardly less than that devoted to sugar beets has been given over to the

* For the detailed calculations, see Supplement Table B.9.

various oilseeds and fiber plants. Among the oilseeds, rapeseed is much the most important. Among the fiber plants (the seeds of which also yield oil) flax is more important than hemp. The total acreage devoted to oilseeds and fiber plants increased from an average of 30,502 hectares during the period 1934–1938, or 37,389 hectares during 1938, to 195,617 hectares in 1955, an increase to 641.3 per cent over the 1934–1938 average. (During 1953 the acreage reached a maximum of 197,144 hectares.) The prewar acreage of sugar beets was 185,645 hectares for the 1934–1938 average. By comparison, the acreage devoted to rapeseed in the Federal Republic in 1955 was 12,000 hectares, less than half the 25,000 hectares so used in the prewar period, and fiber plants, with 3,000 hectares were not only negligible but also only one-third of the prewar average.[27] The calculations of oilseeds and fibers are given in Table 107.

In order to calculate comparable series of tonnage yield, according to West German experts, about 13 per cent of the biological yield must be deducted to arrive at the barn yield for the seed plants. Since no correction figure was found for the fiber plants, no deductions were made, although it is clear that some should have been made; nor were any corrections made for the prewar yield, which was apparently adequately estimated at the time. The figure for deterioration which occurs after the crop has been put into the barn is put at 8 per cent by the Rules of Thumb for Agriculture. As before, seed requirements were deducted before evaluating the total output.

For the various oilseeds, an average seed requirement of 8 kg per hectare was assumed, although the requirements vary anywhere from 4 to 12 kg. For fiber plants, an average of 150 kg per hectare was assumed. This is the upper limit for seeding by drilling machine; 30 per cent should be added for less-mechanized seeding methods. Thus 150 kg per hectare seemed a reasonable approximation to the requirements.

The prices at which the oilseed crops were evaluated were RM 335 per ton for the prewar average and DM 970 per ton for 1950. Both figures refer to received producer prices of oilseeds given by the Statistical Yearbook of the Federal Republic and the Agriculture and Food Handbook. The prices for fibers, which were RM 35.7 per ton in the prewar period and DM 75.2 per ton in 1950 for hemp fiber, and RM 85.4 per ton and DM 181.8 per ton for prewar and 1950, respectively, for flax fiber, had to be estimated from actual prices received in 1953–1954 and an index number of producer prices of oil and fiber plants. Owing to the great difference in the prices of hemp and flax, these two fibers were separately evaluated except for the period 1934–1938, when an average price of RM 60 per ton was assumed, and for 1950, when a price of RM 128.5 per ton was assumed.

The total acreage devoted to oil and fiber plants in 1955 was 647 per cent of 1938, and between 1950 and 1957 it fluctuated around a level of 600 per cent of prewar. However, even in the best year, 1955, output in

Table 107

Acreage, production, sales value, government purchases and forced deliveries of oilseeds and fibers, and possible production of oil and oil cake, East Germany, 1934–1938 average, 1938, and 1950–1958

A. Oilseeds (except oilseeds from fiber plants)

Year	Biological yield, all oilseeds (thousand tons)	Barn yield (87 per cent of biological yield) (thousand tons)	Net yield, all oilseeds (thousand tons)	Acreage, all oilseeds (thousand hectares)	Government Purchases and forced deliveries (thousand tons)
	(1)	(2)	(3)	(4)	(5)
1934–1938 (av.)		33.121		17.623	
1938		50.487		22.616	
1950	163.386	142.146		152.976	170.5
1951	218.513	190.106		152.222	153.6
1952	150.773	131.173		147.296	144.6
1953	176.330	153.407	158.5	166.216	137.9
1954	164.420	143.045	147.9	143.042	125.8
1955	240.603	209.325	222.2	154.012	187.3
1956	200.451	174.392	183.7	143.792	159.8
1957			187.4	150.540	174.6
1958			137.2	148.152	129.1

B. Oilseeds from fiber plants

Year	Biological yield (thousand tons)	Barn yield (87 per cent of biological yield) (thousand tons)	Net yield (thousand tons)	Total available supply (thousand tons)	Sales value (million RM/DM) 1936 Prices (RM 335 per ton)	Sales value (million RM/DM) 1950 Prices (DM 970 per ton)
	(6)	(7)	(8)	(9)	(10)	(11)
1934–1938 (av.)		9.235		37.062	12.416	35.950
1938		8.965		52.491	17.584	50.916
1950	20.165	17.544		141.610	47.439	137.362
1951	19.517	16.980		190.381	63.778	184.670
1952	18.575	16.160		130.128	43.593	126.224
1953	18.864	16.412		150.742	50.499	146.220
1954	27.440	23.873	24.436	146.453	49.062	142.059
1955	23.511	20.455	22.591	204.523	68.515	198.387
1956	19.428	16.902	17.095	169.605	56.818	164.517
1957			10.902	185.310	62.079	179.751
1958			11.487		45.901[a]	132.908[a]

Year	Domestic supplies of oilseeds (thousand tons)	Oil cake available from domestic oilseeds (thousand tons)	Imports of oilseeds (thousand tons)	Oil produced from imports (thousand tons)	Oil cake produced from imports (thousand tons)
	(12)	(13)	(14)	(15)	(16)
1934–1938 (av.)	12.972	20.722			
1938	18.372	29.367			
1950	49.569	78.840	.5	.095	.40
1951	66.633	102.888	95.0	18.050	76.95
1952	45.545	72.413	101.0	19.190	81.81
1953	52.760	83.775	160.7	30.533	128.60
1954	51.259	81.821	197.2	37.487	157.80
1955	71.583	113.534	265.0	50.350	212.00
1956	59.362	89.856	269.1	51.129	215.30
1957	64.859	89.665	320.0	68.000	259.20
1958	47.957[a]	66.298[a]	314.3	59.717	254.58

Table 107 (Continued)

C. *Fiber plants*

Year	Raw fiber yield (thousand tons)	Net yield (thousand tons)	Sales value 1936 Prices (million RM)	Sales value 1950 Prices (million DM)	Acreage (thousand hectares)	Index of acreage 1936 = 100	Index of value, fibers only 1936 Prices 1936 = 100	Index of value, fibers only 1950 Prices 1936 = 100
	(17)	(18)	(19)	(20)	(21)	(22)	(23)	(24)
1934–1938 (av.)	44.929		2.696	5.773	12.879	100.0	100.0	100.0
1938	56.818		3.409	7.301	14.773	114.7	126.4	126.5
1950	103.026	...	7.665	16.299	30.280	235.1	284.3	282.3
1951	91.800	...	6.605	14.039	29.114	226.1	245.0	243.2
1952	94.644	...	6.634	14.100	31.404	243.8	246.1	244.2
1953	88.297	...	6.409	13.625	30.928	240.1	237.7	236.0
1954	128.525	...	9.376	19.933	43.902	340.9	247.8	345.3
1955	119.168	...	8.824	18.762	41.605	323.0	327.2	325.0
1956	104.778	95.858	7.921	16.846	37.654	292.4	293.8	291.8
1957		72.156	5.962	12.681	32.604	253.2	221.1	219.7
1958		84.388	6.973[b]	14.830[b]	31.263	242.7	258.6	256.9

D. *Total sales value, fibers and oilseeds*

Year	1936 Prices (million RM)	1950 Prices (million DM)
	(25)	(26)
1934–1938 (av.)	15.112	41.723
1938	20.993	58.217
1950	55.104	153.661
1951	70.383	198.709
1952	50.227	140.323
1953	56.908	159.845
1954	58.438	161.922
1955	77.339	217.149
1956	64.739	181.363
1957	68.041	192.432
1958	52.874	147.738

Sources: Col. 1: Without seeds from fiber plants. *SJDDR*, 1956, p. 391. Series discontinued in 1957. Cols. 2 and 7: Prewar data: *SHD*, pp. 154–156. Postwar estimates based on advice of Western experts (87 per cent of biological yield). Col. 3: *SJDDR*, 1957, p. 397; 1958, p. 439. Col. 4: *Ibid.*, 1956, p. 391, 1957, p. 397; 1958, p. 459. Col. 5: *Ibid.*, 1956, p. 439, 1957, p. 444; 1958, p. 502. Includes seeds of fiber plants. Col. 6: Same as col. 1. Col. 8: *SJDDR*, 1957, pp. 400–401; 1958, p. 462. Col. 9: Col. 2 + col. 7, less allowance for waste and seed requirements. For details, see Supplement Table B.10. Cols. 10 and 11: Prices given in *SJBR*, 1955, p. 136. Col. 12: 35 per cent of col. 9. Oil content from *LRHBL*, p. 197. Col. 13: Sum of separately calculated oil cake from rapeseed, etc. (55 per cent) and from fiber plants (63 per cent). For details see Supplement Table B.10. Col. 14: *SJDDR*, 1957, p. 520; 1958, p. 576. Cols. 15 and 16: It is assumed that the most important oilseeds imported were soybeans. Technical data from *LRHBL*, p. 197. It was assumed that 19 per cent of imports result in oil and 81 per cent in oil cake; waste is negligible. The figures employed in these calculations are very favorable to East German output. Cols. 17 and 21: *SHD*, pp. 154–155. *SJDDR*, 1956, p. 394; 1958, p. 462. Series for col. 17 discontinued in 1956. Col. 18: *Ibid.*, 1957, p. 400. No data given for years before 1956. Cols. 19 and 20: Sum of separately evaluated sales values of hemp and flax. No allowance was made for waste, seeds, or losses. For details, see Appendix Table B.10. Cols. 22–24: Derived from cols. 19–21. Cols. 25 and 26: Col. 10 + col. 19, and col. 11 + col. 20.

    [a] Assumed to have increased as government purchases and deliveries. 1958 = 73.94 per cent of 1957.

    [b] Assumed to have increased as net yield, 1958 = 116.95 per cent of 1957.

tons was only 551.8 per cent of the 1934–1938 average, and in the worst year, 1952, it was only 351.1 per cent. Productivity certainly did not improve. Even the claimed biological yield of 1,820 kg per hectare in 1955 was less than the prewar average of 1880 kg per hectare (which was a barn yield).[28] (The yield figures refer to winter rapeseed, the most important oilseed crop.)

The reasons for the failure to improve yields are frankly discussed in Statistical Practice. First, the rapid increase in acreage indicated inexperienced growers. Second, phosphate fertilizer supplies were inadequate. Third, the winter rapeseed acreage was not increased sufficiently in spite of the plans to do so. In 1954 "almost 52 per cent of the planted area was destroyed by frost during January and February." "The success of oilseed cultivation depends essentially on the correct timing of seeding, on crop rotation, and on the weather. The supplies of inorganic fertilizers play an important role." While nothing can be done about the weather, the failures are thus officially ascribed to bad planning or at least to bad plan fulfillment.[29]

A comparison of the calculated tonnage with the forced deliveries and government purchases indicates that the deduction of 13 per cent from biological yield to arrive at barn yield may be too small. Thus forced deliveries for 1955 were 168,459 tons, while total yield as calculated was 204,523 tons, about 21 per cent more. It nevertheless seemed preferable to follow expert advice than to raise the loss ratio.

In 1936 prices the total value of oilseeds (including seeds from fiber plants) rose from a prewar average of DM 13.495 million to DM 74.472 million in 1955, by far the best year. The increase is impressive. Yet it is a striking illustration of the absurdity of the autarkic nature of planning. The 196,000 hectares devoted to oilseeds produced DM 74.472 million worth of oilseeds and DM 8.824 million of fibers — together, DM 83.396 million. On the other hand, the 215,000 hectares devoted to sugar beets produced DM 161.910 million worth of sugar beets — twice as much. To be sure, both figures refer to gross receipts, and the net incomes may be quite different. However, sugar beet production, which used to earn foreign exchange, now is at times insufficient to take care of all domestic needs, while clearly it would be better to import oilseeds if bloc organization and central planning made foreign trade easier.

Of the total acreage, an average of 12,879 hectares was given over to fiber-producing plants in the period 1934–1938 and 41,605 hectares in 1955. The tonnage increase in fibers and the increase in acreage are throughout roughly of the same order of magnitude. The yield per acre may even have improved slightly.

In 1936 prices, the total value of oilseeds and fibers rose from the 1934–1938 average of RM 16.191 million to RM 83.296 million in 1955, an increase of 514 per cent. Measured in 1950 prices, the increase was slightly greater — 523 per cent.

It may be presumed that virtually all of the oilseeds and fiber produced go to industrial uses. In the production of oil, however, oil cake is also produced, which flows back to agriculture as feed that agriculture, of course, has to pay for.

Rapeseed, the most important domestic oilseed, yields about 35 per cent oil and about 55 per cent oil cake. The rest appears to be waste. Hemp and flax appear to yield about 35 per cent oil and about 63 per cent oil cake, the waste being small. Imported oilseeds are probably mostly soybeans (from China), which yield about 19 per cent oil and 80 per cent oil cake.[30] On the basis of these conversion figures, domestic production of oil increased from a 1934–1938 average of 2,972 tons to 71,583 tons in 1955 (the best postwar year), and domestically produced oil cake increased from an average of 20,732 tons in 1934–1938 to a peak of 113,534 tons in 1955. In addition, imported seeds probably made the production of another 50,350 tons of oil and an additional 212,000 tons of oil cake possible in 1955. Imports of oilseeds increased substantially after 1955; thus the total supply of oil and oil cake improved despite the drop in domestic production.

Legumes for human consumption

The growth of legumes shows an odd development, although there is some parallelism to the experience of the Federal Republic. Both in East Germany and in the Federal Republic the amounts of legumes grown for human consumption increased sharply shortly after the war and then declined. But, while both acreage and tonnage by 1955 were well below the prewar level in the Federal Republic, the acreage in East Germany remained at more than four times its prewar level, although the tonnage produced in 1955 was much below the 1938 level.

The biological yield data have to be reduced by 20 per cent to arrive at the barn yield. A further deterioration of 3 per cent through loss of water, and so on, after harvesting has to be calculated, and seed requirements of 200 kg per hectare have to be allowed for. The prices at which the crop was evaluated are producer prices of the quantities leaving agriculture for other sectors in the economy as given in the Agriculture and Food Handbook.[31]

The acreage of legumes for human consumption in 1955 was 28,191 hectares and in 1950, it was 81,356 hectares, compared with a prewar average of 25,946 hectares. It seems startling that the available 26,604 tons in 1955 should have been only about two-thirds of the 41,932 tons available in the prewar period. Although there are no references to this poor showing, it is clear that lack of fertilizer and, particularly, lack of labor for such labor-intensive crops account for a good bit of the decrease. The explanation for the fact that the acreage devoted to legumes for human consumption in 1955 remained four and a half times the prewar level can be found only in the difficulties of securing imports. The figures for human consumption of legumes are summarized in Table 108.

Table 108

Acreage, production, sales value, and imports of pulses for human consumption, East Germany, 1934–1938 average, 1938, and 1950–1958

Year	Biological yield (thousand tons) (1)	Barn yield (80 per cent) (thousand tons) (2)	Net yield (thousand tons) (3)	Imports (thousand tons) (4)	Sales value — 1936 Prices (million RM) (5)	Sales value — 1950 Prices (million DM) (6)	Acreage (thousand hectares) (7)	Index of acreage 1938 = 100 (8)	Index of tonnage 1938 = 100 (9)
1934–1938 (av.)		41.932					25.946		
1938		42.616			14.576	20.766	6.247	100.0	100.0
1950	104.537	83.630		6.500	23.346	33.592	81.356	1,302.3	161.8
1951	107.814	86.251		1.480	25.232	36.306	67.388	1,078.7	174.8
1952	58.657	46.926		7.000	13.395	19.274	41.546	665.1	92.8
1953	44.026	35.221	40.471	10.710	10.052	14.464	31.208	499.6	69.7
1954	43.540	34.832	36.932	4.888	9.958	14.328	30.665	490.9	69.0
1955	41.549	33.239	33.904	15.100	9.577	13.781	28.191	451.3	66.4
1956	35.488	28.390	31.240	21.343	8.002	11.514	26.551	425.0	
1957			25.341	9.604	6.490	9.339	27.124	434.1	
1958			26.908	12.893	6.891[a]	9.916[a]	22.760	364.3	

Sources: Col. 1: *SJDDR*, 1956, p. 388. Series discontinued in 1957. Col. 2: Prewar: *ibid*. Postwar adjustment based on advice of Western experts. Barn yield assumed to be 80 per cent of biological yield. Col. 3: *Ibid.*, 1957, p. 395; 1958, p. 520; 1958, p. 576. Cols. 5 and 6: Average producer price RM 360 per ton for 1935/1936–1938/1939 and DM 518 per ton for 1950 for all pulses. Refers only to products leaving agriculture. *SJBR*, 1955, p. 136; see also *SHLE*, p. 109, Table 186.2. 1957 value assumed to change as "net yield": 1957 = 81.1 per cent of 1956. Col. 7: *SJBR*, 1957, p. 389; 1958, p. 457. Col. 8: Derived from col. 7. Col. 9: Derived from col. 2.
[a] Assumed to have changed as net yield; 1958 = 106.18 per cent of 1957.

Table 109

Value of agricultural output for human consumption and industrial use, East Germany, 1934–1938 average, 1938, and 1950–1958

A. 1936 Prices, million RM

Year	Wheat and spelt[a]	Rye[a]	Potatoes for human consumption	Potatoes for industrial use (or export)	Sugar beets	Legumes for human consumption	Oilseeds and fibers	Total	Index 1936 = 100
	(1)	(2)	(3)	(4)	(5)	(6)	(7)	(8)	(9)
1934–1938 (av.)	224.503	188.054	123.648	153.171	179.830	(14.576)[b]	15.112	898.894	100.0
1938	226.696	185.416			209.930	14.576	20.993		
1950	188.608[b]	302.820	180.634	73.606	151.585	23.346	55.104	975.703	108.5
1951	201.346	306.475	173.152	63.213	159.320	25.132	70.383	999.121	111.2
1952	200.756	305.592	149.946	76.787	166.915	13.395	50.227	963.618	107.2
1953	186.267	279.443	149.274	66.394	162.995	10.052	56.908	911.333	101.4
1954	178.105[b]	267.237	142.778	67.738	193.200	9.958	58.438	917.456	102.1
1955	201.494	253.445	136.326	46.771	161.910	9.577	77.339	886.862	98.7
1956	181.163	250.221	135.162	53.267	128.135	8.002	64.739	820.689	91.3
1957	453.730[c]		202.561[c]		194.679	6.490	68.041	925.501	103.0
1958	434.401[c]		193.932[c]		214.497	6.891	52.874	902.595	100.4

B. *1950 Prices, million DM*

Year	Wheat and spelt (10)	Rye (11)	Potatoes for human consumption (12)	Potatoes for industrial use (or export) (13)	Sugar beets (14)	Pulses for human consumption (15)	Oilseeds and fibers (16)	Total (17)	1936 = 100 (18)
1934–1938 (av.)	318.286	290.044	287.040	355.576	256.900	(20.766)^b	41.723	1,570.335	100.0
1938	321.395	285.975			299.900	20.766	58.217		
1950	267.396^b	469.053	419.328	170.872	216.550	33.592	153.661	1,728.452	110.1
1951	285.455	472.690	401.960	146.744	227.600	36.306	198.709	1,769.464	112.7
1952	284.618	471.334	348.088	178.256	238.250	19.274	140.323	1,689.143	107.0
1953	264.077	430.997	346.528	154.128	232.850	14.464	159.845	1,602.889	102.1
1954	252.506^b	412.172	331.448	157.948	276.000	14.328	161.922	1,605.624	102.2
1955	285.665	390.900	316.472	108.576	231.300	13.781	217.149	1,563.843	99.6
1956	256.841	385.927	313.768	123.656	183.050	11.514	181.363	1,456.119	92.7
1957	676.063°		470.231°		278.113	9.339	179.751	1,613.497	102.7
1958	647.263°		450.199°		300.916	9.916	147.738	1,556.031	99.1

Sources: Summarized from Tables 102–108.

^a For wheat, spelt, and rye, only production for human consumption has been evaluated except where noted. For sugar beets, 3 per cent of output is assumed to stay within agriculture as feed. All of pulses for human consumption and of oilseeds have been evaluated. ° Assumed to increase as forced deliveries of wheat and rye. Not separately given.

^b Total production, which is smaller than presumed consumption, has been evaluated.

The value of market crops

The crops dealt with thus far account for the major portion of market crops. What has been omitted is the value of vegetables and fruits.* Since it is our purpose to discover the value of the GNP attributable to agriculture, the following items have been defined as market crops.

1. That part of wheat, spelt, and rye which has been calculated for human consumption, including consumption on the farms themselves. When the total crop was insufficient for human consumption, the total crop was evaluated. Insofar as imports were needed for human consumption they were allowed for in the manner in which the value added of food, drink, and tobacco in Part III was calculated; when needed for fodder, they will be deducted below.

2. The part of potato production calculated for human consumption together with that part calculated to be available for industrial uses (such as potato starch or alcohol).

3. All available sugar beets, except 3 per cent assumed to be animal feed which does not leave the agricultural sector.

4. All legumes for human consumption.

5. All oilseeds and fibers.

6. No allowance is made at this stage for vegetables and fruits or any other minor crops. In the Federal Republic fruit and vegetables accounted for 14.4 per cent of the crops *sold* in 1953–1954 and for 13.7 per cent in 1955–1956. The percentages in East Germany are undoubtedly lower.

The crops used for feeding animals were not evaluated; nor were they deducted from the value of animal products. On the other hand, all imports (except those needed for human consumption) were evaluated and will be deducted below. And, of course, any repurchased feed such as oil cake will be deducted in calculating an approximate value added of agriculture as a whole. Figures for the value of agricultural output for human consumption and industrial use, broken down by crops, are given in Table 109.

In 1936 prices, the value of the market crops (as defined) in 1950 was 8 per cent above the prewar level. It rose to a high of 111.2 per cent in 1951 and by 1955 had fallen off again to slightly above the prewar level. Measured in 1950 prices, the value of market crops reached a level of 112.7 per cent of the prewar average in 1951 and fell to about the prewar level in 1955.

These percentages by themselves clearly are no indication of how the agricultural sector fared. Normally, animal products are a substantially larger part of the total value than vegetable products. It should be pointed out, however, that on a per capita basis the vegetable output is clearly

* See Appendix to this chapter.

still below its prewar level, and, that a decrease after 1953 presumably could mean an improved supply of animal products.

Since West German estimates exclude the consumption by farmers of their own product and evaluate only that part of the crop which is actually sold on the market, it should be stressed that the figures calculated here are not directly comparable with those for West Germany. We have evaluated all consumption whether on or off the farm.

APPENDIX TO CHAPTER XV
A NOTE ON VEGETABLE OUTPUT

Since the only published figures relate to the single year 1955, it was not feasible to estimate the value of vegetables produced. The total land devoted to vegetables increased from 34,156 hectares in 1938 to 47,114 hectares in 1955, an increase of 38 per cent. The total yield increased from 464,350 tons to 890,314 tons, or 91.7 per cent. However, the 1936 figure relates to barn yield, and the 1955 figure to

Table 110

Vegetable production, selected data, East Germany, 1936 and 1955

	1936	1955
Total acreage (thousand hectares)	34.156	47.114 = 138.0 per cent of 1936
Total yield (thousand tons)	464.350	890.314 = 191.7 per cent of 1936

	1936 (thousand hectares)	Yield (100 kilograms per hectare)	Total yield (thousand tons)	1955 (thousand hectares)	Yield (100 kilograms per hectare)	Total yield (thousand tons)
	(1)	(2)	(3)	(4)	(5)	(6)
White cabbage	2.479	294.9	73.110	7.849	308.00	241.718
Red cabbage	1.527	212.6	34.465	1.998	242.50	48.452
Savoy cabbage	1.419	193.6	27.478	n.a.	n.a.	n.a.
Cauliflower	1.709	218.8	37.399	3.123		51.554
Brussels sprouts	1.089	59.0	6.420	1.134	45.10	5.114
Green cabbage	590	111.1	6.555	n.a.	n.a.	n.a.
Kohlrabi	932	158.3	14.753	n.a.	n.a.	n.a.
Peas (green)	3.390	72.2	24.485	2.602	65.60	17.066
Beans	2.896	62.6	18.131	3.296	72.60	23.938
Cucumbers	2.221	144.9	32.174	6.482	185.20	120.035
Tomatoes	838	187.8	15.740	2.184	156.70	34.218
Lettuce, etc.	888	130.7	11.609	n.a.	n.a.	n.a.
Rhubarb	575	217.9	12.532	294	298.20	8.768
Asparagus	8.133	25.8	21.003	831	22.80	1.807
Onions	3.250	226.2	73.520	3.585	131.10	46.999
Turnips, carrots	2.259	252.2	56.976	1.563	183.50	28.678
Celery				1.074	163.40	17.549
Total unaccounted for				11.095	22.03	244.400
Total	34.156	135.9	464.350	47.114	180.00	890.314

Sources: For 1936, *SHD*, pp. 160–167; for 1955, *SJDDR*, 1955, pp. 216–217

biological yield. Probably at least 20 per cent ought to be deducted, which would reduce the 1955 tonnage to 712,251 tons. In addition, there have been substantial changes within the total acreage, away from expensive crops with low yields in kilograms per hectare, such as asparagus, to cheap crops with high yields in kilograms per hectare, such as cabbages of various sorts. There is also a very strange tripling of cucumber acreage. The higher average yield per hectare is thus not only due to the shift from biological to barn yield but also to a shift from "light" to "heavy" vegetables.

The 1938 average price received by farmers for vegetables was RM 190 per ton, and in 1950 it was DM 177 per ton. The prewar output of 464,350 tons would thus be worth RM 50.614 million, or 5.8 per cent of the receipts from the other market crops. Clearly, the area of East Germany was not a great vegetable producer. To allow the same price for the postwar mix of vegetables with its great share of cabbage would greatly overvalue it. Since the acreage devoted to vegetables has increased, some increase in the value is likely to have occurred, but hardly a rise of 91 per cent which is the increase in tonnage. The scanty information is presented in Table 110.

CHAPTER XVI

LIVESTOCK AND ANIMAL PRODUCTS

Traditionally, crops used directly for human consumption and industrial use account for only about one-third of the total value of agricultural output; two-thirds are accounted for by the animal sector. The evaluation of the sales value of the animal sector is somewhat more difficult than that of crops. The procedure followed was, first, to calculate the sales value of the live weight of slaughtered animals; then, to evaluate the sales value in the change of the stock of animals; and, finally, to account for the nonmeat production of animals. Slaughter weights and in general any production of farm products further removed from the farm (for example, meat, or butter, or cleaned wool) have already been implicitly or explicitly treated under industrial production.

LIVE WEIGHT OF SLAUGHTERED ANIMALS

Before the war the Soviet Zone (that is, without East Berlin) had an over-all meat deficit. It produced more pork than it consumed, and more sheep, goat, and chicken meat, but less beef and veal. Berlin, of course, had huge deficits in all categories. Prewar figures show a surplus of pork (including lard) of 29,164 tons, and of "other" meat, 488 tons; a deficit of beef of 42,187 tons, and a deficit of veal of 5,428 tons. The over-all deficit was 17,963 tons (Soviet Zone alone), and that of Berlin was 220,187 tons.[1] These figures refer to 1934–1935, when total consumption was restricted by the depression. Nevertheless, the orders of magnitude remain valid for other years.

During the war, stocks of animals were reduced substantially. Since the war, particularly since 1950, when official figures again became available, the numbers of animals in all categories except horses and goats have increased compared with the prewar base. The increase has been particularly great for pigs and sheep, while the increase in cattle and particularly in the number of cows has been slight. This is, of course, a generally observed phenomenon in poor economies, and a consequence of land reform as well as of the detailed plans for animal keeping (*Viehhaltepläne*).

To estimate the live weight of slaughtered animals, a calculation had to be made for the prewar years for which the slaughter weight is known. Fortunately, technical handbooks give the normal ratios of slaughter weight to live weight for different animals. Unfortunately, an accurate calculation can be made only for 1938.* For this year we know the number of animals slaughtered, broken down into six categories — cattle, calves, pigs, sheep, goats, and horses — and their average slaughter weight in the area of East Germany. It was not possible to allow for slaughtered fowl.

For the years 1950 through 1957, official data are available on the live weight of all animals (including fowl) and, separately, on the live weight of slaughtered pigs. At the same time, the average live weight of pigs and of cattle (without calves) is given separately. Thus the live weight of pigs could be evaluated directly, but a guess had to be made about the composition of the remaining slaughtered animals.

Fortunately, such a guess could be made on the basis of both the official figures and those made available to the author by the Institut für Landwirtschaftliche Betriebslehre in West Berlin, figures which themselves are based on official slaughter statistics for 1954 (see Table 111).

Table 111

Live weight of slaughtered animals, East Germany, 1954

Method of slaughter	Number of animals (thousands)	Average weight (kilograms)	Live weight of slaughtered animals (thousand tons)
	(1)	(2)	(3)
Pigs			
commercial	5,139	116	594
home	1,375	138	190
total	6,514	120[a]	784[a]
Beef cattle			
commercial	510	345	176
home	50	338	17
total	560	344[a]	193
Calves			
commercial	834	54	45
home	198	56	11
total	1,032	54	56

Sources: Figures supplied by the Institut fuer Landwirtschaftliche Betriebslehre, West Berlin.
  [a] These figures are also given in *SJDDR*, 1955, p. 225.

In 1954 the live weight of pigs, beef cattle, and calves combined accounted for 1,033,000 tons, or 91.8 per cent of the total live weight of

* See Supplement Table B.13.

slaughtered animals (including sheep, goats, and fowl), which is given as 1,125,000 tons.[2] It is clear from the development of the stocks of animals that beef and veal must form the overwhelming bulk of the slaughtered animals other than pigs.

This fact permits the valuation of the "other" live weight at average prices for all animals except pigs, prices which are heavily weighted by the price of cattle. The prices for the live weight of slaughtered animals are given in the Agriculture and Food Handbook. For pigs, the 1935–1938 average price was RM 960 per ton, and for 1949–1950 it was DM 2,330 per ton (see Table 112).

Table 112

Prices per ton of live weight of slaughtered animals,
West Germany, 1935–1938 and 1949–1950

	Average 1935–1938 (RM per ton)	1949–1950 (DM per ton)
Beef	660	1,100
Calves	1,050	1,520
Sheep	780	1,120
Pigs	960	2,330
Fowl	1,160	2,000

Source: *SHLE*, p. 10.

After pork, it is clear that beef and veal dominate the meat output. For 1935 through 1938 the above prices are available in reichsmarks per ton of live weight. Allowing a price that is our average of beef and veal alone weighted in proportion to their importance in the 1954 slaughter statistics would give a prewar price of RM 747.75 per ton for all other slaughtered animals. For the period 1945–1950 the price is similarly calculated as DM 1,202.25. This price is slightly below the price of sheep for the prewar period but above it for the postwar period. Since most of the other slaughtered animals not accounted for must be sheep and goats, with an increasing amount of fowl, this average price is, if anything, slightly high. It must be fairly accurate for the postwar period, however. As for Berlin in the prewar period, the usual procedure was followed and one-third of total Berlin slaughtering was allocated to East Berlin. Thus the 1938 base for the total live weight of slaughtered animals was 1,435,331 tons, of which 760,919 tons were pigs and 674,712 tons all other animals (mostly beef). The change is evidenced by the fact that the live weight of slaughtered pigs in 1955 was 70.9 per cent of the weight of all slaughtered animals, while in 1938 it was only 53.01 per cent.*

* These calculations are given in Supplement Table B.13.

Table 113

Tonnage and sales value of live weight of slaughtered animals,
East Germany, 1938 and 1950–1958

A. *Tonnage and sales value*

| | Pigs | | | All other animals | | | | |
| | | Sales value (million RM/DM) | | | Sales value (million RM/DM) | | Combined sales value | |
Year	Live Weight (thousand tons)	1936 Prices (RM 960 per ton)	1950 Prices (DM 2330 per ton)	Live weight (thousand tons)	1936 Prices (RM 747.75 per ton)	1950 Prices (DM 1202.25 per ton)	1936 Prices (million RM)	1950 Prices (million DM)
	(1)	(2)	(3)	(4)	(5)	(6)	(7)	(8)
1938	760.9	730.464	1,772.897	{674.4[a] / 723.6[b]}	{504.283[a] / 561.313[b]}	{810.797[a] / 909.125[b]}	{1,234.747[a] / 1,291.777[b]}	{2,583.694[a] / 2,682.022[b]}
1950	402.4	386.304	937.592	222.3	166.225	267.260	552.529	1,204.852
1951	565.2	542.592	1,316.916	279.9	209.295	336.510	751.887	1,653.426
1952	741.1	711.456	1,726.763	352.9	263.881	424.274	975.337	2,151.037
1953	800.3	768.288	1,864.699	376.6	281.603	452.767	1,049.891	2,317.466
1954	784.1	718.176	1,743.073	341.1	255.058	410.087	973.234	2,153.160
1955	828.8	795.648	1,931.104	340.2	254.385	409.005	1,050.033	2,340.109
1956	834.0	800.640	1,943.220	336.0	251.244	403.956	1,051.884	2,347.176
1957	876.5	841.440	2,042.243	361.2	270.087	434.253	1,111.527	2,458.498
1958	881.6	846.336	2,054.128	370.2	276.817	445.073	1,223.153	2,499.201

B. *Indices*

| | 1936 Prices | | 1950 Prices | |
Year	Excluding fowl	Including fowl	Excluding fowl	Including fowl
	(9)	(10)	(11)	(12)
1938	100.0	100.0	100.0	100.0
1950	44.7	42.8	46.6	44.9
1951	60.9	58.2	64.0	61.6
1952	79.0	75.5	83.3	80.2
1953	85.0	81.3	89.7	86.4
1954	78.9	75.4	83.3	80.3
1955	85.0	81.3	90.6	87.3
1956	85.2	81.4	90.8	87.5
1957	90.0	86.0	95.2	91.7
1958	91.0	86.9	96.7	93.2

Sources: Col. 1: For 1938, see Supplement Table B.13; for postwar years, *SJDDR*, 1957, p. 434; 1958, p. 494. Cols. 2 and 3: Col. 1 multiplied by prices for pigs in Table 112. Col. 4: Same as col. 1. The prewar figure for all other animals excludes fowl; postwar figures include fowl. Cols. 5 and 6: Col. 4 multiplied by average price for live weight of all other animals given in Table 112, but weighted heavily toward beef. Col. 7: Col. 2 + col. 5. Col. 8: Col. 3 + col. 6. Cols. 9–12: Derived from cols. 7 and 8.

[a] Excluding fowl.
[b] Including fowl. The total consumption of fowl in 1936 was 102,000 tons. Allocated according to the population, this gives an estimated consumption in the area of East Germany of 24,582 tons. The prewar price of live fowl was RM 1160 per ton, the postwar price DM 2000 per ton. Assuming that the slaughter weight was 50 per cent of live weight, this permits an estimate of 49,164 tons, valued at RM 57.030 million in 1936 prices and at DM 98.328 million in 1950 prices. Thus the total adjusted value of the live weight of slaughtered animals in 1936 prices was RM 1,291.777 million, and in 1950 prices it was DM 2,682.022 million.

According to the calculations given in Table 113, by 1955 the live weight of slaughtered pigs had increased to 108.9 per cent of prewar, but the live weight of the other slaughtered animals remained at only about half the prewar level. By 1957 the situation had further improved, but without changing the essential features of the situation. In this comparison, the postwar data include, but the prewar data exclude, fowl. If an estimate for fowl is made on the basis of the population and per capita consumption, the total value of the live weight of slaughtered animals declined to 81.3 per cent of the prewar level in 1936 prices, and to 87.3 per cent in 1950 prices. The difference is due to the fact that pig prices more than doubled while other animal prices rose only about 60 per cent. If no allowance for fowl is made in 1938, the decreases in the value are to 85 per cent (1936 prices) and 90.6 per cent (1950 prices).*

Compared with 1950, the increases are more substantial. By 1955, the value of slaughtered animals had increased to 190 per cent of 1950 in 1936 prices and to 194 per cent in 1950 prices. By 1957 there was a further improvement to about twice the 1950 level. It is clear, however, that this substantial improvement was largely due to the small 1950 base. Even by 1957 the prewar production had not quite been reached. Further expansion probably would require substantially increased feed imports.

The figures also make it clear that per capita meat consumption in 1955 could not possibly have been the 43.2 kg claimed by the Statistical Yearbook of the German Democratic Republic,[3] but could very well have been 33.8 kg, a figure also based on official data.[4] Both figures include imported meat and meat products but, presumably, exclude exports (if any) and deliveries to the occupation powers. West German experts believe that exports and deliveries to the occupation authorities might well more than offset imports.

CHANGE IN THE MARKET VALUE OF HERDS OF ANIMALS

The various official East German series on the number of animals start with the year 1950. Other information is available for 1936, 1938, and 1943. It was assumed that the total change in the stock of animals between 1936 and 1938 occurred during 1938, and, similarly, that the total change in the numbers between 1943 and 1950 occurred during 1950. Neither assumption is likely to be correct, but no better procedure suggested itself. It is likely that the effect of this procedure is a substantial understatement of the prewar base, since the number of pigs decreased quite substantially between 1936 and 1938, but the decrease was more than offset by the increase between 1943 and 1950. However, no cumulative error is involved in the procedure.

There is a second bias in favor of East Germany in our calculations of the live weight of the change in the size of the herds, which are based on the average live weight of slaughtered animals, a procedure that undoubtedly exaggerates the weight. The live weight of the change in the size of the herds was valued at the same prices as the live weight of slaughtered animals, except that calves and cattle three months and older

* For estimates of fowl slaughtered, see Table 113, note b.

Table 114

Change in stocks of animals, East Germany, 1936, 1938, 1943, and 1950–1958

Year	Pigs		Cattle				
	Total number (thousands)	Probable live weight of change in stock (thousand tons)	Total number (thousands)	Of which, calves to 3 months (thousands)	Of which, 3 months and over (thousands)	Weight change in stock of calves (thousand tons)	Weight of change in stock of other cattle (thousand tons)
	(1)	(2)	(3)	(4)	(5)	(6)	(7)
1936	6,199.6		3,600.6	299.6	3,301.0		
1938	5,706.9	−137.164	3,653.3	330.0[a]	3,323.3[a]	2,036	11.5960
1943	4,033.0		3,548.8	254.7	3,294.1		
1950	5,704.8	157.985	3,614.7	362.8	3,251.9	6.486	−14.2636
1951	7,088.3	133.646	3,808.3	381.4[a]	3,426.9[a]	1.116	64.7500
1952	9,099.9	271.947	3,936.4	335.9	3,600.5	−2.730	66.6624
1953	8,208.1	−74.911	3,796.2	245.7[a]	3,550.5[a]	−5.412	−18.2500
1954	8,367.1	13.356	3,793.4	297.5	3,495.9	3.108	−18.7824
1955	9,029.3	54.798	3,759.5	283.8	3,475.7	−0.822	−7.0498
1956	8,325.6	−58.618	3,718.5	264.9	3,453.6	−1.134	−7.7350
1957	8,254.6	−7.100	3,744.1	282.1[b]	3,462.0	1.032	−2.9820
1958	7,503.6	−64.135	4,144.9	199.6[b]	3,945.3	−4.455	+17.7012

	Sheep		Horses		Goats		Fowl	
Year	Number (thousands)	Change in tons of live weight (57.8 kg per sheep) (thousand tons)	Number (thousands)	Change in tons of live weight (prewar 520 kg, postwar 500 kg per horse) (thousand tons)	Number (thousands)	Change in tons of live weight (47.5 kg per goat) (thousand tons)	Number (thousands)	Change in tons of live weight (4 kg per fowl) (thousand tons)
	(8)	(9)	(10)	(11)	(12)	(13)	(14)	(15)
1936	1,595.7		814.5		693.4		21,044.0	
1938	1,763.4	9.693	816.0	1.300	678.6	−0.703	21,690.0	2.5840
1943	1,811.5		718.1		734.5		18,201.6	
1950	1,085.3	−41.974	722.9	2.400	1,628.1	42.446	22,725.6	18.0060
1951	1,239.6	8.919	744.7	1.090	1,577.5	−2.404	26,585.4	15.4392
1952	1,427.5	10.861	749.2	2.250	1,327.0	−11.899	27,230.0	2.5784
1953	1,549.8	7.069	726.8	−11.200	1,136.1	−9.068	25,833.9	−5.5844
1954	1,712.1	9.381	694.7	−16.050	961.0	−8.317	26,781.6	3.7908
1955	1,807.4	5.508	669.1	−12.800	859.8	−4.807	27,300.1	2.0740
1956	1,892.8	4.936	641.4	−13.850	764.2	−4.541	28,732.2	5.7284
1957	2,018.7	7.277	623.8	−8.800	693.9	−3.339	31,390.6	10.6334
1958	2,111.4	5.358	606.8	−8.500	625.3	−3.259	33,138.2	6.9904

Sources: Cols. 1, 3, 8, 10, 12, 14: For 1938 and 1950–1957, see *SJDDR*, 1957, p. 421; for 1958, *ibid.*, 1958, p. 482; 1936 and 1943 (including one-third of Berlin), *SHD*, p. 197. Cols. 2, 6, 7, 9, 11, 13, 15: See Supplement Table B.15 for average live weight of slaughtered animals and calculations, as well as additional sources. Cols. 4 and 5: *SP*, March 1957, p. 44, gives detailed data for 1950, 1952, and 1954–1956. For 1953, only figures for cows and heifers are separately shown. *SJDDR*, 1955, p. 221, gives data for all cattle and cows for 1938 and 1950–1955. *SHD*, pp. 196–197, gives data for 1936 and 1943; for 1958, *SJDDR*, 1958, p. 491. ᵃ Data are interpolated. They are probably reasonably correct since herds cannot be built up over night. ᵇ Averaged from quarterly figures.

Agriculture and Forestry

Table 115

Value of change in stocks of animals, East Germany, 1938 and 1950–1958

A. *1936 Prices, million RM*

Year	Pigs	Cattle (excluding calves)	Calves	Sheep	Fowl	Total Excluding horses and goats	Total Including horses and goats
	(1)	(2)	(3)	(4)	(5)	(6)	(7)
1938	−131.677	7.653	2.139	7.561	2.997	−111.327	−111.017
1950	151.666	−9.414	6.810	−32.740	20.991	141.313	176.005
1951	133.100	42.735	1.172	6.957	17.909	201.873	200.717
1952	261.069	43.997	−2.867	8.472	2.991	313.662	305.866
1953	−71.915	−12.045	−5.683	5.514	−6.478	−90.607	−105.072
1954	12.822	−12.396	3.263	7.317	4.397	15.403	−1.677
1955	52.510	−4.653	−0.863	4.296	2.406	53.696	+41.499
1956	−56.273	−5.105	−1.191	3.850	6.644	−52.075	−64.758
1957	−6.816	+1.968	+1.084	5.676	12.355	+14.247	+5.835
1958	−61.570	+11.683	−4.678	4.179	8.109	−42.277	−53.238

B. *1950 Prices, million DM*

Year	Pigs	Cattle (excluding calves)	Calves	Sheep	Fowl	Total Excluding horses and goats	Total Including horses and goats
	(8)	(9)	(10)	(11)	(12)	(13)	(14)
1938	−319.592	12.872	3.096	10.856	5.168	−287.600	−288.256
1950	368.105	−15.833	9.859	−47.011	36.192	351.312	401.516
1951	311.395	71.873	1.696	9.989	30.878	425.831	424.349
1952	633.637	73.995	−4.150	12.164	5.157	720.803	709.974
1953	−174.543	−20.258	−8.226	7.917	−11.169	−206.272	−228.860
1954	31.119	−20.848	4.724	10.507	7.581	33.083	+5.952
1955	127.446	−7.825	−1.249	6.169	4.148	128.689	109.097
1956	−136.580	−8.586	−1.724	5.528	11.457	−130.905	−151.365
1957	−16.593	+3.310	+1.569	8.150	21.267	+17.703	+4.195
1958	−149.435	+19.648	−6.772	+6.001	+13.981	−116.577	−133.695

Sources: The actual calculations on which these figures are based are given in Supplement Table B.15. The prices used are given in Table 112.

and other animal categories were valued separately. For pigs and cattle (except calves) the average live weight for the postwar period is officially given. Prewar data are also available, and they indicate a substantially greater live weight in 1938 than in any postwar year. Since it is (officially) known that calves are not adequately fattened for meat, the live weight of calves for the postwar period was reduced by 10 per cent compared to prewar, a procedure which is still likely to overstate the live weight of calves. For sheep, horses, and goats, prewar West German weights had to be estimated. The weight of fowl was estimated from firsthand experience.

The data presented in Tables 114 and 115 show the following developments:* The weight of the stock of pigs fell substantially from 1936 to 1938; its rise between 1943 and 1952 was even more substantial. During 1952 the total number of pigs reached its highest level, 9,099,900 — 50 per cent above 1936 and even more above 1938. Although the live weight of slaughtered pigs increased until 1952, it did *not* reach the 1938 level. During 1953 (the year of the June uprising) the weight of slaughtered pigs increased substantially and for the first time was above the 1938 level; but the number of pigs fell drastically — by almost 10 per cent. The years 1952 and 1953 also had relatively poor potato crops, a main feed input for pigs. In 1954 and 1955 the number of pigs increased again but still remained 70,000 below 1952; in 1956 it fell below the 1954 level. The live weight of slaughtered animals, on the other hand, fell below prewar during 1954 but rose in 1955 and 1956 to about 10 per cent above prewar.

This account indicates that, even though eventually not only the number of pigs but also the live weight of slaughtered pigs rose to a level above 1938, the economy found it difficult to raise both simultaneously. In fact, between 1952 and 1957, the increase in the live weight of slaughtered pigs was achieved mainly through a reduction in the number and the live weight of the stock of pigs.

The number of cattle increased between 1936 and 1938. In the period 1950–1957, except for 1951 and 1952, the number of cattle (excluding calves) declined steadily until 1956, and the increase during 1957 was slight. The number of calves also increased between 1936 and 1938 and in 1950, 1951, 1954, and 1957; in all other years both number and total weight declined. The live weight of all slaughtered animals, except pigs, increased from 1950 to 1953, then declined steadily to 1956, and increased during 1957 without, however, reaching the postwar high of 1954. Even in 1954 it was only 56 per cent of 1938, and in 1956 it had fallen to slightly under 50 per cent. It is clear that neither the number of cattle nor their meat production could be maintained after 1952.†

* See Supplement Tables B.15 and B.16 for detailed calculations and the weight figures.

† In 1957, official information on the distribution of slaughtered cattle became available in somewhat greater detail. Since it is also of some importance in connection with milk production I have included the following summary.

Statistical Practice, March 1957, p. 44, states that steers and bulls, virtually all of which are slaughtered, in 1956 were only 17.9 per cent of the slaughtered animals. The percentages in 1954 and 1955 are given as 23.9 and 20.7 per cent. On the other hand, in 1954, 1955, and 1956 cows accounted for 54 per cent, 56 per cent, and 58.1 per cent of all slaughtered animals. The average live weight of slaughtered cattle is given as 344 kg

In contrast to cattle, the number of sheep increased during all years except between 1943 and 1950. The number of fowl also increased, except during the year of the June uprising, 1953. The number of horses rose during the period 1950–1953 but then fell, and in 1957 was less than 80 per cent of 1938. The number of goats also fell from 1951 on, but in 1957 it was still as large as in 1938.

When all these developments are added up, it appears that during 1938 the value of the stock of animals fell, and that it rose in all postwar years except in 1953 and again in 1956.

Even when the values of the live weight of slaughtered animals and of the live weight in the change of the number of animals are added, the meat sector in 1957 nevertheless was only 95 per cent of 1938 in 1936 prices; measured in 1950 prices, however, it was 3 per cent above the pre-war level. Perhaps more significant is the fact that, measured in 1936 prices, it passed the 1938 level only during 1952 and, measured in 1950 prices, in 1952, 1955, and again in 1957. However, the fall during 1953 was substantial, and the fall during 1956 was not much smaller. Thus since 1951 there has been no steady improvement, only ups and downs. There is no question that, all efforts notwithstanding, there was not only no growth compared with 1938 but also none to speak of during the First Five Year Plan. I shall return to this point at the end of the present chapter.

ANIMAL PRODUCTS

Milk

The major animal product is fluid milk. There are major difficulties in estimating the milk production. The official statistics have a double valuation of milk, one with a 3.5 per cent fat content and one with a 3.2 per cent fat content. Per capita fluid milk consumption is officially admitted to be only about two-thirds that of 1936, or 84.0 kg per capita in 1955 compared with 127 kg per capita in 1936. At the same time, the number of cows in 1955 was more than 10 per cent above 1936, and the reported yield was only 5 per cent below 1938, a better year than 1936. Undoubtedly the area of East Germany imported milk from the area of the Federal Republic in 1936; so far as is known, there have been no imports either from the Federal Republic or from foreign countries since

---

for 1954 and 349 kg for 1950. In 1956, steers and bulls numbered 183,000. This means that the number of slaughtered cows must have been 594,049, or 28.3 per cent of the cows alive at the end of 1955. This in turn means that the average life expectancy of a cow was only 3½ years compared with 5–6 years in West Germany. During 1955 the number of cows slaughtered must have been (by similar reasoning) 476,091, or 23.2 per cent of the cows alive at the end of 1954. The number of slaughtered cows in 1954 was 454,820, or 22.5 per cent of the stock alive at the end of 1953. In no case did the average age of the cows reach the optimum, and as the result of premature slaughter, "our stock of cows is relatively young and not economical."

the war. Even so, the per capita consumption claimed does not quite agree with the production claimed. This is all the more true as the stock of cows is explicitly stated to be too young and hence uneconomic. The conclusion is unavoidable that something is wrong with the official milk yield data, and corrections will have to be made. Our calculations on milk production in East Germany are given in Table 116.

The official data consist, first of all, of a series giving the total amount of milk in tons, calculated on a fat content of 3.5 per cent. This series also contains goats' milk. The 1938 level, according to this series, was almost reached in 1954; it was exceeded in 1955, and, although it then fell, more milk was produced in 1956 than in 1938.

The share of cows' milk was calculated from the number of cows and the claimed average milk yield per cow; the amount of goats' milk was found as the difference between the total yield and the yield of cows' milk. The amount of cows' milk produced exceeded the prewar level only in 1955. It rose from 1950 to 1952, fell during 1953, and then continued to rise through 1955. The claimed yield per cow reached its highest point of 2,450 kg in 1955, which still left it below the prewar average of 2,549 kg per cow. In 1957 the 1938 average had not yet been reached.

West German experts have doubted that a yield per cow of 2,314 kg could have been reached in 1954, given the shortage of feed and, particularly, of oil cake and other concentrated fodder (*Kraftfutter*), and they have suggested that a figure of 2,200 kg would be nearer the truth. There is now official evidence that the West German criticism was well taken.

The official figures for the milk yield per cow, which had been rising steadily since 1953, show a fall from 2,450 kg per cow in 1955 to 2,371 kg per cow in 1956.

The numerical reduction during 1956 is due to the above-mentioned shortage of fodder. In addition it is also due to the introduction of a new pipette for determining fat content. If the fat content had been determined by the old method, the milk yield per cow would have been 2,437 kg, i.e., only 0.5 per cent less than in 1955.[5]

It is characteristic that the figures for the years preceding the introduction of the new method to determine fat content were not adjusted to make them comparable with the latest figures. Such an adjustment clearly has to be made in order to arrive at a better approximation of the truth. If this is done, the milk yield per cow in 1954 becomes 2,251 kg, only 51 kg more than the already mentioned estimates by West German experts.[6] Although it is likely that the actual milk yield is still smaller, no further correction was made except what was clearly justified on the basis of East German information.

In 1955 the corrected yield was still more than 7 per cent below 1938 and in 1957 it had not quite reached the prewar level. And even though

Table 116

Production, sales value, and government purchases and forced deliveries
of milk, East Germany, 1938 and 1950–1958

Year	Total milk production (3.5 per cent fat content) (thousand tons)	Milk from cows (old yield; thousand tons)	Of which, milk from goats (thousand tons)	Yield per animal (kilograms)	Corrected yield per animal (kilograms)	Number of cows (thousands)	Milk production from cows (3.5 per cent fat content) corrected (thousand tons)
	(1)	(2)	(3)	(4)	(5)	(6)	(7)
1938	5,253.3	4,961.9	291.4	2,549	2,549	1,945.2	4,961.9
1950	3,578.0	2,943.9	634.1	1,935	1,883	1,616.4	2,864.1
1951	4,348.2	3,805.0	543.2	2,201	2,141	1,806.3	3,701.9
1952	4,941.9	4,391.9	550.0	2,303	2,241	1,993.3	4,272.9
1953	4,727.8	4,238.9	488.9	2,109	2,052	2,018.7	4,124.0
1954	5,193.0	4,701.7	491.3	2,314	2.251	2,055.9	4,574.3
1955	5,529.5	5,076.8	452.6	2,450	2,384	2,100.1	4,939.2
1956	5,400.6	4,985.5	415.1	2,367	2,367	2,115.0	4,985.5
1957	5,675.3	5,286.5	388.8	2,508	2,508	2,108.2	5,286.5
1958	6,003.3	5,656.1	347.2	2,676	2.676	2,113.7	5,656.1

Year	"Market production" (including milk from goats thousand tons)	"Market production," corrected (97.29 per cent) (thousand tons)	Estimated farmers' consumption (thousand tons)	Total adjusted sales (including farmers' consumption) (thousand tons)	Sales value of milk sold plus farmers' consumption (million RM/DM) 1936 Prices (RM 140 per ton)	1950 Prices (DM 245 per ton)
	(8)	(9)	(10)	(11)	(12)	(13)
1938	3,637.2	3,637.2	417.4	4,054.6	567.644	993.377
1950	1,779.8	1,731.6	258.9	1,990.5	278.670	487.673
1951	2,381.3	2,316.8	281.1	2,597.9	363.706	636.486
1952	2,753.0	2,678.4	310.3	2,988.7	418.418	732.232
1953	2,752.4	2,677.8	274.9	2,952.7	413.378	723.412
1954	3,133.3	3,048.4	284.4	3,332.8	466.592	816.536
1955	3,377.7	3,286.1	296.0	3,582.1	501.494	877.615
1956	3,301.9	3,301.9	306.6	3,608.5	505.190	884.083
1957	3,586.2	3,586.2	323.6	3,909.8	547.372	957.901
1958	4,240.1	4,240.1	353.0[a]	4,593.1	643.034	1,125.310

Year	Index 1936 = 100	Milk production (corrected: 97.29 per cent; thousand tons)	Index of yield per cow (corrected)	Index of total milk (old series)	Index of total milk (corrected series)
	(14)	(15)	(16)	(17)	(18)
1938	100.0	5,253.3	100.0	100.0	100.0
1950	49.1	3,481.0	73.9	68.1	66.3
1951	64.1	4,230.4	84.0	82.8	80.5
1952	73.7	4,808.0	87.9	94.1	91.5
1953	72.8	4,599.7	80.5	90.0	87.6
1954	82.2	5,052.3	88.3	98.9	96.2
1955	88.4	5,379.7	93.5	105.3	102.4
1956	89.0	5,400.6	92.9	102.8	102.8
1957	96.4	5,675.3	98.4		108.0
1958	113.3	6,003.3	105.0		114.3

Sources: Cols. 1–4: *SJDDR*, 1957, pp. 434–435; 1958, p. 494. Col. 5: *SP*, March 1957, gives yield as 2,371 kg for 1956, but adds that this is due to a new method of calculating the fat content. With the old method, the yield per cow would have been 2.437 kg (*ibid.*, p. 44, table and text). Therefore, the figures for the years 1950 through 1955 have been reduced in the ratio 2371/2437 = 97.29 per cent. Col. 6: *SJDDR*, 1957, p. 421; 1958, p. 494. Col. 7: Col. 5 × col. 6. Col. 8: Government purchases and forced deliveries. Excludes sales on farms and on so-called peasant markets. Includes milk for butter production ordered for the account of the peasant. Cols. 9, 15, and 16: See note to col. 5. Col. 10: Assumed to be proportionate to farm population. Col. 11: Col. 9 + col. 10. Cols. 12 and 13: For prices, see text. Col. 14: Derived from col. 11. Col. 17: Derived from col. 1. Col. 18: Derived from col. 15.

  [a] *SJDDR*, 1958, p. 237 has a completely new series which is not entirely comparable with the old series. Per capita consumption in 1958 is 94.7 liters. With a population of 17.355 million, total consumption would be 1,643.5 million liters. In 1957, per capita consumption is given as 86.0 liters which, with a population of 17.517 million gives a total milk consumption of 1,506.5 million liters. Thus total milk consumption has increased by 9.1 per cent between 1957 and 1958. This percentage has been applied to the 1957 figure of farm consumption.

total cows' milk production in 1956 was slightly, and in 1957 substantially, higher than in 1938 (5,286,500 tons in 1957 compared with 4,961,900 tons in 1938), in 1957 it took about 8.5 per cent more cows to produce 6.5 per cent more milk than in 1938. It was stated in the official Quarterly Journal of Statistics that, "In order to raise milk production the average age of cows is to be improved. The number of cows in their most productive years in 1956 was only 40 per cent." [7]

The second problem concerns the proportion of milk leaving the agricultural sector for final sales or the production of butter, cheese, and so on, which is counted with industrial production. For prewar years, the actual sales of cows' milk are known. The sales were 69 per cent of total production, the rest being used within agriculture, most of it presumably to be fed to animals. No allowance has thus far been made for either the prewar or the postwar years for the human consumption of fluid milk within the agricultural sector. The sales of goats' milk have been estimated at 69 per cent of their production.

For the postwar years the combined amount of forced deliveries and government purchases can be taken to approximate the amounts of milk leaving the agricultural sector. For 1950, 1955, and 1956 the figures are official, calculated from monthly averages given in Statistical Practice. The figures for the other years were made available through the courtesy of the Institut für Landwirtschaftliche Betriebslehre in West Berlin. These amounts (except for the 1956 figure) were corrected to allow for the new determination of fat content. The figure for 1956 presumably had already been measured in the new way and should not be reduced.

From the figures, it appears that the amount of milk leaving the agricultural sector either for final consumption or for further industrial use *fell* about 10 per cent between 1938 and 1955, even though total milk production rose during this span of years. The reason is apparently that too high a percentage of milk — almost 40 per cent in 1956 compared with 30 per cent in 1930 — was used as fodder:

The share of market production in the total production of milk in 1956 was only about 61 per cent. The milk retained within the household of the owner of the cow is too high. This permits the conclusion that too much milk was used for feeding purposes.[8]

Although this increase clearly worries the authorities, who would like to reduce it, it is clear that without increases in oil cake or other concentrated feeds it cannot be reduced without harmful consequences.

Because of the high proportion of milk retained within the agricultural sector and in order to be consistent with the procedures used elsewhere, it was necessary to estimate the amount of milk consumed by peasants. This was done by assuming that (roughly) 20 per cent of total milk consumption is to be allowed to the farms. Milk consumption can be estimated from population data and average milk consumption. Since the latter data are given in liters and for milk of a 3.2 per cent fat content while all other milk data are given in tons and for milk of a 3.5 per cent fat content, estimated milk consumption on the farms had to be calculated.* The estimated milk consumption on farms has to be deducted from the milk used on the farms and added to the milk leaving the agricultural sector. It is this corrected figure that was evaluated as part of agricultural production.

In 1955, total milk production (including goats' milk) was 2.4 per cent and in 1957 about 8 per cent above 1938. But the value of the milk leaving the agricultural sector in 1955 was still 11.6 per cent and in 1957 still 3½ per cent below 1938. During the period of the First Five Year Plan there were, nevertheless, improvements. The yield per cow rose by almost 26 per cent; total milk production rose over 58 per cent; and the sales value of market production (including the farmers' own consumption) increased by 80 per cent.

It should be stressed once more that all calculations are based on official data and that it is likely that our figures overstate the actual production of milk.

Egg production

While the number of laying hens increased substantially, from 10.7 million in 1936 or 11 million in 1938 to just under 14.4 million in 1955, the number of eggs per hen fell so much as to offset the increase. Before the war the yield was about 170. (According to postwar technical handbooks, actual yields vary between 120 and 220.) The postwar number of eggs per hen officially claimed by East Germany for 1955 is 106, which is still substantially below the lower limits of the current yield of hens in West Germany. Even by 1957 the yield per hen was only 132 eggs, and although the total number of laying hens had increased by three-fifths since 1936, egg production was only one-sixth greater. The total number of eggs produced per year up to and including 1957 was found by multiplication. The prewar base is probably too low. Assuming only an average yield of 170 eggs per hen for 1936 would make total egg production in 1956 about 4–5 per cent below 1936 or 1938, but about 20 per cent above prewar in 1957.

Official publications also have a series for total egg production which does not agree with the other data but which is included in Table 117. It may include such products as duck eggs, but this hardly seems to account for the difference. If the claimed number of eggs produced in 1957 were divided by the number of laying hens, the number of eggs per hen would be 171.2, not an impossible number, but much higher than the 132

* See Supplement Table B.17a. On the basis of population figures and per capita milk consumption, it is assumed that milk consumption on farms is 20 per cent of the total.

claimed. Moreover, market production would be only 54 per cent of total production which also is too low. About a third of the eggs would be needed to maintain the stock of laying hens. However, any reader is welcome to adjust the estimates of egg production upward if he does not accept our reasons for believing the lower estimate to be more realistic (see Table 117).

A substantial number of eggs must remain within the agricultural sector. Forced deliveries and government purchases are roughly equivalent to market sales in Western countries. For 1936 and 1938 no figures for the sales of eggs could be found. If it can be assumed that the ratio of forced deliveries and government purchases to the total number of eggs produced is about normal — a ratio of about 2:3 — the 1936 and 1938 market deliveries can be estimated. Actually, the area must have imported eggs on a substantial scale from other parts of the country, for total consumption calculated on the basis of per capita consumption and average population was about 10 per cent above total egg production, to say nothing of market production.

In 1955 market production of eggs was still 15 per cent below the estimates for 1936 (which are probably too low) and even more below 1938. By 1957, however, there was a substantial improvement and market production was 12 per cent above 1936.

The egg production to be evaluated should also include consumption in farmers' households. This is estimated at 20 per cent of market deliveries, based (roughly) on the relative importance of agriculture in the labor force. This appears as a minimum. In addition to the allowance for farm consumption of eggs, the evaluation requires a conversion from numbers to tons. Technical handbooks give as the average weight of an egg 50 g, or 100,000 eggs for 5 tons. This conversion ratio was used.

As in the other cases, prices were taken from the Agriculture and Food Handbook. It should be noted that the 1950 prices used were the highest prices between 1946–1947 and 1957.

It is possible to check the figures against the reported per capita consumption of eggs given in the Statistical Yearbook of the German Democratic Republic.[9] This consumption, it is claimed, was 117 eggs in 1936, and had risen steadily from 63.1 eggs in 1950 to 116.2 eggs per person in 1955. These figures are clearly impossible. They are inconsistent with both total production and the known forced deliveries and government purchases. In order to achieve this per capita consumption, not one egg could have been used in any postwar year to maintain the stock of laying hens; in addition, substantial imports would have had to be purchased, amounting to 50 per cent of total production in 1950. In fact, not one egg was imported in 1950, although later imports rose to substantial amounts. In no case would the claimed consumption have permitted the maintenance of the stock of hens.

If, on the other hand, egg consumption is calculated on the basis of an equally official figure of 18 eggs per capita in 1950 [10] and an index in Statistical Practice for later years, the total consumption of eggs thus calculated is well within the possibilities of the economy. The consump-

Table 117

Output, value, and government purchases and forced deliveries
of eggs, East Germany, 1936, 1938, and 1950–1958

A. *Output and value*

Year	Number of laying hens (thousands)	Eggs per hen	Total number of eggs (millions)	Claimed production of eggs (millions)	Government purchases and forced deliveries (millions)	Government purchases and forced deliveries as per cent of total
	(1)	(2)	(3)	(4)	(5)	(6)
1936	10,675.3	170	1,814.8		1,215.9	67.0
1938	11,003.3	170	1,870.6		1,253.3	67.0
1950	8,725.1			1,208.7	314.3	
1951	10,877.9	95	1,033.4	1,320.0	512.0	49.5
1952	12,904.3	94	1,213.0	1,594.0	760.6	62.7
1953	14,371.3	95	1,365.3	1,921.7	914.1	67.0
1954	13,725.5	109	1,496.1	1,976.5	886.3	59.2
1955	14,362.5	106	1,522.4	2,042.8	1,031.2	67.7
1956	14,933.5	120	1,792.0	2,400.0	1,172.2	65.4
1957	16,012.8	132	2,113.8	2,742.3	1,490.9	70.5
1958	17,326.8	132	2,287.1	3,026.7	1,668.6	73.0

Year	Government purchases and forced deliveries plus 20 per cent farm consumption (millions)	Index of purchases and deliveries plus farm consumption	Weight of eggs (100,000 = 5 tons; thousand tons)	Sales value of egg production (million RM/DM)	
				1936 Prices (RM 1550 per ton)	1950 Prices (DM 3820 per ton)
	(7)	(8)	(9)	(10)	(11)
1936	1,459.1	100.0	72.955	113.080	278.688
1938	1,504.0	103.1	75.200	116.560	287.264
1950	377.2	25.9	18.860	29.233	72.045
1951	614.4	42.1	30.720	47.616	117.350
1952	912.7	62.6	45.635	70.734	174.326
1953	1,096.9	75.2	54.845	85.010	209.508
1954	1,063.6	72.9	53.180	82.429	203.148
1955	1,237.4	84.8	61.870	95.899	236.343
1956	1,406.6	96.4	70.330	109.012	268.661
1957	1,789.1	122.6	89.455	138.655	341.718
1958	2,002.3	137.2	100.115	155.178	382.439

Table 117 (Continued)

B. *Calculation of egg consumption*

Year	Per capita egg consumption		Population (millions)	Total consumption (millions)		Imports of eggs and egg products (millions)
	Claimed	Actual		Claimed	Actual	
	(12)	(13)	(14)	(15)	(16)	(17)
1936	117.0[a]	117.0[a]	16.160	1,890.7	1,890.7	
1938	124.0[a]	124.0[a]	16.569	2,054.6	2,054.6	
1950	63.1	18.0	18.388	1,160.3	331.0	0.0
1951	70.1	31.0	18.351	1,286.4	568.9	46.0
1952	87.5	47.0	18.328	1,603.7	861.4	116.6
1953	107.6	49.0	18.178	1,956.0	890.7	137.7
1954	113.5	47.0	18.059	2,048.6	848.3	216.2
1955	116.2	50.0	17.944	2,085.9	897.2	200.3
1956	144.0		17.716	2,551.1		186.9
1957	163.0		17.517	2,855.3		294.1
1958	181.0		17.355	3,141.3		101.0[b]

Sources: Col. 1: For 1936, total number of fowl from *SHD*, p. 197; for 1938–1957, see *SJDDR*, 1957, p. 421; 1958, p. 482. In 1936: 50.7284 per cent of all fowl assumed to be laying hens. This is the 1938 percentage found in *ibid*. Col. 2: For prewar figures, see *LRHBL*, p. 151. This source gives the number of eggs per hen as between 120 and 220. Here the average is assumed. For postwar figures, see *SJDDR*, 1957, p. 434; 1958, p. 494. Col. 3: Col. 1 × col. 2. Col. 4: *SJDDR*, 1957, p. 434. Col. 5: 1936 and 1938: two-thirds of the total production assumed to go to the market, roughly the percentage of 1955 and 1956. For 1950 through 1957, *SJDDR*, 1957, p. 450; 1958, p. 506. Col. 6: Derived from col. 5. Col. 7: Farmers are assumed to consume an additional 20 per cent, roughly in proportion to their share in the labor force. Col. 8: Derived from col. 7. Col. 9: *LRHBL*, p. 151. The average egg weighs 50 grams. Cols. 10 and 11: Forced deliveries plus farm consumption. The prices are from *SHLE*, p. 110. The 1950 price is the highest of the 1950's. Col. 12: See text. Figures are from *SJDDR*, 1957, p. 218; 1958, p. 237. Col. 13: *Presse-Informationen*, 11 August 1954, No. 92 (1032), and index, *SP*, No. 4 and No. 10, 1955. The plan for 1955 called for 67 eggs per capita, according to *Presse-Informationen*. Col. 14: *SJDDR*, 1958, p. 7. Col. 15: Col. 12 × col. 14. Col. 16: Col. 13 × col. 14. Col. 17: *SJDDR*, 1957, p. 520. The heading specifically states imports to be of "Eggs and Egg Products, Millions of Pieces." Presumably this refers to the "egg equivalent" of dried eggs.
    [a] Refers to average for the Reich.   [b] *SJDDR*, 1958, p. 576. Egg products recalculated as pieces.

tion figures (which presumably include consumption in farmers' households) are of the same order of magnitude as forced deliveries and government purchases. They exceed forced deliveries until 1952, and then fall increasingly below them. All data are found in Table 117.

Wool production

East German wool production can be estimated from the number of sheep and the average yield of raw wool per sheep. The only official figures on raw yield refer to the fact that it rose from 3.8 kg in 1951 to 4 kg in 1955. It must have been lower before 1951. Since the distribution of sheep by breeds is officially known and technical handbooks give average wool yields for various breeds in West Germany, the minimum yield for the prewar years must have been 5 kg. Very likely it was higher.

The East German figures appear extremely low and indicate a great deal of inefficiency. Of the Merino sheep, which are 43.6 per cent of the East German stock of sheep, rams give an average of 7 kg of wool in

West Germany and ewes give 4½ kg. So-called German country sheep, which form another 15.3 per cent of the sheep stock in East Germany, give 6–7 kg and 4 kg for rams and ewes, respectively, in West Germany; and East Frisian milk sheep, which account for another 17.7 per cent of East German stock, are supposed to yield 5 and 4 kg, respectively, in West Germany. High wool-producing breeds thus constitute 76.6 per cent of the East German stock of sheep, less than half of which were ewes.

In spite of the great increase in the number of East German sheep, wool production was even in 1957 at least 14 per cent below 1938, and in 1955 was 18 per cent below 1938. But it was only slightly below 1936 in 1956 and 1957. In 1957 it took 255,300 more sheep than in 1938 to produce 1,178 fewer tons of raw wool. In fact, even though the First Five Year Plan was fulfilled to 100.4 per cent so far as the number of sheep was concerned, the yield plans for wool were fulfilled only in 1954 and 1955.[11]

There is, of course, a great difference between raw wool and cleaned wool. In the case of Merinos, for example, the pure wool content of raw wool is only 36 per cent, on the average, and for German country sheep it is 44 per cent. But the cleaning process is performed in the industrial sector and it has been evaluated there. Here the raw yield is evaluated at West German prices given by the Agriculture and Food Handbook.

The figures for forced deliveries and government purchases are well within the calculated wool yield. In 1954, for example, the difference between the calculated raw wool yield and forced deliveries and government purchases was only 119 tons, but in 1950 it was 630 tons. This probably indicates not so much that the amount of wool retained was rather large but that the calculated yields are probably somewhat too high. All figures are given in detail in Table 118.

Animal products

None of the animal products calculated in the previous section had reached their prewar level in 1956, and only eggs had surpassed it in 1957. Total production in 1956 was about 10 per cent below, and in 1957 almost equal to the prewar level, whether calculated in 1936 or 1950 prices. In 1955 it was still about 13–14 per cent below the prewar level.

There was, of course, a substantial increase between 1950 and 1957. The value of animal products more than doubled. But this increase, achieved only after the First Five Year Plan, barely equaled the prewar level. Since the number of sheep, of laying hens, and of cows was above the prewar level by 1955, this is entirely due to decreased efficiencies. In turn, the poor showing (in spite of the sharp increase since 1950) can be traced back to the lack of concentrated fodder and to insufficient fertilizers and imports.

Table 118

Estimated value and government purchases and forced deliveries
of wool production, East Germany, 1936, 1938, and 1950–1958

Year	Number of sheep (thousands)	Wool yields per sheep (kilograms)	Government purchases and forced deliveries (thousand tons)	Sales value (million RM/DM)		Index 1938 = 100
				1936 Prices (RM 2260 per ton)	1950 Prices (DM 3190 per ton)	
	(1)	(2)	(3)	(4)	(5)	(6)
1936	1,595.7	5 or more	7.9790	18.033	25.435	90.5
1938	1,763.4	5 or more	8.8170	19.926	28.126	100.0
1950	1,085.3	3.5	2.9623	6.695	9.450	33.6
1951	1,239.6	3.8	3.9390	8.902	12.565	44.7
1952	1,427.5	3.8	4.4787	10.122	14.287	50.8
1953	1,549.8	3.8	5.1456	11.629	16.414	58.4
1954	1,712.1	3.8	6.3869	14.434	20.374	72.4
1955	1,807.4	4.0	7.0752	15.990	22.570	80.2
1956	1,892.8	4.0	6.8764	15.541	21.936	78.0
1957	2,018.7	4.0	7.6390	17.265	24.370	86.1
1958	2,111.4	4.0	7.9531	17.974	25.370	90.2

Sources: Col. 1: *SJDDR*, 1957, p. 421; 1958, p. 482; *SHD*, pp. 196–197. Col. 2: For prewar, *Faustzahlen für die Landwirtschaft*, p. 86, gives as an average wool yield for Merino sheep 7 kg per ram and 4.5 kg per ewe; for German country sheep, 6–7 kg and 4 kg, respectively; for East Frisian milk sheep, 5 kg and 4 kg, respectively; and for other sheep, from 2.5 to 6 kg. For postwar, *SP*, 1956, No. 6, p. 75, states that, "Wool yield per sheep has risen from 3.8 kg in 1951 to 4.0 kg in 1955." It also gives the distribution of sheep by breed in 1955 as follows: Merino sheep, 43.6 per cent; German country sheep, 15.3 per cent; East Frisian milk sheep, 17.7 per cent. Thus the three breeds with high wool yield account for 76.6 per cent of the stock. In 1955 less than half the sheep were ewes (47.9 per cent). In 1938, 58.5 per cent were ewes. An average yield of 5+ kg per sheep therefore seems appropriate for the prewar years. Figures for 1950, 1952–1954, 1956, and 1957 interpolated. Pure wool content of yield: Merino sheep, 36 per cent; German country sheep, 44 per cent; East Frisian milk sheep, 70 per cent. Weighted average for the three major breeds is 45 per cent. (*Faustzahlen fuer die Landwirtschaft*, p. 86.) Col. 3: *SJDDR*, 1957, p. 450; 1958, p. 506. Cols. 4 and 5: Prices are from *SHLE*, p. 110. Col. 6: Derived from col. 3.

MARKET VALUE OF THE LIVESTOCK AND ANIMAL PRODUCTS SECTOR

In 1956 the value of the animal sector as a whole (that is, livestock and animal products) remained 10 to 14 per cent below the level achieved before the war (see Table 119). It increased 54.4 per cent (if measured in prewar prices) and 55.1 per cent (if measured in 1950 prices) above the 1950 level; in 1957 the prewar level was about reached. These comparisons do not, however, tell the whole story. The achievement is substantially less than these figures indicate.

In the first place, no real increase was achieved after 1952, when a level of between 95 and 102 per cent of prewar had been achieved (depending on the prices used). But this level could not be maintained, and the value of animal production moved up and down. In 1953 the level of animal production fell drastically, to a level of between three-fourths and four-fifths of prewar. This was undoubtedly both a cause and an effect of the June uprisings in that year. In 1952 the value of the stock

Table 119

Summary: value and indices, animal production, East Germany, 1936, 1938, and 1950–1958

A. 1936 (or prewar) prices

Year	Value of slaughtered animals (million RM)	Value of change in stock of feed animals (million RM)	Value of change in stock of horses and goats (million RM)	Total value of animal production (million RM)	Index (sum, cols. 1–4)
	(1)	(2)	(3)	(4)	(5)
1936					
1938	1,291.777	−111.327	0.310	1,180.760	100.0
1950	552.529	141.313	34.692	728.534	61.7
1951	751.887	201.873	−1.156	952.604	80.7
1952	975.337	313.662	−7.796	1,281.203	108.5
1953	1,049.891	−90.607	−14.465	944.819	80.0
1954	973.234	15.403	−17.080	971.007	82.2
1955	1,050.033	53.696	−12.197	1,091.532	92.4
1956	1,051.884	−52.075	−12.683	987.126	83.6
1957	1,111.527	+14.247	−8.412	1,117.362	94.6
1958	1,123.153	−42.277	−10.961	1,069.915	90.6

Value of animal products

Year	Milk sold (million RM)	Eggs sold plus estimated farm production (million RM)	Total wool (million RM)	Value of animal products (sum, cols. 6–8) (million RM)	Index (col. 9)	Total value of animal sector (million RM)	Index (col. 11)
	(6)	(7)	(8)	(9)	(10)	(11)	(12)
1936		113.080	18.033				
1938	567.644	116.560	19.926	704.130	100.0	1,884.890	100.0
1950	278.670	29.233	6.695	314.598	44.7	1,043.132	55.3
1951	363.706	47.616	8.902	420.224	59.7	1,372.828	72.8
1952	418.418	70.734	10.122	499.274	70.9	1,780.477	94.5
1953	413.378	85.010	11.629	510.017	72.4	1,454.836	77.2
1954	466.592	82.429	14.434	563.455	80.0	1,534.462	81.4
1955	501.494	95.899	15.990	613.383	87.1	1,704.915	90.5
1956	505.190	109.012	15.541	629.743	88.9	1,616.869	85.6
1957	547.372	138.655	17.265	703.292	99.9	1,820.654	96.6
1958	643.034	155.178	17.974	816.186	115.9	1,886.101	100.1

B. 1950 Prices

Year	Value of slaughtered animals (million DM)	Value of change in stock of feed animals (million DM)	Value of change in stock of horses and goats (million DM)	Total value of animal production (million DM)	Index (sum, cols. 13–16)
	(13)	(14)	(15)	(16)	(17)
1936					
1938	2,682.022	−287.600	0.656	2,395.078	100.0
1950	1,204.852	351.312	50.204	1,606.368	67.1
1951	1,653.426	425.831	−1.482	2,077.775	86.8
1952	2,151.037	720.803	−12.311	2,859.529	119.4
1953	2,317.466	−206.272	−22.588	2,088.606	87.2
1954	2,153.160	33.053	−27.131	2,159.082	90.1
1955	2,340.109	128.689	−19.592	2,449.206	102.3
1956	2,347.176	−130.905	−20.460	2,195.811	91.7
1957	2,458.498	+17.703	−13.508	2,462.693	192.8
1958	2,499.201	−116.577	−17.118	2,365.506	98.8

Table 119 (Continued)

Year	Milk sold (million DM)	Eggs sold plus estimated farm production (million DM)	Total wool (million DM)	Value of animal products (sum, cols 18–20) (million DM)	Index (col. 21)	Total value of animal sector (million DM)	Index 1938 = 100
	(18)	(19)	(20)	(21)	(22)	(23)	(24)
1936		278.688	25.453				
1938	993.377	287.264	28.126	1,308.767	100.0	3,703.845	100.0
1950	487.673	72.045	9.450	569.168	43.5	2,175.536	58.7
1951	636.486	117.350	12.565	766.401	58.6	2,844.176	76.8
1952	732.232	174.326	14.287	920.845	70.4	3,780.374	102.1
1953	723.412	209.508	16.414	949.334	72.5	3,037.940	82.0
1954	818.536	203.148	20.374	1,042.058	79.6	3,211.140	86.7
1955	877.615	236.343	22.570	1,136.528	86.8	3,585.734	96.8
1956	884.083	268.661	21.936	1,174.680	89.3	3,370.491	90.8
1957	957.901	341.718	24.370	1,323.989	101.2	3,786.682	102.2
1958	1,125.310	382.439	25.370	1,533.119	117.1	3,898.625	105.3

Sources: Tables 113–118.

of animals increased most sharply; in 1953 it showed a sharp decrease which was almost exactly as big as the increase in the value of the live weight of slaughtered animals. It may be inferred that the rapid build-up of animal stocks led to a shortage of animals for slaughter and hence of meat which in turn affected the uprisings which in turn led to a sharp decrease in the stocks of animals in an attempt to remedy the situation. The stock of animals was built up again during 1954 and even more so during 1955, but during 1956 the gains made during 1955 were again undone.

Second, East German planning was unable simultaneously to build up stocks of animals and to increase the live weight of slaughtered animals to a significant extent except at the beginning of the planning period, when the low base made improvement almost inevitable.

Third, the decline during 1956 indicates not only the effect of changes in agricultural policy (for example, the abolition of compulsory plans for the build-up of stocks), but also real difficulties in increasing agricultural production. The reasons for this are to be sought in the inability to grow or to import sufficient amounts of feed and, one step further back, the inadequate supplies of fertilizers and farm equipment. By 1957, however, production in the animal sector had increased once more as the new policies took effect and imports rose.

These points will come up again presently in more detail when the value of total agricultural production and the cost of imports are discussed.

CHAPTER XVII

THE MARKET PRODUCTION OF AGRICULTURE AND THE COST OF NONAGRICULTURAL INPUTS

THE VALUE OF MARKET PRODUCTION

THE two preceding chapters have evaluated the output of major crops and animals that leaves the agricultural sector. In the crop sector some exports of grains and potatoes to other parts of Germany have not yet been allowed for, nor has an allowance been made for vegetables and fruit; and in the animal product sector the number of beehives and the production of honey have not been evaluated. Clearly, some allowance should be made for the products that have not been calculated separately. But this can be done at best as a total. Table 120 shows the value of agricultural production on the basis of the calculations previously made.

In the Appendix to Chapter 15 it was estimated that the value of vegetables before the war was only about 5.8 per cent of the receipts of market crops. If the value of the postwar crops is increased to about 6 to 7 per cent for the postwar years, the possible increase in vegetable production seems amply allowed for.

For the major kinds of fruit trees a similar comparison can be made between prewar — 1939 in this case — and 1955, no data being available for the intervening years.* Although the area did not produce many vegetables, it was a big fruit producer. In 1939 the value of fruits and berries was RM 210.329 million, 24 per cent of the value of the crop sector when valued in 1935–1938 prices and 18.8 per cent when valued in 1950 prices. In 1955 the tonnage produced had fallen by at least 42 per cent; fruit and berry production was only 14 per cent of crop production in prewar prices and 10.7 in 1950 prices. These are the allowances made for prewar and postwar years, respectively. (See Tables 121 and 122.)

The area of East Germany produces relatively more fruit trees than

* The Statistical Yearbook of the German Democratic Republic, 1957 edition, has made a few additional data available which could not be incorporated.

Table 120

Market value of agricultural production, East Germany,
1934–1938 average, 1938, and 1950–1958[a]

A. 1936 Prices

Year	Crop sector (million RM)	Animal sector (million RM)	Total (million RM)	Index	Crops as per cent of total production	Animal products as per cent of total production
	(1)	(2)	(3)	(4)	(5)	(6)
1934–1938 (av.)	898.894		{2,783.384	{100.0	32.3	67.7
1938		1,884.480				
1950	975.703	1,043.132	2,018.835	72.5	48.3	51.7
1951	999.121	1,379.828	2,371.951	85.2	42.1	57.9
1952	963.618	1,780.477	2,744.095	98.6	35.1	64.9
1953	911.333	1,454.836	2,366.169	85.0	38.5	61.5
1954	917.456	1,534.462	2,451.918	88.1	37.4	62.6
1955	886.862	1,704.915	2,591.777	93.1	34.2	65.8
1956	820.689	1,616.869	2,437.558	87.6	33.7	66.3
1957	925.501	1,820.654	2,746.155	98.7	33.7	66.3
1958	902.595	1,886.101	2,788.696	100.2	34.2	67.6

B. 1950 Prices

Year	Crop sector (million RM)	Animal sector (million RM)	Total (million RM)	Index	Crops as per cent of total production	Animal products as per cent of total production
	(7)	(8)	(9)	(10)	(11)	(12)
1934–1938 (av.)	1,570.335		{5,274.180	{100.0	29.8	70.2
1938		3,703.845				
1950	1,728.452	2,175.536	3,903.988	74.0	44.3	55.7
1951	1,769.464	2,844.176	4,613.640	87.5	38.4	61.6
1952	1,680.143	3,780.374	5,460.517	103.5	30.8	69.2
1953	1,602.889	3,037.940	4,640.829	88.0	34.5	66.5
1954	1,605.624	3,211.140	4,816.764	91.3	33.3	66.7
1955	1,563.843	3,585.734	5,149.577	97.6	30.4	69.6
1956	1,456.119	3,370.491	4,826.610	91.5	30.2	69.8
1957	1,613.497	3,786.682	5,400.179	102.4	29.9	70.1
1958	1,556.031	3,898.625	5,454.656	103.4	28.5	71.5

Sources: Cols. 1 and 7: From Table 109. (See also Supplement Table B.12.) Cols. 2 and 8: From Table 119. (See also Supplement Table B.20.) Col. 3: Col. 1 + col. 2. Col. 4: Derived from col. 3. Cols. 5, 6, 11, and 12: Derived as indicated. Col. 9: Col. 7 + col. 8. Col. 10: Derived from col. 9.

[a] The prewar base for the total market value was derived by adding the 1934–1938 crop value and the 1938 value of the animal sector. This was statistically the only feasible procedure.

the Federal Republic. In West Germany fruits were 15 per cent of the total value of market crops in the 1935–1938 period but only 9.8 per cent in 1955.

Before the war the East German area exported wheat, potatoes, and oats. Figures given by Gleitze indicate that in the year 1934–1935 the Soviet Zone and East Berlin exported 295,600 tons of wheat, 139,800 tons of oats and 129,900 tons of potatoes.[1] (One-third of total Berlin consumption is allocated to East Berlin.) These amounts can be valued at RM

Table 121

Fruit production, selected data, East Germany, 1939 and 1955

	1939			1955		
Specification	Number of trees (millions)	Yield per tree (kilo-grams)	Total yield (thousand tons)	Number of trees (millions)	Yield per tree (kilo-grams)	Total yield (thousand tons)
	(1)	(2)	(3)	(4)	(5)	(6)
Apple trees	12.610	23.1	291.850	12.481		164.714
Tall				9.624	14.6	140.261
Low				2.857	8.6	24.453
Pear trees	5.289	18.0	95.370	4.385	21.8	50.086
Tall				3.662	13.5	44.063
Low				723	8.3	6.023
Plum trees	9.767	11.1	108.530	6.793	4.9	33.007
Sweet cherry trees	2.617	9.3	24.300	2.199	20.5	44.997
Sour cherry trees	3.952	13.8	54.610	4.038	12.9	52.022
Peach trees	848	10.8	9.140	575	7.0	4.012
Apricot trees	...	...	990	130	5.5	714
Walnut trees	...	...	2.860	146	8.2	1.201

Sources: For 1939, see *SHD*, pp. 172 ff. Refers to actual yields. Refers to area of the Soviet Zone without East Berlin. For 1955, see *SJDDR*, 1955, pp. 218–219. Refers to area of East Germany (including East Berlin) and to biological yield. Although the table heading reads "Trees and Bushes in Fruit-Bearing Stage, and Yields (Raw Yields) of Important Kinds of Fruit, by Districts, 1955." A footnote states that the number of trees refers to a 1952 census. The yields apparently refer to 1955.

94.444 million in prewar prices and at DM 135.069 million in 1950 prices (see Table 123). Although more sugar beets were undoubtedly grown than were necessary for the sugar supplies of the area, it is assumed that all went to refineries in the area and that only refined sugar was exported. This is substantially correct. Since there were only negligible exports of agricultural products in the postwar years, only the base period has to be adjusted.*

The acreage devoted to vineyards, important in West Germany, is negligible in East Germany. Although some tobacco is grown, this too can be neglected. The total acreage devoted to tobacco in 1956 was only 4,025 hectares and the vine yield 3,095 tons. In 1951 a peak number of 9,279 hectares was used for tobacco, but the total (biological) yield was only 12,876 tons.[2] Even in the area of the Federal Republic the value of tobacco in the period 1935–1938 was only 2.1 per cent of the total value of

---

* This statement needs qualifications in two respects: Some rye for consumption and some mining props were exported. More important, the Army of Occupation lived off the land, and there may have been shipments to the Soviet Union that are not included with the official statistics on commercial exports.

Table 122

Value of fruits and berries, East Germany, 1939 and 1955, and relative importance of fruit, tobacco, and straw from flax in West German crop sales, selected years

A. *Estimated value of fruits and berries, East Germany, 1939 and 1955*

	Yield (thousand tons)	Value, prewar prices (RM 291 per ton)	Value, 1950 prices (DM 400 per ton)	Index of value in 1935–1938 prices 1939 = 100
	(1)	(2)	(3)	(4)
Total, 1939	722.780	210.329	289.112	100.0
Total, 1955	424.832	123.626	169.933	58.8

B. *Relative importance of fruit, tobacco, and straw from flax in total crop sales, West Germany, prewar and postwar, selected years*

	Years	Per cent
Fruit	1935–1938	15.0
	1949–1950	8.7
	1954–1955	9.8
Tobacco	1935–1938	2.1
	1949–1950	2.4
Straw from flax	1935–1938	less than 0.5
	1949–1950	less than 0.5

Source: *SHLE, passim.*

the market crops, and almost all tobacco before the war was grown in West Germany (in Baden). Finally, the straw from flax, and other minor crops such as hops, can be neglected.

When an allowance is made for exports and for vegetables and fruits, the picture changes. Because of the reversal from exports to imports and the sharp decline in fruit production after the war — which is undoubtedly understated in the calculations made, since prewar figures exclude, but postwar figures include, East Berlin and since postwar figures take account of more fruits than prewar figures do — the sales value of market crops in 1955 was only 87–90 per cent of the prewar level and had not quite reached it even in 1957.

The figures for the animal sector do not require similar adjustments. Only beehives and honey have been omitted, and they are of negligible importance.

The figures for vegetable crops have been given in Table 110. The calculations for major fruits are presented in Tables 121 and 122. The

* See Supplement Table B.23 for calculations.

Table 123

Estimated value of grains and potatoes exported
from East Germany, 1934–1938, average

	Exported (thousand tons)	Value, prewar prices (million RM)	Value, 1950 prices (million DM)
	(1)	(2)	(2)
Wheat	295.6	62.342	88.384
Oats	139.8	26.282	33.175
Potatoes	129.9	5.820	13.510
Total		94.444	135.069

Sources: Col. 1: See Gleitze, *Ostdeutsche Wirtschaft*, pp. 162 ff. See text for exact calculation. Cols. 2 and 3: All prewar prices from *SHLE*, p. 463. For postwar price for wheat and oats, see *SJBR*, 1955 p. 449; for potatoes, see *SHLE*, p. 202.

Price of	1935–1938 (RM per ton)	1950 (DM per ton)
Wheat	210.9	299.0
Oats	188.0	237.3
Potatoes	44.8	104.0

total adjusted sales value of the crop sector* is included in the calculations of the adjusted estimated sales value of total agricultural production in Table 124. Depending on the prices chosen, even in 1955 it was 5 to 10 per cent below prewar. The high level of 1952 had not been reached by 1956, and between 1951 and 1956 there was basically no improvement in total output, only ups and downs.

West German developments afford a sharp contrast. The output of all grains increased by 12.9 per cent between 1935–1938 and 1955, and by 29.1 per cent between 1950 and 1955. The other crops also increased sharply during this period — by 53.6 per cent — over 1935–1938. They decreased by 34.6 per cent between 1950 and 1955. But this decrease is entirely due to the availability of cheaper imports of vegetables and oil-seeds and to a reduction of potato production as diet improved. The output of sugar beets and fruits more than doubled between 1950 and 1955. Thus the crop sector as a whole increased by 35.5 per cent between 1935–1938 and 1955, but it decreased by 20.1 per cent between 1950 and 1955 as cheaper imports became available and diets improved.

In the Federal Republic the live weight of slaughtered animals also increased — by 33.9 per cent between 1935–1938 and 1955 and, even more sharply, by 49.8 per cent from 1950 to 1955. The three major animal products — milk, eggs, and wool — increased 19.4 per cent from 1935–1938 to 1955 and 39.9 per cent from 1950 to 1955, even though wool production — never very important — decreased. The animal sector as a whole (without regard to the increase or decrease in the stock of animals,

* See Supplement Table B. 23 for calculations.

Table 124

Adjusted value of agricultural production, East Germany, prewar and 1950–1958

A. *Prewar prices*

Year	Crop sector[a] (million RM)	Animal sector (million RM)	Total (million RM)	Index	Crop sector as per cent of total	Animal sector as per cent of total
	(1)	(2)	(3)	(4)	(5)	(6)
Prewar	1,263.007	1,884.490	3,147.497	100.0	40.1	59.9
1950	1,180.600	1,043.132	2,223.732	70.7	53.1	46.9
1951	1,208.936	1,372.828	2,581.764	82.0	46.8	53.2
1952	1,165.978	1,780.477	2,946.455	93.6	39.6	60.4
1953	1,102.713	1,454.836	2,557.549	81.3	43.1	56.9
1954	1,110.121	1,534.462	2,644.583	84.0	42.0	58.0
1955	1,072.961	1,704.915	2,777.876	88.3	38.6	61.4
1956	993.033	1,616.869	2,609.902	82.9	38.0	62.0
1957	1,119.856	1,820.654	2,940.510	93.4	38.1	61.9
1958	1,101.166[b]	1,886.101	2,967.267	94.3	36.4	63.6

B. *1950 Prices*

Year	Crop sector[a] (million RM)	Animal sector (million RM)	Total (million RM)	Index	Crop sector as per cent of total	Animal sector as per cent of total
	(7)	(8)	(9)	(10)	(11)	(12)
Prewar	2,094.847	3,703.845	5,798.692	100.0	36.1	63.9
1950	2,034.388	2,175.536	4,209.924	72.6	48.3	51.7
1951	2,082.659	2,844.176	4,926.835	85.0	42.3	57.7
1952	1,977.528	3,780.374	5,757.902	99.3	34.3	65.7
1953	1,886.600	3,037.940	4,924.540	84.9	38.3	61.7
1954	1,889.820	3,211.140	5,100.960	88.0	37.0	63.0
1955	1,840.643	3,585.734	5,426.377	93.6	33.9	66.1
1956	1,713.852	3,370.491	5,084.343	87.7	33.7	66.3
1957	1,899.086	3,786.682	5,685.768	98.1	33.4	66.6
1958	1,898.356	3,896.625	5,796.983	100.0	32.7	67.3

Sources: Preceding tables, Part IV.

a Including value of vegetables and fruit.

b As there is evidence that fruit production has increased significantly in 1958, an allowance of 15 per cent has been made. For vegetables, 7 per cent is allowed, as before.

however) increased by 26.5 per cent from 1935–1938 to 1955 and 44.9 per cent from 1950 to 1955.

Together, the agricultural sector increased continuously from 1935–1938 to 1955, the increase over the whole period being almost 30 per cent

(29.4) and between 1950 and 1955, 14 per cent. Table 125 gives the calculation in detail. Once more we observe that the over-all development is strikingly better in the Federal Republic.

The showing of the Federal Republic is even more striking in light

Table 125

Estimated market value of agricultural production, West Germany, prewar and 1950–1955, in 1935–1938 prices

A. *Market value, million RM*

Year	Rye (RM 181 per ton)	Wheat (RM 206 per ton)	Industrial grains (RM 199 per ton)	Feed grains (RM 169 per ton)	Total grains
	(1)	(2)	(3)	(4)	(5)
1935–1938	244.350	292.520	181.090	6.760	724.720
1949–1950	301.184	234.016	79.600	17.914	632.714
1951	199.100	247.200	99.500	17.745	563.354
1952	239.644	331.042	139.300	17.745	727.731
1953	243.083	362.766	111.639	17.745	735.233
1954	260.459	323.214	159.200	13.520	756.393
1955	338.470	302.408	163.180	12.675	816.733

Year	Potatoes for human consumption (RM 52 per ton)	Potatoes for industrial purposes (RM 36 per ton)	Pulses (RM 360 per ton)	Sugar beets (RM 35 per ton)	Food *Kohlrüben* (RM 30 per ton)	Oilseeds (RM 335 per ton)
	(6)	(7)	(8)	(9)	(10)	(11)
1935–1938	208.520	6.840	3.960	129.500	4.500	12.395
1949–1950	376.636	5.400	11.160	153.160	3.000	41.875
1951	369.564	14.400	5.040	249.515	3.000	23.785
1952	355.056	5.400	3.240	255.150	2.700	25.125
1953	346.580	8.100	2.160	232.400	2.700	16.080
1954	341.276	13.428	2.520	313.495	2.100	9.045
1955	339.404[a]	8.676	2.160	327.320	1.650	4.690

Year	Vegetables (RM 109 per ton)	Fruit (RM 291 per ton)	Grape cider (RM 505 per ton)	Hops (RM 4,440 per ton)	Tobacco (RM 1,350 per ton)	Total crop sector
	(12)	(13)	(14)	(15)	(16)	(17)
1935–1938	133.852	207.192	133.320	39.960	33.750	1,638.510
1949–1950	126.658	171.690	58.580	26.640	32.400	1,639.913
1951	133.089	281.106	138.875	44.440	44.550	1,870.859
1952	103.005	295.656	133.320	57.720	36.450	2,000.553
1953	105.512	393.723	116.150	44.440	31.050	2,034.128
1954	129.601	367.242	105.545	75.480	29.700	2,145.825
1955	96.465	398.670	132.815	62.160	29.700	2,220.443

Table 125 (Continued)

Year	Live weight beef (RM 660 per ton)	Live weight calves (RM 1050 per ton)	Live weight sheep (RM 780 per ton)	Live weight pigs (RM 960 per ton)	Live weight fowl (RM 1160 per ton)	Total animals
	(18)	(19)	(20)	(21)	(22)	(23)
1935–1938	710.820	217.350	28.080	734.280	29.000	1,722.530
1949–1950	555.720	147.000	55.380	568.320	23.200	1,349.620
1951	595.320	170.100	32.760	752.640	29.000	1,579.820
1952	617,100	163.800	29.940	1,034.880	31.320	1,877.040
1953	696.960	190.050	28.080	1,099.200	34.800	2,049.090
1954	807.840	193.200	32.760	1,116.480	41.760	2,191.940
1955	829.620	190.050	25.740	1,261.400	41.760	2,348.570

Year	Milk (RM 140 per ton)	Eggs (RM 1550 per ton)	Wool (RM 2260 per ton)	Subtotal animal products	Total animal sector	Total agricul- ture
	(24)	(25)	(26)	(27)	(28)	(29)
1935–1938	1,596.000	173.600	16.950	1,786.550	3,509.080	5,147.590
1949–1950	1,397.000	125.550	19.662	1,524.212	2,873.832	4,513.745
1951	1,590.400	204.600	15.594	1,810.594	3,390.214	5,261.073
1952	1,713.600	223.200	14.690	1,951.490	3,828.530	5,829.083
1953	1,741.460	223.200	13.786	1,978.446	4,027.536	6,061.664
1954	1,881.320	257.300	12.430	2,151.050	4,342.990	6,488.815
1955	1,834.840	286.750	11.074	2,132.664	4,481.534	6,701.977

B. *Indices*

Year	Animals	Animal products	Animal sector	Crop sector	Total agriculture
	(30)	(31)	(32)	(33)	(34)
Prewar	100.0	100.0	100.0	100.0	100.0
1949–1950	78.4	85.3	81.9	100.1	87.7
1951	91.7	101.3	96.6	114.2	102.2
1952	109.0	109.2	109.1	122.1	113.2
1953	119.0	110.7	114.8	124.1	117.8
1954	127.3	120.4	123.8	131.0	126.1
1955	136.3	119.4	127.7	135.5	130.2

Source: *SHLE*, pp. 109–110.
  [a] Without seed potatoes.

of the fact that the increase in production was achieved by an agricultural labor force which in 1954 was 9.3 per cent smaller than in 1939, 18.5 per cent smaller than in 1949, and 2.9 per cent smaller than in 1953.*[3]

* Since this was written newer figures indicate further increases in West German agricultural output and further substantial decreases in the West German agricultural labor force.

When forestry and fishing are included, as they must be to make the figures comparable with East German figures, agricultural employment between 1939 and 1954 fell by 8.6 per cent, between 1949 and 1954 by 18.8 per cent, and between 1953 and 1954 by 2.9 per cent.

By contrast, employment in agriculture, forestry, and water supply in East Germany rose from 1.704 million in 1939 to 1.983 million in 1950. In 1955 it was still bigger than in 1939 by 4.2 per cent, although by 1956 and 1957 it had fallen below the prewar level.[4]

THE COST OF AGRICULTURAL OUTPUT — THE VARIOUS INPUTS

Procedures

In order to evaluate the value added of agricultural output (which includes consumption by the farmers themselves) the various inputs coming from outside the agricultural sector have to be deducted. It is easiest to account for commercial fertilizers, for which annual official data are available. In addition, farmers buy feed abroad, and they repurchase oil cake and a few other by-products of the industrial processing of agricultural raw materials, such as sugar beets for feed. In addition, oil cake made from imported oilseeds has to be taken into account.

Serious difficulties are encountered in calculating the feed coming from outside the agricultural sector. Imports in tons of wheat, rye, oats, barley, and corn have been published. Unfortunately, this is not the case for other imports. The amount of imported concentrated fodder, such as fish meal, is virtually unknown except that it is reported to be insufficient.

The intermediate products of agriculture, such as fodder beets, need not be calculated except as a check on the availability of fodder. This is also true for manure. In the calculation of the "market" value of agricultural output, care has been taken to include only the output destined for human consumption and industrial use (or export).

There are also, however, a number of nonagricultural domestic inputs, such as electricity, which must be estimated. Official figures for electricity consumption by agriculture are available for 1953 and 1955–1957 and these will have to be extrapolated to other years.[5] Some estimate of gasoline and oil consumed by the MTS will have to be made. And some allowance should be made for other expenditures such as chemical pest controls; but as absolutely nothing is known about these, we have not done so.

On the other hand, the expenditures of agriculture on new housing or barns and other utility structures clearly do not have to be deducted; nor do the expenditures of the MTS on farm machinery. Any such expenditures on construction or machinery must be dealt with in a savings-investment account. They are not a current expenditure relevant to the calculation of value added.

The cost of fertilizers

The use of commercial fertilizers has risen substantially. Conditions in East Germany are very favorable for the production of nitrogen, potash, and calcium fertilizers, but the supply of phosphates presents major difficulties because they must be imported. Deliveries of commercial fertilizers to agriculture increased substantially after 1949–1950, but compared with prewar averages they had risen only 17–20 per cent in the aggregate by 1954–1955 and by 37 per cent by 1956–1957, and the amounts used were, at least in the case of nitrogen and phosphate fertilizers, still below 1938–1939 as late as 1955–1956.

As East German sources stress, the amount of fertilizers supplied might have been sufficient to reach the planned yields per hectare if soils had not been neglected during and immediately after the war. Because of this neglect, however, the planned as well as actual amounts were insufficient. Under East German conditions this shortage appears to be reflected particularly in great variations in yields and a great sensitivity of yields to the weather,[6] especially for beets used as fodder.

All the fertilizer figures used are from official East German sources, which also give prewar figures and by no means flattering comparisons with the Federal Republic. The physical quantities have been evaluated with prewar West German and 1949–1950 prices given in the Agriculture and Food Handbook.

The tonnage of nitrogen fertilizers in the fertilizer year 1954–1955 was below not only the year 1938–1939 but also the year 1951–1952, which saw the highest postwar supply. For the year 1955–1956 the Plan provided for a supply of 364,000 tons, or about 178 per cent of the actual supplies in 1954–1955, but "the actual amounts deviate substantially from the planned amounts."[7] Only during the postwar fertilizer year 1956–1957 did output supplies exceed the prewar level. The characteristic post-1950 development consists of sharp fluctuations in supplies of nitrogen, which run roughly parallel to the fluctuations in the output of the crop sector noted above. There has been no real increase in supplies since the crop year 1950–1951.

The actual supplies of nitrogen fertilizers are well below the reported domestic production which was accepted as actual in the calculations for the industrial sector. Supplies to agriculture in 1950–1951 were only slightly more than 80 per cent of reported production, and in 1955 they were a little over 70 per cent. It is not likely that stockpiling took place. It must be presumed that the remaining 20–30 per cent of fertilizer production was exported — at the expense of domestic agriculture. The failure of nitrogen supplies to reach the desired levels must be due to export commitments or insufficient coordination of production and export plans, or both (see Table 126).

Table 126

Production of nitrogen fertilizers, deliveries to agriculture, amounts available for export, and actual exports, East Germany, 1950–1958

| | | | (Thousand tons of N) | | |
| | | | Exports | | Deliveries to agriculture |
Calendar year[a]	Production	Deliveries to agriculture	Amounts available	Actual	as per cent of production
	(1)	(2)	(3)	(4)	(5)
1950	231.4	187.3	44.1	34.8	80.9
1951	252.2	203.0	49.2	36.3	80.5
1952	256.9	200.4	56.5	41.3	78.0
1953	264.6	189.6	75.0	50.9	71.7
1954	276.7	208.0	68.7	62.6	75.2
1955	293.4	209.7	83.7	83.2	71.5
1956	299.9	206.2	93.7	89.6	68.8
1957	305.4	222.5	82.9	82.6	72.9
1958	320.0	229.0	91.0	95.6	71.6

Sources: Col. 1: For 1950–1955, see *SJDDR*, 1955, pp. 162–163; for 1956–1958, *ibid.*, 1958, p. 344. Col. 2: See *ibid.*, 1955, p. 205, and 1958, p. 476. Col. 3: Col. 1 less Col. 2. Col. 4: *SJDDR*, 1956, p. 520, and 1958, p. 571. Col. 5: Col. 2 ÷ Col. 1.

[a] Figures refer to calendar years, which can be directly compared with production figures. See also Table 130, where figures refer to fertilizer years.

It is interesting to note that even though "the supply plan of nitrogen fertilizers [during the First Five Year Plan] was overfulfilled in every year except 1952/53 . . . the actual supplies are insufficient to reach the planned yields per hectare of the most important crops."[8]

In contrast to East Germany the Federal Republic used one-third more nitrogen in 1954–1955 than before the war (452,000 against 336,000 tons).[9] (For the more important comparison of amounts of fertilizer used per hectare, see Table 129.) Moreover, not only were the planned over-all amounts apparently inadequate in East Germany but also the specific forms were insufficiently supplied. Calcium cyanamide is singled out, since it is important both as a fertilizer and as a means of fighting weeds,* "which, with the present state of our fields, which are full of weeds, should not be overlooked."[10]

East Germany suffers from insufficient imports of phosphates. Although domestic production has increased substantially, it is unlikely that it can ever be expanded sufficiently to take care of domestic needs. In 1955 it was 262.2 per cent of 1936, and it had more than quadrupled between 1950 and 1955, but imports could not be raised sufficiently to meet agricultural needs. As late as the fertilizer year 1955–1956, deliveries of phosphates fell short of prewar averages, and they were only slightly

* Some American experts have questioned the supposed weed control effect of fertilizers; they attribute the statement to a rationalization of the failure to keep the fields in good condition.

more than half the planned deliveries. But by 1956–1957 they finally reached the 1938–1939 level. West German uses of phosphates, on the other hand, rose from 398,000 tons before the war to 519,000 tons (a preliminary figure) in 1954–1955, or about 30 per cent.[11] The data for East Germany, in calendar years, are given in Table 127.

Table 127

Production of phosphates, deliveries to agriculture, and imports, East Germany, 1950–1958

			(*Thousand tons of P_2O_5*)		
				Imports	Deliveries to agriculture
Calendar year[a]	Production	Deliveries to agriculture	Amounts required	Actual	as per cent of production
	(1)	(2)	(3)	(4)	(5)
1950	24.7	100.5	75.8	n.a.	406.9
1951	33.5	70.8	37.3	42.9	211.3
1952	38.1	73.2	35.1	35.1	192.1
1953	72.3	118.4	36.1	51.3	163.7
1954	79.2	139.0	59.8	59.9	175.5
1955	84.6	132.8	48.2	50.4	156.9
1956	111.6	168.5	56.8	60.3	150.9
1957	128.8	186.0	58.2	58.9	144.4
1958	136.3	199.0	62.7	62.2	146.0

Sources: Col. 1: For 1950–1955, see *SJDDR*, 1955, pp. 162–163; for 1956–1958, *ibid.*, 1958, p. 344. Col. 2: *Ibid.*, p. 476. Col. 3: Col. 2 less col. 1. Col. 4: *SJDDR*, 1957, p. 519. *Ibid.*, 1956, p. 523, gives an import of phosphates *not* calculated on a P_2O_5 basis of 407,028 tons. Col. 5: Col. 2 ÷ col. 1.
  [a] See footnote a, Table 126.

If it is true, as Liebig found, that the yields of the soil are ultimately limited by the least available element, phosphates are the ultimate bottleneck among the fertilizers. Deliveries fluctuated during the period of the First Five Year Plan. They reached a fairly high level in 1949–1950, which was not surpassed until 1953–1954.

The seriousness of the problem can be gathered from the fact that East German investigations indicated that only 19 per cent of the soil is by nature well endowed with phosphates while 50 per cent is poorly endowed.

The shortage of potash fertilizers is really surprising. The supply is stated to have been insufficient since 1952–1953 and to have fallen below Plan requirements since that time. East Germany is a major producer of potash. The failure to supply sufficient amounts to domestic agriculture can only be due to export commitments. Supplies used domestically are only one-fourth to one-third of output. Production has increased steadily since 1952, but supplies to agriculture have merely fluctuated around a level of about 430,000 tons a year. The figures for the fertilizer years* are somewhat lower. The use of potash fertilizers increased by about one-

* *Düngejahr.*

fourth from the prewar average to 1954–1955, and by about one-half to the fertilizer year 1955–1956. But even the 457,900 tons used during 1955–1956 fell substantially short of the planned (and required) 574,000 tons. During the same years, West German quantities of potash used increased from a prewar figure of 633,000 tons to 859,000 tons during 1954–1955, an increase of more than one-third. The data for East Germany are given in Table 128.

Table 128

Production of potash, deliveries to agriculture, and exports,
East Germany, 1950–1958 (1,000 tons of K_2O)

Calendar year[a]	Production	Deliveries to agriculture	Actual exports	Deliveries to agriculture as per cent of production
	(1)	(2)	(3)	(4)
1950	1,336	389.9	n.a.	29.2
1951	1,409	356.6	916	25.3
1952	1,346	432.2	842	32.1
1953	1,378	409.5	869	29.7
1954	1,463	448.0	903	30.6
1955	1,552	425.4	1,001	27.4
1956	1,556	445.1	966	28.6
1957	1,604	463.1	976	28.9
1958	1,650	518.5	986	31.4

Sources: Col. 1: Refers to production of raw salts. For 1950–1955, see *SJDDR*, 1955, pp. 162–163; for 1956–1958, *ibid.*, 1958, p. 344. Col. 2: See *ibid.*, p. 476. Col. 3: Refers to exports of raw salts. *Ibid.*, p. 515. For 1950, *SJDDR*, 1956, p. 519, gives exports of 1.382 million tons raw salts, not calculated on K_2O content, 1958, p. 571. Col. 4: Col. 2 ÷ col. 1.

[a] Figures refer to calendar years, which can be directly compared with production figures. See also Table 130, where figures refer to fertilizer years.

The use of calcium fertilizers also rose substantially, but the really significant increase came only from 1953–1954 to 1954–1955, when supplies rose almost one-sixth. West German use fell by about 25 per cent from the prewar years to 1954–1955 (from 823,000 tons to 607,000 tons).

When the various commercial fertilizers are evaluated at West German prices and added, it appears that by 1954–1955 the total supply had increased by only 17 to 20 per cent above prewar, depending on the prices used. During the period of the First Five Year Plan there were violent fluctuations in the amounts supplied but no real increases. The amounts delivered in the fertilizer year 1953–1954 were higher than in 1954–1955, and the amounts used in 1951–1952 were as great. Since the beginning of the Second Five Year Plan, however, the situation has improved noticeably.

Most important is that these amounts fall short of what was allotted to reach the planned yields.

In order to reach the planned yields per hectare, 364,000 tons N, 292,000 tons P_2O_5, and 574,000 tons K_2O were needed. These quantities differ substantially from the planned amounts, particularly for nitrogen and phosphates. . . . In the fertilizer year 1955/56 the mineral fertilizer necessary to fertilize the soil and to raise yields was 571,000 tons P_2O_5 and 837,000 tons K_2O. These amounts of fertilizer cannot be realized in one year. They would have to be delivered during the next five years over and above the plan in order to give our soils a normal composition of nutrients.[12]

Table 129

Commercial fertilizers used per hectare of crop land,
West and East Germany, 1950–1951 through 1954–1955

| Year[a] | Nitrogen fertilizer | | |
	East Germany (kilograms per hectare)	West Germany (kilograms per hectare)	West German use as per cent of East German use
	(1)	(2)	(3)
1950–1951	34.2	35.8	104.6
1951–1952	36.7	38.2	104.0
1952–1953	34.3	42.1	122.7
1953–1954	36.1	44.2	122.4
1954–1955	36.8	45.8	124.4

| Year | Phosphates | | |
	East Germany (kilograms per hectare)	West Germany (kilograms per hectare)	West German use as per cent of East German use
	(4)	(5)	(6)
1950–1951	11.6	41.1	354.3
1951–1952	13.5	46.8	346.6
1952–1953	13.1	37.8	288.5
1953–1954	22.9	44.6	194.7
1954–1955	21.9	52.3	238.8

| Year | Potash fertilizer | | |
	East Germany (kilograms per hectare)	West Germany (kilograms per hectare)	West German use as per cent of East German use
	(7)	(8)	(9)
1950–1951	51.3	28.1	54.7
1951–1952	63.0	35.4	56.1
1952–1953	62.7	41.0	65.3
1953–1954	62.6	47.5	75.8
1954–1955	58.5	50.8	86.8

Source: *SP*, October 1956, p. 150.
   [a] Refers to fertilizer year.

These figures assume that manure was in normal supply. Yet during 1954–1955 only 83.8 per cent of the organic fertilizers needed was available, and during 1955–1956 only 95.7 per cent was available.

Since West Germany has a much higher percentage of pastures than East Germany, comparisons per hectare of all agricultural land are mis-

Table 130

Amounts and value of commercial fertilizers used, East Germany, prewar and 1949–1950 through 1957–1958

	Nitrogen			Phosphates		
		Total cost (million RM/DM)			Total cost (million RM/DM)	
Year[a]	Amount used (thousand tons of N)	1935–1938 Prices (RM 542 per ton)	1950 Prices (DM 932 per ton)	Amount used (thousand tons of P₂O₅)	1935–1938 Prices (RM 285 per ton)	1950 Prices (DM 347 per ton)
	(1)	(2)	(3)	(4)	(5)	(6)
1935–1936	149.1	80.812	138.961	157.5	44.888	54.653
1936–1937	173.7	94.145	161.888	152.4	43.434	52.883
1937–1938	192.7	104.443	179.596	166.8	47.538	57.880
1938–1939	218.2	118.264	203.362	182.0	51.870	63.154
1949–1950	184.4	99.945	171.861	94.7	26.990	32.861
1950–1951	193.2	104.714	180.062	75.9	21.632	26.337
1951–1952	206.3	111.815	192.272	85.8	24.453	29.773
1952–1953	192.5	104.335	179.410	81.4	23.199	28.246
1953–1954	202.4	109.701	188.637	135.4	38.589	46.984
1954–1955	204.7	110.947	190.780	128.8	36.708	44.694
1955–1956[b]	199.9	108.346	186.307	152.4	43.434	52.883
1956–1957	225.4	122.167	210.073	184.0	52.440	63.848
1957–1958	223.7	121.245	208.088	184.4	52.554	63.987

	Potash			Calcium		
		Total cost (million RM/DM)			Total cost (million RM/DM)	
Year[a]	Amount used (thousand tons of K₂O)	1935–1938 Prices (RM 132 per ton)	1950 Prices (DM 224 per ton)	Amount used (thousand tons of CaO)	1935–1938 Prices (RM 19 per ton)	1950 Prices (DM 35 per ton)
	(7)	(8)	(9)	(10)	(11)	(12)
1935–1936	239.3	31.588	53.603	453.0	8.607	15.855
1936–1937	242.7	32.036	54.365	442.5	8.408	15.488
1937–1938	292.5	38.610	65.520	542.7	10.311	18.995
1938–1939	318.2	42.002	71.277	520.0	9.880	18.200
1949–1950	339.0	44.748	75.936	566.8	10.769	19.838
1950–1951	366.2	48.338	82.029	567.4	10.781	19.859
1951–1952	425.6	56.179	95.334	570.8	10.845	19.978
1952–1953	411.0	54.252	92.064	561.5	10.669	19.653
1953–1954	422.6	55.783	94.662	583.7	11.090	20.430
1954–1955	399.7	52.760	89.533	674.2	12.810	23.597
1955–1956	457.9[b]	60.443	102.570	697.3	13.249	24.406
1956–1957	459.6	60.667	102.950	742.2	14.102	25.977
1957–1958	492.6	65.023	110.342	767.8	14.588	26.873

Table 130 (Continued)

| Year[a] | Total cost of fertilizers used | | | |
	1935–1938 Prices (million RM)	1950 Prices (million DM)	Index 1935–1938 prices	Index 1950 prices
	(13)	(14)	(15)	(16)
1935–1936	165.895	263.072		
1936–1937	178.023	284.624	100.0	100.0
1937–1938	200.901	321.991		
1938–1939	222.016	355.993		
1949–1950	182.452	300.496	100.4	103.6
1950–1951	185.465	308.287	102.1	106.3
1951–1952	203.292	337.357	119.2	116.3
1952–1953	192.455	319.373	105.9	110.1
1953–1954	215.163	350.713	118.5	121.0
1954–1955	213.225	348.604	117.4	120.2
1955–1956	225.472	366.166	124.1	126.3
1956–1957	249.376	402.748	137.3	138.9
1957–1958	253.410	409.690	139.5	141.3

Sources: Cols. 1, 4, 7, and 10: For prewar figures, see *SHD*, p. 188; for postwar period figures, *SJDDR*, 1958, p. 476. Planned amounts for 1955–1956 are from *SP*, October 1956. Cols. 2, 3, 5, 6, 8, 9, 11, and 12: Prices are from *SHLE*, p. 115. The 1950 prices of phosphates, potash, and calcium were only about half the prices in subsequent years. Cols. 13 and 14: Derived by addition. Cols. 15 and 16: The prewar average, serving as the base for the indices, has been calculated as follows:

| | Amount (thousand tons) | Value (million RM/DM) | |
		1935–1938 Prices	1950 Prices
N	171.9	93.170	160.211
P_2O_5	158.9	45.287	55.138
K_2O	258.2	34.082	57.837
CaO	479.4	9.109	16.779
Total		181.648	289.965

[a] Years refer to fertilizer years. In Tables 126–129 they are calendar years.

[b] For 1955–1956 the planned amounts of nitrogen were 364,000 tons of N, and of potash 574,000 tons of K_2O.

leading, but the amount of fertilizer available per hectare of crop land is most important. The official figures are given in Statistical Practice (see Table 129).

Except for calcium fertilizers, for which the amounts available per hectare are much larger in East than in West Germany, and potash, for which they have become somewhat larger, the supplies, particularly of the crucial phosphates, are substantially better in West Germany. This situation is reflected in the yields even when the biological yields of East Germany are compared with the barn yields of West Germany as in Statistical Practice. Potato yields per hectare in West Germany in 1955 were 141 per cent of those in East Germany, and sugar beets, 119 per cent. The actual differences in yields are of course bigger when adjustments are made for the differences in the concepts of yield.

Thus, while total fertilizer inputs in East Germany are greater than before the war — they passed the 1951–1952 level only in 1955–1956 — they are insufficient to maintain soil fertility and increase yields, and they fluctuate with crop production as might be expected. The detailed calculations are given in Table 130.

A check of the figures indicates that expenditures on commercial fertilizers in 1936 prices in East Germany before the war were about 6 per cent and in 1954–1955 about 8 per cent of the market value of agriculture. In West Germany, in current prices, they were 7.58 per cent and 8.19 per cent, respectively.[13] The relation of the two percentages probably ought to be the reverse, that is, the area of East Germany before the war probably used more fertilizer relative to the market value of agricultural output (including consumption on the farms themselves) than the area of the Federal Republic. This is probably so because the proportions of pasture land and of cattle were bigger in West Germany. On the other hand, pigs were relatively more numerous in East than in West Germany. If I have underestimated the fertilizer used in East Germany, the prewar as well as the postwar output in the area has been overestimated to the same extent. But, as the closeness of the percentage figures indicates, the error involved cannot be very big.

Purchased feed

Imports of grains. East Berlin of course has always consumed more grain than it produced. The Eastern Zone did, however, have surpluses of wheat and oats of sufficient magnitude in 1934–1935 — the only year for which such detailed figures are available — to yield a surplus of almost 300,000 tons of wheat and 140,000 tons of oats. The area needed substantial rye imports, mostly to East Berlin for human consumption and to the Eastern Zone for fodder. (It is assumed that East Berlin accounts for one-third of the deficit of all of Berlin.)

Gleitze has calculated that in 1934–1935 the Soviet Zone needed 762,-100 tons of wheat, 1,086,600 tons of rye, and 200,100 tons of barley for human consumption.[14] East Berlin needed 83,400 tons of wheat, 100,400 tons of rye, and 20,100 tons of barley. Thus the total tonnage of bread grains needed in 1934–1935 in the area of East Germany was 2,258,700 tons, of which 103,500 were barley. I have calculated the human consumption of wheat and rye for 1934–1938 as 2,155,300 tons,* which is only slightly more than Gleitze's estimate and not sufficiently different to warrant a recalculation, particularly as the estimates refer to slightly different periods. In the calculation of the value of market crops I have assumed that all barley and oats went for fodder, while Gleitze indicates that about 200,000 tons of barley were used for human consumption, and 31,500 tons of oats were used industrially in the area of the Soviet Zone alone.

Therefore, although the calculated value of the market production of crops may be too small, no adjustment appears necessary to allow for barley and oats not used for fodder. If more was available for fodder, less had to be imported; and if market production was smaller by X marks,

* See Supplement Table B.2.

the deductions necessary for fodder are also smaller by X marks. Hence any error cancels.

The amounts of wheat involved changed from a prewar export surplus estimated at 295,600 tons to an import surplus of 606,100 tons in 1956 and 1.078 million tons in 1957. A prewar import surplus of 140,400 tons of rye was increased to an import surplus of 379,000 tons in 1956 and 340,000 tons in 1957. (In 1956, imports of 482,000 tons of rye were offset by unusually large exports of 103,000 tons. In other years, rye exports were negligible.[15]) The estimated export surplus of oats of 139,800 tons changed to an import surplus of 86,700 tons in 1956. In 1956, only the barley and corn import surpluses were smaller than before the war.

These import surpluses were so substantial in 1957 that it was stated that East Germany was importing "more grain for the population than the state gets through forced deliveries and government purchases." [16] Altogether, grain imports (including maize) more than doubled, and this does not allow for any exports in the prewar period.

Oil cake. In addition to grain imports, the agricultural sector purchases oil cake from industry. Some of the oil cake is manufactured domestically; some is made from imported seeds. Since it is not known exactly what oil-bearing seeds are imported or whether oil cakes are imported in any quantity, the amounts involved can only be guessed. Domestic production of oil cake more than quintupled between 1934–1938 and 1955, although here too we cannot see any real upward trend since 1951. On the other hand, the quantity of oil cake which could be made from imported oilseeds (assuming that these were soybeans and that there was only unavoidable waste) not only was more important than oil cake from domestic sources but also increased steadily.

One problem to be solved consists in finding a base for the amount of oil cake purchased by agriculture in the East German area before the war. We know the amounts of oilseed that went into oil and oil cake in 1936 and in 1938 as well as the total amount of oil cake produced. In 1936 the Reich produced 1,056,600 tons of oil cake from imported and domestic seeds, and in 1938, 1,222,800 tons. Both amounts were less than the production in 1933.[17] In addition, net imports were 56,700 tons in 1936 and 185,600 tons in 1938. Since oil cake is fed mainly to cattle, the amount available for the average of 1936 and 1938 may be allocated to the area of East Germany in the proportion of the number of cows. Before the war the area had, on the average, 18.3 per cent of the cattle in the Reich.[18] (The number of cattle in Berlin was negligible.) On the average (of 1936 and 1938), all of Germany had 1,136,548 tons of oil cake available. The share of East Germany can thus be estimated at 207,988 tons.

By 1955, there were 325,523 tons of oil cake available to the economy, an increase of over 55 per cent. By 1957 the supply probably increased to 348,865 tons. Fodder inputs which can be accounted for and which had to be purchased from outside of agriculture trebled by 1957 compared with their prewar level (measured in 1936 prices). The data are given in Table 131.

It is unfortunately impossible to account systematically for other im-

Table 131

Amounts and value of imported fodder, East Germany, 1934–1938 average and 1950–1958

A. *Amounts, thousand tons*

Year	Wheat	Rye	Oats	Barley	Maize	Oil cake
	(1)	(2)	(3)	(4)	(5)	(6)
1934–1938 (av.)	(295.6)ᵃ	140.4	(139.8)ᵃ	472.9	217.2	207.988
1950	250.8		137.2	161.0	4.0	79.240
1951	364.0		...	357.0	43.0	178.888
1952	334.0	49.0	69.0	302.0	50.0	153.213
1953	349.2	65.0	71.4	441.4	88.0	212.375
1954	255.1ᵇ	610.2	30.2	159.0	70.0	239.621
1955	554.9	187.3	40.2	440.0	125.5	325.534
1956	606.1	481.5	86.7	364.7	145.0	310.798
1957	1,078.0	342.0	150.0	387.0	57.0	348.865
1958	1,292.0	207.0	133.0	85.0	143.0	320.878

B. *Value and indices*

	Value (million RM/DM)				Indices of grain imports	
	Grain imports		Oil cake			
Year	Prewar prices	1950 Prices	Prewar prices	1950 Prices	Prewar prices	1950 Prices
	(7)	(8)	(9)	(10)	(11)	(12)
1934–1938 (av.)	129.681	227.706	33.694	65.454	100.0	100.0
1950	109.256	149.278	12.837	24.937	84.2	65.6
1951	147.109	212.633	28.979	56.296	113.4	93.4
1952	152.485	211.571	24.821	48.216	117.6	92.9
1953	187.988	278.469	34.405	66.834	145.0	122.3
1954	201.040	308.702	38.819	75.409	155.0	135.6
1955	249.384	377.112	52.737	102.445	192.3	165.6
1956	307.539	469.219	50.349	97.808	237.2	206.1
1957	392.226	564.802	56.516	109.788	302.5	248.0
1958	341.313	514.525	51.992	100.980	263.2	226.0

Sources: Cols. 1–5: For 1950–1957, see *SJDDR*, 1956, p. 524; 1957, p. 520. For 1958, *SJDDR*, 1958, p. 576. Prewar figures (except for maize) refer to 1934–1935 and are calculated from Gleitze, *Ostdeutsche Wirtschaft*, pp. 162–163. One-third of Berlin has been allocated to East Berlin. The figure for maize comes from *SHD*, p. 396. One-third of the total maize imports for the average 1933–1937 has been allocated to the area of East Germany. No direct figures have been found. Col. 6: For prewar figures, see text, Chapter XVI; for other years, see Table 107. Cols. 7 and 8: Sum of separately calculated imports of individual grains. Col. 6: 1938 average of different kinds of oil cakes. Calculated from *SHD*, p. 464. Col. 10: Export price to Denmark. *SJBR*, 1953, p. 338.

    ᵃ Figures in parentheses are export figures; they are not added in the total value of imported fodder.

    ᵇ Total imports less amounts needed for human consumption. See Supplement Table B.1.

ported fodder inputs (for example, fishmeal) except to state that in 1955 they were clearly insufficient.

Other purchased inputs

The other industrial inputs that can be accounted for are electricity, gasoline, and oil.

Electricity. In 1953, agriculture used 422 million kwhr, and in 1955, 510 million kwhr; both quantities amounted to 1.8 per cent of total electricity consumption. In 1956, agriculture still used only 1.9 per cent of the power generated, but in 1957 there was a jump to 933 million kwhr, or 2.9 per cent. In prewar Germany, 2.4 per cent of the total power generated went to "rural small users," a category which is somewhat more inclusive than the category *Landwirtschaft* but probably not much more. These are the only available figures.[19] For other postwar years it will be assumed that 1.8 per cent went to agriculture. For prewar years it will be assumed, *faute de mieux*, that 2.4 per cent of the power generated in 1936 went to agriculture. Any overestimation implied in the percentage (because of the inclusion of rural nonfarm households) is likely to be more than offset by the fact that by 1938 power generation had increased above the 1936 level.

From these data a reliable series can be calculated that can be evaluated in prices paid by West German farmers, which in 1955 were only

Table 132

Electric power used in agriculture, East Germany, 1936 and 1950–1958

Year	Total generated (million kwhr)	Purchases by agriculture (million kwhr)	Value (million RM/DM)	
			1936 Prices (RM 0.238 per kwhr)	1950 Prices (DM 0.183 per kwhr)
	(1)	(2)	(3)	(4)
1936	14.000	336.0	79.968	61.488
1950	19.466	350.4	83.395	64.123
1951	21.463	386.3	91.939	70.693
1952	23.183	417.3	99.317	76.366
1953	24.427	422.5	100.555	77.318
1954	26.044	468.8	111.574	85.790
1955	28.695	510.0	121.380	93.330
1956	31.310	604.0	143.752	110.532
1957	32.735	933.0	222.054	170.739
1958	34.874	1088.0	258.944	199.104

Sources: Col. 1: *SJDDR*, 1956, pp. 278–279, 1957, p. 294; 1958, p. 344. Col. 2: Figures for 1953 and 1955, absolute amounts given in *SP*, No. 8, 1956. The same percentage (1.8 per cent) was applied to 1950–1952 and 1954. Percentage for 1936 stated to have been 2.4 per cent (*ibid.*). For 1956 and 1957, see *SJDDR*, 1956, p. 301, and 1957, p. 313; 1958, p. 362. Cols. 3 and 4: For price in 1950 and 1951, see *Statistisches Handbuch fuer Landwirtschaft und Ernaehrung*, p. 115; for index or producer price of power and current sold to agriculture, *SJBR*, 1955, p. 436.

77 per cent of 1938 (the base year available). Power is one of the few inputs whose 1950 prices and below the prewar base, although by 1953–1954 the price had risen to slightly above the prewar level.

As Table 132 shows, by 1955 agriculture consumed 51.8 per cent more electric power than in 1936. The actual consumption for 1955, given as 510 million kwhr, seems rather high, since West German consumption is estimated at only 700 million kwhr in 1954–1955. In 1957, farm consumption is supposed to have been as high as 933 million kwhr. However, consistency with the general practice in this study has induced us to accept these rather high figures.

Gasoline and oil. With increasing mechanization of agriculture, the inputs of gasoline and diesel oil have become increasingly important. As mentioned before, there is an asymetry in the fact that as horses become less important the decrease in their number is reflected as a decline of agricultural output while increasing mechanization leads to increased purchases from other sectors of the economy.

Mechanization in the East German economy as elsewhere in communist economies is concentrated in the Machine Tractor Stations (MTS), which are treated as investment by agriculture and hence not deducted from gross output as a cost. This is consistent with our aim of finding the gross national product attributable to agriculture rather than developing a balance sheet of agriculture or otherwise determining changes in the wealth and welfare of the agricultural sector.

The first problem consists in finding the quantities of tractors and other agricultural machinery available in the area of East Germany. We assumed that the average horsepower available per hectare of agricultural land was the same in East and West Germany, namely, 3.4 hp per hectare.[20] It was probably higher in East Germany because the percentage of crop land is higher. No adjustment could be made, however. In 1939 the agricultural land in the area of the Eastern Zone was 6.59 million hectares, that in Berlin being negligible. Assuming that each tractor had 25 hp (the average per tractor in the area of the Federal Republic), we arrive at an estimate for 1935–1938 of 8,962 tractors.[21]

The basic postwar figure is for the year 1949. The Statistical Yearbook of the German Democratic Republic gives the number of tractors in 1949 as 23,311; although the horsepower of the tractors is not mentioned, it presumably averages 30 hp, the standard on which the other statistics are based. For the later postwar years we have the number of tractors only for MTS and nationalized farms. These two sets of figures are given for tractors of all kinds and for tractors recalculated on the basis of 30 hp. The MTS and nationalized farms own an increasing number of tractors as well as an increasing percentage of the total stock. No data have been found for other owners, such as production cooperatives or the few private peasants.

The stock of tractors was estimated as follows: It was assumed that the scrappage is 4 per cent a year, that is, that the life expectancy of tractors is about 25 years. Although this seems high, difficulties of replacement would induce as many repairs as possible and the longest possible use. Total production of new tractors, as well as imports known to have gone to agriculture rather than the army or the police, is assumed to go to agriculture. For 1951, Professor Kramer estimated tractor horsepower per hectare as 15, which gives the figure of 32,950 tractors with an average of 30 hp that we accepted. If the method just sketched had been used, the stock of tractors would have been calculated as 32,395, a very close approximation. Calculated in this manner, by 1955 the total number of tractors with an average of 30 hp had increased to 186.9 per cent of 1950, which is more than 575 per cent of the prewar average. West German development increased even more. In terms of horsepower, by 1954 it had increased to 230.5 per cent of 1950, and to 1,506 per cent of the prewar average (1935–1938). By July 1955 the number of tractors had increased to 423,000, another 14 per cent above 1954. By July 1956 the number was 492,000. It should be observed that the horsepower per hectare in West Germany increased from 3.4 hp in 1935–1938 to 23.1 hp in 1950, and to 52.8 hp in 1955. In East Germany it rose from the same 3.4 in 1935–1938 to 12.7 hp in 1950, and to 23.9 hp in 1955. That is, in 1955 East Germany was about where West Germany was in 1950.

Considering the fanfare surrounding the mechanization of agriculture, this is a surprisingly meager result. It becomes even more meager when one considers that the proportion of crop land to total agricultural land is much higher in East than in West Germany. This much more favorable development of agricultural mechanization in West Germany is admitted by East German sources,[22] although they treat it as a bad sign of necessity imposed on West German agriculture by a labor shortage. According to such sources, "the essential difference in the mechanization of agriculture between East and West Germany lies in the fact that in our republic mechanization helps not only large socialized farms but also small peasant holdings because the state makes the machines available, a condition which also ensures a full utilization of the stock of machines whereas in capitalist agriculture only large farms can utilize machines fully, and small farms can use machinery only to a limited extent and only at substantially higher cost."[23] Complaints in East German newspapers and journals do not entirely bear out the claims to full utilization of machinery under the MTS system, but this situation, being outside our more narrow interest, will not be pursued further here.

More interesting is the fact that the average horsepower of tractors in West Germany decreased from 25 hp in 1935–1938 to 23.5 hp in 1950 to 20.3 hp in 1954. East German tractors, on the other hand, are likely to be larger than 30 hp, although no exact calculation can be made. This is certainly true for the tractors owned by both MTS and socialized farms. The average horsepower for MTS-owned tractors in 1950 was 32.3, and in 1957, 35.6; in 1955, for tractors owned by MTS and socialized farms, 38.1.

The figures suggest strongly that, as with industry, preference is given to "large" items; that size is expected to make up for numbers and perhaps even for quality. The figures are certainly consistent with the development of agricultural output in East and West Germany and with the need for a large number of people in the agricultural sector, as noted in Part I — this in the face of a labor shortage that is certainly much more acute in East Germany than in the Federal Republic.

In addition to tractors, some trucks are used on farms. No average figure has been found for 1935–1938, but the number of trucks used then must have been negligible. Either tractors or, more likely, horses and oxen were used. For the postwar period the total number of MTS-owned trucks is available since 1950, and the number of state-farm-owned trucks for the years 1952 through 1955. Cooperatives undoubtedly also own trucks, but no published figures are available. The total number involved is very small — 3,427 in 1955. Undoubtedly, most transport is allocated to the transport sector. The scanty data on tractors and trucks are given in Table 133.

In addition to trucks and tractors, only self-propelled combines use gasoline or diesel fuel. Threshing machines, milking machines, sorting machines, and others use either electricity (already accounted for) or coal through steam engines, the amount of which is presumably negligible. It is not clear what proportion of the existing modern combines are self-propelled. The total number of combines owned by MTS has increased sharply, from 127 in 1951 to 2,260 in 1955 and 3,702 in 1957.[24] (It is unlikely that there are other owners, except perhaps state farms.) Because of the uncertainty as to what proportion are self-propelled, no fuel consumption was calculated. However, since the number of combines is small and the number of hours they are used is certainly substantially smaller than for trucks, the amounts involved cannot be large.

In order to calculate fuel consumption it is necessary to get some idea of how much the farm machinery is run. East German sources have developed a measure called "hm" which is the amount of work needed to plow one hectare of average crop land 20–25 cm deep (*Hektar mittleren Pflügens*). According to the Rules of Thumb for Agriculture it takes a tractor of between 20 and 30 hp about 4 hours to plow one hectare 20–25 cm deep.[25] This is the conversion ratio used although it appears to be a minimum. Another source states that a 30-hp tractor has to work 4.2 hours with two plow attachments to plow one hectare of average-quality soil to the depth of a seed row.[26]

The East German information relates only to tractor services of the

Table 133

Tractors and trucks in agriculture, East Germany, 1935–1938 average and 1949–1958

Year	Tractors in agricultur[a]	MTS[b] Tractors All types	MTS[b] Tractors Recalculated to 30 hp	MTS[b] Trucks, all types	VEG[c] Tractors All types	VEG[c] Tractors Recalculated to 30 hp	VEG[c] Trucks, all types	Production of tractors	Imports of tractors
	(1)	(2)	(3)	(4)	(5)	(6)	(7)	(8)	(9)
1935–1938 (av.)	8,962								
1949	23,311								
1950	27,549	10,834	11,668	675	1,830			5,170	...
1951	32,950	14,342	16,639	970	2,321			5,946	...
1952	37,135	18,419	22,185	1,191	2,831	3,278	149	5,526	1,130
1953	42,905	23,042	28,686	1,830	3,597	4,472	290	5,729	2,210
1954	48,148	27,884	33,988	2,225	3,914	5,019	459	7,041	3,460 Plan
1955	51,495	31,531	37,546	2,859	4,185	5,312	568	6,459	...
1956	n.a.	33,866	39,415	3,069	n.a.	n.a.	n.a.	5,345	
1957	n.a.	34,617	41,121	3,259	n.a.	n.a.	n.a.	3,146	
1958	n.a.	37,076	n.a.	3,607	n.a.	n.a.	n.a.	4,139	

Sources: Col. 1: 1935–1938 average calculated from *SHLE*, p. 38. For 1949, see *SJDDR*, 1955, p. 199 (horsepower unknown, presumably 30 hp). 1950–1955: Calculations based on 4 per cent scrapping rate for tractors each year. According to Professor Daniel Suits, University of Michigan, the scrapping rate in the United States varies between 4 and 5 per cent. Total production of tractors is considered as going to agriculture. According to this method we would have 32,395 tractors in 1951 compared to 32,950 as based on the horsepower per hectare calculations given in Kramer, *Die Landwirtschaft*, p. 35. The series reproduced in Col. 3 has been discontinued, and another one in "15 PS Zughaken" has been substituted back to 1955. No definition of the new measure is given. Cols. 2–4: *SJDDR*, 1957, p. 356; 1958, p. 426. Cols. 5–7: *Ibid.*, 1955, p. 198. This information has been dropped from later editions. Col. 8: *Ibid.*, pp. 164–165, and 1957, p. 300; 1958, p. 350. Refers to wheeled tractors only. Col. 9: For 1952, see "Caterpillars and Tractors" in *Der Aussenhandel der sowjetischen Besatzungszone Deutschlands 1952* ("*Materialien*"), Bonn, n.d., pp. 26 and 53. For 1953–1954, see *Der Aussenhandel der sowjetischen Besatzungszone Deutschlands 1953 und Plan 1954* ("*Materialien*"), Bonn, n.d., p. 14.
ᵃ 1935–1938: 25 hp; 1949–1957: 30 hp.   ᵇ MTS: Machine Tractor Stations.   ᶜ VEG: *Volkseigene Güter* (socialized farms).

MTS, which increased from 648 hours in 1950 to 1330 hours in 1955. For 1936 we assumed a use of 800 hours per year. For 1950 the Rules of Thumb for Agriculture suggest a normal use of 1,000 hours a year. Prewar usage was probably smaller.[27] For the other years it is assumed that MTS tractor utilization is typical of all tractors. Any error involved becomes progressively less as the percentage of MTS tractors in the total increases.

Diesel fuel consumption can be calculated at 1 kg for each 10 rated horsepower, while about 5 g of lubricating oil are needed per horsepower-hour.[28] Because of the increasing use made of the tractors, the amount of diesel fuel and lubricating oil used about doubled between 1935–1938

Table 134

Diesel fuel, gasoline, and lubricating oil used in agriculture,
East Germany, 1936 and 1950–1955

A. *Tractors*

Year	Number of tractors	Number of hours used per year per tractor	Fuel used per tractor per year (kilograms)	Lubricating oil used per tractor per year (kilograms)	Total diesel fuel used (thousand tons)	Total lubricating oil used (thousand tons)
	(1)	(2)	(3)	(4)	(5)	(6)
1936	8,962	800	2,000	100.0	17.924	0.896
1950	27,549	648	1,944	97.2	53.555	2.678
1951	32,950	780	2,340	117.0	77.103	3.855
1952	37,135	792	2,376	118.8	88.233	4.412
1953	42,905	1,204	3,612	180.6	154.972	7.748
1954	48,148	1,180	3,540	177.0	170.444	8.522
1955	51,495	1,330	3,990	199.5	205.465	10.273

B. *Trucks*

Year	Number of trucks	Gasoline per truck with 30,000 km average mileage per year (liters)	Total consumption (million liters)	Oil used for lubrication (thousand tons)
	(7)	(8)	(9)	(10)
1936				
1950	675	6,000	4.0	0.20
1951	970	6,000	5.8	0.29
1952	1,340	6,000	8.0	0.40
1953	2,120	6,000	12.7	0.63
1954	2,684	6,000	16.1	0.81
1955	3,426	6,000	20.6	1.03

Table 134 (Continued)

C. *Value of fuels and lubricating oil used by trucks and tractors, million RM/DM*

	Diesel fuel		Lubricating oil	
Year	1936 Prices (RM 196 per ton)	1950 Prices (DM 286 per ton)	1936 Prices (RM 1660 per ton)	1950 Prices (DM 2000 per ton)
	(11)	(12)	(13)	(14)
1936	3.513	5.126	1.477	1.780
1950	10.497	15.317	4.764	5.740
1951	15.112	22.051	5.212	6.280
1952	17.294	25.235	7.985	9.620
1953	30.375	44.322	13.911	16.760
1954	33.407	48.747	15.488	18.660
1955	40.271	58.763	18.758	22.600

	Gasoline		Gasoline, diesel fuel, and lubricating oil combined	
Year	1936 Prices (RM 0.33 per liter)	1950 Prices (DM 0.46 per liter)	1936 Prices	1950 Prices
	(15)	(16)	(17)	(18)
1936			4.990	6.906
1950	1.320	1.840	16.581	22.897
1951	1.941	2.668	22.265	30.999
1952	2.640	3.680	27.919	38.535
1953	4.191	5.842	48.477	66.924
1954	5.313	7.406	54.208	74.813
1955	6.798	9.476	65.827	90.839

Sources: Col. 1: From Table 133, col. 1; 25 hp per tractor assumed for 1936, 30 hp for postwar years. Col. 2: *SJDDR* 1955 ed., p. 198. Conversion ratio of 1 hectare average plowing used as in East Germany. The work for 1 ha average plowing is 4 hours, *FL*, p. 63. For 1936, 800 hours were assumed per annum. Col. 3: Calculated with 250 gram/hr hp.; 40 per cent load = 0.1 kg/hr hp. See *ibid.*, p. 65. Col. 4: 4-cycle diesel engine uses 3–6 gram/ hr hp, *ibid.*, p. 65; estimated, 5 grams. Col. 5: Col. 1 × col. 3. Col. 6: Col. 1 × col. 5. Col. 7: Trucks of MTS and VEG only. See text and Table 133. Number of trucks in 1936 not available, but probably negligible. Col. 8: Gasoline use of medium trucks assumed to be 20 liters per 100 km. In East Germany smaller truck types probably prevail. Col. 9: Col. 7 × col. 8. Col. 10: Assumed about 5 per cent of fuel used. Cols. 11–16: 1950 prices of diesel fuel and lubricating oil from *FL*, p. 64. Gasoline price of DM 0.60 retail less a third reduction for agriculture assumed. Prewar prices calculated with index in *SJBR*, 1953, p. 494. 1938 = 100; 1950 = 120; 1936 assumed to be equal to 1938. Cols. 17 and 18: Found by adding col. 11 + col. 13 + col. 15 and col. 12 + col. 14 + col. 16 respectively.

(or 1950) and 1955. On the other hand, the total tonnage of diesel fuel required almost trebled from 1935–1938 to 1950, and by 1955 it was 384 per cent of 1950 (and 1,146 per cent of 1935–1938). Although appearing as a cost item, it is of course a measure of the success of building up both the number of tractors and their utilization.

The estimation of gasoline consumption by trucks is explained in the notes to Table 134. Altogether, the value of gasoline, diesel fuel, and lubricating oil used by the agricultural sector rose from just under RM 5 million in 1935–1938 to DM 66 million in 1955 in 1936 prices, or 1,319 per cent; in 1950 prices the rise was slightly less, 1,315 per cent.

THE COST OF INPUTS AND VALUE ADDED

OF AGRICULTURE (EXCLUDING FORESTRY)

Table 135 summarizes the findings of the earlier calculations. The total value of agricultural inputs, which fell slightly from the prewar base to 1950, rose substantially during the period of the First Five Year Plan.

Table 135

Inputs into agriculture, East Germany, prewar and 1950–1958 (million RM/DM)

A. *In 1936 prices*

Year	Fertilizers	Electricity	Fuels	Grain imports	Oil cake	Sum
	(1)	(2)	(3)	(4)	(5)	(6)
Prewar	181.648[a]	79.968	4.990	129.681	33.694	429.981
1950	182.452	83.395	16.581	109.256	12.837	404.521
1951	185.465	91.939	22.265	147.109	28.979	475.757
1952	203.292	99.317	27.919	152.485	24.821	507.834
1953	192.455	100.555	48.477	187.988	34.405	563.880
1954	215.163	111.574	54.208	201.040	38.819	620.804
1955	213.225	121.380	65.827	249.384	52.737	702.553
1956	225.472	143.752	69.118[b]	307.339	50.349	796.030
1957	249.376	222.054	72.090[b]	392.226	56.516	992.262
1958	253.410	258.944	76.560[b]	341.313	51.982	982.209

B. *1950 prices*

Year	Fertilizers	Electricity	Fuels	Grain imports	Oil cake	Sum
	(1)	(2)	(3)	(4)	(5)	(6)
Prewar	289.965[a]	61.488	6.906	227.706	65.454	651.519
1950	300.496	64.123	22.897	149.278	24.937	561.731
1951	308.287	70.693	30.999	212.633	56.296	678.908
1952	337.357	76.366	38.535	221.571	48.216	722.045
1953	319.373	77.318	66.924	278.469	66.834	808.918
1954	350.713	85.790	74.813	308.702	75.409	895.427
1955	348.604	93.330	90.839	377.112	102.445	1,012.330
1956	366.166	110.532	95.381[b]	469.219	97.808	1,139.106
1957	402.748	170.739	99.482[b]	564.802	109.788	1,347.559
1958	409.690	199.104	105.650[b]	514.525	100.980	1,329.949

Sources: Tables 130–134.

  [a] Average, 1934–1938, calculated. See Table 130, note to cols. 15 and 16.

  [b] Assumed to have increased between 1955 and 1956 and from 1956 to 1957 as the number of MTS tractors (105 per cent and 104.3 per cent). Calculated from *SJDDR*, 1956, p. 356, and 1957, p. 364. Increase from 1957 to 1958 (measured by "15 pull hooks HP") was 106.2%; measured by numbers: 107.1%. The lower number has been used; *SJDDR*, 1958, p. 426.

In prewar prices, 1950 inputs were at a level of 94.8 per cent of the 1935–1938 average, but by 1955 they were at 172.4 per cent of 1950 and at 163.4 per cent of 1935–1938. By 1957 the cost of inputs had more than doubled. In 1950 prices, the decline between 1935–1938 and 1950 was much greater, namely, to 86.9 per cent. The rise between 1950 and 1955 to 178.9 per cent was greater, but the rise to 155.4 per cent between 1935–1938 and 1955 was smaller than when measured in 1935–1938 prices.

The increased costs reflect, of course, the shift toward greater mechanization (and greater use of commercial fertilizers). They also reflect very importantly, however, the shift from a crop to an animal economy. The cost of purchased feed stuffs — whether imported grain or oil cake — in 1935–1938 was about 38.4 per cent of total inputs. By 1955 these two categories amounted to 42.5 per cent. The importance of fertilizers, on the other hand, declined sharply — from almost 42 per cent in 1935–1938 to 30.6 per cent in 1955.

The value added of agriculture, as calculated (and without making an allowance for forestry) can be estimated for 1935–1938 as RM 2,717.516 million (see Table 136). The 1953 edition of the Statistical Yearbook of the Federal Republic set the net social product of agriculture (presumably including forestry) for 1936 and in 1936 prices at RM 2.5 billion.[29] Mr. Sanderson, on the other hand, estimated the gross national product of agriculture, forestry, and fisheries to have been RM 3.1 billion,[30] an estimate which is quite close to the one adopted here. To anticipate the next section somewhat, the combined GNP of agriculture and forestry (but excluding fisheries) is calculated at RM 2,911.322 million for the prewar average. Thus our estimate is roughly of the same order of magnitude as the two other estimates quoted, the bases of whose calculations, however, are unknown to me.

By 1950 the value added of agriculture (without forestry and in 1936 prices) was RM 1,819.211 million, which is only two-thirds of prewar. Mr. Sanderson's calculations, which include forestry and fisheries, indicate a 1950 level which is three-fourths of 1936; when forestry is included in our calculations, the level reached in 1950 is 70.1 per cent of 1936. By 1952, the last year for which Sanderson has published an estimate, he estimates the GNP of agriculture, forestry, and fisheries at 3.0 billion, or 97 per cent of 1936. My own estimate is that in 1952 the level of agricultural output including forestry was only 91.1 per cent of 1936, and, excluding forestry, 90 per cent. By 1955 the output of agriculture excluding forestry was definitely below the 1952 level, and it was only three-fourths of 1936. The GNP attributable to agriculture, whether including forestry or not, did not approach the prewar level even in 1957, although the market value did.

Calculations in 1950 prices are much more favorable to East Germany, but even in 1950 prices agriculture produced only about 86 per cent of

Table 136

Value added in agriculture, East Germany, prewar and 1950–1958 (million RM/DM)

A. *1936 Prices*

Year	Sales value		Sum of crop production and animal production[a]	Cost of inputs	Wood production	Value added			
	Crop production	Animal production				Agriculture without forestry	Agriculture and forestry	Index without wood	Index including wood
	(1)	(2)	(3)	(4)	(5)	(6)	(7)	(8)	(9)
Prewar	1,263.007	1,884.490	3,147.497	429.981	193.806	2,717.516	2,911.322	100.0	100.0
1950	1,180.600	1,043.132	2,223.732	404.521	224.444	1,819.211	2,043.655	66.9	70.2
1951	1,208.936	1,372.828	2,581.764	475.757	256.222	2,106.007	2,362.229	77.5	81.1
1952	1,165.978	1,780.477	2,946.455	507.834	208.626	2,438.621	2,647.247	89.7	90.9
1953	1,102.713	1,454.836	2,557.549	563.880	221.328	1,993.669	2,214.997	73.4	76.1
1954	1,110.121	1,534.462	2,644.583	620.804	208.201	2,023.779	2,231.980	74.5	76.7
1955	1,072.961	1,704.915	2,777.876	702.553	192.424	2,075.323	2,267.747	76.4	77.9
1956	993.033	1,616.869	2,609.902	796.030	177.290	1,813.872	1,991.162	66.7	68.4
1957	1,119.856	1,820.654	2,940.510	992.262	173.476	1,948.248	2,121.724	71.7	72.9
1958	1,101.166	1,886.101	2,967.267	982.209	171.300	1,985.058	2,156.358	73.0	74.1

B. *1950 Prices*

Year	Sales value			Cost of inputs	Wood production	Value added			
	Crop production	Animal production	Sum of crop production and animal production[a]			Agriculture without forestry	Agriculture and forestry	Index without wood	Index including wood
	(10)	(11)	(12)	(13)	(14)	(15)	(16)	(17)	(18)
Prewar	2,094.847	3,703.845	5,798.692	651.519	428.284	5,147.173	5,575.457	100.0	100.0
1950	2,034.388	2,175.536	4,209.924	561.731	515.802	3,648.193	4,163.995	70.9	74.7
1951	2,082.659	2,844.176	4,926.835	678.908	599.263	4,247.927	4,847.190	82.5	86.9
1952	1,977.528	3,780.374	5,757.902	722.045	489.734	5,035.857	5,525.591	97.8	99.1
1953	1,886.600	3,037.940	4,924.540	808.918	519.930	4,115.622	4,635.552	80.0	83.1
1954	1,889.820	3,211.140	5,100.960	895.427	491.610	4,205.533	4,697.143	81.7	84.2
1955	1,840.643	3,585.734	5,426.377	1,012.330	458.489	4,414.047	4,872.536	85.8	87.4
1956	1,713.852	3,370.491	5,084.343	1,139.106	423.143	3,945.237	4,368.380	76.6	78.4
1957	1,899.086	3,786.682	5,685.768	1,347.559	413.804	4,338.209	4,752.013	84.3	85.2
1958	1,898.358	3,898.625	5,796.983	1,329.949	411.580	4,467.034	4,878.614	86.8	87.5

Source: Preceding tables in Part IV and Table 137.
[a] For statistical reasons the combined value of crop and animal production for the prewar period is the sum of the value of crop production for the average of the years 1934–1938, and of the value of animal production for the year 1938. The evidence suggests that the value of the crop sector in 1938 was substantially higher than the average of the preceding four years.

its prewar output in 1955, and output was also substantially below the 1952 level.

It is necessary to preface any interpretation with a word of caution: the structure of agriculture has changed considerably. Yet, having said so, I should like to point out also that all figures rest on official data, and that only known inputs have been deducted, and that, on the other hand, almost all conceivable products were evaluated. In spite of all the caution one may wish to exercise, the conclusion seems to be (to put it mildly) that East German agricultural production has not been a success. In spite of more efficient use of more tractors and of increased use of fertilizer since 1950, there is no evidence that agricultural production increased since 1951 or 1952. The output of 1952 has not been reached in any subsequent year. Clearly, the costs of planning and of attempted agricultural reforms are very high. So are the costs of the division of the country and a forced development of industry (which nevertheless was rather slow) without sufficient attention to reintegration into a world economy. And so are the costs of neglecting investments in agriculture and of neglecting the use of incentives.

One further point should be made. Between 31 December 1952 and 31 December 1953, total employment in agriculture, forestry, and the supply of water fell from 1,701,673 to 1,673,180. But by December 31, 1955 it had risen above the 1952 level to 1,774,747, 6 per cent above the 1952 low. Agricultural output (including forestry but excluding the supply of water) rose from 1953 to 1955 by 2 per cent; in 1955 it was 12 per cent below 1952. Clearly, output per man not only did not improve but fell in spite of increased mechanization. Only in 1956 and 1957 was there some indication of an increase in agricultural productivity. These were years in which planning was reformed, prices became somewhat more favorable to the farmers, and some of the excessive detail of planning was eliminated.

Once more it should be stressed that the results are all based on official data and are plausible. Even if one should object to the corrections made to transpose from biological to barn yields — and some corrections must be made — and even if some of the increases in prewar yields suggested by West German statistical usage are not made, it remains true that the official figures for wheat, barley, oat, and potato crops in 1955 were below the 1934–1938 average, and in some cases substantially so. Even though the numbers of animals are above their prewar level, their average weights and their yields are much below it. Hence, while it is debatable precisely how much allowance should be made for losses between the field and the barn, it is beyond dispute that agricultural output was still below the prewar average in 1956, an admittedly poor year, and in 1957, a much better year.

Unfortunately, it was impossible to make the same kind of calculations for forestry as for agriculture. There are no official figures for the various inputs although the number of acres worked, fertilized, and so on are given for the years 1950 through 1957. Nor did it prove feasible to evaluate the change in the value of standing timber. It is known that the Nazis had already overcut badly; hence the sharp increase in wood production until 1947 is certainly offset, and possibly more than offset, by reductions in the value of standing timber. And vice versa, the sharp decline in cuttings after 1948 is almost certainly to be interpreted as a good sign and is almost certainly offset, or more than offset, by increases in the value of standing timber. Hence the fluctuations in the value of wood production are not indicative of the production of the forest sector.

The only calculation that could be made is for wood production. Table 136 gives figures for the combined value added of agriculture and market value of wood production, but this combined figure is less reliable than that for the value added of agriculture alone.

Even the calculations for wood production are uncertain. For the postwar years, the Statistical Yearbook of the German Democratic Republic gives total cuttings in so-called *Festmeter*.* This figure is broken down by various categories of which the major subclassifications of interest here are firewood and wood for other uses (such as boards, poles, and mining props). Some figures are available for reforestation; since they refer to acreage rather than to volume, however, they are useless for our purpose.

The official figure for total wood production in 1935–1936 are given in Table 137.[31]

The 1935–1936 figure may probably be considered a normal yield of forests. As early as 1939, when cuttings were 12.220 million cu m, there was some overcutting, which by 1947 undoubtedly had reached the catastrophic proportions of 21.024 million cu m. Ever since that date cuttings have been reduced, and they show a systematic downward trend since 1951. Nevertheless, cuttings fell below the 1935–1936 level only during 1955, which implies some overcutting even in 1954 and 1955.

In 1955 the reduction in wood output, which in the aggregate was about 88.1 per cent of 1936, reflects in part the exhaustion of forests through consistent overcutting after the Nazis took over. But it also reflects serious attempts at reforestation and at achieving some sort of forest equilibrium. Hence the larger wood production until 1954, compared with 1936, undoubtedly reflects capital consumption while, possibly since 1952 or 1953, reductions in wood production are partially or even wholly offset by the building up of forests.

* A *Festmeter* is defined as a solid cubic meter of wood without air spaces.

Table 137

Wood production and value, East Germany, 1935–1936 average, 1939, and 1946–1958

A. *Production, million fm*[a]

Year	Firewood	Timber	Total of firewood and timber (*Derbholz*)[b]
	(1)	(2)	(3)
1935–1936	4.612	7.183	11.795
1939	2.479	9.741	12.220
1946	6.834	11.517	18.351
1947	10.561	10.463	21.024
1948	6.567	10.548	17.115
1949	4.282	9.599	13.881
1950	3.280	9.485	12.765
1951	2.654	11.444	14.098
1952	1.979	9.422	11.401
1953	2.060	10.018	12.079
1954	1.676	9.572	11.249
1955	1.119	9.090	10.209
1956	957	8.417	9.375
1957	961	8.222	9.183
1958	666	8.279	8.945

B. *Value, million RM/DM*

Year	1936 Prices			1950 Prices		
	Firewood (RM 11.20 per fm)	Timber (RM 19.79 per fm)	Firewood and timber combined	Firewood (DM 17.70 per fm)	Timber (DM 48.26 per fm)	Firewood and timber combined
	(4)	(5)	(6)	(7)	(8)	(9)
1935 = 1936	51.654	142.152	193.806	81.632	346.652	428.284
1939	27.765	192.774	220.539	43.878	470.101	513.979
1946	76.541	227.921	304.462	120.961	555.810	676.771
1947	118.283	207.063	325.346	186.930	504.944	691.874
1948	73.550	208.745	282.295	116.235	509.046	625.281
1949	47.958	189.964	237.922	75.791	463.248	539.039
1950	36.736	187.708	224.444	58.056	457.746	515.802
1951	29.725	226.477	256.222	46.976	552.287	599.263
1952	22.165	186.461	208.626	35.028	454.706	489.734
1953	23.072	198.256	221.328	36.462	483.468	519.930
1954	18.771	189.430	208.201	29.665	461.945	491.610
1955	12.533	179.891	192.424	19.806	438.683	458.489
1956	10.718	166.572	177.290	16.939	406.204	423.143
1957	10.763	162.713	173.476	17.010	396.794	413.804
1958	7.461	163.839	171.300	11.792	399.788	411.580

Sources: Cols. 1–3: For 1935–1936 and 1951–1958, see *SJDDR*, 1958, p. 477 for 1939, see *SHD*, p. 186; and for 1946–1950, see *SJDDR*, 1955, p. 220. Firewood in 1935–1936 prorated according to 1939 percentage of total wood. Timber in 1935–1936 found as the residual between total wood and firewood. Cols. 4–9: For prices, see notes to Supplement Table B.31.

[a] Fm: *Festmeter*, i.e., one cubic meter of solid wood, without air spaces.

[b] *Derbholz*: Wood with a diameter of more than 7 cm; branches and stems, but not twigs and roots.

The exhaustion of the forests is reflected in the proportion of firewood (including bark) to other wood. In 1936, firewood comprised 20.2 per cent of cuttings. By 1947 it amounted to 50.2 per cent, by 1950 the percentage was down to 25.7 per cent, and by 1955 it had fallen to 11.9 per cent. Clearly, the reduction of wood production primarily affected firewood, which in turn can be linked both with the greater availability of coal for heating purposes after 1950 and the attempts at reforestation and allowing trees to grow to reasonable size.

In the calculations, firewood and other timber were separately valued. For 1936 the price of firewood may be estimated at RM 11.20 per cu m, and for 1950 at DM 17.70 per cu m. This price had to be estimated in a rather roundabout manner: a retail price per 50 kg is known, half of which is assumed to be the price received by the forest owner, which is, if anything, too high. The conversion of kilograms into cubic meters was made on the basis of technical information found in *Neue Hütte* (one cubic meter of firewood is assumed to weigh about 500 kg).[32]

The price for timber was probably RM 19.79 per cu m in 1936 and DM 48.26 per cu m in 1950. These prices were arrived at from averages for various types of wood, weighted by their importance in East Germany in 1955.*

The combined sales value of firewood and other timber in 1936 can be estimated in 1936 prices at RM 193.806 million, and in 1950 prices at DM 428.284 million, a fairly substantial amount. By 1950, wood output was 17 per cent above 1936 but only about 2 per cent above 1939. By 1955 it had fallen to a level of 91.6 per cent of 1936 and 78.5 per cent of 1950 (all measured in 1936 prices). Measured in 1950 prices, the decline from 1936 to 1955 was only 6.6 per cent. It should be stressed once more that this decline in wood production must be interpreted as a "good" development.

This decline is overwhelmingly due to the fall in firewood output. Other timber cut in 1955 was only 2.8 per cent below 1936, whether measured in 1936 or in 1950 prices. The decline between 1950 and 1955, especially between 1951 and 1955, was more substantial. However, the fact that cuttings of "other" timber were almost as great in 1955, after decades of overcutting, as in 1936, when the composition of forests was more normal, indicates that even in 1955 some overcutting must have taken place.

* For details, see notes to Table 137.

IS ENOUGH FODDER AVAILABLE?

It is possible to check roughly on the calculations for fodder at least to the extent of indicating whether the reported production figures are possible or not. This check was done first by converting the available fodder into so-called grain units,* and, second, by calculating (roughly, of course) the fodder needs, also valued in grain units, of the various groups of animals. In this method of checking, no allowance is made for the fact that only within limits are various types of fodder substitutes for each other.

The major difficulty to be solved is determining how much animals are actually fed in East Germany. We started with the actual fodder input in the Federal Republic. This ought to overestimate the feed requirements in East Germany, since cattle in particular are known to be about 40 per cent lighter in East than in West Germany and pigs are known to be slightly lighter. (See Chapter XVI.)

The fodder intakes per animal have been taken from Liebe,[33] except that for horses, which seemed too high, where the value given in the Agriculture and Food Handbook[34] was substituted. These fodder intakes per animal were multiplied by the number of animals and totaled. Thus calculated, the total need for fodder in 1955 amounted to 14,449,000 tons of grain or its equivalent.

On the supply side, the available amounts of grains, potatoes, oil cake, sugar beets, and milk (calculated above, Chapter XVI) were converted into grain values with the appropriate figures. In addition, the various fodder crops which are used entirely within the agricultural sector and were therefore not evaluated above are included in the calculations. Although all such calculations have to be taken with more than the proverbial grain of salt, the evaluation of pasture output is particularly hazardous — but fortunately it is not very important. For 1955 the sum of the fodder available and calculable is 13,545,574 tons of grain units. We thus come within about 6.5 per cent of what is needed.

Although this margin of error is in itself reasonable, considering the data used, it probably can be explained away completely by the fact that fodder requirements were calculated for the much heavier animals in West Germany. All data on fodder are given in Tables 138 through 141.

* A grain unit is the food value of one kilogram of grain.

Table 138

Fodder available, East Germany, 1950–1955 (million tons)

	Year	Clover	Hay	Intermediate crop	Fodder beets	Fodder legumes
		(1)	(2)	(3)	(4)	(5)
Conversion ratio for grain values[a]		0.4	0.4	0.15	0.1	1.5
	1950	2.059	2.899	1.889	5.643	0.095
	1951	3.307	4.191	2.589	6.718	0.133
	1952	2.501	3.316	3.245	6.435	0.161
	1953	3.095	3.921	5.261	7.885	0.125
	1954	3.306	3.747	8.005	10.958	0.134
	1955	4.390	4.421	11.245	10.380	0.112
Grain values, 1955		1.756	1.768	1.687	1.038	0.168

	Year	Wheat	Rye	Mixed grains	Oats	Barley	Potatoes
		(6)	(7)	(8)	(9)	(10)	(11)
Conversion ratio for grain values[a]		1.0	1.0	1.0	1.0	1.0	0.25
	1950	0.286		0.205	0.850	0.446	
	1951			0.291	1.201	0.578	2.964
	1952			0.278	1.098	0.527	2.372
	1953	0.380	0.164	0.277	1.154	0.641	2.813
	1954			0.252	0.948	0.614	4.169
	1955	0.565	0.544	0.267	1.133	0.747	2.566
Grain values, 1955		0.565	0.544	0.267	1.133	0.747	0.641

	Year	Sugar beets	Oil cake	Sugar beets for fodder	Milk	Maize
		(12)	(13)	(14)	(15)	(16)
Conversion ratio for grain values[a]		1.0	1.4	0.25	0.7	1.0
	1950	0.371	0.079	0.287	1.491	
	1951	0.391		0.302	1.633	
	1952	0.409		0.317	1.819	
	1953	0.400	0.212	0.309	1.657	
	1954	0.473	0.240	0.367	1.720	
	1955	0.397	0.326	0.307	1.798	0.132
Grain values, 1955		0.397	0.456	0.077	1.258	0.132

Sources: Col. 1: Clover, clovergrass, alfalfa, serradella grasses. *SJDDR*, 1955, pp. 214–215. Col. 2: Estimation of fodder values derived from pastures. Total pastures in 1955 were 389,700 ha (*ibid.*, p. 201), to which may be added one-half of the 7,100 ha which alternate between being used as meadow and as pasture. This gives a total pasture area of 393,300 ha. Since 2.5–3 cows can graze on each hectare of average pasture (*FL*, p. 214), assuming 3 cows per hectare, 1,180,000 heads of cattle could be fed on the available pasture land. The pasture season extends normally in the North from May 15 through October 15. This implies that the available pasture can feed 491,665 heads of cattle for a full year, which permits an estimate of fodder available from pasture of 748,314 tons of grain value. As a check, the following calculation can be made. According to *SJDDR*, 1955, p. 215, 1.73 million tons of hay were harvested from pasture. The grain value is 692,000 tons. If 2.8 cows per hectare had been assumed, instead of 3, the fodder requirements would have been almost identical with the 692,000 tons of grain value available from pastures. An alternative explanation to make requirements and availability agree lies in underfeeding, which probably also has taken place. Col. 3: *Ibid.*, p. 215. Col. 4: *Ibid.*, p. 213. Col. 5: *Ibid.*, p. 208. Cols. 6, 7, 11–13, and 16: See various preceding tables. Col. 8: *SJDDR*, 1955, p. 207. Cols. 9 and 10: *Ibid.*, p. 206. Col. 14: 15 per cent of crop. See Hans Liebe, "Die Entwicklung der Landwirtschaft in der sowjetischen Besatzungszone seit 1945 und der augenblickliche Stand der Versorgung mit Nährungsmittel," in *Wirtschaftsforschung und Wirtschaftsführung*, West Berlin, Duncker & Humblot, 1956, p. 173. Col. 15: Total production (adjusted) less market production and estimated consumption by farmers. (See Supplement Table B.17.)

[a] Grain values given in *SHLE*, p. 213.

Table 139

Feed and fodder needed per animal per year, West Germany (kilograms)

	Concentrated feed[a]	Hay and green fodder	Straw	Milk of all kinds	Total
	(1)	(2)	(3)	(4)	(5)
Horses	941	1,509	290		2,740
Cattle	150	1,123	90	159	1,522
Sheep	30	223	29		292
Goats	20	459			479
Poultry	15			1	16
Pigs (grown)	620			83	703
Fodder necessary to raise one pig	538			73	611

Sources: Col. 1: For horses, see *SHLE*, p. 72. Hans Liebe, "Die Entwicklung der Landwirtschaft in der sowjetischen Besatzungszone seit 1945 und der augenblickliche Stand der Versorgung mit Nährungsmittel" in *Wirtschaftsforschung und Wirtschaftsführung*, p. 175, gives a value of 1,500 kg. The lower official West German value of 940 kg was used in our calculations. It is likely that hay and pasture are less available in East Germany; thus the need for concentrated feed should be higher. The total fodder in grain values in West Germany is 2,740 kg per horse. For cattle, sheep, goats, and poultry, see Liebe, *op. cit.*, p. 175. The two figures for pigs are actual amounts fed to pigs in the Federal Republic, 1954–1955, given in *SHLE*, p. 72. Liebe, *op. cit.*, p. 174, mentions that 500–600 kg grain values will result in 100 kg live weight in pigs. Cols. 2–5: *SHLE*, p. 72.

[a] Includes bread grains, fodder grains, legumes, oilseeds, potatoes, and sugar and other beets.

Table 140

Estimated amount of feed and fodder needed, East Germany,
1936, 1938, and 1950–1956 (thousand tons of grain value)

Year	Goats	Poultry	Horses	Cattle	Sheep	Pigs	Total
	(1)	(2)	(3)	(4)	(5)	(6)	(7)
1936	332.1	336.7	2,231.7	5,479.5	463.0	3,788.0	12,631.0
1938	325.0	347.0	2,235.8	5,560.3	514.9	3,486.9	12,470.0
1950	779.9	363.6	1,980.7	5,501.6	316.9	3,485.6	12,428.0
1951	755.6	425.4	2,040.5	5,796.2	361.9	4,330.9	13,710.0
1952	635.6	435.7	2,052.8	5,991.2	416.8	5,560.0	15,092.0
1953	544.2	413.3	1,991.4	5,777.8	452.5	5,015.1	14,194.0
1954	460.3	428.5	1,903.5	5,773.6	499.9	5,112.3	14,178.0
1955	411.8	436.8	1,833.3	5,721.9	527.8	5,516.9	14,449.0
1956			1,757.4	5,659.6	552.7	5,086.9	

Calculated from Tables 114 and 139.

Table 141

Fodder balance sheet, East Germany, 1955 (thousand tons of grain value)

	Feed and fodder available		Feed and fodder required[a]
Clover	1,756	Goats	412
Hay	1,768	Poultry	437
Pasture	748	Horses	1,833
Intermediate crops	1,687	Cattle	5,722
Beets for fodder	1,038	Sheep	528
Pulses for fodder	168	Pigs	5,517
Wheat	565		
Rye	544		
Mixed grains	267		
Oats	1,133		
Barley	747		
Potatoes	641		
Sugar beets, direct	692		
Sugar beets, shavings	397		
Oil cake	456		
Milk	1,258		
Maize	132		
Total fodder available	13,997		
Deficit (possibly explained by underfeeding below West German standards)	452		
	14,449		14,449

Sources: Table 138 and Table 140.

[a] Based on West German requirements.

PART FIVE

CONSTRUCTION, TRANSPORTATION
AND COMMUNICATIONS,
AND TRADE

CHAPTER XVIII

CONSTRUCTION

Sufficient data do not exist for the other economic sectors to make possible as detailed calculations as for industry and agriculture. The calculations presented in the preceding parts of this volume can claim a substantial degree of reliability. Particular judgments by the author can no doubt be questioned, but, with so much detail available, even substantial errors in one sector will hardly affect the total outcome significantly; and there is no reason to assume either that cumulative errors have occurred or that all individual industrial outputs, say, have been systematically undervalued. In fact, if anything, industrial production has been overvalued because until 1955 East German figures included rejects under output.

The measurement of the value added of construction is difficult even for a governmental statistical agency. Thus the Production Statistics of 1936 states explicitly that its estimates of construction figures are extremely rough,[1] presumably because of the difficulties not only of deciding what the main construction industry is as distinct from auxiliary construction trades (*Bauhauptgewerbe,* such as masons or bricklayers, and *Baunebengewerbe,* such as plumbers and electricians) but also where industry ends and artisans begin.

THE AVAILABLE DATA

For the postwar years, the first *Statistical Yearbook GDR* gives three sets of figures :[2]

1. The major information relates to the construction *industry*,[3] which, by definition, excludes artisans and architects' offices. Its performance is defined as follows:

Construction work including the value of materials used in the main building trades (bricklaying, excavating, roadwork, clearing of rubble, etc.) and auxiliary building trades (painting, plumbing, roofing, tiling, etc.). The setting up and taking down of the building site is included. Also included is construction work undertaken by the construction units of firms in other economic sectors, who execute construction work with their own labor.[4]

The 1957 edition of the Statistical Yearbook of the German Democratic Republic adds that the manufacture and erection of prefabricated houses and barracks is not a part of the building industry except for the preparation of the foundation. Also excluded are the erection of steel constructions for buildings, installation of generating equipment, and a few other minor categories.[5]

Aside from such information as the number of employees and the number of establishments by size, the chief relevance of this section for us is the total construction value (as defined) in thousands of East marks for the years 1950 through 1955 and a breakdown of these figures by major types of construction (for example, industrial, dwelling, road) for the years 1953 through 1957. The limitations of these figures are threefold: first, they refer only to the construction *industry;* secondly, they are once more too "gross"; and, thirdly, it is quite unclear what prices are used, whether current, constant 1950 prices or *Messwerte.* It seems most likely that some kind of constant prices were used, but one cannot be sure.

2. A second set of data appears in the section on "Artisans and Small Industry," [6] where the "Production and Services" of the following groups of artisans and small businessmen are given: bricklayers, roadbuilders, excavators (*Tiefbauer*) in the main construction trades, and plumbers, roofers, painters, and glaziers in the auxiliary construction trades.[7] All figures are in unspecified marks and refer only to the years 1952 through 1955. The information available for later years is even less detailed.

The production and services of these artisans are quantitatively important. In 1955 their production amounted to DM–O 1.111 billion, compared with DM–O 2.944 billion credited to the construction industry proper, that is, almost 38 per cent. The 1957 figures are DM–O 1.686 billion and DM–O 3.663 billion respectively, or 46 per cent. The unusually great importance of artisans is in part due to the fact that, while as a rule small industry and artisan shops may not employ more than 10 people, the limit for many construction-artisan shops is 20 and for others it is 15. Since the construction trades normally operate on a relatively small scale, shops employing up to 20 persons make up a substantial part of the industry (in the broader sense). Unfortunately, this information is incomplete.

3. The third place in which construction figures appear is in the context of national accounting.[8] The East German figures on gross product, amount of material used up, and net product have been given above.* The combined gross product (East German definition) of the construction industry (including small industry and artisans) is given as DM–O 4,632 million for 1955, its net product as DM–O 2,925 million. Gross and net product are supposedly measured in constant 1950 prices. The gross product of 1955 is almost DM–O 600 million greater than the sum of the

* See Part II, Chapter IV, Table 17.

products given in the sections on construction and on artisans. As already suggested, this may be due to omissions of important small industries and artisans engaged in construction; it may, however, also be due to the use of different prices. The latter is suggested by the fact that for 1955 the production and services of the total construction performed by small industries and artisans is given as DM–O 1,396 million, which still leaves about DM 292 million to be accounted for.[9] (By 1957 the spread between the gross product of construction, DM–O 5.711 billion, and the combined gross products of the construction industry and of construction artisans, DM–O 5.349 billion, had narrowed to DM–O 362 million*.)

If the DM 292 million are allocated to differences between 1950 and 1955 prices, the 1950 price level is computed to be 93.7 per cent of the 1955 level. This is quite possible.

The official figures claim that the gross product of construction, with all the double countings it includes had risen by 1955 to 193.9 per cent of 1950, and net production (which presumably has eliminated all double countings) to 185.2 per cent. In 1955, wage payments in construction were only DM–O 1,750 million and had risen to only 179 per cent of 1950, with the average monthly payment rising from DM–O 267 in 1950 to DM–O 372 in 1955, or 139 per cent. This implies that employment had risen 29 per cent. This increase agrees roughly with the calculations presented in Chapter III, Table 13, which indicate a rise in employment (as measured by the number of people employed rather than by man-hours) of 25 per cent between 1950 and 1955 or 1957.

THE PROCEDURES ADOPTED

It is clear from the summary of the official figures available that they do not suffice to calculate the GNP attributable to construction. They might possibly enable us to picture the development from 1950 on, but they are insufficient to link these figures to prewar data or to give absolute values which might be put into a meaningful context with the GNP calculated for industry and agriculture.

Therefore, since no figures are available comparable to the American series on housing starts[10] or on, say, the number of cubic meters of factories or meters of roads put in place, two methods suggested themselves.

One method essentially involves the assumption that total construction put in place varies in some manner with the labor employed. Taking employment figures and correcting them for changes in productivity would give an index that could be applied to the estimated GNP of construction in 1936 in the area of East Germany. The figures mentioned above on average monthly wages, payrolls, and increases in employment suggest only a minimal increase in productivity between 1950 and 1955. But before

* Figures in current East marks.

any conclusions can be drawn not only is it necessary to be quite clear why there is such a big difference between the DM–O 1.750 billion payrolls and the DM–O 2.925 billion net product of construction but it is also advisable first to describe and use another method of estimating the productive contribution of construction.

The second estimating method, on which major reliance will be placed in this chapter, reasons that construction output must vary with available building materials. Hence an index of *available* materials was constructed and applied to the 1936 base given in Production Statistics of 1936. This is essentially the method used by Sanderson,[11] who describes his procedure as follows: "Projected by multiplying the 1936 estimate by an index of building materials (cement, bricks, and window glass) *output;* with cement weighted at 37 per cent, bricks at 59 per cent, and glass at 4 per cent of the 1936 total." [12]

The method adopted here is basically a refinement of Sanderson's approach. First, the *availability* of building materials was considered more relevant than output. The difference between output and availability is significant. For the prewar period (specifically, for 1938) we have data that show that the area of East Germany excluding Berlin used 421.1 million pieces of roofing tile and that all of Berlin used another 55 million. Allocating one-third of Berlin to the East German sector (as we have throughout) raises the total of roofing tile used to 439.4 million pieces, of which only 224.8 million pieces or 51.2 per cent were locally supplied. With ordinary bricks, the discrepancy was slight. The area of East Germany used an estimated 2,485.5 million pieces (again allowing one-third of total Berlin consumption to East Berlin) while it produced 2,556.6 million pieces. There was thus a small surplus of about 4 per cent. The Berlin area apparently did not produce either roofing tiles or bricks. In addition, the area used a substantial amount of wall boards, which are manufactured from cement and other materials. The area of East Germany apparently consumed 176,193 cu m of these boards but produced only about 64,334 cu m, or 36.5 per cent.[13] The area of the Eastern Zone (excluding Berlin) in 1944 produced 20.2 per cent of all window glass or 7.420 million sq m;[14] but for 1936 the Statistical Yearbook of the German Democratic Republic gives 2.153 million sq m as the amount produced.[15]

No figure is available for the amount of glass consumed in the area of East Germany before the war. But we do have the total consumption of window glass in the Reich as a whole. It seems reasonable to allocate 30 per cent of total window glass production to the area of East Germany in order to calculate a base of the available glass to which postwar construction figures can be linked, since it corresponds roughly to the percentage of ordinary bricks used within the area. The result is that 7.421 million sq m of glass were probably used although production was only 2.153 million sq m.

The effect of using available rather than produced materials as the base thus had the effect of making the basis of any index constructed larger than the comparable basis used by Sanderson. The increase is substantial.

For the postwar years, however, the change from production to availability has the effect of reducing the level of the index in later years. This is so because it is known that cement in particular was exported in substantial quantities.

The question of weights was handled differently from the method employed in Sanderson's calculations. The index we constructed is based upon five series: bricks, roofing tiles, window glass (flat glass), cement, and cement products. (The inclusion of both cement and cement products is necessary since both are used in construction.) Although postwar figures for such items as roofing (tar) paper and ceramic building products are available, they could not be linked to any prewar estimate.

Instead of assigning fixed percentage weights to the series, we evaluated them individually at prewar and postwar West German prices. Since the 1936 prices used to evaluate the prewar production of wallboards differs from the 1936 price used to evaluate the postwar output of cement products, the two weighting methods do not yield the same results (as one might perhaps think). This procedure seemed necessary to arrive at a sensible result, because the nature of cement products has changed drastically as building methods have changed. Official figures show that by 1955 bricks and roofing tile had recovered to only 53.5 per cent and 60.6 per cent, respectively, of their 1936 level. Undoubtedly bricks proved a bottleneck in postwar years. With recent changes in building methods the substantial expansion of cement must have greatly eased this particular bottleneck.

Before the war, *Leichtbauplatten* undoubtedly referred to cement products used primarily for interior construction and they were probably rather expensive. The development of cement construction took place primarily in the postwar years. Most of postwar cement construction probably uses large cement blocks and prefabricated parts such as stairs, all of which are relatively inexpensive. So far as I know, the pouring of cement or construction using reinforced concrete was not customary in East Germany during the years under discussion. Hence the series "products made of concrete, etc." available for the postwar years was linked to the prewar base of *Leichtbauplatten,* but with different postwar and prewar prices. It is regrettable that the other series available for the postwar years could not be linked to a prewar base even by such a roundabout method.

ESTIMATED OUTPUT OF CONSTRUCTION

According to official statements, by 1955 the production of cement had risen to 215.4 per cent of 1936 and that of window glass to 663.3 per cent, but that of bricks and roofing tile had fallen to only 53.5 per cent and 60.6 per cent, respectively. The production of bricks is officially given as "bricks of normal size," while Gleitze's figures refer to larger bricks. Hence the figures for the number of bricks used also has to be adjusted to the East German "normal size." *

Only two other adjustments had to be made. Some of the prewar figures refer to 1938. These were prorated back to 1936 on the basis of the number of bricks used in 1936 compared with 1938. And, second, the amount of cement used for the production of cement blocks and other cement products was deducted since they are separately evaluated.†

There can be no doubt that the inputs of all major building materials declined between 1936–1938 and 1957, with two exceptions, window glass and cement products. Available bricks in 1955 were 55.7 per cent of 1936, tiles were 41.2 per cent, and cement, 79.2 per cent. As late as 1957, available bricks were only about three-fifths, and roofing tiles less than half the amount used in 1936; and even cement used was still slightly below 1936. But the value of cement products and glass in 1955 was 793 per cent and 153 per cent, respectively, of 1936 and increased substantially further to 1957. However, their total weight in the index, measured by the total value (shown in Table 142), did not change sufficiently to raise the 1955 level of construction above 1936 or 1938.

Table 142

Relative importance of value of various building materials inputs,
East Germany, 1936 and 1955 (per cent)

	1936	1955	Sanderson
	(1)	(2)	(3)
Bricks	37.4	23.9⎫	59
Tiles	11.6	5.5⎭	
Cement	43.9	31.5⎫	37
Cement products	3.6	32.7⎭	
Glass	3.6	6.4	4

Sources: Cols. 1 and 2: Calculated from values in 1936 prices. See Supplement Table C.2. Col. 3: See Fred Sanderson, in *Trends in Economic Growth: A Comparison of the Western Powers and the Soviet Bloc*, a study prepared for the Joint Committee on the Economic Report by the Legislative Reference Service of the Library of Congress, Joint Committee Print, 83d Congress, 2d Session, Washington, D.C., 1955, p. 292.

The net result is that by 1955 construction had probably not reached more than 85 per cent of its (very high) 1936 level if measured in 1936 prices, and only about 77 per cent if measured in 1950 prices. By 1957,

* See Supplement Table C.1.
† For these calculations, see Supplement Table C.2.

however, construction had passed its prewar level. From what is known about housing, the state of roads, and labor productivity, it is doubtful whether construction had reached much more than 40 per cent of the 1936 level by 1950. This compares with the level of about two-thirds of prewar construction estimated by Sanderson.[16] For 1952, Sanderson estimated a level of construction of five-sixths the 1936 level; our estimate is only a little more than one-half.

The difference in the estimates is primarily due to the fact that we made an adjustment for the availability of material and also that our method of estimating allows for changes in the importance of individual inputs. For 1936 the results obtained from both methods are similar, but for 1955 they differ substantially.

One special problem consisted in finding the gross value added of construction in 1936 in the area that is now East Germany. For 1936 the total sales value of construction for the Reich as a whole is estimated as RM 6.265 billion, of which RM 1.605 billion are allocated to the area of East Germany exclusive of East Berlin and RM 289.8 million are allocated to Berlin.[17] Allowing our customary one-third of the total Berlin value to East Berlin, we arrived at an estimated value of the construction industry in the area of East Germany in 1936 (in 1936 prices) of RM 1.701 billion, 60 per cent of which is presumed to be value added.[18] In this way the value added for 1936 is estimated at RM 1.021 billion. The 1936 value added in 1950 prices was found by adjusting its 1936 value with the ratio of the 1936 value of inputs in 1950 prices to the 1936 value of inputs in 1936 prices. The figure derived is DM 1.955 billion.

This is the only figure based on an official source. It is not entirely clear to what extent artisans were included. The Production Statistics of 1936 makes it clear that, since its purpose was to establish capacities of industries in case of war, "industry" is rather widely defined throughout; no comments are made as to what is included under construction as they are for other industries.

Our figure is somewhat smaller than the RM 1.2 billion given by Sanderson, who based his estimate on a table in the Statistical Yearbook of the Federal Republic for 1954. Since that table was dropped after 1955 and was inconsistent with a table apparently covering the same data in earlier editions, it was undesirable to use it here.

Our estimate indicates that the value added of construction was about one-seventh of the GNP of industry, roughly 13.2 per cent. In 1936 in West Germany the ratio was 13.9 per cent. Possibly this indicates some slight undervaluation.

The comparison of developments in the two parts of Germany after the war is extremely unfavorable to East Germany. In West Germany (in 1936 prices) the GNP of construction had risen by 1955 to 190.8 per cent of 1936, and in 1950 it was already 114.3 per cent of the prewar level;[19] comparable figures for East Germany are 77–85 per cent for 1955 and 42–44 per cent for 1950.

Compared with 1950, the East German showing is substantially better. Construction about doubled during the period of the First Five Year Plan while it rose by only two-thirds in West Germany. But the East German growth, of course, was from a smaller base in 1950, and the faster growth between 1950 and 1955 in East Germany still left it substantially behind the Federal Republic.

Our calculations for the development between 1950 and 1955 are extremely close to official claims. In 1950 prices, our calculations indicate an increase in output by 1955 to 184.7 per cent of 1950, and in 1936 prices to 194.0 per cent. Officially, gross output is claimed to have risen during the same period to 193.9 per cent of 1950, and net output to 185.2 per cent (see Table 143).

Table 143

Indices of construction, West and East Germany, 1936 and 1950–1958

	East Germany				
	Value added		Official gross product	Official net product	West Germany value added
Year	1936 Prices	1950 Prices			
	(1)	(2)	(3)	(4)	(5)
1936	229.4	239.8			87.5
1950	100.0	100.0	100.0	100.0	100.0
1951	121.1	122.1	142.8	138.0	113.7
1952	128.7	129.7	158.7	152.1	119.1
1953	151.1	149.9	173.5	165.2	141.5
1954	167.4	161.9	181.2	172.5	150.3
1955	194.0	184.7	193.9	185.2	167.0
1956	239.0	222.1			
1957	296.1	270.7			
1958	325.7	296.6			

Sources: Cols. 1 and 2: Calculated from Supplement Table C.2. Cols. 3 and 4: Calculated from *SJDDR*, 1955, p. 90. These series cannot be brought up to date because later editions of the *SJDDR* give figures only in current prices (e.g., see 1957, p. 159). Col. 5: Refers to net value added. Calculated from *SJBR*, 1956, p. 520.

The similarity between the changes in the calculated and the official figures for construction is not surprising. Unlike industry, in which there are many intermediate stages, in construction there is relatively little possibility of artificially blowing up the figures (without actually falsifying returns, of course). There are few intermediate products; and purchases of bricks, cement, and other materials are made directly. Moreover, it is likely that in many cases (those in which artisans work for accounts other than their own and with materials other than their own) the value of the materials used is not calculated as a part of the production of artisans.

Hence it is clear that the absolute value of construction as officially given by East German sources should be much greater than the GNP of construction, but the changes of output should not differ very much — always assuming that there is no deliberate falsification of data.

Table 143 summarizes the results of our calculations and also compares the GNP attributable to construction in East Germany with the official figures for both the Federal Republic and East Germany.

The changes of employment in construction provides some check on the reasonableness of the results reached by what we may call the "input method." In Part I of this study, year-end figures were given for the years 1950 through 1957. (See Tables 12 and 13.) The annual averages, which are available for workers and employees alone, differ only very slightly from these figures. For the prewar years an official figure for 1939 is available.

The estimated employment for 1936 was arrived at as follows. In the area of East Germany exclusive of Berlin, employment in the construction *industry* (without artisans) and in other industries not elsewhere specified was 364,249 persons.[20] It is known that of this number 59,300 persons were employed in the aircraft industry.[21] On the other hand, we must allocate one-third of the total Berlin employment to East Berlin and deduct the numbers employed there in the aircraft industry. This gives an estimate of 320,317 persons employed in the construction *industry*.*

In order to estimate the number employed as artisans in construction, it was assumed that the ratio of total employment in the main and the auxiliary building trades to employment in the main building trades only was the same in the area of postwar East Germany as in the Reich as a whole. This ratio was found to have been 1.35:1.† Using this ratio, total employment in construction may be estimated at 432,428. In this calculation, a few categories like chimney sweeps and administrative personnel were omitted. If they were to be included, estimated employment for 1936 would be raised to 475,350. Since the latter group probably are not included

---

* Calculated as follows: construction and other employment in the Soviet Zone: 364,429 plus one-third of Berlin (19,208) equals 383,637, less zonal employment in aircraft (59,300) less one-third of aircraft employment in East Berlin (3,840) equals 320,317.

† Derived as follows:

Employment in main building trades (1939)	1,522,538
Engineers and architects	32,609
Employment in auxiliary building trades	500,054
Total	2,055,201

Source: Statistical Handbook of Germany, p. 242 (2,055,201: 1,522,538 = 1.35: 1).

Table 144

Employment and output per man in construction, East Germany, 1936 and 1950–1958

Year	Employment			Index of output		Output per man indices			
	Number	Index				1936 Prices		1950 Prices	
		1936 = 100	1950 = 100	1936 Prices 1936 = 100	1950 Prices 1936 = 100	1936 = 100	1950 = 100	1936 = 100	1950 = 100
	(1)	(2)	(3)	(4)	(5)	(6)	(7)	(8)	(9)
1936	432,428	100.0	90.5	100.0	100.0	100.0	253.1	100.0	265.0
1950	391,148	90.5	100.0	43.6	41.7	48.1	100.0	46.1	100.0
1951	482,484	111.6	123.4	52.8	50.9	47.3	98.1	45.6	98.9
1952	484,885	112.1	124.0	56.1	54.1	50.0	103.8	48.3	104.6
1953	508,366	117.6	130.0	65.9	62.5	56.0	116.2	53.1	115.3
1954	477,545	110.4	122.1	73.0	67.5	66.1	137.1	61.1	132.6
1955	487,601	112.8	124.7	84.6	77.0	75.0	155.6	68.3	148.1
1956	484,911	112.1	123.9	104.2	92.6	93.0	193.3	82.6	179.2
1957	494,120[a]	114.3	126.3	129.1	112.9	112.9	234.7	98.8	214.3
1958	497,948	115.2	127.3	142.0	123.7	123.3	256.3	107.4	233.0

Sources: Col. 1: For 1936 estimate, see text; for 1950–1958, see Table 13. Col. 4: Recalculated from Table 143. Other columns derived from cols. 1 and 4.
[a] Revised figure.

in construction in East German methodology, we have used the lower figure* even though it is possible that it does not include some workers on public works projects of an emergency nature who should logically be included.

If the figures are accepted, they indicate that by the end of 1955, 12.8 per cent more persons were engaged in construction than in 1936, and 24.7 per cent more than in 1950. The greatest number employed, however, was in 1953. The figures clearly indicate a sharp rise in productivity, or, rather, output per man, from 1950 to 1955 and particularly from 1953 to 1955. If construction output is measured in 1950 prices, the increase in "productivity" was 56.8 per cent between 1950 and 1955; measured in 1936 prices, it was 66.9 per cent, which is entirely plausible. By 1957, output per man may have more than doubled that of 1950. No official productivity index for construction has been found. However, employment in construction in 1957 was 127.3 per cent of 1950, and gross production East German definition — was 219.9 per cent, which gives an increase in "productivity" by 1957 to 172.7 per cent of 1950. Unfortunately, the employment figures exclude "the employed persons in construction units of firms in other economic sectors," while these units themselves certainly and their output apparently are included in the figures for construction.[22]

But, compared with 1936, the result is substantially worse. In 1955 the "productivity" measured as output per man was only three-quarters or two-thirds of 1936, depending on whether output is measured in 1936 or 1950 prices. This result of course may be due in part to differences in hours worked, to a greater degree of seasonality (for example, because of worse weather), and undoubtedly also to a different product mix. Nevertheless, it seems entirely plausible from what is known that, in general, production per man was only about 75–85 per cent of prewar owing to shortages of materials, interrupted flows of materials, imperfect planning, and so on. This suggests that any underestimation of the true output of construction in our calculations is likely to be minor. By 1957, however, output per man seems to have reached or perhaps even surpassed the prewar level, and this too is plausible. The figures are summarized in Table 144.

HOUSING AND NONHOUSING CONSTRUCTION

The 1956 edition of the Statistical Yearbook of the German Democratic Republic for the first time gives the number of dwelling units constructed and repaired.[23] Elsewhere it is stated that housing construction in the construction industry alone (that is, not including artisans) was 17.7 per cent, 20.6 per cent, and 21.6 per cent, respectively, of the total output of the construction industry in 1953, 1954 and 1955.[24] By comparison, residential construction in the United States is about one-half of total postwar construction.

* In Part I the higher figure of 481,300 persons engaged in construction and "other" industries is higher chiefly because aircraft employment has not been deducted.

According to one source, during the entire period of the First Five Year Plan, 198,230 units were built. But if this figure is realistic, it must include a substantial number of repairs. During the years 1953–1955, fewer than 100,000 units were built. That the much higher figure of dwelling units "constructed" from 1950 on includes units made livable by relatively minor repairs has now been confirmed by the 1957 edition of the Statistical Yearbook of the German Democratic Republic. By comparison, the net addition of dwelling units in the Federal Republic (exclusive of West Berlin) during 1955 alone was 527,159 units; including West Berlin, it was 547,534 units.[25]

For 1936 a rough estimate is given in the Statistical Handbook of Germany. It indicates that about 81,750 dwelling units were added in the area of East Germany (including East Berlin), compared with 171,715 in the Federal Republic (exclusive of West Berlin) or 182,912 including West Berlin.[26]

Since prewar dwelling units were undoubtedly larger than postwar units, and present West German apartments are also somewhat larger than those now constructed in East Germany, the prewar and postwar figures are clearly not directly comparable. Nevertheless, they do suggest that before the war the net addition of dwelling units in East Germany was about 45 per cent of that in West Germany, while in 1955 it was less than 10 per cent.

Although there may be some doubt as to the exact figures, the total picture must be substantially correct. Thus the value of housing erected by the construction *industry* alone in 1955 in East Germany was DM–O 635.257 million.[27] Even if the contribution of artisans is valued at another DM–O 300 million, and 20 per cent of repairs, or roughly DM–O 75 million are allocated to housing, the total would come to roughly DM–O 1 billion. In the Federal Republic in 1955, somewhat more than DM 10 billion of housing was erected by the housing sector of construction, and another DM 1.250 billion of housing was erected by the nonhousing sector of construction.[28] Assuming that prices were not very different, the value of East German construction in 1955 accounted for between 8 and 9 per cent of that in West Germany. No imaginable price difference could get East German housing construction to a level comparable to the West German performance. The meager information is presented in Table 145.

It is possible to get some idea of the relative size of dwelling units in East and West Germany by considering some input figures. According to a newspaper report in 1956, 240 million bricks, 12 million roofing tiles, 96,000 tons of cement, and 240,000 tons of cement products are needed to produce 11,000–12,000 new dwelling units.[29] This amounts to about 20,000–21,800 bricks per unit in East Germany compared with a probable 115,000 in West Germany before the war,[30] to about 1,000–1,100 roofing

Table 145

Dwelling units made available, East and West Germany, 1936 and 1949–1958

	East Germany				
Year	Number of dwelling units	Total floor space (thousand square meters)	Floor space per dwelling unit (square meters)	West Germany,[a] number of dwelling units	East Germany as per cent of West Germany
	(1)	(2)	(3)	(4)	(5)
1936	81,750			182,912	44.7
1949	17,428				
1950	17,541	1,800	58.1	973,200	5.5
1951	18,627	3,565	58.4		
1952	17,643	2,882	60.6	436,252	4.0
1953	32,296	1,991	61.6	520,770	6.2
1954	34,740	2,237	64.4	550,835	6.3
1955	32,830	2,157	65.7	547,534	6.0
1956	32,849	2,109	64.2	568,604	5.8
1957	61,125	3,714	76.1	534,201	11.4
1958	63,466	3,750	59.1		

Sources: Col. 1: 1936: Calculated from *SHD*, p. 341; for 1949–1952, see *SJBR*, 1954, p. 547; for 1953–1957, *SJDDR*, 1957, p. 334; 1958, p. 385. For 1950–1952, *SJDDR*, 1957, p. 334, gives the following numbers: 1950 = 30,992; 1951 = 61,040; 1952 = 47,589, but states that the dwelling units were overwhelmingly those made livable by repairs. All postwar figures refer to both new and repaired dwelling units. Col. 2: *SJDDR*, 1957, p. 334; 1958, p. 385. Col. 3: Col. 2 ÷ col. 1. Col. 4: 1936: Calculated from *SHD*, p. 341; for 1949–1955, see *SJBR*, 1957, p. 258; 1958, p. 225; 1959, p. 220. Figures for 1949–1952 exclude and those for 1953–1955 include West Berlin. Refers to net additions of dwelling units.

[a] Includes West Berlin.

tiles compared with 4,575 in West Germany; to about 8–8.7 tons of cement and about 20–22 tons of cement products in East Germany, compared with about 20 tons of cement in West Germany. Although no West German figure for cement products was found, it is certain that West Germany uses a per-unit minimum of 56 cu m of wooden construction parts (which in part take the place of prefabricated concrete products) and at least 5 tons of steel against an estimated 0.8 tons in East Germany and 4,500 plaster boards against 280 in East Germany.[31]

An official East German source states that an average apartment of 40 sq m and about 2.80 m in height requires 14,000 bricks, 1,400 roofing tiles, and 8 tons of cement.[32] The figures seem low even for so small an apartment. The West German "index house" has a total ground floor area of 160 sq m and has two upper floors. It has six dwelling units, two on each floor, each with an area of 80 sq m. The inputs per square meter are therefore about the same in East and West Germany. But there is little doubt that the actual housing unit in East Germany is smaller by about one-third to one-half.

The real interest in these figures, however, lies not in a proof that

housing in East Germany lags seriously behind that in West Germany —
even a casual visit to East Berlin will confirm that fact. Rather, the information enables us to calculate the construction activity of sectors other
than that of housing. This will be done by estimating the amount of
materials needed for dwellings and deducting this figure from the total
available materials in order to calculate an index of other construction
from which inferences about investments can be made.

To estimate the inputs for housing in 1936, it was assumed that one-
sixth of the amount of material used for the index house was used for each
dwelling unit. This seems reasonable, as the following calculation indicates: in 1936 in all Germany the total investment in housing was RM
2.207 billion,[33] or 35.23 per cent of the total value of construction of RM
6.265 billion.[34] Of the total value we allocated to the area of East Germany,
including East Berlin, about RM 1.701 billion. Assuming the ratio of investment in housing to the total value of construction was the same in the
area of East Germany as in the Reich as a whole, we arrive at an estimate
of RM 599 million for housing. This yields an average value for the 81,750
dwellings allocated to the area of East Germany of RM 7,332, which in
turn is the cost of a 3-room apartment or a 3-room one-family house in a
medium-sized to small town, which in turn corresponds to the West German standard dwelling unit.[35]

Unfortunately it was impossible to obtain either prewar or postwar
input data for glass or to get comparable data for concrete products. Our
index was therefore calculated wholly on the basis of bricks, tiles, and
cement. It indicates that by 1955 East German housing construction was
less than half the 1936 level, although by 1957 it had jumped to about
four-fifths. These ratios are consistent with the number of dwelling units
provided in the various years on which the index was based.* If anything
it is slightly high.

Two procedures seemed possible from here on. To judge the development of nonhousing construction, the amounts of cement, brick, and
tiles needed for housing could be deducted from the total available, and
another index could be calculated on the basis of the remaining materials.
An alternative was to estimate by means of the housing index the investment in housing in value terms, and to deduct this from the total
amount of GNP attributable to construction or from the total sales value
of construction. The latter course seems preferable since the index of
construction (and its estimated value) is based on more information than
was available for the housing index.

As indicated above, housing in 1936 in the Reich was 35.23 per cent
of total construction. Hence we may estimate the total value of (or investment in) housing as about RM 599 million and the total value of (or

* For calculations, see Supplement Table C.3.

Table 146

Gross investment in housing and other construction, East Germany, 1936 and 1950–1958

A. *1936 Prices*

Year	Total value of construction (million RM)	Of which, housing (million RM)	Of which, all other (million RM)	Indices	
				Housing 1936 = 100	All other 1936 = 10
	(1)	(2)	(3)	(4)	(5)
1936	1,701.424	599.412	1,102.012	100.0	100.0
1950	741.821	139.962	601.858	23.4	54.6
1951	898.352	148.654	749.698	24.8	68.0
1952	954.499	139.163	815.336	23.3	73.9
1953	1,121.238	257.747	863.491	43.0	78.4
1954	1,242.039	276.928	965.111	46.2	87.6
1955	1,439.404	261.943	1,177.461	43.7	106.8
1956	1,772.884	261.943	1,458.196	43.7	137.1
1957	2,196.538	487.921	1,708.617	81.4	155.0
1958	2,416.022	506.503	1,909.519	84.5	173.3

B. *1950 Prices*

Year	Total value of construction (million DM)	Of which, housing (million DM)	Of which, all other (million DM)	Indices	
				Housing 1936 = 100	All other 1936 = 100
	(6)	(7)	(8)	(9)	(10)
1936	3,326.283	1,171.850	2,154.150	100.0	100.0
1950	1,387.060	252.065	1,134.995	21.5	52.7
1951	1,693.078	267.251	1,425.427	22.8	66.2
1952	1,799.519	250.893	1,548.626	21.4	71.9
1953	2,078.927	464.053	1,614.874	39.6	75.0
1954	2,245.241	499.208	1,746.033	42.6	81.1
1955	2,561.238	472.255	2,088.983	40.3	97.0
1956	3,080.275	472.255	2,608.020	40.3	117.2
1957	3,755.374	878.888	2,876.488	75.0	133.5
1958	4,114.612	938.852	3,175.760	80.1	147.4

Sources: Cols. 1 and 6: For 1936, see Gleitze, *Ostdeutsche Wirtschaft*, p. 185. All of East Zone area plus one-third of Berlin. See Supplement Table C.2 for details. Cols. 2 and 7: See text. For 1936, 35.23 per cent of total construction was allocated to housing. Cols. 3 and 8: Col. 1 less col. 2, and col. 6 less col. 7, respectively. Other columns: Derived from cols. 2, 3, 7, and 8.

investment in) all other construction as RM 1.102 billion.* The gross value added of construction was about 60 per cent of sales value in 1936 and may

* In the United States in 1939, residential housing was 56.3 per cent of total construction; in 1936 it was 48.5 per cent; in 1956 it was 45.9 per cent; and in 1953, 46.1 per cent. (Council of Economic Advisors, *Economic Indicators,* prepared for the Joint Committee on the Economic Report, Washington D.C., various issues, and Historical Supplement.

therefore be estimated at about RM 360 million for housing and about RM 660 million for all other construction.

Table 146 presents the calculation of the total gross value for both housing and other construction; the major interest centers not on gross value added but on the total value of construction, which corresponds to gross fixed investment. It is clear that by 1955 the gross investment in construction other than housing had about recovered to its prewar level. Measured in 1950 prices it was slightly below, but measured in 1936 prices it was slightly above the prewar level and by 1957 was 30 to 50 per cent above it. Gross fixed investment outside of housing, as well as housing construction, just about doubled between 1950 and 1955 (measured in 1936 prices). But the rapid increase in housing is due to the low base, and even by 1957 it had not yet recovered to its prewar level. The share of housing in total construction, which had been 35.23 per cent in 1936, was only 19.7 per cent in 1950 and had risen by 1955 to only 23.8 per cent, which was still substantially below prewar. The share of housing in total construction had not changed further by 1957.*

AN ESTIMATE OF GROSS INVESTMENT FOR 1955

For the years 1952 through 1955, the Statistical Yearbook of the German Democratic Republic gives fairly detailed breakdowns of the East mark values of construction by types. In 1955, total construction above ground (*Hochbau*), including housing, accounted for 44.7 per cent of the total value of construction. Since housing accounted for 21.6 per cent, this leaves 23.1 per cent for other construction above ground, such as public buildings, "cultural buildings," and agricultural structures. This category almost certainly also includes factories, although 18.6 per cent of construction in 1955 was attributed to "industry construction," which presumably means construction other than factories on and below but not above the ground. Repairs, with 12.5 per cent in 1955, were the third largest category. The other categories were relatively small: construction relating to the supply of water, 6.3 per cent; road construction, 4.6 per cent; railroad construction, 5.2 per cent; bridges, 1.6 per cent; other construction below ground level (*Tiefbau*), 4.1 per cent; and cleaning of rubble (*Enttrümmerung*), 2.3 per cent.

It is clear from these figures that the bulk of all investment went into

---

* These percentages come surprisingly close to the claims of the Statistical Yearbook of the German Democratic Republic (1955, p. 181). In 1955, 21.6 per cent of the total contribution of the building *industry* (without artisans) was attributed to housing, and another 12.5 per cent was attributed to repairs. If 21.6 per cent of the repairs are allocated to housing, corresponding to the importance of housing in total construction, another 2.7 per cent of total construction should be attributed to housing, which comes to 24.3 per cent. It has already been argued that in the case of construction the degree of double counting and its disturbing influence ought to be substantially smaller than for industry and agriculture.

industry proper. We can allocate to investment in fixed plant at least 18.6 per cent of "industrial construction." Of the 23.1 per cent construction above ground which is not housing, we have guessed that at least 15 per cent was industrial construction, the rest being schools, public buildings of various sorts, and so on. (It should be stressed, however, that this is a pure guess with no basis whatsoever in statistics. All the "other building below ground" amounting to 4.1 per cent, and the 9.8 per cent for repairs not allocated to housing should be included here. This would give an *industrial* investment in fixed plant of 47.5 per cent, or about RM 684 million in 1955 (but measured in 1936 prices).

If only housing expenditures, including the 2.7 per cent of repairs allocated to it, plus the expenditures for clearing of rubble and for road-building and public buildings are deducted, we can calculate an amount corresponding to the American usage of expenditures on fixed plant (which also includes transportation equipment but not roadbuilding). This calculation indicates that in 1955, 60.1 per cent of total construction, or DM 865.1 million (in 1936 prices), was investment outside of housing as the term is understood in the United States. The American classification differs, however, from the prewar German classification, in which roads as well as railroads, were classified as investment in transportation.

It is estimated that during the postwar period investment in fixed plant in the United States has been about 23 per cent of the total expenditures on fixed plant and investment, whereas in 1925 it was about 44 per cent.[35] This means that in the postwar period the expenditures on machinery have been about three times the expenditures on plant. West German experts estimate the West German ratio of plant to machinery expenditures *in manufacturing industry alone* as 1:4, which seems quite plausible.

If we take 47.5 per cent of all construction, that is, of DM 684 million, to be construction in manufacturing industry (including, however, mining in 1955) and apply to it the 1:4 ratio, we can estimate the expenditures on machinery at DM 2,736 million. If we take total investments in plant to include the transportation sector (excluding roads), that is RM 865.1 million, and apply to it the American ratio 1:3, we arrive at an estimate of total equipment purchased of RM 2,655.3 million.

Our previous calculations of the output of engineering construction that the total sales value of engineering construction, electrical equipment and supplies, fine mechanics and optics, and road vehicles (exclusive of bicycles but including trucks and tractors) in 1955 (in 1936 prices) was RM 3,790.766 million; when iron and steel products are added — as they must be, since they include wires, nuts and bolts, and other industrially necessary products — it was RM 4,124.199 million. This means that investment is manufacturing industry, estimated at DM 2,736 million in 1955, was 66.3 per cent of the total production of the industry groups just enumerated; and total investment may similarly be estimated at 64.4 per cent of the output of the enumerated industries in 1955. The rest presumably went to consumers and primarily to export.

Although the calculations are obviously very rough, the results are nevertheless plausible and of interest. For 1955, in 1936 prices, the GNP attributable to industry, mining, power generation, agriculture, and construction in East Germany can be estimated at DM 13.010 billion, as follows:

	(Billion DM)
Industry, mining, power	10.092
Agriculture (excluding forestry)	2.054
Construction	.864
Total	13.010
Total (including forestry)	13.186

Investment in plant and equipment was perhaps DM 3,420–3,520 billion, and in housing, DM 342 million. Thus gross fixed investment may be estimated at DM 3.762–3.862 billion, or about 29 per cent of the GNP attributable to the three major productive sectors. This figure seems reasonable. When the GNP attributable to trade and transportation are added, the gross investment ratio are substantially reduced.

The primary purpose of these calculations was to check on the reasonableness of the calculations made previously. The more detailed estimates of the way in which national income is spent will be treated in Chapter XX.

CHAPTER XIX

TRANSPORTATION AND COMMUNICATIONS, AND TRADE

TRANSPORTATION

THE publication of the Statistical Yearbook of the German Democratic Republic in 1956, 1957, and 1958 has made data available not only on the total tonnage of goods shipped, but also on the "output" of transportation in terms of ton-kilometers, total number of persons transported, and total number of person-kilometers. These data are broken down by railroad, canal and river traffic (*Binnenschiffahrt*), ocean traffic, and trucks and buses. In terms of both tons shipped and ton-kilometers "produced," the railroads are of overwhelming importance.

Data on city traffic, also very important, are separately available. One of the most important Berlin city transportation networks, the so-called S-Bahn, is part of the Reichsbahn.

In addition to the aggregate figures, data have been published on the major commodity groups shipped by the Reichsbahn and inland (East) German shipping. Truck transportation is broken down into short- and long-distance shipments (long distance defined as more than 50 km by air), and for 1955 and 1956 a breakdown by major goods shipped is also available. Figures on passenger bus traffic (excluding city buses) are available for the years 1951 through 1956, and, for 1956 and 1957 only, passenger traffic on city conveyances is given for the major cities.

These data are sufficient to calculate with fair accuracy the development of the transportation sector. The major problems to be solved were the development of an index of transportion output that could be linked to the 1936 base, the finding of proper prices and rates, the establishment of a reasonable base for 1936, and the calculation of a proper ratio of value added to total output.

The 1936 base in 1936 prices

Since our estimate of the 1936 base differs from that of other writers, it is necessary to explain each step in detail.

Railways and freight. As our basis we took the average of total shipments and receipts in 1936 for the following railway districts: Mecklenburg, excluding harbors, and the provinces of Brandenburg, Magdeburg, Merseburg, Thuringia, Saxonia, and Leipzig. To this we added one-third of the total for the Baltic harbors from Rostock to Flensburg (since the more important harbors are not in the area now East Germany) and *all* of Berlin. All of Berlin was included rather than one third, as in the previous calculations of the other economic sectors, because almost all railway terminals are in the Eastern sector, and even now rail transportation from West Berlin to the Federal Republic has to start in East Berlin. (In fact, interzonal traffic earns foreign exchange for East Germany.) This prewar average amounts to 96.714 million tons.*

In 1936 goods were shipped an average distance of 153.6 km,[1] which gives an estimated output of 15.116 billion ton-km. This estimate is consistent with the figures given in the Statistical Yearbook of the Federal Republic[2] but not with Dr. Seidel's much higher estimates of 131.204 million tons and 22.052 billion ton-km.[3] Obviously, Dr. Seidel included in his estimate for the Soviet Zone not only Berlin but also the areas east of the Oder-Neisse. The total number of ton-kilometers he allocated to the railroads of the Federal Republic and East Germany (whose railroads still use the name of Reichsbahn) equals the total ton-kilometer output of the Reichsbahn in all Germany in 1936.

Before the war the German railroads shipped a substantial part of their freight at a special low tariff. The goods shipped at this exceptional tariff included coal and coke, cement, ores, potatoes, fertilizers, and grains. These heavy goods made up 47.285 million tons or 48.9 per cent of the total tonnage shipped.† We assume that the total ton-kilometers were distributed among heavy and light goods in East Germany in the same proportion as in the Reich. This means 7.392 billion ton-km was heavy freight paid for at low rates, and 7.724 billion ton-km was paid for at higher rates.

The low rate can be calculated at 2.693 pf per ton for 1936 and the high rate at 4.924 pf per ton.[4] Using our 1936 figures for heavy and light freight, we estimate the total receipts from low rate shipments at RM 183.581 million, and from higher-rate shipments at RM 408.643 million, giving an estimated gross value (that is, receipts) for the railway freight in 1936 prices for 1936 at RM 592.224 million.

Passenger traffic. In 1936 the total output for all German railways was 36.887 billion passenger-kilometers (without the important Berlin and Hamburg city traffic), with a revenue of RM 948.6 million.[5] The average revenue per passenger-kilometer can thus be calculated at 2.57 pf. It may be estimated that 25 per cent of the passenger-kilometers were in East Germany. This corresponds to the percentage of persons traveling in East

---

* See calculations in Supplement Table D.1.
† See Supplement Tables D.2 and D.3.

Germany in the total number of railway travelers in the Reich, or the percentage of railway passenger cars or freight cars.[6] The estimate amounts to 9.221 billion passenger-kilometers, giving a revenue of RM 236.980 million.

In addition, the output of the Berlin S-Bahn in 1936 was 5.819 billion passenger-kilometers, with an average revenue of 1.4 pf per passenger-kilometer,[7] adding another RM 81.466 million to receipts. Total railway receipts from passenger traffic can thus be estimated at RM 318.446 million for 1936.

Shipping. In 1936 shipments on East German inland waterways amounted to 11.169 million tons.[8] This tonnage is 11.8 per cent of railway goods shipments, which is a reasonable relationship, as the following quotation indicates: [9]

In *Saxony* and *Central Germany, Brandenburg,* and *Silesia,* the *Elbe and Oder Regions* as well as the waterways of the *Mark Brandenburg,* Bavaria right of the Rhine on the waterways of the Main river and the Danube, the railroads carry the overwhelming bulk of traffic. In *Brandenburg* and Silesia, inland waterways carried as much as 16 per cent of the respective rail freight traffic; in *Saxony* and *Central Germany* and in Bavaria right of the Rhine, only 6 per cent.*

The average distance of freight shipments on inland waterways was 225 kilometers,† which allows an estimated output of 2.513 billion ton-kilometers.[10]

We were unable to locate a tariff schedule for barges, but we know that the bulk of waterways shipments must have been heavy goods, for which the low railway tariff was probably charged. We therefore assume an average rate of 3 pf per ton-kilometer, which means that roughly 90 per cent or slightly less of the shipments were at the low railway rates, and 10 per cent were at the higher rates. Given this average rate of 3 pf per ton-kilometer, we estimate the gross revenue from freight earned on inland waterways at RM 75.390 million.

Since East Germany has no major seaports, ocean shipping cannot be of major importance. In 1936 the area received ocean shipments of only 1.091 million tons and shipped out 1.250 million tons. We took as the base for our calculations the average of 1.175 million tons.[11] For German ocean shipping as a whole, the average distance shipped was 4,810 km for overseas shipments and 560 km for coastwise shipments.[12] Neither figure is acceptable for the calculation of a base. The ports of the Baltic coast that were important were Stettin, now in Poland; Königsberg, now Russian and

---

* See Supplement Table D.1. The italicized names refer to areas presently within the area of East Germany. Before the war the term "Central Germany" — now used in West Germany to designate East Germany — referred to the area around Magdeburg, specifically in the present context to the counties in the Regierungsbezirke Magdeburg-Anhalt and Merseburg-Erfurt.

† In spite of the greatly changed geographic structure, even in 1956 the average distance of shipments on inland waterways was 195 kilometers.

renamed Kaliningrad; and Lübeck, now in West Germany. Wismar, Warnemünde, Stralsund, and Sassnitz (Rügen) were all minor ports. Swedish ores went to the area of West Germany or to Stettin and up the Oder River. Most shipments in the area of the Soviet Zone must have been coastwise in the Baltic only, with a small amount going across to Sweden. An average distance of 325 kilometers seems all that is justified.*

On this basis, the output of ocean shipping was 382 million ton-km. We assumed the same rate per ton-mile shipped for ocean traffic as for inland waterways, 3 pf per ton-km, although a lower rate is possible, depending on the nature of the shipment. The bulk shipments to the area of East Germany did not come by ocean to any ocean ports of East Germany, but, rather, by rail or by barge up the Elbe and Havel (from Hamburg) or the Oder (from Stettin). The total revenue of ocean shipments was at most RM 11.460 million, or 1.9 per cent of rail traffic receipts.

Trucking. The contribution of trucking must be largely guessed at for 1936, but fortunately any error will be of minor importance because trucking did not amount to much at the time. Long-distance trucking (that is, for distances of more than 50 kilometers, roughly 30 miles) probably accounted for 894 million ton-km in 1936. The area of East Germany exclusive of Berlin received 3.641 million tons and shipped 3.800 million tons; Berlin received 1.535 million tons and shipped 0.615 million tons.[13] Allocating one-third of Berlin to East Germany and averaging, we estimate the tonnage at 4.005 million tons; the average distance can be calculated at 219.2 km.[14]

No figures could be found for local trucking. In 1936 it was undoubtedly more important than long-distance trucking. Even in the postwar period in East Germany the ton-mile output of local trucking has been three to four times the ton-mile output of long-distance trucking. We arbitrarily assumed an output of 1.5 billion ton-km, which is almost certainly too small.

The rates charged for trucking are equally uncertain. No official figure could be found, but we know that truck rates were strictly controlled so as to offer little competition to the railways. In addition, bulk shipments were not made by trucks. Rates could never go below railway rates legally and on local hauls they were higher. We assumed a rate of 6 pf per ton-kilometer for trucking, which seems to be reasonable and perhaps slightly low. On this basis, total trucking revenue can be estimated at RM 143.640 million.

Streetcars and buses. In 1936 the streetcar lines of the Soviet Zone (that is, without East Berlin) transported 370 million people and bus

---

* It should be pointed out that taking a higher figure would raise the estimate for the 1936 performance of ocean shipping in the area of East Germany considerably and thus lower the postwar development compared with the prewar base. Any error introduced must be favorable to East Germany.

lines transported another 88 million. In all of Berlin 789 million passengers were transported on streetcars and 170 million people in buses.[15] Allocating one-third of Berlin to the Eastern sector, we can estimate the number of East Berlin passengers at 320 million people and the total number of persons carried on streetcars and buses at 778 million.* Although no data were found, the average distance traveled was assumed to be 6 km† (a reasonable distance, which is probably slightly low for Berlin), giving 4.668 billion passenger-kilometers, with an average revenue of about 3 pf per passenger-kilometer.[16] The estimated revenue is therefore RM 140.040 million.

Summary: The 1936 base in 1936 prices. Thus the total gross revenue from freight shipments can be estimated at RM 822.714 million and from passenger traffic (including municipal railways, subways, streetcars, and buses) at RM 458.486 billion, a total of RM 1,281.200 million.

Table 147

Ton-kilometers, passenger-kilometers, and revenues, all transportation media, East Germany, 1936, in 1936 prices

	Freight		Passengers	
	Ton-kilometers (billions)	Revenue (million RM)	Passenger-kilometers (billions)	Revenue (million RM)
	(1)	(2)	(3)	(4)
Railways (without Berlin)	15.116	592.224	9.221	236.980
Inland waterways	2.513	75.390		
Trucks	2.394	143.640		
Ocean shipping	0.382	11.460		
Berlin railways			5.819	81.466
Streetcars and buses			4.668	140.040
Total	20.405	822.714	19.708	458.486

Sources: For derivation of figures, see text and Supplement Tables D.1–D.8.

This figure needs to be adjusted once more, however. In 1936 the Reichsbahn earned a total of RM 3.985 billion, of which traffic revenues alone were RM 3.706 billion. Thus 5.79 per cent was earned through such other services as storage of goods. We adjusted the calculated value by the factor 1.0579, and therefore assumed that other transportation services

* While the S-Bahn and U-Bahn now run between East and West Berlin, and the S-Bahn even runs outside of East Berlin into the Zone proper, no bus or streetcar crosses from West to East Berlin and vice versa.

† This figure was suggested by my memory. In the 1957 edition of the Statistical Yearbook of the German Democratic Republic, published in the summer of 1958, it is stated (p. 476) that 1.443 billion passengers rode trolleys for 214.172 million km, which gives about 6.7 km per passenger as an average.

on the average had as much extra earnings as the railroads. For shipping, the earnings were probably relatively higher; for municipal streetcars and others they were undoubtedly much lower.

The final base adopted for 1936 for the transportation sector is RM 1,355.481 million. The data are summarized in Table 147.

Evaluation of the 1936 base in 1950 prices. The prices and rates used to evaluate the 1936 ton-kilometers and passenger-kilometers in 1950 prices are all taken from West German sources. (These are specified in the footnotes to the Supplement Tables.) Railroad rates for heavy freight increased more than rates for light freight probably in connection with the steel and coal community, which induced the Federal Republic to give up the special rates for coal discriminating in favor of shipments to German destinations. After the adjustment for nontransportation services, the total revenue of the transportation sector is estimated at RM 1,898.183 million. Table 148 summarizes the results of our calculations.*

Table 148

Gross receipts of the transport sector, East Germany,
1936, in 1950 prices (million DM)

	Freight	Passengers
	(1)	(2)
Railways (without Berlin)	769.521	355.931
Inland waterways	117.608	
Trucks	201.096	
Ocean shipping	17.878	
Berlin railroads		122.199
Streetcars and buses		210.060
Total	1,106.103	688.190

Sources: For derivation, see Supplement Tables D.1–D.8.

Estimating procedure

Because of the changed industrial structure of East Germany, with its emphasis on mining and heavy industries, shipments of heavy goods have become a much larger and more important part of total freight shipped. Data available for railroad shipments (shown in Table 149) indicate that the tonnage of heavy goods rose from 45.1 per cent in 1936 to 56.1 per cent in 1950 and to 59.6 per cent in 1956.

At the same time, total railway shipments were larger than total domestic shipments because of receipts from abroad. We have import figures in tons for some of the materials that undoubtedly paid lower rates. We do not know what quantity was shipped by rail and what by barge. On

* Details are given in the Supplement Tables D.1–D.8.

Table 149

Shipments of "heavy" goods on East German railroads, 1936 and 1950–1958[a] (million tons)

	1936	1950	1951	1952	1953	1954	1955	1956	1957	1958
Coal and coke	30.670	50.677	57.916	61.666	71.994	75.777	85.648	87.751	92.521	92.662
Cement	1.498	...	1.452	1.765	2.137	2.421	2.839	3.072	3.025	2.863
Potatoes	1.361	...	1.484	1.511	1.703	1.533	1.511	1.347	1.257	1.183
Sugar beets	2.580	2.448	2.987	2.976	3.228	3.311	3.161	2.561	3.441	3.896
Ores	0.378	...	0.714	1.244	2.255	2.251	2.144	1.947	1.822	1.894
Fertilizers	6.221	5.734	6.338	6.349	6.680	7.138	7.934	8.277	8.295	8.679
Grains, legumes, and oilseeds	0.943	...	1.793	2.001	2.023	1.900	1.781	1.771	1.486	1.301
Total	43.651	—	72.684	77.512	90.020	94.331	105.018	106.726	111.847	112.478

Sources: for 1936, see Supplement Table D.2; for postwar years, *SJDDR*, 1956, p. 254; 1957, pp. 462, 463; 1958 pp. 516–517.

[a] For postwar years, normal gauge only, without shipments from abroad.

the whole, for most years, imports of those heavy goods for which we can account were about 80 per cent of total imports carried by rail (see Table 150). We also have to account for the few narrow-gauge railroads. It is reasonable to assume that most of them are connected with factories and lignite or iron ore mines, and that at least 80 per cent of im-

Table 150

Known imports of "heavy" goods into East Germany, 1950–1958 (million tons)

	1950	1951	1952	1953	1954	1955	1956	1957	1958
Lignite	3.8	3.7	4.0	4.2	4.4	4.1	4.6	4.2	5.2
Soft coal	3.5	3.5	3.9	6.0	6.5	6.3	5.6	5.8	7.4
Soft coal coke	1.7	1.6	1.9	2.1	2.6	2.6	2.3	2.7	2.5
Subtotal	9.0	8.8	9.8	12.3	13.5	13.0	12.5	12.7	15.1
Iron ore	...[a]	0.10	0.40	0.60	0.80	1.20	1.80[b]	2.10[b]	
Pyrites	0.10	0.20	0.20	0.30	0.20	0.20	0.20[b]	0.40[b]	
Wheat	0.25	0.36	0.33	0.35	0.33	0.56	0.61	1.08	1.29
Rye	0.00	0.00	0.05	0.07	0.61	0.19	0.48	0.34	0.21
Oats	0.14	0.00	0.07	0.07	0.03	0.04	0.09	0.15	0.13
Barley	0.16	0.36	0.30	0.44	0.16	0.44	0.37	0.39	0.09
Corn	...[a]	0.04	0.05	0.09	0.07	0.13	0.15	0.06	0.14
Rice	...[a]	...[a]	0.02	0.02	0.03	0.08	0.05	0.06	0.06
Oilseeds	...[a]	0.10	0.10	0.16	0.20	0.27	0.27	0.32	0.31

Sources: *SJDDR*, 1956, pp. 523–524; 1957, pp. 519–520; 1958, p. 576.

[a] Negligible.

[b] Figures given only in tons of iron or sulfur content. Tonnage estimated.

ports and of narrow-gauge railroad freight traffic is made up of heavy goods.

The percentages of heavy and light goods shipped thus found were then applied to the ton-kilometers of rail shipments given and evaluated with the 1936 rates for the two types of shipment. Because of the increased importance of heavy shipments in the total, the value of rail freight shipments had increased by 53.2 per cent between 1936 and 1955 and by 65.9 per cent between 1936 and 1956 (all in 1936 prices), compared to an increase in ton-kilometers of 66.9 per cent and 60.8 per cent, respectively.* For the other carriers and for passenger transportation no special adjustment was needed. They have all been evaluated both in terms of the 1936 prices discussed above and in terms of 1950 prices, the sources of which are given in the footnotes to the tables.†

The total gross receipts of all transportation services performed were added to arrive at the total sales value of the transportation sector. The only additional adjustment was to allow in 1936 an additional 5.79 per cent for earnings from nontransportation services, such as storage as already indicated. For the postwar period this figure was reduced to 4 per cent. The nontransportation services were certainly smaller after the war, for inventories were kept to an absolute minimum, turn-around time for cars was reduced, and some efficiencies (and shortages) effected (if this may be said of a shortage). The 4 per cent adjustment is, if anything, slightly high.

From the sales value, that is the gross receipts, the value added was calculated by the following method. In 1936 the Reichsbahn earned RM 3,984.788 million. Wages and other payments to persons (including substantial pension payments) amounted to RM 2,356.335 billion. The surplus was 471.818 million. Both are clearly part of the GNP attributable to the transport sector. Material expenses (*sächliche Ausgaben*) for coal, water, gas, electricity, and other inputs amounted to RM 1,149.596 million.[17] Thus the value added in Germany as a whole was $3.985 - 1.150/3.985 = 2.835/3.985 = 71.14$ per cent. This figure was applied to the sales value for 1936.

In the postwar period, value added was almost certainly a smaller fraction of gross receipts. For the Federal Republic we can calculate roughly the value added as a percentage of the total value of production for transportation and communications combined, as in Table 151. (Communications cannot be separated from transportation.)

To be sure, the West German figures are in current prices and include communications. But in communications, payments to other sectors are certainly smaller than for railways while wage payments are relatively higher. On the other hand, the railroad system in the Federal Republic has been modernized, and diesel engines have been introduced on a large scale, whereas in East Germany the locomotive stock is old, and lignite briquets have been substituted for soft coal. Consequently, the inputs must have gone up more than proportionately. It is possible, however, that some other efficiencies have been introduced which offset the increased and

---

* Details are given in Supplement Tables D.3 and D.4.
† See Supplement Tables D.5 — D.8.

Table 151

Production value and value added, transport and communications,
West Germany, 1950–1958, in current prices (million DM)

Year	Total value	Payments to other sectors	Value added	Value added as per cent of total value
	(1)	(2)	(3)	(4)
1950	10,470	3,280	7,190	68.7
1951	12,773	4,458	8,315	65.1
1952	14,528	5,170	9,358	64.4
1953	14,846	5,148	9,698	65.3
1954	15,719	5,270	10,449	66.5
1955	19,250	6,865	12,385	64.3
1956	21,356	7,656	13,700	64.2
1958	23,347	8,522	14,825	63.5

Source: *SJBR*, 1959, p. 483.

less efficient use of lignite (see Table 152). Furthermore, the inland shipping sector, although relatively small, probably has a higher value added ratio, while trucking probably has a lower one. Altogether, it seems plausible to allow for the postwar period a value added ratio of only 70 per cent, which is still higher than the ratio of the Federal Republic for any year in the period 1950–1955 (see Table 153). To apply the even higher prewar ratio for the postwar years would certainly substantially overestimate the value added.* The results thus arrived at are given in Table 154 and discussed below.

COMMUNICATIONS

In Germany even before the war, mail, telephone, telegraph, and radio were governmentally controlled by the post office.

A substantial amount of information is available on the numbers of radios and television sets licensed,[18] the numbers of post offices, telephones, letters sent, amounts of postal savings, numbers of newspapers sent, and so forth. This is interesting information but it is clearly not suitable for calculating an index of GNP attributable to communications on this sort of basis.

Instead, the output of the communications sector is presumed to have varied with the number of employees. The postal service in the fiscal year 1935–1936 had 371,688 employees, and in fiscal 1936–1937, it had 381,866 employees, with an average employment for the calendar year 1936 of 376,777. Of these we can allocate 24.1 per cent to the area that became East Germany, corresponding to its share in the total German population in 1936. This gives an estimated 90,800 East German postal employees in 1936. By 1956 this number had risen to 125,517.

* For an alternative assumption, see Table 157.

Table 152

Volume of transport services, East Germany, 1936 and 1950–1958

A. *Freight traffic*

Railways

Year	Total goods transported (million tons)	Goods transported at low tariff, per cent	Goods transported at high tariff, per cent	Total ton-km (billions)
	(1)	(2)	(3)	(4)
1936	96.714	48.9	51.1	15.116
1950	128.504	56.1	43.9	15.064
1951	153.214	54.4	45.6	17.291
1952	158.287	56.6	43.4	19.077
1953	182.257	57.5	42.5	22.112
1954	191.437	57.8	42.2	23.182
1955	207.514	59.5	40.5	25.222
1956	210.207	59.6	40.4	27.334
1957	220.335	60.1	39.9	28.635
1958	227.199	59.1	40.9	30.101

Shipping and trucking

Year	Goods transported by inland shipping (billion ton-km)	Goods transported by ocean shipping (billion ton-km)	Goods transported by trucking (billion ton-km)
	(5)	(6)	(7)
1936	2.513	0.382	2.394
1950	1.579	. . . [a]	1.945
1951	1.797	. . . [a]	2.201
1952	1.707	. . . [a]	2.404
1953	1.738	0.034	2.569
1954	1.742	0.046	2.945
1955	2.168	0.480	3.194
1956	2.268	0.412	3.492
1957	2.498	0.833	3.916
1958	2.398	3.758	4.147

B. *Passenger traffic (billion passenger-kilometers)*

Year	Railway (Reichsbahn) without city railway, Berlin	City railway, Berlin	Streetcars and buses
	(8)	(9)	(10)
1936	9.221	5.819	4.668
1950	12.768	5.808	3.814
1951	13.332	6.195	4.468
1952	14.715	6.086	4.972
1953	15.021	5.508	4.850
1954	16.522	6.110	5.655
1955	16.844	6.061	6.750
1956	16.458	6.102	7.665
1957	16.567	6.217	10.111
1958	15.372	6.027	n.a.

Sources: For 1936 estimates, see text; for postwar years, *SJDDR*, 1957, pp. 461, 465, and 478; 1958, pp. 518–519.

[a] Not available, but probably negligible.

Table 153

Gross receipts and value added, transport sector, East Germany,
1936 and 1950–1958[a] (million RM/DM)

	Freight traffic		Passenger traffic		Total transport	
	Railway, ships, trucks, gross receipts		Total railway, buses, streetcars, gross receipts		Passenger and freight, gross receipts	
Year	1936 Prices	1950 Prices	1936 Prices	1950 Prices	1936 Prices	1950 Prices
	(1)	(2)	(3)	(4)	(5)	(6)
1936	809.886	1,056.804	458.486	688.190	1,268.372	1,744.994
1950	717.279	977.350	523.870	786.443	1,241.149	1,763.793
1951	827.531	1,123.224	563.402	845.770	1,390.933	1,968.994
1952	893.920	1,217.518	612.540	919.545	1,506.460	2,137.063
1953	1,012.446	1,380.058	608.652	913.729	1,621.098	2,293.787
1954	1,072.890	1,463.590	679.805	1,020.534	1,752.695	2,484.124
1955	1,178.206	1,617.479	720.245	1,081.209	1,898.451	2,698.688
1956	1,272.394	1,746.167	738.349	1,108.346	2,010.743	2,854.513
1957	1,360.430	1,872.523	816.140	1,225.038	2,176.570	3,097.561
1958	1,518.179	2,104.728	808.606	1,208.488	2,319.785	3,313.216

	Total transport adjusted for other services[b]		Value added of transportation[c]	
Year	1936 Prices	1950 Prices	1936 Prices	1950 Prices
	(7)	(8)	(9)	(10)
1936	1,341.811	1,846.029	954.564	1,313.265
1950	1,290.795	1,834.345	903.557	1,284.042
1951	1,446.570	2,047.754	1,012.599	1,433.428
1952	1,566.718	2,222.545	1,096.703	1,555.782
1953	1,685.942	2,385.538	1,180.159	1,669.877
1954	1,822.803	2,583.489	1,275.962	1,808.442
1955	1,974.389	2,806.635	1,382.072	1,964.645
1956	2,091.172	2,968.693	1,463.820	2,078.085
1957	2,263.633	3,221.463	1,584.533	2,255.024
1958	2,412.576	3,445.745	1,688.803	2,412.022

[a] For detailed calculations, see Supplement Tables D.3–D.8.
[b] In 1936 the Reichsbahn in all Germany earned RM 3.985 billion, of which RM 3.706 billion were earned through passenger and goods transport. Thus 5.79 per cent was earned through other services. For later years this percentage is likely to be lower; we estimate 4 per cent. For the 1936 value, see *SJR, 1938*, p. 211.
[c] 70 per cent of sales value. For derivation, see text.

On the basis of the figures given in Table 154, the average total value added for the calendar year 1936 was estimated at RM 1,735.4 million. In 1936 the postal services employed 376,777 persons in all Germany, which gives a value added per employee of RM 4,605.90.

The value added for the postwar years in 1936 prices is assumed to vary in proportion to the number of employees. This is the best assumption that could be made. It implies that the average productivity of the postal services has not changed, which is not likely; but no reasonable correction suggested itself. Any error introduced, however, must be relatively minor.

To estimate the 1936 value added in 1950 prices was even more difficult. Since the usual procedure — to evaluate the 1936 output in 1950 prices —

Table 154

Value added per employee in the German postal services, prewar (million RM)

	1935–1936	1936–1937
Wage and salary payments (*persönliche Kosten*)	1,118.5	1,144.4
Capital and interest payments	32.0	35.0
Depreciation	184.9	202.3
Reserves (*Zuweisungen zu Vermögen*)	43.5	71.6
Payments to the Reich	104.3	148.8
	1,671.4	1,799.4

Source: *SJR*, 1937, p. 197.

was not feasible, we calculated the actual 1950 value added per postal employee in the Federal Republic and moved the total value added in 1950 prices parallel to this value. This procedure, which implies that the 1950 technical relations also held in 1936, is less satisfactory than the one followed in the calculations for the other sectors. Table 155 gives the

Table 155

Value added, postal services, West Germany,
1950, in 1950 prices[a] (million DM)

Payments to persons	1,324.8
Payments to the Federal Republic	143.3
Profits	234.6
	1,702.7

Source: *SJBR*, 1954, p. 361.
   [a] Omitted were payments for running the office (*Betriebsführung*), maintenance, and renovation, which were assumed to be payments to other sectors.

relevant calculations. With 294,353 employees, the 1950 value added per employee can be estimated at DM 5,784.6.

VALUE ADDED OF THE TRANSPORTATION AND COMMUNICATIONS SECTORS

Whether measured in constant 1936 or 1950 prices, by 1950 the value added of transportation in East Germany had almost recovered to the 1936 level, while the value added of the communications sector had slightly surpassed that level. Altogether, the 1950 level of transportation and communications was 98–100 per cent of the prewar level. By 1955 the level reached was 141.9 per cent (at 1936 prices) or 145.5 per cent (at 1950 prices); and by 1956 there was a further increase to 148.7 per cent (1936 prices) and 152.5 per cent of 1936 (1950 prices). Since 1950 the calculated development has been slightly faster (see Table 156).

Table 156

Value added and official gross and net product, transportation and communications, East Germany, 1936 and 1950–1958; net national product transportation sector, West Germany, 1936 and 1950–1955; and gross domestic product, transport and communications, West Germany, 1936 and 1950–1958

A. *Value added, East Germany, and net national product, West Germany, in 1936 prices*

	East Germany,					
	Transportation (adjusted)			Postal services and communications		
		Indices			Indices	
Year	Million RM	1936 = 100	1950 = 100	Million RM	1936 = 100	1950 = 100
	(1)	(2)	(3)	(4)	(5)	(6)
1936	954.564	100.0	105.6	418.216	100.0	94.9
1950	903.557	94.7	100.0	440.660	105.4	100.0
1951	1,012.599	106.1	112.0	466.808	111.6	105.9
1952	1,096.703	114.9	121.3	515.529	123.3	117.0
1953	1,180.159	123.6	130.5	506.976	121.2	115.0
1954	1,275.962	133.7	141.2	560.759	134.1	127.2
1955	1,382.072	144.8	152.9	565.305	135.2	128.3
1956	1,463.820	153.3	161.9	578.118	138.2	131.1
1957	1,584.533	166.0	175.3	596.109	142.5	135.2
1958	1,688.803	176.9	186.8	600.098	143.5	136.1

	East Germany, total of transport, postal services and communications			West Germany, net national product		
		Indices			Indices	
Year	Million RM	1936 = 100	1950 = 100	Million RM	1936 = 100	1950 = 100
	(7)	(8)	(9)	(10)	(11)	(12)
1936	1,372.780	100.0	102.1	3,256	100.0	75.6
1950	1,344.217	97.9	100.0	4,307	132.3	100.0
1951	1,479.407	107.8	110.1	4,524	138.9	105.0
1952	1,612.232	117.4	119.9	4,921	151.1	114.2
1953	1,687.135	122.9	125.5	5,058	155.3	117.4
1954	1,836.721	133.8	136.7	5,348	164.3	124.2
1955	1,947.377	141.9	144.9	6,151	188.9	142.8
1956	2,041.938	148.7	151.9			
1957	2,180.642	158.8	162.2			
1958	2,288.903	166.7	170.3			

Table 156 (Continued)

B. *Value added, East Germany, and gross domestic product, West Germany, 1950 prices*

East Germany

	Transportation (adjusted)			Postal services and communications		
		Indices			Indices	
Year	Million DM	1936 = 100	1950 = 100	Million DM	1936 = 100	1950 = 100
	(13)	(14)	(15)	(16)	(17)	(18)
1936	1,313.265	100.0	102.2	525.242	100.0	94.9
1950	1,284.042	97.8	100.0	553.430	105.4	100.0
1951	1,433.428	109.1	111.6	586.269	111.6	105.9
1952	1,555.782	118.5	121.2	647.459	123.3	117.0
1953	1,669.877	127.2	130.1	636.717	121.2	115.0
1954	1,808.442	137.7	140.8	704.263	134.1	127.2
1955	1,964.645	149.6	153.0	709.973	135.2	128.3
1956	2,078.085	158.2	161.8	726.066	138.2	131.3
1957	2,255.024	171.7	175.6	748.660	142.5	135.2
1958	2,412.022	183.7	187.8	753.670	143.5	136.1

	East Germany, total of transportation, postal services and communications			West Germany, gross domestic product, transportation, and communications		
		Indices			Indices	
Year	Million DM	1936 = 100	1950 = 100	Million DM	1936 = 100	1950 = 100
	(19)	(20)	(21)	(22)	(23)	(24)
1936	1,838.507	100.0	100.1	5,419	100.0	75.6
1950	1,837.472	99.9	100.0	7,168	132.3	100.0
1951	2,019.697	109.9	110.0	7,863	145.1	109.7
1952	2,203.241	119.8	119.9	8,049	148.5	112.2
1953	2,306.594	125.5	125.6	8,295	153.1	115.7
1954	2,512.705	136.7	136.8	8,858	163.5	123.6
1955	2,674.618	145.5	145.6	9,998	184.5	139.5
1956	2,804.151	152.5	152.7	10,828	199.8	151.0
1957	3,003.684	163.4	163.6	11,295	208.4	157.5
1958	3,165.692	172.2	172.4	11,185	206.4	156.0

Table 156 (Continued)

C. *Official gross and net product, East Germany, in 1950 East German prices*

Year	Gross product		Net product	
	Million DM-O	Index 1950 = 100	Million DM-O	Index 1950 = 100
	(25)	(26)	(27)	(28)
1936				
1950	1,847	100.0	1,203	100.0
1951	2,148	116.3	1,421	118.1
1952	2,425	131.3	1,587	131.9
1953	2,706	146.5	1,852	153.9
1954	2,923	153.3	1,788	148.6
1955	3,123	169.1	1,829	152.0
1956	3,148	170.4	1,834	152.5
1957	3,305	178.9	1,926	160.1
1958	n.a.	n.a.	n.a.	n.a.

Sources: Cols. 1 and 13: Table 153. Cols. 2, 3, 5, 6, 8, 9, 14, 15, 17, 18, 20, and 21: Calculated from appropriate columns. Cols. 4 and 16: For 1936 value added, see Tables 154 and 155. Other years calculated by assuming the value added of postal services and communications moved as employment. (See Table 13.) Col. 7: Col. 1 + col. 4. Col. 10: *SJBR*, 1956, p. 520. Figures after 1955 not available. The figures refer to net national product at factor cost and are therefore comparable with the calculated but not with the official East German figures, which are in market prices, including indirect taxes. Cols. 11 and 12: Calculated from col. 10. Col. 19: Col. 13 + col. 16. Cols. 22, 23, 24: Calculated from West German figures in 1954 prices, *SJBR*, 1958, p. 179. For method of adjustment to 1950 prices and for estimate of the 1936 value, see Table 163, note[a]. Cols. 25 and 27: For 1950-1955, see *SJDDR*, 1955, p. 90. This series has been discontinued in later editions. The 1956 edition, pp. 143 f. gives new figures in 1955 prices as follows (million DM-O):

	1955	1956	1956 as per cent of 1955
Gross product	5,086	5,125	100.8
Net product	3,158	3,167	100.3

The 1956 figures have been calculated with these percentages. The 1957 edition, pp. 154 and 156, gives figures for 1950-1957 in current prices as follows (million DM-O):

	1956	1957	1957 as per cent of 1956
Gross product	5,125	5,381	105.0
Net product	3,167	3,326	105.0

The 1957 figures in these columns have been calculated with these percentages. It will be noticed that the 1956 figures are the same in 1955 and 1956 prices, which may indicate an inaccurate description of the tables in *ibid.*, pp. 153 ff. The 1957 figures are preliminary. Cols. 26 and 28: Calculated from cols. 25 and 27.

This development is very good; it probably overestimates the extent of expansion. If the postwar ratio of value added to gross receipts had been reduced in the same proportion as in the Federal Republic, the development would have been substantially less favorable, as Table 157 indicates.

A comparison with official East German claims indicates that the ratio of value added to gross receipts is likely to have fallen more than the 70 per cent assumed in Table 156 and discussed above. But it is unlikely to have moved as the West German figure did. The East German railroads are known to use relatively more labor, although this does not prove that the ratio of value added to gross receipts is high, since they also use poorer fuel. However, fuel does not represent a very high percentage of cost — only about 10 per cent in West Germany before the war.

Official East German data claim an increase of 52 per cent in the

Table 157

Value added, East German transport sector, using West German ratios of value added to gross receipts, and using a constant 70 per cent ratio, 1936 and 1950–1957, in 1936 prices

Year	East German value added, assumed at 70 per cent of gross receipts (million RM)	West German ratios of value added to gross receipts	East German value added, assumed at ratios to gross receipts given in col. 2 (million RM)	Index of East German value added 1936 = 100	1950 = 100
	(1)	(2)	(3)	(4)	(5)
1936	954.564		954.564	100.0	107.6
1950	903.557	68.7	886.776	92.9	100.0
1951	1,012.599	65.7	950.396	99.6	107.2
1952	1,096.703	64.4	1,008.966	105.7	113.8
1953	1,180.159	65.3	1,100.920	115.3	124.1
1954	1,275.962	66.5	1,212.164	127.0	136.7
1955	1,382.072	64.3	1,269.532	133.0	143.1
1956	1,463.820	. . .	1,344.624[a]	140.9	151.7
1957	1,584.533	. . .	1,455.516[a]	152.5	164.2

Sources: Col. 1: See Table 156. Col. 2: See Table 151. Col. 3: Gross receipts (Table 153) × col. 3. Cols. 4 and 5: Derived from col. 3.
   [a] Ratio of 64.3 per cent assumed as in 1955.

transportation and communication sector between 1950 and 1955, and 52.5 per cent between 1950 and 1956. Our own calculations (using the 70 per cent ratio of value added to gross receipts) are below the East German figures until 1955 but agree with them in 1956. Moreover, the East German figures indicate that the net product of the transportation and communications sector declined from a high point in 1953 and had not yet quite recovered to that level in 1956. Our own calculations (using the 70 per cent ratio) do not indicate such a fluctuation. An index calculated for the combined transportation and communications sector with varying ratios of value added to gross receipts would show an increase by 1956 to only 144.9 per cent of 1950.

The result is consistent with East German claims. Since there are too many unknowns in the East German calculations and in the actual workings of the transportation sector, we did not feel justified in making further adjustments to bring the results of our calculations any closer to East German figures.

Our result is, of course, consistent with the actual increase in ton-miles of goods moved and passenger-miles of persons transported. It is also consistent with the West German findings that the net product (not the gross product, which unfortunately is not available in constant prices at the time of writing) of the transportation sector, which probably also includes communications (the German term is *Verkehr*), increased by almost 89 per cent between 1936 and 1955 and by almost 43 per cent between 1950 and 1955. When we compare 1955 with 1936, the increase (in *net* product) in West Germany is substantially larger than in East Germany, but the increase is about the same when 1955 is compared with 1950, when the level in West Germany was already one-third above prewar.

One test of the reasonableness of this result is to compare the increase in the transportation sector with the change in industrial production. From 1950 to 1955 the index of production in the Federal Republic rose to 175 per cent (and by 1956 the new index had risen to 192.2 per cent, a gross value added figure of course). By 1955 the net product of the transportation sector had risen to 142.8 per cent.

We calculated industrial production in East Germany in 1955 to have been 162.7 per cent of 1950, transportation alone 152.9 per cent, and transportation and communications 144.9 per cent (all in 1936 prices). In both parts of Germany transportation and communications rose substantially less than industrial production, but in East Germany the transportation sector rose relatively more. This, too, is quite reasonable. The industrial economy of East Germany has in great part shifted from light to heavy goods, which is reflected in the proportion of heavy goods in the total amount of goods transported. Another reason is the much greater importance of the railroads in transporting goods in East Germany.

In 1936, 74.1 per cent of the total ton-kilometers shipped were moved by rail in the East German area, another 12.3 per cent by inland waterway, 11.7 per cent by truck, and only 1.9 per cent by ocean shipping (probably mostly coastwise). By 1956 the railroads were responsible for 81.6 per cent of all ton-kilometers of freight moved, inland waterways moved only 6.8 per cent, trucks only 10.4 per cent, and ocean shipping 1.2 per cent. By comparison, the railroads of the Federal Republic in 1956 moved only 55.3 per cent of all ton-kilometers, inland shipping 28.8 per cent, and long-distance trucking 15.9 per cent.

Thus the results are reasonable although probably less certain than the calculations of the industrial and agricultural value added. Another way of stating the result is to say that East Germany must put relatively more resources into transportation than the Federal Republic, partly because of the change in the industrial structure away from "light" toward "heavy" goods and partly because it is less favored than the area of the Federal Republic with such excellent natural highways as the Rhine River and the lower Elbe River near its mouth.

TRADE

Trade is the last sector that will be estimated in detail. It completes the list of all sectors which in East German terminology are considered "productive" except one, the water economy, which is of very minor importance in East Germany.

Here trade refers to wholesale and retail trade and to restaurants and publishing, which both before and after the war were included in this sector. Before the war it included some other groups such as jobbers and brokers, the functions of which have been taken over by the various East German state trading organizations. In addition, banking and insurance services were included before the war. Since the war, however, these services have apparently not counted as productive, although in the 1950 population census, not published until November 1957, banking and insurance were included with trade, and restaurants were grouped with transportation and communications.

The degree of socialization is very high in wholesale trade, much lower in retail trade. On June 30, 1953, there were 282,509, or 35.7 per cent, of a total of 790,665 persons working in retail trade employed in private retailing, but only 26,353 of a total of 211,576 in wholesale trade or 12.5 per cent, in private wholesaling. On December 31, 1956 the corresponding figures were 295,824 of the total 929,551, or 31.8 per cent, in retailing, and 49,587 of 287,785, or 16.7 per cent, in wholesale trade. In terms of gross product (communist definition), in 1955 over 95 per cent of wholesale trade was socialized.[19]

It would have been desirable to calculate the GNP attributable to trade by some sort of physical measure and some data are available on the tonnage of various amounts of both foodstuffs and manufactured consumer goods shipped to retail stores. Although, the information is interesting and fills several pages in the Statistical Yearbook of the German Democratic Republic, it turned out to be insufficient for estimating the GNP attributable to trade.

Instead, two alternative methods were used. In the first it was assumed that the contribution of the trade sector to the GNP varies with the amount of employment. This is probably a fairly accurate assumption for the last years of our estimating period, say from 1955 on, since by that time the amount of goods supplied to the population had increased and employees in retail and wholesale trade presumably were not idle. The fact that employment in trade increased substantially after 1950 may possibly indicate an increase in productivity. Nonetheless, since the supply of goods to be turned over was exceedingly meager, there must have been a substantial amount of underemployment in trade.

The method of using employment to estimate the GNP of trade therefore assumes that the effectiveness of labor after the war was about the same as before. This assumption may be accepted for 1955 and later years, but for the early years of the 1950's it certainly was not so. Hence the increase from 1950 to 1955 or 1956 calculated by this method probably understates the real growth somewhat because the base was too big, while the change from 1936 to 1955 and later is probably correct.

The other method consisted in deflating East German figures for the gross product of trade by an East German price index. The gross product of trade is defined as the "markup, including sales taxes and excises, unless these are already included in factory received prices." [20] This procedure corresponds methodologically to our value added in market prices. This figure is given in 1950 (East German) prices for the years 1950 to 1955. The valuations for 1956 and 1957 changed, but, assuming that the gross production of trade would have changed about the same from 1955 to 1956 and from 1956 to 1957 whether measured in 1950 or 1955 East German prices, the calculations can be linked to 1955.

The 1936 Base

Both methods involve finding a 1936 base which is reasonably accurate for a sector for which such estimates are difficult to make. For 1936 no figures exist on which such estimates could be based: the only reichsmark figures for trade turnover come from the turnover tax statistics for 1935, the employment figures refer to 1933 and 1939, and all we have is an index of retail and wholesale turnover between 1935 and 1936 of 110.6 per cent.

Since the first of our methods is based on the movement of employment and the average gross value added per employee, the employment estimate for 1936 has to be explained in detail. In 1933, trade, transportation, and communications combined in all Germany employed 5,932,069 persons, of whom restaurants and trade employed 3,986,996, or 67.2 per cent.[21] On May 17, 1939 employment in the trade, transportation, and communications sector in Germany within the 1936 boundaries was 6.07 million, an increase of 137,931 persons.[22] Assuming that the increase was about the same year by year — and we have no real alternative — allows an estimate of an increase of 68,965 persons between 1933 and 1936, of which 67.2 per cent was in the trade sector (that is, 46,344 persons). Presumably the employment in trade in different areas is proportional to population — probably a safe assumption. Thus, of the increase of 46,344 persons employed in trade in all Germany between 1933 and 1936 (or 1936 and 1939), 24.1 per cent or 11,169 may be allocated to the postwar area of East Germany (including East Berlin).

In Part I we estimated the 1939 employment in trade in the area of East Germany as 940,000, which allows an estimate of 928,831 persons for 1936.* So much for the estimate of employment in 1936. The estimate of value added is also complicated.

First, we know the turnover figures for all Germany for 1935. These are given in Table 158. In addition, banks and insurance companies had

* I am of course aware that the precision down to the last employee is fictitious. But I have let the figure stand for purposes of calculation. It must be roughly correct between the limits of 928,000 and 929,000.

Table 158

Trade turnover,[a] Germany, 1935 (million RM)

Wholesale	36,424.9
Retail	16,604.5
Restaurants	4,352.1
Publishing and brokerage firms	2,785.3
	60,166.8

Source: *SJR*, 1938, p. 546.

  [a] Includes both taxable and nontaxable turnover.

a turnover of RM 1.073 billion, which is not included in Table 158 because they are now treated as nonproductive.

On the basis of figures given in the Reichs Statistical Yearbook, 1937,[23] trade turnover had presumably increased by another 10.5 per cent by 1936. (This is the increase for retail trade only. It appears as a minimum. Wholesale trade probably increased by more, but no over-all figure was found. Wholesale turnover of shoes and household goods increased much more; that of textiles and restaurants was of the same order of magnitude.[24]) We thus arrive at a 1936 estimate of RM 66.544 billion (as defined in the enumeration above) for all Germany, of which 24.1 per cent, or RM 16.037 billion, may be allocated to the East German area according to its population.

Unfortunately, I was unable to locate any prewar figure for the ratio of value added to turnover. We do know that the net value added at factor cost (*Wertschöpfung*, or value creation) of trade in the area of the Federal Republic (excluding West Berlin) was RM 4.188 billion. If it was proportionate to the population, this would allow a net value added at factor cost in 1936 in the area of East Germany (including East Berlin) of RM 1.740 billion.

For the Federal Republic for 1950 we can also estimate that the ratio of value added at market prices to net value added at factor prices was 1.32, and that it remained at about this ratio in the years after 1950.[25] Assuming that this ratio also holds for 1936 gives a 1936 estimate of the GNP attributable to trade in the area of East Germany of RM 2.296 billion.

An alternative derivation starts with the ratio of GNP to turnover, which in 1950 was about 13.22 per cent. (The similarity of this figure to the 1.32 ratio mentioned in the preceding paragraph is purely coincidental.) With an estimated turnover in the area of East Germany in 1936 of RM 16.037 billion, by this method we may estimate the value added of trade as RM 2.120 billion — which is very close to our first result. In the calculations which follow, the average of the two, RM 2.208 billion, will be assumed to be the most reasonable estimate we can get for the 1936 value added in 1936 prices.

In order to evaluate the 1936 value added in 1950 prices, we used the estimates made by the Statistische Bundesamt in Wiesbaden on the net value added at factor cost of trade for 1950 both in 1936 and in 1950 prices. When calculated in this manner, the price rise is 174.8 per cent. The calculations are summarized in Table 159. From these figures, the

Table 159

Net value added of trade at factor cost, West Germany,
in 1936 and 1950 prices (billion RM/DM)

	1936 Prices	1950 Prices
Retail	2.035	3.531
Wholesale	2.209	3.904
Restaurants	0.492	0.829

Sources: For estimate in 1936 prices, see *SJBR*, 1956, p. 520; for estimate in 1950 prices, *ibid.*, p. 516.

value added of trade in 1936 in 1950 prices is estimated at DM 3.860 billion.

The employment method

If the GNP attributable to trade is assumed to vary with employment, it had just about recovered to the 1936 level by 1956 or 1957, and in 1950 it was less than 80 per cent of the prewar level. The 1956 or 1957 results seem reasonable. Industrial production had gone up by 16 per cent, but the manufacture of consumer goods certainly had not increased by much more than 10 or 15 per cent. Agricultural output and construction (where wholesale trade is not so important) were down. Hence it is questionable where the turnover could have come from and what goods were sold. To be sure, perhaps selling bad and cheap rayon requires as many people as selling the same amount of good woolens. But on the whole, total production of the trade sector between 1936 and 1956 or 1957 cannot have increased much more than our calculations indicate. However, since even the not-very-good situation in 1955 or 1956 was a substantial improvement over 1950, it is likely to have increased much more between 1950 and 1955 or 1957 than the calculated index shows.

Official East German figures indicate an increase in trade turnover in (East German) 1950 prices of 40.7 per cent between 1950 and 1955, which does not seem unreasonable. I have nevertheless refrained from adjusting the figures for the years 1950 through 1955 on that basis.

A test of the reasonableness of the results may be provided by the following facts. In 1939 employment in trade in the area of East Germany was 26.5 per cent of employment in industry and producing artisans;

in 1955 this ratio was 27.0 per cent. On the other hand, the calculated
GNP of trade in 1936 was 28.7 per cent of industrial GNP, while in 1955
it was only 21.3 per cent. Some of this decline may be due to the decline
in the importance of artisans,* that is, to the fact that in the postwar
figures industrial output includes some things that before the war were
produced by artisans and are therefore excluded from the calculations.
This cannot, however, be the whole story. Since investments go mainly
to industry, and perhaps since trade is in any case more difficult to ra-
tionalize, there must have been a decline in the productivity of trade
compared with industry.

The deflation method

The basic data for the "gross product" of trade — which unlike the
gross product data of industry do not contain double counting by Western
standards but closely approximate in concept the Western concept of gross
value added — are available in 1950 East German prices for 1950 through
1955, in 1955 prices for 1955 and 1956, and in current prices for 1950
through 1957. For the years 1950 through 1956 East Germany has also
published a retail price index broken down by major categories, based on
1936.

This retail price index itself is based on 550 commodities, and it includes, of course, indirect taxes which were and are substantial. This is
not the place to analyze price changes in East and West Germany and
to compare real wages in the two parts of Germany. (An attempt will be
made below to calculate per capita consumption.) Rather, I shall deflate
the gross product of trade in constant 1950 East marks by the retail price
index of 1950, using a 1936 base; in 1950 this index stood at 418.6 per
cent of 1936, and it fell thereafter to 272.9 per cent of 1936 in 1956, largely
because of reductions in the turnover tax. The method assumes that
wholesale prices changed as retail prices did, which may or may not be
true. No information on this point was found.

Using this method, our calculations indicate that the GNP of trade
in 1950 was about 10 per cent below 1936 and in 1955, 30 per cent above
it. This, incidentally, would be an increase exactly matching the increase
in industrial production between 1936 and 1955 measured in 1936 prices;
but it would be almost twice the increase of industrial production measured in 1950 prices. Altogether this increase is quite unlikely. It also
implies that the 1950 level of trade was 92.5 per cent of 1936 while that
of industrial output was only 80 per cent, which is improbable. I do not
believe this estimate to be as good as the one arrived at by using employment figures. One reason I do not believe the deflation method
to be particularly relevant is the fact that the "gross product" figures for
trade given in the various Statistical Yearbooks of the German Demo-

* See Part III for a discussion of the methodology relevant to this point.

Table 160

Employment, value added, and "gross production" in trade, East Germany, in 1950 and current East German prices, and East German retail price index, 1936 and 1950–1958[a]

A. *Employment method*

| | Employment | | Value added | |
Year	Total	Index	1936 Prices (million RM)	1950 Prices (million DM)
	(1)	(2)	(3)	(4)
1936	928,831	100.0	2,208.000	3,859.584
1950	736,103	79.3	1,750.944	3,060.650
1951	716,326	77.1	1,702.368	2,975.739
1952	836,008	90.0	1,987.200	3,473.626
1953	864,803	93.1	2,055.648	3,593.273
1954	889,752	95.8	2,115.264	3,697.481
1955	903,879	97.3	2,148.384	3,755.375
1956	929,551	100.1	2,210.208	3,863.444
1957	931,887	100.3	2,214.624	3,871.163
1958	925,517	99.6	2,199.168	3,844.146

B. *Deflation method*

| | Gross production[b] (million DM-O) | | Retail price index 1936 = 100 | Deflated gross production | | Index of deflated gross production | |
Year	1950 Prices	Current prices		1936 Prices (million RM)	1950 Prices (million DM)	1936 = 100	1950 = 100
	(5)	(6)	(7)	(8)	(9)	(10)	(11)
1936			100.0	2,208	3,859	100.0	108.1
1950	8,555	6,118	418.6	2,043	3,571	92.5	100.0
1951	9,862	8,474	368.8	2,356	4,118	106.7	115.4
1952	10,360	9,917	329.9	2,475	4,326	112.1	121.2
1953	10,938	11,733	307.9	2,613	4,568	118.3	127.9
1954	11,428	8,730	284.1	2,730	4,772	123.6	133.6
1955	12,036	8,520	274.0	2,875	5,026	130.2	140.8
1956	12,782	9,064	272.9	3,053	5,336	138.3	149.5
1957	n.a.	9,323	270.0				
1958		n.a.					

Sources: Col. 1: For 1936 estimate, see text; for 1950–1957, Table 13. Col. 2: Derived from col. 1. Cols. 3 and 4: For derivation, see text. Col. 5: For 1950–1955, see *SJDDR*, 1955, p. 90. Figure for 1956 calculated with index given in *ibid.*, 1956 ed., p. 145 (1955 = 100, 1956 = 106.2). Col. 6: See *ibid.*, 1957 ed., p. 154. Series discontinued in 1958. A recalculation gives substantially different results. Col. 7: Price index for retail trade, based on East German market basket in 1955, given in *ibid.*, p. 216. Series discontinued in 1958. Cols. 8 and 9: Col. 5 deflated by index, col. 7. Cols. 10 and 11: Derived from cols. 8 and 9.

[a] If figures given in col. 6 were deflated by index in col. 7, the results would be quite different. The deflated gross product of trade for 1950 in 1936 prices would be only RM 1.462 billion; it would reach a maximum of RM 3.805 billion in 1953, fall drastically to RM 3.073 billion in 1954, and then rise gradually to RM 3.457 billion in 1957. It is difficult to say whether this absurdity is due to the retail price index or to the gross product of trade in current prices, which, it will be further noticed, differs substantially from the gross product in 1950 prices, although in that year the prices were supposedly identical. The precise meaning of the altered definition is also unclear.

[b] Gross production of trade in 1950 prices: "Nur Handelsspanne mit Verbrauchsabgaben und Akzise soweit diese nicht bereits im Industrieabepreis enthalten sind." (Only trade markups including excise taxes and turnover taxes, unless they were already included with the factory received prices.) See *SJDDR*, 1955, p. 93. Gross production of trade in current prices: "Erträge, Verbrauchsabgaben und Akzise sowie Gesamtwert der industriellen Bruttoproduktion der Binnenhandelsbetriebe — einschliesslich Gaststätten, jedoch ohne Handwerksbetriebe — abzüglich Subventionen." (Receipts, turnover taxes and excise taxes, and total value of the industrial gross production of domestic trade firms — including restaurants but without artisan firms — less subsidies.) See *ibid.*, 1957, p. 152.

cratic Republic do not agree even when supposedly expressed in the same prices. Table 160 gives the latest series available to me that illustrate the point. Considering how employment has moved, this estimate is based on the assumption that rationalization in trade has been as effective as in industry, or, rather, that any deterioration in productivity in trade was no greater than in the industrial sector, which of course may be the case but is not likely. The calculations and results are found in Table 160.

For the years 1936, and 1950 through 1955, there are West German calculations in 1936 prices for the net value added at factor cost. The figures, reproduced in Table 161, indicate that by 1955 the net contribu-

Table 161

Net value added of trade sector at factor cost, West Germany,
1936 and 1950–1955, in 1936 prices

Year	Wholesale (billion RM)	Retail (billion RM)	Restaurants (billion RM)	Total (billion RM)	Indices 1936 = 100	Indices 1950 = 100
	(1)	(2)	(3)	(4)	(5)	(6)
1936	1.800	1.816	0.572	4.188	100.0	88.7
1950	2.205	2.025	0.492	4.722	112.8	100.0
1951	2.408	2.152	0.581	5.145	122.9	109.0
1952	2.477	2.285	0.665	5.427	129.6	114.9
1953	2.756	2.538	0.764	6.058	144.7	128.3
1954	3.072	2.699	0.862	6.633	158.4	140.4
1955	3.473	2.953	0.943	7.369	176.0	156.0

Source: *SJBR*, 1956, p. 520.

tion of trade (as defined) had increased to 176 per cent of 1936 and to 156 per cent of 1950. It is not likely that gross value added would have behaved very differently. The point is not so much that trade in West Germany expanded more than in East Germany, as has every other major sector; rather, the point to be made is that the net product of trade increased much less than that of industry. To use the "deflation method" to calculate the value added of East German trade would lead to the conclusion that trade in East Germany expanded about as much or more than the output of the industrial sector, which is extremely unlikely. A comparison with West Germany, important in itself, adds one more reason that the results of the "employment method" are more reasonable. The results of both methods are presented for the use of those readers who do not feel convinced by my reasoning.*

---

* East German practice itself also rejects the deflation method for finding the net product of trade in constant prices. See above, Part II.

SERVICES

The sectors calculated do not exhaust the available and the employed labor supply; nor do they exhaust production as this term is used in the West. "Non-productive" employment — the major items of, which are personal services of various kinds, government services, banking, and insurance — in 1936 was about 1.145 million. By 1957 it had increased to 1.218 million. Assuming that on the average services had about the same value added per capita in 1936 as trade — RM 2,377 in 1936 prices — and assuming that the value added of this sector increased parallel to employment, we can estimate a 1936 value added of RM 2.721 billion in 1936, RM 2.769 billion in 1955, and RM 2.868 billion in 1956, a very small increase. From the communist standpoint, perhaps the smallness of this increase is not to be construed as a failure. Rather, since this employment is not considered productive though useful, the fact that it increased at all may (or may not) be considered bad. The rough calculations are given in Table 162.

Table 162

Employment and value added, "nonproductive" sector,
East Germany, 1936 and 1950–1958

Year	Total employment	Value added	
		1936 Prices (million RM)	1950 Prices (million DM)
	(1)	(2)	(3)
1936	1,145,000	2,721	3,374
1950	1,136,459	2,701	3,349
1951	1,119,075	2,660	3,298
1952	1,065,664	2,533	3,141
1953	1,082,756	2,574	3,191
1954	1,192,820	2,835	3,515
1955	1,165,064	2,769	3,433
1956	1,206,359	2,868	3,556
1957	1,217,545	2,894	3,589
1958	1,187.252	2,822	3,499

Sources: Col. 1: 1936 adjusted from 1939 figure, assuming that employment in services moved parallel to employment in trade. For 1939, 1950, and 1951, see Table 13; for 1952–1956, *SJDDR*, 1956, p. 166; and for 1957, see *ibid.*, 1957, p. 176. Col. 2: Calculated with value added per person engaged in trade in 1936 = RM 2377. Value added per person assumed to be the same for trade and for services. Col. 3: 1950 value added raised by a factor of 1.24 as calculated for services for the Federal Republic in 1936 and 1950 prices. See *SJBR*, 1956, pp. 517 and 520.

The purpose of this quick calculation is, first, to get comparable estimates with West German data and coverage; second, to get an estimate of GNP in East Germany for 1936 comparable with the Sanderson estimate. Sanderson estimates total GNP (West German coverage, including services) to have been RM 17.5 billion.[26] Our own estimates add up to RM 15.2 billion without services and RM 18.0 billion with services, which is reasonably close to his result.

There is one further comment on the nonproductive sector that should be made even though time and the scarcity of data make an exhaustive treatment impossible.

As time has passed, the East German concept of what is productive and what is nonproductive labor, and hence what effort makes a contribution to national income and what effort requires — in Western terminology — transfer income have changed. The East German concept has approached Western usage. The outstanding example is, perhaps, the inclusion of all transportation and communications services since 1956. In 1955, passenger transport and communications services for the government and the population at large were still excluded, and only freight transportation and communication for "business" were part of national income, a practice apparently still followed in Poland and in other satellites.

Is it unreasonable to assume that at some future date the Communist concepts will change further in the direction of capitalist usage? The borderline between what is production and what is a transfer will, of course, always remain somewhat fuzzy; and a good case could be made for the exclusion of government services on the ground that they are only indirectly influenced by and subject to the market mechanism.

On the other hand, even in primitive societies it is recognized that education and measures to improve the health of the population are essential to increase productivity, and that resources channeled into these areas will pay ample dividends. In advanced economies, among which the economy of East Germany must assuredly be included, technical education and advanced research must surely become more and more important. What sense is there in continuing to pretend that teachers' services are unproductive while trade services are the "continuation of production in the sphere of circulation"? Why should the dead hand of Adam Smith be so much heavier in communist economies than in market economies while his living ideas have not penetrated beyond the iron curtain?

Perhaps we shall see the time when teachers' and governmental services will be described as the "beginning of production in the sphere of planning and organization," to paraphrase the heavy-handed jargon of Marxism. If so, what might be involved? Officially, we have census data only for 31 August 1950. Of the 1,159,316 persons who can clearly be identified as nonproductive,[27] 368,741 were employed in public administration; 234, 241 in medicine, hygiene, and sport; 146,943 in teaching, research, and religion; 145,379 in political, social, and economic organizations, and 139,044 as domestic servants. The arts employed 50,867 persons (including "exhibitors," possibly film operators), and banking 34,942 persons. Of the remaining categories only insurance (excluding social insurance), with 17,185 persons, employed more than 10,000 persons; all other areas employed fewer.

No such breakdown exists for other years. We can calculate that in 1957, there were 159,963 persons in full-time teaching and research, including libraries,[28] but this is all the information available except for a figure for the professions practiced by the private sector (49,774) that is, without doctors employed in the socialized sectors. The lack of data seems strange since such information is freely published in the Polish Statistical Yearbook.

PART SIX

THE GROSS NATIONAL PRODUCT
OF EAST GERMANY

CHAPTER XX

THE GROSS NATIONAL PRODUCT
OF EAST GERMANY

OVER-ALL DEVELOPMENT

THE preceding discussion has presented detailed calculations, sector by sector, for East Germany's GNP (gross national product). The concepts and methodology we have employed are Western, but the coverage has conformed to East German usage. To complete the picture, a rough calculation has also been made for those services which in Communist terminology are "areas outside of material production," covering mainly government services, private and social insurance, banking, defense services, and professional and domestic services. In order that West German calculations of GNP be made comparable with East German concepts, actual and imputed rents have also to be deducted.

Measured in 1936 prices, the East German GNP in 1936 was RM 15.299 billion without personal services and RM 18.020 billion including personal services, which is slightly higher than the Sanderson estimate given in Chapter XIX but sufficiently close to warrant considerable confidence.

Depending on whether personal services are included in the estimates of GNP, the level reached in 1955 was 111–113 per cent of 1936 and in 1957, 120–122 per cent. For reasons explained above, the estimate of the GNP attributable to trade calculated by the employment method is preferable to the one calculated by the deflation method, and hence only the lower estimate was added in the final calculations of the GNP. Anyone wishing to use the higher estimate, however, can easily enough recalculate the corresponding GNP.

Between 1950 and 1955 the increase was 40 to 50 per cent, and between 1950 and 1957 it was 55 to 66 per cent. Measured in 1950 prices, the increase between 1936 and 1955 was only about 6 per cent, but between 1950 and 1955 the increase was slightly higher than if it had been measured in 1936 prices — 45 to 50 per cent.

This is not a bad showing between 1950 and 1955 or 1957, but it is a very poor showing for the whole span of the period. Moreover, the increase between 1950 and 1955 was so large simply because the level in 1950 was so extremely low. It should be remembered that employment also rose quite substantially between 1950 and 1955 even though the labor force did not. Employment in 1950 was only 7,419,236, although the total labor force in August 31, 1950, according to census figures published in 1956, was 8,477,159 including the temporarily unemployed (*Berufstätige einschliesslich der zeitweise Arbeitslosen*).[1] The same source gives the number of independents and persons not in the labor force as 2,612,123; in addition, there were 7,298,890 dependent persons not in the labor force, adding up to a total population of 18,388,172.[2] These figures confirm the statement made in Part I that unemployment must have been considerable. By the end of 1955, total employment (including self-employment) had risen to 8,231,808, or 11 per cent above 1950, and by 1956 it was 8,178,343.[3] Thus some of the increase in output was due to increases in the labor force, but there must also have been some increase in productivity both between 1950 and 1955, and even between 1936 and 1955.*

The sectors that had expanded from their 1936 level by 1955 were industry and transportation. Agriculture and construction decreased, and trade may have stayed the same or may have increased somewhat. "Nonmaterial" services increased slightly. By 1956 all sectors except agriculture had risen above their prewar levels. Agriculture alone remained below the 1936 level in 1957.

It is possible to make a rough over-all comparison with developments in the Federal Republic. From the published figures of the West German GNP in constant 1936 prices I deducted the *net* value added at factor cost of the sectors mentioned in the first paragraph of this chapter (the so-called value creation, or *Wertschöpfung*). No adjustment was made for the balance of trade. The absence of any further adjustment implies that all indirect taxes and all depreciation allowances are attributable to the sectors included in the East German version of the GNP. This procedure does not involve a large error. In 1955, for example, the sectors covered paid in current prices DM 23.607 billion of a total DM 25.898 billion in taxes (less subsidies) and DM 12.138 billion of a total depreciation of DM 15.428 billion.[4] (The greatest part of the depreciation not covered is attributable to housing, of course.)

By 1955 the GNP of the Federal Republic, thus adjusted, had risen to 180.3 per cent of 1936 and to 163.5 per cent of 1950. Employment (exclusive of the self-employed) rose between 1950 and 1955 from 13.827 million to 17.175 million, or 24 per cent, but an allowance for the self-employed would make the percentage increase much smaller. The increase in productivity was therefore substantial and in many but not all years greater than in East Germany.

---

* The labor force declined steadily from 1954 on, but there was an increase again during 1957.

When the East German GNP is calculated with the West German coverage (but exclusive of imputed or paid rents), the East German GNP in 1936 prices between 1936 and 1955 rose 10.4 per cent, and from 1950 to 1955 it rose 40.6 per cent. The comparable West German GNP rose in the same time span 80.3 per cent and 63.5 per cent, respectively. Regardless of the adjustments one wishes to make and the qualifications one wishes to voice for all such calculations, adjustments, and comparisons, there can be little doubt that the over-all performance of the Federal Republic was substantially better whether 1955 is compared with 1936 or with 1950, and that the improvement in the performance per worker was substantially better in West Germany between 1936 and 1955 and slightly better between 1950 and 1955. The latter statement should be understood properly: Without any intent to belittle what has been achieved in East Germany, it is a fact that both output per man and total output grew slightly faster in West Germany than in East Germany in spite of the higher level on which the increases in the West German GNP are based. The figures are given in Table 163.

For the years 1950 through 1955 we also have figures for the East German gross and net product in 1950 prices. These are reproduced above in Part II. The official figures that have been available for gross and net product and for depreciation allowances in current prices for the years 1950 through 1957 allow the calculation of implicit price indices and the estimate of a GNP using East German 1950 prices. The calculations as well as the basic data are given in Table 164. The increase in the GNP thus estimated is 63.3 per cent between 1950 and 1955, which is slightly more than the increase in East German calculations for the net product

Table 163

Gross national product by major sectors, and indices, East Germany, 1936 and 1950–1958, in 1936 and 1950 prices; and West Germany, 1936 and 1950–1955, in 1936 prices, and 1936 and 1950–1958, in 1950 prices

A. *East Germany, 1936 prices (million RM)*

Year	Agriculture (including forestry)	Industry	Construction	Transportation and communications	Trade (employment method)	Gross national product, East German coverage
	(1)	(2)	(3)	(4)	(5)	(6)
1936	2,911.322	7,786.399	1,020.854	1,372.780	2,208.000	15,299.355
1950	2,043.655	5,863.832	445.092	1,344.217	1,750.944	11,447.740
1951	2,362.229	6,838.070	539.011	1,479.407	1,702.368	12,921.085
1952	2,647.247	7,417.964	572.699	1,612.232	1,987.200	14,237.342
1953	2,214.997	8.577.292	672.742	1,687.135	2,055.648	15,207.814
1954	2,231.980	9,323.925	745.223	1,836.721	2,115.264	16,253.113
1955	2,267.747	9,898.350	863.642	1,947.377	2,148.384	17,125.500
1956	1,991.162	10,426.787	1,063.730	2,041.938	2,210.208	17,733.825
1957	2,121.724	10,952.291	1,317.973	2,180.642	2,214.624	18,787.254
1958	2,156.358	11,585.552	1,449.613	2,288.903	2,199.168	19,979.594

Gross National Product

Table 163 (Continued)

Year	Services (rough estimate)	Gross national product (West German coverage)[a]	Trade (deflation method)	Indices			
				GNP, East German coverage		GNP, West German coverage	
				1936 = 100	1950 = 100	1936 = 100	1950 = 100
	(7)	(8)	(9)	(10)	(11)	(12)	(13)
1936	2,721	18,020	2,208	100.0	133.7	100.0	127.4
1950	2,701	14,149	2,043	74.8	100.0	78.5	100.0
1951	2,660	15,581	2,356	84.5	113.0	86.5	110.2
1952	2,533	16,772	2,475	93.1	124.5	93.1	118.6
1953	2,574	17,782	2,613	99.4	132.9	98.7	125.7
1954	2,835	19,088	2,730	106.2	142.0	105.9	134.9
1955	2,769	19,895	2,875	111.9	149.6	110.4	140.6
1956	2,868	20,602	3,053	115.9	154.9	114.3	145.6
1957	2,894	21,681	3,457	122.8	164.2	120.3	153.2
1958	2,822	22,502	n.a.	130.6	174.6	124.9	159.1

B. *East Germany, 1950 prices* (*million RM*)

Year	Agriculture (including forestry)	Industry	Construction	Transportation and communications	Trade (employment method)	Gross national product, East German coverage
	(14)	(15)	(16)	(17)	(18)	(19)
1936	5,575.457	15,668.999	1,995.770	1,838.507	3,859.584	28,938.317
1950	4,163.995	10,472.226	832.236	1,837.472	3,060.650	20,366.579
1951	4,847.190	12,242.140	1,015.846	2,019.697	2,975.739	23,100.612
1952	5,525.591	13,406.815	1,079.711	2,203.241	3,473.626	25,688.984
1953	4,635.552	15,573.300	1,247.356	2,306.594	3,593.273	27,356.075
1954	4,697.143	16,944.316	1,347.145	2,512.705	3,697.481	29,198.790
1955	4,872.536	17,770.079	1,536.743	2,674.618	3,755.375	30,609.351
1956	4,368.380	18,684.433	2,233.267	2,804.151	3,863.444	31,903.675
1957	4,752.013	19,685.176	2,253.224	3,003.684	3,871.163	33,565.260
1958	4,878.614	20,797.187	2,468.767	3,165.692	3,844.146	35,154.406

Year	Services (rough estimate)	Gross national product (West German coverage)[a]	Trade (deflation method)	Indices			
				GNP, East German coverage		GNP, West German coverage	
				1936 = 100	1950 = 100	1936 = 100	1950 = 100
	(20)	(21)	(22)	(23)	(24)	(25)	(26)
1936	3,374	32,312	3,859	100.0	142.0	100.0	136.2
1950	3,349	23,716	3,571	70.4	100.0	73.4	100.0
1951	3,298	26,399	4,118	79.8	113.4	81.7	111.3
1952	3,141	28,830	4,320	88.8	126.1	89.2	121.5
1953	3,191	30,547	4,568	94.5	134.2	94.5	128.7
1954	3,515	32,714	4,772	100.9	143.3	101.2	137.9
1955	3,433	34,042	5,026	105.8	150.3	105.4	143.6
1956	3,556	35,460	5,336	110.2	156.5	109.7	149.5
1957	3,589	37,154	5,359	116.0	164.8	115.0	156.7
1958	3,499	39,153		121.5	172.6	121.2	165.1

Table 163 (Continued)

C. *West Germany, 1936 prices* (*billion RM*)

Year	Gross national product	Index 1936 = 100	Index 1950 = 100	Adjusted gross national product	Index 1936 = 100	Index 1950 = 100
	(27)	(28)	(29)	(30)	(31)	(32)
1936	47.928	100.0	87.4	41.188	100.0	90.7
1950	54.845	114.4	100.0	45.445	110.3	100.0
1951	62.734	130.9	114.4	53.058	128.8	116.8
1952	66.664	139.1	121.6	56.573	137.4	124.6
1953	71.556	149.3	130.5	60.996	148.1	134.3
1954	77.520	161.7	141.3	66.536	161.5	146.4
1955	85.805	179.0	156.4	74.271	180.3	163.5

D. *West Germany, 1950 prices* [b] (*billion DM*)

Year	Agriculture and forestry	Mining, electricity, gas, and industry	Construction	Trade	Transportation and communications	Gross national product, East German coverage
	(33)	(34)	(35)	(36)	(37)	(38)
1936	10.093	38.596	4.688	11.419	5.419	70.215
1950	9.790	43.342	5.356	12.885	7.168	78.541
1951	11.873	49.399	5.591	13.700	7.863	89.226
1952	12.005	54.538	6.040	14.464	8.049	95.096
1953	12.230	57.775	7.314	15.599	8.295	103.213
1954	12.404	65.600	7.728	16.758	8.858	111.348
1955	12.108	76.495	8.812	18.535	9.998	125.948
1956	11.977	81.369	9.369	20.187	10.828	133.730
1957	12.005	85.925	8.884	21.643	11.295	139.752

Year	Services	Gross national product, West German coverage	GNP, East German coverage 1936 = 100	GNP, East German coverage 1950 = 100	GNP, West German coverage 1936 = 100	GNP, West German coverage 1950 = 100
	(39)	(40)	(41)	(42)	(43)	(44)
1936	10.245	80.460	100	89.4	100	85.3
1950	15.749	94.290	111.9	100.0	117.2	100.0
1951	16.787	106.013	127.1	113.6	131.8	112.5
1952	18.091	113.187	135.4	121.0	140.7	120.1
1953	19.042	122.255	147.0	131.4	151.9	129.6
1954	20.109	131.457	158.6	141.7	163.4	139.4
1955	21.486	147.434	179.4	160.3	183.2	156.3
1956	22.917	156.647	190.5	170.2	194.7	166.1
1957	24.438	164.190	199.0	177.8	204.1	174.1

Sources: A and B (Cols. 1–26): Summary of preceding tables. C (Cols. 27–29): *SJBR*, 1956, p. 520. C (Col. 30): Total gross national product as given in *ibid.* less net social product at factor cost of banking, private insurance, house rents, public administration (including social security but without public enterprises), defense, and professional, households, and other services. All indirect taxes and all depreciation allowances have therefore been imputed to the other sectors. No adjustment has been made for the balance of trade. D (Cols. 33–44): *SJBR*, 1956, p. 520, and 1958, p. 479.

ª Trade included as estimated by employment method, col. 5. Does not include paid and imputed rents for which no estimate was made.

ᵇ West German figures refer to the gross *domestic* product. They are given in current and in 1954 prices. The calculations in 1950 prices have been made by calculating implicit price indices, and then deflating each sector individually, as given in the figures in 1954 prices. The implicit price indices for the individual sectors are (1954 = 100): agriculture and forestry, 93.86; mining, electricity, and gas, 74.17; industry, 92.79; construction, 89.74; trade, 82.23; transport and communications, 84.73. The indices for the service sectors are: banks and private insurance, 91.16; house rents, 98.32; government, 74.51; all other services, 80.76. The 1936 figures were estimated by assuming that the change of each sector between 1936 and 1950 would have been the same in 1950 prices as the actual change of the *net* value added of each sector was in 1936 prices.

ᶜ But excluding house rents.

Table 164

East German gross national product (West German definition), 1950–1955,
in 1950 East German prices; and net product and depreciation,
1950–1957, in current East German prices (billion DM–O)

Year	Net product current prices	Net product 1950 prices	Implied price index	Depreciation current prices	Depreciation 1950 prices	Gross national product 1950 prices	Index gross national product 1950 prices
	(1)	(2)	(3)	(4)	(5)	(6)	(7)
1950	30.829	30.662	100.75	1.318	1.308	31.970	100.0
1951	38.371	36.513	105.09	1.551	1.476	37.989	118.8
1952	43.966	39.745	110.62	1.735	1.568	41.313	129.2
1953	47.032	41.521	113.27	1.953	1.724	43.245	135.3
1954	50.987	46.365	109.97	2.316	2.106	48.471	151.6
1955	52.214	49.819	104.81	2.503	2.388	52.207	163.3
1956	54.629			2.710			
1957	58.629			2.915			

Sources: Cols. 1 and 4: *SJDDR*, 1957, p. 158. Figures for 1957 are preliminary. In 1958, the figures were substantially revised downward for the years 1950 through 1954 (*SJDDR*, 1958, p. 176). Col. 2: See above, Table 17. Col. 3:
Col. 1 ÷ col. 2. Col. 5: Col. 4 ÷ col. 3. Col. 6: Col. 2 + col. 5. Col. 7: From col. 2.

and not much more than our calculated increase. The differences are not
so great that they could not be imputed to the distorted price structure
used in the official calculation of the East German figures. Thus the official East German claims make our own calculations seem very reasonable.*

Table 165 indicates to what extent the increases in GNP have been
due to increases in the labor force.

INVESTMENT AND THE GROWTH OF THE ECONOMY

In the chapter on construction, a rough estimate of investment for
1955 was made. In the present section I shall attempt to develop a series
for investments and to indicate further — very roughly, for this is all that
is possible — the share of gross investment in GNP and the relation of
investment to the growth of output. West German estimates of East German investments were published in 1957, but they refer only to investments in industry. It may be most useful to start with a brief comment
on East German methodology and with a description of the available
East German figures. We have given above (Part I, Table 17) the data
on the use of the total product of society as published in the first Statistical Yearbook of the German Democratic Republic. Since then, slightly
different figures have been published, and in the 1957 edition a change in

* The real difference between developments of total output (measured by GNP) in
the Federal Republic and in East Germany is: the aggregate GNP in East Germany in
1950 was at least 25 per cent below the 1936 level, and probably even less, while in the
Federal Republic it was about 10 per cent above prewar. Strenuous developments in East
Germany since then have not succeeded in narrowing the gap that existed at the starting
point. See Part II for a detailed description of East German methodology.

Table 165

Annual percentage increases in gross national product, in employment
and in output per employed person, West and East Germany, 1951–1958

A. *West Germany*

Increase during	Gross national product (1936 prices)	Gross national product (1954 prices)	Gainfully employed persons	Output per employed persons
	(1)	(2)	(3)	(4)
1951	14.4	11.8	3.0	8.5
1952	6.3	6.8	1.7	5.0
1953	7.3	7.8	2.7	5.0
1954	8.3	7.1	3.3	3.6
1955	10.7	11.8	3.6	7.9
1956		6.4	3.6	2.6
1957		5.0	2.5[a]	2.5[a]
1958		2.8	1.5[a]	1.3[a]

B. *East Germany*

Increase during	Gross national product (1936 prices) West German coverage	Gross national product (1936 prices) East German coverage	Gainfully employed	Output per employed West German coverage	Output per employed East German coverage
	(5)	(6)	(7)	(8)	(9)
1951	10.1	12.9	2.6	7.3	10.0
1952	7.6	10.3	3.2	4.3	6.9
1953	6.0	6.8	1.3	4.6	5.4
1954	7.3	6.9	3.7	3.5	3.1
1955	4.2	5.4	−0.2	4.4	5.6
1956	3.6	3.6	−0.8	4.4	4.4
1957	5.2	5.9	0.7	4.5	5.2
1958	3.8	6.3	−0.7	4.5	7.0

Sources: Col. 1: Calculated from *SJBR*, 1955, p. 521. Cols. 2–4: *Monthly Report of the Deutsche Bundesbank*, February 1959, p. 3. Cols. 5–6: Calculated from Table 164. Col. 7: See Table 13 for figures and sources. Cols. 8–9: Calculated from preceding columns.
  [a] Preliminary.

methodology is foreshadowed that would bring East German usage into closer conformity with what is apparently the usage in the Soviet Union and the other satellites. Unlike the data presented in Table 17, individual consumption in later editions is defined to include expenditures on house construction also. For the years 1955 through 1957 (but not for preceding years) the 1957 edition of the Statistical Yearbook of the German Democratic Republic gives two percentages for the share of "accumulation" in the domestically available national income (not the GNP). One figure refers only to "productive" investment and the increase in inventories. The second figure (presented only in a footnote) also refers to "productive and unproductive accumulation," which includes "investment and other expenditures for the construction and maintenance of dwelling space . . . [previously] included in individual consumption" and "additions to and major repairs of societal institutions." [5] The latter usage corresponds methodologically to Western concepts.

Since there are no figures for balance of payments, it is unfortunately difficult, if not impossible, to arrive at a figure even in East marks for the domestically available national income — to say nothing of an estimate in West German prices.*

My own estimates for gross fixed investment start with the calculations made above for the value of construction. I assumed that the values of construction put in place and of equipment must bear a reasonable fixed relationship. The first step was to separate the total value of housing from the value of construction. According to an East German source quoted by a West German author, investment in building was 34 per cent of total state-financed investment in plant and equipment in 1955, and in earlier years it was probably as high as 40 per cent.[6] Consequently I assumed in my calculations that the value of equipment during the years 1950 through 1952 was one-and-one-half times the value of nonhousing construction put in place, and in 1953 and subsequent years twice that value. The 2 to 1 ratio of equipment to investment which I used, is closer to American experience than to either prewar or postwar German experience, both of which are higher. The lower figure was adopted for three reasons. First, it corresponds to official East German claims. Since the East German price distortions are less within the investment sector than between the investment and consumption sectors I felt the estimate to be acceptable. Second, the emphasis on heavy industry and mining in East Germany would in any case make construction a relatively large part of total investment. Third, my estimate of the construction portion of fixed investment also includes nonindustrial construction, and this too ought to lower the ratio of equipment (which is predominantly industrial) to construction.

The figure for the value of fixed plant and equipment thus arrived at was then increased by the value of housing construction to arrive at an estimate of total gross fixed investment. The figures presented in Table 166 indicate a steady increase in the value of investment, with a jump in 1953, a slight slowing down in 1954, and rapid increases thereafter. As Table 167 indicates, the estimates are certainly reasonable. Thus my estimate of the value of equipment investment for 1950 is DM 903 million, while the total value of investment goods production (defined as the

* The Statistical Yearbooks of the German Democratic Republic give figures for total imports and exports in rubles or marks, but unfortunately the figures are valued in either case f.o.b. the border *shipping* country. On the other hand, the unpublished figures for the domestically available national income are stated to be valued at domestic prices in East Germany, including the domestic East German price for imports and exports.

Table 166

Fixed investment and investment in inventories (including state reserves and forests), East Germany, 1950–1958[a]

A. *Gross fixed investment, 1936 prices (billion RM)*

Year	Value of nonhousing construction	Value of equipment[b]	Value of fixed plant and equipment	Value of housing	Gross fixed investment
	(1)	(2)	(3)	(4)	(5)
1950	601.858	0.903	1.505	0.140	1.645
1951	749.698	1.125	1.874	0.149	2.023
1952	815.336	1.223	2.038	0.139	2.177
1953	863.491	1.727	2.590	0.258	2.848
1954	965.111	1.930	2.895	0.277	3.172
1955	1,177.461	2.355	3.532	0.262	3.794
1956	1,510.941	3.022	4.533	0.262	4.795
1957	1,708.617	3.417	5.126	0.488	5.614
1958	1,909.519	3.819	5.729	0.507	6.236

B. *Gross fixed investment, 1950 prices (billion DM)*

Year	Value of nonhousing construction	Value of equipment[b]	Value of fixed plant and equipment	Value of housing	Gross fixed investment
	(6)	(7)	(8)	(9)	(10)
1950	1,134.995	1.702	2.837	0.252	3.089
1951	1,425.427	2.138	3.564	0.267	3.831
1952	1,548.626	2.323	3.872	0.251	4.123
1953	1,614.874	3.230	4.845	0.464	5.309
1954	1,746.033	3.492	5.238	0.499	5.737
1955	2,088.983	4.178	6.267	0.472	6.739
1956	2,608.020	5.216	7.824	0.472	8.296
1957	2,876.488	5.753	8.629	0.879	9.508
1958	3,175.760	6.352	9.528	0.939	10.467

C. *Inventory accumulation, 1936 and 1950 prices; percentage in domestically available national income*

Year	Fixed productive investment[e]	Increment in institutions of societal consumption	Total (col. 11 + col. 12)	Inventory accumulation[d]	Ratio of inventory accumulation to total (col. 14: col. 13)	Estimate of inventory accumulation 1936 Prices (col. 3 × col. 15)	Estimate of inventory accumulation 1950 Prices (col. 8 × col. 15)
	(11)	(12)	(13)	(14)	(15)	(16)	(17)
1950	3.0	1.5	4.5	3.0	66.67	1.003	1.891
1951	3.3	1.6	4.9	3.7	75.51	1.415	2.691
1952	3.8	1.7	5.5	3.9	70.91	1.445	2.746
1953	5.2	1.6	6.8	3.6	52.94	1.371	2.565
1954	5.4	1.1	6.5	0.6	9.23	0.267	0.483
1955	7.3	1.1	8.4	1.2	14.29	0.505	0.896
1956	10.1	1.3	11.4	1.5	13.16	0.597	1.030
1957	10.1	1.2	11.3	2.1	18.58	0.952	1.603
1958	10.9	1.1	12.0	5.3	44.17	2.530	4.209

Sources: Cols. 1, 4, 6, 9: Table 146. Cols. 11–15: *SJDDR*, 1957, p. 160. Other columns calculated as indicated.

[a] *SJDDR*, 1958, p. 182 presents new figures which indicate that inventory accumulation was throughout bigger. The 1958 calculation refers to this new calculation. The figures in Col. 15 would throughout be bigger by about three percentage points.

[b] For the years 1950 through 1952, estimated at 1½ times the value of nonhousing construction; for 1953–1957 at 2 times. For justification of this procedure, see text.

[e] "Increment in basic means and unfinished investments."

[d] "Increment in material means of circulation, forests, and state reserves."

Table 167

Production of equipment (sales value), investment in equipment,
and amounts available for other purposes, East Germany, 1950–1956

A. *1936 Prices, billion RM*

Year	Investment in equipment	Production of equipment[a]	Investment in equipment as per cent of production	Presumed exports and other uses	
				Sales value	As per cent of output
	(1)	(2)	(3)	(4)	(5)
1950	0.903	1.870	48.3	0.967	51.7
1951	1.125	2.171	51.8	1.046	48.2
1952	1.223	2.416	50.6	1.193	49.4
1953	1.727	3.258	53.0	1.531	47.0
1954	1.930	3.667	52.6	1.737	47.4
1955	2.355	3.960	59.5	1.605	40.5
1956	3.022	4.405	68.6	1.383	31.4

B. *1950 Prices, billion DM*

Year	Investment in equipment	Production of equipment[a]	Investment in equipment as per cent of production	Presumed exports and other uses	
				Sales value	As per cent of output
	(6)	(7)	(8)	(9)	(10)
1950	1.702	3.872	44.0	2.170	54.0
1951	2.138	4.429	48.3	2.291	51.7
1952	2.323	4.938	47.0	2.615	53.0
1953	3.230	6.621	48.8	3.391	51.2
1954	3.492	7.421	47.1	3.929	52.9
1955	4.178	8.004	52.2	3.846	47.8
1956	5.216	8.874	58.8	3.658	41.2

[a] Engineering, road vehicles (except bicycles and motor cycles), electrical equipment, fine mechanics and optics.

sales value of machinery construction, road vehicles [except bicycles and motor cycles], electrical products, and fine mechanics and optics) was DM 1.8 billion (both calculated in 1936 prices), which indicates that domestic uses of investment goods were about half of total production, with the other half presumably exported except for a minor part domestically consumed. By 1956 the estimated investment in equipment was about DM 3.417 billion, or about three-fourths of the total production of equipment, which also seems reasonable although perhaps slightly high. The ratio of gross fixed investment in the GNP is, of course, of major interest. In 1950 this percentage was 11.6, and in 1953, 16 per cent. In 1956, however, it had risen to 23.2 per cent, a figure comparable to West German percentages.

We may also venture to make estimates of investment in inventories. As stated above, the 1957 edition of the Statistical Yearbook of the German Democratic Republic gives a detailed percentage distribution of the uses of the domestically available national income from 1950 through 1957. For 1950 through 1954 we cannot separate housing investment from individual consumption by using these East German statistics, but, as stated, it is possible to do so for later years. As late as 1956, however, housing expenditures were extremely small. On the other hand, the percentage of the additions to the investment of "societal consumption" are given for all years since 1950. If we can make the assumption that inventory accumulation bore the same relation to the combined "productive" accumulation plus the increase in investment for societal consumption as their percentages in the domestically available income, we can arrive at an estimate for investment in inventories. The figures, which are presented in Table 166, are inherently plausible. During the years 1950 through 1953 the increase in inventories is officially stated to have been between 3 and 4 per cent of the domestically available income, or one-half to three-fourths of the total fixed investment (accumulation). In 1954, inventory accumulation dropped precipitously to less than one-tenth of fixed investment, undoubtedly as the result of the 1953 uprising, but even in 1957 it was less than 15 per cent of the combined productive and nonproductive fixed investment outside of housing. On the basis of these percentages it is possible to estimate that investment in inventories (in 1936 prices) rose from just under RM 1 billion in 1950 to just under RM $1\frac{2}{8}$ billion in 1952 and 1953, but then dropped off to only one-quarter of a billion reichsmark in 1954, and was still less than half a billion in 1956. During 1958, however, they seem to have jumped to RM $2\frac{1}{2}$ billion. Two points should be stressed. One is that the method of calculation is obviously rough and subject to large errors. The second, however, is that the results are inherently plausible since the East German economy was starved for circulating capital and had to build up inventories and reserves. The third point is that the building up of forests is included with inventory accumulation and that it is possible that imports temporarily swelled state reserves.

Table 167 gives the estimated investment in equipment and a comparison with the production of equipment. As the calculations indicate, the percentage of domestic production of investment goods domestically invested rose from somewhat less than 50 per cent in 1950 to almost 70 per cent in 1956, while presumed exports fell correspondingly from slightly more than 50 per cent to slightly more than 30 per cent. These figures certainly are plausible.

More interesting, perhaps, are the figures giving the value of fixed investment as a percentage of the GNP. The figures in Table 168 define GNP in the communist manner to exclude the value of personal, govern-

Table 168

Gross investment in construction and equipment, West and East Germany,
in 1936 and 1950 prices, 1950–1958

A. *East Germany, 1936 prices (billion RM)*

Year	Value of construction	Value of equipment	Total	Gross national product (East German coverage without services)	Gross fixed investment as per cent of gross national product
	(1)	(2)	(3)	(4)	(5)
1950	0.742	0.903	1.645	11.448	14.4
1951	0.898	1.125	2.023	12.921	15.7
1952	0.954	1.223	2.177	14.237	15.3
1953	1.121	1.727	2.878	15.208	18.9
1954	1.242	1.930	3.112	16.253	19.1
1955	1.439	2.355	3.794	17.126	22.2
1956	1.773	3.022	4.795	17.734	27.0
1957	2.197	3.417	5.614	18.787	29.9
1958	2.417	3.819	6.236	19.980	31.2

B. *East Germany, 1950 prices (billion DM)*

Year	Value of construction	Value of equipment	Total	Gross national product (East German coverage without services)	Gross fixed investment as per cent of gross national product
	(6)	(7)	(8)	(9)	(10)
1950	1.387	1.702	3.089	20.367	15.2
1951	1.693	2.138	3.831	23.101	16.6
1952	1.800	2.323	4.123	25.689	16.0
1953	2.079	3.230	5.309	27.356	19.4
1954	2.245	3.492	5.737	29.199	19.6
1955	2.561	4.178	6.739	30.609	22.0
1956	3.080	5.216	8.296	31.904	26.0
1957	3.755	5.733	9.488	33.565	28.3
1958	4.115	6.352	10.477	35.154	29.8

C. *West Germany, 1936 prices*[a] *(billion RM)*

Year	Gross national product, adjusted[b]	Gross fixed investment[c]	Gross fixed investment as per cent of gross national product
	(11)	(12)	(13)
1950	45.445	9.992	22.0
1951	53.058	10.739	20.2
1952	56.573	10.942	19.3
1953	60.996	12.566	20.6
1954	66.536	14.078	21.2
1955	74.271	16.791	22.6

Table 168 (Continued)

D. *West Germany, 1950 prices*[a] (*billion DM*)

Year	Gross national product, adjusted[b]	Gross fixed investment[c]	Gross fixed investment as per cent of gross national product
	(14)	(15)	(16)
1950	78.541	18.455	23.6
1951	89.226	19.203	21.5
1952	95.096	20.492	21.5
1953	103.213	23.609	22.9
1954	111.348	26.772	24.0
1955	125.948	31.756	25.2
1956	133.730	34.100	25.5
1957	139.752	31.992	22.9

Sources: For A and B, see preceding tables and text. For C, col. 11, see *SJBR*, 1956, p. 520; for col. 12, *ibid.*, p. 521. For D, col. 14, see Table 163, col. 38; for col. 15, *SJBR*, 1958, p. 482. Gross investment in plant and equipment in 1954 prices, deflated by implied price index (83.13%).

[a] In interpreting the figures, it should be remembered that, although inventory accumulations are relatively smaller than in East Germany, there were in each year (except 1950) sizable export surpluses not included.

[b] Total GNP less banks, private insurance, rents (housing), public administration, defense, and professions, domestic, and other services.

[c] Only plant and equipment, without inventories.

mental, and other services. The GNP in the Federal Republic was adjusted to the East German coverage by deducting the value of banks, private insurance, rents (housing), public administration, defense, and professional, domestic, and other services. It can be seen that gross fixed investment in the Federal Republic was quite steadily about 20 per cent or more of the GNP thus adjusted. The East German percentages were undoubtedly substantially lower until 1953, but by 1955 they were certainly roughly of the same order of magnitude. The differences in the investment ratios may well account for the fact that the annual increment in the GNP of East Germany has been declining while the increment in the Federal Republic, after declining until 1952, has increased steadily. There is some expectation, however, that the greater increase in investment in 1956 and 1957 will raise the rate of increase of the East German GNP again. The data on the annual increases in GNP in the two parts of Germany are presented in Table 169.

The data also permit us to compute marginal capital-output ratios, but their meaning is obscured even more than usual by the fact that we have data for only a few years and that, moreover, the early years of the period were in every respect abnormal. During the early 1950's, it was undoubtedly possible to raise output by relatively small investments in repairs or in the easing of special bottlenecks.

The figures presented in Table 170 compare gross fixed investment alone and gross fixed investment plus inventories with the increase in GNP with

Table 169

Annual percentage increases in gross national product (West German coverage),
West and East Germany, 1951/1950–1958/1957

Year	West Germany		East Germany	
	1936 Prices	1954 Prices	1936 Prices	1950 Prices
	(1)	(2)	(3)	(4)
1951/1950	14.4	11.8	10.1	11.3
1952/1951	6.3	6.8	7.6	9.2
1953/1952	7.3	7.8	6.0	5.9
1954/1953	8.3	7.1	7.3	7.1
1955/1954	10.7	11.8	4.2	4.1
1956/1955		6.4	3.6	4.1
1957/1956		5.0[a]	5.2	4.8
1958/1957		2.8[a]	3.8	5.4

Sources: Col. 1: *SJBR*, 1956 ed., p. 521. Col. 2: Calculated from *ibid.*, 1959, p. 482. We have given the increases in 1954 prices because the figures are available and it seemed desirable to include some estimates in postwar prices. Cols. 3 and 4: From Table 163.
  [a] Preliminary.

a one-year lag. (Investment during 1950 was divided by the increase in GNP during 1951.) The table brings out two facts. One is that the lagged incremental capital-output ratios of East Germany increased from a low of between 1 and 2 to a figure of about 6 and fell again to about 5. During the last available period it seems to have risen to 8. The second is that the incremental capital-output ratios calculated in an identical manner for the Federal Republic remain rather low. Since the same price system was used to calculate the capital-output ratios in both East and West Germany, the explanation must be sought elsewhere. Part of the explanation lies, of course, in the known predilection of the East German planners for heavy industry. But we may infer that in part at least West German investments were handled more efficiently and that there must have been more than the inevitable waste in East Germany.

During the whole period 1950 through 1955, East Germany invested 15.659 billion marks (in 1936 prices) in gross fixed investment alone, and 21.532 billion marks in gross fixed investments and inventory accumulation; the GNP increased during the same six years by DM 5.746 billion, measured in the same prices, giving an average incremental capital-output ratio of 2.73 and 3.75, respectively, depending on whether inventories are excluded or not. Gross investment excluding inventories between 1950 and 1957 amounted to 20.068 billion marks of 1936 purchasing power, and including inventories to 33.623 billion marks, while GNP increased 8.353 billion marks between 1950 and 1958. This gives average incremental capital-output ratios of 3.12 and 4.03, respectively, perhaps indicating a substitution of capital for labor as the labor ceiling is reached.

For the Federal Republic, gross fixed investments during the same period were 75.108 billion marks of 1936 purchasing power, and gross

Table 170

Postwar capital-output ratios, lagged by one year,[a]
West and East Germany, 1950–1956, in 1936 prices

	A. *East Germany*				
Year	Gross fixed investment during the year (billion RM)	Increase in GNP during the year (billion RM)	Capital-output ratio lagged by one year	Gross investment including inventories (billion RM)	Capital-output ratio
	(1)	(2)	(3)	(4)	(5)
1950/1951	1.645	1.432	1.15	2.648	1.85
1951/1952	2.023	1.191	1.70	3.438	2.89
1952/1953	2.177	1.010	2.16	3.622	3.59
1953/1954	2.848	1.306	2.18	4.219	3.23
1954/1955	3.172	0.807	3.93	3.439	4.26
1955/1956	3.794	0.707	5.37	4.299	6.08
1956/1957	4.795	1.079	4.44	5.392	5.00
1957/1958	5.614	0.821	6.84	6.566	8.00
1958	6.236			8.766	

	B. *West Germany*				
Year	Gross fixed investment during the year (billion RM)	Increase in GNP during the year (billion RM)	Capital-output ratio lagged by one year	Gross investment including inventories (billion RM)	Capital-output ratio
	(6)	(7)	(8)	(4)	(10)
1950/1951	9.992	7.889	1.27	10.680	1.35
1951/1952	10.739	3.930	2.73	13.554	3.45
1952/1953	10.942	4.892	2.24	13.156	2.69
1953/1954	12.566	5.964	2.11	14.610	2.45
1954/1955	14.078	8.285	1.70	16.327	1.97
1955/1956	16.791			18.791	

Sources: East Germany: as calculated in preceding tables. West Germany: *SJBR*, 1956, p. 520.
[a] Investment in year x divided by increase in GNP during year x + 1.

investments (including inventory accumulation) 87.118 billion. The GNP rose from 1950 to 1955 by 30.960 billion marks, giving average incremental capital-output ratios of 2.43 and 2.81, respectively. Thus over the whole period the ratios were not very different, although still noticeably smaller than in East Germany.

It is possible to make similar calculations with the recently published West German figures in 1954 prices, adjusted to a 1950 price basis. The lagged capital-output ratios, comparing gross fixed investment only (that is, without inventories) with the increase in the GNP with East German coverage (that is, without personal services) during the following year, give a slightly different picture. The figures, which the reader can easily calculate from the preceding tables, indicate that from 1950 to 1952 and in 1957 East German capital-output ratios were smaller, but in other years they were the same or larger than in West Germany. During the whole period 1950 through 1957 the East German GNP (with East German coverage) increased by DM 13.875 billion, measured in 1950 prices, with total gross fixed investments during the years 1950 through 1956 amounting to DM 37.124 billion. This gives an average incremental capital-output ratio for East Germany of 2.68. For West Germany the corresponding figure for the gross domestic product, adjusted to East German coverage and to West German 1950 prices, was DM 61.211 billion. With gross fixed investments of DM 174.387 billion, this gives a West German average incremental capital-output ratio of 2.85.

When only gross fixed investments are considered, the capital-output ratios are thus not too different in the two parts of Germany, the West German ratio being somewhat greater. When inventory accumulations are included, however, the picture is reversed. During the years 1950 through 1956, gross investments including inventories were DM 48.953 billion in East Germany and DM 197.700 billion in West Germany, giving an average incremental capital-output ratio of 3.53 for East Germany and 3.23 for West Germany.

CONSUMPTION AND THE STANDARD OF LIVING

It would have been desirable to have estimated consumption as a share in GNP by a method utilizing the actual supplies of consumer goods to the population. However, the data to make such a method practical are insufficient in spite of all the interesting information published in the Statistical Yearbooks of the German Democratic Republic. Instead, we were forced to make our estimate of consumption by a roundabout method which starts with East German data on wage and salary payments.

The average monthly gross earnings of industrial wage earners before taxes are not very different in the two parts of Germany but they appear to be somewhat higher in West Germany. Both parts of Germany publish retail-price and cost-of-living indices, but they are only very roughly comparable since the commodity basket entering the retail price index is undoubtedly inferior in East Germany and the housing component in the cost-of-living index in East Germany reflects both very much lower housing standards and rents controlled at the prewar level. In 1956 the retail price index in West Germany stood at 183 per cent of 1938, while the East German index stood at 272 per cent of 1936. (The difference between the two base years is negligible.) This in itself would indicate that the average real income in East Germany would be about 70 per cent that of West Germany in 1956 and much less in the preceding years. The cost-of-living index in West Germany in 1956 stood at 176 per cent of 1938 and in East Germany at 191 per cent of 1936. Thus, measured even in terms more favorable to East Germany, West Germany was noticeably although less spectacularly better off.

The relevant data for industrial gross wages before taxes and the calculation of real income deflated by either the cost-of-living or the retail

Table 171

Average monthly wages of industrial workers, West and East Germany, in current marks and in marks of 1936 purchasing power, deflated by cost-of-living index and by retail price index, 1950–1958

A. *West Germany*

Year	Average gross weekly wages (DM)	Average gross monthly wages (4 × col. 1) (DM)	Cost-of-living index 1938 = 100	Average real monthly wages (DM)	Retail-price index 1938 = 100	Average real monthly wages (DM)
	(1)	(2)	(3)	(4)	(5)	(6)
1950	60.54	242.16	156	155.2	172	140.8
1951	68.52	278.08	168	165.5	188	147.9
1952	74.00	296.00	171	173.1	188	157.4
1953	77.87	311.88	168	185.6	180	173.3
1954	80.99	323.96	169	191.7	179	181.0
1955	86.85	347.40	172	202.0	180	193.0
1956	92.96	371.84	176	211.3	183	203.2
1957	98.75	395.00	180	219.4	188	210.1
1958	103.91	415.64	186	223.5	192	216.5

B. *East Germany*

Year	Average gross monthly wages (DM–O)	Cost-of-living index (1936 = 100)	Average real monthly wages (DM–O)	Retail-price index (1936 = 100)	Average real monthly wages (DM–O)	East Germany as per cent of West Germany
	(7)	(8)	(9)	(10)	(11)	(12)
1950	265	306.9	86.3	418.6	63.3	45.0
1951	298	242.2	123.0	368.8	80.8	54.6
1952	318	222.1	143.2	329.9	96.4	61.2
1953	344	211.3	162.8	307.9	111.7	64.5
1954	376	196.4	191.1	284.1	132.3	73.1
1955	386	191.9	201.1	274.0	140.9	73.0
1956	396	191.0	207.3	272.9	145.1	71.4
1957	409	187.9	217.6	270.0	151.5	72.1
1958	421[a]	184.6[b]	228.1	263.6[b]	159.7	73.8

Sources: Col. 1: *SJBR*, 1959, p. 445. Refers to all industry without mining. Wages including mining are higher. Col. 2: Four times value in col. 1. Col. 3: *SJBR*, 1959, p. 430. Col. 4: Col. 2 ÷ col. 3. Col. 5: *SJBR*, 1959, p. 430. Col. 6: Col. 2 ÷ col. 5. Col. 7: *SJDDR*, 1958, p. 213. Col. 8: *Ibid.*, p. 217. Col. 9: Col. 7 ÷ col. 8. Col. 10: *SJDDR*, 1957, p. 216. Col. 11: Col. 7 ÷ col. 10. Col. 12: Col. 11 ÷ col. 6.

[a] Preliminary.

[b] The old series have been discontinued, and a new "Index of retail and service prices and of the purchasing power of the German Mark" has been substituted which is based on the turnover structure of 1958 and takes account of the abolition of the double price system. It has been assumed that the change in the old indices would have been the same as the actual change in the new index. *SJDDR*, 1958, p. 231.

price indices are presented in Table 171. The fact that the West German indices are based on 1938 while the East German indices are based on 1936 does not make much difference. More important is the fact that the published West German wage figures refer to average weekly earnings that have been multiplied by four to approximate average monthly wage income. This too underestimates gross monthly wages in the Federal Republic and hence somewhat overstates the East German as compared with the West German standard of living.

It is obvious that because of the changed structure of consumption in East Germany the figures cannot be taken at face value. As stated, the East German index is based on the commodity basket of 1955 although the Statistical Yearbook of the German Democratic Republic states that for each year qualities typical for that year were selected. Even as late as 1956 the East German commodity basket was much inferior to that of West Germany. The breakdown of the indices (which are not reproduced here) indicates that food, drink, and tobacco and manufactured household goods and clothing are much more expensive in East than in West Germany. On the other hand, house rents, fuel and electricity, transportation, and toilet articles are cheaper in East Germany, but they are also much inferior and, in part, rationed. Hence the differences in the standards of living are much greater than the differences in the indices indicate.

A complete analysis of the indices cannot be undertaken here although such an analysis would be quite interesting. Rather, we attempted to arrive at real consumption by a process of deflation which will now be described in detail.

We started out with the figures for the total wage bill in current East marks. These figures were then adjusted for the number of the self-employed. It was assumed that the average earnings of the self-employed equal the average wage and salary payments. This assumption is, I believe, the best that can be made with the existing information, although the results are probably slightly high. The bulk of the independent income earners are in agriculture or in retail trade and are not likely to have as high an income as the average of industrial or socialized farm workers. Moreover, the number of more highly paid independent writers, professionals, and so on is hardly sufficient to raise the average income of the independent group. Basically, since direct taxation plays a very subordinate role in the East German tax system, this figure is the disposable income of consumers. The only further adjustments that should be made are for savings by the population. Since individuals do not have checking accounts, I took as net savings by individuals the annual increases in savings accounts and also adjusted the disposable income for the difference between payments and benefits of social and other insurance.

The result of the adjustment is assumed to be expenditures on consumption in current East marks. If anything, it is an overestimate of the consumption expenditures because it must be presumed that independent farmers and retailers make some investments out of their income and that some investments, for example, in housing, are also made by other population groups. Since there was no information whatsoever to permit even a rough guess at the amount of such investments, we did not adjust the consumption figures further. The figures were deflated by the official retail price index mentioned. The calculations are presented in Table 172. In this table we also deflated consumption by the cost-of-living index,

Table 172

Estimated consumption in gross national product, East Germany, 1936 and 1950–1958, in current marks and in marks of 1936 purchasing power

Year	Wage bill (billion DM–O)	Net savings during year (billion DM–O)	Benefits minus premiums paid into insurance funds other than social security (billion DM–O)	Net payments of social security funds (billion DM–O)	Total (billion DM–O)
	(1)	(2)	(3)	(4)	(5)
1936	7.845	n.a.	n.a.		
1950	15.250	−0.176[a]	−0.186	−0.089[a]	14.799
1951	17.436	−0.176	−0.219	−0.089	16.952
1952	19.422	−0.578	−0.300	+0.356	18.900
1953	21.575	−0.512	−0.346	+0.118	20.835
1954	24.697	−1.165	−0.405	+0.061	23.188
1955	25.530	−1.226	−0.454	+0.135	23.985
1956	26.198	−1.135	−0.512	−0.122	24.429
1957	27.880	−2.833	−0.595	+0.549	25.001
1958	28.569	−2.274	−0.360	+0.796	26.731

Year	Per cent of wage and salary earners in the labor force	Wage bill adjusted for independent income earners (billions)	Retail-price index 1936 = 100	Cost-of-living index 1936 = 100
	(6)	(7)	(8)	(9)
1936	n.a.	n.a.	100.0	100.0
1950	76.5	19.345	418.6	306.9
1951	[76.5][b]	22.159	368.8	242.2
1952	77.0	24.545	329.9	222.1
1953	79.7	26.142	307.9	211.3
1954	80.9	28.663	284.1	196.4
1955	80.8	29.684	274.0	191.9
1956	81.9	29.828	272.9	191.0
1957	83.0	30.122	270.0	187.9
1958	84.8	31.522	263.6[c]	184.6[c]

Table 172 (Continued)

Year	Real consumption in 1936 prices (adjusted wage bill, col. 7) (billion RM)		Population (millions)	Per capita real consumption (RM)	
	Deflated by retail-price index	Deflated by cost-of-living index		Deflated by retail-price index col. 10: col. 12	Deflated by cost-of-living index col. 11: col. 12
	(10)	(11)	(12)	(13)	(14)
1936	10.816	10.816	16.160	669.00	669.00
1950	4.621	6.303	18.388	251.32	342.79
1951	6.008	9.149	18.351	327.42	498.56
1952	7.440	11.051	18.328	405.94	602.97
1953	8.490	12.372	18.178	467.07	675.03
1954	10.089	14.594	18.059	558.60	808.14
1955	10.834	15.469	17.944	603.74	862.04
1956	10.930	15.617	17.716	616.96	881.51
1957	11.156	16.031	17.517	636.88	915.16
1958	11.958	17.076	17.355	689.02	983.92

Year	Gross national product 1936 prices (billion RM)	Consumption as per cent of gross national product	
		Deflated by retail-price index	Deflated by cost-of-living index
	(15)	(16)	(17)
1936	18.020	60.0	60.0
1950	14.149	32.6	44.5
1951	15.581	38.6	58.7
1952	16.772	44.4	65.9
1953	17.782	47.7	69.6
1954	19.088	52.9	76.5
1955	19.895	54.5	77.8
1956	20.602	53.1	75.8
1957	21.681	51.5	73.9
1958	22.502	53.1	75.9

Sources: Col. 1: *SJDDR*, 1956, p. 193; 1957, p. 208; 1958, p. 211. Col. 2: *Ibid.*, 1956, p. 204 (calculated from total deposits); 1957, p. 219; 1958, p. 250. Col. 3: *Ibid.*, 1957, p. 220 and 1958, pp. 252, 253 (persons and property insurance). Col. 4: *Ibid.*, 1957, p. 529; 1958, p. 246. Col. 5: Sum of cols. 1 through 4. Col. 6: Calculated from Table 13. Members of cooperatives are included with wage and salary earners. Col. 7: Col. 5, col. 6. Col. 8: *SJDDR*, 1957, p. 216. Col. 9: *Ibid.*, p. 217. Cols. 10 and 11: Independent estimate for 1936. Col. 12: See Table 4. Col. 13: Col. 10 ÷ col. 12. Col. 14: Col. 11 ÷ col. 12. Col. 15: See Table 163. Col. 16: Col. 10 ÷ col. 15. Col. 17: Col. 11 ÷ col. 15.   a Assumed the same as 1951.   b Change in coverage.   c See note b to Table 171.

which raises estimated consumption in East Germany by roughly 50 per cent compared with the estimate arrived at by means of the retail-price index. We believe, however, that the use of the cost-of-living index is really not justifiable for this particular purpose. It contains a high percentage of rationed goods in short supply. Moreover, since our estimate of the GNP does not include any house rents (imputed or actually paid) it also seemed illogical and undesirable to use the cost-of-living index, which is so greatly influenced by rents.

For 1936, the base year, consumption was estimated directly by assuming that the share of private consumption of GNP was the same in East Germany as in the Federal Republic, namely, 60.5 per cent. The calculations indicate that, measured in 1936 prices, consumption deflated by the retail price index was about one-third of GNP in 1950 and still not quite 55 per cent of GNP in 1955. It fell to slightly more than half by 1957. By contrast, consumption in the Federal Republic, although also a smaller share of GNP than in 1936, in most years since the war has been quite close to the prewar percentage. The calculations and results are given in Table 172.

THE REMAINING USES

The uses of the GNP which we have not calculated include the government as this term is understood in the West and also the export balance, which in the early postwar years must have been substantial because of reparations. It is unfortunately impossible at this time to make any reasonable estimate for the balance of payments. Data on foreign trade indicate that in either rubles or East German marks of a specified gold content East Germany had an import surplus in 1950, 1952, and 1953 and export surpluses in all other years, the export surplus in 1957 being about DM-O 430 million, or about 780 million rubles. Unfortunately these figures are valueless for our purposes. In the years up to 1953, exports did not include reparation payments, and the valuation for both imports and exports is the foreign trade price of the commodities including freight and other incidental costs to the border of the *delivering* country. No information whatsoever could be found on transportation and other similar costs; nor was I able to find sufficient information on the valuations actually employed.

The uses of the gross national product in the Federal Republic and in East Germany

When these estimates for fixed investments, inventory accumulation, and consumption are combined, they permit some comparisons between the uses of GNP in the Federal Republic and in East Germany, which in turn suggest conclusions as to the relative efficiencies of the two economies. As we have been at pains to point out, the calculations are rough, and the figures for East and West Germany are not perfectly comparable. Nevertheless, the order of magnitude must be correct, and our own calculations of the East German performance are largely confirmed by the official East German figures.

Consider just the shares of various uses of GNP given in Table 174, derived from the figures summarized in Table 173.

Table 173

Uses of gross national product,[a] West and East Germany, 1936 and 1950–1958, in 1936 prices (billion RM)

	1936	1950	1951	1952	1953	1954	1955	1956	1957	1958
A. West Germany										
1. Private consumption	28.986	33.250	35.870	38.751	42.475	45.861	50.998	55.435	57.985	59.937
2. Gross investments:	8.972	10.680	13.554	13.156	14.610	16.327	18.918	18.956	19.637	20.405
Gross fixed investments	(6.900)	(9.992)	(10.739)	(10.942)	(12.566)	(14.078)	(16.791)	(18.034)	(18.084)	(18.862)
Inventory accumulation	(2.072)	(0.688)	(2.815)	(2.214)	(2.044)	(2.209)	(2.127)	(1.006)	(1.595)	(1.595)
3. Other (government and export balance):	9.970	10.915	13.310	14.757	14.471	15.332	15.889	17.049	18.558	18.449
Export balance	(0.000)	(0.460)	(1.979)	(1.916)	(1.756)	(1.836)	(1.988)	(2.734)	(3.161)	(2.651)
Defense expenditures (current)	...	(2.335)	(2.446)	(2.780)	(2.333)	(2.334)	(2.286)	...	...	...
Defense expenditures (investments)	...	(0.251)	(0.535)	(0.921)	(0.692)	(0.737)	(0.651)	...	...	...
4. Aggregate gross national product	47.928	54.845	62.734	66.664	71.556	77.520	85.805	91.297	95.844	98.561
B. East Germany										
1. Individual consumption	10.898	4.621	6.008	7.440	8.490	10.089	10.834	10.930	11.156	11.958
2. Gross investment:	3.368	2.648	3.438	3.622	4.219	3.439	4.299	5.392	6.566	8.766
Fixed (including housing)	...	(1.645)	(2.023)	(2.177)	(2.848)	(3.172)	(3.794)	(4.795)	(5.614)	(6.236)
Housing	...	(0.140)	(0.149)	(0.139)	(0.258)	(0.277)	(0.262)	(0.262)	(0.488)	(0.507)
Inventories	...	(1.003)	(1.415)	(1.445)	(1.371)	(0.267)	(0.505)	(0.597)	(0.952)	(2.530)
3. Other (residual)	3.754	6.880	6.135	5.710	5.073	5.560	4.762	4.280	3.959	1.778
4. Aggregate gross national product	18.020	14.149	15.581	16.772	17.782	19.088	19.895	20.602	21.681	22.502

Sources: For the East German figures, see the preceding tables, 163 ff. For the 1936 and 1950–1955 West German figures, see *SJBR*, 1956, p. 520. 1956 to 1958 estimated on the assumption that increases in 1936 prices are the same as increases in 1954 prices as calculated by *ibid*, 1959, p. 488. Because of method of calculation details will not add to total precisely. [a] The concept of GNP employed for the East German calculations differs from that of the official West German calculations only in that the latter include, while the East German calculations exclude rents for housing. All other services have been allowed for, at least roughly.

Table 174

Percentage distribution of uses of gross national product,[a] West and East Germany, 1936 and 1950–1958, in 1936 prices

	1936	1950	1951	1952	1953	1954	1955	1956[b]	1957[b]	1958[b]
A. West Germany										
1. Private consumption	60.5	60.6	57.1	58.1	59.3	59.2	59.4	60.0	59.8	60.1
2. Gross investments:	18.7	19.5	21.6	19.7	20.4	21.1	22.0	23.8	23.4	23.7
Fixed	...	(18.2)	(17.1)	(16.4)	(17.6)	(18.2)	(19.6)	(22.4)	(21.4)	(21.7)
Inventory accumulation	...	(1.3)	(4.5)	(3.3)	(2.9)	(2.8)	(2.5)	(1.4)	(2.0)	(2.0)
3. Other:	20.8	19.9	21.2	22.1	20.2	19.8	18.5	16.2	16.8	16.2
Export balance		(0.8)	(3.2)	(2.9)	(2.5)	(2.4)	(2.3)	(3.6)	(4.0)	(3.2)
B. East Germany										
1. Individual consumption	60.5	32.7	38.6	44.4	47.7	52.9	54.5	53.1	51.5	53.1
2. Gross investments:	18.7	18.7	22.1	21.6	23.7	18.0	21.6	26.2	30.3	39.0
Gross fixed investment	...	(11.6)	(13.0)	(13.0)	(16.0)	(16.6)	(19.1)	(23.2)	(25.9)	(27.7)
Inventory accumulation	...	(7.1)	(9.1)	(8.6)	(7.7)	(1.4)	(2.5)	(2.9)	(4.4)	(11.2)
3. Other	20.8	48.6	39.4	34.0	28.5	29.1	23.9	20.8	18.3	7.9

Sources: Same as Table 173. [b] Distribution of West German GNP of 1956 to 1958 refers to calculations in 1954 prices, *SJBR*, 1958, p. 488.
[a] See note to Table 173.

The major differences between the uses of the GNP in the East and West German economies lie in the "other" uses. By 1955, consumption was 54 per cent of GNP in East Germany and 59 per cent in West Germany. It took the East German economy the whole of the First Five Year Plan to reach a point where the share of consumption in GNP was at least of the same order of magnitude as the share which consumption has held throughout the postwar years in the Federal Republic.

Perhaps more startling is the fact that gross fixed investment was undoubtedly a smaller portion of GNP from 1950 through 1952 or 1953 in East Germany than in the Federal Republic. By 1955 the ratios had become approximately the same; and by 1957, the East German ratios surpassed those in West Germany. The share of total gross investment including inventory accumulation in the GNP was, however, the same or somewhat larger in the East German than the West German economy throughout the whole period. Thus from 1950 through 1953, the East German economy found it necessary to use many times the portion of GNP to accumulate inventories than the Federal Republic. From 1954 on, however, there was a dramatic fall, and the inventory accumulation fell to a smaller share than in West Germany, a trend once more reversed in 1957 and 1958.

Since it is known that there were continuous shortages of raw materials, interrupting smooth flows of production and presenting bottlenecks, the high rate of inventory accumulations is startling. The phenomenon of comparatively high inventory accumulation, however, is not unknown in other satellite economies and, indeed, in many underdeveloped countries. In East Germany there was certainly a great need to accumulate stocks, but the inference is inevitable that inventory accumulations were bigger than planned — why else should there have been complaints about insufficient flows of material — and that the figures (which are based on official claims) reflect tendencies toward hoarding, apparently common to planned economies that use too much physical planning and such odd indices as the gross production index discussed above to measure plan fulfillment and productivity.*

* They also lend some credence to the continual East German complaints that the inefficiencies of trade rather than the insufficiencies of production were responsible for shortages of consumer goods. (Needless to say, this cannot be the whole explanation of low consumption!)

Since this discussion was written, R. W. Campbell's article on "A Comparison of Soviet and American Inventory-Output Ratios" has appeared. His calculations and interpretations parallel ours. He concludes that:

"It is highly likely that the Soviet system requires higher stocks in relation to flows than does the U. S. economy. This conclusion contradicts Soviet statements on the subject, but with regard to industry, at least, is not at all inconsistent with what is known about the operation of economy. In particular the poor operation of the supply system makes hoarding almost a rule of economic rationality for the Soviet factory manager. . . . The implications of these high inventory requirements are not hard to see. The difference between the American ratios and the Soviet ratios represents a tying up of resources in

The high ratio of GNP going to "other" uses from 1950 through 1952 need cause no surprise. There must be a substantial export surplus on reparations accounts included with this item, but how much it is impossible to say. By 1955 the share of "other" uses in the GNP was down to a reasonable figure, which, though larger than in the West, was at least of the same order of magnitude.

Whatever similarities in the uses of GNP appear between East and West Germany, when the share of the various uses in GNP is considered, the similarities disappear if the figures are put on a per capita basis as in Table 175. Even in 1957, per capita consumption cannot have been back to the 1936 level in East Germany, while in the Federal Republic it was certainly already above it in 1952. All the substantial increases in per capita consumption since the First Five Year Plan, which was inaugurated in 1950, cannot hide the fact that even in 1955, at the end of the First Plan, per capita consumption in East Germany was only 60 per cent of that in West Germany. Nor did the gap narrow in 1956 or 1957, although by 1958 the relative position of the average East German may have improved somewhat.

The showing of East Germany is only a little better when per capita investment is considered. The Federal Republic had already risen above the 1936 level in 1951 (and with fixed investment only, in 1950). East Germany reached the level of prewar per capita investment only in 1953, and had to retreat temporarily from that level during 1954 in response to the pressures for higher consumption following the uprising of 17 June 1953. Except for 1953, when East German per capita gross investment reached a level of 81 per cent of the corresponding West German figure, it remained much closer to three-fifths of the West German level; but in 1957 it almost reached the West German level.

Only inventory accumulations and the "other" uses required more GNP per capita in East than in West Germany until 1953 and again in 1956 and 1957 — and that is a dubious distinction.

The differential in per capita GNP for East and West Germany in the postwar years was also much bigger than it had been in 1936. The area which became East Germany always had slightly lower average wages than the Western areas of Germany. Our calculated differential in the per capita GNP for 1936 is about 10 per cent, which is probably too high. But the postwar figures indicate that throughout the whole postwar period per capita GNP in the East German area has remained fairly constantly at a level of about two-thirds of the West German per capita GNP.

---

the Soviet economy that could well be used elsewhere. And from another point of view, one particularly relevant to the Soviet case, they represent a burden on economic growth. The excessive inventory increments associated with expanding production are greater than they need to be, and represent a deduction from resources available for investment in fixed capital." (*American Economic Review* [September 1958], Vol. XLVII, No. 4, pp. 564–565.)

Table 175

Per capita expenditures, consumption, investment, and other uses of gross national product,[a] West and East Germany, 1936 and 1950-1958, in 1936 prices

	1936	1950	1951	1952	1953	1954	1955	1956	1957	1958
A. *West Germany*										
1. Private consumption	759	700	746	799	867	926	1020	1132	1149	1165
2. Gross domestic investment:	235	225	282	271	298	330	378	381	389	397
Fixed	(181)	(210)	(223)	(226)	(256)	(284)	(336)	(362)	(358)	(367)
Inventory accumulation	(54)	(14)	(59)	(46)	(42)	(45)	(43)	(20)	(32)	(31)
3. Other:	261	230	277	304	295	310	318	342	367	359
Export surplus	(0)	(10)	(41)	(40)	(36)	(37)	(40)	(55)	(63)	(52)
4. Gross national product	1255	1155	1304	1375	1460	1566	1716	1833	1899	1916
B. *East Germany*										
1. Individual consumption	674	251	327	406	467	559	604	617	637	689
2. Gross investment:	208	144	193	203	240	192	240	304	375	505
Fixed		(89)	(110)	(119)	(157)	(176)	(211)	(271)	(320)	(359)
Inventory accumulation		(55)	(83)	(84)	(83)	(16)	(29)	(33)	(55)	(146)
3. Other	232	374	334	312	279	308	265	242	226	103
4. Gross national product	1115	769	849	915	978	1057	1109	1163	1238	1297
C. *East Germany as per cent of West Germany*										
1. Individual consumption	89	36	44	51	54	60	59	54	55	59
2. Gross investment:	89	64	68	75	81	58	63	80	96	127
Fixed		(42)	(49)	(53)	(61)	(62)	(63)	(75)	(89)	(98)
Inventory accumulation		(393)	(141)	(183)	(198)	(36)	(67)	(165)	(172)	(471)
3. Other	89	163	121	103	95	99	83	71	62	29
4. Gross national product	89	67	65	67	67	67	65	63	65	68

Sources: Same as Table 173.
[a] See note to Table 173.

Again, although the particular figure may be criticized as too high or too low, it is beyond reasonable doubt, first, that the per capita GNP is significantly lower in East than in West Germany, and, second, that the differential has not narrowed.

To explain these phenomena brings us back to our introductory comments. The East German economy has performed more poorly than the West German economy by whatever tests one wishes to apply. It is, however, next to impossible to determine quantitatively how much of the poorness of the performance is to be attributed to each of various contributing causes. The continuous loss of trained people must put a strain on East German resources. Soviet exploitation, as shown by the per capita GNP spent on "other" uses, must bear a major part of the blame.

But this cannot be the whole story. Per capita GNP in East Germany rose no more than in West Germany in spite of the increases in relative amounts spent on investments. Hence the figures point to a relative inefficiency of investments in East Germany compared to West Germany, for which the attempts to expand heavy industries and to minimize the importance and change the structure of foreign trade are probably partly responsible. But at this stage of our knowledge of the East German foreign trade or of the distribution of investments among various types of industries, we can neither prove the statement nor assess its quantitative importance.

BIBLIOGRAPHY

NOTES

INDEX

BIBLIOGRAPHY

A. PRE 1945 PUBLICATIONS

Die Deutsche Industrie. Gesamtergebnisse der amtlichen Produktionsstatistik, Schriftenreihe des Reichsamtes fuer wehrwirtschaftliche Planung. Berlin: 1939.

Loesch, August. "Die Leistung der Seeschiffahrt im Vergleich zu den Leistungen der uebrigen Guetertransportmittel (Binnenschiffahrt, Eisenbahn, Kraftfahrzeug und Flugzeug)," in *Nauticus 1941; Jahrbuch fuer Deutschlands Seeinteressen*. Adm. Gottfried Hansen, ed., 24th edition. Berlin: E. S. Mittler und Sohn, 1941.

Statistik der Eisenbahnen im Deutschen Reich. Published at the request of the Reichswerksministerium. Berlin: Reich Printing Office, 1937 (E. S. Mittler und Sohn, distributors.)

Statistisches Reichsamt. *Statistisches Jahrbuch des Deutschen Reiches*. 1935, 1938, and 1939–1940 editions. Berlin.

———— *Wirtschaft und Statistik*. Berlin: 1938 (Monthly).

B. EAST GERMAN PUBLICATIONS

1. JOURNALS AND NEWSPAPERS

a. Miscellaneous

Der Aussenhandel und der innerdeutsche Handel. (Published under the auspices of the Ministry for Foreign and Inner-German Trade). Berlin: Verlag Die Wirtschaft (Biweekly journal since 1950).

Deutsche Finanzwirtschaft; Zeitschrift fuer das gesamte Finanzwesen. Berlin: Verlag Die Wirtschaft (Monthly).

Gesetzblatt der Deutschen Demokratischen Republik (Official Gazette).

"Internationale Niederschachtofentagung in Leipzig," *Neue Huette.* Berlin: V.E.B. Verlag Technik, Vol. I, 1955/56, No. 4.

Kohlmey, Guenther. "Spaltungsdisproportionen und Aussenhandel," *Wirtschaftswissenschaft,* 1958, No. 1.

Ministerium fuer Finanzen. *Das neue Preisrecht.* Berlin (Loose leaf collection).

Moeke, S. "Die Bewertung der Industrieproduktion," *Die Wirtschaft.* Berlin: April 29, 1955.

Mostertz, Walter. "Spezialisierung und Koordinierung im Maschinenbau zwischen den sozialistischen Laendern," *Wirtschaftswissenschaft.* Berlin: Vol. VI, No. 5, July–August, 1958.

Oelssner, Fred. "Staat und Oekonomie in der Uebergangsperiode," *Wirtschaftswissenschaft.* Berlin: Vol. V, No. 3, April–May, 1957.

Taegliche Rundschau (Daily).

Vajda, Imre. "Einige Bemerkungen ueber die Preisbasis auf dem sozialistischen Weltmarkt," *Aussenhandel.* Berlin: Vol. 8, No. 22, November 27, 1958.

Die Wirtschaft; Zeitung fuer Politik, Wirtschaft und Technik. Berlin (Weekly).

b. Einheit

Zentralkomitee der sozialistischen Einheitspartei Deutschlands, *EINHEIT;* Zeitschrift fuer Theorie und Praxis des wissenschaftlichen Sozialismus. Berlin: Dietz Verlag, 1958 (Monthly official organ of the Central Committee of the SED).

Apel, Erich. "Unsere oekonomische Hauptaufgabe und die Weiterentwicklung unserer Industrie," Vol. 13, August 1958, pp. 1108–1121.

Henke, Georg and Rouscik, Lothar. "Eine neue Etappe der wirtschaftlichen Zusammenarbeit im sozialistischen Lager," Vol. 13, June 1958, pp. 821–836.

c. Neues Deutschland

Neues Deutschland. Berlin (Daily; official organ of the Socialist Unity [Communist] Party of the German Democratic Republic).

Rau, Heinrich. Speech given at the Warnow shipyards. 1957, February 2.

Ulbricht, Walter. "Die Rolle der DDR im Kampf um ein friedliches und glueckliches Leben des deutschen Volkes," (Speech given at the 25th meeting of the Central Committee of the Socialist Unity [Communist] Party of Germany). 1955, October 30, No. 255.

d. Statistische Praxis

Staatliche Zentralverwaltung fuer Statistik bei der staatlichen Plankommission der Regierung der Deutschen Demokratischen Republik. *Statistische Praxis.* Berlin: V.E.B. Deutscher Zentralverlag, various years, up to and including the first half of 1956.

Draheim, Gerhard. "Entwicklung der Hektarertraege im ersten Fuenfjahrplan," April 1956.

Lange, Ursula. "Kritische Bremerkungen zu den repraesentativen Untersuchungen in der Landwirtschaft," June 1955.

Raehse, Hans. "Die Auswahlmethode fuer die repraesentativen Betriebsuntersuchungen in der Landwirtschaft," July, 1955.

Staatliche Zentralverwaltung fuer Statistik beim Ministerrat der Deutschen Demokratischen Republik. *Statistische Praxis.* Berlin: V.E.B. Deutscher Zentralverlag, second half of 1956 and following years.

Forbrig, G. "Zur Ermittlung der industriellen Bruttoproduktion," March, 1957.

Hentschel, Martin. "Die Berechnung des Aufkommens und der Verwendung des gesellschaftlichen Gesamtproduktes und des Nationaleinkommens im zweiten Fuenfjahrplan," Vol. XII, August and September, 1958.

Janakieff, Rumen. "Kritische Bemerkungen zur Anwendung der Kennziffer Bruttoproduktion fuer die Einschaetzung der Produktionsarbeit des Industriebetriebes," Part I, May 1957; Part II, June 1957. (English translation in International Economic Papers, Vol. VIII, 1957.)

"Rohstoffverbrauch und Rohstoffversorgung der Textilindustrie," 1957, No. 2.

Schlecht, Rolf. "Die Elektroenergieerzeugung und -versorgung im ersten Fuenfjahrplan," 1956, No. 8.

Schmidt, Erich. "Der Einfluss der Kooperationsbeziehungen auf den Nachweis des Produktionsvolumens der Industrie," December, 1956.

Schulz, Hans-Juergen. "Bemerkungen zur Problematik betrieblicher und volkswirtschaftlicher Leistungsziffern," Part I, Febr. 1959, No. 2.

2. OFFICIAL EAST GERMAN PUBLICATIONS

Anlage 1 zur zweiten Anordung zur Vorbereitung des Volkswirtschaftsplanes 1956; Ordung der Materialplanung (Verzeichnis der Kontingenttraeger) ab 1956. Teil I: Industrieerzeugnisse (ohne Nahrungsgueter, Stand Mai 1955), Gesetzblatt der Deutschen Demokratischen Republik. Berlin: Sonderdruck No. 90, July 15, 1955.

Anordnung ueber die Ordnung der Materialplanung (Verzeichnis der Kontingenttraeger) ab 1956. Teil II: Nahrungsgueter, (Stand Dezember 1955), Gesetzblatt der Deutschen Demokratischen Republik. Berlin: Sonderdruck No. 149, January 30, 1956.

Direktive fuer den zweiten Fuenfjahrplan zur Entwicklung der Volkswirtschaft in der Deutschen Demokratischen Republik, 1956 bis 1960. Berlin: Dietz Verlag, 1956.

"Der Fuenfjahrplan des friedlichen Aufbaus," *Dokumente der Deutschen Demokratischen Republik.* No. 13, Berlin: 1951.

Ministerium fuer Planung, Statistisches Zentralamt. *Allgemeines Warenverzeichnis.* Berlin: August 1950.

Presseamt beim Ministerpraesidenten der Regierung der Deutschen Demokratischen Republik. *Presse-Informationen.* Berlin: Various issues.

Staatliche Verwaltung fuer Statistik. *Statistisches Jahrbuch der Deutschen Demokratischen Republik,* 1955, 1956, 1957 and 1958 editions. Berlin: V.E.B. Deutscher Zentralverlag.

Staatliche Zentralverwaltung fuer Statistik. *Vierteljahreshefte zur Statistik der Deutschen Demokratischen Republik.* Berlin: Various issues.

Zweite Anordung zur Vorbereitung des Volkswirtschaftsplanes 1956; Ordnung der Planung 1956. Teil I: Materialplanung vom 1. Juni 1955, Gesetzblatt der Deutschen Demokratischen Republik. Berlin: Sonderdruck No. 88.

3. OTHER EAST GERMAN PUBLICATIONS

a. Diskussionsbeitraege

Diskussionsbeitraege zu Wirtschaftsfragen. Berlin: Verlag Die Wirtschaft.
Goll, Guenter. "Ueber Begriffe des Rechnungswesens der volkseigenen Industriebetriebe," 1955, No. 20.
Hessel, Hans. "Die Bilanzierung in der Planung der Volkswirtschaft der DDR," 1953, No. 11.
Koziolek, Helmut. "Zur marxistisch-leninistischen Theorie des Nationaleinkommens," 1953, No. 9.
Schmidt, Margarete. "Probleme bei der Ermittlung der industriellen Bruttoproduktion," 1953, No. 12.
Zimmermann, Horst. "Bilanzierung der Geldeinnahmen und-ausgaben der Bevoelkerung in der Deutschen Demokratischen Republik, ihren Bezirken und Kreisen," 1954, No. 15.

b. Miscellaneous

Deutsches Wirtschaftsinstitut. *Zur Entwicklung der Krise in den USA.* Bericht 11/12, Vol. VI, June 1955.
Kindelberger, Albert. *Die statistische Berichterstattung der privaten Wirtschaft.* Berlin: Verlag Die Wirtschaft, 1955.
Koziolek, Helmut. *Grundfragen der marxistisch-leninistischen Theorie des Nationaleinkommens; Sozialismus.* Berlin: Verlag Die Wirtschaft, 1957.
Oelssner, Fred. *Die Uebergangsperiode vom Kapitalismus zum Sozialigmus in der Deutschen Demokratischen Republik.* Deutsche Akademie der Wissenschaften zu Berlin, Vortraege und Schriften. Berlin: 1955, No. 56.
Rudolph, Johannes und Friedrich, Gerd. *Grundriss der Volkswirtschaftsplanung.* Berlin: Verlag Die Wirtschaft, 1957.
Ulbricht, Walter. *Die Entwicklung des deutschen volksdemokratischen Staates, 1945–1958.* Berlin: Dietz Verlag, 1958.
——— Der Fuenfjahrplan und die Perspektiven der Volkswirtschaft. Berlin: Dietz Verlag, 1950.

4. TRANSLATIONS FROM THE RUSSIAN

Akademie der Wissenschaften der UdSSR, Institut fuer Oekonomie. *Politische Oekonomie — Lehrbuch.* Berlin: Dietz Verlag, 1955 (official Russian text on economics).
Joffe, J. "Die Planung der Industrieproduktion," *Sowjetwissenschaft.* Berlin: Verlag Die Wirtschaft, special issue No. 4 (the original article in Russian was published in 1948).
Notkin, A. I. *Die Bestimmung des oekonomischen Nutzeffekts von Investitionen; Aus sowjetischer und volksdemokratischer Wirtschaftsliteratur.* Berlin: Verlag Die Wirtschaft, 1955.

C. WEST GERMAN PUBLICATIONS

1. BUNDESMINISTERIUM FUER GESAMTDEUTSCHE FRAGEN

a. Bonner Berichte aus Mittel und Ostdeutschland, Bonn.

Abeken, Gerhard. "Das Geld- und Bankwesen in der sowjetischen Besatzungszone und im Sowjetsektor von Berlin von 1945 bis 1954," 1955.
"Die Bevoelkerungsbilanz der sowjetischen Besatzungszone 1939–1949," 1951.

"Bilanz der Arbeitskraefte und Arbeitsmarktlage in der sowjetischen Besatzungszone," n.d.

"Die chemische Industrie in der sowjetischen Besatzungszone," Gemeinschaftsarbeit der Aussenstelle Berlin des Instituts fuer Raumforschung und einer Arbeitsgruppe des Bundesministeriums fuer gesamtdeutsche Fragen, 1952.

Faber, Dorothea. "Einkommensstruktur und Lebenshaltung in der sowjetischen Besatzungszone," 1953.

Haas, Gerhard und Leutwein, Alfred. "Die rechtliche und soziale Lage der Arbeitnehmer in der SBZ," 1954.

Kitsche, Albert. "Die oeffentlichen Finanzen im Wirtschaftssystem der sowjetischen Besatzungszone Deutschlands," 1954.

Kramer, Matthias. "Die Landwirtschaft in der sowjetischen Besatzungszone," 1953.

――― "Die Landwirtschaft in der sowjetischen Besatzungszone," Sonderdruck des Anlagenteiles und des dokumentarischen Anhangs, n.d.

Leutwein, Alfred. "Die sozialen Leistungen in der SBZ," 1955.

Meimberg, Rudolf und Rupp, Franz. "Die oeffentlichen Finanzen in der sowjetischen Zone und im Sowjetsektor von Berlin," n.d.

"Die Reparationen der sowjetischen Besatzungszone in den Jahren 1945 bis Ende 1953," 1953.

Rupp, Franz. "Die Reparationsleistung der sowjetischen Besatzungszone," 1951.

Walther, Otto. "Verwaltung, Lenkung und Planung in der Wirtschaft in der sowjetischen Besatzungszone," 1953.

b. Materialien zur Wirtschaftslage der sowjetischen Besatzungszone. Bonn.

"Der allgemeine und spezielle Maschinenbau in der sowjetischen Besatzungszone."

"Der Aussenhandel der sowjetischen Besatzungszone Deutschlands, 1949–1950."

"Der Aussenhandel der sowjetischen Besatzungszone Deutschlands, 1951, 1952 Plan."

"Der Aussenhandel der sowjetischen Besatzungszone Deutschlands, 1952, Plan 1953."

"Der Aussenhandel der sowjetischen Besatzungszone Deutschlands, 1953 I-III, und Plan 1954."

"Der Aussenhandel der sowjetischen Besatzungszone Deutschlands, 1953, Plan 1954, und 1. Halbjahr 1954."

"Der Einzelhandel in der Versorgung der Bevölkerung der sowjetischen Besatzungszone."

"Die eisenschaffende Industrie in der sowjetischen Besatzungszone."

"Die elektrotechnische Industrie in der sowjetischen Zone Deutschlands."

"Die Entwicklung der Industrieproduktion der sowjetischen Besatzungszone, 1951, Planziffern fuer 1952."

. . . 1. Halbjahr 1951."

. . . 1. Quartal 1952."

. . . 1. Halbjahr 1952."

. . . 1952, Planziffern fuer 1953."

. . . 1953, I. Quartal."

. . . 1953, I. Quartal und Plan 1953 II. Quartal."

. . . 1953, III. Quartal."

. . . 1953 und Plan 1954.

"Der Fahrzeugbau in der sowjetischen Besatzungszone Deutschlands."

"Feinmechanik und Optik in der sowjetischen Besatzungszone."

"Die Investitionen in der sowjetischen Zone 1951 und 1952 nach staatlichen Plaenen."

Karden, Erich. "Der Bergbau in der sowjetischen Besatzungszone."

Kinzel, Eduard and Steinberg, Herbert. "Die chemische Industrie in der sowjetischen Besatzungszone."

Kinzel, Eduard. "Die Elektrizitaetswirtschaft in der sowjetischen Besatzungszone."

—— "Die Nicht-Eisen Metallindustrie in der sowjetischen Besatzungszone."

"Die Kraftwirtschaft in der Sowjetzone, ihre Quellen und Reserven."

Luv, Herbert. "Die pharmazeutische Industrie in der sowjetischen Besatzungszone."

"Die Maschinen-Traktoren-Stationen (MTS) in der sowjetischen Besatzungszone."

"Der Schiffbau in der sowjetischen Besatzungszone."

"Der Schwermaschinenbau in der sowjetischen Besatzungszone."

Seidel, Wolfgang. "Verkehrswirtschaft und Verkehrspolitik in der Sowjetzone."

"Die sowjetischen Entnahmen aus dem Produktionsaufkommen der Sowjetzone im Jahre 1951."

"Die Stellung der SAG in der Wirtschaft der Sowjetzone im Jahre 1951."

"Die Textil- und Lederindustrie in der sowjetischen Besatzungszone."

"Der Uranbergbau in der sowjetischen Besatzungszone."

c. Miscellaneous

Gleitze, Bruno. *Die Wirtschaftsstruktur der Sowjetzone und ihre gegenwaertigen sozial- und wirtschaftsrechtlichen Tendenzen.* Bonn, 1951.

Die SBZ von 1945–1954. Bonn: 1956.

Thalheim, Karl C. and Propp, Peter D. *Die Entwicklungsziele fuer die gewerbliche Wirtschaft der sowjetischen Besatzungszone in der zweiten Fuenfjahrplan-Periode.* Bonn: 1957.

2. Other Official West German Publications

Bundesministerium fuer Ernaehrung, Landwirtschaft und Forsten. *Statistisches Handbuch der Landwirtschaft und Ernaehrung,* Section VI, Planning and Economic Reporting, under the direction of Dr. K. Haefner; Redactor, Dr. G. Thiele. Hamburg and Berlin: Paul Parey, 1956.

Deutsche Bundesbank. *Monthly Report of the Deutsche Bundesbank,* previously called Monthly Report of the Bank Deutscher Laender. Frankfurt/Main.

Spormann, Kurt. "Der permanente Fluechtlingsstrom," *Bulletin des Presse- und Informationsdienstes der Bundesregierung.* Bonn: Jan. 17, 1959.

Statistisches Bundesamt, Wiesbaden. *Der Aussenhandel der Bundesrepublik Deutschland.* Various editions. Stuttgart: W. Kohlhammer.

Statistisches Bundesamt, Wiesbaden. "Die industrielle Produktion, 1951–1955. Jahreszahlen," *Die Industrie der Bundesrepublik Deutschland.* Stuttgart: W. Kohlhammer, Special Issue, 1956, No. 11.

Statistisches Bundesamt, Wiesbaden. "Der Interzonenhandel der Bundesrepublik Deutschland mit der SBZ und der sowjetischen Zone von Berlin," *Statistische Berichte,* (mimeo).

Statistisches Bundesamt, Wiesbaden. "Neuberechnung des Index der industriellen Nettoproduktion," *Die Industrie der Bundesrepublik Deutschland.* Stuttgart: W. Kohlhammer, Special Issue, 1956, No. 8.

Statistisches Bundesamt, Wiesbaden. *Statistisches Jahrbuch fuer die Bundesrepublik Deutschland,* 1953, 1954, 1955, 1956, 1957 and 1958 editions. Stuttgart: W. Kohlhammer.

Statistisches Landesamt Berlin. *Berlin in Zahlen.* Berlin: 1951.

Statistisches Landesamt Berlin. *Statistisches Jahrbuch von Berlin.* Berlin: 1951.

3. PUBLICATIONS FROM THE DEUTSCHES INSTITUT
FUER WIRTSCHAFTSFORSCHUNG

Die deutsche Wirtschaft zwei Jahre nach dem Zusammenbruch. Berlin: Albert Nauck & Co., 1947.

"Industrie- und Energiewirtschaft der sowjetischen Besatzungszone (SBZ) und der osteuropaeischen Laender," *DIW Mitteilungen,* 1952, No. 1.

"Industrie- und Energiewirtschaft der SBZ, der Laender Osteuropas und des Fernen Osten," *DIW Mitteilungen,* 1953, No. 5.

"Der Kalibergbau in der SBZ Deutschlands in den Jahren 1945–1951," *DIW Bericht,* Jan. 1952.

Kohlenbergbau und Kohlenwirtschaft im Gebiete der Sowjetzone Deutschlands, Einzelschrift No. 51, 1951.

Kupky, H. "Die langfristige Entwicklung der Bruttoanlageeinvestitionen der mitteldeutschen Industrie von 1924–1955," *Vierteljahreshefte zur Wirtschaftsforschung,* 1957, No. 4.

Ostchronik, Chronik der wirtschaftlichen und sozialen Gesetzgebung der SBZ. (Discontinued since 1959.)

Otto, Heinz. *Entwicklung und Probleme des sowjetzonalen Verkehrswesens.* Sonderheft, Reihe B, Vortraege No. 36.

Statistisches Kompendium ueber die Sowjetische Besatzungszone, n.d. (mimeo).

Vierteljahreshefte zur Wirtschaftsforschung. (Quarterly journal since 1948.)

"Wirtschaft und Finanzen im sowjetischen Besatzungsgebiet waehrend der Vorbereitungsperiode des Fuenfjahrplanes," *DIW Bericht,* 1951.

Wirtschaftsprobleme der Besatzungszonen. Berlin: Duncker & Humblot, 1948.

Wochenberichte (Weekly since 1950.)

"Zahlen zur Energiewirtschaft der sowjetischen Besatzungszone Deutschlands vor und nach 1945," *DIW Mitteilungen,* Special Issue, June 25, 1953.

4. MITTEILUNGEN AUS DEM INSTITUT FUER RAUMFORSCHUNG

Institut fuer Raumforschung, *Mitteilungen aus dem Institut fuer Raumforschung.* Bonn.

"Die eisen- und stahlerzeugende Industrie in der SBZ," No. 10, n.d.

"Die Fahrzeugindustrie der SBZ," Part I, 1953, No. 22.

"Die Fahrzeugindustrie der sowjetischen Besatzungszone Deutschlands," Part II and III, 1954, No. 25.

"Die Gaswirtschaft in der SBZ," No. 3, n.d.

"Der Maschinen- und Apparatebau in der SBZ und Ostberlin," No. 5, n.d.

"Die Versorgung mit Elektroenergie in der SBZ," 1953, No. 1.

"Die Zuckerindustrie in der SBZ," 1951.

Ipsen, Guenther. "Die Bevoelkerung Mittel- und West-Deutschlands bis 1955," *Informationen,* 1954, Nos. 27–29, July 2.

5. PUBLICATIONS BY VORSTAND DER SOZIALDEMOKRATISCHEN
PARTEI DEUTSCHLANDS (SOPADE).

Die Erzeugung von Elektroenergie in der Sowjetzone, Denkschrift No. 42, n.d.

Die Forstwirtschaft in der Sowjetzone, Denkschrift No. 58, n.d.

Die Reichsbahn in der Sowjetzone, Denkschrift No. 43, n.d.

6. PUBLICATIONS BY BERLINER ZENTRALBANK

Meimberg, Dr. Rudolf. *Wirtschaft und Waehrung Westberlins zwischen Ost und West.* Berlin: Duncker & Humblot, 1950.

────── *Die wirtschaftliche Entwicklung in Westberlin und in der sowjetischen Zone,* 2nd. edition. Berlin: 1952.

7. MISCELLANEOUS BOOKS AND PAMPHLETS

Abeken, Gerhard. "Die sowjetzonale Wirtschaftsexpansion," in *Wirtschaftsforschung und Wirtschaftsfuehrung.* Berlin: Duncker & Humblot, 1956.

Boettcher, Bodo. *Industrielle Strukturwandlungen im sowjetisch besetzten Gebiet Deutschlands.* Osteuropa Institut an der Freien Universitaet Berlin, Wirtschaftswissenschaftliche Veroeffentlichungen. Berlin: 1956, No. 4.

Deutscher Ammoniak Vertrieb, landwirtschaftliche Abteilung. *Faustzahlen fuer die Landwirtschaft.* 3rd. edition. Bochum: 1951.

Eik, Juergen. *Die wirtschaftlichen Folgen der Zonengrenzen.* Hamburg: Union Verlag, 1948.

Foerster, Wolfgang. "Die Rolle der Kosten in der ostzonalen Wirtschaftspolitik (Kostenpolitik)," *Berichte des Osteuropa Instituts an der Freien Universitaet Berlin.* Berlin: 1952, No. 1.

Gleitze, Bruno. *Ostdeutsche Wirtschaft,* Deutsches Institut fuer Wirtschaftsforschung. Berlin: Duncker & Humblot, 1956.

────── *Das Problem der gespaltenen Wirtschaft Deutschlands,* Wirtschaftswissenschaftliches Institut der Gewerkschaften. Koeln, 1954, Febr.-March.

IFO Institut. *Statistisches Handbuch der Bauwirtschaft.* Munich: 1949.

Koziolek, Helmut. "Probleme der Wirtschaftsentwicklung der Deutschen Demokratischen Republik in der Zeit von 1950 bis 1955," *Kieler Vortraege,* New Sequence. Kiel, 1957, No. 11.

Kramer, Matthais. Unpublished manuscript on East German agriculture.

Laenderrat des amerikanischen Besatzungsgebietes. *Statistisches Handbuch von Deutschland, 1928–1944.* Munich: 1949.

Liebe, Hans. "Die Entwicklung der Landwirtschaft in der sowjetischen Besatzungszone seit 1945 und der augenblickliche Stand der Versorgung mit Nahrungsmittel," in *Wirtschaftsforschung und Wirtschaftsfuehrung.* Berlin: Duncker & Humblot, 1956.

Mehnert, Klaus and Schulte, Heinrich. *Deutschland Jahrbuch 1949.* Essen: West Verlag, 1949.

────── *Deutschland Jahrbuch 1953.* Essen: West Verlag, 1953.

Padberg, K. and Nieschulz, A. "Produktion, Verkaufserloese und Betriebsausgaben der Landwirtschaft im Bundesgebiet," *Agrarwirtschaft,* Zeitschrift fuer Betriebswirtschaft und Marktforschung. Bonn: A. Strohte, Vol. VI, No. 2, Febr. 1957.

Pfuehl, Eberhard. "Das allgemeine Vertragssystem in der volkseigenen Wirtschaft der sowjetischen Besatzungszone Deutschlands," *Berichte des Osteuropa Instituts an der Freien Universitaet Berlin.* Berlin: 1952, No. 4.

Thimm, Gerhard. "Die Preis- und Kostenstruktur in der Industrieproduktion der Sowjetzone," Part I, *Berichte des Osteuropa Instituts an der Freien Universitaet Berlin.* Berlin: 1956, No. 24.

Varga, E. "Das Geld im Sozialismus," *Weltwirtschaftliches Archiv,* Vol. 78, No. 2. (English translation appeared in *International Economic Papers,* Vol. VIII, 1958.)

Waggershausen, Otto. *Landwirtschaftliche Richtzahlen und Hinweise (Faustzahlen) fuer den Berater und praktischen Landwirt,* 3rd. revised edition, Dr. Gisbert Vogel, ed. Stuttgart: Eugen Ulmer, 1956. Under the auspices of the Institut fuer landwirtschaftliche Betriebs- und Arbeitslehre der Universitaet Kiel.

D. OTHER PUBLICATIONS

1. TECHNICAL BOOKS AND PRICE CATALOGUES

Automotive and Aviation Manufacturing. *Automotive Industries,* 37th Annual Statistical Issue, Vol. 112, No. 6. A Chilton Publication, March 15, 1955.

J. T. Baker Chemical Co., Phillipsburg, N. J. *Baker Analyzed Reagents and Other Chemicals,* Specification Catalogue and Price List, No. 54.

Cotton Facts, 1927 ed. New York, Shepperson Publishing Company, 1928.

Dammer, Otto. *Chemische Technologie der Neuzeit,* Vol. II, Part II, Second edition, Franz Peters and Hermann Grossmann, eds. Stuttgart: Verlag Ferdinand Enke, 1933.

Dubbel, Prof. H. *Taschenbuch fuer den Maschinenbau,* Vols. I and II. Berlin: Verlag Julius Springer, 1953.

Merck, E. Darmstadt. *Preisverzeichnis,* J, 1950, No. 16. (price list).

Riedel- de Haen, A. G. Seelze bei Hannover. *Reagenzien, De Haen's* . . . , R2/ 1952.

Sinner, Georg, ed. *Huette, Des Ingenieurs Taschenbuch,* 27th edition. Akademischer Verein "Huette," E. V., Berlin. Berlin: Wilhelm Ernst und Sohn, 1950.

United States Steel Company, United States Steel Corporation Subsidiary. *The Making, Shaping and Treating of Steel,* 26th edition. Pittsburgh: June 1951.

2. UNITED STATES PUBLICATIONS ON GERMANY

Office of the Military Government for Germany (U. S.), Economic Division. *A Year of Potsdam,* n.d.

———— *Economic Data on Potsdam Germany,* Special Report of the Military Governor, September, 1947.

3. OTHER UNITED STATES GOVERNMENT PUBLICATIONS

Bureau of Mines, *Minerals Yearbook,* Vol. III, 1952. Washington, D. C.: United States Government Printing Office, 1955.

———— *Minerals Yearbook,* Vol. II, 1953. Washington, D. C.: United States Government Printing Office, 1956.

Sanderson, Fred. in *Trends in Economic Growth: A Comparison of the Western Powers and the Soviet Bloc.* A Study prepared for the Joint Committee on the Economic Report by the Legislative Reference Service of the Library of Congress, Joint Committee Print, 83rd Congress, 2nd Session. Washington, D. C.: United States Government Printing Office, 1955.

United States Department of Commerce, Bureau of the Census. Biennial *Census of Manufactures,* Part I. Washington, D. C. United States Government Printing Office, 1937.

———— *Census of Manufactures: 1937.* Washington, D. C.: United States Government Printing Office, 1939.

———— *Census of Manufactures 1947,* Vol. II, Statistics by Industry. Washington, D. C.: United States Government Printing Office, 1949.

———— *Statistical Abstract of the United States 1950.* Washington, D. C.: United States Government Printing Office.

United States Department of Commerce, Industrial Reference Service, Part 12, *Textiles and Related Products.* Washington, D. C.: United States Government Printing Office, April 1941, No. 20.

4. O.E.E.C. PUBLICATIONS

"The Chemical Industry in Europe," *Trends in Economic Sectors*. Paris: Dec. 1954, Sept. 1955, Dec. 1955.

"The Electricity Supply Industry in Europe," *Trends in Economic Sectors*. Paris: Jan. 1955.

Fuel Consumption of Thermal Power Stations; First Enquiry 1952–1958. Paris: Febr. 1953.

Fuel Consumption of Thermal Power Stations; Third Enquiry 1952–1958. Paris: Jan. 1955.

"The Non-Ferrous Metal Industry in Europe," *Trends in Economic Sectors*. Paris: January 1955.

"The Textile Industry in Europe," *Trends in Economic Sectors*. Paris: February 1956.

5. OTHER PUBLICATIONS CONSULTED

Bergson, Abram. *Soviet National Income and Product in 1937*. New York: Columbia University Press, 1953.

Djilas, Milovan. *The New Class*. New York: Praeger Co., 1958.

Economic Commission for Europe. *Economic Bulletin for Europe*. Geneva: Miscellaneous issues.

—— *Economic Survey of Europe in 1954*. Geneva: 1955.

—— *Economic Survey of Europe in 1955*. Geneva: 1956.

—— Food and Agriculture Organization of the United Nations. *Handbook for the Preparation of Food Balance Sheets*. Washington, D. C., April 1949.

Gerschenkron, Alexander. *Description of an Index of Italian Industrial Output 1881–1913*. Rand Corporation Publication R-187, April 6, 1951 (mimeo).

Gerschenkron, Alexander, with the assistance of Ehrlich, Alexander. *A Dollar Index of Soviet Machinery Output 1927–1928 to 1937*. Rand Corporation Publication R-197, 1951.

Gerschenkron, Alexander. *A Dollar Index of Soviet Electric Power Output*. Rand Corporation Publication, 1954.

Gould, J. M. *Output and Productivity in the Electric and Gas Utilities 1899–1942*. New York: National Bureau of Economic Research, 1946.

Hayes, Samuel P. "Potash Prices and Competition," *Quarterly Journal of Economics*, 1942, p. 31 ff.

Iverson, Carl. "Economic Development and Economic Policy in Denmark," *Quarterly Review*, Skandinaviska Banken A. B., April, 1955.

Jackson, E. F. "Social Accounting in Eastern Europe," in *Income and Wealth*, Series IV. London: International Association for Research into Income and Wealth, 1955.

Krause, Heinz. *Economic Structure of East Germany and its Position within the Soviet Bloc*, Parts I and II. Washington, D. C.: Council of Economic and Industrial Research Inc.

Kurrelmayer, L. K. *The Potash Industry*. Albuquerque: 1951.

Lange, Oskar. "Outline of a Reconversion Plan for the Polish Economy," *International Economic Papers*, Vol. VII, 1957, English translation. (Originally appeared in *Zycie Gospodarcze* [Warsaw], July 16, 1956.

Machinery and Allied Products Institute. *Capital Goods Review*. Chicago: May 1950, No. 2.

Maddison, A. "East-West Trade," *Bulletin of the Oxford Institute of Statistics*, Vol. 16. Oxford: Basil Blackwell, Febr.–March, 1954, Nos. 2 and 3.

Nettl, John P. *The Eastern Zone and Soviet Policy in Germany 1945–50*. London and New York: Oxford University Press, 1951.

Nettl, John P. *Die deutsche Sowjetzone bis heute*. Frankfurt: 1953. (Translation from the English and brought up to date.)

S.B.Z. Archiv. Dokumente, Berichte, Kommentare zu gesamtdeutschen Fragen. Koeln: Verlag fuer Politik und Wirtschaft G.m.b.H., miscellaneous issues.

Stolper, Wolfgang F. "The Labor Force and Industrial Development in Soviet Germany," *Quarterly Journal of Economics*, Vol. LXXI, November 1957.

United Nations. *Yearbook of International Trade Statistics*, 1957 ed., Vol. I. New York: 1958.

Zimmermann, Erich W. *World Resources and Industries*. New York: Harper & Brothers, 2nd. ed., 1951.

Zur Muehlen, "Die Pankower Sowjetrepublik und der Deutschen Westen," *Rote Weissbuecher*, 1953, No. 10.

NOTES

SHORT FORMS OF TITLE USED IN THE NOTES AND TABLES

Direktive — Direktive für den zweiten Fünfjahrplan zur Entwicklung der Volkswirtschaft in der Deutschen Demokratischen Republik, 1956 bis 1960
DJ — Deutschland Jahrbuch
FL — Faustzahlen für die Landwirtschaft
LRHBL — Landwirtschaftliche Richtzahlen und Hinweise (Faustzahlen) für den Berater- und praktischen Landwirt
Materialien — Materialien zur Wirtschaftslage in der Sowjetischen Zone
Neuberechnung — Neuberechnung des Index der Industriellen Nettoproduktion
Produktionsstatistik, 1936 — Gesamtergebnisse der amtlichen Produktionsstatistik
SHD — Statistisches Handbuch von Deutschland, 1928–1944
SHLE — Statistisches Handbuch für Landwirtschaft und Ernährung
SJBR — Statistisches Jahrbuch für die Bundesrepublik Deutschland
SJDDR — Statistisches Jahrbuch der Deutschen Demokratischen Republik
SJR — Statistisches Jahrbuch des Deutschen Reiches
SP — Statische Praxis
VHS — Vierteljahreshefte zur Statistik

PREFACE

1. Milovan Djilas, *The New Class* (New York: Praeger, 1958).
2. Carl Iverson, "Economic Development and Economic Policy in Denmark," *Quarterly Review* (Skandinavska Bankens, A. B.), April 1955.
3. *Presse-Informationen,* 18 February 1959, No. 21 (1704), p. 5.
4. *Presse-Informationen,* 20 February 1959, No. 22 (1705).
5. Oskar Lange, "Outline of a Reconversion Plan for the Polish Economy," *International Economic Papers,* 1957, Vol. VII, appearing originally in *Zycie Gospodarcze* [Warsaw] 16 July 1956.
6. E. Varga, "Das Geld im Sozialismus," *Weltwirtschaftliches Archiv,* [1957], Vol. 78, No. 2, pp. 223–288; an English translation appeared in *International Economic Papers,* 1958, Vol. VIII.
7. Official German figures from *SJDDR,* 1955, pp. 242 ff.; 1956, pp. 518 ff.; 1957, p. 515; for the Russian statistics see United Nations, *Yearbook of International Trade Statistics,* 1957, Vol. I, p. 576.
8. E. Varga, *op. cit.*
9. Günther Kohlmey, "Spaltungsdisproportionen und Aussenhandel," *Wirtschaftswissenschaft,* 1958, No. 1, p. 72.
10. Imre Vajda, "Einige Bemerkungen über die Preisbasis auf dem sozialistischen Weltmarkt," *Der Aussenhandel und der Innerdeutsche Handel* [East Berlin], 27 November 1958, No. 22, pp. 775–778.
11. Walter Mosterz, "Spezialisierung und Koordinierung im Maschinenbau zwischen den sozialistischen Ländern," *Wirtschaftswissenschaft,* [East Berlin], July–August 1958, Vol. VI, No. 5, p. 664.
12. *Ibid.,* p. 663, my italics.
13. *Ibid.*
14. Georg Henke and Lothar Rouscik, "Eine neue Etappe der wirtschaftlichen Zusammenarbeit im sozialistischen Lager," *Einheit* [East Berlin], June 1958, Vol. XIII, No. 6, pp. 821–836.

CHAPTER I. Population and the Labor Force

1. *SJBR*, 1956, p. 13.

2. *SJDDR*, 1955, p. 9.

3. *Ibid.*, p. 37.

4. zur Mühlen, "Die Pankower Sowjetrepublik und der Deutsche Westen," *Rote Weissbücher*, 1953, No. 10, p. 52.

5. *DIW, Wochenbericht*, 24 February 1956, No. 8.

6. Günther Ipsen, "Die Bevölkerung Mittel- und West-Deutschlands bis 1955," *Informationen, Institut für Raumforschung*, 2 July 1954, No. 27–29, p. 425. (Unless specifically stated, all translations are mine.)

7. Walter Ulbricht, *Der Fünfjahrplan und die Perspektiven der Volkswirtschaft* (East Berlin, Dietz, 1950), p. 51. It is not clear whether Ulbricht is referring to all women workers or to women employees only.

8. Deutsches Institut für Wirtschaftsforschung, *Ostchronik*, Sec. M, No. 5, refers to *Gesetzblatt der Deutschen Demokratischen Republik*, 1951, p. 973.

9. *SJDDR*, 1955, p. 104.

10. Figures for employment are from *SJBR*, 1956, p. 13. It is assumed that one-third of Berlin employment was in the Eastern sector.

11. As quoted by Prof. Bruno Gleitze in "Das Problem der gespaltenen Wirtschaft Deutschlands," *Mitteilungen des Wirtschaftswissenschaftlichen Instituts der Gewerkschaften*, February–March 1954, Vol. VIII, No. 2/3, p. 30.

12. Gleitze, *op. cit.*, p. 31.

13. *SP*, July 1956, p. 90.

14. *Ibid.*

15. Gleitze, *op. cit.*, p. 31.

16. *SP*, July 1956, p. 91.

CHAPTER II. Employment by Economic Sectors and Industries

1. *SJDDR*, 1955, p. 106.

2. *Politische Oekonomie, Lehrbuch* (East Berlin: Dietz, 1955) pp. 587–588. (My translation of German edition of Russian text by Soviet Academy of Sciences.)

3. E. F. Jackson, *Social Accounting in Eastern Europe* "Income and Wealth," Series IV (London: International Association for Research in Income and Wealth, 1955), pp. 246–248. For footnote (a), see note 1, p. 247; for (b) see p. 248, note 1; other footnotes have been omitted.

4. See Martin Hentschel, "Die Berechnung des Aufkommens und der Verwendung des gesellschaftlichen Gesamtproduktes und des Nationaleinkommens im zweiten Fünfjahrplan," *SP*, August 1958, pp. 151–155; September 1958, pp. 178–182.

5. *SP*, August 1958, p. 153.

6. *SHD*, p. 481.

7. *SP*, August 1956, pp. 108–109.

8. *Ibid.*

9. Franz Rupp, *Die Reparationsleistung der Sowjetischen Besatzungszone* (Bonn, 1951). (*Bonner Bericht.*) See also, Anonymous, *Die Reparationen der Sowjetischen Besatzungszone in den Jahren 1945 bis Ende 1953*, a continuation of the Rupp study (Bonn, 1953).

10. *SJDDR*, 1955, p. 184, introductory note.

11. *Ibid.*, p. 106.

12. Anonymous, "Zur Entwicklung der Krise in den USA," Deutsches Wirtschaftsinstitut, (East) Berlin, *Bericht*, Vol. VI, No. 11/12 (June 1955).

CHAPTER III. National Accounting and the East German Index of Gross Production

1. Fred Sanderson, in *Trends in Economic Growth: A Comparison of the Western Powers and the Soviet Bloc*, a study prepared for the Joint Committee on the Economic Report by the Legislative Reference Service of the Library of Congress, Joint Committee Print, 83rd Congress, 2d Session, Washington, D. C., 1955, p. 292.

2. *SJDDR*, 1955.

3. *Ibid.*, pp. 90, 93. See also Table 17.

4. *Ibid.*, p. 120–170.

5. Ibid., 1957, pp. 154–160. For the data on net national product, see Table 164.

6. This is implied in the discussion of Martin Hentschel, "Die Berechnung des Aufkommens und der Verwendung des gesellschaftlichen Gesamtproduktes und des Nationaleinkommens im zweiten Fünfjahrplan," *SP*, August 1957, pp. 151–155.

7. Hans-Jürgen Schulz, "Bemerkungen zur Problematik betrieblicher und volkswirtschaftlicher Leistungsziffern," *SP*, February 1959, p. 30.

8. Dr. Margarete Schmidt, *Probleme bei der Ermittlung der industriellen Bruttoproduktion* (East Berlin: Verlag Die Wirtschaft, 1953), *Diskussionsbeiträge zu Wirtschaftsfragen*, No. 12, p. 19.

9. *Ibid.*

10. *Ibid.*, pp. 19–20 (italics in the original.)

11. *SJDDR*, 1955, p. 120.

12. Dr. Margarete Schmidt, *op. cit.*, pp. 22–23 (italics in the original).

13. *Ibid.*, p. 39.

14. *Ibid.*, pp. 40–41, and note 44 on p. 41.

15. *Ibid.*, p 68–69.

16. *Ibid.*, p. 46.

17. *Ibid.*, p. 51.

18. *Ibid.*, p. 61.

19. *SJDDR*, 1957, p. 222; Hentschel, *op. cit.*, pp. 151–152.

20. Rumen Janakieff, "Kritische Bemerkungen zur Anwendung der Kennziffer Bruttoproduktion für die Einschätzung der Produktionsarbeit des Industriebetriebes, Part I," *SP*, May 1957, p. 96. Part II appeared in June 1957. (An English translation of the article has been published in *International Economic Papers*, 1958, Vol. 8, pp. 179–200.)

21. *SJDDR*, 1955, p. 120.

22. Dr. Margarete Schmidt, *op. cit.*, p. 86.

23. Ibid., pp. 86, 87, and notes 96 and 97 on p. 87. A. Kindelberger, *Die statistische Berichterstattung der privaten Wirtschaft* (East Berlin, 1955), p. 36, states that the *Messwerte* were based on plan prices which in turn were based on the average of actual prices in 1947–1948.

24. Dr. Margarete Schmidt, *op. cit.*, p. 89.

25. *Ibid.*, pp. 89–90.

26. *Ibid.*, p. 91.

27. *Ibid.*, p. 92.

28. *Ibid.*, p. 93.

29. Fred Oelssner, Die *Übergangsperiode vom Kapitalismus zum Sozialismus in der Deutschen Demokratischen Republik* (East Berlin, 1955), pp. 50–51.

30. *Ibid.*, p. 34.

31. *Ibid.*, pp. 66–67.

32. *SJDDR*, 1955, p. 120.

33. See Janakieff, *op. cit.*, Part I.

34. Walter Ulbricht, "Die Rolle der Deutschen Demokratischen Republik im Kampf um ein friedliches und glückliches Leben des deutschen Volkes," Speech given at the 25th meeting of the Central Committee of the Socialist Unity (Communist) Party of Germany. *Neues Deutschland*, 30 October 1955, No. 255, p. 5.

35. *Ibid.*, p. 3.

36. Oskar Lange, "Outline of a Reconversion Plan for the Polish Economy," *International Economic Papers*, 1957, Vol. VII, pp. 145–155. This article originally appeared in *Zycie Gospodarcze* [Warsaw], 16 July, 1956.

37. G. Forbrig, "Zur Ermittlung der industriellen Bruttoproduktion," *SP*, March 1957, pp. 47–51.

38. *Ibid.*, p. 49.

39. *Ibid.*, p. 50.

40. *Ibid.*, p. 51.

41. "During the Second Five Year Plan, we may expect an increased specialization in the metalworking industries. As gross production is measured at present, this would lead to an overestimate of gross production. In light industries we may count on the

formation of combines so that here the increase in the volume of gross production would be insufficiently expressed. Even if these changes were to offset each other . . . the share of individual industry branches in gross production would be changed. . . ." (Erich Schmidt, "Der Einfluss der Kooperationsbeziehungen auf den Nachweis des Produktionsvolumens der Industrie," *SP* December 1956, p. 193.)

42. Janakieff, *op. cit.*

43. *Ibid.*, Part I, p. 97.

44. *Ibid.*

45. *Ibid.*, p. 110.

46. *SJDDR*, 1957, p. 223.

47. *Ibid.*, 1955, Notes, p. 93.

48. Martin Hentschel, *op. cit.*, August 1957, p. 153.

49. *Ibid.*

50. All accounts for the deflation procedures used during the First Five Year Plan come from Helmut Koziolek, *Grundfragen der marxistisch-leninistischen Theorie des Nationaleinkommens-Sozialismus* (East Berlin, Verlag Die Wirtschaft, 1957), pp. 56–57.

51. Hentschel, *op. cit.*, September 1957, p. 179. Koziolek, *op. cit.*, p. 57, claims that a recalculation for the construction industry was made until 1954–55 without stating how, and that producer prices were used to deflate the performance of construction artisans.

52. Hentschel, *op. cit.*, Sept. 1957, p. 179.

53. Koziolek, *op. cit.*, p. 57.

54. Hentschel, *op. cit.*, Sept. 1957, p. 180.

55. *Ibid.*

56. "The recalculation of trade on a 1950 price base was done by taking for every year the actually realized trade markups. It was necessary, however, to add each year the subsidies and impositions realized by trade in 1950." Koziolek, *op. cit.*, p. 57. This reads as if trade markup in *current* prices had been combined with the turnover tax, etc. in 1950.

57. Hentschel, *op. cit.* Sept. 1957, p. 180.

58. *Ibid.* My italics.

59. *Ibid.*

60. *Ibid.*, p. 182.

CHAPTER V. Mining and Gas

1. Erich Karden, *Der Bergbau in der Sowjetischen Besatzungzone, Materialien* (Bonn, n.d.), p. 44.

2. Gerhard Thimm, *Die Preis-und Kostenstruktur in der Industrieproduktion der Sowjetzone*, Berichte des Osteuropa Instituts an der Freien Universität Berlin, Berlin 1956, *passim*.

3. *SJDDR*, 1955, p. 162, and 1956, p. 279.

4. Eduard Kinzel and Herbert Steinberg, *Die chemische Industrie in der sowjetischen Besatzungszone, Materialien*, (Bonn, n.d.), pp. 63–64.

5. Eduard Kinzel, *Die Elektrizitätswirtschaft in der sowjetischen Besatzungszone, Materialien*, (Bonn, n.d., probably 1954), App. 7, p. 38. Unfortunately, the table does not give the date to which the listing refers.

6. SoPaDe Informationsdienst, *Die Erzeugung von Electroenergie in der Sowjetzone*, Memorandum No. 42, p. 23, App. 4. It is also stated that 18 SAG stations had a capacity of 1,424 MW, 79 mining-associated stations had a capacity of 570 MW, 1,215 other industrial stations had a capacity of 795 MW, and 129 public generating stations had a capacity of 1,930 MW. (*Ibid.*, App. 4 and 4a.)

7. Deutsches Institut für Wirtschaftsforschung, *Kohlenbergbau and Kohlenwirtschaft im Gebiete der Sowjetzone Deutschlands* (Berlin, October 1951), footnote 1, p. 28. Monograph No. 51.

8. *Neue Hütte*, Special Issue, Internationale Niederschachtofentagung in Leipzig (East Berlin, VEB Verlag Technik, February 1956), p. 219.

9. *Ibid.*, p. 217.

10. *Produktionsstatistik*, 1936, p. 44.

11. Prof. H. Dubbel, *Taschenbuch für den Maschinenbau*, 6th ed. (Berlin, Julius Springer, 1935), p. 539.

12. *Die Gaswirtschaft in der Sowjetischen Besatzungszone Deutschlands,* p. 4. *Mitteilungen aus dem Institut für Raumforschung* No. 3 (Bad Godesberg, 1950), p. 4.

13. *SJDDR,* 1956, p. 523.

14. Dubbel, *op. cit.,* p. 540.

15. According to *Die Gaswirtschaft,* p. 6, it was not possible to get the maximum amounts producible in the early days because of the inefficiency of the small plants.

16. Figures are from *SHD,* various pages, and *SJBR,* 1955, p. 218.

17. An analysis of the various ores found in East Germany was published in *Neue Hütte, op. cit.,* p. 194. According to this source, many of these ores are too acid and of too low a quality to be used in ordinary blast furnaces. However, the new low-shaft furnaces can handle some of these ores.

18. Karden, *op. cit.,* p. 19.

19. Bruno Gleitze, *Ostdeutsche Wirtschaft* (Berlin, Duncker and Humblot, 1956), p. 191.

20. *Ibid.,* p. 191; Eduard Kinzel, *Die Nicht-Eisen Metallindustrie in der sowjetischen Bezatzungszone, Materialien,* (Bonn, 1955), pp. 8–9; and *Direktive,* p. 22. It might be added that such ores appear well within the range that would be considered exploitable in the United States.

21. *Produktionsstatistik, 1936,* note 5, p. 44.

22. Samuel P. Hayes, "Potash Prices and Competition," *Quarterly Journal of Economics,* November 1942, pp. 31 f. "Potash is sold as a highly standardized product, muriate of potash (potassium chloride, from 80 to 98 per cent pure), priced on the basis of the amount of K_2O (potassium oxide) that could be obtained from them" (*ibid.,* p. 31). "Moreover, 80 per cent is used for fertilizer, and variations in other contents than K_2O are apparently irrelevant for most purposes" (*ibid.,* p. 32). See also, L. K. Kurrelmayer, *The Potash Industry* (Albuquerque, 1951).

23. *SJBR,* 1953, p. 250, and 1955, p. 218.

24. *Direktive,* p. 22.

25. *Produktionsstatistik,* 1936, p. 44.

26. *SJBR,* 1955, pp. 227, 230.

27. *SJDDR,* 1955, p. 104.

CHAPTER VI. Electric Power

1. *SP,* August 1956. Since this was written, a further breakdown for 1955 through 1958 has been published in *SJDDR,* 1956, 1957, and 1958. Although the figures for 1955 differ from the data given above, the differences are too small to warrant a recalculation. The figures are given as follows:

Energy sources of electric power generation,
East Germany, 1955, 1956, and 1957

(Per cent of total)

	1955	1956	1957	1958
Soft coal	6.1 (5.9)	5.2	4.5	4.6
Raw lignite	63.2	66.3	68.3	69.3
Lignite briquets	9.0 (88.2)	8.5	7.4	6.8
Lignite coke	14.4	12.7	12.7	12.0
Dry coal (*Trockenkohle*)	0.7	0.7	0.5	0.5
Water power	1.7 (2.6)	1.7	1.5	1.8
Oil	0.1	0.1	0.1	0.1
Gases	4.7 (3.3)	4.6	4.8	4.7
Other	0.1	0.2	0.2	0.2
Total	100.0	100.0	100.0	100.0

The figures in parentheses are given in *SP,* June 1956, p. 106; 1955 and 1956 figures are given in *SJDDR,* 1956, p. 301, the 1957 figures in 1957, p. 313, and 1958 in 1958, p. 362.

2. Jacob Martin Gould, *Output and Productivity in the Electric and Gas Utilities, 1899–1942* (New York, National Bureau of Economic Research, 1946), p. 58.

3. Calculated from data presented in OEEC, *Fuel Consumption of Thermal Power Stations,* 3d Enquête, p. 18.

4. *Ibid.,* p. 19.

5. *Ibid.,* p. 20.

6. Prof. H. Dubbel, *Taschenbuch für len Maschinenbau* (6th ed. Berlin, Julius Springer, 1935), Vol. 1, p. 502. Figures are always the "lower heat value."

7. *Ibid.*

8. Information from the Department of Mechanical Engineering, Massachusetts Institute of Technology.

9. OEEC, *op. cit.,* p. 17.

10. Deutsches Institut für Wirtschaftsforschung, *Zahlen zur Energiewirtschaft in der sowjetischen Besatzungszone Deutschlands vor und nach 1945, Mitteilungen,* Special Issue, June 25, 1953, Part II, pp. 19, 19a, and 19b.

11. *Neue Hütte,* Special Issue, Internationale Niederschachtofentagung in Leipzig (East Berlin, VEB Verlag Technik, February 1956), p. 232.

12. Eduard Kinzel, *Die Elektrizitätswirtschaft in der sowjetischen Besatzungszone, Materialien* (Bonn, n.d., (probably 1954), p. 13.

13. Professor Helmut Koziolek of East Berlin stated in a talk at the University of Kiel that in "1936, using equipment 3,000–3,500 hours per year was considered bearable. . . . Today our generating stations run 5,600–5,700 hours, those of the Federal Republic 4,500 hours. . . . Fast repairs help to keep the stations in order. Of course we shall reduce the number of hours run as capacities are increased, but it will always lie substantially above 1936." H. Koziolek, "Probleme der Wirtschaftsentwicklung der Deutschen Demokratischen Republik in der Zeit von 1950 bis 1955" *Kieler Vorträge,* 1957, n.s., No. 11, p. 11.

14. *SP,* August 1956.

15. *SHD,* p. 337.

16. *Ibid.,* p. 335; *Produktionsstatistik, 1936,* p. 55.

17. *SJBR,* 1955, p. 435.

18. *Produktionsstatistik, 1936,* p. 55.

19. *Ibid.,* p. 29.

20. Rolf Schlecht, "Die Elektroenergie-Erzeugung und Versorgung im ersten Fünfjahrplan," *SP,* August 1956, p. 107.

21. *Ibid.*

22. *Ibid.,* p. 106. The maximum capacity in East Germany is given as follows (megawatts):

	Total	Increase	Percentage increase over preceding year
1950	3,709		
1951	3,869	160	4.3
1952	4,040	171	4.4
1953	4,250	210	5.2
1954	4,930	680	16.0
1955	5,186	256	5.2
1957	5,484.5	298.5	5.8
1958	5,993.6	509.1	8.5

Figures for 1950–1955, *ibid.,* pp. 105–106; for 1957, *SJDDR,* 1957, p. 318, for 1958, *ibid.,* p. 368.

Figures refer to maximum output with the installed capacity, given its state of repair. Installed capacity has increased less than maximum capacity because of repairs. *SJDDR,* 1957, p. 318, gives the following figures:

      installed capacity: 6,415.4 megawatts (i.e., nominal capacity)

      fahrbare Leistung: 5,484.5 megawatts (i.e., maximum capacity)

      verfügte Leistung: 4,935.0 megawatts (i.e., power delivered to the distribution network)

   hours of *fahrbare Leistung* used: 5,969

   installed capacity used: 85.5 per cent

For 1958, *ibid.*, 1957, p. 368, gives the following figures:

installed capacity:	6769.6
fahrbare Leistung:	5993.6
verfügte Leistung:	5375.9
hours used:	n.a.
installed capacity used:	88.5 per cent.

CHAPTER VII. Metallurgy

1. *Die eisenschaffende Industrie in der sowjetischen Besatzungzone, Materialien* (Bonn, 1953), p. 24.

2. *Ibid.*

3. Otto Dammer, *Chemische Technologie der Neuzeit,* 2nd. ed., Hermann Grossmann, ed. (Stuttgart: Ferdinand Enke, 1933), Vol. II, Part 2, p. 83.

4. *SJBR*, 1955, p. 453.

5. The inputs required are based on information given the author by Professor Thomas B. King of the Department of Metallurgy, Massachusetts Institute of Technology.

6. The amount of these inputs as well as the amount of electricity and coke used is also based on information given the author at the Massachusetts Institute of Technology.

7. *SJBR*, 1955, p. 452. For details see the notes to the Tables in the Supplement.

8. *SJDDR*, 1956, pp. 278–279.

9. *Direktive*, p. 79.

10. *Ibid.*, p. 2.

11. *Ibid.*, p. 20.

12. *Ibid.*, p. 21.

13. Dr. Gerhard Thimm, *Die Preis- und Kostenstruktur in der Industrieproduktion der Sowjetzone. Berichte des Osteuropa Instituts an der Freien Universität Berlin* (West Berlin, 1956) Part I, p. 124.

14. *SJBR,* 1955, p. 223.

15. ECE, *The Non-Ferrous Metal Industry in Europe* (Paris, January 1955), p. 76.

16. *SJBR,* 1955.

17. "The production of magnesium is to start anew." (*Direktive*, p. 23.) In 1955 West Germany produced 4,150 tons of magnesium and magnesium alloys.

18. U. S. Department of Commerce, Bureau of the Census, *Statistical Abstract of the United States, 1950* (Washington, Government Printing Office, 1951), p. 1156.

19. *SJBR,* 1956, p. 429.

20. *Neuberechnung,* p. 61. These data refer to the *new* index based on 1950 relationships. In Table A.23 of the Supplement the *old* index has been retained. Like our own calculations it is based on the 1936 relationship.

CHAPTER VIII. Engineering Construction

1. Alexander Gerschenkron, "Description of an Index of Italian Industrial Output, 1881–1913" (hectograph).

2. Information obtained from Professor Milton C. Shaw, Massachusetts Institute of Technology.

3. Dr. Wolfgang Seidel, *Verkehrswirtschaft und Verkehrspolitik in der Sowjetzone, Materialien* (Bonn, n.d. p. 91) gives a list of plants producing trucks in 1951, none of which was more than 3 tons. The distribution of tires by size (*ibid.*, p. 123) also indicates primarily that small trucks are being built. However, it is not known how the program has changed since 1951, but it is virtually certain that to use a 3-ton truck as the average errs, if at all, on the high side.

4. *SJBR,* p. 437. In 1936 the dealer price was about RM 5,400, and in 1954 it was DM 9,000. Allowing for a 15 percent markup, this reduces to RM 4,590 and DM 7,650, respectively. (If the price index is applied, the 1936 price would be DM 3,530, which is known to be too low. The known price for 1936 has been kept, but for the other years the price index has been applied to the 1950 price.)

5. *Ibid.*, p. 222.

6. *Automotive Industries,* 37th Annual Statistical Issue, 15 March 1955, p. 158.

7. Bruno Gleitze, *Ostdeutsche Wirtschaft*, (Berlin, 1956, Duncker and Humblot) p. 177.

8. *SJBR*, p. 233.

9. U. S. Department of Commerce, Bureau of the Census, *Census of Manufactures: 1937* (Washington, Government Printing Office, 1939), pp. 1196, 1203, and 1209.

10. Deutsches Institut für Wirtschaftsforschung, *Wochenbericht*, 31 May 1957, p. 89.

11. "Until 1948 the agricultural machinery industry concentrated on repairs. In 1950 the value of agricultural machinery was only 35% of 1936. During the first years of the [First] Five Year Plan, agricultural machinery building received insufficient attention. . . . Since 1953 there has been a considerable improvement, however. Production of agricultural machinery was concentrated primarily on attachments. . . ." H. Koziolek, "Probleme der Wirtschaftsentwicklung der Deutschen Demokratischen Republik in der Zeit von 1950 bis 1955," *Kieler Vorträge*, 1957, n.s., No. 11, p. 18.

12. *SJR*, 1935, p. 148.

13. *SJBR*, 1955, p. 438.

14. Calculated from *Produktionsstatistik, 1936,* p. 47, and Gleitze, *Ostdeutsche Wirtschaft*, p. 181.

15. Prof. Rumen Janakieff, "Kritische Bemerkungen zur Anwendung der Kennziffer Bruttoproduktion für die Einschätzung der Produktionsarbeit des Industriebetriebes," Part I, *SP*, May 1957, p. 98.

16. Ibid., Part II, *SP*, June 1957, p. 110. (An English translation of the two parts of this article has been published in *International Economic Papers*, 1958, Vol. VIII, pp. 179–200.)

17. *SJDDR*, 1955, p. 128.

18. *SP*, May 1956, p. 61.

19. Gleitze, *Ostdeutsche Wirtschaft*, p. 181.

20. Bodo Böttcher, *Industrielle Strukturwandlungen im sowjetisch besetzten Gebiet Deutschlands*, (West Berlin, Duncker and Humblot) 1956, p. 131.

21. *SP*, May 1956, p. 61.

22. *Die Elektrotechnische Industrie in der Sowjetischen Zone Deutschlands, Materialien* (Bonn, n.d.) pp. 7–8.

23. Employment figures are from *SJDDR*, 1955, p. 128. Output figures refer to our calculations.

24. West German figures from *SJBR*, 1955, pp. 209, 228.

25. Böttcher, *op. cit.*, p. 13.

26. *SJBR*, 1955, p. 436.

27. *Feinmechanik und Optik in der sowjetischen Besatzungszone, Materialien* (Bonn, n.d.) p. 7.

28. *SJDDR*, 1955, pp. 166–167.

29. *SJBR*, 1958, p. 188. *SP*, May 1956, p. 61 gives a West German output of 266.4 per cent.

CHAPTER IX. Chemicals

1. *SJBR*, 1955, p. 454.

2. Dr. Gerhard Thimm, *Die Preis- und Kostenstruktur in der Industrieproduktion der Sowjetzone, Berichte des Osteuropa Instituts an der Freien Universität Berlin* (West Berlin, 1958).

3. Bruno Gleitze, *Ostdeutsche Wirtschaft*, (Berlin, Duncker and Humblot, 1956), p. 183.

4. SHD, p. 259. Employment figures refer to "technical units," 1939, groups 1102 and 1104.

5. *Ibid.*, p. 267.

6. *Produktionsstatistik*, 1936, p. 50.

7. Thimm, *op. cit.*, p. 315.

8. SHD, p. 309. Figure includes both Thomas phosphates and superphosphates.

9. *DJ*, 1949, p. 143.

10. *Produktionsstatistik, 1936*, p. 99.

11. SHD, p. 187.

12. *Ibid.*

13. Dr. Matthias Kramer, *Die Landwirtschaft in der sowjetischen Besatzungszone, Bonner Berichte* (Bonn, 1953), p. 29.

14. *Ibid.*

15. These statements are based on data given by Gleitze, *Ostdeutsche Wirtschaft,* p. 205.

16. *Ibid.,* p. 179.

17. *Produktionsstatistik,* 1936, p. 52.

18. Increase of continuous-filament rayon, 186; of staple rayon, 189; of average "raw and spinning materials" (which in West Germany also include imported cotton and wool), 183. *SJBR,* 1955, p. 442.

19. *SP* (May 1956, p. 62) gives the following table:

Production of continuous-filament rayon (1,000 tons)

	East Germany	West Germany
1936	12.4	26.3
1950	9.0	48.6
1955	22.3	68.6

That is, according to the East German source, continuous-filament rayon production increased in East Germany by 179.8 per cent and in the Federal Republic by 260.8 per cent between 1936 and 1955. Nevertheless, the article adds: "With (continuous-filament) rayon production, the increase during the First Five Year Plan was greater in the German Democratic Republic than in West Germany and by 1955 reached a level of 247.3 per cent while West German rayon production increased only 141.2 per cent compared to 1950."

20. *Direktive,* p. 14.

21. *Produktionsstatistik, 1936,* Group II, p. 44.

22. *Direktive,* p. 13.

23. Deutsches Institut für Wirtschaftsforschung, *Wochenbericht,* 1957, No. 24, p. 96.

24. Prof. H. Dubbel, *Taschenbuch für den Maschinenbau* (Berlin: Julius Springer, 1935). For details, see Supplement Table A.49.

25. Gleitze, *Ostdeutsche Wirtschaft,* p. 175.

26. *Ibid.,* p. 192.

27. *Ibid.,* p. 206.

28. *Ibid.,* p. 183.

29. *SHD,* pp. 312–313.

30. *Ibid.*

31. Gleitze, *Ostdeutsche Wirtschaft,* p. 183.

32. *SJDDR,* 1956, pp. 520 and 523, and 1957, pp. 516 and 519.

33. The weights were kindly supplied by the Boston District Office of the Goodyear Tire and Rubber Company. Bicycle tire weights have been estimated. See notes to Supplement Table A.51 for details.

34. Based on Gleitze, *Ostdeutsche Wirtschaft,* p. 206. In East Germany, sales of motor car tires were 6.6 per cent; of tubes, 5.8 per cent; of bicycle tires and tubes, negligible. Therefore, the 5 per cent estimate errs on the low side.

35. In 1936 the value added of rubber and asbestos in all Germany was RM 270.392 million (*Produktionsstatistik, 1936,* p. 44); sales in East Germany were 16.54 per cent (Gleitze, *Ostdeutsche Wirtschaft,* pp. 174 f.). This gives an estimated value added of RM 44.723 million less RM 4.358 million attributable to tires and tubes. This leaves RM 40.365 million for goods not separately specified.

CHAPTER X. Building Materials, Wood, Paper and Printing

1. Calculated from Bruno Gleitze, *Ostdeutsche Wirtschaft,* (Berlin, 1956, Duncker and Humblot), p. 202.

2. *Ibid.,* p. 181.

3. *Produktionsstatistik, 1936,* p. 48.

4. All figures in this paragraph are from *ibid.,* pp. 49–50.

5. Gleitze, *Ostdeutsche Wirtschaft,* p. 183.

6. Dr. Gerhard Thimm, *Die Preis- und Kostenstruktur in der Industrieproduktion der Sowjetzone, Berichte des Osteuropa Instituts an der Freien Universität Berlin* (West Berlin, 1956), p. 329.

7. Deutsches Institut für Wirtschaftsforschung, *Wochenbericht,* 1950, No. 23.

8. *SJBR,* 1955, p. 440.

9. Gleitze, *Ostdeutsche Wirtschaft,* p. 183.

10. *Neuberechnung,* p. 73.

11. *SJDDR,* 1955, p. 129.

12. *Ibid.,* pp. 166–167.

13. Value added in all Germany: RM 47.541 million (*Produktionsstatistik 1936,* p. 49). According to Gleitze (*Ostdeutsche Wirtschaft,* p. 202, note 4.), at least 80 per cent was produced in West Germany. This given 65,400 cubic meters sold elsewhere. According to *SHD,* p. 274, sales east of the Oder-Neisse were RM 16.211 million, while those in the Soviet Zone were only RM 4.238 million, or 20.7 per cent of all sales outside of West Germany. This would give an estimated production of 13,537 cubic meters for the Soviet Zone. A calculation based on price estimates gave 12,420 cubic meters.

14. *Die Entwicklung der Industrieproduktion der sowjetischen Besatzungszone 1953–54, Materialien* (Bonn, n.d.), p. 27.

15. *Produktionsstatistik, 1936,* p. 51; Gleitze, *Ostdeutsche Wirtschaft,* p. 183. The gross sales values given by Gleitze are slightly below the gross production of the official *Produktionsstatistik, 1936.* It has been assumed that the percentages given by Gleitze could be applied to the official data. The difference is obviously due to consumption within integrated firms.

16. *SJBR,* 1955, p. 441.

17. *Ibid.*

18. *Neuberechnung,* pp. 73 and 78.

CHAPTER XI. Textiles, Clothing, Leather, and Shoes

1. *SJDDR,* 1955, pp. 166–167.

2. See Bruno Gleitze, *Ostdeutsche Wirtschaft* (Berlin, Duncker and Humbolt, 1956), p. 179, for the sales values.

3. *Cotton Facts, 1927* (New York: Shepperson Publishing Co., 1928), p. 192.

4. U. S. Department of Commerce, Industrial Reference Service, Part 12, *Textiles and Related Products,* No. 28, June 1941, p. 3. (1.66301 sq yds per pound, or 3.0654008 sq m per kg.)

5. *SP,* December 1947.

6. "Rohstoffverbrauch und Rohstoffversorgung der Textilindustrie," *SP,* February 1957, p. 25.

7. *SP,* December 1947.

8. *Ibid.*

9. Gleitze, *Ostdeutsche Wirtschaft,* p. 208; *SP,* December 1947.

10. U. S. Department of Commerce, Industrial Reference Service, Part 12, *Textiles and Related Products,* April 1941, No. 20. Figures refer to 1937. American figures show only half that weight, with an average of 9.0416 sq m per kg of rayon cloth, almost the same weight as British cotton but almost twice the yardage of German cotton weaves. It is assumed that German rayon is also heavier.

11. In 1936, silk cloth manufacturing establishments in all Germany used 3,841 tons of cotton, 18,603 tons of rayon, and only 1,222 tons of natural silk. *SHD,* p. 325.

12. Gleitze, *Ostdeutsche Wirtschaft,* p. 208, gives the following figures (thousand tons)

		1936	1938	1943	
Filament rayon,	all Germany	45.212	67.700	95.600	
Of which, Soviet Zone		13.046	17.300	90.983	
Staple rayon,	all Germany	43.603	157.200	294.400	
Of which, Soviet Zone		17.127	68.300	144.349	
Woolens,	all Germany	139.3	102.2	75.6	(1944)
Of which, Soviet Zone		83.5	61.2	49.2	(1944)
Cotton cloths,	all Germany	233.3	269.7	153.2	(1944)
Of which, Soviet Zone		32.0	36.9	30.6	(1944)

13. *Ibid.*

14. *SHD*, p. 326. This figure includes some usable waste. It refers to "value of total production for the producers' own account." The total sales value is given in Gleitze, *Ostdeutsche Wirtschaft*, p. 179, as RM 820.771 million. The *Bruttoproduktionswert* is given in *Produktionsstatistik, 1936,* p. 53, as RM 814.074 million. The first figure has been adopted for the calculations because this source is the only one with the detail necessary for our calculations.

15. *Die Textil- und Lederindustrie in der sowjetischen Besatzungszone* (Bonn, 1955) p. 12. *"Materialien."*

16. *SJBR,* 1955, p. 464. *Damenschlüpfer,* medium quality, size 44, rayon. All other prices given refer to woolen garments, which are certainly not typical for the postwar period.

17. Gleitze, *Ostdeutsche Wirtschaft*, p. 208.

18. *SHD,* p. 326. Figure given in 1,000 dozen pairs.

19. On the basis of these figures we arrived at an average 1936 price of RM 0.74536 per pair, which is obviously an average producer price for 1936. The 1950 price was found by applying the price change of women's cotton or rayon stockings between 1938 and 1950 of 226.55 per cent to the 1936 price. (Women's stockings, cotton with seam and double sole, size 9½, rayon, medium quality. In 1938, RM 1.77 per pair; in 1950 DM 4.01 per pair. The price falls substantially in subsequent years. *SJBR,* 1955, p. 464.) For knitwear the corresponding price increase is 212.06 per cent.

20. Gleitze, *Ostdeutsche Wirtschaft,* pp. 134–135.

21. *Ibid.,* p. 179.

22. *Ibid.,* pp. 134–135.

23. According to Gleitze RM 524.144 million of the total RM 820.771 million sales value of hosiery and knitwear originated in the area of East Germany, that is, about 63.86 per cent. The value added of the industry for 1936 was derived by applying this percentage to the total value added of Germany as a whole, RM 428.733 million. This gives RM 273.789 million as the 1936 value added in 1936 prices produced in East Germany.

The 1936 value added in 1950 prices was found by multiplying the 1936 value added in 1936 prices by the ratio of the 1936 sales value in 1950 prices to the 1936 sales value in 1936 prices as found by our calculations. For differences in the 1936 figures in *ibid.* (p. 179), *SHD* and *Produktionsstatistik, 1936,* see note 14 above.

24. Gleitze, *Ostdeutsche Wirtschaft,* p. 179.

25. Fred Oelssner, "Staat und Oekonomie in der Übergangsperiode," *Wirtschaftswissenschaft,* April–May 1957, Vol. V, No. 3, p. 328.

26. *SJDDR,* 1955, p. 129.

27. Gleitze, *Ostdeutsche Wirtschaft,* p. 179, and *SHD,* p. 275. However, *SHD,* on p. 326 estimates the share of the area of East Germany, east of the Oder-Neisse, and the Saar to have been approximately 60 per cent. This would give a minimum of 50 per cent for the area of East Germany alone. The former figure, based on *Produktionsstatistik, 1936,* is used here even though the latter information seems more plausible.

28. *SHD,* p. 326.

29. *Neuberechnung,* p. 79.

30. *SJDDR,* 1955, p. 166.

31. Gleitze, *Ostdeutsche Wirtschaft,* p. 207.

32. Statistisches Bundesamt, Wiesbaden, *Die industrielle Produktion, 1951–1955: Jahreszahlen* in *Die Industrie der Bundesrepublik Deutschland,* Special Issue No. 11 (Stuttgart: W. Kohlhammer, April 1956).

33. *SJR,* 1939–1940, p. 333.

34. Since the price changes of stiff and soft leather between 1936 and 1938 almost exactly offset each other, as shown by the quotation from *SJR, 1939–1940,* p. 333, the price index in the 1955 edition of *SJBR* (p. 441), based on 1938, was used to calculate the price change between 1936 and 1950.

35. Gleitze, *Ostdeutsche Wirtschaft,* p. 207.

36. *SJDDR,* 1955, p. 166; *SP,* May 1956, p. 62. Both the article in *SP* and Gleitze, *Ostdeutsche Wirtschaft,* p. 107, give West German production of leather shoes in 1936 as 67.2 million pairs, *SP* omitting the note, however, that the Saar area is included.

37. *SJBR*, 1955, p. 446.

38. Calculated from *Lederstrassenschuhe, SJBR,* 1954, p. 339.

39. *SJBR*, 1955, p. 466.

40. *Ibid.,* p. 441.

41. *SJBR*, 1954, p. 239.

42. *Produktionsstatistik, 1936,* p. 52.

43. Gleitze, *Ostdeutsche Wirtschaft,* p. 179.

44. *SJBR*, 1955, p. 441.

45. This figure is given only in *Karteiblatt* in *SP,* May 1956. *SJDDR,* 1955, p. 129, shows data from 1950 through 1955 only for clothing, leather, and shoes combined. Leather and shoes are shown separately only from 1953 through 1955 *(Ibid.,* p. 130).

CHAPTER XII. Fats and Oils, Food, Drink, and Tobacco

1. Base, 1938 = 100. No price change occurred between 1936 and 1938. *SJBR*, 1955, pp. 442–443.

2. Statistisches Bundesamt, Wiesbaden, *Die industrielle Produktion, 1951–1955: Jahrezahlen, Die Industrie der Bundesrepublik Deutschland,* Special Issue, No. 11. (Stuttgart: W. Kohlhammer, April 1956), p. 73.

3. *Direktive,* p. 14.

4. *SJR, 1939–1940,* p. 398.

5. *SJBR*, 1955, p. 499.

6. *Ibid.*

7. *SHD,* p. 397, which states that the average import price was RM 230.8 per ton.

8. *SJR, 1939–1940,* p. 398.

9. *Ibid.*

10. Bruno Gleitze, *Ostdeutsche Wirtschaft,* (Berlin: Duncker and Humblot, 1956), p. 46.

11. *Presse Informationen,* 11 August 1954, No. 92 (1032).

12. *SP,* May 1957.

13. Courtesy of the firm of Johannes Röskamp, Leer-Loga, Germany.

14. U. S. Department of Commerce, Bureau of the Census, *Census of Manufactures: 1937,* (Washington: Government Printing Office, 1939), Part I, pp. 1209–1311. The 1936 ratio given by *Produktionsstatistik, 1936* is 61 per cent; the 1950 ratio is 48 per cent.

CHAPTER XIII. All Other Industries

1. *SHD,* p. 308, gives sales values as follows: 1936, RM 82.273 million; 1939, 106.683 million. The tonnage of sales in 1939 was 79,173 tons.

2. Bruno Gleitze, *Ostdeutsche Wirtschaft,* (Berlin: Duncker and Humblot, 1956), p. 203.

3. *SJBR*, 1956, p. 434.

4. Fred Oelssner, "Staat und Ökonomie in der Übergangsperiode," *Wirtschaftswissenschaft,* April–May 1957, Vol. V, No. 3, p. 329.

5. Gleitze, *op. cit.,* p. 185.

6. *SP,* October 1953.

7. ECE, *Economic Survey of Europe: 1954* (Geneva, 1955), p. 267.

8. *SJBR*, 1956, p. 437.

CHAPTER XIV. The Development of Industrial Production in East Germany

1. Fred Sanderson, in *Trends in Economic Growth: A Comparison of the Western Powers and the Soviet Bloc,* a study prepared for the Joint Committee on the Economic Report by the Legislative Reference Service of the Library of Congress, Joint Committee Print, 83d Congress, 2d Session (Washington: Government Printing Office, 1955), p. 292, Table XII.1.

2. Gerhard Abeken, "Die Sowjetzonale Wirtschaftsexpansion" in *Wirtschaftsforschung und Wirtschaftsführung* (Berlin: Duncker and Humblot, 1956), p. 191.

3. *SJBR*, 1955, p. 542.

4. For the preliminary results, see W. F. Stolper, "The Labor Force and Industrial

Development in Soviet Germany," *Quarterly Journal of Economics,* November 1957, Vol. LXXI, pp. 518–545.

5. All comments in this paragraph are based on *Produktionsstatistik, 1936,* p. 12.

6. *SJBR,* 1955, p. 533.

7. *SJDDR,* 1957, p. 156.

8. West German figures are from *SJBR,* 1956, p. 516.

CHAPTER XV. The Crop Sector

1. *SJDDR,* 1956, p. 8; Dr. Matthias Kramer, *Die Landwirtschaft in der sowjetischen Besatzungszone, Bonner Berichte* (Bonn, 1953), Appendix p. 3.

2. *SJDDR,* 1955, pp. 200–201; Kramer, *Die Landwirtschaft,* p. 9.

3. From an unpublished manuscript of Professor Kramer's, which he kindly permitted me to see and to quote (herinafter referred to in the reference notes as Kramer, unpublished manuscript).

4. Gerhard Draheim, "Entwicklung der Hektarerträge im ersten Fünfjahrplan" *SP.* April 1956, pp. 41, 42.

5. Dr. Hans Raehse, "Die Auswahlmethode für die repräsentativen Betriebsuntersuchungen in der Landwirtschaft," *SP,* July 1955, p. 106. See also Ursula Lange, "Kritische Bemerkungen zu den repräsentativen Untersuchungen in der Landwirtschaft" *SP,* June 1955, pp. 86–90.

6. *SP,* July 1955, p. 100.

7. *Gesetzblatt der Deutschen Demokratischen Republik,* 11 June 1957, Part II, No. 26, p. 192.

8. See also Food and Agriculture Organization of the United Nations, *Handbook for the Preparation of Food Balance Sheets,* Washington, D. C., April 1949.

9. *SHLE,* Table 91, note 5, p. 53.

10. *Ibid.,* p. 463.

11. *SJBR,* 1955, p. 449.

12. *SHLE,* p. 463.

13. Kramer, unpublished manuscript, Appendix VIII.4.

14. All import figures are from *SP,* May 1957, or *SJDDR,* 1957, p. 520.

15. Kramer, unpublished manuscript, Appendix VIII.4.

16. *SJDDR,* 1955, p. 207.

17. Fred Oelssner, "Staat und Ökonomie in der Übergangsperiode," *Wirtschaftswissenschaft,* April–May 1957, Vol. V, No. 3, p. 329. This is a revised version of a speech given before the 30th Plenum of the Central Committee of the Socialist Unity (Communist) Party. Mr. Oelssner has since been dismissed.

18. *Ibid.*

19. See Draheim, *op. cit.,* pp. 41 ff.

20. *Ibid.,* pp. 43–44.

21. *SHLE,* p. 68.

22. *SHD,* pp. 150–151.

23. *SP,* April 1957, p. 43.

24. Oelssner, "Staat and Ökonomie."

25. *Landwirtschaftliche Richtzahlen,* p. 195.

26. ECE, *Economic Survey of Europe in 1953,* Geneva, 1954, p. 273, and *Economic Survey of Europe in 1954,* Geneva, 1955, p. 267.

27. Figures from *SHLE,* pp. 59–60.

28. *SJDDR,* 1955, p. 208.

29. *SP,* April 1956, pp. 42–43.

30. Technical data from *Landwirtschaftliche Richtzahlen,* p. 197.

31. *SHLE,* p. 109.

CHAPTER XVI. Livestock and Animal Products

1. Bruno Gleitze, *Ostdeutsche Wirtschaft,* (Berlin, Duncker and Humblot, 1956), p. 165.

2. *SJDDR,* 1955, p. 225.

3. *Ibid.,* p. 103.

4. This figure was arrived at on the basis of a 1950 base figure of 15.3 kg. given in *Presse-Informationen,* 11 August 1954, No. 92 (1032); an index in *SP,* October 1954; and a figure given in *Neues Deutschland,* 4 February 1956, p. 2.

5. *SP,* March 1957, p. 44.

6. Specifically, the Institut für Landwirtschaftliche Betriebsforschung, West Berlin.

7. *VHS,* 1957, Vol. I, No. 1, p. 8.

8. *Ibid.*

9. *SJDDR,* 1957, p. 218.

10. *Presse-Informationen,* 11 August 1954, No. 92 (1032).

11. *SP,* June 1956, p. 75.

CHAPTER XVII. The Market Production of Agriculture and the Cost
of Nonagricultural Inputs

1. Bruno Gleitze, *Ostdeutsche Wirtschaft* (Berlin, Duncker and Humblot, 1956), pp. 162 ff.

2. *SJDDR,* 1956, p. 404.

3. *SHLE,* p. 30.

4. See Table 13.

5. *SP,* August 1956; also *SJDDR,* 1956, p. 301, and 1957, p. 313.

6. *SP,* October 1956, pp. 140 ff.

7. *Ibid.,* p. 151.

8. *Ibid.,* p. 149.

9. *SHLE,* p. 115.

10. *SP,* October 1956, p. 149.

11. *SHLE,* p. 115.

12. *SP,* October 1956, p. 151.

13. East German figures calculated from Tables 124 and 130. West German figures calculated from *SHLE,* Tables 185 and 186, pp. 108–110 and 115.

14. Gleitze, *Ostdeutsche Wirtschaft,* pp. 162 ff.

15. *SJDDR,* 1957, p. 518.

16. Heinrich Rau, in a speech at the Warnow Shipyards, published in *Neues Deutschland,* 2 February 1957.

17. *SHD,* p. 327.

18. *SHLE,* p. 229.

19. All figures are from *SP,* August 1956 pp. 107–108; *SJDDR,* 1956, p. 301, and 1957, p. 313.

20. *SHLE,* p. 38.

21. *Ibid.*

22. *SP,* June 1956, p. 79.

23. *Ibid.*

24. *SJDDR,* 1957, p. 365.

25. *FL,* p. 63.

26. *Landwirtschaftliche Richtzahlen,* p. 60.

27. *FL,* p. 63.

28. Both figures are from *FL,* p. 65.

29. *SJBR,* 1953, p. 580. (This table bears the note that the concepts are not directly comparable with West German usage; it was dropped a few years later.)

30. Joint Committee on the Economic Report, *Trends in Economic Growth: A Comparison of the Western Powers and the Soviet Bloc,* a study prepared by the Legislative Reference Service of the Library of Congress, Joint Committee Print, 83d Congress, 2d Session, Washington, D. C., 1955, p. 292.

31. *SJDDR,* 1957, p. 415.

32. *Neue Hütte,* Special Issue, Internationale Niederschachtofentagung in Leipzig (East Berlin: VEB Verlag Technik, 1956), pp. 916–919.

33. Hans Liebe, "Die Entwicklung der Landwirtschaft in der sowjetischen Besatzungszone seit 1945 und der augenblickliche Stand der Versorgung mit Nahrungsmitteln," in *Wirtschaftsforschung und Wirtschaftsführung,* (West Berlin, Duncker and Humblot, 1956), p. 175.

34. *SHLE,* p. 72.

CHAPTER XVIII. Construction

1. *Produktionsstatistik,* 1936, p. 35; see also p. 55, note 24.

2. *SJDDR,* 1955, pp. 171–183, 188–189.

3. *Ibid.,* Part XII, pp. 171–183, and 1957, Part XVIII, pp. 319–338.

4. *SJDDR,* 1955, p. 171.

5. *SJDDR,* 1957, p. 319.

6. *SJDDR,* 1955, Part XIII, pp. 184–193, and 1957, pp. 339 ff.

7. *SJDDR,* 1957, Part XVIII, pp. 319–338.

8. *SJDDR;* 1955, Part IX, pp. 90–103.

9. *Ibid.,* p. 191.

10. *Ibid.,* p. 230, and 1957, p. 476. These figures refer only to the length of the road, railroad, and canal network.

11. Fred Sanderson, in *Trends in Economic Growth: A Comparison of the Western Powers and the Soviet Bloc,* a study prepared for the Joint Committee on the Economic Report by the Legislative Reference Service of the Library of Congress, Joint Committee Print, 83d Congress, 2d Session, Washington, D. C., 1955, p. 292.

12. *Ibid.,* p. 292, note 4 (italics mine).

13. All figures are from *SHD,* p. 307.

14. *Ibid.*

15. *SJDDR,* 1955, p. 162.

16. Sanderson, *op. cit.,* p. 292.

17. Bruno Gleitze, *Ostdeutsche Wirtschaft* (Berlin, Duncker and Humblot, 1956), p. 185.

18. According to *Produktionsstatistik, 1936,* p. 29.

19. Calculated from *SJBR,* 1956, p. 520.

20. *SHD,* p. 272.

21. Gleitze, *Ostdeutsche Wirtschaft,* p. 184.

22. *SJDDR,* 1957, p. 320, table and notes.

23. *SJDDR,* 1956, p. 327, and 1957, p. 334. Figures are also given for estimated floor space.

24. *SJDDR,* 1956, p. 318.

25. *SJBR,* 1957, p. 258.

26. *SHD,* p. 341.

27. *SJDDR,* 1955, p. 181.

28. *SJBR,* 1957, p. 257.

29. *Neues Deutschland (East Berlin),* 18 December 1956. All calculations were made on the basis of 11,000 dwelling units.

30. IFO Institut, *Statistisches Handbuch der Bauwirtschaft* (Munich, 1949), p. 74. Refers to a West German standard house.

31. *Informationsbureau West (West Berlin),* bulletins dated Berlin, 28 and 31 May 1957 (mimeograph).

32. *Presse Informationen,* 14 November 1956, No. 131 (1372).

33. *SHD,* p. 606.

34. Gleitze, *Ostdeutsche Wirtschaft,* p. 185.

35. For source, see IFO Institut, *Statistisches Handbuch,* p. 74.

36. Machinery and Allied Products Institute, *Capital Goods Review* (Chicago), May 1950, No. 2, Chart 2.

CHAPTER XIX. Transportation and Communications, and Trade

1. Calculated from data in *SJR, 1938,* p. 212.

2. *SJBR,* 1955, p. 17.

3. Dr. Wolfgang Seidel, *Verkehrswirtschaft und Verkehrspolitik in der Sowjet Zone, Materialien* (Bonn, n. d.), p. 34.

4. These figures were calculated as follows: Receipts from coal shipments at exceptional tariffs, RM 109.165 million; from other carload shipments at exceptional tariffs, RM 525.580 million; coal shipments, 22.710 billion ton-km; other exceptional rate shipments, 19.436 billion ton-km; receipts from carload shipments at normal rates, RM 841.012 million; total carload shipments at normal rates, 17.078 billion ton-km. *Statistik*

der Eisenbahnen im Deutschen Reich, published at the request of the Reichswerksministerium (Berlin: Reich Printing Office, E. S. Mittler und Sohn, distrib., 1937), pp. 118–119.

5. Wirtschaft und Statistik, 1938, pp. 347–348.

6. Calculated from Bruno Gleitze, Ostdeutsche Wirtschaft (Berlin, Duncker and
Humblot, 1956), p. 211. Since the figures refer only to the Reichsbahn exclusive of
Berlin, we have included one-third of Berlin. The important Berlin city railroad (S-Bahn),
also run by the Reichsbahn, was evaluated separately. Including one-third of Berlin,
persons traveling in East Germany accounted for 25 per cent of the Reich total; railway
passenger cars, 24.8 per cent; and railway luggage cars, 24.1 per cent.

7. Wirtschaft und Statistik, 1938, pp. 347–348.

8. Calculated from ibid., pp. 52–53.

9. Ibid.

10. August Lösch, "Die Leistung der Seeschiffahrt im Vergleich zu den Leistungen der
übrigen Gütertransportmittel (Binnenschiffahrt, Eisenbahn, Kraftfahrzeug und Flugzeug),"
in Nauticus 1941: Jahrbuch für Deutschlands Seeinteressen, edited for the Naval High
Command by Admiral Gottfried Hansen, 24th ed. (Berlin: E. S. Mittler und Sohn, 1941),
p. 333.

11. SJBR, 1955, pp. 16–17.

12. Lösch, op. cit., p. 333.

13. Figures from SHD, p. 375.

14. Calculated from data in SHD, p. 374. In all Germany, 18.252 million tons were
shipped over 18.252 billion ton-km. Lösch, op cit., p. 333, gives as the average distance
for long-distance trucking 216 km.

15. SJBR, 1955, p. 17.

16. No source was found, but this is what my memory of subway, bus, and trolley
trips in Berlin indicates.

17. Statistik der Eisenbahnen im Deutschen Reich, pp. 126–127.

18. See SJDDR, 1957, p. 477.

	Radios licensed	Television sets licensed
1950	3,489,100	None
1954	. . .	2,313
1957	5,306,300	159,490

19. SJDDR, 1956, pp. 508–509; for additional figures, see SP, May 1956.

20. SJDDR, 1955, p. 93, notes.

21. SJR, 1937, p. 25.

22. SJBR, 1957, p. 13.

23. SJR, 1937, p. 374.

24. Ibid., p. 373.

25. SJBR, 1957, p. 559.

26. Fred Sanderson, in Trends in Economic Growth: A Comparison of the Western
Powers and the Soviet Bloc, a study prepared for the Joint Committee on the Economic
Report by the Legislative Reference Service of the Library of Congress, Joint Committee
Print, 83d Congress, 2d Session, Washington, D. C., 1955, p. 292, Table XII.1.

27. SJDDR, 1955, p. 26, Table 17, rows 52 (publishing) through 63 (domestic services).

28. Calculated from SJDDR, 1957, pp. 108 ff.

CHAPTER XX. The Gross National Product of East Germany

1. SJDDR, 1956, p. 154.

2. Ibid.

3. Ibid., p. 166.

4. SJBR, 1957, p. 559.

5. SJDDR, 1957, p. 160.

6. H. Kupky, "Die langfristige Entwicklung der Bruttoanlageinvestitionen der mit-
teldeutschen Industrie von 1924–1955," Vierteljahreshefte zur Wirtschaftsforschung, 1957,
No. 4, p. 396, quoting Rudolph and Friedrich, eds., Grundriss der Volkswirtschaftsplanung
(East Berlin: Verlag Die Wirtschaft, 1957), p. 339.

INDEX

BOOKS FROM THE CENTER FOR INTERNATIONAL STUDIES
Massachusetts Institute of Technology

PUBLISHED OR DISTRIBUTED BY HARVARD UNIVERSITY PRESS

The Chinese Family in the Communist Revolution
   by C. K. Yang, Technology Press of MIT and Harvard, 1959

A Chinese Village in Early Communist Transition
   by C. K. Yang, Technology Press of MIT and Harvard, 1959

The Structure of the East German Economy
   by Wolfgang F. Stolper, Harvard, 1960

Bloc Politics in the United Nations
   by Thomas Hovet, Jr., Harvard, 1960

FROM OTHER PUBLISHERS

The Dynamics of Soviet Society
   by W. W. Rostow, Alfred Levin, et al., Norton, 1953; Mentor Books, 1954

The Prospects for Communist China
   by W. W. Rostow, et al., Technology Press of MIT and Wiley, 1954

Soviet Education for Science and Technology
   by Alexander G. Korol, Technology Press of MIT and Wiley, 1957

The Economics of Communist Eastern Europe
   by Nicholas Spulber, Technology Press of MIT and Wiley, 1957

A Proposal: Key to an Effective Foreign Policy
   by M. F. Millikan and W. W. Rostow, Harper, 1957

China's Gross National Product and Social Accounts: 1950–1957
   by William W. Hollister, Free Press, 1958

Scratches on Our Minds: American Images of China and India
   by Harold R. Isaacs, John Day, 1958

Forging a New Sword: A Study of the Department of Defense
   by William R. Kintner, with Joseph I. Coffey and Raymond J. Albright,
   Harper, 1958

Changing Images of America: A Study of Indian Students' Perceptions
   by George V. Coelho, Free Press, 1958

*Industrial Change in India: Industrial Growth, Capital Requirements, and
Technological Change, 1937–1955*
   by George Rosen, Free Press, 1958

The American Style: Essays in Value and Performance
   edited by Elting E. Morison, Harper, 1958

Handbook for Industry Studies
   by Everett E. Hagen, Free Press, 1958

The Japanese Factory: Aspects of Its Social Organization
by James C. Abegglen, Free Press, 1958

The Passing of Traditional Society: Modernizing the Middle East
by Daniel Lerner, with Lucille W. Pevsner (co-sponsored by the Bureau
of Applied Social Research, Columbia University), Free Press, 1958

Industrial Growth in South India: Case Studies in Economic Development
by George B. Baldwin, Free Press, 1959

Financing Economic Development: The Indonesian Case
by Douglas S. Paauw, Free Press, 1960

The Religion of Java
by Clifford Geertz, Free Press, 1960

Postwar Economic Trends in the United States
edited by Ralph E. Freeman, Harper, 1960

The United States in the World Arena
by W. W. Rostow, Harper, 1960

The Question of Government Spending: Public Needs and Private Wants
by Francis M. Bator, Harper, 1960

The United Nations and U.S. Foreign Policy
by Lincoln P. Bloomfield, Little, Brown, 1960.